# COOKING
# GLUTEN-FREE!

### A Food Lover's Collection of Chef and Family Recipes
### Without Gluten or Wheat

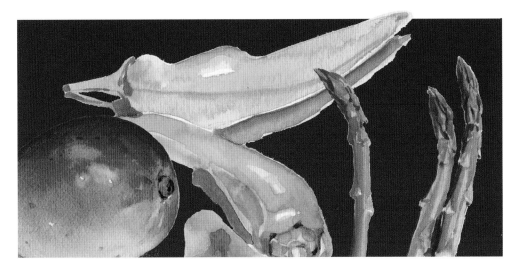

## Karen Robertson
### Illustrated by J. Diane Robertson

Celiac Publishing, Seattle, Washington

First Edition

Published by Celiac Publishing, Seattle, Washington

Design by DD Dowden
Printed in South Korea

10   9   8   7   6   5   4   3   2   1

Library of Congress Control Number: 2002092249

    Robertson, Karen
        Cooking Gluten-Free!
        A Food Lover's Collection of Chef and Family Recipes Without Gluten or Wheat / Karen
            Robertson; watercolors by J. Diane Robertson
        1. Gluten-free diet—Recipes.

        ISBN   0-9708660-0-3

Celiac Publishing
P.O. Box 99603
Seattle, WA  98199
celiacpublishing@earthlink.net

*With Love to Carmen and Sam*

———————❤———————

# CONTENTS

# ACKNOWLEDGMENTS

So many people have played a part in making this book possible. My sincere thanks go to everyone who took the time to make a contribution.

I owe a great deal to my husband, Alan, who endured many years of cookbook writing and happily took on the role of supreme taste tester (along with our gluten intolerant children, Carmen and Sam). He also deserves credit for both teaching me how to cook and contributing many of the grill recipes. The book was brought to life with the gorgeous watercolors generously donated by Alan's mother, Diane Robertson. Without her efforts, this book would be missing a very important element. Thank you, Diane!

I also owe many thanks to both my editors and my designer. Barbara Figueroa, a former chef and restaurant owner, has brought her talents to this book through editing, rewriting, recipe contribution, and consulting. Her tireless efforts significantly improved the manuscript! And a special thank you to Kathy Winkenwerder for providing a "fresh set of eyes" and great insight during the important final edit. DD Dowden designed a beautiful, functional book, and cheerfully kept me on track every step of the way. I was very lucky to find these talented people. Many thanks also go to Chris Cauble for overseeing the printing and design work. It would have been impossible to achieve my goal without him.

The gathering of recipes from renowned chefs across the country was greatly facilitated through the efforts of many people. Josh Raynolds (Rosenthal Wine Merchants), Larry Stone (Master Sommelier at Rubicon), and Dan Phillips (The Grateful Palate) all connected me to some of the best chefs in America. I am especially honored to know Dan McCarthy of McCarthy & Schiering Wine Merchants, who aided tremendously in this effort, and who also selected the wine pairings for many of the recipes throughout the book.

A special note of gratitude goes to Christopher Kimball and Ludger Szmania, two chefs who believed in this book from the beginning and made it possible for me to get my project off the ground. Thanks also go to the many contributing chefs who took the time to create recipes for the home cook: Gerry Hayden, Hans Bergmann, Christian Svalesen, Tom Douglas, Lynne Vea, Ludger Szmania, Todd Gray, Suzanne Goin, Kathy Casey, Erol Tugrul, Barbara Figueroa, Charlie Trotter, Dennis Leary, Bob Kinkead, Linda Yamada, Michael Kornick, Christopher Kimball, Thoa Nguyen, and Marcella Rosene.

Goldie Caughlan and Marilyn McCormick are credited with inspiring me to learn more about the food we consume. I thank them both for having faith in my ability to teach gluten-free cooking classes. I also give special thanks to Cynthia Lair, Karol Redfern Hamper, and Linda Carlson as my mentors throughout the book publishing process.

I have been very fortunate to know and work with Bette Hagman, the pioneer of gluten-free cooking. She has graciously answered my many questions, and has supported my efforts in writing this book.

Joanne VanRoden, Amy Bogino Eernissee, Debra Daniels-Zeller, Edel Amundson, Jerry and Julie Hawkins, Heather Shaw, Diane Robertson, Marian Robertson, Bill Bassett, Lorna Sass, Wendy Wark, Cynthia Lair, Judy Bullock, and Bill Fredericks have all earned kudos for the recipes they contributed.

The top-quality baked goods in this book would not be possible without Wendy Wark's superior flour mix. I owe her much gratitude for allowing me to use this formula as the basis of all of my baked goods. And thanks to Rebecca Reilly for developing some excellent gluten-free recipes in her book. Once I tasted a few recipes from these two women, I knew there was hope for delicious gluten-free treats!

Cynthia S. Rudert, M.D., F.A.C.P., is to be credited with penning the book's foreword. She is one of the foremost authorities on celiac disease in the United States today. I am indeed blessed to have met her, and appreciate her eagerness to take part in the writing of this book.

My gratitude goes out to Shelley Case, R.D., who specializes in celiac disease, for helping me understand the finer points of the gluten-free diet. I am also fortunate to know Cynthia Kupper, C.R.D., Executive Director of the Gluten Intolerance Group. She has been a tremendous resource for me over the years in putting this book together with the most accurate information available. Her unrelenting work for GIG and her efforts to join the various celiac groups in North America together with one voice are to be commended.

A final thank-you goes to all the Gluten Intolerance Group members, especially Michele Benson and Jennifer Smith, for their encouraging feedback on my gluten-free recipes and their insightful recommendations for this book.

# FOREWORD

CELIAC DISEASE IS THE MOST COMMON INHERITED GENETIC ILLNESS IN AMERICA. Fortunately, it is a condition that will generally show marked improvement through strict adherence to a lifelong gluten-free diet. Upon eliminating wheat, oats, rye, and barley, the microscopic damage to the small intestine will immediately begin to improve. There are ongoing studies evaluating the safety of oats in the diet of celiac patients. At the present time, oats are not recommended for patients in the United States, where cultivation in fields cross-rotated with wheat is permitted. Dermatitis herpetiformis patients must observe the same dietary guidelines. Individuals with DH almost always have underlying celiac disease, though they might exhibit few, if any, gastrointestinal problems.

In our country, we are just beginning to realize how common celiac disease is. The University of Maryland's Center for Celiac Research is conducting an ongoing multi-center serologic study, and has tested over 10,000 individuals in order to better understand its prevalence in the United States. Preliminary data indicates that it may affect one out of every 170 Americans in the general population. In fact, if you have a relative with the disorder, the chance that you also have it may be as high as one in twelve.

It has recently come to light that if you adhere strictly to a gluten-free diet, you will decrease the likelihood of developing another associated autoimmune disease, such as Addison's disease, B-12 deficiency, myasthenia gravis, Raynaud's disease, scleroderma, Sjogren's syndrome, lupus erythematosus, thyroid disease, or autoimmune chronic active hepatitis. (For example, the incidence of Type I Diabetes, or insulin dependent diabetes mellitus, in people with CD/DH is believed to be twice that of the general population.) Anyone with ongoing gastrointestinal symptoms should be evaluated for celiac disease, now thought to occur in one out of every thirty individuals referred to a gastroenterologist for any reason.

In my experience, the most common symptom associated with the disorder is fatigue. In fact, many of my patients have been misdiagnosed with chronic fatigue syndrome before celiac disease was discovered to be the actual cause. Interestingly, symptoms may vary depending on the individual. Some patients suffer from unexplained abdominal pain, gas, or bloating; others may have constipation or diarrhea. By the time extensive damage has been done to the small intestine, malnutrition, weakness, and weight loss is inevitable. Certain individuals may actually have difficulty losing weight. A gluten-free diet is a healthy diet, and it is wonderful to be able to treat celiac patients without submitting them to a life-long medication regimen. Of course, it is important to address other coexisting problems, such as vitamin and mineral deficiencies. Chronic malabsorption of calcium can lead to osteopenia or osteoporosis, even in adolescence.

The vast majority of patients note substantial improvement and even total resolution of their symptoms on a gluten-free diet. If their symptoms continue, or recur, I would be concerned about inadvertent gluten ingestion.

Please turn to your physician for testing if you are the relative of a celiac patient. It is not unusual for the condition to be misdiagnosed as "irritable bowel syndrome" or "spastic colon." The initial phase involves screening for antigliadin IgG and IgA antibodies, antiendomysial antibodies, tissue transglutaminase, and serum IgA level. It is also necessary to have a biopsy obtained from several portions of the small intestine during a procedure called endoscopy (esophagogastroduodenoscopy), as blood tests may be normal in up to twenty percent of individuals with celiac disease, and therefore cannot be relied upon for conclusive results.

If you are diagnosed with celiac disease, you should be under the care of a physician with related experience, in order to manage continued or recurrent symptoms and other coexisting medical disorders. I urge you to join support groups and play an active role in your recovery. Finally, read this book; a gluten-free diet for life can be both therapeutic and absolutely delicious!

*Cynthia S. Rudert, M.D., F.A.C.P.*
*Medical Advisor, Celiac Disease Foundation*
*Medical Advisor, Gluten Intolerance Group*
*Medical Director, Gluten Sensitive Support Group of Atlanta*
*Founding Member, Celiac Standardization Group*

The Medical Quarters, Suite 312
5555 Peachtree Dunwoody Road, NE
Atlanta, Georgia  30342
(404) 943-9820

# PREFACE

*COOKING GLUTEN-FREE!* was written for people with a gluten or wheat intolerance and for those who dine with them daily. Gluten intolerance is known as celiac disease and/or dermatitis herpetiformis. A person with gluten intolerance must avoid wheat, oats, rye, barley, spelt, triticale, and kamut or risk intestinal damage. The standard American diet is dominated by these forbidden grains, which makes a gluten-free diet a tremendous challenge. Gluten is also "hidden" in many foods that contain malt or malt flavoring, modified food starch, hydrolyzed vegetable protein, etc.

A special diet causes great frustration and a huge life change, so it is helpful to know that gluten-free food can be absolutely delicious; it is simply a matter of using quality recipes and ingredients. This book was designed to help you wade through the jungle of gluten-free recipes so you won't have to waste your time and money on the bad ones. Included are proven recipes for such essentials as desserts, flour tortillas, breads, hamburger buns, breadsticks, pancakes, waffles, and sweet breads; there are also recipes with which to compose wonderful menus for your weekly repertoire. Recommended mail order pastas, crackers, and snacks are also listed. There is hope!

The great chefs rely heavily on fresh ingredients, so that much of what they cook is gluten-free (excluding bread and pasta); they also possess the know-how to make gluten-free substitutions when necessary. In developing this book I asked some of the finest chefs in America to contribute gluten-free meals that would be easy for you to prepare at home.

When our children were diagnosed with celiac disease, I decided it was easier to cook one gluten-free meal for the whole family rather than feed our children differently. The key was getting organized with gluten-free ingredients and finding recipes combining ease of preparation with taste appeal. Our entire family now has a healthier diet and we have amassed a collection of recipes with which to make delectable meals and treats. Cooking gluten-free involves some initial "start up" time while you learn what to buy and how to cook without gluten.

Positive thinking is quite powerful. Once you understand the basics and have some experience, you will be pleased with what you can create. Cooking is a great way for families to reconnect at the end of the day; it brings people together and makes a house a home. There is no doubt that other activities will need to be rearranged or put on hold awhile. Your top priority must be support of the gluten intolerant person, especially in the first year following diagnosis.

A chapter is included to help parents of gluten-intolerant children cope with the many challenges they face. An optimistic outlook and a commitment to your role as a personal chef/dietician are very important.

Trying to figure out what to have for dinner requires creativity. This book does the creative thinking for you and quickly solves the "what's for dinner?" dilemma. A variety of quick meals (⏲) are included, though most entrées with side dishes can be prepared within 30-45 minutes from start to finish.

Since a gluten-free diet is stricter than a wheat-free diet, the book's content is tailored to the former. Anyone on a wheat-free diet will find the book very beneficial as well.

You will notice recipes including healthy flours such as brown rice, amaranth, and quinoa. Other recommended ingredients include organic shortening, tofu, fruit puree sweeteners, etc. Try to incorporate these ingredients for a healthier overall diet. Some recipes include alternative flours. Amaranth, quinoa, buckwheat, teff, and millet are gluten-free providing you can find a pure source (grown in dedicated fields and processed on dedicated equipment). You can research this issue further by contacting the Gluten Intolerance Group, Celiac Sprue Association/USA, Canadian Celiac Association, and Celiac Disease Foundation.

Everyone wants to experience a good meal that is satisfying to both eyes and tummy and is easy to prepare. This book provides recipes and guidance to achieve this goal.

# INTRODUCTION

THE ENTRÉE RECIPES in this volume are arranged by season so you can take advantage of fresh produce at its peak, and because seasons tend to dictate our "food moods." However, you will find some items such as tomatillos, which are plentiful in summer, used in a winter recipe. Many foods are available year round, thanks to our global economy, and it is refreshing to have a taste of summer even in wintertime.

Some meals are labeled "quick" for those nights when time is at a premium. You will find ways to shorten your time in the kitchen as cooking becomes a part of your life. Rest assured that you won't have to spend each day cooking from scratch! Your homemade gluten-free food can be stored in the freezer for those "no time to cook" nights of the week, while on other nights you can create a simple dinner such as gluten-free pasta with fresh vegetables. Most recipes for each meal can be prepared in 30-45 minutes, and you will learn how to prepare certain parts in advance to ease the stress of getting dinner on the table when everyone is hungry.

Since the book is written with the novice cook in mind, directions are provided for very simple recipes, and cooking terms are defined in the glossary.

### Accompaniments

Salads, vegetables, and other side dishes are covered here. Most entrées include a suggested accompaniment from this section.

## Breads

Essentials such as sandwich breads, tortillas, pizza crusts, sweet breads, muffins, etc. fill this chapter.

## Sweets

Recipes include scrumptious cakes, cookies, pies, elegant fruit desserts, and chocolate confections.

## Chef Recipes

Throughout the book, you will find recipes contributed by celebrated chefs and well-known cookbook authors throughout the country.

The appendix is a wealth of information for anyone who must remove gluten or wheat from his or her diet.

## Warning

Since a gluten-free diet is the "prescription" for those with celiac disease, a strict caveat is in order. Given the numerous recommendations by allergists and naturopaths to eliminate wheat from the diet, it is important that the patient know the pitfalls of eliminating wheat before ruling out celiac disease. A traditional wheat-free diet does not address foods containing hidden gluten. Any gluten consumption will depress the immune system of a celiac patient.

As many allergists and naturopaths are unfamiliar with the condition, you must enlist the help of a knowledgeable gastroenterologist, who will run a simple diagnostic blood screening test. In order for test results to be accurate, only a qualified lab should run the test, and the patient should still be consuming wheat at a normal level. Many people have undermined their chances for a proper diagnosis by embarking on a wheat-free or gluten-free diet prior to testing. (Call any of the celiac organizations for lab names and recommended physicians.)

Patients with untreated celiac disease have an increased risk for developing: lupus, thyroid disease, Addison's disease, scleroderma, Grave's disease, Sjogren's syndrome, and diabetes. This is not a complete list. Please contact the Gluten Intolerance Group, Celiac Sprue Association, Canadian Celiac Association, or Celiac Disease Foundation to learn more about celiac disease, and to get all the facts from a qualified source.

# HOW TO GET STARTED

You will find it easier to begin by relying heavily on prepackaged gluten-free food, and by devoting your energies to researching brand names and availability. The multiple tasks of cooking and baking throughout the week may become overwhelming unless you plan with expediency in mind. As most people get tired of "fast food" after awhile, there is much incentive to acquire an ever-broadening repertoire of cooking skills. (Before meeting my husband, I was not much of a cook, testament that anyone can become quite proficient with the right instruction!) A big challenge with gluten-free cooking is weeding through the many recipes available and determining which are worthwhile. Recording a list of favorites will assist you in your efforts.

The right tools in the kitchen can make cooking easy and successful. Good quality cookware, knives, and a few gadgets can really save time. Many American kitchens are outfitted with thin cookware that burns food easily and knives that are dull, lightweight, and uncomfortable. In *The Cook's Bible*, Christopher Kimball gives his recommendations for basic cookware and utensils. Buy his book, or check it out from the library; it will help you buy the right equipment and teach you so much about cooking! My list of preferred kitchenware is shown in the Appendix of this book.

If fat is a concern, be aware that packaged gluten-free foods have many of the same unhealthy characteristics as the regular grocery store fare. A case in point is the addition of refined sugar as a flavor enhancer. Simple carbohydrates, unless utilized for energy, quickly turn to glucose in the bloodstream and are stored as fat. When you cook your own food, you know the exact ingredients, and can save the sugar (in small amounts) for dessert. If you balance your daily intake from the basic food groups and exercise daily, you can still eat great gluten-free sweets in moderation while maintaining your desired weight. The key word is balance. Many of the healthier flours, such as quinoa, amaranth, and brown rice flour are used in this book, and make for healthier treats than those based on white flour.

The key to cooking gluten-free is setting oneself up with all the necessary resources. This may seem like a daunting task at first, but once you are set up it is simple to maintain and you will feel like a pro! Take it slow at first so that you don't exhaust yourself—it is difficult enough to adapt to this huge change in your life, but with time and practice you will be an excellent cook!

## Pantry Basics

It is time to reorganize your pantry. This will be an ongoing process as you try the various recipes in this book. You may not have a bottle of Madeira in your cabinet right now, but the bottle you buy for a particular recipe will serve you well for a number of other dishes. Don't avoid a recipe because of a bare-bones cupboard. Buy the ingredients and expand your horizons! Review pantry basics in the Appendix, but don't rush out to buy everything right away. Take your time and add to your pantry week by week.

It is helpful to have a cabinet near your stove top to hold the variety of cooking wines, oils, vinegars, and spices you will need while cooking. A separate shelf for all the special gluten-free flours and baking ingredients is also good to have. It is, of course, advantageous to have your foodstuffs grouped together logically so that you can see when you need to restock. Keep a shopping list, categorized by source (store or mail order house), and reorder promptly, allowing for delivery time, when any given item runs low.

## Cookware and Utensils

Try to buy the best utensils and cookware you can afford. You are making an investment in your future, since celiac disease is a lifelong condition. It will represent a sizeable initial expense, but you will save money in the long run as you enjoy your own fine cooking rather than eating out or buying convenience foods. One item, the Kitchenaid mixer, stands out above all others as a recommended purchase. Gluten-free baked goods are a different beast altogether, and proper mixing of the batter or dough depends on a heavy-duty standing mixer for success.

## Where to Shop?

### Produce

If the chain groceries in your neighborhood don't have good produce, try to find a specialty grocer or farmer's market. Since the gluten-free diet is so restrictive, it pays to find a place with fresh, appetizing fruits and vegetables (frozen is a good alternative for some items). Make a point of befriending the produce person at your store, who can direct you to ingredients that you might otherwise have trouble finding. It is terribly time-consuming to shop by reading all the produce signs in search of an unfamiliar item; however, once you learn to recognize it by sight, the process will go much faster. If you have access to them, use organic fruits and vegetables; it is the way to go for long-term health.

### Mail Order

There are many good mail order sources for gluten-free food. Contact them all to discover which products you like best (some are listed in the Appendix). Since beans are a great source of nutrients for people on a gluten-free diet, and the standard grocery store line is pretty humdrum, check out specialty catalogs (or organic markets) for interesting fresh varieties.

### Specialty Food Stores = Quality and Freshness

If you are fortunate enough to have a fish market, butcher, gourmet market, or farmers market nearby, take advantage of what they have to offer. You can more readily get answers to your questions about freshness, organic growing methods, or freedom from hormones. The knowledgeable staff at these stores can also tell you whether shrimp or scallops are packed in a wheat slurry, or whether sausages and lunch meat contain gluten. Frequenting these shops also helps you avoid the additives found in lower-grade products. In order to make all the "store hopping" a bearable task, keep in mind that this is how the Europeans shop, and that you are getting the freshest, highest quality gluten-free food possible.

### Outdoor Grilling In All Seasons

It may sound crazy (and if you live somewhere with snow on the ground throughout the winter, it is crazy), but many people grill outdoors 12 months a year. In Seattle, the climate is fairly temperate, so we have an outdoor grill set up under cover and use it all year long. Many stores do not stock charcoal throughout the winter, so you may need to stock up in the fall or find a wood stove store that carries charcoal all year round. Charcoal grilling is the best by far, but there are some good gas grills to which you can add wood chips for better flavor. Try apple wood, cherry wood, alder wood, etc. for a variety of aromas.

### Plan Your Time

This is easier said than done; however, make this your number one goal and you'll be glad you did. Before you begin to cook, read each recipe you will be preparing. In this way, you can make your grocery list, determine how much time you will need, know what you can chop up in advance, and prioritize the steps involved. Try to sit down and plan three meals at a time so you don't end up at the grocery store every day. Finding the time to do this is difficult, but it makes life much easier knowing what is on the menu and having all your ducks in line. If your upcoming week is a busy one, consider spending time on the weekend making pizza crusts, soups, or sauces, and freeze them for use during the week.

Designate a day to bake bread, and make a special treat every other week for the cookie jar or the lunch box. (I find it helpful to have extra brownies frozen individually, so that if our children are invited to a birthday party, they can each take a brownie to eat while the other kids are having wheat flour cake.) Stock your kitchen with five pounds each of the types of flour you use most often, as well as an ample supply of xanthan gum.

## Mise en Place

This is a French term for having everything ready up to the point of cooking. The most time-consuming part of cooking is the chopping, grating, and other prep work that must be done prior to combining the ingredients (which is why you rarely see it demonstrated start to finish on a cooking show). Buy a variety of glass bowls, chop up everything needed for the recipe ahead of time, and place the ingredients in the bowls. By doing this you insure against last minute mistakes. If you freeze your meat, take defrosting time into consideration too. Be sure any marinade you use is made early enough so the meat has time to marinate. If you use a charcoal grill, light it in advance so that the coals are ready when you need them. These steps seem obvious, but they are easily overlooked when one is pressed for time.

Think about each recipe in the meal, and take the cooking time of each element into account so that everything is ready at the same time and nothing is overcooked. (For example, start the chicken entrée, and begin steaming the broccoli during the last ten minutes of cooking time.) It takes a bit of practice, but after cooking a meal once or twice you will begin to get the hang of it and learn to anticipate potential problems. After doing this for a while, you will be a pro at pulling together a meal quickly, and your hard work will have paid off.

## Ingredient and Resource Notes

Fresh ground pepper and sea salt are my choices, as are the fresh herbs now available in most grocery stores. It is best to choose unprocessed vegetable oils such as corn, olive, canola, walnut, sesame, sunflower, and safflower. Butter is a better choice than margarine, which is rarely used in gourmet kitchens. Organic shortening is a healthy new product that you might try instead of regular shortening, which contains artery-clogging hydrogenated oils (as does margarine). Products that may be difficult to find in the average grocery store are listed in the Appendix, along with mail order sources.

## Cookbooks and Classes

Expand your knowledge base by taking some cooking classes. Many talented chefs offer cooking classes in their restaurants. Many natural food stores offer some of the best classes around. I have even taken an excellent chocolate truffle-making class through a university extension program.

One cookbook I recommend for people with multiple sensitivities is Carol Fenster's *Special Diet Solutions*, which offers good substitution ideas for those who must avoid gluten, dairy, eggs, yeast, or refined sugar. Bette Hagman covers the subject of gluten-free bread in great detail in her book, *The Gluten-Free Gourmet Bakes Bread*. Wendy Wark has developed my favorite flour mix of all in her book, *Living Healthy with Celiac Disease*. Wendy has graciously permitted me to use several of her recipes, including her All Purpose Gluten-Free Flour Mix (found on page 181). Another indispensable resource for the novice cook is *The New Food Lover's Companion* by Sharon Tyler Herbst. The book is a comprehensive guide of over 4000 food, wine and culinary terms published by Barron's. I have found this volume to be as fascinating as it is informative.

*Cook's Illustrated* magazine is a great monthly resource. There are no advertisements, just page after page of great cooking ideas and "how to" tips.

### Eating Out

If you enjoy fine dining, you will likely find a chef willing to cook gluten-free once you explain the diet to him or her during an off-peak period. However, be aware that most short order restaurant cooks cannot avoid hidden gluten, since much of the food they use is prepackaged and frozen. Even a simple hamburger may have been bought as a frozen patty with fillers (a common purchasing specification in many such restaurants). Also, short order cooks are usually in a hurry, and may overlook cross-contamination potential on preparation and cooking surfaces. As a family, we find it easier, less expensive, and safer to cook gluten-free at home most of the time. Since both of our children are still young, and it is imperative to keep their gluten intake as close to zero as possible, I am able to ensure their health through knowledge of every ingredient used in making their dinner.

Over the years, I have made note of the problems most people have with gluten-free cooking, and have attempted to resolve them in this book. Here's hoping it addresses your own challenges, either potential or actual, and that you find it both helpful and easy to use.

# BREAKFAST

# Granola Cereal

This granola is lighter and fresher than others we have tried. It is a good cereal or yogurt topping. A small food processor makes grinding the nuts and seeds effortless.

## ingredients:

2 cups unsweetened coconut

1 cup chopped or coarsely ground walnuts
   or almonds

⅔ cup chopped or coarsely ground
   pumpkin seeds or sunflower kernels

2 cups coarsely ground soy nuts

2 tablespoons flax seed,
   finely ground (optional)

2 cups gluten-free brown rice crisp cereal
   (see Sources)

½ cup honey

2 teaspoons vanilla

½ cup vegetable oil

## comment:

Nuts contain high-quality fats that are especially beneficial for active children and adults. 90 percent of the fat in nuts is unsaturated fat, which is heart-healthy and can lower LDL (bad) cholesterol. Nuts and seeds are rich sources of protein, fiber, B vitamins, calcium, minerals, and Vitamin E.

## makes 8 cups

Preheat oven to 225°F. Lightly oil two large jelly roll pans (12½ x 17½-inch) with a bit of vegetable oil.

Combine coconut, walnuts, pumpkin seeds, soy nuts, flax seed, and cereal in a medium bowl. In a small saucepan mix honey, vanilla, and oil. Bring to a boil, stirring constantly. Quickly remove from heat when mixture begins to bubble. Pour honey mixture over granola and stir until thoroughly moistened. Spread mixture in an even layer on prepared pans. Bake for 1½ hours, stirring every 30 minutes.

# Granola Bars

Make the granola one day and granola bars the next day for a freezer full of quick snacks.

## ingredients:

8 cups granola (page 16)

¾ cup semi-sweet chocolate chips

1 cup chopped dried dates, figs, raisins,
   or cranberries

1½ cups peanut butter or almond butter

1¼ cups dark corn syrup

## comment:

Soy nuts are a great way to add the benefits of soy into your diet. Flax seed provides calcium, iron, niacin, phosphorous, and vitamin E, as well as omega-3 fatty acids. Both soy and flax seed are rich in phytoestrogens (plant hormones) that appear to decrease menopausal symptoms, lower cholesterol, increase bone density, and protect against cancer. Be sure to refrigerate or freeze flax seed, and only grind enough for what you plan to use each day.

## makes 45-50 granola bars

In a large bowl, mix granola with chocolate chips and dried fruit. Heat peanut butter and corn syrup over low heat in a medium saucepan, stirring occasionally, until texture is smooth and consistency becomes thinner. Equally divide granola mix into two large bowls. Pour ½ peanut butter syrup over one bowl of granola, stirring well. Repeat this step with second bowl of granola mix and remaining peanut butter syrup. With your hand in a plastic bag, spread mixture evenly ¾-inch thick into a lightly oiled 12 ½ x 17 ½-inch jelly roll pan. Refrigerate for an hour, then cut into bars. Wrap and freeze individual bars for quick on-the-go snacks. If you include flax seed, granola bars should be refrigerated or frozen.

## variations:

If you decide to omit the chocolate chips, add ¼ cup each of peanut butter and corn syrup to the mixture.

Gluten-free brown rice syrup is a good substitution for corn syrup; you may also try a concentrated fruit juice sweetener.

# Fruit Smoothies

For breakfast on the run, get the day started with a quick, healthy smoothie.

## ingredients:

1 banana, peeled

½ cup berries, frozen or fresh

½ cup orange juice or other juice

⅓ cup plain yogurt or silken tofu

1 tablespoon maple syrup or honey

1 teaspoon flax seed, freshly ground
   (optional)

Protein powder to taste (optional)

## makes 12 ounces

Place all ingredients in a blender. Blend on high speed until smooth.

# Smoked Salmon Potato Pancakes with Dill Yogurt Cheese

A nice addition to a Sunday brunch, this recipe also makes a great appetizer.

### ingredients:

*One recipe of Dill Yogurt Cheese (page 27)*

*One recipe of Potato Pancakes (page 144)*

*4 ounces thinly sliced smoked salmon*
*(such as lox)*

*2 tablespoons capers in distilled vinegar,*
*drained*

### 4 servings

To serve, spread 1-2 tablespoons cheese mixture on each potato pancake. Top with a slice of smoked salmon and a few capers.

# Pancakes and Waffles

Pure maple syrup, warmed and poured over a stack of pancakes, is a weekend indulgence!
Try sprinkling raisins, dried cherries, cranberries, fresh blueberries, or thin slices of a tart, juicy apple onto pancake batter while it cooks to add variety.
This recipe is adapted from Wendy Wark's *Living Healthy with Celiac Disease* (AnAffect 1998). Use the same recipe for waffles.

## ingredients:

1 cup buckwheat flour

1 cup Wendy Wark's gluten-free flour
   mix (page 181)

½ teaspoon salt

1 teaspoon cream of tartar

½ teaspoon baking soda

2 teaspoons baking powder

¼ cup sugar

½ cup melted butter or vegetable oil

3 eggs

1½ cups milk

## 4 servings

Heat a non-stick griddle or a heavy-bottomed frying pan to 350°-375°F.

Whisk together flours, salt, cream of tartar, baking soda, baking powder, sugar, butter, and eggs in a medium bowl. Stir just enough to dampen the batter, do not overbeat. Cautiously add milk until you reach desired consistency. (You may not need all the milk.) Pour ¼ cup of batter onto the cooking surface. Cook until the pancake is full of bubbles on top and the underside is lightly browned, then flip with a spatula and cook the other side until it is lightly browned. Remove from griddle or pan and set aside on a warm plate while cooking the remaining pancakes. Serve with warm maple syrup.

*Note: The amount of milk determines the thickness of these pancakes.*

# French Toast

## ingredients:

3 eggs

½ cup milk

¼ teaspoon each of cinnamon and nutmeg

8 slices day old gluten-free bread

½ cup pure maple syrup, warmed

## 4 servings (two slices per serving)

Heat a non-stick griddle to 350°-375°F.

Whisk together eggs, milk, and cinnamon in a bowl large enough to lay a slice of bread flat. Dip both sides of bread into egg mixture, coating completely. Place on griddle and cook until browned on both sides. Repeat with each slice of bread, keeping cooked slices warm in a 200°F. oven. Serve with warm maple syrup.

## variation:

Top each slice with a ½ tablespoon of roasted tahini. Tahini is a creamy paste made from hulled sesame seeds, and it adds a nice dimension to French toast.

# Cinnamon Rolls

Every now and then you must treat yourself to a cinnamon roll! Packing them tightly into a baking dish helps to keep them moist throughout. Adapted from Wendy Wark's *Living Healthy with Celiac Disease* (AnAffect, 1998).

## ingredients:

1 recipe Workable Wonder Dough (page 169)

3 tablespoons butter, melted

⅔ cup brown sugar

3 tablespoons ground cinnamon

½ cup raisins

1 ⅓ cups confectioners' sugar

3-4 tablespoons milk

## makes nine 2-inch rolls

Butter an 8-inch round cake pan.

Roll out dough to a 9 x 18-inch rectangle, approximately ½-inch in thickness. Brush dough with 3 tablespoons melted butter. Sprinkle sugar, cinnamon, and raisins evenly over the dough. Beginning at one of the 9-inch sides, roll dough into a log shape. Using a sharp, clean knife, cut log into 9 equal pieces. Arrange rolls in prepared pan, packing tightly together and keeping the swirl side up. Cover with a warm, wet towel and let rise one hour. Bake at 400°F. for 15-20 minutes. While cinnamon rolls are baking, whisk together confectioners' sugar and milk in a small bowl. Drizzle mixture over hot, baked cinnamon rolls.

# Old Fashioned Cake Donuts

A special treat! Serve donuts with a dusting of powdered sugar or a Chocolate Glaze (page 198).

## ingredients:

1 egg, lightly beaten

½ cup milk

½ cup sugar

2 teaspoons baking powder

¼ teaspoon nutmeg

½ teaspoon salt

1 tablespoon butter, melted

1¾-2 cups Wendy Wark's gluten-free
   flour mix* (page 181)

¾ teaspoon xanthan gum

Vegetable oil for frying

Confectioners' sugar or Chocolate Glaze

*Amount of flour needed depends on humidity

## makes twelve 3-inch donuts

Mix egg, milk, sugar, baking powder, nutmeg, salt, and butter in a medium bowl. Combine flour and xanthan gum in a small bowl. Add flour mix until just incorporated. The dough will be very soft. Cover and refrigerate for one hour.

On a lightly floured surface, gradually work additional flour into the dough until it is no longer sticky. Roll out to ½-inch thickness and cut out 3-inch rounds with a well-floured cookie cutter or a knife. Cut out a 1-inch hole from the middle of each and save to make donut holes. Place donuts and donut holes on a sheet of wax paper on a baking sheet. Allow to air-dry for 10 minutes to help reduce oil absorption while frying. In a heavy-bottomed pan or a deep fryer, heat 3-4 inches of vegetable oil to 360°F. Fry 2-3 donuts at a time, turning once to brown on both sides, for about 6 minutes. Drain on paper toweling. Dust with confectioners' sugar or glaze with chocolate before serving.

Notes: You may substitute cocoa for ¹/2 cup of the flour mix to make chocolate donuts. Feel free to experiment with other flavors by adding spices or by mixing in lemon or orange zest.
All ingredients should be room temperature.

# APPETIZERS

# Hummus

This recipe is from Cynthia Lair's *Feeding the Whole Family* (Moon Smile Press, 1997), which offers wonderful whole foods recipes for babies, young children, and their parents. Cynthia's book is a great way to start cooking with healthy, tasty ingredients that you may not have tried before, such as sea vegetables, various beans, and soy products. This recipe is very quick if you have a pressure cooker. I have recently purchased one of the new, safer pressure cookers from Kuhn Rikon, and it is wonderful. Canned beans can replace chickpeas as a variation on the theme.

## ingredients:

2 cups cooked chickpeas (garbanzo beans)

5 tablespoons tahini

½ tablespoon sea salt

⅓ cup freshly squeezed lemon juice
    (juice of 1½-2 lemons)

2-3 cloves garlic

3 tablespoons extra virgin olive oil

¼ cup (approximately) cooking liquid from
    beans (or water)

Chopped parsley (optional)

Paprika (optional)

## makes 2¾-3 cups

Place cooked chickpeas in food processor or blender with tahini, salt, lemon juice, garlic, and olive oil. Blend until smooth. Add cooking liquid from beans or water to desired consistency. Garnish with chopped parsley or paprika if desired. Stores well, refrigerated, for at least a week.

### For babies 10 months and older

Reserve some plain cooked chickpeas and mash. Some may enjoy picking up and eating plain cooked chickpeas; be sure they are well cooked.

## variation for children

Hummus may be too spicy; try reducing lemon juice and garlic by half.

*Comment: Hummus is a traditional Middle Eastern dish that is great as either a dip or a sandwich spread. The combination of chickpeas and tahini adds up to a high-protein formula. (Tahini is a creamy paste made from hulled sesame seeds.)*

# Mexican Salsa

This salsa is among the most popular in Mexico, and it combines cooked and uncooked ingredients, resulting in a more complex flavor.

## ingredients:

2 cups water

3 jalapeños, stemmed

2 plum tomatoes

2 medium tomatillos, husks removed and
   sticky exterior washed

2 small onions, peeled and quartered

6 cloves garlic

½ teaspoon salt

15 sprigs fresh cilantro, chopped

## makes 2 cups

Bring water to a boil in a medium saucepan. Add 2 whole jalapeños, tomatoes, tomatillos, 1 onion, and 4 cloves garlic. Boil for 15 minutes, remove from heat, and let cool a bit.

In the bowl of a food processor, place 1 halved jalapeño, 2 quartered garlic cloves, 1 onion, and salt. Chop coarsely. Add chopped cilantro and gradually add cooked vegetables to the fresh mixture in the food processor and blend. Add a little cooking water if necessary to thin the sauce.

# Cheese Board

An array of cheese, pears, apples, figs, and dates can serve as either an appetizer or as a course to precede dessert. It is both fun and easy to put together. When tasting, try different combinations (such as blue cheese with pears and dates, a wonderful harmonization of flavors).

## ingredients:

1 pound of assorted cheeses, such as pecorino
   (an Italian sheep's milk cheese),
   Camembert, Brie, and blue cheese
6-7 dried figs or dates, quartered
3-4 fresh pears, cored and sliced
   (choose from D'Anjou, Bartlett, or Bosc)
10 ounces rice crackers

## 6 servings

Arrange cheese, dried figs or dates, and pears on a wooden cutting board and serve.

## variation:

Tart apples make a nice substitution for the pears.

## wine suggestion:    Italian Pinot Grigio

# Artichoke Pesto

A tasty dip with crackers.

## ingredients:

1 can (13 ounces) whole artichoke hearts
(drained, with 3 tablespoons liquid reserved)

½ cup grated Parmesan cheese

Juice from 1 lemon

1 small garlic clove, passed through a
garlic press or minced

2 tablespoons olive oil

## makes 1 ¼ cups

Combine artichoke hearts, reserved liquid from artichokes, Parmesan, lemon juice, and garlic in the bowl of a small food processor. Pulse on high for a minute, then slowly drizzle in olive oil while machine is running until well incorporated.

# Dill Yogurt Cheese

A good low-fat substitute for sour cream or cream cheese. This recipe combines it with sour cream for a tangier flavor.

## ingredients:

8 ounces non-fat plain, gluten-free yogurt,
drained of liquid (see Note)

½ cup gluten-free sour cream

¼ cup chopped fresh dill

## makes 1 ½ cups

Combine drained yogurt with sour cream and dill. Mix well.

Note: Once the liquid is drained from yogurt it becomes yogurt cheese. Donvier makes a yogurt strainer that is easy to use. Simply place the yogurt in the mesh basket, cover, and refrigerate. The liquid will drain out in about 2 hours. You can fashion your own strainer by suspending a mesh sieve over a bowl.

# Baked Cheese Wafers

This recipe is adapted from the *Pasta & Co. By Request* cookbook by Marcella Rosene (Pasta & Co., 1991). Pasta & Co. is Seattle's premier, upscale take-out food shop with five locations.

### ingredients:

6 ounces Monterey jack cheese,
    cut into sixteen ¼-inch slices
1 heaping teaspoon Pasta & Co. House
    Herbs or herbes de Provence

### makes 16 wafers

Preheat oven to 400°F.

Arrange 8 cheese slices with plenty of space in between on a non-stick baking sheet. Sprinkle with herbs. Bake exactly 10 minutes. Lift each cheese wafer onto a cooling rack covered with paper towels. Repeat process with remaining 8 slices.

*Note: Herbes de Provence is found in the spice section in large grocery stores. It includes basil, fennel, lavender, marjoram, rosemary, sage, summer savory, and thyme, all of which are commonly used in southern France.*

# Roasted Pumpkin Seeds

Pumpkin seeds, also known as pepitas, are popular in Mexican cooking. Sprinkle roasted pumpkin seeds over salads, use as a garnish, or eat as a healthy snack. Stores that offer organic produce often sell pumpkin seeds in bulk.

### ingredients:

Olive oil
1-2 cups pumpkin seeds, raw and unsalted

### makes 1-2 cups

Preheat oven to 250°F.

Lightly coat or spray a large jelly roll pan or baking sheet with oil. Scatter pumpkin seeds evenly over the pan and season with salt. Bake for 1-2 hours (the latter makes for a crunchier result). Cool and store in an airtight container.

# Tapenade

Marian Robertson introduced this tapenade to our family, and we are grateful! All ingredients can be kept on hand for last minute preparation.

## ingredients:

1 jar (7 ounces) roasted red peppers,
    drained
1 can (6 ounces) whole artichokes,
    drained and quartered
½ cup fresh parsley, large stem removed
½ cup grated Parmesan

¼ cup olive oil
3 cloves garlic, finely chopped or
    passed through a garlic press
1 tablespoon lemon juice
¼ cup gluten-free capers, drained

## makes 2 cups

Place all ingredients in a food processor. Mix until well blended. Serve on gluten-free crackers or bread.

## wine suggestion:    Italian Dolcetto d'Alba

# Channa Dal Spread

Debra Daniels-Zeller teaches a Bean Cuisine cooking class at our local natural foods market, PCC Natural Markets.
Her class is a wealth of information on beans and cooking how-to. Beans provide many of the nutrients that people on a gluten-free diet may lack.
They are high in protein, low in fat, and are good sources of calcium, iron, B vitamins, niacin, and zinc. They are also rich in soluble fiber.
A special benefit for diabetics is the gradual release of the glucose in beans into the bloodstream, which helps stabilize sugar levels.

## ingredients:

1 cup channa dal, soaked overnight

1 strip kombu, cut into small pieces

4 cups water

3 tablespoons chopped sun-dried tomatoes

½ cup hot water or water used for
   cooking beans

½ tablespoon olive oil

1 medium onion, chopped

2 jalapeños, seeded and minced

2 cloves garlic, minced

2 teaspoons chili powder

½ teaspoon cumin

Generous dash of cayenne (optional)

Salt to taste

⅓ cup chopped cilantro

## makes 3 cups

Place soaked beans, kombu, and water in a soup pot. Bring to a boil, then reduce heat. Cover and simmer for 45 minutes, or until beans are very tender.

While beans are cooking, soak sun-dried tomatoes in hot water until softened.

Heat a heavy skillet over medium heat. Add olive oil, onion, and jalapeños. Stir briefly, then reduce heat, cover, and cook until onions are soft. Add garlic, chili powder, cumin, and cayenne if desired. Continue to cook until vegetables are very soft.

When beans have finished cooking, drain, reserving liquid. Puree beans and jalapeño mixture in a food processor or blender with the sun-dried tomatoes (using more of the bean cooking liquid if needed) until it forms a smooth paste. Season to taste with salt and pepper. Pulse in chopped cilantro at the end.

Spoon into a serving bowl. It can be used as a spread, or you can add a bit more water and make a dip.

## wine suggestion:   California Sauvignon Blanc

*Comment: You will find this nutty spread to be downright delicious. Channa dal beans are hulled and split baby garbanzo beans. They can be found in natural food markets, specialty food stores, and through mail order houses (see Sources). Garbanzo, red, or pinto beans are possible substitutes, but the flavor will not be the same.*

# Spicy Shrimp Skewers

Our neighbor, Bill Bassett, likes to cook, and comes up with interesting creations all the time.
He made this one night as an appetizer to accompany my Lopez Taquitos (page 50). They were great together!

### ingredients:

1 pound medium shrimp, shelled, rinsed,
   and deveined

1½ tablespoons cumin (or less to taste)

1 medium jalapeño, stemmed and
   finely chopped

2-3 tablespoons olive oil

1 lime, cut in half

### 6 servings

Prepare an outdoor grill. Thread shrimp onto bamboo skewers. In a small bowl, combine cumin, jalapeño, and olive oil. Brush shrimp skewers with seasoning mixture. When coals are hot, sprinkle skewers with salt and pepper and arrange in an even layer on the grill. Cook shrimp until just opaque in the center, squeezing the juice of half a lime over each side while grilling. Serve immediately.

### wine suggestion:   French Chablis

# Peach Salsa

This is an unusual yet tasty salsa for chips. It would be fun and interesting over halibut as well.

### ingredients:

4 Italian plum tomatoes, cut into ¼-inch dice

1 cup (¼-inch dice) fresh, peeled peaches

½ cup finely diced red onion

16 large basil leaves, finely chopped

4 teaspoons balsamic vinegar

¼ cup extra-virgin olive oil

### makes 2 cups

Combine tomatoes, peaches, onion, basil, balsamic vinegar, and olive oil in a large bowl. Season with salt and pepper. Serve.

### wine suggestion:   French Sancerre

# Tomatillo Salsa

A salsa to serve as an appetizer or as an accompaniment to an omelet. When buying tomatillos, look for firm fruit with tight fitting husks. If the fruit has started to shrink in the husk, it is aging. Tomatillos are available year round; however, the smaller fruit found during the winter months will necessitate buying ten or eleven for this recipe.

## ingredients:

*7 medium tomatillos, husks removed and*
*   sticky exterior washed*
*Salt and freshly ground pepper*
*½ cup chopped parsley or cilantro*
*¼ cup olive oil*
*1 tablespoon lime juice*
*2-3 tablespoons diced sweet onion*
*Half of a medium cucumber, diced*
*1 medium avocado, diced*

## makes 2 cups

In the bowl of a small food processor, puree 3 tomatillos with salt, pepper, and parsley. Slowly add olive oil. Chop the remaining tomatillos and toss with the lime juice, onion, cucumber, and tomatillo puree. Add the avocado and gently mix. The salsa can be used right away, or covered and refrigerated for about one hour.

# SPRING

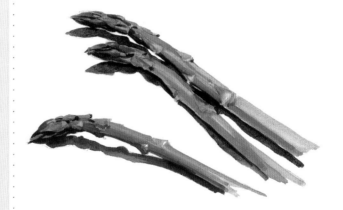

🕐 – indicates a quick meal

# Chiles Rellenos with Mango Salsa

This is a great meatless meal, with flavors that go wonderfully together. Make a large batch to guarantee leftovers for lunch the next day. Serve with black beans for a nice color contrast, or with refried beans.

## ingredients:

### mango salsa

2 cups peeled, chopped mango
   (about 2 whole mangoes)
½ cup chopped red onion
1 cup chopped red bell pepper
3-4 tablespoons finely chopped fresh cilantro
3 tablespoons lime juice

### chiles

9 ounces Monterey Jack cheese, grated
12 ounces mozzarella cheese, grated
7 ounces feta cheese, crumbled
8 poblano or Anaheim chiles, or
   4 cans (7 ounces each) whole green chiles

## 4 servings (two per person)

For Mango Salsa: Mix all ingredients in a nonreactive bowl. Cover and refrigerate.

Preheat oven to 400°F.

Combine cheeses in a medium bowl and mix well.

Roasting Fresh Chiles: To prepare, char peppers under the broiler, turning periodically to blacken on all sides. Transfer peppers to a paper bag and seal. When peppers are cool, remove the blackened skins, which will come off easily.

Cut a slit in each chile and remove seeds and membranes. Fill each chile with a handful of cheese mixture. Place chiles on a baking sheet and top with remaining cheese mixture. Bake until cheese melts and chiles are heated through (about 5 minutes). Transfer chiles to plates and spoon salsa over each.

**wine suggestion:**    California Sauvignon Blanc

*Note: The poblano chile is a dark green to black variety; its flavor is somewhat earthy rather than spicy. Peak season is summer to early fall, although many markets sell them year round. Anaheims are lighter green and milder in flavor.*

*Variation for Children:* # Quesadillas

### *4 servings*

Substitute 8 corn tortillas for the chiles in the recipe on the preceding page.

Place four corn tortillas on a non-stick baking sheet, cover with cheese mixture, and place another tortilla on top of each. Sprinkle with more of the cheese mixture and cook as directed for chiles rellenos. Cut each tortilla into six equal wedge-shaped pieces.

*If you are not familiar with mangoes, they can be quite difficult to work with, thanks to the large, flat seed inside. Sunfresh brand mangoes are a good alternative to fresh mangoes; they are sliced and vacuum packed in jars, and are usually found in the refrigerated section of grocery stores near the produce. Fresh mangoes in season (around midsummer) are wonderful. Look for skin that is either orange or red with a little green. Fruit should be soft and unblemished. Large mangoes are better, since they yield a greater proportion of fruit. To prepare, first peel the fruit, then score the outside all the way around. With the knife tip, slice off the mango squares, cutting through until you feel resistance from the seed.*

# Fried Rice with Cashews and Snow Peas

A quick meal that is satisfying. Serve with Miso Soup (page 89) or as a one-dish meal.

## ingredients:

¾ cup cashews

4 servings of cooked rice

2 eggs

¼ teaspoon salt

2 tablespoons peanut oil

3 scallions, chopped

1 pound chicken or pork tenderloin, sliced
    ¼-inch thick in 1-inch pieces

½ teaspoon minced fresh ginger or
    ginger juice (see Sources)

1 teaspoon toasted sesame oil

1 cup snow peas, stringed, or
    frozen green peas

2 tablespoons gluten-free tamari or gluten-
    free soy sauce

## 4 servings

Preheat oven to 325°F.

Spread cashews out on a baking sheet. Bake for 5-10 minutes until light golden in color. Watch carefully to avoid burning.

Have cooked rice ready before starting. Beat eggs with salt in a small bowl. Heat 1 tablespoon of peanut oil in a large skillet or wok. Add scallions and eggs and stir-fry until set. Remove from pan and set aside. Heat another tablespoon of oil. Add meat and briefly cook over high heat. Add ginger, sesame oil, peas, and cashews. Stir-fry for 2 minutes. Stir in tamari, eggs, and rice, mixing together gently to combine ingredients. Heat through and serve.

## variations:

Carrots, asparagus, or green beans can be added or used in place of the peas.

Tofu is a good substitution for chicken or pork. Frozen tofu provides the best texture for this dish. Be sure to thaw tofu completely. Drain tofu by placing it on a plate, resting another plate on top, and setting a 1-pound weight atop the second plate. After 10 minutes or so discard excess water. Chop tofu into ½-inch cubes, substitute for the meat in the recipe.

# Spinach Chèvre Pasta with Marinara Sauce

This comforting entrée features a wonderfully light, low-fat creamy marinara sauce with spinach. The sauce is adapted from a recipe in Marcella Rosene's *Pasta & Co. By Request* cookbook (Pasta & Co., 1991). Pasta & Co. is Seattle's premier upscale take-out food shop with five locations. They have also begun to stock gluten-free pasta.

## ingredients:

### Marinara Sauce

3 tablespoons olive oil

1 teaspoon red pepper flakes or dash of chili oil

3 cloves of garlic, finely chopped or passed
   through a garlic press

2 cups dry white wine

2 cans (28 ounces each) high quality
   crushed tomatoes

2 ounces tomato paste

½ teaspoon salt

Black pepper to taste

2-3 tablespoons fresh basil

2-3 tablespoons fresh oregano


1 pound gluten-free penne pasta
   (Tinkyada or Bi-Aglut is best)

2 ounces fresh spinach, washed and dried

5 ounces soft creamy goat cheese (chèvre)

## 4 servings

Heat olive oil in a medium saucepan over moderate heat. Add red pepper flakes and garlic. Cook for one minute, stirring frequently and being careful not to brown the garlic. Add wine and simmer for 10 minutes until reduced by half. Add tomatoes and tomato paste, cover, and simmer on low heat for 20 minutes, stirring occasionally. Taste sauce for seasoning, adding salt, pepper, and sugar as needed. Add fresh herbs. Simmer a few minutes longer.

Prepare pasta according to package directions. Place cooked pasta on a dinner plate, top with a handful of fresh spinach, ladle marinara sauce on top of spinach (the heat from the sauce and pasta will lightly wilt the spinach), and top with goat cheese. Serve immediately.

## wine suggestion:   Italian Pinot Bianco


*Marinara Sauce: This flavorful sauce can be easily made with 10 minutes of preparation time and 30 minutes of cooking time. If you like a lighter sauce, omit the tomato paste. The sauce will keep frozen for several months; you can make several double batches and freeze for future use.*

# Pan-Fried Chicken with Leeks

A very quick meal with a nice twist to the typical chicken dinner. Serve with Master Recipe for Long Grain White Rice (page 151), it is the best method I've discovered for cooking rice perfectly every time. To keep things simple, the vegetable accompaniment consists of thick slices of ripe, juicy tomato.

## ingredients:

*3 large leeks*

*1 tablespoon olive oil*

*2 cloves garlic, finely minced or*
  *passed through a garlic press*

*1 whole boneless, skinless chicken breast,*
  *cut into 2-inch strips*

*3-4 boneless, skinless chicken thighs,*
  *cut into 2-inch strips*

*½-¾ cup gluten-free chicken stock*

*¼ cup cream*

## 4 servings

Rinse leeks well and cut off the root ends. Slice white part diagonally into ¾-inch pieces.

Heat oil in a large skillet over low heat. Add garlic and leeks. Cook, stirring occasionally, until leeks are softened. Remove from skillet and set aside. Increase heat to high. Add chicken to skillet and cook, stirring, until lightly browned. Add chicken stock and reduce by half. Add cream. Season with salt and pepper. Scrape the browned bits from the bottom of the skillet, using a wooden spoon, and stir until cream is well incorporated. Serve over rice.

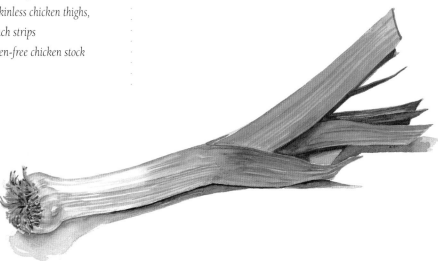

# Savory Crustless Tart with Artichokes and Bacon

Be sure to save stale gluten-free bread to make bread crumbs for this recipe. Serve with either Basil Spinach Salad (page 121) or Apple Sauté (page 135). Recipe adapted from *Breakfast in Bed*, Carol Frieberg (Sasquatch Books, 1990).

## ingredients:

8 slices bacon

½ medium onion, chopped

1 can (13 ounces) of whole artichoke hearts, chopped (plus ¼ can reserved liquid)

6 eggs, slightly beaten

⅓ cup grated Parmesan cheese

⅓ cup gluten-free bread crumbs

Grated Monterey Jack cheese

Chopped chives or parsley for garnish

## 4 servings

Preheat oven to 325°F.

Butter a 9-inch quiche or pie plate.

Cook bacon over low heat until crisp in a medium skillet. Remove from pan and drain on paper toweling. Remove all but 2 tablespoons of bacon fat from skillet. When bacon cools, crumble into small pieces.

Cook onion in bacon fat over low heat, stirring occasionally, until translucent. Add artichokes and reserved artichoke liquid. Heat for 2 minutes, stirring and scraping skillet with a wooden spoon to deglaze. In a large bowl, lightly beat eggs; add Parmesan cheese, bread crumbs, artichoke mixture, and bacon. Mix well and place in prepared dish. Bake for 25 minutes, or until just set. Sprinkle top with grated cheese and bake for 5 minutes more. Garnish with chopped chives or parsley.

# Northwest Paella

### Chef Barbara Figueroa — Seattle, Washington

Barbara Figueroa is a former executive chef and restaurateur who has spent her career in such kitchens as Spago, Le Cirque, and the Sorrento Hotel. She is currently the director of food and beverage at the Warwick Hotel, and has been a contributor to various publications as well as the editor of this book.

## ingredients:

3 tablespoons olive oil

2 medium onions, diced

2 large red bell peppers, diced

3 pounds chicken thighs

3 cloves garlic, minced

1½ pounds rice, preferably basmati or Texmati

1 quart (generous) rich gluten-free chicken stock
   (about 20 ounces)

2 cups canned plum tomatoes
   (seeded and coarsely chopped),
   plus 1½ cups of their juice, strained

1 pound gluten-free chorizo, cut in ½-inch rounds
   (may substitute with gluten-free spicy sausage)

½ teaspoon saffron

2-3 bay leaves

4 pounds assorted seafood (prawns, mussels,
   clams, squid, cubes of salmon or halibut fillet,
   crab or whatever is seasonally available), cleaned

1½ pounds snow peas or sugar snaps, stringed
   (snow peas may be cut in half diagonally)

¼ cup (rounded) chopped Italian parsley

Additional sprigs of Italian parsley for garnish

## chef's comments:

*A one-dish perennial favorite of both young and old. The flavors marry well over a few days' time, lending the recipe to "big batch" production.*

## 12 servings

Heat olive oil in a large heavy pot over moderate flame. Add onions and peppers. Sauté until onions barely begin to soften. Add chicken thighs and garlic. Cook until chicken is seared on all sides. Add rice. Lower heat. Cook, stirring, over moderate low heat, until grains take on a translucent appearance. Add 1 quart of the stock, tomatoes, and tomato juice. Bring to a boil. Add chorizo, saffron, and bay leaves. Reduce heat to low. Cover and simmer, stirring occasionally, until rice is barely cooked. Season with salt and pepper. Immediately turn out onto a flat pan to cool.

Cook peas until crisp-tender in boiling salted water. Drain and shock in ice water. Drain again thoroughly.

To serve, reheat rice mixture in a moderate (about 350°F.) oven, covered with foil. When rice is reheated, bring remaining stock to a simmer. Add seafood, cover, and steam until done, removing pieces as they finish cooking. Toss seafood (and its steaming liquid, which should be minimal), peas, and parsley with rice mixture. Garnish with parsley sprigs.

## wine suggestion:

A white Rioja is a classic with this dish, but you might want to try a French Sauvignon Blanc from the Loire Valley, or a northern Italian Pinot Grigio.

# Dungeness Crab Caesar Salad

This is one of the few recipes that include a store-bought salad dressing. I prefer to make my own dressings, however, the best Caesar dressings made at home include a raw or briefly cooked egg. With young children in the house, I am hesitant to serve egg in this manner. One of the chef contributors to this book is Ludger Szmania. His bottled Caesar Salad Dressing is superior to any others we have tried. Distribution in stores is limited to the Northwest (see Sources). Annie's Caesar Dressing is a good alternative and is available through Mrs. Roben's catalog (see Sources) and in many natural food stores.

## ingredients:

4 large slices gluten-free bread, cubed

1 head romaine lettuce, washed and dried

Szmania's Caesar Salad Dressing

Parmesan cheese, grated

½ pound fresh Dungeness crab meat,
   picked over to remove bits of shell

## 4 servings

Preheat oven to 400°F.

Spread cubed bread in an even layer on a large baking sheet. Bake for 10 minutes until croutons are crispy.

Tear romaine into bite-sized pieces and transfer to a large salad bowl. Toss dressing with romaine until well coated. Add croutons and Parmesan and toss again. Serve salad on individual plates and top with fresh crab. Season with salt and pepper to taste.

## wine suggestion:   Alsatian Pinot Blanc

*Note: An alternative to baking the bread cubes is to sauté them in butter in a skillet. I have tried both methods, and baking the croutons produces a crispier crouton that also takes the flavor of the Caesar dressing better.*

# Pacific Rim Flank Steak

An easy marinade to tenderize and flavor a tougher cut of meat. If you plan to serve this on a weeknight be sure to marinate the meat early in the day. (It takes only about five minutes to put the marinade together.) When serving, cut thin slices across the grain of the meat for a more tender result. Serve with Fresh Artichokes (page 138) and Tinkyada fettuccine. Toss each pound of pasta with 4-5 tablespoons of Homemade Pesto (page 69), or with butter and Parmesan cheese.

## ingredients:

1½–2 pounds flank steak

### Marinade:

¾ cup vegetable oil

¼ cup gluten-free tamari or
gluten-free soy sauce

3 tablespoons honey

2 tablespoons red wine vinegar

1 clove garlic, finely minced or
passed through a garlic press

One 1-inch piece of ginger, minced

## 4 servings

Place flank steak in a nonreactive dish. Combine all marinade ingredients and pour marinade over the meat. Cover and refrigerate for at least 5 hours, turning meat several times.

Preheat grill.

Cook flank steak two inches above hot coals, 4-5 minutes on each side. (You may also broil it for about the same amount of time.)

## wine suggestion:   Washington Merlot

*Note: Hot coal test: you will be able to hold your hand above the grate for only 2 seconds.*

# Chicken Fajitas with Sweet Peppers

A fairly quick meal; once you make the tortillas a few times the process will be faster. While the chicken is marinating, you can slice the onions and peppers and make the tortillas in about 15 minutes. Serve fajitas with Homemade Refried Beans (page 153) for a more complete meal.

## ingredients:

1½ pounds boneless, skinless chicken breast,
   cut into thin 2-inch strips
⅓ cup olive oil or cilantro oil
   (found in gourmet markets)
⅓ cup chopped fresh cilantro
Juice of one lime
1½ tablespoons ground cumin
4 cloves garlic, finely chopped or
   passed through a garlic press
1 recipe of Homemade Tortillas (page 167)
⅓ cup sliced onions
1½ cups sliced assorted sweet peppers

## 4 servings

In a nonreactive medium bowl, combine chicken, oil, cilantro, lime juice, cumin, and garlic. Refrigerate.

Prepare flour tortillas (see recipe).

While tortillas are being held in the oven, heat a large skillet. Remove chicken from marinade and stir-fry until cooked through. Add sweet peppers and onions, seasoning with salt and pepper. Serve in warm tortillas with your favorite salsa and sour cream. (NOTE: If you prefer to grill the chicken, simply sauté the peppers and onions in a small amount of olive oil. When chicken is cooked through, slice into 2-inch strips and serve.)

## wine suggestion:   French Côtes du Rhône

# Braised Tuna with Ginger and Soy

## Chef Christopher Kimball

Founder, editor, and publisher of *Cook's Illustrated* magazine.* Author of *The Cook's Bible* and *The Yellow Farmhouse Cookbook*
Recipe adapted from *The Cook's Bible* (Little Brown, 1996)

### ingredients:

5 tablespoons rice wine vinegar

⅓ cup tamari (gluten-free soy sauce)

⅓ cup white wine

⅛ teaspoon ground cardamom

½ teaspoon sugar

3 tablespoons peanut oil

4 fresh tuna steaks

1 small onion, diced

1 tablespoon peeled and minced gingerroot

3 cloves garlic, minced

2 teaspoons toasted sesame oil (see Sources)

2 scallions, diced

### chef's comments:

*Roasted (or toasted) sesame oil is available in health food stores. It has a great deal more flavor than regular sesame oil, which should not be substituted in this recipe. If you cannot find it, simply omit it from the recipe. Serve with Master Recipe for Long Grain White Rice (page 151).*

### 4 servings

Preheat oven to 375°F.

Combine vinegar, tamari, wine, cardamom, and sugar in a small bowl. Put 2 tablespoons peanut oil into a Dutch oven or flameproof casserole dish over medium-high heat. When oil is hot, add tuna steaks (in batches if pan is crowded) and sear for about 2 minutes. Turn tuna over and cook for 1 minute more. Remove steaks from pan and keep warm.

Add remaining tablespoon of peanut oil to pan. Cook onion and ginger over medium heat, stirring frequently, for 4 minutes. Add garlic and cook, stirring frequently, for another 3 minutes. Add the reserved vinegar mixture and bring to a boil. Add the tuna steaks, cover, and bake in preheated oven until done (about 7 minutes, depending on the thickness of the steaks). Check after 4-5 minutes to avoid overcooking. Remove steaks from pan and keep warm.

Place pan on top of stove and reduce liquid over medium-high heat for 1 to 2 minutes. Add sesame oil and scallions. Season with salt and pepper. Continue cooking for another minute, or until reduced and flavorful. Pour liquid over tuna steaks and serve.

### wine suggestion:

Pinot Blanc. Try two winners from the *Cook's Illustrated* May/June 1999 issue taste test: the 1997 Steele Bien Nacindo Vineyard or the 1997 Lockwood.

*Cook's Illustrated is a wonderful magazine for seasoned cooks as well as those just learning. Each month well-researched and tested recipes are featured to provide you the best way to prepare the dish. Another good source from Christopher Kimball is The Cook's Bible, a fabulous book with over 400 recipes for just about anything you want to cook. It is like having a cooking instructor constantly at your side.

# Pork Tenderloin Medallions

An easy, flavorful dinner you will enjoy time and again. Serve with Oven Roasted Red Potatoes (page 139) and Fried Sage Green Beans (page 139); it is also nice served over Tinkyada gluten-free fettuccine.

## *ingredients:*

2 pounds pork tenderloin

4 heaping tablespoons gluten-free
   Dijon mustard

3 teaspoons green peppercorns

1 tablespoon olive oil

2 cloves garlic, finely minced or passed
   through a garlic press

2 tablespoons butter

6 tablespoons white wine

4 tablespoons whipping cream

## *4 servings*

Slice the pork tenderloin into round slices ¼-inch thick. Arrange slices side by side and sprinkle with salt and pepper. Spread mustard on one side of each slice. Using either a mortar and pestle or the back of a spoon in a small bowl, thoroughly crush the green peppercorns and set aside.

Heat the oil in a large, heavy-bottomed skillet on high heat. Add the garlic and heat for a moment without allowing garlic to brown. Add the meat and cook for a few minutes on each side until golden brown. (The bottom of the pan will develop a crust as the meat and mustard brown.) Add the crushed peppercorns and butter, stirring well to incorporate. Once meat is cooked, remove to a plate and keep covered to retain heat.

Over high heat, deglaze pan by adding the wine and reducing by half, scraping the bottom of the pan to loosen browned meat and mustard bits stuck to the pan. Add the cream and incorporate well. Return meat to the pan, coating thoroughly with the sauce.  Serve immediately.

## *wine suggestion:*   Oregon Pinot Noir

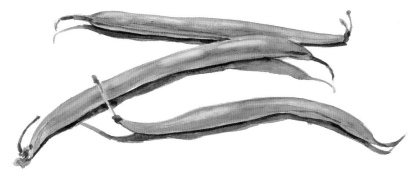

# Pan-Fried Crab Cakes with Tomato Coulis and Cilantro Oil

### Chef Christian Svalesen, 36° – Dallas, Texas

Chef Svalesen was featured in the 1998 *Wine Spectator* as a hot young chef. When Chris heard of this book, he enthusiastically put together some easy and scrumptious recipes. These crab cakes are fabulous! Chris uses Jonah crab from Maine. Dungeness crab from Alaska is an excellent substitution. Find a good source for seafood and enjoy! Serve with salad of daikon and radish sprouts.

## ingredients:

### Cilantro Oil

1 cup cilantro oil (if not available at your
   market, use olive oil)
1 bunch cilantro, washed with stems removed
2 cloves of garlic, finely minced or passed
   through a garlic press

### Tomato Coulis

6 Roma tomatoes, chopped
2 cloves garlic, finely minced or passed
   through a garlic press

### Crab Cakes

1 pound crab meat, picked over for shells
1 egg, slightly beaten
½ cup gluten-free mayonnaise
½ cup gluten-free bread crumbs
¼ cup finely chopped red and
   green bell peppers
¼ cup finely chopped onion
1 tablespoon Worcestershire sauce
8 shots of Tabasco
⅛ cup finely chopped cilantro
1 tablespoon olive oil
1 tablespoon butter

## 4 servings (two crab cakes per person)

**For Cilantro Oil:** Puree olive oil, cilantro, and garlic together in a small food processor or in a blender. Season with salt and pepper.

**For Tomato Coulis:** Puree tomatoes and garlic in a food processor. Place in a medium saucepan and simmer until thickened (about 30-40 minutes). Strain out excess liquid in a fine mesh strainer. Season with salt and pepper.

**For Crab Cakes:** In a medium bowl, mix together crab, egg, mayonnaise, bread crumbs, peppers, onion, Worcestershire sauce, Tabasco, and cilantro. Season with salt and pepper. Form eight patties weighing two ounces each. (Extra crab cakes can be frozen.)

In a medium broiler-safe skillet, pan-fry crab cakes over medium heat in olive oil and butter. Brown one side, then place under broiler to brown the other side for 2 minutes. Place a portion of tomato coulis on a dinner plate next to two crab cakes and drizzle with cilantro oil.

**wine suggestion:** Shiraz (the name given the Syrah grape in Australia, where it is a popular varietal)

*Note: Save extra cilantro oil to toss with pasta or a salad for another meal.*

# Butterflied Leg of Lamb

So easy and delicious, and not as challenging as it sounds. Ask your butcher to butterfly the lamb for you. This recipe comes from Joanne VanRoden, owner of Wellspring Cookbooks. Her daughter is a friend of mine, and dinner at Anne's house is always an occasion to remember! Serve as a spring holiday meal with Roasted Vegetables (page 149), Garlic Mashed Potatoes (page 140), and Gorgonzola–Pear Salad (page 121). Conclude with the Cheese Board (page 26).

## ingredients:

4-5 pounds butterflied leg of lamb

¼ cup gluten-free tamari or gluten-free
   soy sauce

¾ cup red wine
   (a Burgundy or a full-bodied Syrah)

3 tablespoons honey

1 tablespoon gluten-free Dijon mustard

3 cloves garlic, passed through a
   garlic press or minced

3 tablespoons fresh rosemary
   (or 2 teaspoons dried rosemary)

¼ teaspoon freshly ground pepper

Juice and zest of 1 orange and 1 lemon

1 cup gluten-free beef broth

## 8 servings

Place meat in a large nonreactive baking dish. In a small bowl, whisk together tamari, red wine, honey, mustard, garlic, rosemary, pepper, juice, and zest. Pour marinade over the meat and refrigerate overnight, or for at least 12 hours.

Prepare an outdoor grill by mounding the charcoal about 6 inches below grating at its highest point. Preheat the grill. Reserve the marinade and pat the meat dry. Cook meat over hot coals (about 12 minutes per side for meat that is 1½ -2 inches thick, or until internal temperature is 130º-135ºF. for medium rare). Cover with foil and let rest for 5-8 minutes on cutting board.

Make a sauce for the meat by reducing reserved marinade and beef broth by half in a small pot. Taste, seasoning with salt and pepper as necessary.

To serve, cut lamb diagonally across the grain in ½-inch thick slices. Place several slices in the center of a warm plate and spoon sauce over and around the lamb.

## wine suggestion:    French Red Rhône

Notes: Zesting an orange or lemon can be done with a zester or with a very fine grater. The grater is a quicker method. Grate over a large bowl to capture the flavorful orange and lemon oils that are released as you grate. By removing the shank bone and ball joint from the leg of lamb, the butcher can create a flat piece of meat that is easy to grill.

# Roasted Asparagus Quesadillas with Cactus Salsa

My friend Edel has a son with multiple allergies. She faces many of the same challenges as gluten intolerant people but in different food categories. She must check ingredients with manufacturers and watch everything that her son eats or contacts. Through it all she has developed interesting recipes, including this one. Serve as a good weekend lunch or a quick on-the-go dinner. Cactus salsa is sold in specialty grocery stores.

## ingredients:

1 bunch of asparagus (thin stalks)
Olive oil
1 cup white sharp cheddar cheese, grated
½ cup cactus salsa or green salsa
8 corn tortillas

## 4 servings

Preheat oven to 400°F.

Wash and dry asparagus. Holding a stalk of asparagus, bend until it snaps in two, discarding the lower portion. Repeat with remaining stalks. Place asparagus in one layer on a baking sheet, spray (or brush) lightly with olive oil, and season with salt and pepper. Roll stalks to coat with oil and seasoning on all sides. Bake for 10 minutes (or 20 minutes for thick asparagus).

Heat a skillet or griddle and warm a tortilla on each side. Place 4 asparagus stalks, 2 tablespoons cheese, and 2 tablespoons salsa on one half of tortilla. Fold tortilla over to cover ingredients. Repeat steps to fill other tortillas. You might also like to top with additional cheese, melting cheese briefly under the broiler.

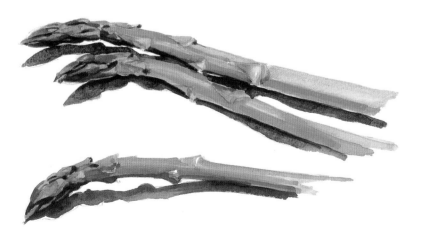

# Roast Chicken

I consider this the best way to cook a whole chicken, as it is very easy and the chicken will be quite succulent.

There will also be plenty of leftovers to use in a chicken salad later in the week.

You will need an upright poultry roasting column; this item is made of stainless steel, clay, or other material, and can be purchased in gourmet cookware shops.

## ingredients:

1 whole chicken
  (weighing between 3½ and 5 pounds)
2-3 tablespoons of lemon juice
2-3 fresh sprigs each of rosemary, thyme,
  and sage (or 2-3 tablespoons each of
  dried rosemary, thyme, and sage,
  tied in a cheesecloth bag)
1 tablespoon butter, melted

**Recipe requires an hour or more preparation/cooking time.**

## 4 servings

Preheat oven to 400°F. Be sure you have pulled any extra racks out of the oven before they get hot. (The lowest rack is probably the only one you will need.) Use a shallow baking pan with an easy to clean surface, and have a roasting column ready.

Remove the giblets and neck of the chicken. Rinse the chicken inside and out, and pat dry with a paper towel. Place chicken in baking pan, pour the lemon juice inside the cavity, and season both cavity and exterior of chicken with salt and pepper. Place herbs on top of the roasting column and insert the column into the bird (neck up and legs down). Tie the legs together with cooking twine. Baste chicken with melted butter (use lemon juice for low-fat basting).

Pour 1½ cups water into the baking pan. Roast chicken for one hour, or until a meat thermometer inserted into the thickest part of the thigh reads 170°–175°F. Let rest 20 minutes before carving.

**wine suggestion:**    Spanish Rioja

Note: Save carcass for homemade chicken stock, freezing in a freezer bag for future use.

# Lopez Taquitos

"Taquito" actually means little taco, but you often find them in Mexican restaurants in the form of a corn tortilla wrapped tightly around a meat filling and deep-fried until crisp. We pan-fry our taquitos in a small amount of oil, and the end result is quite similar with less mess and fewer calories.
This recipe was created by Diane Robertson, who painted the watercolors for this book.

Make-ahead steps include cooking and shredding the chicken, assembling the taquitos, preparing the salsa, and cooking the beans before refrying them.
Serve with Mexican Salsa (page 25), Homemade Refried Beans (page 153), and rice.

## ingredients:

1½ quarts of water, lightly salted

4 chicken breasts, boneless and skinless

6 garlic cloves

1 cup red bell pepper, finely chopped

1 cup green bell pepper, finely chopped

1 medium onion, sliced

3-4 garlic cloves, finely chopped or
     passed through a garlic press

1 cup mushrooms, finely chopped

2 tablespoons olive oil

20 corn tortillas

¾ cup Parmesan cheese

Vegetable oil

**Recipe requires an hour or more preparation/cooking time.**

## 6 servings

Place water, chicken, and garlic cloves in a large saucepan. Bring water to a boil, then remove pan from heat and let chicken and garlic sit in the water, covered, for 20 minutes. Remove chicken from water. Let cool, then shred into bite size pieces.

In a large saucepan or skillet, sauté chicken with red and green peppers, onion, garlic, and mushrooms in the olive oil. Season with salt and pepper.

Heat a large skillet over medium low heat, and add enough oil to cover the bottom of the pan. Dip a corn tortilla into oil and coat completely. (This softens the tortilla for filling and rolling.) Place on a paper towel to drain. Spread a few tablespoons of chicken mixture down the middle of the open tortilla, sprinkle with some Parmesan, and roll up tightly. (This step can be done a day ahead.)

When ready to serve, heat ¾-inch of oil in a large skillet. Over medium-high heat, fry the taquitos until crisp and heated through, about 3 minutes per side. Drain well on paper toweling. Keep taquitos warm in a 250°F. oven until ready to serve.

**wine suggestion:**     Dry French Rosé

# Vegetarian Lasagna

My sister-in-law Heather Shaw, an excellent cook, gave me this recipe. Her lasagna, made with a vegetarian sauce, tastes fresh and, we think, much better than lasagna made with meat. Gluten-free pasta does not lend itself to freezing, so plan to eat this the day you make it.

## ingredients:

### Sauce

*1 medium onion, chopped*

*2 cloves garlic, finely chopped or passed through a garlic press*

*¼ cup olive oil*

*3 zucchini, sliced ⅛ inch thick*

*1 can (28 ounces) whole tomatoes, chopped (including the juice, seeds strained out)*

*1 can (6 ounces) tomato paste*

*¼ cup each of Italian flat leaf parsley and basil, finely chopped (or 1 tablespoon each dried parsley and basil)*

*1 package (5 ounces) gluten-free lasagna noodles (Ener-G Foods brand is recommended, see Sources)*

*8 ounces gluten-free ricotta cheese*

*8 ounces mozzarella cheese, grated*

*4 ounces Parmesan cheese, grated*

**Recipe requires an hour or more preparation/cooking time.**

## 4 servings

Butter a 12-cup baking dish.

Lightly sauté onions and garlic in olive oil. Add zucchini and cook for 10 minutes, or until zucchini softens a bit. Add tomatoes (with juice) and tomato paste. Add parsley and basil. Season with salt and pepper. Mix well and simmer for 30 minutes.

Preheat oven to 350°F.

Cook lasagna noodles very al dente. (They will cook further in the oven.) Arrange a layer of cooked noodles in the buttered baking dish. Spread half the sauce over the noodles. Sprinkle half the mozzarella and a third of the Parmesan cheese over the sauce. Drop half the ricotta cheese by tablespoons over the mozzarella and Parmesan. Add another layer of cooked noodles, remaining sauce, remaining mozzarella, another third of the Parmesan, and remaining ricotta. Arrange final layer of cooked noodles and top with remaining Parmesan cheese. Bake for 30 minutes.

Note: Freezing gluten-free pasta dishes will cause the pasta texture to change. However, you can make extra sauce and freeze it for a future quick meal.

**variation for meat sauce:** Substitute ½ pound of ground meat and ½ pound sweet Italian sausage for the zucchini.

**wine suggestion:** Italian Valpolicella

*(continued on next page)*

🕐 – *indicates a quick meal*

# SUMMER

**Mexican Green Soup** ...... 68
Chef Christian Svalesen

**Pizza** ...... 69

**Sautéed Salmon with Caramelized Onion-Strewn Grits and Portobello Mushroom-Red Wine Sauce** ...... 70
Chef Charlie Trotter

**Mustard Crusted Black Cod with White Asparagus, Black Trumpet Mushrooms, Leek-Potato Puree, and Seville Orange Vinaigrette** ...... 72
Chef Dennis Leary

**Slow Barbecue Baby Back Ribs** ...... 74

# Chicken Salad

Chicken salad is an easy, satisfying summer meal; it is easier yet when using leftover chicken. Try the variation with apples, or create your own interesting combination. Wrap in Homemade Tortillas (page 167) and serve with fresh sliced peaches.

## ingredients

2 cups cooked chicken, chopped

½ cup red cabbage, chopped

½ cup red pepper, chopped

3 scallions, chopped

3-4 tablespoons gluten-free mayonnaise

## 4 servings

Combine chicken, cabbage, red pepper, scallions, and mayonnaise in a medium bowl. Season with salt and pepper and serve.

**wine suggestion:**   Chianti Classico

## variation:
### Granny Smith Chicken Salad

Substitute one large organic Granny Smith apple, cored and cubed, for cabbage and pepper. Substitute one finely chopped shallot for scallions. Instead of fresh peaches, serve with watermelon slices.

# Grilled Mahi-Mahi with Tomatillo Sauce

### Chef Bob Kinkead, Kinkead's – Washington D.C.

In 1983, *Food & Wine* magazine named Bob Kinkead one of the nations' most promising culinary talents. He has lived up to that title over the years with multiple nominations and awards from the James Beard Foundation. Countless magazines, from *Esquire* to *Gourmet*, have featured Chef Kinkead. He has served as executive chef and partner at 21 Federal in Nantucket and Twenty-One Federal in Washington D.C. He now owns Kinkead's, where he continues to work his magic.

Serve with Jicama Slaw (page 134) and black beans.

## ingredients:

### Tomatillo Sauce

6 scallions

6 tomatillos, husked

1 poblano chile

2 Anaheim chiles

1 small onion, quartered

Olive oil

5 cloves garlic, peeled and minced

1 tablespoon whole cumin seed, toasted

Juice of 4 limes

1 jalapeño, finely minced

1 bunch cilantro leaves, stems removed

Six 5-ounce mahi-mahi fillets,
    skinned and boned

Cilantro sprigs and lime wedges for garnish

## 6 servings

Preheat an outdoor grill.

Chop scallion greens, leaving the white part whole for grilling. Toss white scallion bottoms, tomatillos, poblanos, Anaheims, and onion in a bit of olive oil and season with salt and pepper. Grill vegetables on a hot grill and remove when cooked on all sides. Place the chiles in a plastic bag and seal. When chiles are cool enough to touch, peel and dice.

In a blender, place white scallion bottoms, tomatillos, Anaheim chiles, garlic, cumin, and lime juice. Puree until smooth. Season with salt and pepper. Empty mixture into a nonreactive (glass or plastic) container. Without cleaning out the blender, add the scallion greens, poblanos, grilled onion, jalapeño, and cilantro leaves. Puree until smooth. Season with salt and pepper. Empty mixture into a separate container. (The sauces are pureed separately to keep a nice bright green color.)

Lightly oil the mahi-mahi fillets and season with salt and pepper. Cook on a hot grill for 4 minutes on the first side, then turn and cook for 2-3 minutes on the other side, or until just done in the middle.

To finish the sauce, bring the tomatillo puree to a boil. Add the cilantro puree. Remove from heat when heated through. Adjust seasoning and pour sauce onto 6 warm plates. Top with a mahi-mahi fillet. Garnish with a cilantro sprig and lime wedge.

## wine suggestion: California Chardonnay

# Barbecued Tri Tip

This triangle cut of meat is from the sirloin tip. Slow grilling is the trick. Wood chips and charcoal make this a wonderfully flavorful meal.
Serve with Pasta Salad (page 126) and Green Beans (page 139).

### ingredients:

1-2 pound tri tip steak

Seasoned salt (Lawry's is recommended)

2 cups large wood chips (cherry wood,
    apple wood, or hickory wood chips)

### 4 servings

Sprinkle meat lightly on both sides with seasoned salt. Refrigerate.

Prepare an outdoor grill by mounding the charcoal about nine inches below the grating at its highest point. Preheat the grill. While grill is preheating, soak wood chips in water. Once coals are hot (you should be able to hold your hand above the grating for only 2 seconds), spread them out in an even layer. Drain wood chips and place a handful on the hot coals. Put grating in place, heat for a few minutes, then clean with a wire brush. Place meat on grill and cook, turning once, for about 45 minutes (or until internal temperature is 120ºF-130ºF. for rare beef, 130ºF-135ºF. for medium-rare beef).

### wine suggestion:    Washington Merlot

# Halibut and Chips

Though not deep-fried, here's a quick homemade version of fish and chips that will satisfy your craving and is actually much better than any fish and chips you could buy. A tartar sauce recipe is included if you want to use it though halibut and ling cod are delicate fish. Serve with "chips" (Homemade Fries page 148) and Cole Slaw (page 128).

## ingredients:

**4 servings**

2 pounds fresh halibut cheeks or ling cod
¼ cup gluten-free flour mix
1 tablespoon vegetable oil
3 tablespoons butter
Lemon wedges

Lightly dust halibut with gluten-free flour. In a medium skillet, heat oil and butter over moderate high heat. Sauté halibut, turning once, until the center is no longer translucent (about 8-9 minutes per inch of halibut thickness). Serve with lemon wedges.

**wine suggestion:**    Oregon Pinot Gris or Chardonnay

## Tartar Sauce:   makes 3/4 cup

Combine mayonnaise, vinegar, capers, and herbs. Keep refrigerated.

¾ cup mayonnaise
1 tablespoon distilled white vinegar
2 teaspoons gluten-free capers
2 teaspoons finely chopped fresh chives
1 teaspoon finely chopped fresh dill
1 teaspoon finely chopped fresh
   Italian parsley

# Jerk Chicken with Cilantro Mango Salsa

The island of Cayman Brac is a paradise for scuba divers, though, at the time of our visit very few restaurants existed. One evening we found "the" place for locals. They were having a big party, and jerk chicken was the main attraction. It was fabulous! This tasty recipe is quite a faithful interpretation. Try the Cilantro Mango Salsa for a nice foil to the spicy chicken. A serving of brown rice and Sugar Peas (page 143) completes the meal. For a true island presentation, serve with red beans and plantains.

## ingredients:

### Cilantro Mango Salsa

2 cups peeled, chopped mango
¼ cup chopped red onion
2 tablespoons finely chopped cilantro
Juice from 1 lime

2 whole chicken breasts, boneless,
    skinless, and halved
½ teaspoon crushed red pepper flakes
1 teaspoon garlic powder
1 teaspoon paprika
½ teaspoon ground cloves
½ teaspoon ground cinnamon
½ teaspoon ground allspice
½ teaspoon ground ginger
2 teaspoons salt
1 teaspoon freshly ground pepper
2 teaspoons dried thyme
¼ cup brown sugar, tightly packed

## 4 servings

Combine mango, onion, cilantro, and lime juice. Keep refrigerated.

Preheat an outdoor grill.

Pound the chicken to ½-inch thickness. Combine spices and sugar in a small bowl and rub the mixture evenly into each chicken breast before grilling. Cook chicken over a medium-hot fire (about 3 minutes per side) until cooked but still plump and juicy.

### wine suggestion:   Washington Syrah

# Grilled Swordfish Steak over Grilled Eggplant Tapenade with Basil Oil

### Chef Christian Svalesen, 36° – Dallas, Texas

In the middle of Texas, Chef Christian Svalesen has fresh fish flown in daily to his Net Result seafood market and 36° Restaurant next door. Chris creates some of the finest fare in the region. Most large cities have first-rate fish markets; take the time to find one in your area and savor this wonderful dish! Serve with a side of Creamy Polenta (page 148).

## ingredients:

### Basil Oil Puree

*1 cup basil leaves*
*2 cloves garlic, roughly chopped*
*1 cup olive oil*

### Tapenade

*1 small eggplant, sliced ¼-inch thick*
*1 zucchini, sliced ¼-inch thick*
*1 yellow squash, sliced ¼-inch thick*
*1 each red, green, and yellow bell peppers,*
*    quartered, seeds and veins removed*
*3 tablespoons olive oil*
*1 tablespoon fresh oregano or*
*    1 teaspoon dried oregano*

*Four 6-ounce swordfish steaks*

## 4 servings

Using a small food processor or blender, puree basil, garlic, and olive oil. Set aside.

Preheat outdoor grill. Brush vegetables lightly with 1 tablespoon olive oil, season with salt and pepper, and grill until tender but still firm. Transfer vegetables from grill to cutting board and cut into ¼-inch dice. Place diced vegetables into a medium bowl and add 1 tablespoon olive oil, oregano, and 1 tablespoon basil oil puree. Stir well and let sit at room temperature. (You can also roast the vegetables in a 400°F. oven on a large baking sheet for 20 minutes.)

Brush swordfish lightly with 1 tablespoon olive oil and season with salt and pepper. Grill for two minutes, then turn over and grill for another 2 minutes, or until swordfish is opaque in the center but still springy and moist.

Serve swordfish on a bed of the tapenade. Finish with a drizzle of the basil oil puree over the swordfish.

**wine suggestion:**   Pinot Noir

# Beef Kebabs

## ingredients:

2½ pounds Spencer or top sirloin steak
    cut into 1-inch cubes

1-2 tablespoons olive oil

Garlic pepper or garlic salt (to taste)

12 ounces cherry tomatoes

8 ounces button mushrooms

1 green pepper, cut in 1½-inch pieces

1 sweet onion, quartered

### 4 servings

Using bamboo or metal shish kebab skewers, form kebabs, alternating meat cubes with vegetables and pushing tightly together. Brush kebabs with olive oil and season with garlic salt or garlic pepper. Preheat an outdoor grill. Grill over hot coals for about 5 minutes per side. Use tongs to turn the skewers.

### wine suggestion:    French Rhône Syrah Grenache Blend

Note: Hot coal test: you will be able to hold your hand above the grate for only 2 seconds.

# Red Sauce with Sweet Butter Clams and Pasta

This excellent meal can be made in the time it takes to boil the pasta. If fresh clams are unavailable, you can use a 10-ounce can of baby clams (typically from Thailand, they are fairly consistent in quality). However, if you have access to live clams in the shell, by all means use them; their flavor and visual appeal make this a great meal for entertaining. Serve with Seasonal Greens and Garden Cucumbers (page 128).

## ingredients:

½ cup olive oil

½ medium onion, finely chopped

2 tablespoons minced garlic

1 teaspoon red pepper flakes

1 cup dry white wine, room temperature

16 ounces bottled clam juice

1 can (28 ounces) diced tomatoes

2 tablespoons tomato paste

½ cup butter

4 tablespoons finely chopped parsley

2 pounds live butter, Manila, or
    littleneck clams, thoroughly scrubbed

1 pound gluten-free pasta,
    spaghetti or linguine

## comment:

If you dig the clams yourself, be sure to clean them well. Place clams in a large bucket of cold water mixed with cornmeal (6 tablespoons for every 4 cups of water) for a few hours. The clams siphon the cornmeal, which purges them of sand. (Salt may be substituted in equal quantities for the cornmeal.)

## 4 servings

In a large skillet with a lid, sauté onion in olive oil until translucent. Add garlic and red pepper flakes. Cook, stirring frequently, for one minute. (Do not let garlic brown.) Add wine, bring to a boil, and reduce by half. Add clam juice and reduce again by one third. Add tomatoes and tomato paste and stir well. Simmer, covered, for 15 minutes. While sauce is simmering, cook pasta according to package directions. Add butter and parsley to sauce, stirring until butter is incorporated. Add clams and cover for 5 minutes. Clams will open when cooked. (Discard any clams that do not open.) Transfer cooked clams to a bowl. Toss sauce with pasta and divide between 4 plates. Arrange clams on and around the pasta for a striking presentation.

**wine suggestion:**   Vernaccia di San Gimignano

*This recipe is adapted from Pasta & Co. By Request (1991). Pasta & Co. is Seattle's premier upscale take-out food shop with five locations. They also stock gluten-free pasta.*

*Notes: If using canned clams, drain and pick over, discarding shell fragments. Add clams to sauce at the same time as butter and parsley. Heat until clams are warmed through.*

# Yellow Tomato Soup with Avocado, Red Onion, and Mint

### Chef Todd Gray, Equinox – Washington, D.C.

Equinox is one of this city's premier fine dining establishments, offering sophisticated, pure American cuisine. Chef Gray uses fresh, local organic ingredients whenever possible. He is a James Beard Award Nominee for Chef of the Year, Mid-Atlantic, in 2001, and has won various "top table" awards from *Condé Nast, Bon Appétit, Esquire,* and *Gourmet* magazines.

Serve with Red Snapper Fillet with Spaghetti Squash, Saffron, and Tomato Cream (page 82) and Grand Marnier Semifreddo with Bittersweet Chocolate Sauce and Local Blackberries (page 206).

## ingredients:

⅓ cup grapeseed oil or olive oil

2 Vidalia onions, peeled and sliced

6 garlic cloves, crushed

10 yellow tomatoes, quartered

3 cups heavy cream

1 quart vegetable stock

3 avocados, peeled and chopped

1 red onion, minced

½ garlic clove, minced

¼ bunch mint, chopped

A few mint leaves for garnish

## 6 servings

Heat grapeseed oil in a large saucepan until hot. Add onions and garlic. Sauté for 3 minutes. Add yellow tomatoes and cook for five minutes. Season with salt and pepper. Add cream and stock. Simmer for 30 minutes.

To make guacamole, mash avocado in a small bowl. Add red onion, garlic, and mint. Combine well, cover tightly, and chill.

Remove soup from heat, puree in a blender, and pass through a fine mesh sieve. Chill soup for two hours.

Chill six large bowls in the refrigerator.

To serve, ladle soup into chilled bowls and place a large dollop of guacamole in the center. Garnish with a fresh mint sprig. Serve immediately.

# Apple Cider-Dijon Salmon

A wonderful meal that requires little effort. Once you have done the minimal prep work for the side dishes, you can devote your attention to grilling the salmon.
Serve with Spinach Sautéed with Garlic and Lemon (page 146) and Oven Roasted Baby Red Potatoes (page 139).

### ingredients:

*2 tablespoons apple cider*

*1 tablespoon gluten-free Dijon mustard*

*3 tablespoons brown sugar*

*4 tablespoons olive oil*

*2 pounds fresh king salmon fillet*

### 4 servings

Preheat an outdoor grill placing coals eight inches below the cooking grate. Combine apple cider, Dijon mustard, and brown sugar. Slowly drizzle in 2 tablespoons olive oil, stirring constantly with a wire whisk. Brush skin side of salmon with remaining olive oil. Turn fish over and spread cider glaze evenly over the flesh side of the salmon. Season with salt and pepper.

Place salmon flesh side down and cook for 5-7 minutes. Using a large metal spatula, turn salmon over (skin side down) and cook until barely translucent in the center. (Total cooking time is about 8-9 minutes per inch of thickness in the fillet).

### wine suggestion:    French Chablis

## Glaze Variation: Honey Mustard Glaze

### makes 1/2 cup of glaze

*½ cup honey*

*½ tablespoon gluten-free Dijon mustard*

*½ tablespoon lemon juice*

*2 tablespoons butter*

*½ teaspoon coriander*

*½ small garlic clove, finely chopped*

In a small saucepan, heat honey, mustard, lemon juice, butter, coriander, and garlic just until the butter melts. Spread mixture on salmon. Cook as directed above.

*Note: You may broil the salmon instead if you prefer.*

# Thyme-Marinated Flank Steaks

Serve with French New Potato Salad with Summer Herb Coulis (page 127).

## ingredients:

6 sprigs fresh thyme

2 cloves of garlic, finely chopped or
    passed through a garlic press

1 tablespoon freshly ground pepper

¼ cup olive oil

3 tablespoons red wine vinegar

2 pounds flank steak

## 4 servings

Whisk all marinade ingredients together. Place flank steaks in a nonreactive glass dish and pour marinade over the meat. Cover dish and refrigerate for at least 5 hours, turning meat over several times. Preheat an outdoor grill or prepare a broiler pan. Grill two inches above hot coals or cook under the broiler, 4-5 minutes on each side (until internal temperature is 120°F–130°F for rare meat, 130°F-135°F for medium rare). When serving, cut thin slices across the grain of the meat for a more tender result.

### wine suggestion:   California Cabernet

# Seared Sea Scallop-Green Papaya Salad with Cranberry Essence

### Chef Linda Yamada, The Beach House Restaurant — Kauai, Hawaii

The Beach House is a favorite restaurant for our family vacations on Kauai. Consistently voted near the top of the Zagat Restaurant Survey each year, The Beach House offers fresh island flavor by using locally grown ingredients as the focal point of their menu.

## ingredients:

### Cranberry Essence

2 cups red wine

2 cups sugar

2 cups cranberry juice

1 cup fine julienne green papaya

¼ cup fine julienne carrot

1 teaspoon finely chopped garlic

2 teaspoons finely chopped fresh cilantro

2 tablespoons fresh lime juice

1 teaspoon Thai fish sauce (see Sources)

Pinch of sugar

12 large sea scallops
   (about 10 scallops per pound)

3 tablespoons olive oil

5-6 ounces salad greens

Fried corn tortilla strips (optional)

## 4 servings

In a nonreactive pot, bring wine and 1 cup sugar to a boil. Simmer until mixture achieves a thin syrup consistency (about 230°F. on a candy thermometer). Meanwhile, in a separate nonreactive pot, bring cranberry juice and remaining sugar to a boil and simmer to a thin syrup consistency. Combine the wine syrup and cranberry syrup together. Set aside at room temperature until ready to use. If syrup begins to harden, you can soften it again by placing the pot of syrup in a warm water bath. (Syrups take about 10-15 minutes to make.)

Mix green papaya, carrot, garlic, cilantro, lime, fish sauce, and sugar. Set aside.

Season scallops with sea salt and cracked black pepper. Heat a sauté pan until hot. Add olive oil and sear scallops on both sides until browned and the center is no longer translucent.

Place salad greens in the center of each plate and top with papaya salad. Arrange 3 scallops around plate and drizzle with Cranberry Essence. Fried corn tortilla strips can be used for garnish.

## wine suggestion:   Loire Valley Sancerre

*Note: Be careful not to cook the Cranberry Essence too long, or you will end up with a hard candy.*

# Pan-Fried Chicken and Black Bean Salad

The chicken recipe is good even without the Marsala, and is quite versatile. Serve it over rice, or as part of a salad as shown here.
The sweetness of balsamic dressed greens complements the heat of the jalapeños in the Black Bean Salad.

## ingredients:

One recipe Black Bean Salad (page 130)

2 whole chicken breasts, boneless, skinless,
    and halved

1 tablespoon olive oil

2 small garlic cloves, thinly sliced

1 shallot, finely minced

3 tablespoons Marsala

Juice from one lemon

One head of red leaf lettuce, rinsed and dried

2 tablespoons balsamic vinegar

2 tablespoons olive oil

## 4 servings

Cut chicken into 2-inch long strips. Heat oil in a large frying pan until medium hot. Sauté garlic and shallots until soft, stirring frequently. Increase heat to high, add chicken, and stir-fry quickly until browned. Add Marsala and lemon juice, and season with salt and pepper. Stir to coat chicken and reduce liquid a bit. Remove from heat. Toss red leaf lettuce with balsamic vinegar and olive oil. Divide salad between four plates. Top each with a serving of chicken and Black Bean Salad.

**wine suggestion:**    French Rhône Valley Red

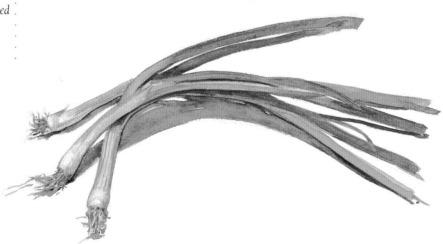

# Mexican Green Soup

### Chef Christian Svalesen, 36° — Dallas, Texas

36° offers the flavors of modern Texas cooking, combining such ingredients as chile peppers and cilantro with French technique.
The result is a wonderfully unique way with Chris' signature fish and seafood dishes. This bouillabaisse-type fish stew is one of Chef Svalesen's best-loved recipes.

## ingredients:

12 littleneck clams

12 mussels

12 large scallops

8 large shrimp (peeled and deveined)

1½ pounds assorted fish
  (halibut, salmon, snapper, sole, etc.)

2 Maine lobsters
  (halved, stomach and intestine removed)

1 cup poblano chiles, pureed

½ cup fresh cilantro leaves, stems removed

¼ cup olive oil

2 teaspoons chopped shallots

2 teaspoons chopped garlic

4 cups dry vermouth
  (Note: Use the best quality you can afford)

2 tablespoons butter

## 4 servings

Thoroughly wash all seafood. Cut assorted fish into 2 ounce pieces.

Roast poblano chiles over a gas flame or under a broiler until blackened on all sides. Peel and remove seeds and veins. Place in the bowl of a food processor and puree.

In the bowl of a small food processor, puree cilantro, olive oil, shallots, and garlic. (Recipe can be prepared in advance up to this point. Refrigerate ingredients until ready to finish the bouillabaisse.)

In a Dutch oven or large heavyweight pan, combine poblano chile puree, cilantro oil mixture, vermouth, and butter. Season with salt and pepper. Bring to a boil over medium heat and reduce liquid by half.

Add seafood, layered in the following order: halved and cleaned lobster, large chunks of fish, shrimp, scallops, mussels, and clams. Bring liquid to a boil again, then simmer just until clams and mussels open (about 8-10 minutes). Discard any unopened clams and mussels. Serve immediately.

## wine suggestion:    Riesling or Pinot Grigio

*Tip: Ask the fish market personnel to split and remove the stomach and intestines from the lobster.*

# Pizza

This pizza has a good yeast-risen crust that is the closest thing I have tasted to a thick wheat flour crust.
Be sure to make big batches of pesto, tomato sauce, and crusts for freezing; you can then enjoy fresh gluten-free pizza in less time than it takes to have a pizza delivered.
If you are making the pesto, sauce, and crust in one day, prepare each recipe in the order shown for the most efficient use of time.

## ingredients:

### Homemade Pesto

¼ cup pine nuts
1 cup fresh basil, stemmed
⅛ cup olive oil
½ cup grated Parmesan
6 cloves garlic, finely chopped or
    passed through a garlic press

### Scratch Pizza Sauce

¼ cup olive oil
2 medium onions, finely chopped
2 large cloves garlic, finely chopped or
    passed through a garlic press
2 cans (28 ounces each) crushed tomatoes
2 tablespoons sugar
4-5 tablespoons fresh basil leaves,
    finely chopped

> **Recipe requires an hour or more preparation/cooking time.**

Thick Pizza Crust recipe (page 171)

### Suggested toppings

  (for one 13-inch pizza)

½ cup sun-dried tomatoes, chopped
1 can (14 ounces) whole artichoke hearts,
    well-drained and chopped
3-4 tablespoons homemade pesto
12 ounces mozzarella cheese, grated
¼ cup Parmesan cheese, grated

*Note: Muir Glen Organics makes a good pizza sauce. However, if you have the time, try making it yourself and taste the difference. Be sure to cook the sauce down to a thick, rich consistency. (A watery sauce and a gluten-free crust do not go together well at all.)*

### comment:

Prior to going gluten-free, this pizza was a favorite at our local pizzeria, Romio's. It is called the G.A.S.P., which stands for garlic, artichokes, sun-dried tomato, and pesto. They use much more garlic and it tends to take your breath away (gasp!). This version is much smoother and probably appeals to more people. My daughter said this is the only "adult pizza" she likes. For a spicier pizza, sprinkle with red pepper flakes

**Pesto:** Finely chop pine nuts in a small food processor. Remove nuts from bowl and set aside. Place basil and olive oil in the food processor. Gently pulse until most of the leaves are chopped. Add Parmesan and garlic and pulse a few more times. Add pine nuts and process until well blended. Let stand for one hour at room temperature. Recipe makes about 1 cup and freezes well.

**Sauce:** In a large saucepan, heat olive oil over medium-high heat. Add onions and garlic and sauté until onions are translucent. Stir in tomatoes, sugar, and basil. Season with salt and pepper. Cover and simmer for 30 minutes, or until nicely thickened. Makes enough sauce for four 13-inch pizzas and freezes well.

Make pizza crusts and cover each with tomato sauce. Prepare pizza toppings as stated above and arrange on pizza in order listed. Bake for 20 minutes.

### wine suggestion:
    a dry Northern Italian white wine

# Sautéed Salmon with Caramelized Onion-Strewn Grits and Portobello Mushroom-Red Wine Sauce

### Chef Charlie Trotter, Charlie Trotter's – Chicago, Illinois

Charlie Trotter's offers highly personal cuisine combining impeccable products, French techniques, and Asian influences. Charlie's restaurant and cookbooks are well known across the country. The restaurant's list of awards ranges from Relais Gourmand to the *Wine Spectator*, the James Beard Foundation, AAA—the list goes on and on. Recipe with permission from *Charlie Trotter's Seafood*, (Ten Speed Press, 1997).

## ingredients:

1 red onion, julienned

3 tablespoons butter

2 tablespoons chopped chives

1 tablespoon lemon juice

2 cups cooked white grits

2 roasted portobello mushrooms (page 150)

½ cup Red Wine Jus (page 71)

Four, 4-ounce pieces salmon, skin on

2 tablespoons canola oil

**Recipe requires an hour or more preparation/cooking time.**

## chef's comments:

Leaving the skin on the salmon in this dish creates a crispy, crackly layer that melts into the flesh with each bite. The buttery, sweet mound of grits with the caramelized red onion makes an interesting textural contrast. To further push this preparation into soul-satisfying territory, it is paired with an earthy yet refined Portobello Mushroom-Red Wine Sauce. This combination of flavors and textures would satisfy even the most avid meat lover.

## 4 servings

Cook red onion in a sauté pan over moderate heat with 1 tablespoon of the butter for 5-8 minutes, or until golden brown and caramelized. Fold the caramelized onion, chives, and lemon juice into the cooked grits and season to taste with salt and pepper.

Coarsely chop one of the roasted mushrooms. Place in a blender with the Red Wine Jus and puree for 2 minutes, or until smooth. Place the mushroom puree in a small saucepan and warm over medium heat. Whisk in the remaining 2 tablespoons of butter and season to taste with salt and pepper.

Season the salmon with salt and pepper and score the skin side with a sharp knife. Place skin side down in a hot sauté pan with the canola oil and cook for 2-3 minutes per side, or until golden brown and cooked to the medium stage.

continued:

**Sautéed Salmon with Caramelized Onion-Strewn Grits and Portobello Mushroom-Red Wine Sauce**

Thinly slice the remaining roasted mushroom. Place a small mound of grits in the center of each plate and top with some of the sliced portobello. Place a portion of salmon on top and spoon the Portobello Mushroom-Red Wine Sauce around the plate. Sprinkle with freshly ground black pepper.

**wine suggestion:** An earthy, aromatic red Burgundy will bring this dish to another level. Vosne-Romanée by producers such as Mongeard-Mugneret or Jean Gros will heighten the flavors of the caramelized onion and mushroom, but still allow the rich salmon to shine through.

# Red Wine Jus

This intense reduction is compatible with fish as well as meat and poultry.

## ingredients:

1½ cups chopped onions

1 cup chopped carrots

1 cup chopped celery

2 tablespoons canola oil

1 Granny Smith apple, chopped

1 orange, peeled and chopped

6 cups Burgundy wine

3 cups port

## makes 1 ½ cups

In a medium saucepan, cook the onions, carrots, and celery in the canola oil over medium heat, stirring frequently, for 10 minutes, or until golden brown and caramelized. Add the remaining ingredients and simmer over low heat for 1 hour. Strain through a fine mesh sieve and return to the saucepan. Simmer for 30-45 minutes, or until reduced to 1½ cups. Season with salt and pepper.

# Mustard Crusted Black Cod with White Asparagus, Black Trumpet Mushrooms, Leek-Potato Puree and Seville Orange Vinaigrette

### Chef Dennis Leary, Rubicon — San Francisco, California

Drew Nieporent's Rubicon showcases the culinary talents of Dennis Leary and the formidable wine knowledge of Master Sommelier Larry Stone. Larry is a legend in wine circles. Dennis was named the Best Rising Star Chef in San Francisco, 2001 and was featured as one of the Ten Best New Chefs in *Food & Wine* magazine in 1994. The restaurant has received accolades for food and wine selection from the *Wine Spectator* and the James Beard Foundation.

## ingredients:

### Mustard Crust

1 egg
¾ cup grapeseed oil
¾ ounce brown mustard seed, ground
   (a little less than 2 tablespoons)
1 ounce hazelnuts, lightly toasted
Juice of ½ lemon
1 teaspoon white wine vinegar
1 ounce water

### Seville Orange Vinaigrette

1 Seville orange
1 Valencia orange
1 shallot, peeled and diced
½ cup extra virgin olive oil
3 drops white wine vinegar
2 tablespoons water
Pinch of sugar

### Vegetables

16 stalks white asparagus
2 tablespoons salted butter
12 ounces fresh black trumpet mushrooms,
   rinsed thoroughly
2 tablespoons vegetable oil
12 stalks celery

### Leek-Potato Puree

10 large leeks (about 1½ pounds)
4 ounces (1 stick) butter
2¼ pounds Yellow Finn potatoes

Four, 6-ounce Black Cod fillets
½ cup finely ground gluten-free
   bread crumbs

Black trumpet mushrooms have a distinct aroma and an elegant buttery flavor. You will find them from midsummer through the middle of fall in specialty produce markets. Seville oranges are typically used to make liqueurs such as Cointreau, Grand Marnier, and Triple Sec. The flesh is tart, bitter, and has a high acid content.

## chef's comments:

It is best to make the mustard crust ahead of time (24 hours or more) to allow the flavor to develop. Prepare Seville Orange Vinaigrette six hours prior to serving for better flavor.

## 4 servings

**Mustard Crust:** Place egg in a food processor and add oil in a slow stream. Add ground mustard, hazelnuts, lemon juice, vinegar, and water. Season with salt and pepper. The consistency should be that of thin mayonnaise, but still spreadable.

*continued:*

**Mustard Crusted Black Cod with White Asparagus, Black Trumpet Mushrooms, Leek-Potato Puree and Seville Orange Vinaigrette**

*Recipe requires an hour or more preparation/cooking time.*

**Seville Orange Vinaigrette:** Juice Seville orange into a small bowl. Juice ½ of the Valencia orange into the same bowl and add shallot, olive oil, vinegar, and water. Season with salt and pepper. (The vinaigrette should be pleasantly tangy; add sugar if necessary to adjust acidity.) Set aside.

**Vegetables:** Peel asparagus, leaving tips intact. Cook in a large pot of salted boiling water until barely tender, about 2 minutes. Brush with butter while still hot and set aside.

Preheat oven to 350°F.

Toss trumpet mushrooms in two tablespoons vegetable oil and a generous pinch of salt. Roast uncovered for 5 minutes, or until some of their moisture has evaporated. Do not overcook, or they will shrink excessively. Drain on paper toweling and set aside.

Peel celery stalks and cut into 2-inch pieces. Cook in generously salted boiling water for 30 seconds until bright green. Immediately plunge celery into a bowl of ice water for 10 seconds. Remove and drain thoroughly. Set aside.

**Leek-Potato Puree:** Slice leeks in half lengthwise, then chop finely. Rinse well and drain. Place leeks in a shallow sauté pan with half the butter and cook, covered, over low heat until tender. Watch carefully to avoid browning or burning.

Peel potatoes and cook in boiling salted water until soft.

Combine leeks, potatoes, and remaining butter in a food processor. Puree until uniformly smooth. The puree should be slightly stiff but have no traces of fiber, and it should not be gummy. Add a little hot water to correct the consistency if necessary. Set aside in a warm place.

To serve, preheat oven to 375°F. Bake cod fillets for 7 minutes, or until almost cooked through. Remove from oven and brush each fillet with a liberal amount of mustard crust. Briefly warm the asparagus, mushrooms, and celery in the oven. Spoon warm leek-potato puree onto four warmed plates. Arrange vegetables around the puree and drizzle them with a small amount of vinaigrette.

Just before serving, sprinkle cod fillets with gluten-free bread crumbs and brown briefly under the broiler. Place on top of the leek puree and serve at once.

*wine suggestion:*   Duckhorn Vineyards Sauvignon Blanc

# Slow Barbecue Baby Back Ribs

Some of the best baby back ribs you will taste!
This recipe allows for a ½ rack per person (about a pound). Serve with Tomato Bread Salad (page 131) and Green Beans (page 139).

## ingredients:

4 pounds baby back pork ribs
Lawry's Seasoned Salt
2 cups large mesquite wood chips

**Recipe requires an hour or more preparation/cooking time.**

## 4 servings

Cover ribs with a light sprinkling of seasoned salt on all sides.

Prepare an outdoor grill by mounding the charcoal about nine inches below the grating at its highest point. Preheat the grill. While grill is preheating, soak wood chips in water. Once coals are hot (you should be able to hold your hand above the grating for only 2 seconds), spread them out in an even layer. Drain wood chips and place a handful on the hot coals. Put grating in place, heat until temperature is 225°F., then clean with a wire brush. Place ribs on grill and smoke for 45-60 minutes (turning ribs once) until well browned on both sides. Remove ribs and wrap tightly in two layers of regular aluminum foil. Return to grill for 30-45 minutes. Remove foil packet from grill and let ribs rest in the foil for 15 minutes before serving.

### wine suggestion:   California Zinfandel

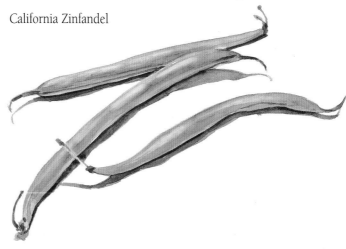

# FALL

# Assorted Sausages and Mustards

Many butcher shops sell wonderful sausages made without gluten. Find your favorites and try this easy meal. Present it family style so everyone has a chance to sample the variety of sausages. Serve with Garlic Mashed Potatoes (page 140) and Butter Lettuce with Caramelized Nuts (page 122).

*ingredients:*

*2 kielbasa*

*2 hot (spicy) Italian sausages*

*2 bockwurst*

*2 knackwurst*

*2 cups or more water*

*2-3 tablespoons butter*

*Assorted gluten-free mustards*

*4 servings*

Place sausages in a large skillet. Pour 1 cup of water over sausages and cook over medium-high heat until water evaporates. Allow sausages to brown lightly on both sides, then add another cup of water to the skillet. The browned bits stuck to the pan will be released (a process called deglazing). Simmer until water cooks down again and repeat until sausages are cooked through (about 20 minutes). Lower heat to medium. Add butter to the skillet and melt. Brown sausages on all sides. Serve with your favorite gluten-free mustards.

*wine suggestion:* French Syrah

*Note: Not all sausage is gluten-free, check with the manufacturer.*

# Leek and Saffron Soup with Sautéed Shrimp

### Chef Michael Kornick, mk – Chicago, Illinois

Michael is a nationally recognized leader in the culinary arts. His distinguished career began at New York's legendary restaurant, The Quilted Giraffe. Since then, he has received numerous accolades during his tenure as executive chef at Aujord'hui in Boston and various Chicago restaurants including Gordon, Marche, and Red Light. Michael is now consultant/partner of Nine in Chicago and Exec Chef/partner at mk.

## ingredients:

½ cup chopped, fresh Italian parsley

½ cup olive oil

4 chopped garlic cloves

18 uncooked medium shrimp, peeled, deveined, and halved lengthwise

6 tablespoons (¾ stick) butter

5 chopped medium leeks, about 3 cups (use pale green and white parts only)

One 8-ounce russet potato, peeled and chopped (about 1½ cups)

¼ teaspoon (scant) crumbled saffron threads

5 cups gluten-free chicken stock or canned low-salt chicken broth

1 tablespoon whipping cream

1 small bunch chives, cut into 1-inch pieces

## comment:

This soup is a real treat, with outstanding flavors and a lovely presentation. Serve either as a first course or as a light meal with a salad.

## 6 servings

Combine parsley, oil, and one garlic clove in food processor. Blend until parsley is coarsely chopped. Transfer ¼ cup parsley-garlic oil to medium bowl. Add shrimp and toss to coat. Pour remaining parsley-garlic oil into a cup. Cover shrimp and remaining oil separately and refrigerate.

Melt butter in a large heavy pot over medium-high heat. Add leeks and sauté until tender and wilted, about 5 minutes. Add potato, remaining 3 garlic cloves, and saffron. Sauté for 2 minutes. Add chicken stock and bring to a boil. Reduce heat to medium-low. Cover and simmer 30 minutes.

Working in batches, puree soup in blender or processor until smooth. Return to pot. Add cream and season with salt and pepper.

Heat a heavy medium skillet over low heat. Add shrimp and sauté until just opaque in center. Ladle soup into heated bowls with 6 shrimp halves per serving. Garnish with chives and several drops of remaining parsley-garlic oil and serve.

## wine suggestion: French Sancerre

*Notes: If using frozen shrimp, inquire if it was frozen in a wheat slurry (to prevent individual pieces from sticking to one another).*

# Spicy Tomato and Sausage Pasta

The spiciness of the pasta dish is nicely complemented by the sweetness of the Gorgonzola–Pear Salad (page 121). This will not be a high calorie meal if individual servings are moderate in size.

## ingredients:

4 large gluten-free Italian sausages
  (2 hot and 2 mild)

1½ cups dry white wine or water

1 medium onion, chopped

2 cloves garlic, finely chopped or
  passed through a garlic press

2 tablespoons olive oil

5 ounces mushrooms, sliced

1 can (28 ounces) crushed tomatoes

1 can (28 ounces) whole tomatoes, chopped
  (use tomatoes only, discarding the juice)

3 tablespoons fresh basil, very finely chopped
  (or 3 teaspoons dried basil)

¾ pound gluten-free penne pasta

Freshly grated Parmesan cheese

## 4 servings

In a large saucepan, cook sausages in ¾ cup of white wine over high heat until wine evaporates. Add another ¼ cup of wine to deglaze the saucepan. Cook sausages for a few minutes longer, turning occasionally, until lightly browned. Remove sausages and cut in ¼-inch slices (they should be pink inside). Set aside, along with any remaining liquid.

In the same saucepan, sauté onion and garlic in olive oil until onions are translucent. Add mushrooms and cook until limp. Add cooking liquid from sausages and remaining wine to the saucepan. Reduce liquid by half over medium-high heat. Add sliced sausage, crushed tomatoes, chopped whole tomatoes, and basil. Season with salt and pepper. Simmer for about 30-40 minutes, stirring occasionally.

Cook pasta to al dente stage in boiling salted water, drain, and toss with sauce. Serve with Parmesan cheese.

### wine suggestion:    Valpolicella or Chianti Classico

Notes: Your community very likely has a high quality meat market where you can purchase top-grade gluten-free sausages. An inferior product will translate into a poor sauce. If finding crushed tomatoes proves difficult, you may substitute 1 can (28 ounces) diced tomatoes and 1 can (14 ounces) tomato sauce for the crushed tomatoes.

# Cream of Yellow Squash Soup

### Chef Erol Tugrul, Café Margaux – Cocoa, Florida

A recent Zagat Restaurant Survey describes Café Margaux as a "great little French café," and bestows upon it the title of Most Popular Restaurant on the Atlantic Coast.

## ingredients:

10 yellow crookneck squash, halved, seeds
    scooped out, chopped

1 large carrot, chopped

3 celery ribs, chopped

1 medium onion, chopped

½ cup chopped leeks

1 tablespoon olive oil

3 quarts gluten-free chicken stock

1 tablespoon butter

1 tablespoon potato starch flour

2 cups heavy cream

## comment:

A delicately flavored soup that can be made vegetarian if a quality vegetable stock is substituted for chicken stock. Enjoy this soup either as a first course or as a light meal with a salad.

## 4 servings

Over medium-high heat, sauté squash, carrot, celery, onion, and leeks in olive oil until softened. Working in batches, puree vegetables in a blender, adding stock as needed. Combine vegetable puree and remaining stock in a heavy pot. Reduce by half over medium heat, stirring occasionally (about 30 minutes).

Meanwhile, melt butter in a small saucepan. Add flour. Cook over low heat, stirring frequently, for about 10 minutes. (This mixture is known as a roux.) Mix some of the soup into the roux, stirring constantly with a wire whisk until smooth, then whisk mixture back into the rest of the soup. Simmer, stirring frequently, until soup is lightly thickened. Add cream, combine thoroughly, and serve.

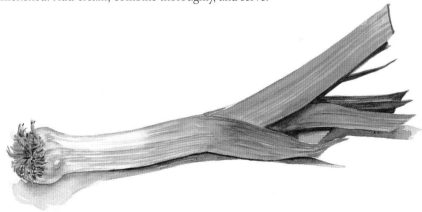

# Homemade Tacos

Some version of tacos is served at our house at least once a month. It is a hassle to fry up your own tortillas, but they are much better than anything store bought. Buy two dozen corn tortillas so that you have extra on hand if a few don't turn out. Serve with Banana-Pineapple Sauté (page 135) and Homemade Refried Beans (page 153—canned beans can also be substituted).

## ingredients:

### homemade taco seasoning

2 teaspoons arrowroot

1 teaspoon ground red pepper

2 teaspoons ground cumin

2 teaspoons garlic salt

1 teaspoon paprika

2 pounds ground beef or boneless, skinless
   chicken breast cut into 1-inch pieces

2 ripe tomatoes, sliced

1 cup shredded iceberg lettuce

1 cup grated cheddar cheese

Olives, guacamole, gluten-free sour cream,
   other toppings

1 dozen corn tortillas (experiment until you
   find your favorite brand, as quality varies)

Vegetable oil for frying

### 4 servings (3 tacos per person)

Combine arrowroot, red pepper, cumin, garlic salt, and paprika in a small bowl.

Brown ground beef and drain excess oil (or pan-fry chicken in a bit of oil). Add taco seasoning and 1½ cups water. Stir well. Bring to a boil, reduce heat, and simmer for 10 minutes. Place prepared tomatoes, lettuce, cheese, and taco toppings in small bowls for serving.

Fry taco shells ten minutes before serving. To prepare, heat ½-inch vegetable oil until shimmering, in a large skillet, over high heat. Using long-handled tongs, submerge a flat tortilla in the oil. Let it cook for about a minute until puffy, turn it over, and cook other side. Pick up one side of the tortilla with the tongs, fold in half to form a taco shell, and cook for about a minute more. Remove to a plate lined with paper toweling to drain. Repeat with remaining tortillas. (Note: The longer you fry the tortillas, the crisper they become. The first tortilla or two may not turn out if the oil is either too hot or not hot enough. It's a bit tricky, but will come more easily with practice.)

Assemble tacos and enjoy!

# Roasted Pork Tenderloin

Another very easy, tasty meal! The pork tenderloin may also be grilled for this dish. Serve with Sweet Sautéed Yams (page 142) and Classic Spinach Salad (page 123).

## ingredients:

2 pounds pork tenderloin

2 cloves garlic, finely minced or
   passed through a garlic press

## 4 servings

Preheat oven to 400°F. Place tenderloin on a rack in a shallow baking pan. Rub with garlic and season on all sides with salt and pepper. If one side has more fat on it, place the fatty side up.

Roast for about 30 minutes. Be careful not to overcook; the trick is to take it out of the oven while the center is just a bit pink (internal temperature will read 150°F. on a meat thermometer). Cover with foil and let rest for 5 minutes, then slice and serve.

## Variation:
## Roasted Pork Tenderloin with Pinot Noir Sauce

After tenderloin has finished cooking, remove from roasting pan. Add 2 cups chicken stock to the pan. Reduce by half. Add 1 cup Pinot Noir and reduce again by half. Off the fire, finish by stirring in 2 tablespoons whole grain gluten-free mustard. Serve this sauce with the tenderloin.

**wine suggestion:**   Oregon Pinot Noir

# Red Snapper Fillet with Spaghetti Squash, Saffron, and Tomato Cream

### Chef Todd Gray, Equinox - Washington, D.C.

Equinox is one of this city's premier fine dining establishments, offering sophisticated, pure American cuisine. Chef Gray uses fresh, local organic ingredients whenever possible. He is a James Beard Award Nominee for Chef of the Year, Mid-Atlantic, in 2001, and has won various "top table" awards from *Condé Nast, Bon Appétit, Esquire,* and *Gourmet* magazines. Serve with starter Yellow Tomato Soup with Avocado, Red Onion, and Mint (page 63) and for dessert Grand Marnier Semifreddo with Bittersweet Chocolate Sauce and Local Blackberries (page 206).

## *ingredients:*

1 medium spaghetti squash

6 red snapper fillets, cleaned

1 tablespoon grapeseed oil or olive oil

1 cup white wine

1 cup heavy cream

2 tablespoons butter

Juice from ½ lemon

1 teaspoon saffron threads

4 Italian plum tomatoes, diced and seeded
   (or 2 medium beefsteak tomatoes)

## *6 servings*

Spaghetti squash can be steamed quickly in a microwave. Pierce the skin with a fork, cut squash in half down the middle, and cover with plastic wrap. Microwave for 8-12 minutes, or until tender. (To cook in the conventional manner, bake at 400°F. for about 30-40 minutes, or until skin is easily pierced with a knife.) When cool enough to handle, remove seeds. Using a fork, scrape out the flesh, which will have the texture of spaghetti. Divide "spaghetti" among 6 dinner plates.

Season snapper fillets with salt and pepper. Heat grapeseed oil to medium temperature in large sauté pan. Sauté fish skin side down for 2 minutes. Turn fish and finish cooking.

In a saucepan over medium heat, reduce white wine to one quarter its original volume. Add cream and reduce by half. Whisk in butter, then lemon juice and saffron, stirring well to combine. Pass sauce through a fine mesh strainer and return to the saucepan. Add diced tomatoes and stir. Season with salt and pepper.

Divide sauce between six serving plates and place a red snapper fillet in the middle of each plate. Serve immediately.

## *wine suggestion:*   Pine Ridge Chenin Blanc Viognier, California 1999

# Vegetable Tofu Stir-Fry

Although the list of ingredients seems long, this recipe does not take much time to prepare. Freezing the tofu gives it a chewier texture, which is desirable for this dish. Serve with Master Recipe for Long Grain White Rice (page 151).

## ingredients:

1 package traditional firm tofu,
    previously frozen

### marinade

2 tablespoons peanut oil
1 tablespoon sesame oil
1 tablespoon grated ginger or ginger juice
    (see Sources)
1 clove garlic, minced or
    passed through a garlic press

1 tablespoon peanut oil
¼ small red onion, chopped
2 scallions, chopped
1 tablespoon grated ginger or ginger juice
1 clove garlic, thinly sliced
2 medium carrots, peeled and
    sliced diagonally ¼-inch thick
½ medium cauliflower, cut in 1-inch pieces
1 cup asparagus, cut in 2-inch long pieces
4-6 large leaves bok choy, chopped
1 tablespoon sesame oil
½ cup peanuts, toasted
Gluten-free tamari to taste

## 4 servings

Drain tofu by placing it on a plate, resting another plate on top, and setting a 1-pound weight atop the second plate. After 10 minutes or so discard excess water. Chop tofu into ½-inch cubes and place in a glass dish. Combine marinade ingredients and pour over tofu cubes. Cover and refrigerate for an hour or so.

Preheat oven to 400°F.

Remove tofu cubes from marinade. Spread in a single layer on a baking sheet. Bake for 10-15 minutes.

Heat peanut oil in a wok over medium-high heat. Add red onion and scallions. Cook, stirring, for 1 minute, then add ginger and garlic. Cook, stirring, for 1 minute more. Add carrots and cauliflower. Stir-fry for 3 minutes. Add asparagus, bok choy, and sesame oil. Stir-fry until vegetables are crisp tender. Add peanuts and season with salt and pepper. Mound stir-fried vegetables on a bed of rice. Top with baked tofu.

# Tomato Basil Soup

This soup is a great way to preserve the wonderful taste of summer with fresh tomatoes and basil. You may need to add a tablespoon of tomato paste when using fresh tomatoes.
Serve with Baked Cheese Wafers (page 28) and spinach greens topped with Tomatillo Salsa (page 32).
This recipe is adapted from *Pasta & Co. By Request* by Marcella Rosene (Pasta & Co., 1991). Pasta & Co. is Seattle's premier, upscale take-out food shop with five locations.

## ingredients:

¼ cup olive oil

1 large onion, chopped

2-3 garlic cloves, chopped or
    passed through a garlic press

1 can (28 ounces) crushed tomatoes (or 4
    garden tomatoes, skinned and chopped)

1 can (15 ounces) whole tomatoes (or 2
    garden tomatoes, skinned and chopped)

2 cans (14.5 ounces each) low salt,
    gluten-free chicken stock

3 ounces fresh basil leaves, finely chopped

¾ teaspoon sugar

½ teaspoon pepper

½ teaspoon thyme

## makes 8 cups

Heat olive oil in a large soup pot. Add onions and garlic. Cook until soft without letting garlic brown. Stir in tomatoes, stock, basil, sugar, pepper, and thyme. Simmer for 20 minutes. Remove from heat and puree in a food processor in small batches to avoid splattering.

## wine suggestion:   Italian Chianti Classico

*Notes: A quick way to remove the skins of fresh tomatoes is to briefly blanch the tomatoes in boiling water. Once skin splits, remove from boiling water and immerse in cold water for a few minutes. Skins should slip off easily.*

# Pan-Fried Chicken in Marsala

We enjoy the simplicity of this dish. Serve with Roasted Asparagus (page 137) and gluten-free pasta tossed with butter and Parmesan.

## ingredients:

2 whole chicken breasts, boneless, skinless,
    and halved

1 cup gluten-free flour mix

1 teaspoon salt

½ teaspoon pepper

3 teaspoons olive oil

½ medium onion, chopped

2 cloves of garlic, finely chopped or passed
    through a garlic press

¼ cup dry white wine

½ cup sweet Marsala wine

## 4 servings

Place chicken between two pieces of plastic wrap and pound to ¼-inch thickness. (If breast is fairly thick, use a sharp knife to cut slits into the underside of breast to flatten it out a bit first, as it is important to pound it out very thinly.) Place gluten-free flour mix, salt, and pepper in a plastic bag or on a plate. Dredge chicken pieces in the flour to coat evenly, shaking off excess.

In a large, heavy skillet, heat 1 teaspoon olive oil and add onions and garlic. Sauté until onions are translucent but not browned. Remove onions from skillet. Add wine to skillet, deglaze, and pour wine over onions. Set aside. Rinse skillet or wipe out with a paper towel.

Replace skillet over high heat. When hot, add 1 teaspoon olive oil and half the chicken pieces. Cook quickly on both sides until they begin to brown. Remove to a warm plate and cook remaining chicken in another teaspoon of oil. Remove chicken, add Marsala to skillet, and reduce briefly. Return chicken to skillet, add reserved onions with their liquid and coat chicken with the sauce. Serve immediately.

**wine suggestion:**   Salice Salentino

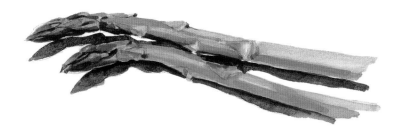

# Moroccan Chickpea Stew

### Chef Tom Douglas, Dahlia Lounge, Etta's Seafood, and Palace Kitchen — Seattle, Washington

Tom Douglas is a winner of the James Beard Award, considered the Academy Award of the culinary world! He is known for his wonderful restaurants and his Rub with Love meat rubs that add great flavor to salmon, pork, and chicken (see Sources).

## ingredients:

2 tablespoons olive oil

1 medium onion, peeled and sliced

1 teaspoon minced garlic

½ teaspoon ground cumin

½ teaspoon ground coriander

1 tablespoon curry powder

1 cinnamon stick

2 cups canned crushed tomatoes

⅓ cup dry white wine

1 red bell pepper, roasted, peeled,
    seeded, and chopped

¼ teaspoon gluten-free harissa (or to taste),
    or substitute Tabasco

1 cup cooked chickpeas (garbanzo beans)

## chef's comment:

This Moroccan-inspired vegetarian stew is seasoned with a little harissa, which is a traditional Moroccan hot sauce. (Try the "Dea" brand.) Tabasco is a fine substitution for harissa; you can also use cayenne pepper or red chili flakes. At the Dahlia Lounge, this stew is served with couscous, but brown rice is used to make the dish gluten-free. Serve with Curry Roasted Vegetables (page 143) and Brown Rice with Pine Nuts and Currants (page 152).

## 4 servings

Heat olive oil in a large skillet over medium heat and sauté onions until soft and caramelized, about 15-20 minutes. Add garlic, cumin, coriander, curry powder, and cinnamon stick, and sauté for a couple of minutes. Add tomatoes, white wine, and red bell pepper. Simmer for 15-20 minutes. Remove mixture from skillet and discard cinnamon stick. Puree the stew semi-smooth in a food processor or blender, working in batches if necessary. (Leave a little bit of a chunky texture). Return stew to skillet and season to taste with harissa (or Tabasco), salt and pepper. Add chickpeas and reheat the stew. Serve hot.

## wine suggestion:   Washington Lemberger or a Zinfandel

*Note: Canned roasted red bell pepper and chickpeas are perfectly acceptable, and will save you much preparation time.*

# Buttermilk Chicken

This is the very best "fried chicken" we have ever had. It is less caloric than regular fried chicken, since the recipe uses skinless white meat (although you may use dark meat if you wish). A year-round favorite, it makes great picnic and back yard fare. Serve with Spinach Basil Kumquat Salad (page 124) and a wild rice mix (see Sources).

## ingredients:

3 large, whole, boneless, skinless
   chicken breasts, cut into 2-inch pieces

1 quart buttermilk

3-4 cups vegetable oil for frying

2-3 cups gluten-free flour mix or rice flour

2 teaspoons salt

1 teaspoon pepper

## 4 servings (with leftovers)

In a large glass dish, soak chicken overnight in the buttermilk.

The next day, preheat frying oil to 400°F. in a deep fryer or heavy skillet. Mix flour with salt and pepper. Put flour mixture on a plate or in a large plastic bag. Dredge chicken pieces in flour, shaking off excess. Fry chicken in batches so as not to overcrowd the fryer. (Doing so will lower the temperature of the oil and make the chicken greasy.) Each batch will cook to a nice golden brown in approximately 5-7 minutes. (You might want to test a piece for doneness by cutting into the center.) Drain on paper toweling. Serve either hot or cold.

## wine suggestion:   Spanish Rioja

# Simple Sushi

This is a fun family project. You may choose your favorite ingredients from the list below, or substitute if you wish.
Serve with pickled ginger, tamari, and Miso Soup (opposite page). Have all ingredients ready before making rice.

## ingredients:

2½ cups hot, cooked sushi rice or
   short grain white rice
¼ cup seasoned rice vinegar
5 nori sheets, cut 4 x 6½-inches
Wasabi, gluten-free
¼ pound cooked shrimp or prawns
¼ pound cooked crabmeat,
   picked over for shells
2 large carrots, thinly sliced in 6-inch strips
1 large cucumber, thinly sliced in
   6-inch strips
1 medium avocado, thinly sliced lengthwise
Pickled ginger, gluten-free
Bamboo rolling mat
Tamari, gluten-free

*Note: Some fish markets have sashimi grade ahi (yellow fin tuna), albacore, and other top-grade raw seafood; however, I prefer to put cooked seafood in our sushi when feeding the children.*

## comment:

Bamboo rolling mats, nori (sheets of seaweed for making rolls), pickled ginger, and wasabi (Japanese horseradish) can all be found in the Asian food section of most supermarkets.

### 4 servings (with leftovers) – 10 rolls (60 pieces)

Place cooked rice in a large, flat-bottomed, nonmetallic bowl. Using a flat rice paddle or rubber spatula, spread an even layer of rice on the bottom of bowl. Make a hollow in the center and pour some, but not all, of the vinegar into the hollow. Using a slicing motion, lift and mix the rice (as opposed to stirring); this technique is known as folding. Your goal is to evenly blend the vinegar into the rice so that the rice is slightly sticky. Gradually add remaining vinegar if needed. (Do not add too much, or the rice will become mushy.)

Once rice and vinegar are combined and have cooled to body temperature, cover with a warm, damp towel to hold rice at this temperature. If rice becomes colder, it will harden and become difficult to work with.

## rolling sushi:

Position nori in the middle of the bamboo rolling mat. (Lower edge of nori should be about 1-inch from the bottom edge of the mat.) With damp hands, take a golf ball-sized handful of sushi rice and spread evenly from left to right in the center of the nori, forming a log shape. (Be sure to leave a ¾-inch strip of nori uncovered on the upper edge of the sheet.) Form a channel down the center of the rice to help keep the filling in place. Spread ⅛ teaspoon of wasabi from left to right across the surface of the rice. Place a few tablespoons of seafood and vegetables (from ingredient list) in the channel. While holding filling in place with your fingers, use your thumbs to lift up the edge of the bamboo rolling mat closest to you. Wrap mat around nori and roll away from you while pressing down evenly. The ¾-inch strip of nori at the end of the sheet will adhere to the outside of the roll and form a seal. Apply firm pressure down the length of the roll to seal end to end, then gently roll once more to restore a cylindrical shape. With a sharp, clean knife, slice roll into six equal pieces to form bite size pieces of sushi.

## wine suggestion:

Sake or Italian Soave

# Miso Soup

This recipe is from Cynthia Lair's cookbook, *Feeding the Whole Family* (Moon Smile Press, 1997), a whole foods cookbook for babies and young children (and their parents). It is a great book for anyone interested in getting their children off to a healthy start in life. The book includes good vegetarian meals, recipes to incorporate more legumes into your diet (providing nutrients that the typical gluten-free diet lacks), and ideas for using quinoa, brown rice, tofu, sea vegetables, greens, and alternative sweeteners.

## ingredients:

4-inch piece of wakame
  (a sea vegetable found in the Asian
  section of most supermarkets)
6 cups water
1 tablespoon grated gingerroot
¼ pound firm tofu, cut in cubes
4 tablespoons light or
  mellow unpasteurized miso
1-2 scallions, thinly sliced for garnish

## comment:

Miso is a salted paste made from cooked and aged soybeans. The soybeans are mixed with various grains and other ingredients to produce a variety of flavors. Be sure you buy a miso that is gluten-free. Look for it in the refrigerated section of your store.

## 4 servings

Place wakame in a small bowl of water. Soak for 5 minutes. Put 6 cups of water in a 3-quart pot and bring to a simmer. Remove wakame from water and chop into small pieces, removing the spine. Add chopped wakame to water. Simmer for 10 minutes, adding gingerroot and tofu cubes during the last minute or two of cooking time. Pour a bit of broth into each serving bowl and dissolve 1 tablespoon (or less, according to taste) of miso into each bowl. Fill bowl with soup, stirring gently. Garnish each bowl with a light sprinkling of sliced scallions.

## for babies
## 10 months and older:

Remove a little of the cooked wakame from the soup. Chop very finely and add to pureed cereal or vegetables you are serving the baby. Wakame is a source of calcium and other minerals.

# Omelets

This recipe makes one large omelet to split between two people. Though this is an unconventional way to make an omelet,
it is ultimately quicker and allows the family to sit down to eat together. Serve with Apple Sauté (page 135).

### ingredients:

4-5 large eggs
½ tablespoon butter
⅓- ½ cup grated cheddar cheese
⅛ cup chives or scallions, chopped

### comment:

**2 servings**

To this basic omelet recipe you may add any number of ingredients. I like to add crumbled cooked bacon inside the omelet and top it with avocado slices and tomato salsa. Try your own combinations with mushrooms, onions, sausage, peppers, herbs, etc. For a fluffy omelet, beat the yolks and whites separately until light and airy (the whites should stand in firm but not stiff peaks), and fold together before cooking.

In a small bowl, lightly whisk the eggs. Over medium heat, melt butter in a non-stick skillet. When butter is fragrant and sizzling, pour eggs into pan. As eggs begin to set, use a plastic spatula to gently move the cooked eggs away from the edges of the skillet and let the uncooked eggs run underneath. When eggs are almost completely set, add cheese, scallions, and other fillings. Continue to cook over medium heat while cheese melts then flip one side of omelet over onto the other side so it is folded in half and serve.

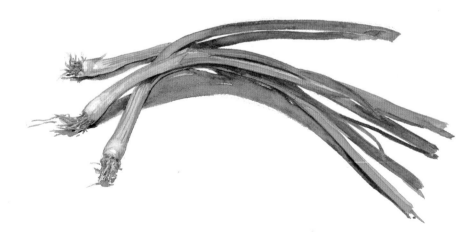

# Pan-Fried Pork Chops with Lime Juice

A quick, flavorful meat entrée. Serve with brown rice and Baby Lettuces with Beets, Pumpkin Seeds, and Pesto (page 123).

## ingredients:

1-2 teaspoons vegetable oil

Four pork chops, cut ¾-inch thick

Juice of 1 lime

## 4 servings

Heat oil in a large skillet over high heat, sear the chops 4-5 minutes per side until browned and cooked through. (Be careful not to overcook; chops should still be juicy in the center.) Add lime juice to deglaze the pan. Pour over the chops.

**wine suggestion:**  French Red Burgundy

# Coconut Chicken

### Chef Thoa Nguyen, Chinoise Café — Seattle, Washington

Chinoise is an Asian grill and sushi bar that has become a weekly destination for many Seattleites. Although the entire menu is mouth-watering, this dish has become my personal favorite. I am grateful to Thoa for taking so much time to adjust the recipe for home use. Fish sauce and coconut milk can be found in the Asian food section of most supermarkets. Serve with Edamame (page 152), jasmine rice, or sliced fresh cucumbers.

## ingredients:

### marinade

⅓ cup fish sauce (see Sources)

⅔ cup coconut milk

1½ tablespoons yellow curry powder

½ cup sugar

⅓ cup water

1 tablespoon vegetable oil

3 pounds chicken thighs (boneless and
    skinless), pounded to ¼-inch thickness

### Coconut Dipping Sauce

14 ounces coconut milk

⅓ cup creamy peanut butter

½ teaspoon yellow curry powder

2 tablespoons sugar

2 tablespoons fish sauce

## serves 6

Combine all marinade ingredients in a large bowl and mix well. Submerge chicken thighs in marinade, cover, and refrigerate for at least 2 hours.

Preheat oven to 425°F. Remove chicken from marinade and arrange in a single layer in a shallow baking pan. Reduce oven to 375°F. and bake chicken for about 20 minutes, or until golden brown. (If you prefer, you may grill the chicken instead.)

While chicken is cooking, bring all sauce ingredients to a boil and mix well. Serve in small warm bowls, presenting one with each plate for dipping.

Instead of wine, try green tea with this dish.

# "Groovy" Gnocchi with Portobello Mushroom Carpaccio

## Chef Ludger Szmania, Szmania's – Seattle, Washington

Szmania's is a warm, inviting neighborhood restaurant in Seattle that has earned accolades in *Zagat*, *Gourmet* magazine, and *Food & Wine* magazine. Ludger is such a talented chef, and we are thankful to have his excellent restaurant in our neighborhood! The gnocchi is "groovy" because of the grooves impressed upon each one with a fork or gnocchi board. Make a double or triple batch of gnocchi if you wish to freeze some for quick weekday meals.

## ingredients:

### Gnocchi

2 large russet potatoes,
    unpeeled and scrubbed
1½ cups gluten-free flour mix
½ teaspoon xanthan gum
2 egg yolks
Dash of nutmeg

### Portobello Mushroom Carpaccio

3 large portobello mushrooms
¼ cup olive oil
¼ cup red wine vinegar
2 tablespoons butter
2 tablespoons shallots, finely chopped
1 cup white wine
½ cup gluten-free chicken stock
2 tablespoons chèvre (goat cheese)
4 tablespoons herbs (parsley and chives),
    finely chopped
Olive oil
Asiago cheese, grated, to taste

## 4 servings

**Gnocchi:** Bake the potatoes in a 400ºF. oven for 45 minutes. Let cool and cut in half. With a spoon, scoop the soft cooked flesh into a bowl. Pass cooked potato through a potato ricer. Combine the "riced" potato with the flour, egg yolks, and nutmeg. Season with salt and pepper. Blend with a wooden spoon, dusting with flour every so often to prevent the dough from sticking.

On a smooth, floured surface, roll out the dough into a long ½-inch cylinder. Cut lengthwise into 1-inch pieces and "groove" the gnocchi with either fork or gnocchi board. It's a good idea to do this over a floured tray so the gnocchi do not stick to the counter or to each other. Once formed, boil gnocchi in salted water until they float. Remove from heat, drain, and shock in an ice water bath.

(To freeze, spread uncooked gnocchi in a single layer on a lightly floured baking sheet. Wrap tightly and freeze until gnocchi are hard, then package in freezer bags.)

**Portobello Mushroom Carpaccio:** Marinate the mushrooms with olive oil and vinegar. Cook either on the grill or in a skillet over low to medium heat. Cool.

Heat butter in a skillet over low heat. Sauté shallots until brown. Add white wine and reduce by half. Add chicken stock and again reduce by half. Lastly, add the goat cheese and herbs, mixing well.

Slice the cooked portobellos very thinly on the bias and arrange on each plate. Sauté the gnocchi in a bit of olive oil, adding salt, freshly ground pepper, and Asiago. Place atop sliced mushrooms and drizzle with the sauce.
Garnish with fresh herbs and enjoy.

**wine suggestion:** French White Burgundy

*Recipe requires an hour or more preparation/cooking time.*

(continued on next page)

🕐 – indicates a quick meal

# WINTER

# Caramelized Cremini Mushroom Soup with Fresh Rosemary

### Chef Gerry Hayden, Aureole – New York, New York

This starter complements Gerry's Pan-Roasted Pork Tenderloin with Fennel, Radish, and Arugula Salad (following page) and his dessert
Floating Islands with Caramel Blood Oranges (page 212).

## ingredients:

2 tablespoons butter

1 pound cremini mushrooms, cleaned
   and sliced

½ cup shallots, sliced

2 cups water or gluten-free chicken stock

½ tablespoon finely chopped rosemary

2 tablespoons extra virgin olive oil (optional)

Freshly ground white pepper

## 4 servings

In a heavy-bottomed soup pot, heat butter to a light brown color. Stir in mushrooms, reserving a few nice slices for garnish. Add sliced shallots and continue to cook until mushrooms and shallots are a deep golden brown. Pour in water or chicken stock and add rosemary. Season with salt and freshly ground white pepper. Simmer for 10 minutes.

Puree mixture in a blender until very smooth and adjust seasoning. Ladle soup into heated bowls and garnish with reserved mushroom slices and a drizzle of olive oil. A fresh grind of white pepper completes the dish.

# Pan-Roasted Pork Tenderloin
# with Fennel, Radish, and Arugula Salad

### Chef Gerry Hayden, Aureole - New York, New York

Charlie Palmer's Aureole is revered as a paradigm of progressive American cuisine. It is one of New York's finest restaurants. Restaurant critic Bob Lape says of Aureole, "An elegant dining experience packed with punch … boldly flavored seasonal dishes … theatrically inspired three-dimensional desserts serve to delight all the senses." Chef de cuisine Gerry Hayden taps his experience from some of the finest kitchens in America: the critically acclaimed River Café, Marguery Grill, Tribeca Grill, and Aqua.

## ingredients:

¼ cup balsamic or red wine vinegar

¼ cup extra virgin olive oil

1 fennel bulb, trimmed, washed,
    and sliced thin

1 bunch arugula, washed and julienned

10 red radishes, washed and sliced into circles

1½ pounds fresh pork tenderloin

2 tablespoons canola oil

3 tablespoons butter

¼ cup water

## chef's comments:

Serve Caramelized Cremini Mushroom Soup with Fresh Rosemary (previous page) as a first course, and serve Floating Islands with Caramel Blood Oranges (page 212) for dessert.

## 4 servings

In a small bowl, whisk together 1 tablespoon of the vinegar and 3 tablespoons of the olive oil. Season with salt and pepper. Set aside. In a separate larger salad bowl, combine the fennel, arugula, and radishes.

Season the pork tenderloin with salt and freshly ground pepper. In a heavy bottomed sauté pan over medium-high heat, sear tenderloin in canola oil until light brown on all sides. Lower heat slightly and add 2 tablespoons butter to pan. Baste tenderloin with butter for 3-4 minutes (internal temperature 150°F.) Remove tenderloin from pan, cover with foil, and let rest on cutting board for 5-8 minutes.

Pour excess grease out of pan and return to heat. Pour in water to deglaze any pan drippings, scraping them up with a wooden spoon if necessary. Pour in remaining vinegar and reduce by half. Whisk in 1 tablespoon butter and 1 tablespoon olive oil. Remove pan from heat and adjust seasoning of sauce.

Toss vegetables with the reserved vinaigrette and adjust seasoning. Arrange salad on plates. Slice pork and arrange on top of each salad, spooning sauce around the plate.

## wine suggestion:    1998 Frog's Leap Sauvignon Blanc

# Bathing Rama

This dish's curious name is of Thai origin. Essentially, it consists of pan-fried chicken strips with a peanut sauce, served over rice and spinach. This quick, satisfying meal is ideal for a busy schedule.

## ingredients:

¾ cup coconut milk

2 teaspoons ginger juice or grated fresh ginger

¼ cup gluten-free tamari or
    gluten-free soy sauce

2 teaspoons brown rice vinegar

¼ cup chili oil

2 tablespoons sesame oil

1 cup peanut butter (cashew or almond
    butter may be substituted)

½ cup (or less) water

2 whole chicken breasts, boneless and skinless

2 teaspoons peanut oil

1-2 cloves garlic, minced

4 servings hot, cooked white rice
    (try sushi or pearl rice)

4 handfuls of washed spinach leaves

## 4 servings

Combine coconut milk, ginger, tamari, vinegar, chili oil, sesame oil, and peanut butter in a blender. With motor running, add water gradually until mixture reaches desired consistency. (The heat from the rice is enough to warm this sauce, but, if you prefer, you may heat the sauce briefly in a saucepan before serving.)

Cut chicken into strips ½-inch wide. Heat oil in a skillet over medium-high heat; when hot, add chicken and garlic. Season with salt and pepper. Cook, stirring, until chicken is nicely browned. (It should be moist and not overcooked.)

To serve, make a bed of the rice and spinach leaves on four warmed dinner plates. Heap chicken strips on the rice and spinach. Top with peanut sauce and serve immediately.

Green tea, rather than wine, is recommended for this dish.

*Note: Ginger juice is a great item to keep on hand.
Made by The Ginger People, it can be substituted for fresh grated ginger
in the same quantities without the extra work. (see Sources)*

# Supper Nachos with Homemade Corn Tortilla Chips

This is a family recipe that is especially appealing when prepared in a baking dish made of glazed Mexican pottery. This one-dish meal lends itself to preparing ahead for parties. If time is short, you may prefer to use your favorite gluten-free packaged tortilla chips instead of making them yourself.
Serve with margaritas; many margarita mixes are gluten-free, as is most tequila.

## ingredients:

½ pound ground beef

½ pound gluten-free pork sausage

1 large onion, chopped

1 can (12 ounces) gluten-free refried beans
    (or recipe on page 153)

1 can (7 ounces) chopped green chilies

2 cups of grated cheddar and
    Monterey Jack cheese

8 ounces gluten-free green or red taco sauce

10-15 corn tortillas

¾ cup vegetable oil

## Garnishes:

(choose several to suit your taste)

⅛ cup chopped fresh chives

⅛ cup chopped black olives

Avocado, sliced or made into guacamole

Gluten-free sour cream

## 6 servings

Preheat oven to 400°F.

In a large skillet, brown the ground beef and sausage over medium-high heat. Add chopped onion and cook, stirring frequently. Drain fat and season meat with salt and pepper to taste. Using the back of a spoon, spread the refried beans evenly in a shallow 13 x 9-inch baking dish. Spread meat mixture over the beans and sprinkle with the chopped green chilies. Cover evenly with grated cheese. Drizzle taco sauce over the cheese. Bake uncovered for 20-25 minutes.

While the supper nachos are baking, stack 4-5 corn tortillas on top of each other and slice through the stack to cut each tortilla in half, then slice each half stack of tortillas into thirds (triangular-shaped chip size). Heat oil on high heat until very hot (shimmering) in a large, heavy, skillet. Oil should be deep enough to cover tortilla chips as they cook. Add about 8 tortilla chips to the oil. Cook quickly until they firm up. Using long-handled tongs, remove chips to a bowl lined with paper towels. Drain briefly.

Top supper nachos with your choice of garnishes and serve with homemade chips.

# Meat Loaf

Great comfort food to have from time to time. Although it is not necessary to sauté the onions first, it will lightly caramelize them, thereby enhancing their flavor. My mom always covered the top lightly with ketchup, which may seem quirky, but old habits and memories die hard. Serve with Potato Pancakes (page 144) and Sugar Peas (page 143).

## ingredients:

1 tablespoon olive oil

1 clove garlic, finely chopped or
    passed through a garlic press

½ large onion, chopped

1 tablespoon chopped fresh sage (optional)

1 pound ground beef

1 tablespoon Worcestershire sauce

1 tablespoon gluten-free Dijon mustard

1 egg, slightly beaten

¾ teaspoon salt

¼ heaping teaspoon pepper

½ cup gluten-free bread crumbs

Ketchup (optional)

## 4 servings

Preheat oven to 350°F.

Sauté garlic and onion in olive oil until onions are translucent. If using sage, add and cook for 1 minute more. Let cool completely. Butter a 5 x 9-inch baking dish. In a large bowl combine ground beef, cooled onions, Worcestershire, Dijon mustard, egg, salt, pepper, and bread crumbs. Mix ingredients well with your hands, taking care to avoid overworking the mixture. Place meat in prepared baking dish and form into a loaf shape. Using the back of a spoon, spread ketchup over the top of the meat loaf. Bake for 35-40 minutes, until internal temperature is 135°F., medium rare. Slice and serve.

## wine suggestion:   California Syrah

# Stuffed Quail with Spinach, Pine Nuts, and Fresh Chanterelle Mushrooms

*Chef Ludger Szmania, Szmania's - Seattle, Washington*

Szmania's is a warm, inviting neighborhood restaurant in Seattle that has earned accolades in *Gourmet* magazine, the *Zagat* survey, and *Food & Wine* magazine. I enjoy stopping in for a seat at the counter to watch the chef and learn new techniques. Serve this meal with wild rice or Creamy Polenta (page 148).

## ingredients:

1 bunch spinach

3 tablespoons olive oil, plus additional
  for roasting quail

½ large onion, finely diced (reserve
  2 tablespoons for chanterelles)

1 clove garlic, finely chopped

½ cup Asiago cheese, grated

½ cup pine nuts, toasted

4 boneless quail (all bones are removed
  except those in the wings and legs)

4 tablespoons butter, softened

3 cups fresh chanterelle mushrooms,
  cleaned and sliced

¾ cup dry white wine

2 tablespoons parsley, coarsely chopped

## chef's comments:

The quail for this recipe are available in many grocery stores, but you may need to place a special order a few days in advance. They are very small, so if you are serving big eaters, you may want to prepare two quail per portion.

### 4 servings

Preheat oven to 350°F.

Cut off root end of spinach, leaving stems on, and wash thoroughly. Blanch for a few seconds in boiling water, then immerse in ice water to stop it from cooking further. Drain spinach and dry on paper toweling. Cut up coarsely.

In a medium skillet, heat 3 tablespoons of olive oil over moderate heat. Add diced onions (reserve 2 tablespoons) and sauté until golden brown. Add the garlic and spinach. Sauté for 3-4 minutes more. If the pan gets too dry, add a little olive oil.

Remove spinach from skillet and put on a plate, pouring any excess liquid back into skillet. Reduce liquid to a honey-like consistency. Add the spinach, Asiago, and pine nuts to the reduction.

Stuff the quail with the spinach mixture. (If preparing in advance, allow the stuffing to cool thoroughly in the refrigerator before stuffing). Using cooking twine, tie legs together to secure the stuffing. Season with salt and pepper.

**Stuffed Quail with Spinach, Pine Nuts, and Fresh Chanterelle Mushrooms**

In a large skillet over high heat, sear the stuffed quail on all sides in a bit of olive oil. Turn quail on their backs and roast in the oven for 15 minutes (they should be pink within when finished). Remove from oven and let stand for a few minutes before serving.

While quail is roasting, heat 1 tablespoon of the butter in a medium skillet over moderate heat. Add the reserved 2 tablespoons of onion and sauté until golden brown. Add chanterelles and sauté (a lot of moisture will come out). Cook until pan is almost dry, then add white wine. Turn heat to high and reduce liquid by half, seasoning with salt and pepper. Add parsley and remaining butter, mixing thoroughly.

To serve, remove twine from quail. Ladle chanterelles onto center of each serving plate and place quail on top.

**wine suggestions:**   Pinot Noir or Syrah

**Tips:** Toasting pine nuts: Preheat oven to 325°F. Spread pine nuts out in an even layer on a baking sheet. Bake for 5-10 minutes, or until light golden in color. Watch carefully to avoid burning.

**Cleaning mushrooms:** Never soak mushrooms in water to clean them, as they will absorb it like a sponge. Use a damp paper towel to wipe them, or, if absolutely necessary, rinse quickly and dry immediately.

# Gnocchi Sautéed with Rosemary, Sage, and Almonds

### Chef Lynne Vea — Seattle, Washington

Lynne is a talented rising star in the culinary world. Her years as a chef on the Pacific Coast have given her the opportunity to explore and celebrate the diversity of the culinary world. Lynne's creations are a taste sensation, and I always look forward to attending her cooking classes in the Seattle area. She is a food stylist and also works with Chef John Sarich (of Chateau Ste. Michelle winery fame) as his production assistant for the television show, *Best of Taste*.

## ingredients:

½ cup Italian Bread Crumbs (page 168)
½ teaspoon gluten-free celery salt
¼ teaspoon ground white pepper
1 recipe of Ludger's Groovy Gnocchi
   (page 93), made in advance and frozen
2 tablespoons butter
1 tablespoon olive oil
¼ cup slivered almonds
2 cloves garlic, minced
4-5 fresh sage leaves, finely sliced
1 sprig fresh rosemary
2 tablespoons chopped Italian parsley
Spicy Winter Tomato Salad (page 129)
Lemon wedges or Truffle Oil with
   Capers (page 129)

## chef's comments:

Gnocchi, little poached pillows made of potato and flour, make a perfect alternative to the usual pasta dish. Sage is a classic Tuscan addition. This dish is made especially appealing when arranged on rustic plates around a bed of spicy Winter Tomato Salad.

## 4 servings

In a small bowl combine the bread crumbs, celery salt, and white pepper. Set aside.

Bring a large pot of salted water to a boil. Drop in handfuls of gnocchi and cook until they float. Remove with a slotted spoon and shock in an ice water bath. Drain and set aside.

In a non-stick skillet, heat the butter and oil. Add the almonds and cook, stirring, for 1-2 minutes, or until lightly golden. Add the garlic and herbs and stir briefly. Toss in gnocchi and stir to coat. Sprinkle in the bread crumb mixture evenly and stir-fry until each little pillow is crusty and lightly browned, 3-4 minutes. Keep warm.

To serve this meal, place about ⅓ cup of Spicy Tomato Salad in a tight mound in the center of each plate. Arrange the gnocchi in a spiral pattern around the salad. Sprinkle the almonds around the plate. Drizzle lightly with lemon juice (or Truffle Oil with Capers) and garnish with fresh herbs and shaved pecorino cheese if desired.

## wine suggestion:   a good Italian Chianti

*Note: If you can find gluten-free frozen gnocchi, buy them; otherwise try Ludger's "Groovy" Gnocchi. Take some time on the weekend to double the batch and freeze it so you can make this a quick meal during the week. Kids love to make this, so you can turn production into a fun family project.*

# Apricot Pecan Chicken

This is an excellent, nutty chicken dish. Serve with Mushroom Mélange (page 146) and Spinach Sautéed with Garlic and Lemon (page 146).
Recipe adapted from *Bay and Ocean: Ark Restaurant Cuisine,* Main and Lucas, (Ladysmith Limited, 1986).

## *ingredients:*

½ cup white wine

½ cup thinly sliced dried apricots

2 whole chicken breasts, boneless,
    skinless, and halved

2 cups pecans, finely chopped

¼ teaspoon paprika

½ teaspoon white pepper

1 teaspoon curry powder

1 egg

¼ cup milk

¼ cup gluten-free flour mix

2 tablespoons butter

2 tablespoons olive oil

1 teaspoon minced garlic

Juice of ½ lemon

Few dashes of Tabasco or chili oil

½ cup Madeira

½ cup gluten-free chicken stock

½ cup heavy cream

## *4 servings*

Cover apricots with wine and set aside.

Remove tenderloins from chicken breasts and pound chicken to ¼-inch thickness.

Mix together pecans, paprika, white pepper, and curry powder in a shallow bowl. Lightly beat egg and milk in another shallow bowl to make an egg wash. Dredge chicken breasts lightly in flour. Dip floured chicken breasts in egg wash, allowing excess to drip off, then roll in pecan mixture, coating thoroughly.

Simmer apricots and wine in a small nonreactive saucepan until apricots are tender. Meanwhile, in a large, heavy skillet over medium heat, melt butter and olive oil. Add pecan coated chicken and cover. Cook until browned (about 3 minutes per side). Remove chicken to a warmed serving dish.

Add garlic, lemon juice, Tabasco, Madeira, and chicken stock to the skillet and reduce by half. Add cream and reduce a bit until well blended. Pour sauce over chicken and garnish with apricots.

## *wine suggestion:*  California Pinot Noir

# Cannelloni in Marinara Sauce

Part of this recipe was adapted from Amy Bogino Eernissee's collection of old family recipes that she compiled into a book and gave to friends one year during the holidays. I use her wonderful little book a lot. Serve with a green salad.

## ingredients:

1 recipe Marinara Sauce (page 37)

6 ounces gluten-free lasagna noodles
  (see Sources)

15 ounces gluten-free ricotta cheese

¾ cup grated Parmesan cheese

¾ cup finely chopped flat leaf
  Italian parsley (about ½ bunch)

1 egg, lightly beaten

Grated Parmesan cheese

## 4 servings

Preheat oven to 350°F.

If you have the marinara sauce prepared and frozen, this recipe can be made more quickly. Defrost the sauce in a medium saucepan on low heat. (You can also make the sauce and plan on adding 30 minutes or so to your preparation time.)

Cook lasagna noodles until they are al dente (offer some resistance when bitten into), as pasta will cook further when placed in the oven later on. Drain in colander and rinse in cold water. Drain well. Remove lasagna noodles from colander and lay side by side on a clean work surface.

Combine ricotta, ¾ cup Parmesan, parsley, and egg in a medium bowl, seasoning with salt and pepper. Cover the bottoms of two 9 x 12-inch baking dishes with a thin even layer of the sauce. Place a few tablespoons of ricotta mixture on top of each lasagna noodle, roll up into a tube shape. Place "cannelloni" in baking dishes. Cover with remaining marinara sauce. Bake for 20-25 minutes. Remove from oven and top with grated Parmesan cheese. Return to oven for an additional 5 minutes.

## wine suggestion:   Chianti Classico

Comments: Amy's original recipe is for stuffed shells but I have yet to find gluten-free pasta in a large shell form. With this recipe lasagna noodles are wrapped around the cheese filling to make little cannelloni. If you are able to find large gluten-free shell pasta, use that instead, as it will be easier! Although homemade gluten-free pasta is time consuming, and the results often leave much to be desired, Bette Hagman's Bean Flour Pasta from the Gluten-Free Gourmet (Revised Edition) is well worth trying. I have had success using her recipe to make both ravioli and this dish.

# Butternut Squash Soup with Roasted Chestnuts

### Chef Hans Bergmann, Cacharel – Arlington, Texas

Cacharel is a great restaurant situated between Dallas and Fort Worth. The restaurant has received top restaurant status in *Zagat, Condé Nast Traveler*, and *Gourmet* magazine.

This is by far the best butternut squash soup we have ever had. It is very smooth and creamy, a wonderful addition to many fall and winter meals.
Double the recipe and freeze it for future meals. To serve this on a weeknight as a quick soup, bake the squash the day before.
Enjoy this soup either as a first course or as a light meal with salad or Breadsticks (page 165).

## ingredients:

1 small butternut squash (about 20 ounces)

2 tablespoons butter

1 small onion, diced

½ stalk celery, diced

1 small piece of leek, diced (white part only)

2 garlic cloves, peeled

4 thyme sprigs

½ bay leaf

4½ cups gluten-free chicken stock

10 fresh chestnuts

¾ cup whipping cream

Dash of allspice

## 4 servings

Preheat oven to 375°F.

Poke a few holes in the squash with a knife or fork, place on a baking sheet, and bake for 45 minutes to one hour, or until soft. Cut cooked butternut squash in half. Using a spoon, remove seeds and discard. Spoon out all meat and discard skin.

Melt butter in a soup pot over medium heat. Add onions, celery, leeks, garlic, thyme, and bay leaf. Sweat vegetables by placing a sheet of foil or parchment directly on top and tightly covering the pot (a procedure which allows the vegetables to soften without browning) for two minutes. Add cooked butternut squash and chicken stock. Bring to a boil, then lower heat and simmer for 30 minutes.

Meanwhile with a small sharp knife, slash a deep X through the tough skin of the chestnuts. Spread out on a baking sheet, sprinkle with water, and roast in the preheated oven for 15-20 minutes, or until they can be easily pierced with a small knife. Remove chestnuts from the oven and pull the skins off while they are still hot. (If you have a rubber garlic peeler, it will make the job easier.) Roughly chop peeled chestnuts.

Remove thyme and bay leaf from soup and process soup in a blender until smooth. Bring soup back to a boil, add whipping cream, and season with allspice, salt, and pepper. Add chopped roasted chestnuts and simmer for one more minute. Ladle soup into heated bowls and serve with a salad.

*Notes: You may pressure cook the butternut squash rather than baking it, which will take considerably less time. An alternative to sweating the vegetables is roasting them in the oven, which allows their natural sugars to caramelize and enhances the flavor of the soup. If you plan to freeze the soup for later consumption, do not add the chestnuts until ready to serve.*

# Pork Tenderloin with Pancetta and Brussels Sprouts in Madeira

Fuller's Restaurant in the Sheraton Seattle Hotel and Towers teamed up with McCarthy and Schiering Wine Merchants one evening to present a winemakers' dinner. The meal was delicious, and inspired me to try to duplicate the entrée. It is a fairly accurate interpretation, although pork tenderloin (which is both more readily available and less expensive) has been substituted for the veal loin served at Fuller's. Serve with Garlic Mashed Potatoes (page 140).

## ingredients:

2 pounds boneless pork tenderloin

2 cloves garlic, finely minced or
    passed through a garlic press

½ ounce pancetta

2 teaspoons olive oil

2 shallots, finely minced

1½ cups Madeira

1 cup gluten-free chicken stock

12 small Brussels sprouts, quartered

## 4 servings

Preheat oven to 400°F.

Rub pork tenderloin with garlic on all sides, seasoning with salt and pepper. Place on a rack in a shallow roasting pan with the fatty side up.

Roast for 30 minutes, or until the internal temperature reads 150°F. on a meat thermometer. Remove from oven, cover with foil, and let rest for 5 minutes.

While the tenderloin is cooking, sauté pancetta until crisp. Remove from pan and drain on paper toweling, then chop and set aside. Over medium-high heat, add olive oil and shallots to the pan and cook until translucent. Increase heat to high and add Madeira. Reduce by half. Add chicken stock and reduce again until rich and flavorful. Strain the Madeira sauce through a small sieve and keep warm.

Meanwhile place Brussels sprouts in a steamer basket over a pot of boiling water. Steam until tender when pierced with a thin sharp knife, being careful not to overcook.

To serve, slice tenderloin and place a few slices on each plate with some pancetta and Brussels sprouts. Ladle sauce over and around the pork.

**wine suggestion:** Oregon Pinot Noir

# Cumin-Seared Tofu with Corn and Baby Lettuces

Tofu is low in calories, high in protein, and has a slightly nutty taste. We try to have one meal a week in which tofu is substituted for meat.
The flavors and colors of this meal have a bright Southwest flair, lending both visual and taste appeal.

## ingredients:

*2 pounds firm tofu, drained*

*3 tablespoons vegetable oil*

*3 cloves of garlic, halved*

*½ teaspoon ground cumin*

*2 tablespoons Worcestershire sauce,*
*  or more to taste*

*2½ cups frozen corn*

*5-6 ounces mixed baby lettuces*

*3 tablespoons olive oil*

*1 tablespoon rice wine or brown rice vinegar*

*2 tablespoons chives, cut into 1-inch lengths*

*Squeeze of lime (optional)*

## 4 servings

Drain tofu by placing it on a plate, resting another plate on top, and setting a 1-pound weight atop the second plate. After 10 minutes or so discard excess water.

Slice tofu into twelve, ¼-inch thick triangle shaped pieces. Heat oil in a large skillet. Sauté garlic for a minute. Add tofu triangles, cooking in batches until nicely browned. (Add more oil if needed to prevent sticking.). Season tofu with cumin and Worcestershire.

Remove tofu to a warm plate. Add corn to skillet and heat through, scraping up and incorporating the browned bits on the bottom of the pan. Season with salt and pepper. Remove corn from heat.

Toss lettuce with oil and vinegar. Divide lettuce equally between serving plates and top with several tofu triangles and corn. Garnish with chopped chives. Try a squeeze of lime juice over the plate for a little extra zip.

### wine suggestion:    California Sauvignon Blanc

*Note: If you have a Trader Joe's near you, try their pre-washed bag of baby spring mix.*
*It contains a great variety of young lettuces: red and green romaine, oak leaf, lollo rosa, tango, frisée, radicchio,*
*mizuna, arugula, red chard, and spinach. Any combination from among these options will work fine.*

# Minestrone Genovese

Minestrone soup is satisfying; this version is quite fresh and is superb when made with a bounty of garden vegetables at their peak.
Enjoy this soup either as a first course or as a light meal with salad or Breadsticks (page 165).

## ingredients:

⅓ to ½ cup basil leaves, washed,
 dried, and finely chopped

⅓ cup freshly grated Parmesan cheese

¼ cup tomato paste

3 cloves garlic, finely chopped or
 put through a garlic press

¼ cup extra virgin olive oil

½ cup gluten-free orzo (see Sources)

½ cup freshly grated Romano cheese

6 cups water

2 teaspoons salt

2 cups carrots, peeled and cut into ¼-inch dice

1 cup onion, cut into ¼-inch dice

1 cup celery, cut into ¼-inch dice

2 cups red potatoes, skins on and
 cut into ½-inch dice

½ cup green bell pepper, cut into ¼-inch dice

½ cup zucchini, unpeeled, cut into ¼-inch dice

¼ cup gluten-free bread crumbs

½ teaspoon hot paprika

10 grinds fresh black pepper

Very small pinch saffron (optional)

2 cups water

1 can (8 ounces) kidney beans,
 well rinsed and drained, or 3 cups
 fresh green beans, washed and cut
 diagonally into 1-inch pieces

1 can (14.5 ounces) diced tomatoes in
 rich puree, or 2 cups fresh tomatoes,
 diced (including juice)

½ cup frozen peas or corn
 (add to soup frozen) or
 fresh corn cut from the cob

½ cup finely chopped Italian parsley

Parmesan cheese,
 grated by hand at the table
 (Parmigiano-Reggiano if possible)

**comment:** Pasta & Co. is Seattle's premier, upscale take-out food shop with five locations in the area. They feature unique food items from all over the world and carry gluten-free pasta as well. This recipe is from *Pasta & Co. By Request* (Pasta & Co., 1991)

## makes 13 cups

In a medium bowl, whisk together basil, Parmesan, tomato paste, and garlic into a thick paste. Slowly drizzle in olive oil until incorporated. Set aside.

Cook orzo in a large amount of boiling water until al dente. Drain well and fold into olive oil mixture. Fold in Romano and set aside.

In a large soup pot, bring 6 cups of water and salt to a boil. Add carrots, onion, and celery. Cook 5 minutes. Add potatoes and cook 5 minutes more. Add bell pepper, zucchini, bread crumbs, paprika, black pepper, and saffron and cook 5 minutes more.

Turn off heat and ladle a couple of cups of the soup into orzo mixture. Stir well and pour back into the soup pot. Add 2 cups water, kidney beans, tomatoes, frozen peas or corn, and parsley. Stir to mix.

Serve topped with additional freshly grated Parmesan.

## wine suggestion: Vernaccia di San Gimignano

# Beef Fajitas with Pico de Gallo

It is great to be able to enjoy flour tortillas again! With a little practice you can roll out and cook 8 flour tortillas in about 15 minutes. In order to complete this meal within the 45-minute preparation time frame, you will need to pulse the pico de gallo ingredients in a food processor rather than chopping them with a knife, and the marinade will need to be made the night before. It also helps if you have someone else working the grill, but it is not critical. Serve everything family style so you can enjoy the bright display of colors created by this bountiful meal.

### ingredients:

4 skirt steaks (about 2 pounds)

### Marinade:

¼ cup lime juice

1 cup olive oil or cilantro oil

6 garlic cloves passed though a garlic press

1 teaspoon freshly ground pepper

### Pico de Gallo:

6 medium roma tomatoes, chopped

½ medium onion, chopped

¼ cup finely chopped cilantro

Juice of one lemon

Juice of one lime

Salt and freshly ground pepper to taste

3-4 jalapeño peppers, chopped

### Other ingredients:

1-2 avocados, mashed in a bowl with a
  dash of lemon juice

Gluten-free refried beans, either canned
  or homemade (page 153)

Homemade Flour Tortillas (page 167)

### 4 servings

Place meat in a nonreactive bowl. Combine marinade ingredients and pour over meat. Marinate for at least 5 hours, and up to 24 hours.

Combine pico de gallo ingredients in a medium-sized, nonreactive bowl and set aside. Refrigerate if preparing ahead.

Preheat an outdoor grill; while the coals are heating, make the flour tortillas.

Once tortillas are made and warming in the oven, remove meat from marinade. Grill 1-2 minutes per side, or to desired doneness. Slice into bite sized pieces. Wrap meat in a flour tortilla together with pico de gallo and avocado. Serve with refried beans.

### wine suggestion:    California Zinfandel

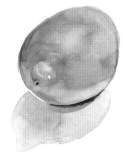

# Roasted Root Vegetables over Warm Goat Cheese Medallions

*Chef Lynne Vea — Seattle, Washington*

## ingredients:

2 Dungeness or other sweet carrots, peeled

2 parsnips or beets, peeled

1 sweet onion, peeled

4-5 Jerusalem artichokes, peeled

4-5 small potatoes (baby reds, yellow Finn,
   Yukon gold), scrubbed

1 red bell pepper, seeded and
   membranes removed

½ cup hazelnuts, with skin on

¼ cup extra virgin olive oil, divided

Juice of ½ lime

Splash of Tabasco

3 tablespoons chopped fresh basil and
   Italian parsley

¼ cup dried sour cherries

1 tablespoon maple syrup

2 tablespoons sherry wine vinegar

### Cheese Medallions:

6 ounces creamy goat cheese

4 ounces cream cheese, softened

½ cup fine Italian Bread Crumbs (page 168)

Olive oil

## chef's comments:

Roasting brings out the natural sweetness of vegetables and deepens and enhances their colors. To complement this transformation, I have added earthy hazelnuts and bright sour cherries in a slightly sweet vinaigrette base. The creamy cheese medallions add the touch of elegance that this beautiful mixture deserves.

## 4 servings

Preheat oven to 425°F. Coarsely chop all vegetables into ¾-inch cubes. Toss vegetables and hazelnuts with 2 table-spoons olive oil, lime juice, Tabasco, salt and pepper. Spread the mixture in an even layer on two large baking sheets and roast for 15-20 minutes or until the potatoes are tender and the vegetables are caramelized around the edges.

Place roasted vegetables into a large metal bowl and add chopped herbs, sour cherries, maple syrup, sherry vinegar, and remaining olive oil. Season to taste with salt and pepper. Keep in a warm oven while preparing the cheese medallions.

Mix goat cheese and cream cheese together. (*Note: You may use only goat cheese if you wish, substituting 10 ounces of goat cheese for the quantities given.*) Form cheese into 8 equal balls, then flatten until each is a ½-inch thick disk. Press firmly into the bread crumbs on both sides. Let rest in the refrigerator until ready to cook. (*As the warmth from your hands may make the cheese quite soft, you can place the medallions in the freezer for a few minutes to firm them up before cooking.*)

Heat a little olive oil in a heavy skillet over medium heat. Sear the cheese medallions quickly on each side until golden and hot.

Place 2 medallions on each plate. Scatter the roasted vegetables over and around the medallions. Top with sprigs of fresh herbs or a garnish of thinly sliced red peppers.

## variation:

Place Braised Winter Greens with Garlic (page 147) in a tight mound in the center of each plate and prop the goat cheese medallions at a rakish angle against them. What a gorgeous foil for the more subdued tones of the roasted vegetables.

## wine suggestion:

a bold Washington Chardonnay

# Enchiladas Cazuela

A family favorite and easy one-dish meal that travels well to parties.

## ingredients:

½ pound pork sausage

½ pound ground beef

1 can (16 ounces) tomato sauce

1 cup water

1 tablespoon chili powder

½ teaspoon ground cumin

½ teaspoon salt

8 corn tortillas

Vegetable oil for frying

2 cups grated cheddar cheese

½ cup scallions, chopped

1 can (2¼ ounces) sliced black olives

1 cup gluten-free sour cream

## 4–6 servings

Preheat oven to 350°F.

Brown sausage and ground beef in a large skillet, draining excess fat. Stir in tomato sauce, water, chili powder, cumin, and salt. Simmer for 10 minutes.

Over high heat in another large skillet, heat ¼-inch oil until hot and shimmering. Fry tortillas until soft and puffed. Drain on paper toweling.

In a 10 x 7 x 3-inch baking dish, layer ingredients (reserving ¼ cup cheese) as follows: tortillas, meat sauce, cheese, scallions, and olives. Repeat layers until all tortillas are used. Sprinkle reserved cheese on top.

Bake uncovered for 20-25 minutes.
Top with sour cream.

## wine suggestion:

California Zinfandel

# Hearty Spaghetti Sauce

This was recorded as my husband was creating his favorite sauce, a concoction designed to please hearty eaters.
You will want to make plenty to freeze for another meal. Serve with Tinkyada or Bi-Aglut pasta.

## ingredients:

¾ pound ground beef

¾ pound ground gluten-free Italian sausage

5 cloves garlic, finely chopped or
    passed through a garlic press

1 medium onion, chopped

2 tablespoons olive oil

10 white or button mushrooms, sliced

1 can (28 ounces) whole tomatoes,
    drained and chopped (reserve liquid)

1 can (15 ounces) tomato sauce

1 can (12 ounces) tomato paste

1½ tablespoons dried oregano

1 tablespoon dried basil

¾ cup red wine

¾ cup Parmesan cheese

**Recipe requires an hour or more
preparation/cooking time.**

## 4 servings

Over high heat in a large deep skillet with a cover (or a Dutch oven) brown the meat. Remove meat from pan, drain well, and set aside. In the same skillet over medium-high heat, sauté garlic and onion in oil until onions are translucent. Add mushrooms. Cover and cook until slightly softened. Add tomatoes, tomato sauce, tomato paste, oregano, basil, red wine, and Parmesan. Season with salt and pepper. If additional liquid is needed, use the reserved liquid from the tomatoes. Simmer for several hours, checking seasoning about 10 minutes from end of cooking time. Serve over gluten-free pasta.

## wine suggestion:   Italian Sangiovese or Chianti

# Sautéed Lamb Chops with Goat Cheese on a Roasted Red Bell Pepper Sauce with Sun-Dried Tomatoes

### Chef Hans Bergmann, Cacharel – Arlington, Texas

Cacharel is a great restaurant situated between Dallas and Fort Worth.
The restaurant has received top restaurant status in *Zagat Restaurant Survey* as well as in *Condé Nast* and *Gourmet* magazines.

Serve with Butternut Squash Soup with Roasted Chestnuts (page 107), Turnip Timbale Soufflé (page 141), and Cranberry Soufflé (page 208).
Although these recipes comprise a complete menu, the fledgeling cook may want to start by trying one at a time with simple accompaniments.

## ingredients:

2 red bell peppers

3 ounces olive oil

½ onion, diced

2 garlic cloves

1 thyme sprig

1 bay leaf

2 cups gluten-free chicken stock

4 tablespoons sun-dried tomatoes

Cayenne pepper

2 racks of lamb (ask butcher to scrape the
    bones and cut them into 12 chops)

2 ounces goat cheese,
    rolled into 12 balls of equal size

**Recipe requires an hour or more
preparation/cooking time.**

## 4 servings

Split red bell peppers in half lengthwise. Remove the core, seeds, and white membrane. Cut into 1-inch dice. Heat a sauté pan, pour in 2 ounces olive oil and heat until almost at the smoking point. Add red bell pepper and sauté for 1 minute. Add onion and garlic cloves. Sauté for another 3 minutes, stirring occasionally. Add thyme and bay leaf, deglaze pan with chicken stock, and simmer for 10 minutes. Remove thyme and bay leaf. Pour sauce into blender, blend until smooth, and strain through a sieve.

Cut sun-dried tomatoes into strips and sauté in 1 tablespoon olive oil for 1 minute then add red bell pepper sauce and simmer for 2 minutes. Season with salt, pepper, and cayenne to taste.

Preheat oven to 500ºF. Season lamb chops with salt and pepper. In an oven-safe pan over high heat, add one tablespoon olive oil, then quickly sear chops on both sides. Press a goat cheese ball on top of each lamb chop. Place pan in the oven and cook to desired doneness (see below). Ladle sauce onto warmed plates, arrange 3 lamb chops on top of sauce, and serve.

**Doneness of Lamb Chops:** Europeans prefer rare lamb, which is very tender and full of delicious juices. In America, doneness is more a matter of personal preference. When using a meat thermometer, lamb is medium rare at 135ºF. and well done at 170ºF. As it is difficult to use a meat thermometer with small chops, you may use this rule of thumb instead: Medium Rare 1-inch chops, 3-4 minutes per side; 1½-inch chops, 5-6 minutes per side.

**wine suggestion:** Cain 5, a California meritage, or wine made from a proprietary blend of various grapes (this excellent example includes five varietals).

# Chicken a la Margaux

## Chef Erol Tugrul, Café Margaux – Cocoa, Florida

Café Margaux is a recommended restaurant that is frequented by Gluten Intolerance Group members when attending conferences in Florida. *Zagat* consistently awards Café Margaux with "Top Restaurant" status as well.

Serve with Grilled Garlic-Studded Portobello Mushrooms with Roasted Tomato-Basil Sauce (page 136) and Cream of Yellow Squash Soup (page 79).

## ingredients:

*Six 5-ounce chicken breasts (skinless and boneless), pounded ¼-inch thick*
*6 slices smoked ham, very thinly sliced*
*6 medium asparagus stalks, blanched*
*1 large carrot, cut in 3-inch julienne*
*6 ounces spinach, steamed*
*12 thin slices gluten-free bacon*

### Wild Mushroom Sherry Sauce

*1½ cups wild mushrooms, sliced (cèpes, also called boletus mushrooms or porcini, work well)*
*1½ tablespoons olive oil*
*1½ tablespoons amontillado sherry*
*6 small bouquets of fresh sage, dill, and bay leaves*
*1½ tablespoons chopped fresh sage and parsley*

> **Recipe requires an hour or more preparation/cooking time.**

## 6 servings

Preheat oven 350°F.

Place one slice of ham, one asparagus stalk, a few julienned carrots, and 1 ounce of spinach onto a flattened chicken breast and roll chicken tightly around filling. Wrap 2 slices of raw bacon around rolled chicken so that the chicken is completely covered. (The rolled chicken bundle is called a roulade.) Repeat procedure with remaining chicken breasts. Season with salt and pepper.

Place roulades in a large skillet and cook over medium heat, rotating each roulade at least four times to crisp bacon on all sides. Strain rendered bacon fat by straining through a paper filter or a double thickness of cheesecloth, set aside. Bake roulades in oven for 20 minutes while preparing sauce.

Sauté mushrooms in olive oil, adding sherry toward the end. Season with salt and pepper.

Slice the chicken roulades and place three slices on each plate. Top with cèpes and ladle some of the natural chicken juices and clear rendered bacon fat over both the chicken and mushrooms. Garnish the dish with a bouquet of herbs and a sprinkling of the chopped herbs.

**wine suggestion:**   Beaux Freres Pinot Noir-Oregon

# Sunday Slow-Cooked Roast Beef with Half a Bottle of Wine and a Cup of Garlic

*Chef Kathy Casey, Kathy Casey Food Studios® – Seattle, Washington*

Kathy Casey is celebrated as a pre-eminent chef who has paved the way for the emergence of women chefs and Northwest cuisine on a national level. She received her first acclaim as executive chef of Fuller's restaurant in Seattle, where *Food & Wine* magazine named her as one of the 25 "hot new American chefs." Casey's talent for innovation continues to be recognized today. As owner of Kathy Casey Food Studios®, a culinary mecca for food, beverage, and concept consulting, she opens her doors to the public for classes and special events. In addition to running her business, she pens a monthly feature column called "Dishing" for *The Seattle Times*.

Serve with Yukon gold mashed potatoes and Buttermilk Biscuits (page 170).

## ingredients:

3-3½ pounds beef chuck roast
1 tablespoon kosher salt
½ teaspoon black pepper
2 tablespoons vegetable oil
1 large onion, peeled and cut into 8 wedges
1½ cups sliced mushrooms
½ bottle (about 1½ cups) red wine

3 tablespoons sweet rice flour
20 peeled cloves garlic
5 sprigs of fresh thyme
4 carrots, cut in 1½-inch pieces
4 celery ribs, cut in 1½-inch pieces
1 tablespoon chopped fresh basil (optional)

**Recipe requires an hour or more preparation/cooking time.**

## makes about 6-8 generous servings

Preheat oven to 325°F. Pat roast dry with paper towels. Rub with salt and pepper.

Heat oil in a large Dutch oven or other heavy pot over a high flame. Add roast. Sear on all sides until well browned. Remove meat to a platter. Add onions and mushrooms to the pot. Cook, stirring, for a few minutes, or until onions and mushrooms are softened. Set roast back in the pot, pulling the onion and mushroom mixture up from under the roast.

Whisk together the wine and flour until smooth (add wine gradually to the flour to avoid clumps) and add to the Dutch oven along with the garlic and thyme. Bring to a simmer. Cover and transfer to the preheated oven. Add carrots and celery during the last 45 minutes of cooking time. Roast for about 2½ to 3 hours, turning roast occasionally, or until meat is fork-tender.

Stir basil into sauce and serve.

*Note: If you desire a thicker sauce, make a cornstarch slurry with 1 tablespoon cornstarch mixed with 2 tablespoons water. Drizzle and whisk the slurry into simmering sauce a little at a time until desired thickness is reached.*

## Salads

*(continued on next page)*

# ACCOMPANIMENTS

# Basil Spinach Salad

## ingredients:

*¼ bunch fresh spinach*

*¼ head red leaf lettuce*

*1 medium tomato, sliced*

*12 fresh basil leaves, finely chopped*

*2-3 tablespoons olive oil or basil oil*
*(page 60)*

*2 tablespoons balsamic vinegar*

### 4 servings

Wash and dry spinach and lettuce. Tear into bite size pieces and place in salad bowl. Add tomato and chopped basil to bowl. Drizzle basil oil and balsamic vinegar over salad and toss well, seasoning with salt and pepper.

# Gorgonzola-Pear Salad

An excellent recipe from talented home cook Amy Bogino Eernissee.

## ingredients:

*1 head of bibb lettuce*

*2 ripe pears, cut into bite size pieces*
*(Bosc or Anjou pears are recommended)*

*2-4 ounces crumbled Gorgonzola,*
*French feta, or chèvre goat cheese*

*¼ cup olive oil*

*3 tablespoons balsamic vinegar (or to taste)*

*¼-½ cup walnut halves*

### 4 servings

Wash and dry lettuce. Tear into bite size pieces. Combine lettuce, pears, and cheese with oil and vinegar, tossing well. Top salad with walnuts and a grating of fresh black pepper.

# Butter Lettuce with Caramelized Nuts

Butter lettuce can yield small heads under certain growing conditions. Adjust oil and vinegar accordingly.

## ingredients

1 cup pecans or walnuts

½ cup confectioners' sugar

⅓-½ cup vegetable oil

2 tablespoons brown rice vinegar

3 tablespoons olive oil

1 head butter lettuce, washed, dried,
   and torn in bite-size pieces

## 4 servings

Place nuts in a steamer basket over boiling water and steam for 3 minutes. In a medium bowl mix sugar and steamed nuts, stirring well to coat the nuts with sugar. Heat ½-inch of vegetable oil in a small skillet and place half the sugared nuts in the oil. Cook until sugar caramelizes (about 30 seconds). Remove nuts with a slotted spoon. Repeat steps with remaining nuts. Let dry, spread out in a single layer, before serving.

Whisk the vinegar and olive oil together, seasoning with salt and pepper. Toss with lettuce. Serve sprinkled with caramelized nuts.

*Note: This recipe works well for pecans or walnuts. Make an entire batch, and store the extra in an airtight container in the refrigerator. They are so tasty you may end up serving them as a snack.*

# Classic Spinach Salad

This salad involves some prep work. It is a good one to try on a night when the rest of the meal is easy.

### ingredients:

½ bag of washed spinach greens
  (about 3 ounces)
2 hard-boiled eggs
4 strips of thick sliced bacon,
  cooked and crumbled
3 tablespoons olive oil
1 tablespoon balsamic,
  raspberry or red wine vinegar

### 4 servings

Place all prepared ingredients in a salad bowl, seasoning with salt and pepper.

Toss gently but thoroughly and serve.

*Tip: To make a perfect hard-boiled egg, place egg in a small saucepan and cover with cold water by about 1-inch. Bring to a boil, then simmer for 12 minutes. Plunge egg into cold water. Once cooled, peel shell and chop up egg for salad.*

# Baby Lettuces with Beets, Pumpkin Seeds, and Pesto

If you have a Trader Joe's near you, try their pre-washed bag of baby spring mix. It contains a great variety of young lettuces: red and green romaine, oak leaf, lollo rosa, tango, frisée, radicchio, mizuna, arugula, red chard, and spinach. Any combination from among these options will work fine.

### ingredients:

1 tablespoon pesto, (page 69)
3 tablespoons olive oil
2 tablespoons balsamic vinegar
5 ounces mixed baby lettuces
1 medium roasted beet (page 142)
½ cup roasted pumpkin seeds (page 28)

### 4 servings

Whisk pesto, olive oil, and balsamic vinegar together to make a dressing, seasoning with salt and pepper. Mix remaining ingredients in a salad bowl. Add dressing. Toss together and serve.

# Spinach Basil Kumquat Salad with Raspberry Vinaigrette

The kumquat is a small orange citrus fruit, either oval or round in shape. The entire fruit is edible, and can be sliced and served raw in salads.
Kumquats are a good source of potassium, vitamin A, and vitamin C. If you are unable to find them, substitute thinly sliced oranges with the skin and pith removed

## ingredients

### Raspberry Vinaigrette

⅓ cup olive oil

4 tablespoons raspberry vinegar

3 tablespoons crème frâche (page 209)

½ bunch spinach or ½ bag prewashed
   spinach (about 2 ounces)

2 tablespoons fresh basil,
   leaves torn into pieces

¼ small red onion, thinly sliced

3 kumquats, thinly sliced

½ cup roasted pumpkin seeds
   (page 28) or toasted pine nuts

## 4 servings

### Raspberry Vinaigrette:

Whisk oil, vinegar, and creme frâche together until smoothly combined. (Note: Chilling the ingredients, bowl, and whisk will help keep the vinaigrette emulsified and prevent separation.) Season with salt and pepper.

Combine spinach, basil, onion, kumquats, and pumpkin seeds in a salad bowl. Add just enough vinaigrette to lightly coat the spinach leaves. Toss gently but thoroughly. Serve on room temperature plates.

# Warm Winter Scallop Salad with Shiitake Mushrooms and Apples

## Chef Lynne Vea – Seattle, Washington

Lynne is a talented rising star in the culinary world. Her years as a chef on the Pacific Coast have given her the opportunity to explore and celebrate the diversity of the culinary world. Lynne's creations are a taste sensation, and I always look forward to attending her cooking classes in the Seattle area.
She is also working with Chef John Sarich (of Chateau Ste. Michelle winery fame) as his production assistant for the television show, *Best of Taste*.

### ingredients:

2 tablespoons olive oil combined with
    1 teaspoon sesame oil
1 pound sea scallops (20-24 size)
1 cup rinsed leeks, cut into thirds, halved
    horizontally, and sliced lengthwise
    in julienne strips
4 ounces shiitake mushrooms
    (stems removed), sliced
1 teaspoon fresh rosemary, finely chopped
2 Pink Lady or Braeburn apples,
    cored and thinly sliced
½ cup gluten-free chicken broth
½ cup gluten-free hard cider or
    fresh pressed cider
¼ cup rich coconut milk
½ teaspoon red curry paste (see Sources page)
1 tablespoon gluten-free cranberry chutney
1 tablespoon sherry wine vinegar
4-6 cups loosely packed bright
    winter lettuces, washed and dried
Snipped chives and fresh rosemary for garnish

### chef's comment:

Although this seems an unlikely combination, you will be amazed at how the earthy and fruity flavors complement each other.

### 4 servings

Preheat oven to 200°F.

In a large, heavy, non-stick skillet, heat the oil over a medium-high heat until quite hot. Carefully add the scallops. Cook 3-4 minutes on each side until golden and just cooked through (they will appear opaque). Remove to an ovenproof platter and keep warm in the oven.

Place the pan back on the heat. Add the leeks, mushrooms, and rosemary. Cook, stirring, for one minute. Add apples. Cook, stirring, for 3 minutes. (You may need to add a little oil to the pan if it is too sticky from the scallops.) Turn the heat to high and stir in the broth and cider. Cook, stirring and scraping to deglaze the pan juices, until reduced by half. Add the coconut milk, curry paste, chutney, and sherry wine vinegar. Season with salt and freshly ground black or white pepper. Simmer for 1 minute, blending the curry paste well into the mixture.

To serve, divide the greens between four large plates, piling the greens in a tight mound in the center of the plate. Arrange the scallops around the outside of the lettuces and top each one with a tiny rosemary sprig. Drizzle the dressing over the greens and around the scallops. Garnish with snipped chives.

Substitutions: You may use mango chutney instead of cranberry chutney, in which case you will want to substitute basil or cilantro for the rosemary.

### wine suggestion:    Oregon Pinot Noir

*Note: 20-24 is "fish lingo" for the size of the scallops. It translates as 20-24 scallops per pound.*

# Pasta Salad

The key to this recipe is the quality of the gluten-free pasta; we like the brand Tinkyada.

### ingredients:

8 ounces rotelle (or other spiral shape)
    or penne gluten-free pasta

12 ounces mozzarella, cut into ½-inch cubes

4 ounces gluten-free salami,
    cut into ½-inch cubes

14 ounces whole artichoke hearts,
    cut into 1-inch pieces

10 oil cured, sun-dried olives, finely chopped

½ cup sun-dried tomatoes, chopped

1 teaspoon roasted garlic or
    granulated garlic (or to taste)

4 tablespoons olive oil

2 tablespoon balsamic or red wine vinegar

1-2 teaspoons fresh oregano or basil,
    finely chopped

### comment:

Mariani makes sun-dried tomatoes, packaged in a resealable bag, that are soft and ready to use. They are very good and worth the search. See Sources in the Appendix for Mariani's address and ask your local grocer to stock them. They also produce apricots, prunes, and other dried fruit that is great for on-the-go snacking or other recipes.

### 6 servings

Prepare pasta according to package directions. Drain and rinse pasta with cold water. Drain thoroughly and set aside. Combine mozzarella, salami, artichoke hearts, olives, and tomatoes in a medium serving bowl. Add garlic, olive oil, vinegar, and herbs, adjusting to taste. Season with salt and pepper. Add pasta and mix well. Serve at room temperature.

Note: Whole artichokes are a better quality than quartered artichokes. Avoid marinated artichokes.

# French New Potato Salad with Summer Herb Coulis

## Chef Lynne Vea – Seattle, Washington

Lynne has graciously contributed many recipes throughout this book!

### ingredients:

2 pounds new potatoes, washed

1 cup loosely packed basil leaves

½ cup flat leaf parsley, stems removed

1 sprig tarragon, leaves only

3-4 garlic cloves

½ cup white or sherry wine vinegar

¼ cup hazelnuts, toasted and
   skins removed*

¼ cup dry white wine,
   (a Washington Sauvignon Blanc is good)

¾ cup extra virgin olive oil

Summer greens (sorrel, arugula,
   butter lettuce, frisée, etc.)

Accompaniments listed in recipe

### chef's comment:

My favorite summer crop by far is the lowly potato. I can hardly wait each year as the moment arrives to begin digging in the warm ground for the first little treasures. Silky and moist, a tiny new potato is indeed a gift from the earth. Our local farmer's markets offer a dazzling variety as the summer progresses. This recipe, in the French fashion, dresses them lightly and with respect!

### 4 servings

Cut potatoes in half or into bite sized pieces. Simmer gently in salted water for 20 minutes, or until tender. Drain. (If you plan to dress the potatoes later in the day, toss potatoes with about ⅛ cup olive oil and season with salt and pepper immediately after cooking and draining. Refrigerate.)

While potatoes are cooking, combine basil, parsley, tarragon, garlic, vinegar, hazelnuts, and wine in a food processor. Process until well blended. Add olive oil gradually while blending. Process until relatively smooth. Pour over warm potatoes and toss gently.

Arrange summer greens around the perimeter of each plate. Place a mound of potato salad in the center of each plate and arrange any combination of the following accompaniments around the plate:
   Smoked oysters or smoked trout; Nicoise, Picholine, and/or Moroccan olives; Roasted red peppers;
   Sugar peas in the shell, lightly blanched; Thin slices of sweet Walla Walla or Vidalia onions;
   Goat cheese; Fresh mozzarella cheese.

### wine suggestion:  Washington Sauvignon Blanc

Notes: *If you can find the thin-skinned Duchilly, you can skip the step of removing the skin. To skin hazelnuts, spread on a baking sheet in an even layer. Roast at 350° F. for 10-15 minutes, or until skins begin to flake. Place a handful of hazelnuts in a dish towel and rub together until most of the skin is removed. Repeat with remaining hazelnuts.

# Seasonal Greens and Garden Cucumbers

### ingredients:

1 small garlic clove

½ teaspoon salt

1 head butter lettuce, rinsed, dried, and
   torn into bite-sized pieces

1 large garden fresh cucumber, sliced

4 tablespoons olive oil

1½ tablespoons brown rice vinegar

### 4 servings

Place salt and garlic clove in a wooden salad bowl. Rub the salt and clove into the bowl to season.

Toss lettuce, cucumber, oil, and vinegar together. Season with salt and pepper.

# Cole Slaw

The illustrator of this book (my mother-in-law) kindly donated the watercolors and this recipe!

### ingredients:

½ head green cabbage, chopped

¼ head red cabbage, chopped

2 carrots, grated

8 ounce can crushed pineapple, drained

1 cup raisins or currants

2 scallions, finely chopped

⅓ cup gluten-free mayonnaise

### 4 servings

Combine cabbage, carrots, raisins, scallions, and mayonnaise in a medium bowl. Season with salt and pepper.

# Spicy Winter Tomato Salad

### Chef Lynne Vea — Seattle, Washington

Lynne has graciously contributed many recipes throughout this book!

## ingredients:

1½ cups chopped vine-ripened
   winter tomatoes
2 tablespoons extra virgin olive oil
2 teaspoons balsamic vinegar or
   1 teaspoon sherry vinegar
1 teaspoon sugar or maple syrup
Dash each cinnamon, cloves, and coriander
¼ teaspoon chipotle powder
¼ cup thinly sliced green onions
Pecorino cheese for garnish
A drizzle of Truffle Oil with Capers (optional)

## Truffle Oil with Capers:

⅓ cup Spanish or Italian salted capers,
   soaked in water for 10 minutes
   and rinsed several times
3-5 large basil leaves
½ cup truffle-infused olive oil
Juice from ½ lemon

## comment:

The key to this salad is to have the tomatoes chopped and ready to go for quick assembly and heating.

## 4 servings

Mix all ingredients except the onion together in a medium bowl. Season with salt and freshly ground white pepper. In a medium skillet over high heat, sauté the onion in a bit of olive oil for one minute. Add other salad ingredients, heating through for one minute more. Remove immediately from skillet and serve.

## Truffle Oil with Capers: makes 1/2 cup

This oil adds an interesting dash of flavor that you must try at least once. Check Sources (page 228) on how to find the capers and truffle oil.

Place capers and basil leaves on cutting board. Cover with 1 tablespoon truffle-infused olive oil and finely chop. In a small bowl, combine lemon juice and remaining truffle oil. Add capers and basil and mix well. Set aside until ready to serve.

# Black Bean Salad

### ingredients:

2 cans (15 ounces each) black beans,
    rinsed and drained

4 scallions, finely chopped

1 cup chopped red and green peppers

1 cup frozen corn kernels

4 tablespoons finely chopped fresh cilantro

1-2 jalapeño or serrano chiles, finely minced

Juice of two limes

2 avocados, diced

### 4 servings

Combine beans, scallions, sweet peppers, corn, cilantro, jalapeños, and lime juice. Season with salt and pepper. Gently toss avocado into the salad and serve.

# Tomato Bread Salad

This recipe works well with the recommended bread. If you have found a good gluten-free Italian bread, you may use it instead. Recipe provided by talented home cook, Amy Bogino Eernissee.

## ingredients:

4-5 fresh, ripe tomatoes
  (try different varieties)
1-2 medium sweet onions, sliced
  (Vidalia, Oso, Rio, or Walla Walla)
1 cup fresh basil leaves, lightly packed
¾ cup olive oil or more to taste
¼ cup balsamic or red wine vinegar
½ loaf stale, gluten-free Brown Rice Bread
  or Quinoa Bread (pages 163-64)
3 garlic cloves

## 6 servings

Cut tomatoes into wedges and combine in a large salad bowl with onions, basil, ½ cup of olive oil, and vinegar. Season with salt and pepper. Cover tightly and refrigerate overnight to let the flavors marry.

Two hours before you plan to serve salad, remove from refrigerator to bring to room temperature. Slice bread 1-inch thick, brush with remaining olive oil, and toast under broiler. Remove bread from oven and rub one side of each slice with garlic cloves. Dice bread into 1-inch cubes and combine with tomato mixture. Taste, adding more oil, vinegar, or seasoning as needed. Serve at room temperature.

# Spinach Salad with Dried Cranberries and Roasted Pumpkin Seeds

This recipe lends itself to substitution. Dried cherries can stand in for the cranberries, and both are available year round. Toasted pine nuts, walnuts, or pecans work well if you have no pumpkin seeds on hand.

## *ingredients:*

1 bunch of spinach (about 10 ounces)
   washed and trimmed of coarse stems

½ cup dried cranberries or
   dried sour cherries

¼ cup roasted pumpkin seeds
   (see page 28)

4 tablespoons olive oil

1 tablespoon brown rice vinegar

## 4 servings

Toss all ingredients together in a salad bowl and serve.

# Warm Beet Salad with Walnuts

Serve with a winter holiday meal such as prime rib.

## ingredients:

½ head of red leaf lettuce, washed and dried

½ head of butter lettuce, washed and dried

3 ounces blue cheese or feta, crumbled

½ cup chopped walnuts, toasted

2-3 medium beets, cooked and still warm

4 tablespoons walnut or olive oil

1½ tablespoons brown rice vinegar

## 4 servings

Tear lettuce into bite size pieces and place in a large salad bowl. Add crumbled cheese and walnuts.

Just before serving the meal, toss warm beets with walnut oil and vinegar. Season with salt and pepper. Toss beets with salad and serve.

Note: To cook beets, do not remove the skin, and leave one inch of root intact.
Either pressure cook according to pressure cooker directions or boil the beets for 40 minutes.
Once cooked, a fork pierces the beet easily and the skin can be removed.
Slice beets into rounds, then julienne (cut them in strips 1/8-inch thick). Keep beets warm until ready to serve the salad.

# Jicama Slaw

### Chef Bob Kinkead, Kinkead's - Washington D.C.

In 1983, *Food & Wine* magazine named Bob Kinkead one of the nations' most promising culinary talents. He has lived up to that title over the years with multiple nominations and awards from the James Beard Foundation. Countless magazines, from *Esquire* to *Gourmet*, have featured Chef Kinkead. He has served as executive chef and partner at 21 Federal in Nantucket and Twenty-One Federal in Washington D.C. He now owns Kinkead's, where he continues to work his magic.

## ingredients:

2 large jicama, peeled and julienned

12 radishes, julienned

6 scallions, finely chopped

3 oranges, sectioned

1 cup cilantro leaves, loosely packed

¼ cup lime juice

2 teaspoons red wine vinegar

1 teaspoon sugar

2 poblano chiles (optional), roasted,
   peeled, and julienned

1 medium red onion, julienned

## makes 1 quart, plus extra

Toss everything together in a stainless steel bowl, season with salt and pepper, and serve.

# Banana-Pineapple Sauté

A sweet complement to many Mexican dishes.

### ingredients:

2-3 bananas, peeled and sliced

½ fresh pineapple, cut in chunks, or 1 can
(16-ounces) chunk pineapple, drained

2 tablespoons butter

2 teaspoons cinnamon

### 4 servings

Melt butter in a medium skillet. Add bananas and pineapple.
Sauté briefly, then add cinnamon. Cook for 5-10 minutes,
until softened and lightly browned.

# Apple Sauté

This is an all time favorite at our house. We use it as a side dish with eggs, pork, or sausages.
If you like, you may add a dash of brandy or sherry while cooking the apples.

### ingredients:

3-4 Golden Delicious apples, peeled,
cored and sliced

2-3 tablespoons butter

1-2 tablespoons sugar

1-2 teaspoons cinnamon

### 4 servings

Melt butter in large skillet. Add apples, sugar, and cinnamon.
Cook for 15 minutes, or until apples are tender and golden brown.

# Grilled Garlic-Studded Portobello Mushrooms with Roasted Tomato-Basil Sauce

*Chef Erol Tugrul, Café Margaux – Cocoa, Florida*

Café Margaux is a recommended restaurant that is frequented by Gluten Intolerance Group members when attending conferences in Florida. Zagat consistently awards Café Margaux with "Top Restaurant" status as well. This dish would make a nice quick meal paired with a salad, provided you are able to marinate the mushrooms early in the day.

## ingredients:

*1 cup olive oil (scant)*
*4 large portobello mushrooms*
*¼ cup balsamic vinegar*
*¼ cup chopped shallots*
*5 sprigs fresh rosemary*
*2 sprigs fresh thyme*
*8 garlic cloves, peeled*

### Tomato Basil Sauce:

*8 ripe Italian plum tomatoes*
*1 medium onion, quartered*
*1 teaspoon garlic, chopped*
*1 teaspoon shallots, chopped*
*2 tablespoons olive oil*
*½ cup fresh basil, chopped*
*¼ cup heavy cream*

## 4 servings

Rub 4 tablespoons (1 tablespoon per mushroom) olive oil into mushrooms until absorbed. Combine ½ cup olive oil, vinegar, shallots, rosemary, and thyme. Pour marinade over mushrooms and marinate for eight hours.

Preheat oven to 300°F. Cover the bottom of a small roasting pan with 3 tablespoons olive oil, add garlic cloves, and roast for 20 minutes, or until tender. Turn garlic cloves in pan occasionally to make sure they do not burn. When done, cut garlic into small slivers and set aside.

Preheat an outdoor grill. Grill mushrooms for 3-4 minutes per side. Cut a few slits in the top of each mushroom and insert garlic slivers into the slits. Serve immediately with Tomato Basil Sauce.

**Tomato Basil Sauce:** Preheat oven to 400°F.

Roast whole tomatoes, onion, garlic, and shallots in oil in a shallow roasting pan for 15 minutes, or until tomatoes are soft and "saucy." Puree mixture in a blender, then pour into a saucepan. Set saucepan over low heat. Add fresh basil and cream. Heat through. Season with salt and pepper.

To serve, pour basil sauce onto four warm serving plates.
Top with grilled garlic-studded mushrooms.

# Roasted Asparagus

This is an unusual preparation method for many home cooks but is easy and heightens the vegetable's flavor.
Roasted asparagus is best served immediately, as it tends to soften after cooking.

## ingredients:

1 bunch asparagus

Olive oil

### 4 servings

Heat oven to 400°F.

Wash and dry asparagus. Holding a stalk of asparagus, bend until it snaps in two, discarding the lower portion. Repeat with remaining stalks. Place asparagus in one layer on the baking sheet, spray (or brush) lightly with olive oil, and season with salt and pepper. Roll stalks to coat with oil and seasoning on all sides. Bake for 10-15 minutes, then serve right away.

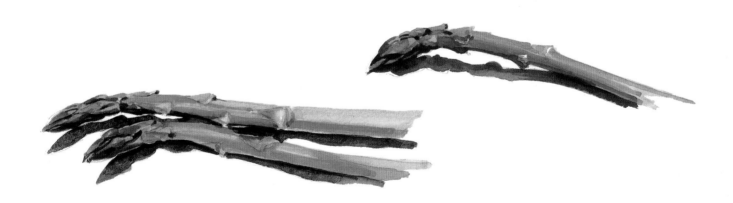

# Fresh Artichokes

In the spring, artichokes are at their peak, and are delicious when treated with simplicity. They take awhile to boil but are otherwise effortless. Most people eat fresh artichokes as an appetizer, but we like to serve them as part of the entrée. Look for dark green artichokes with tight, unblemished leaves. If you own one of the new pressure cookers your cooking time will be cut in half. Follow pressure cooker directions for amount of water and cooking time.

## ingredients:

4 globe artichokes

4 quarts water

4 tablespoons melted butter or
   gluten-free mayonnaise

## 4 servings

Bring a large pot of water to boil and add salt. While waiting for the water to boil, prepare artichokes by slicing 1-inch off the pointed end and about ¼-inch off the stem end. Using kitchen scissors, snip the prickly end of each leaf off with a straight cut. You may also want to strip a few of the large, coarse leaves from the stem. Place artichokes into the boiling water, and cook for 30-40 minutes. When a leaf pulls off easily, the artichoke is ready; you may also want to try piercing the stem and bottom with a fork to test for tenderness. Remove artichokes from water and drain upside down. Serve with butter or mayonnaise.

### tip for eating an artichoke:

Remove a leaf and dip the wide meaty end into butter or mayonnaise. Scrape the leaf with your teeth to get the soft, succulent part. Once you finish the leaves, the cone shaped prickly "choke" remains; it is inedible. At the bottom of the choke is the tender artichoke bottom or "heart", recognizable by its cup shape once separated from the choke. Cut the bottom off, discard the choke, and savor the meaty heart. You may wish to save the stem to dice and add to a salad.

# Oven Roasted Red Potatoes

### ingredients:

2 pounds baby red potatoes, quartered
Olive oil

### 4 servings

Preheat oven to 400°F. Brush a baking sheet with olive oil and arrange potatoes on sheet. Season with salt and pepper. Bake for 30 minutes, stirring occasionally, or until crisp and lightly browned.

# Fried Sage Green Beans

The process of frying sage is quick and adds a new dimension to green beans, potatoes, asparagus, etc.

### ingredients:

¼ cup vegetable oil
1 ounce large sage leaves
¾ pound green beans, trimmed

### 4 servings

Heat oil over medium heat in a small skillet. Add sage leaves. Cook for about 10 seconds (leaves should be lightly crisped). Remove with a slotted spoon and drain on paper toweling.

Cook green beans quickly in boiling salted water until crisp tender. Drain well. Toss with butter and season with salt and pepper. Top with fried sage leaves immediately before serving.

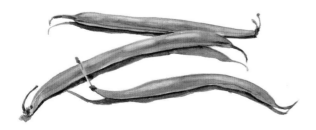

# Garlic Mashed Potatoes

I don't bother with a potato ricer, as we like our mashed potatoes with a rougher texture, and often use unpeeled organic potatoes.

## ingredients:

4 medium potatoes, peeled and quartered

4 tablespoons butter

2 garlic cloves, finely chopped or
    passed through a garlic press

¼ cup heavy cream, warmed

Fresh chives, cut into 1-inch pieces

## 4 servings

Place potatoes in a large pot of water and bring to a boil. When potatoes are easily pierced with a fork (about 20 minutes cooking time), turn off the heat. Place cooked potatoes, butter, and garlic in the bowl of a heavy-duty stand mixer. Using the paddle attachment, mix for a minute or two. Add cream and blend until smooth. Season with salt and pepper. Serve with chives as garnish.

# Oven Roasted Butternut Squash

## ingredients:

1 large butternut squash

½ tablespoon olive oil

1 tablespoon unsalted butter

4 teaspoons brown sugar

## 4 servings

Heat oven to 400°F. Cut butternut squash in half lengthwise and scrape seeds out with a spoon. Brush flesh of each squash half with olive oil and place cut side down on a roasting pan. Bake for 15 minutes. Turn and season with salt and pepper. Fill each cavity with a piece of butter and 2 teaspoons of brown sugar. Bake for about 45 minutes, brushing with butter-sugar mixture in the squash cavities every 15 minutes, until flesh is golden brown and tests done with a fork. Cut each squash in half again to make four pieces and serve.

# Turnip Timbale Soufflé

## Chef Hans Bergmann, Cacharel – Arlington, Texas

Cacharel is a great restaurant situated between Dallas and Fort Worth.
The restaurant has received top restaurant status in *Zagat Restaurant Survey* as well as in *Condé Nast* and *Gourmet* magazines.

### ingredients:

1 pound turnips

2 eggs

1 egg yolk

½ cup whipping cream

Nutmeg

2 tablespoons butter, softened

### makes 6 timbales (2 ½ ounces each)

Peel and cook turnips in boiling water (or pressure cook) until easily pierced with a fork. Once cooked, drain and place a weight on the turnips to remove excess water. Preheat oven to 300°F.

Weigh ½ pound of cooked turnips and place in a blender. Add eggs, egg yolk, and cream. Season with salt, pepper, and nutmeg. Blend until smooth. Brush timbale forms or soufflé ramekins with soft butter and fill the timbales with the mixture.

Fill a shallow roasting pan with an inch or so of water and place the timbales or ramekins in the water. (The French call this a water bath, or bain-marie, and it allows the timbales to cook in gentle heat without breaking or curdling them.) Place water bath in the oven and bake for 45 minutes to an hour (they will be firm but still springy, not hard). Unmold and serve.

### variation:

Instead of turnips you can use red beets. For a great color contrast, fill the timbales with half turnip and half red beet mixture.

**Turnips:** Turnips are white-fleshed, with a white skin and purplish top. When shopping, look for a small size and a relatively heavy weight, as these younger specimens will have a delicate, slightly sweet flavor. Store turnips at 55°F. in a well-ventilated area. They should be washed, trimmed and peeled before using. Peak season is October-February.

**Beets:** Beets range in color from the familiar garnet red to white, and are available year round. The green, leafy tops are also edible and very nutritious. Be sure to cut them off before storing, as they leach moisture from the bulb. Choose beets that are firm and have smooth skin. Be careful not to puncture the thin skin, which can cause nutrient and color loss, and always leave about 1-inch of stem to prevent the same during cooking. Peel beets after they have cooked. An easy way to peel cooked beets is by holding the beet in a paper towel, using the paper towel to rub off the skin.

# Sweet Sautéed Yams

*ingredients:*

*3 medium yams*

*2 tablespoons olive oil*

*2 tablespoons butter*

### 4 servings

Peel the yams and cut into ¼-inch round slices. In a large, heavy bottomed pan, heat the oil and butter over a medium-high flame. Add the sliced yams. Cook for a few minutes, stirring frequently, then lower heat to medium low. Season with salt and pepper. Cook, covered, for 10-15 minutes, stirring occasionally, until yams are tender.

# Roasted Beets

*ingredients:*

*4 medium beets*

### 4 servings

Preheat oven to 425°F. Wash beets, but do not peel. Leave an inch or two of the stem intact, which will help to retain the nutrients while cooking. In a shallow baking dish, place beets and ½ cup water. Cover dish and bake until fork tender (about 30-60 minutes, depending on number and size of beets). Remove from oven and cool, uncovered. Remove skin and stem. Cut into ¼-inch slices. Refrigerate until ready to use.

*(Note: You may also use a pressure cooker, which will cut the time in half.)*

# Sugar Peas

**ingredients:**

¾ pound sugar peas, stringed

**4 servings**

Just before the rest of the meal is served, bring a medium pot of water to boil. Drop peas into the boiling water. Cook for a minute or two until color brightens. Drain thoroughly. Add salt and pepper to taste, toss, and serve immediately.

# Curry Roasted Vegetables

*Chef Tom Douglas, Dahlia Lounge, Etta's Seafood, and Palace Kitchen — Seattle, Washington*
Tom Douglas is a winner of the James Beard Award, considered the Academy Award of the culinary world!
He is known for his wonderful restaurants and his Rub with Love meat rubs that add great flavor to salmon, pork, and chicken.

**ingredients:**

2 carrots, peeled and
    cut on an angle into ¼-inch thick slices
½ small acorn squash,
    seeded and cut into ¼-inch thick
    "half moon" slices (leave skin on)
1 medium potato, peeled and
    cut into ¼-inch thick slices
½ small head cauliflower,
    broken into clumps about 1½-inches wide
2 tablespoons olive oil
2 teaspoons curry powder

**4 servings**

Preheat oven to 425°F. Put all vegetables in a bowl and toss with olive oil, curry powder, salt, and pepper. Spread vegetables on a baking sheet and roast in oven for 20 minutes, turning once with a spatula. When vegetables are tender and slightly browned around the edges, remove from oven and serve.

# Potato Pancakes

A crunchy, soul-satisfying side dish. Potato pancakes are great with lox and cream cheese, topped with gluten-free capers or chives, for a Sunday brunch.

## ingredients:

⅓ cup gluten-free flour mix
⅛ teaspoon salt
1 large egg
½ cup milk
2 medium potatoes, peeled and grated
⅓ cup vegetable oil

### 4 servings, 2 pancakes per person

In a small bowl combine the flour and salt. Using a wire whisk or fork, beat in the egg and milk until almost smooth. Set batter aside. In a skillet over medium heat, heat 2 teaspoons oil. Add ¼ cup grated potato. Spread grated potato in a very thin layer and cook until golden brown on one side. Pour 1 tablespoon of batter over the cooked potato, trying to keep batter within the confines of the cooked potato. Cook 2 minutes until top is set and bottom is browned, then turn over and cook the other side. Longer cooking time results in crispier potato pancakes. Repeat steps to make seven more pancakes. Keep warm until ready to serve.

# Caramelized Ginger Carrots

## ingredients:

6 medium carrots, peeled and sliced
2½ tablespoons butter
¼ cup loosely packed brown sugar
1 teaspoon minced ginger or ginger juice

### 4 servings

Place carrots, butter, and brown sugar in a medium saucepan. Pour in just enough water to cover the carrots. Cook over medium-high heat, covered, for about 30 minutes. When all water is absorbed and carrots are caramelized to a golden brown color, remove from heat and serve.

# Green Beans with Pecan Paste

### Chef Lynne Vea — Seattle, Washington

Lynne is a talented rising star in the culinary world. Her years as a chef on the Pacific Coast have given her the opportunity to explore and celebrate the diversity of the culinary world. Lynne's creations are a taste sensation, and I always look forward to attending her cooking classes in the Seattle area.

She is also working with Chef John Sarich (of Chateau Ste. Michelle winery fame) as his production assistant for the television show, *Best of Taste*.

## ingredients:

¼ cup toasted pecans, finely chopped

2 tablespoons finely chopped Italian parsley

1 clove garlic, finely minced

Splash Tabasco

Squeeze lemon juice

½ cup freshly grated
   Parmigiano Reggiano cheese

Extra virgin olive oil to hold it together
   and form a paste

¾ pound green beans, trimmed

## chef's comment:

The paste can be made the day before and refrigerated.

## 4 servings

Blend together all ingredients up to and including Parmigiano Reggiano. Add just enough olive oil to hold the mixture together and form a paste.

Quickly cook green beans in a pot of boiling salted water. Drain well, toss with pecan paste, and serve right away.

## Alternative pecan paste preparation:

Once ingredients are combined, roll mixture into a log wrapped in plastic wrap. Refrigerate until firm, then cut into medallions. Serve as a garnish on top of vegetables, grilled fish, etc.

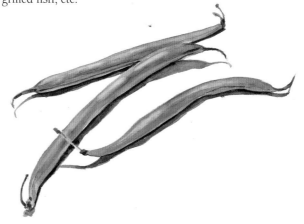

# Mushroom Mélange

A quick, earthy side dish that complements an entrée such as Apricot Pecan Chicken (page 105).

### ingredients:

4 tablespoons butter

2 tablespoons olive oil

1 shallot, chopped

3 cups of sliced shiitake, oyster,
  and cremini mushrooms

### 4 servings

Melt butter and oil together in skillet over medium heat. Add shallot and cook for a minute. Add mushrooms and cover skillet while turning heat to low. Cook for about 10 minutes. Mushrooms will release their moisture and become tender. Remove to a warm covered dish until ready to serve.

# Spinach Sautéed with Garlic and Lemon

This has become a favorite at our house. One would never believe that this recipe would appeal to children, but ours now prefer spinach prepared this way, and request it often.

### ingredients:

4 tablespoons butter

4 tablespoons olive oil

2 cloves garlic, finely chopped

10-12 ounces spinach, coarse stems removed

1 tablespoon lemon juice

### 4 servings

Melt butter with the oil. Cook garlic, stirring frequently, for one minute. (Do not allow it to brown.) Add spinach and cook until it wilts (a minute or two). Add lemon juice, mix well, and serve.

This dish cooks up quickly. Prepare it a few minutes before you sit down to eat, in order to prevent it from cooling while waiting for the other items.

# Braised Winter Greens with Garlic

Chef Lynne Vea – Seattle, Washington

Lynne has graciously contributed many recipes throughout this book!

### ingredients:

4-5 cups loosely packed young winter
    braising greens (chard, kale, spinach,
    or broccoli rabe)
1-2 teaspoons sesame oil
3 cloves garlic, peeled and minced
Splash of sherry vinegar

### 4 servings

Wash and dry the greens, leaving a bit of moisture still clinging to the greens.
Chop coarsely.

Heat oil in a heavy pan over medium-high heat. Add garlic. Stir briefly and add the greens.
Stir again to coat greens with oil and cover pan. Cook for 3-5 minutes, stirring occasionally, until the leaves have wilted and turned darker green. Season with sherry vinegar, salt, and pepper. Serve immediately.

Note: If you have access to a specialty import shop, look for fig-infused balsamic vinegar
as a substitute for the sherry vinegar; it is a real treat.

# Corn on the Cob

### ingredients:

4-8 ears fresh corn, shucked and trimmed

### 4 servings

In a large pot of boiling water, cook corn for 3-5 minutes. Serve immediately, buttered and seasoned with salt and pepper.

To grill corn, place shucked and trimmed corn directly on a hot grill. Turn each cob to cook evenly on all sides. Total cooking time is 3-4 minutes.

# Creamy Polenta

This method is a convenient way to make polenta, as only 15 minutes is spent stirring over the flame and the remaining cooking time is in the oven. The process of combining the cornmeal with some of the cold water or stock is better than pouring the cornmeal directly into the boiling water or stock, as it will prevent lumps from forming.

### ingredients:

**4 servings**

2 tablespoons butter

¼ cup finely chopped onions

4 cups water (salted), vegetable stock, or chicken stock

1 cup cornmeal

2 ounces mozzarella cheese, grated

2 ounces Reggiano Parmesan cheese, grated

Preheat oven to 350°F. Melt butter in a large heavy saucepan. Add onion and cook, stirring frequently, until translucent. Add 3 cups water or stock and bring to a boil. Combine cornmeal and 1 cup of cold water or stock. Gradually stir into boiling liquid. Reduce heat to low and stir constantly with a wooden spoon for 15 minutes, or until thickened.

In a buttered 1½-2 quart baking dish, alternate half the thickened cornmeal mixture with half the grated mozzarella and Parmesan cheese, spreading in even layers. Repeat with remaining cornmeal mixture and cheese. Bake for 35 minutes until top is browned. Let stand for 10 minutes, then serve right away while piping hot.

# Homemade Fries

### ingredients:

**4 servings**

2-3 medium russet potatoes,

4 tablespoons olive oil

1 teaspoon dried basil

1 teaspoon dried oregano

Preheat oven to 400°F. Slice potatoes into strips about 3 inches long and ¼ to ½-inch thick. Place potatoes in a large bowl. Add olive oil and herbs, tossing until well coated. Arrange potatoes in one layer on a baking sheet. Bake for 30 minutes, or until crisp and nicely browned.

# Roasted Vegetables

An easy and elegant way to serve vegetables.

## ingredients:

1 bunch asparagus

3 medium leeks

2 medium crookneck yellow squash

1 large red bell pepper

Olive oil

## 4 servings

Preheat oven to 400°F. Wash and dry asparagus. Holding a stalk of asparagus, bend until it snaps in two, discarding the lower portion. Repeat with remaining stalks. Wash leeks thoroughly and remove root end and dull green tops. Slice leeks in half lengthwise and cut crosswise into 4-inch pieces. Slice squash into several lengthwise 4-inch pieces. Cut pepper in half lengthwise and remove stem, membrane, and seeds. Slice pepper into ½-inch strips.

Place vegetables in a large bowl and drizzle with a few tablespoons of olive oil to lightly coat vegetables. Season with salt. Arrange vegetables on one or two large baking sheets in an even layer. Bake for about 20 minutes, stirring occasionally, or until crisp-tender.

Note: Thin asparagus and leeks cook more quickly (in about 10 minutes); you may want to put them on a separate baking sheet.

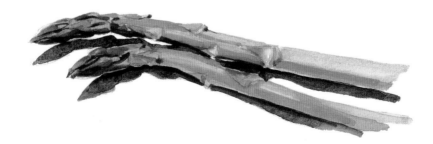

# Roasted Mushrooms

### Chef Charlie Trotter, Charlie Trotter's – Chicago, Illinois

Charlie Trotter's offers highly personal cuisine combining impeccable products, French techniques, and Asian influences.
Charlie's restaurant and cookbooks are well known across the country. The restaurant's list of awards ranges from Relais Gourmand to the *Wine Spectator*,
the James Beard Foundation, AAA—the list goes on and on. Recipe with permission from *Charlie Trotter's Seafood*, (Ten Speed Press, 1997).

## ingredients:

2½ cups cleaned and stemmed mushrooms

2 sprigs thyme or rosemary

½ cup chopped onion

1 tablespoon olive oil

⅓ cup water

## chef's comment:

The juices that come out of the mushrooms make a great sauce with a little bit of butter.

## makes 1½ cups

Preheat oven to 325°F.

Place all ingredients in an ovenproof pan and season to taste with salt and pepper. Cover and roast for 30-40 minutes, or until tender. Cool in the juices and refrigerate for up to 4 days.

# Master Recipe for Long Grain White Rice
## (Modified Stovetop Method)

Chef Christopher Kimball

Founder, editor, and publisher of *Cook's Illustrated* magazine – Author of *The Cook's Bible* and *The Yellow Farmhouse Cookbook*

### ingredients:

2 cups long grain white rice

2 cups water or gluten-free chicken stock

4 teaspoons olive oil

1 teaspoon kosher salt

   (or ⅔ teaspoon regular salt)

### chef's comments:

For years, I used the basic stovetop recipe found on the back of the box, but when testing recipes for cooking kasha, I became interested in the notion of sautéing rice with a bit of oil and then cooking with less water. This recipe only uses 1 cup of water to 1 cup of rice, half the amount of water usually called for, and it makes great rice. Also note the rice has to sit for at least 10 minutes after cooking. This time is needed to finish the cooking and to let the grains "set" so they do not become sticky. If you are using commercial chicken stock, you will not need to add salt. Be sure to use a low-sodium brand.

### 4 servings

Heat oil over medium heat in a medium saucepan and add rice. Stir for 1 minute. Add water and bring to a boil. Reduce heat to low, cover, and simmer for 10 minutes. Check after 3 or 4 minutes to make sure that the water is at a slow simmer, not at a rapid boil. Remove from heat and let stand covered for 15 minutes, fluff with a fork and serve.

# Brown Rice with Pine Nuts and Currants

## Chef Tom Douglas, Dahlia Lounge, Etta's Seafood, and Palace Kitchen — Seattle, Washington

Tom Douglas is a winner of the James Beard Award, considered the Academy Award of the culinary world! He is known for his wonderful restaurants and his Rub with Love meat rubs that add great flavor to salmon, pork, and chicken.

### ingredients:

1 cup long grain brown rice

2 cups water

½ teaspoon salt

1 tablespoon olive oil

¼ cup pine nuts, toasted

¼ cup currants, steeped in hot water
    and drained

2 tablespoons chopped fresh cilantro

### 4 servings

Place brown rice, water, salt, and olive oil in a heavy bottomed saucepan with a tight fitting lid. Bring to a boil over high heat, then cover and reduce heat to low. Cook for 45 minutes, or until rice is tender and all the water is absorbed. Remove from heat and fluff with a fork. Gently stir in pine nuts, currants, and cilantro.

# Edamame

Pronounced ed-a-ma-me, these green soybeans are sold in many grocery stores in the frozen food aisle, either shelled or in the fuzzy green pod. If you can't find them at your local grocery, try an Asian market. Edamame has a wonderful nutty flavor and is a great way to add the benefits of soy to your diet. Many Japanese restaurants serve edamame as an appetizer.

I like to use edamame in the pod. Prepare according to package directions (which is generally boiling the beans for 5 minutes, then draining in a colander). Place beans in a serving dish, salt, and serve. To eat, pop the beans out of the shell and into your mouth. Some of the salt on the outside of the pod will be consumed as well.

# Homemade Refried Beans

There are a variety of methods for soaking and preparing beans. The traditional overnight method is used here. Beans are soaked to replenish moisture, reduce cooking time, and remove the complex sugars that cause flatulence. While canned refried beans are my standard, due to the convenience factor, I like to make refried beans from scratch every now and then. If you own one of the new, safer pressure cookers, you can dramatically reduce the cooking time. Double the recipe and freeze in meal size servings.

## ingredients:

1 pound pinto beans or black beans

7 cups water

1 inch strip of kombu (optional)

2 tablespoons plus ¼ cup vegetable oil

3 garlic cloves, peeled

½ medium onion, chopped

2 teaspoons salt

## 6 servings

Cover beans with water and soak overnight (4 cups of cold water for every cup of beans). The next day, drain and rinse beans, discarding water.

In a large pot, place 7 cups of water, soaked beans, 2 tablespoons oil, and kombu. Bring water to a brief boil, then let beans simmer for 1-1½ hours. If necessary, add more boiling water during cooking time. Add salt to beans when they have started to soften, but before they are tender. To test for doneness, remove a few beans and blow on them; if the skin breaks, they are done. Remove kombu and discard.

Puree half the beans in a food processor, or mash them well by hand. With the side of a large chef's knife, flatten garlic cloves. Heat ¼ cup oil in a large skillet and add garlic. Brown garlic lightly, stirring frequently, then discard. Add onion and cook until translucent and lightly browned. Add mashed beans, cooked whole beans, and salt. Cook until beans thicken and serve.

*Note: Kombu is a sea vegetable sold in most stores with sushi ingredients.*
*It naturally tenderizes the beans and makes them more digestible (reduces flatulence).*
*Kombu will also reduce the cooking time by 15 minutes and enhance the flavor of the beans.*
*Cut kombu in one-inch strips, and it will melt away into the bean mixture.*

**Recipe requires an hour or more preparation/cooking time.**

# Macaroni and Cheese

This takes just a few more minutes to assemble than the boxed stuff, but it is so much better! For a quick meal, serve with organic frozen peas.

## ingredients:

8 ounces gluten-free macaroni or penne
   (see Sources)
8 ounces cheddar cheese, sliced
½ cup half and half

### 4 servings

Butter an 8 x 8-inch glass baking dish. Preheat oven to 350°F.

Cook macaroni for a little less time than package directions indicate so that it stays slightly undercooked. Drain and rinse macaroni in cold water. Spread half the macaroni evenly in the baking dish and top with half the cheese. Layer remaining macaroni, then remaining cheese, on top. Pour in half and half. Bake, uncovered, for 15 minutes, or until heated through.

### variation:

Try substituting Monterey Jack cheese for all or part of the cheddar cheese.

Chicken Stock ...... 156

Chicken Noodle Soup ...... 156

Nine Bean Soup ...... 157

Smoky Chipotle Chili with Roasted Red Peppers ...... 158

Split Pea Soup ...... 160

*(Quick soups are found in seasonal sections.)*

# LONG SIMMERING SOUP, CHILI, *and* STOCK

# Chicken Stock

It is hard to find the time to make this, but the price of chicken stock is high and many are not gluten-free.
The quality of the soup you make from homemade stock is far superior to that of soup with a base of canned stock.
Start a collection of roasted poultry carcasses, necks, and leftover bones in the freezer, and make up a big pot of stock when you have accumulated enough.
Trimmings and leftovers from onions, celery, carrots, leeks, parsley, and mushrooms should be saved as well; all but the onions and leeks can be frozen.

## ingredients:

2 pounds of chicken bones
   (Note: If you have whole carcasses,
   break them into smaller pieces)
10 cups cold water
1 onion, peeled and quartered
2-3 carrots, trimmed and cut in thirds
3 stalks of celery with leaves, cut in thirds
1 bay leaf
2-3 large cloves of garlic, cut into pieces
1-2 teaspoons freshly ground pepper
1 teaspoon each of dried basil and thyme
1 cup fresh flat leaf parsley

## makes 5-6 cups

Wash the chicken parts if raw (omit this step if cooked) and put them in a large stockpot. Add water, vegetables, seasonings and additional water necessary to cover chicken pieces and vegetables. Bring to a boil, reduce heat to medium low, and simmer. Skim off any film or impurities that might appear on the surface; do this regularly to prevent emulsification with the stock. Simmer partially covered for 4-5 hours. Strain through a colander. Cool, uncovered, in an ice bath, stirring frequently. You may also cool the stock in a flat pan in the refrigerator. Do not cover while still warm, or it may turn sour.

**Tip:** A basic stock should not be salted until it is used as an ingredient in another recipe.

*Notes: Do not remove the layer of fat on top of the stock until you are ready to use it, as this will act as a preservative seal.*

# Chicken Noodle Soup

Save a few cups of chicken stock and add chopped up pieces of the cooked chicken pieces, carrots, celery, and onions used for making the stock. Add salt and pepper to taste and some cooked gluten-free noodles. It is so nice to have this on hand, especially if you are sick and need some comfort food!

# Nine Bean Soup

A great soup for a cold winter evening. Serve with Cornbread (page 166).

## ingredients:

2 cups of mixed beans (see list below)

1 medium ham hock (about 1½ pounds)
   with lots of meat

1 large onion, chopped

1 can (28 ounces) crushed tomatoes
   (including liquid)

1 teaspoon chili powder

Juice of two fresh lemons

### 10-12 servings

Wash beans and place in a large bowl. Cover beans with water (4 cups of cold water for every cup of beans) and let sit overnight. (Add more water if necessary to keep beans covered.)

The next day, drain and rinse beans, discard soaking water. Place beans in a soup pot with the ham hock and 2 quarts of water. Bring to a boil, then simmer for one hour, stirring occasionally.

Remove ham hock and cool for a few minutes on a plate. Once cool, remove tasty ham pieces from the fat and bones. Set aside the ham pieces, discarding fat and bones. Continue to simmer soup.

Add ham pieces, onion, tomatoes, chili powder, and lemon juice to the soup pot. Season with salt and pepper and simmer for 30 minutes more or longer if desired, stirring occasionally.

**wine suggestion:**    Côtes-du-Rhône

**beans:**    Buy a bag of each kind of bean at the store, then mix them all together in a large container. An airtight glass canister is a nice display case for the bright array of colors. Buy your beans in a store with high volume and quick turnover to get the best quality beans for your soup.

| | |
|---|---|
| Pinto beans | Split green peas |
| Navy beans or Great Northern beans | Lentils |
| Small red beans | Kidney beans |
| Black-eyed peas | Black turtle beans |
| Split yellow peas | |

# Smoky Chipotle Chili with Roasted Red Peppers

Lorna Sass has several books dedicated to pressure cooking. This recipe is adapted from her book, *The Pressured Cook* (William Morrow, 1999).
Smoky chipotle chilies, roasted red peppers, lime juice, and cilantro make this chili exceptional.
If you don't own one of the new, safe pressure cookers, instructions are also included for regular stockpot cooking.

## ingredients:

### Cilantro-Lime Cream

1 cup sour cream
½ cup tightly packed chopped fresh cilantro
1 tablespoon freshly squeezed lime juice
¼ teaspoon salt, or more to taste

1 cup red kidney beans, picked over,
    rinsed, and soaked overnight
2 tablespoons olive oil, or more if needed
2 pounds well-trimmed boneless beef chuck,
    cut into ½-inch pieces
2 cups coarsely chopped onions
2 teaspoons whole cumin seeds
2 tablespoons mild chili powder,
    or more to taste
2 cups beef or chicken broth
1 large green bell pepper, seeded and diced
¼ teaspoon ground cinnamon
2 dried chipotle chiles, stemmed, seeded,
    and finely chopped
    (or substitute ⅛ teaspoon cayenne)
3 tablespoons tomato paste
2 large cloves garlic, finely chopped or
    passed through a garlic press
1 teaspoon dried oregano leaves
2 large red bell peppers, roasted (page 34),
    seeded and cut into ½-inch squares
1 tablespoon freshly squeezed lime juice,
    or more to taste

## 4-6 servings

Make cilantro-lime cream by combining sour cream, cilantro, lime juice, and salt in a nonreactive bowl. Keep refrigerated until ready to use.

Drain and rinse soaked beans. Set aside.

Heat a tablespoon of oil in the pressure cooker over medium-high heat. Brown beef in small batches, adding more oil if needed. Set the beef aside on a plate. Heat another tablespoon of oil. Add onions and cumin and cook for 1 minute, stirring frequently. Return beef to the pot. Add chili powder, stir to completely coat beef, and cook for an additional minute. Add broth and stir well, scraping up any browned bits stuck to the bottom of the pot. Stir in beans, green pepper, cinnamon, and chipotle chiles.

**Pressure cooker instructions:** Lock lid of pressure cooker in place. Bring to high pressure over high heat. Lower heat while maintaining high pressure and cook for 15 minutes. Allow pressure to come down naturally; if short on time, use the quick-release method. Unlock the lid, lifting up and tilting away from you to allow any excess steam to escape. If the meat and/or beans are not fork tender, simmer over medium heat until done, or return to high pressure for 5 minutes more.

*continued:*

## Smoky Chipotle Chili with Roasted Red Peppers

*Regular stockpot cooking instructions:* Bring to a boil, then turn down heat. Cook covered at a gentle simmer until meat is tender, about 1-1½ hours. If chili becomes dry as the stew cooks, stir in a bit more broth.

Blend tomato paste into chili. Add the garlic and oregano. Season with salt and pepper. Taste for seasoning, stirring in more chili powder if needed. Simmer for a few minutes more over medium heat until flavors mingle and garlic loses its raw taste. If the chili is too soupy, add about ½ cup of mashed beans and stir in.

Minutes before serving, stir in the roasted red peppers and cook for another minute. Stir in lime juice to enhance the flavors. Top each portion with a generous spoonful of Cilantro-Lime Cream.

*wine suggestion:*  California Syrah

# Split Pea Soup

When we brought our first child home from the hospital, my mother-in-law brought over a big pot of this soup.
I did not think I liked split pea soup, but it was the perfect meal on a cold November day for two very sleep deprived parents. Now our children ask for it all winter long.
Although it is not necessary to sauté the onion, carrots, oregano, and garlic, the end result will be a more flavorful soup. Serve with cornbread.

## ingredients:

2 tablespoons butter

1 medium onion, chopped

3-4 medium carrots, sliced

1 teaspoon dried oregano

2 cloves garlic, finely chopped or
    passed through a garlic press

3 quarts of water

1 package (16 ounces)
    split green peas, rinsed

1 medium ham hock
    (about 1½-2 pounds) with lots of meat

1 bay leaf

## 6 servings (1 ½ cup serving size)

In a large soup pot, sauté onion, carrots, and oregano in butter for a few minutes until onion appears translucent. Add garlic and sauté for one minute more. Add water, peas, ham hock, and bay leaf. Bring to a boil, then turn heat down to low. Simmer for at least one hour, preferably 2 hours. Stir occasionally. After one hour of cooking, remove ham hock and remove all meat from the bones. Discard bones, cut meat into bite size pieces, and return meat to the soup pot. Continue cooking for another hour to marry flavors further, or serve as is.

**wine suggestion:**    California Chardonnay

*Note: This recipe freezes well; you may want to make a double batch,
freezing the extra for another meal.*

# BREAD

# Bread Making

BAKING GLUTEN-FREE BREAD CAN BE CHALLENGING. This section offers high quality recipes for the basic necessities.

A common problem exists in gluten-free bread making. A perfect loaf of bread emerges from the oven, only to collapse while cooling. I have found two elements to cause this unfortunate experience: a) too much liquid in the recipe during periods of high humidity, or b) the type of flour.

I have tested many bread recipes, and have had my greatest success with those provided here; they turn out perfect loaves every time, and are favorites in my cooking classes. They also possess versatility; for instance, the sandwich bread recipe can be used to make hamburger buns as well.

The texture of brown rice flour, amaranth flour, buckwheat flour, or quinoa flour actually seems to prevent the bread from collapsing. You will want to reduce the liquid of all gluten-free bread recipes by ⅛–¼ cup until you learn how to recognize when the batter is the right texture and when it is too wet.

A stand mixer is essential for gluten-free bread making, as it aerates the batter, producing lighter bread with a fine crumb and more height. It is a far better choice than a bread machine, as only a few brands can produce satisfactory gluten-free bread. If you absolutely have your heart set on a bread machine, call Red Star Yeast for recommended models (see Sources).

The variety of flours used in gluten-free baking is tremendous. Read Gluten-Free Flours (page 231) to learn more about each type. This knowledge will help as you venture forth with your own recipes.

If you are lactose intolerant, dairy-free substitutions can be found in the Appendix.

Sweet breads are excellent with quinoa, amaranth, or buckwheat flour substituted for up to one half of the flour in a recipe.

# Brown Rice Bread

So far, this is the best gluten-free bread we have tried, and it makes a good hamburger bun as well. Recipe adapted from Barbara Emch's, a fellow celiac.

## ingredients:

3 large eggs

¼ cup vegetable oil

1 teaspoon lemon juice

1¼ cups warm water (105°-115°F.)

4 tablespoons sugar, divided

1½ tablespoons active dry yeast

2 cups tapioca starch flour

2 cups fine brown rice flour

⅔ cup instant non-fat dry milk powder

2 teaspoons xanthan gum

1 teaspoon salt

2 tablespoons ground flax seed (optional)

## comment:

Quinoa flour is a great source of protein, calcium, and phosphorus, and can be substituted for some of the brown rice flour (see variation on next page).

## makes one loaf

Bring all refrigerated ingredients to room temperature. Grease a 5 x 9-inch loaf pan.

In the bowl of a stand mixer, combine eggs, oil, and lemon juice. In a large measuring cup, combine water, 1 tablespoon sugar, and yeast; let stand for 5 minutes, or until foamy. In a medium bowl, combine tapioca starch flour, brown rice flour, dry milk powder, xanthan gum, salt, flax seed, and 3 tablespoons sugar. Add yeast mixture to the egg mixture, then slowly add dry ingredients a little at a time until completely incorporated. Mix batter on high speed for 3½ minutes, then pour into prepared pan.

Cover bread with foil and place in a cold oven. Set a pan of hot water on a lower shelf underneath the bread. Leave for 10 minutes with oven door closed. (This will cause the bread to rise quickly.) Remove bread from oven (do not uncover) and place in a warm place in the kitchen. Preheat oven to 400°F. Bread will continue to rise as oven preheats.

Uncover bread and bake for 10 minutes to brown the top. Cover bread with foil and continue to bake bread for 30 minutes. Turn bread out onto a cooling rack. When completely cooled, wrap tightly to maintain freshness for as long as possible.

**Tips:** If humidity is high, reduce the amount of water in the recipe to avoid overrising. Many gluten-free bakers experience the frustrating situation in which a beautiful loaf of bread deflates once removed from the oven. You will need to experiment a little to get just the right amount of water in your bread depending on the humidity in the air. If in question, use less water than the recipe calls for.

You may use rapid rise yeast instead of regular yeast. If doing so, eliminate the cold oven rise method with a pan of hot water, follow yeast package directions instead for rise time. *(continued on page 164) continued from page 163:*

**Variations:** **Quinoa Bread, Amaranth Bread, or Buckwheat Bread**

Using the Brown Rice Bread recipe, substitute the following combination of flours for straight brown rice flour and tapioca flour:

*1½ cups tapioca starch flour*

*1½ cups brown rice flour*

*1 cup quinoa flour, amaranth flour, or buckwheat flour*

Be certain you are using flour that is considered completely gluten-free (meaning that it is grown in dedicated fields and processed on dedicated equipment). See Sources.

**Hamburger Buns**

Pour batter into English muffin rings, follow directions above. Bake for just 15 minutes.

Once completely cooled these buns freeze well. Always serve buns warmed, otherwise they will be crumbly.

*Note: Buckwheat is a great source of B vitamins and high-quality protein.*
*Buckwheat appears to help lower cholesterol as well.*

# Breadsticks

Wendy Wark's recipe for breadsticks is the best gluten-free version I have ever had. Once you make them a few times, it becomes quite easy to do them quickly and well. These breadsticks are quite versatile, as you can mix in garlic salt, herbs, Parmesan cheese, or cinnamon sugar (2 tablespoons sugar with 2 teaspoons cinnamon), creating a wide range of variety from a single recipe. Recipe from *Living Healthy with Celiac Disease* (AnAffect, 1998).

## ingredients:

2 teaspoons unflavored dry gelatin

2¼ teaspoons active dry yeast

⅔ cup warm water (105°-115°F.)

2 tablespoons sugar

2½ cups Wendy Wark's gluten-free
   flour mix (page 181)

2½ teaspoons xanthan gum

¼ cup instant non-fat dry milk powder

½ teaspoon salt

2 eggs

3 tablespoons olive oil

Seasoning additions (see ideas above)

Melted butter to taste

## makes 24

Preheat oven to 400°F.

Combine gelatin, yeast, water, and sugar in a large measuring cup. Let stand 5 minutes. In the bowl of a stand mixer, combine flour, xanthan gum, milk powder, salt, and the seasoning additions of choice. Add eggs and oil to dry mixture, then beat in yeast mixture.

On a floured surface (tapioca flour works well), roll out dough into a large rectangle 5 x 18 inches. Cut into strips 5 inches long and ¾-inch wide. Twist each strip a couple times and place on a lightly oiled baking sheet, pressing ends down onto the baking sheet. Brush generously with melted butter. Bake 7-8 minutes until lightly golden.

# Cornbread

This is my grandmothers' cornbread recipe. (She always served it with butter and honey.)
Until I tried this recipe with Wendy Wark's flour mix, my gluten-free version did not taste right.
Her mix makes this taste just like the wheat flour cornbread my grandmother made.
The original recipe calls for shortening, though I prefer butter. Using buttermilk instead of milk creates a moister cornbread.

## ingredients:

½ cup sugar

1 teaspoon baking soda

½ teaspoon salt

¼ teaspoon xanthan gum

½ cup Wendy Wark's gluten-free
   flour mix (page 181)

1 cup corn meal

2 tablespoons butter or
   organic shortening, melted

1 large egg

1 cup buttermilk or milk

## 16 servings

Preheat oven to 400°F. Butter an 8-inch baking dish.

Combine sugar, baking soda, salt, xanthan gum, flour mix, and corn meal in a medium bowl. Combine butter, egg, and buttermilk in a small bowl. Slowly add the egg mixture to the flour mixture until blended. Pour batter into prepared baking dish. Bake for 20-25 minutes, or until toothpick tests clean.

# Homemade Flour Tortillas

This is the best gluten-free flour tortilla we have tasted. Recipe adapted from Wendy Wark's, *Living Healthy with Celiac Disease* (AnAffect, 1998)

## ingredients:

2 cups Wendy Wark's
  gluten-free flour mix (page 181)

¾ teaspoon salt

1½ teaspoons xanthan gum

1½ teaspoons baking powder

2½ tablespoons vegetable oil

¾ cup water

## makes eight, 8-inch tortillas

Mix dry ingredients together, then add oil and water. (This works well in a Kitchenaid stand mixer, using the paddle attachment instead of the dough hook) Mix on high speed for a few minutes until dough is well blended and forms a smooth ball. Let dough rest for 10 minutes, then divide into 8 equal sized balls. Flatten each portion slightly and roll out on a floured work surface (tapioca flour works nicely). Heat an ungreased griddle until very hot. Using a large spatula, place rolled-out tortilla on griddle, and cook for a minute or so on each side.

**Tip:** Depending on the weather, you may want to vary the amount of water until you get the right consistency. Try holding back ⅛ to ¼ cup water in the beginning. Flour tends to absorb moisture from the air during periods of high humidity, while on dryer days you may need to add another tablespoon or so of water.

Makes great communion wafers.

*Note: Wendy suggests keeping the cooked tortillas covered with a warm, damp towel;*
*you can also wrap the tortillas in foil and keep warm in a 200° F. oven.*
*(Tortillas can be frozen and reheated on a griddle.*
*Quickly steaming each side is another good trick to "bring them back to life.")*

# Italian Bread Crumbs

You may substitute dried herbs in this recipe. Remember that 1 tablespoon of finely chopped fresh herbs equals 1 teaspoon of dried herbs.

## ingredients:

2 slices stale gluten-free bread
¾ tablespoon finely chopped fresh rosemary
½ tablespoon finely chopped fresh oregano
¾ tablespoon finely chopped fresh thyme
1 tablespoon finely chopped fresh basil

## makes 1 cup

Place bread in a small food processor and process into fine crumbs. Transfer crumbs to a bowl. Add herbs and toss until well combined.

# Workable Wonder Dough

You will probably find many uses for this good, user-friendly dough. Recipe from Wendy Wark's *Living Healthy with Celiac Disease* (AnAffect, 1998). Wendy uses this for pretzels, breadsticks, cinnamon rolls, and pizza crust. Use it as a substitute for wheat flour dough in your favorite recipes.

## ingredients:

2 teaspoons unflavored dry gelatin

2¼ teaspoons active dry yeast

⅔ cup warm water (105°-115°F.)

2 tablespoons sugar

2½ cups Wendy Wark's gluten-free
    flour mix (page 181)

2½ teaspoons xanthan gum

¼ cup instant non-fat dry milk powder

½ teaspoon salt

3 tablespoons vegetable oil

2 eggs

## makes 1 ½ pounds dough

Combine gelatin, yeast, water, and sugar together in a 2-cup glass measure. Let stand for 5 minutes, or until foamy. In the bowl of a stand mixer, add flour mix, xanthan gum, milk powder, and salt. Mix briefly, then add oil and eggs, followed by yeast mixture. Beat on high speed for 2 minutes, using the paddle attachment until a soft dough forms. Use dough in your favorite recipe.

# Buttermilk Biscuits

Try these today and celebrate the return of a quick, scrumptious bread to your evening meal!

## ingredients:

1¾ cups Wendy Wark's gluten-free
  flour mix (page 181)

½ teaspoon xanthan gum

½ teaspoon salt

1 teaspoon baking powder

⅛ teaspoon baking soda

½ cup (1 stick) cold butter, unsalted

¾ cup buttermilk

## comment:

Larger bits of cold butter in the dough, and the process of turning and folding the dough, result in a biscuit with a layered, flaky texture.

## makes 8 biscuits

Preheat oven to 500°F. Combine flour, xanthan gum, salt, baking powder, and baking soda in a medium bowl. Cut in cold butter with a pastry blender until butter pieces are the size of peas. Add buttermilk, folding gently with a rubber spatula to make a soft dough.

Roll out dough between two sheets of wax paper into a 4 x 5-inch rectangle of about ¾-inch thickness. Peel wax paper away from dough several times to prevent sticking. Fold dough like a letter into thirds, give the dough a quarter turn, and roll out again to same dimensions. Repeat, folding once more. Wrap dough in the wax paper and refrigerate for 20 minutes.

Using two fresh sheets of wax paper, roll dough out into a ½-inch thick rectangle. Fold and turn once more. Cut out biscuits with a 2½-inch round cookie cutter. You will get a higher-rising biscuit if you dip the cutter in flour before each cut, and if you use a straight down and up motion rather than twisting. Transfer biscuits to a baking sheet lined with parchment.

Bake for 4 minutes at 500°F., then lower temperature to 375°F. Continue baking until golden brown, about 15 to 20 minutes. (Cover biscuits with foil if they brown too quickly before they are done in the center.) Serve warm.

# Thick Pizza Crust

This recipe is adapted from Bette Hagman's first book, *The Gluten-Free Gourmet* (Henry Holt, 1990).
The tricks I have learned over the years to produce a perfect crust are part of the recipe.
You may use all brown rice flour if you can't find the amaranth or quinoa flour, although the health benefits of these latter two make them well worth the search.

## ingredients:

1½ cups brown rice flour

½ cup amaranth or quinoa flour

2 cups tapioca flour

⅔ cup instant non-fat dry milk powder

3 teaspoons xanthan gum

1 teaspoon salt

1 cup water (105°-115°F.)

2 tablespoons active dry yeast

1 tablespoon sugar

½ cup warm water

3 tablespoons olive oil

4 egg whites at room temperature

Olive oil for spreading pizza dough

## makes two 13-inch pizzas

Grease two 13-inch pizza pans, using organic shortening.

In the bowl of a stand mixer, combine the flours, milk powder, xanthan gum, and salt. In a large measuring cup, combine the 1 cup water, yeast, and sugar. Let stand until yeast proofs (becomes foamy). In another measuring cup, combine the ½ cup water and 3 tablespoons olive oil. Add olive oil-water mixture to dry ingredients, then egg whites, mixing well after each addition. Finally add yeast mixture and beat on high speed for 4 minutes.

Divide dough into two equal portions. Place each portion on a prepared pizza pan. Cover your hand with a clean plastic bag. Drizzle about a tablespoon of olive oil over your hand and one portion of dough. Spread the dough out evenly over the pizza pan, forming a ridge around the edge to contain the pizza toppings. Repeat process for second portion of dough. Let dough rise for about 20 minutes. Preheat oven to 400°F. Bake pizza crusts for 7 minutes (until lightly golden) and remove from oven. At this point you can either cool the crusts, wrapping and freezing them for future use, or you can spread tomato sauce on the crust and top with your favorite toppings (see Scratch Pizza Sauce and topping suggestions, page 69).

# Chocolate Zucchini Bread

Here is a quick recipe for a goodie to keep on hand in the freezer. It's especially convenient to take along to the office, or to pack with your child's lunch. You might want to prepare the dry ingredients in advance for a quick mix to use later. (Be sure to refrigerate any prepared dry mixes.)
Recipe adapted from *Breakfast in Bed,* Carol Frieberg (Sasquatch Books, 1990).

## ingredients:

3 eggs plus 1 egg white

1 cup vegetable oil (or ½ cup applesauce
   and ½ cup oil)

2 teaspoons vanilla extract

2 cups sugar

3 cups grated zucchini

2⅓ cups Wendy Wark's gluten-free
   flour mix (page 181)

½ teaspoon xanthan gum

½ cup unsweetened cocoa

2 teaspoons baking soda

1 teaspoon cinnamon

1 teaspoon salt

¼ teaspoon baking powder

¾ cup chocolate chips

## makes 2 loaves

Preheat oven to 350°F. Butter two 5 x 9-inch loaf pans.

Combine eggs, oil, vanilla, and sugar in a large bowl. Add zucchini, mixing well. In a medium bowl, sift flour, xanthan gum, cocoa, baking soda, cinnamon, salt, and baking powder. Slowly add sifted mix to the zucchini mixture. Blend well and stir in chocolate chips.

Divide mixture between the two prepared loaf pans and bake for 50-55 minutes, until a toothpick inserted near the center comes out clean with a few crumbs clinging to it. Remove bread from pans and cool completely on a wire rack.

*Notes: Slices of bread freeze well wrapped individually.*
*If using a standard gluten-free flour blend, add ½ teaspoon xanthan gum to the dry ingredients.*

# Pumpkin Bread

One day I was trying to use up my remaining supply of a standard gluten-free flour blend, and wanted to add some quinoa flour to the mix.
This recipe is the result. Although the glaze is a great way to gild the lily, it is perfectly good on its own.
If you prefer, you can substitute Wendy's gluten-free flour mix for all of the flour in this recipe while reducing the xanthan gum by half.

## ingredients:

¾ cup vegetable oil

4 eggs

One can (15-ounces) pumpkin puree

1¾ cups sugar

¼ cup orange juice

½ cup quinoa flour

2 cups standard gluten-free flour blend
(page 181)

¾ cup sweet rice flour

¼ cup cornstarch

1¾ teaspoons xanthan gum

2 teaspoons baking powder

2 teaspoons baking soda

¾ teaspoon salt

½ teaspoon ground cloves

1 teaspoon cinnamon

1 teaspoon nutmeg

1 cup chopped pecans

### Glaze

1 cup confectioners' sugar

¼ teaspoon nutmeg

¼ teaspoon cinnamon

⅓ cup orange juice

### makes 2 loaves

Preheat oven to 350°F. Butter two 5 x 9-inch loaf pans.

Blend oil, eggs, and pumpkin puree together in a large bowl. Gradually add sugar, mixing well. Stir in orange juice.

Sift together flours, cornstarch, xanthan gum, baking powder, baking soda, salt, cloves, cinnamon, and nutmeg in a medium bowl. Slowly add sifted ingredients to the pumpkin mixture until well combined. Stir in pecans.

Pour batter into prepared pans and bake for 55 minutes, or until a toothpick inserted near the center comes out clean with a few crumbs clinging to it. Remove bread from pans. If you want to glaze the bread, whisk sugar, nutmeg, cinnamon, and orange juice together in a small bowl. Pour glaze over each loaf of warm pumpkin bread and allow it to soak in for a minute. Cool loaves completely on a wire rack.

*Note: The addition of sweet rice flour and cornstarch provides a smooth texture to the otherwise gritty standard gluten-free flour blend.*

# Carrot Bread

A tasty, hearty sweet bread, so good that you will never miss the wheat! Make muffins from this recipe for a quick on-the-go snack.
You can substitute amaranth or quinoa flour for up to half of the flour mix.
Recipe adapted from *Breakfast in Bed*, Carol Frieberg (Sasquatch Books, 1990).

## ingredients:

3 eggs plus 1 egg white
½ cup vegetable oil
½ cup unsweetened applesauce
2 teaspoons vanilla extract
2 cups finely grated carrots
2 cups grated unsweetened coconut*
1 cup raisins or currants
1 cup chopped walnuts
2 cups Wendy Wark's gluten-free
   flour mix (page 181)
¾ teaspoon xanthan gum
1 cup sugar
1 teaspoon baking powder
1 teaspoon baking soda
1 teaspoon ground cinnamon
½ teaspoon salt

*Ask the folks at Ener-G Foods about their coconut. It is not on the price list, but they sometimes sell it in bulk. Their coconut is more finely grated than the brands in the local grocery store, and it is guaranteed gluten-free.

## makes one loaf or 18 muffins

Preheat oven to 350°F. Butter a 5 x 9-inch loaf pan or 18 muffin cups.

In a large bowl, beat eggs until yolks and whites are well combined. Add oil, applesauce, and vanilla, mixing well. Stir in carrots, coconut, raisins, and walnuts.

Sift flour, xanthan gum, sugar, baking powder, baking soda, cinnamon, and salt in a medium bowl. Add sifted mix to carrot mixture gradually until thoroughly combined.

Pour batter into prepared pan or muffin tin. Bake loaf for 1 hour, muffins for 30 minutes. (A toothpick inserted near the center should come out clean with a few crumbs clinging to it.) Remove bread from pan and cool completely on a wire rack.

*Note: If using a standard gluten-free flour blend, add ¹/₂ teaspoon xanthan gum to the dry ingredients.*

# Blueberry Muffins

These muffins are easy to make fresh in the morning. They take about 10 minutes to mix and about 20 minutes to bake.
To make a healthier muffin, try substituting at least ½ cup of amaranth or quinoa flour for the flour mix.

## ingredients:

1½ cups Wendy Wark's gluten-free
   flour mix (page 181).
½ teaspoon xanthan gum
¾ cups sugar
2 teaspoons baking powder
1 teaspoon cinnamon
¼ teaspoon salt
1½ teaspoons lemon zest
   (grated lemon peel)
½ cup milk
½ cup vegetable oil
1 large egg
1 cup fresh or frozen blueberries

## makes 12 muffins

Preheat oven to 350°F. Use a non-stick muffin tin if available; if not, butter 12 standard muffin cups.

In a medium mixing bowl, combine flour, xanthan gum, sugar, baking powder, cinnamon, and salt. Make a well in the center of the flour mix and add lemon zest, milk, vegetable oil, and egg. Blend thoroughly with a fork until smooth, then fold in the berries. (Be very careful not to over mix.) Divide batter into prepared muffin cups.

Bake for 20-25 minutes, or until a toothpick inserted near the center comes out clean with a few crumbs clinging to it. Cool muffins in the tin for a few minutes. Remove muffins and serve warm, or cool completely on wire rack and keep on hand for breakfast on the run.

Note: If using a standard gluten-free flour blend, add ¹/₄ teaspoon xanthan gum to the dry ingredients.

# Banana Bread

If you do not have time to make the bread right away, freeze your ripe bananas for later use in this recipe.

## ingredients:

½ cup unsalted butter, softened

1 cup sugar

1 teaspoon vanilla extract

2 eggs

4 medium, ripe bananas, peeled and mashed

1 teaspoon milk

2 cups Wendy Wark's flour mix (page 181)

½ teaspoon xanthan gum

1 teaspoon baking soda

¼ teaspoon salt

## makes one loaf

Preheat oven to 350°F. Butter a 5 x 9-inch loaf pan.

Cream butter, sugar, and vanilla on high speed until pale in color and light in texture. Beat in eggs one at a time until well blended. With a fork, mix bananas and milk in a small bowl and set aside. In another small bowl, combine the flour, xanthan gum, baking soda, and salt. Blend dry ingredients into the creamed mixture alternately with banana mixture.

Turn batter into prepared pan and bake for 1 hour, until a toothpick inserted near the center comes out clean with a few crumbs clinging to it. Remove from pan and cool completely on a wire rack.

Note: If using a standard gluten-free flour blend, add ¼ teaspoon xanthan gum to the dry ingredients.

# Hazelnut Zucchini Bread

Each year our garden overflows with zucchini, thus the need for a variety of zucchini bread recipes in our home.
Hazelnuts add a wonderful flavor; if you can find the thin-skinned Duchilly variety, you can save yourself the trouble of roasting them and rubbing off the skin.

## ingredients:

2 cups Wendy Wark's gluten-free
    flour mix (page 181)
¾ teaspoon xanthan gum
1 teaspoon baking soda
¾ teaspoon baking powder
¼ teaspoon salt
1¼ cups sugar
2 large eggs
½ cup vegetable oil
⅓ cup orange juice
2 teaspoons orange zest
2 teaspoons ginger juice or
    peeled grated ginger root
1 teaspoon vanilla extract
1½ cups grated zucchini
½ cup finely chopped hazelnuts,
    bitter skin removed*

*To remove the skin, spread hazelnuts on a
baking sheet in an even layer. Roast at 350°F.
for 10-15 minutes, or until skins begin to
flake. Place a handful of hazelnuts into a dish
towel and rub the nuts until most of the skin
is removed. Repeat with remaining hazelnuts.

### makes one loaf or 18 muffins

Preheat oven to 350°F. Butter a 5 x 9-inch loaf pan or 18 muffin cups.

Sift flour, xanthan gum, baking soda, baking powder, salt, and sugar into a large bowl. Whisk eggs, oil, orange juice, zest, ginger, and vanilla together in a small bowl. Stir the egg mixture into the flour mixture until combined. Gently stir in zucchini and hazelnuts.

Pour batter into prepared pan or muffin tin. Bake for 45-50 minutes (20-25 minutes for muffins), or until a toothpick inserted near the center comes out clean with a few crumbs clinging to it. Cool in the pan for 10 minutes, then turn out onto a wire rack to cool completely.

*Note: If using a standard gluten-free flour blend, add
1/4 teaspoon xanthan gum to the dry ingredients.*

# SWEETS

# Sweets

This chapter is the home of decadent treats. If you take the time to bake for yourself, you will no longer feel deprived. Whether you believe it or not, you have the ability to make delicious, tempting baked goods. There is no need to eat dry, tasteless gluten-free duds. If you are going to eat something fattening, it should taste fabulous. (Make it worth the indulgence!). If you freeze your baked goods, you will always have something on hand when time is short. Keep in mind that children find it very important to have terrific gluten-free goodies on hand.

Home baking allows you to control the ingredients for the healthiest possible baked goods. You can both exclude saturated fats and include nutritious flours such as quinoa, amaranth, and buckwheat. Try using unrefined sugar as much as possible. See Sources in the Appendix for sugar substitutes and the new organic shortening available in many natural food markets.

Quinoa, amaranth, and buckwheat flours are great in sweet breads, pancakes, carrot cakes, and some cookies. When using these flours substitute them for up to one half of the flour in a recipe.

Substitutions for the lactose intolerant are found on page 217.

Don't be concerned if a recipe seems to have a lot of ingredients. Mixing the many dry ingredients takes just five minutes longer than opening up a prepackaged mix, and your results will be far superior in taste, quality, and healthfulness.

Be sure to keep gluten-free flours in airtight containers, as the flour will absorb moisture from the air, affecting the outcome of your baked goods.

Many of the recipes suggest using parchment lined baking sheets. You may grease your baking sheets with organic shortening instead, but parchment provides for much easier cleanup.

# Recommended Flours

This mix makes the best gluten-free baked goods. It produces a tender, moist end product that I have not found with any other formula. Triple the measurements to have a large supply on hand for all your baking. It should be refrigerated in an airtight container to keep the brown rice flour fresh.

## Wendy Wark's Gluten-Free Flour Mix

Flour mix recipe from Wendy Wark's book, *Living Healthy with Celiac Disease* (AnAffect, 1998). This book is full of recipes and resources. Wendy has graciously allowed me to include several of her recipes in my book. To order her book, see the Appendix.

1 cup brown rice flour

1¼ cup white rice flour*

¼ cup potato starch flour

⅔ cup tapioca starch flour

¾ cup sweet rice flour

⅓ cup cornstarch

2 teaspoons xanthan or guar gum

*\* I like to omit the white rice flour and use all brown rice flour (2¼ cups).*

## Alternative Flour Base
### (Standard Gluten-Free Flour Blend)

This blend is available from several gluten-free mail order sources. Recipes in this book using Wendy's flour mix show a xanthan gum addition for readers who choose to use this standard gluten-free flour blend.

2 parts rice flour*

⅔ part potato starch flour

⅓ part tapioca starch flour

*\* I highly recommend using brown rice flour for the best results.*

## Xanthan Gum

You can revise your favorite recipes by using this guideline for adding xanthan gum. Xanthan gum replaces gluten and acts as a binding agent. It must be an ingredient in all baked goods based on gluten-free flour. When using Wendy Wark's flour, use this guideline but reduce the xanthan gum just a bit, since her mix already includes some.

Bread     1 teaspoon per cup of flour mix

Cakes     ½ teaspoon per cup of flour mix

Cookies    ¼ teaspoon per cup of flour mix

# Almond Quinoa Cookies

We have really missed the flavor, texture, and nutrition of oatmeal cookies. After some experimentation, I have recreated an "oatmeal cookie" with quinoa flakes and ground almonds. The cookies are fabulous! Guittard chocolate chips are optional; any gluten-free chocolate chip will work, but in taste testing conducted at our home and at *Cook's Illustrated* magazine, Guittard chocolate chips were the number one choice. I use Ancient Harvest quinoa flakes (see Sources).

## ingredients:

1 cup unsalted butter, softened

1 cup granulated sugar

1 cup packed brown sugar

2 eggs plus one egg white

1 teaspoon vanilla extract

2 cups Wendy Wark's gluten-free
   flour mix (page 181)

½ teaspoon xanthan gum

1½ cups almonds or pecans, finely ground

1⅛ cups quinoa flakes

7 ounces finely grated Guittard bulk
   chocolate

½ teaspoon salt

1 teaspoon baking powder

1 teaspoon baking soda

12 ounces Guittard chocolate chips or raisins

## makes 5 dozen cookies

Preheat oven to 375°F. In a large bowl, cream butter and sugars on high speed until light in texture. Add eggs and vanilla, mixing well. Combine flour, xanthan gum, ground nuts, quinoa flakes, grated chocolate, salt, baking powder, and baking soda in a medium mixing bowl. Slowly add flour mixture to creamed butter, mixing until well incorporated. Add chocolate chips and mix well.

Drop by rounded teaspoonfuls on a cookie sheet lined with parchment and bake for 8–10 minutes. Remove to a cooling rack.

*variation:* You may substitute quinoa flakes for the almonds and omit the grated chocolate. This version tastes a lot like oatmeal cookies and is less time consuming.

*Notes: If using a standard gluten-free flour blend, add ½ teaspoon xanthan gum to the dry ingredients.*
*A rotary grater makes the task of grating chocolate much easier.*
*A Hershey bar may be substituted for the Guittard bulk chocolate.*

# Macaroons

This is a yummy sweet to add to your holiday cookie assortment. I have found that these are the ones that usually disappear first!
The texture of unsweetened coconut is preferred, though it can be difficult to find. If you use unsweetened coconut, triple the amount of sugar in the recipe.

## ingredients:

½ cup sugar

4 cups sweetened coconut

3 large egg whites

Pinch of salt

2 tablespoons unsalted butter, melted

1 teaspoon vanilla extract

4 ounces semi-sweet chocolate

½ teaspoon organic shortening

### makes 35 pyramid-shaped macaroons

Using your hands, mix together sugar, coconut, egg whites, and salt in a large bowl. Add butter and vanilla, mixing well. Refrigerate mixture for at least an hour.

Preheat oven to 350°F. Line two baking sheets with parchment paper. Run cool water over your hands, shaking off excess water, and shape coconut mixture by tablespoons into pyramid forms. Place macaroons on prepared baking sheets, spacing 1-inch apart. Bake for 15 minutes, or until edges are golden brown. Transfer baking sheet to a wire rack. Let macaroons cool completely before removing.

Melt chocolate and shortening in the top of a double boiler, stirring occasionally. Dip top of each macaroon in the melted chocolate to a depth of ½-inch. Let chocolate set until firm before serving. (Brief refrigeration will hasten the process.)

# Chocolate Chip Cookies

This is the basic recipe on the back of most chocolate chip bags. You can use the standard gluten-free flour blend, though Wendy's flour mix will yield a better result.

## ingredients:

2 sticks (1 cup) unsalted butter, softened

¾ cup granulated sugar

¾ cup packed brown sugar

2 eggs

1 teaspoon vanilla extract

2¼ cups Wendy Wark's gluten-free
    flour mix (page 181)

½ teaspoon xanthan gum

1 teaspoon baking soda

1 teaspoon salt

1 cup chopped walnuts

2 cups chocolate chips

## makes 5 dozen cookies

Preheat oven to 375°F.

Cream butter and sugars on high speed until light in texture. Add eggs and vanilla, mixing well. Combine flour, xanthan gum, baking soda, and salt in a medium bowl. Add gradually to the creamed mixture until well incorporated. Add walnuts and chocolate chips, mixing well.

Drop mixture by rounded teaspoonful onto an ungreased baking sheet and bake for 8 minutes. Remove baking sheet from oven. Let stand for a few minutes before transferring cookies to a cooling rack.

# Molasses Cookies

Every year during the holidays, my grandma made "from scratch" cookies and peanut brittle. The molasses cookies were always my favorite. Luckily for all of us, Grandma's recipe was handed down through the family. This recipe does not use eggs, has a higher proportion of spices than other molasses cookie recipes, and uses cold coffee for a big flavor punch. As the standard gluten-free flour blend is a bit too grainy for this recipe, I highly recommend using Wendy Wark's flour mix.

## ingredients:

1½ cups granulated sugar

1 cup organic shortening

½ cup molasses

½ cup cold coffee

3¾ cups Wendy Wark's gluten-free
    flour mix (page 181)

½ teaspoon xanthan gum

2 teaspoons baking soda

1 teaspoon ground cloves

1 teaspoon ginger

1 teaspoon cinnamon

Granulated sugar

## makes 6 dozen small cookies

Preheat oven to 375°F.

Cream sugar and shortening on high speed until pale in color and light in texture. Add molasses and coffee, mixing well. In a medium bowl, combine flour, xanthan gum, baking soda, cloves, ginger, and cinnamon. Slowly add flour mixture to molasses mixture until well incorporated. Chill dough for 20 minutes.

Roll cookie dough into balls the size of walnuts and dip one side into sugar. Place sugar side up on a parchment lined baking sheet. Bake for 7 minutes.

*Notes: These cookies make a great cheesecake crust.*
*If using a standard gluten-free flour blend, add ¹/₂ teaspoon xanthan gum to the dry ingredients.*

# Cut-out Cookies with Royal Icing

Gluten intolerant children really enjoy having holiday cookies to roll, cut out, and decorate.
The recipe was adapted from Carol Fenster's version found in a back issue of *Living Without*. (See Sources for more information on this helpful magazine.)

## ingredients:

¼ cup unsalted butter, softened

2 tablespoons honey

½ cup sugar

1 tablespoon vanilla

2 teaspoons grated lemon peel

1½ cups Wendy Wark's gluten-free
     flour mix (page 181)

½ teaspoon salt

1 teaspoon baking powder

½ teaspoon baking soda

2-3 tablespoons water

## Royal Icing

½ cup organic shortening

4 cups confectioners' sugar

¼ cup water

Food coloring

## makes thirty 3-inch cookies

Cream butter, honey, and sugar on high speed until pale in color and light in texture; scrape the bowl periodically while creaming. Add vanilla and grated lemon peel, combining thoroughly. Sift flour, salt, baking powder, and baking soda. Gradually add flour mixture to creamed mixture. Once combined, add water as needed to form a soft dough. Gather dough into a ball, wrap tightly in plastic wrap, and chill in the refrigerator for 30 minutes.

Preheat oven to 325°F. Line two baking sheets with parchment paper.

Remove half of the dough from the refrigerator. Roll out dough to ¼-inch thickness between two sheets of wax paper. Cut out cookies with a cookie cutter, then lift cookies off wax paper with a spatula and transfer to prepared baking sheet. Place baking sheet in the refrigerator while rolling out the second half of the dough.

Bake for 10-12 minutes. Cool on baking sheet for a few minutes, then turn out onto a wire rack to cool completely before frosting.

### Royal Icing:

In a small bowl, combine shortening and sugar with a fork. Add water gradually to a spreading consistency. Mix in food coloring to desired tint. Fill a pastry decorating bag with icing (or use a sandwich size plastic bag with one corner snipped off). Squeeze icing out in a decorative pattern.

# Gingersnap Cookies

When you roll out these cookies, the dough will seem terribly crumbly, and you may wonder if you have gone wrong somewhere.
Don't worry; they will hold together beautifully and make a delicious, crispy ginger snap. This recipe makes good "gingerbread people."

## ingredients:

6 tablespoons unsalted butter

½ cup sugar

2 tablespoons light corn syrup

1½ cups Wendy Wark's gluten-free
  flour mix (page 181)

¼ teaspoon xanthan gum

2 teaspoons ground ginger

½ teaspoon baking soda

### Icing

½ cup confectioners' sugar

2 teaspoons water

## makes 8 large cookies (using 6-inch cookie cutters)

Preheat oven to 350°F. Grease two cookie sheets or line them with parchment paper.

Melt butter, sugar, and corn syrup in a heavy-bottomed saucepan, stirring occasionally. Remove from heat when butter is melted and ingredients are well combined. Let cool while mixing dry ingredients.

Sift flour, xanthan gum, ginger, and baking soda in a medium bowl. Make a well in the center of the flour mixture. Pour melted butter mixture into well and mix thoroughly with a wooden spoon.

Using your hands, form the dough into a ball. Roll out dough on a lightly floured surface to ¼-inch thickness. Cut out cookies with cookie cutter. Carefully lift each cookie with a spatula and transfer to prepared cookie sheet.

Bake for 10-12 minutes. Cool cookies on baking sheet for a few minutes before transferring to a wire rack. Let cool 5 minutes longer.

### Icing:

While cookies are cooling, sift confectioners' sugar into a small bowl. Add water and beat until smooth. Spoon icing into a pastry bag with a small decorating tip (or spoon into a clean plastic bag with one corner snipped off). Decorate cookies and let icing set for one hour, or until hardened.

Note: If using a standard gluten-free flour blend, add ⅛ teaspoon xanthan gum to the dry ingredients.

# Mexican Wedding Cakes

My sister-in-law has made these cookies a Christmas tradition.
Present them on a beautiful platter with other assorted holiday cookies such as macaroons, cut-out cookies decorated with icing, shortbread, or any of your family favorites.
The secret of converting the original recipe to a gluten-free version is the substitution of either sour cream or cream cheese for some or all of the butter.

## ingredients:

¾ cup unsalted butter, softened

¼ cup gluten-free sour cream or
  cream cheese, room temperature

½ cup confectioners' sugar

1 teaspoon vanilla extract

2 cups Wendy Wark's gluten-free
  flour mix (page 181)

Scant ½ teaspoon xanthan gum

¼ teaspoon salt

¼ cup jam, raspberry or boysenberry

## makes four dozen 1 1/2-inch cookies

Preheat oven to 400°F.

Cream butter, sour cream, and sugar together on high speed until light and airy in texture. Add vanilla and mix well. Sift flour, xanthan gum, and salt into a small bowl. Gradually add flour mixture to creamed butter, mixing well. (Dough will look like a coarse meal.) Continue to beat on high speed long enough for the butter to soften and the dough to form a soft mass.

Shape the dough by tablespoons into balls. Place onto an ungreased baking sheet. Make a thumbprint impression in each ball and fill with a bit of jam. Refrigerate cookies for 15 minutes prior to baking. Bake cookies for 11-12 minutes, or until lightly browned. Remove to a wire rack to cool completely, then sprinkle lightly with confectioners' sugar.

# Rocky Road

Another holiday favorite that is especially easy for children learning how to cook.
If you have gluten intolerant children, introduce them to the kitchen early in life to develop a love of cooking.

## ingredients:

*8 ounces semi-sweet chocolate*

*1 cup gluten-free miniature marshmallows*

*½ cup chopped walnuts*

### makes 35 bite-sized pieces

Microwave chocolate in a glass bowl on high heat for 20 seconds. Stir with a rubber spatula. Repeat heating in 10-20 second increments, stirring each time, until chocolate is melted. (The repeated stirring will prevent burning.) Stir in marshmallows and nuts until thoroughly coated.

Spread mixture evenly onto a baking sheet. Cover and refrigerate to harden (about 30 minutes). Bring candy to room temperature, then cut into bite-size pieces.

# Java Chocolate Truffles

Prior to writing this cookbook, I was known within the Gluten Intolerance Group as the gluten-free chocolate truffle lady.
The truffles are so fresh they rival those purchased at the fancy chocolate shops. This is a quick home version that anyone can handle.
If you would like to hand dip your truffles, rent a Sinsation tempering machine to simplify that process. Fine European chocolate is recommended for the best results.
Recipe provided by Bill Fredericks, The Chocolate Man, purveyor of fine chocolates and truffle-making supplies (see Sources).

## ingredients:

8 ounces milk chocolate

¼ cup mocha coffee beans

⅔ cup cream

1 cup cocoa for coating

## makes 3 dozen

Place chocolate in a glass bowl. Heat in a microwave oven for 30 seconds. Remove and stir until smooth. If some bits of chocolate remain, microwave in 10-20 second increments until completely melted.

Grind coffee coarsely, then pass through a sieve to remove fine particles. (This will prevent a gritty texture in the truffle mixture.)

Mix cream and ground coffee together in a small saucepan. Bring to a simmer and remove from heat. For a stronger coffee flavor, simmer for a few minutes.

Pour cream into a small bowl through a sieve to catch the coffee grounds. When chocolate and cream have cooled to lukewarm, combine and whisk together thoroughly. This mixture is called ganache. Once ganache has cooled, cover with plastic wrap and chill to set.

Scoop ganache into balls, using a 1-inch scoop with a release lever. (You may also form a 1-inch piece with a spoon and roll into a ball with your fingers). Drop each ganache ball into a shallow bowl of cocoa and roll about until thoroughly coated. Shake off excess and arrange on a serving plate.

*Notes: Oils can be used to flavor the ganache, as opposed to the liqueurs commonly used.*
*Since it is difficult to determine the gluten-free status of liqueurs, flavored oils are a better choice (see Sources).*
*For the dark chocolate lover, try substituting 4 ounces of bittersweet and*
*4 ounces of semi-sweet chocolate for the milk chocolate.*

# Chewy Brownies with Raspberry Sauce

There are many ways to make brownies, but we prefer the kind that are chewy and crackled on top. Although many brownie recipes have passed through my test kitchen, this is the best one yet. Raspberry sauce and a scoop of vanilla ice cream can transform a brownie into an elegant dessert. The contrasting flavors work very well together.

## ingredients:

½ cup (1 stick) unsalted butter

4 ounces unsweetened chocolate

1 cup Wendy Wark's gluten-free
   flour mix (page 181)

½ teaspoon xanthan gum

¼ teaspoon salt

2 tablespoons cocoa powder

1½ cups sugar

2 teaspoons vanilla extract

3 large eggs

1 cup walnuts, coarsely chopped (optional)

## Raspberry Sauce

2 cups raspberries

½ cup sugar

½ cup water

1 teaspoon lemon juice

## makes 16 brownies (2-inches square)

Preheat oven to 350°F. Butter an 8-inch square glass baking dish. Line the bottom with parchment and then butter the parchment.

Melt butter and chocolate in the top of a double boiler. Remove from heat, stir, and let cool. In a separate medium bowl, sift flour, xanthan gum, salt, and cocoa.

Add sugar and vanilla to the chocolate mixture, mixing well. Add eggs one at a time until thoroughly blended. Add the dry ingredients slowly until well incorporated. Stir in nuts. Pour into the prepared baking dish, scraping bowl well.

Bake for 35-40 minutes, or until a toothpick comes out clean with a few crumbs clinging to it. Set the dish on a wire rack until cool enough to handle. Run a knife between the walls of the dish and the baked brownie mixture and invert onto a flat surface to release. Peel off the parchment and place brownie sheet on the rack to cool completely.

When completely cool, place brownie sheet on a cutting board. Using a thin, sharp knife, cut into 16 squares, wiping the knife between cuts to ensure smooth, clean edges. Brownies can be frozen in individual serving sizes; wrap each tightly in plastic wrap, then seal in a large freezer bag.

**Raspberry Sauce:** Bring raspberries, sugar, and water to a boil in a nonreactive saucepan, stirring occasionally. Remove from heat. Stir in lemon juice. Puree in a blender. Strain through a sieve, pushing on the solids and discarding the seeds. Adjust quantity of sugar or lemon juice if necessary.

Note: If using a standard gluten-free flour blend, add ¹/₂ teaspoon xanthan gum to the dry ingredients.

# Yellow Butter Cake with Chocolate Frosting

This simple cake with chocolate frosting is a birthday classic. As with all cakes made with Wendy's flour mix, this cake will stay moist for several days — if it lasts that long!

## ingredients:

8 tablespoons (1 stick) unsalted butter,
    softened

1 cup sugar

4 eggs, separated, plus one egg white

½ cup cold water

1 teaspoon vanilla extract

2 cups Wendy Wark's gluten-free
    flour mix (page 181)

½ teaspoon xanthan gum

½ teaspoon salt

4 teaspoons baking powder

## Chocolate Frosting

2 ounces unsweetened chocolate

1 tablespoon butter

⅓ cup milk

2 cups confectioner's sugar, sifted

1 teaspoon vanilla extract

## comment:

The Chocolate Frosting recipe makes enough for an 8-inch or 9-inch two-layer cake. This is a smooth, spreadable frosting. If you like a thick layer of frosting, you will want to double the recipe.

### makes two, 8-inch rounds or 18 cupcakes

Preheat oven to 350°F. Butter and lightly flour two 8-inch round cake pans.

In a large bowl, beat the butter and sugar until pale in color and light in texture. Add egg yolks and cold water, mixing well. Add vanilla and blend. In a medium bowl, combine flour, xanthan gum, salt, and baking powder. Add to the butter mixture. In a small bowl, using an electric mixer, beat the egg whites until stiff but not dry. Carefully fold egg whites into the cake batter. Pour batter into prepared pans. Bake for 20-25 minutes, until a toothpick inserted near the center comes out clean with a few crumbs clinging to it. Let cake rest in pans for 5-10 minutes, then turn out onto a cooling rack. Cool completely before frosting.

If making cupcakes, use a non-stick muffin tin or butter 18 muffin cups. Divide batter into muffin cups and bake for 12-13 minutes, until the toothpick test shows them to be done. Allow cupcakes to cool for 5 minutes in the tin before turning out onto a cooling rack.

**Chocolate Frosting:** In a double boiler, melt chocolate, butter, and milk together. Remove from heat and cool to lukewarm. Add sugar and vanilla. Beat with an electric mixer to a spreading consistency.

*Note: If using a standard gluten-free flour blend, add ½ teaspoon xanthan gum to the dry ingredients.*

# Sour Cream Coffee Cake

This is an old family recipe that we make throughout the year. It is also part of our Christmas morning breakfast each year.
My husband is from a family of accomplished cooks, and they could not believe I made the cake with gluten-free ingredients. It is fantastic!

## ingredients:

½ cup organic shortening

¾ cup sugar

1 teaspoon vanilla extract

3 eggs

2 cups Wendy Wark's gluten-free
   flour mix (page 181)

½ teaspoon xanthan gum

1 teaspoon baking powder

1 teaspoon baking soda

1¼ cups gluten-free sour cream

6 tablespoons unsalted butter, softened

1 cup brown sugar

2 teaspoons cinnamon

1 cup chopped nuts (walnuts or pecans)

## makes one 10-inch cake

Preheat oven to 350°F. Butter a 10-inch tube pan, then line with parchment cut to cover the bottom and sides. Butter inner surface of parchment.

In a large bowl, beat shortening and sugar until pale in color and light in texture. Add vanilla, then add eggs one at a time, beating well after each addition.

Sift flour, xanthan gum, baking powder, and baking soda in a medium bowl. Add sifted mix to creamed mixture alternately with sour cream, blending after each addition. Spread half the batter in prepared tube pan. Using a pastry blender or a fork, combine butter, brown sugar, cinnamon, and nuts in a medium bowl. Sprinkle half of the nut mixture over the batter, then cover nut mixture with remaining batter. Sprinkle remaining nut mixture on top.

Bake for 50-55 minutes, until a toothpick inserted near the center comes out clean with a few crumbs clinging to it. Allow cake to cool in the pan for 15 minutes. Invert cake and place on a cooling rack. Let cake cool completely before slicing.

*Notes: If using a standard gluten-free flour blend, add ½ teaspoon xanthan gum to the dry ingredients.
You may substitute regular shortening for organic shortening,
although the latter is strongly recommended as it is much healthier.*

# Lemon Cake

Many lemon cakes are too sweet and heavily glazed. This version has a nice lemon flavor and a light glaze. It is an excellent and easy-to-make recipe. Recipe adapted from *The Silver Palate Cookbook*, Rosso and Lukins (Workman Publishing, 1982).

## ingredients:

½ pound (2 sticks) unsalted butter,
    room temperature
2 cups sugar
3 large eggs plus 1 egg white
3 cups Wendy Wark's gluten-free
    flour mix (page 181)
1 teaspoon xanthan gum
½ teaspoon baking soda
½ teaspoon salt
1 cup buttermilk
1 tablespoon grated lemon peel
2 tablespoons fresh lemon juice

## Lemon Glaze

1 cup confectioners' sugar
6 tablespoons unsalted butter,
    room temperature
1 tablespoon grated lemon peel
¼ cup fresh lemon juice

### makes one 10-inch cake

Preheat oven to 325°F. Butter and flour a 10-inch tube pan or a 12-cup Bundt pan.

In a large bowl, beat butter and sugar on medium-high speed until pale in color and a light texture. Add eggs one at a time, mixing well after each addition.

Sift together flour mix, xanthan gum, baking soda, and salt in a medium bowl. Add flour mixture to egg mixture a little at a time, alternating with buttermilk, until all is well incorporated. Add grated lemon peel and juice.

Pour batter into prepared pan and bake for 1 hour and 5 minutes, or until a toothpick inserted near the center comes out clean with a few crumbs clinging to it. Cool for 12 minutes in the pan before turning out onto a wire rack. Prepare Lemon Glaze.

Lemon Glaze: In a small mixing bowl, beat butter and sugar on medium-high speed until light and creamy. Add grated lemon peel and juice, mixing well. Spread glaze over the top of warm cake. (The icing will soak in a little, and it will crystallize at room temperature.)

*Note: If using a standard gluten-free flour blend, add ¼ teaspoon xanthan gum to the dry ingredients.*

# Pound Cake

Known affectionately in the Robertson family as a sandtorte, this cake has gone through much testing to get the gluten-free version right.
Serve with fresh, local strawberries and vanilla ice cream for a fantastic dessert!

## ingredients:

1 cup unsalted butter, room temperature

3 cups sugar

6 eggs

3 cups Wendy Wark's gluten-free
   flour mix (page 181)

1 teaspoon xanthan gum

¼ teaspoon baking powder

1 cup gluten-free sour cream

1½ teaspoons vanilla extract

Confectioners' sugar for dusting top of cake

## makes one 10-inch cake

Preheat oven to 350°F. Butter and flour a 10-inch tube pan or a 12-cup Bundt pan.

Cream butter and sugar in a medium bowl on high speed until pale colored and light in texture. Add eggs one at a time, blending well after each addition.

Sift flour, xanthan gum, and baking powder in a small bowl. Add flour mixture to creamed mixture, alternating with sour cream. Add vanilla and mix well.

Bake for 1 hour and 30 minutes, or until a toothpick inserted near the center comes out clean with a few crumbs clinging to it. Let cake stand for 10-15 minutes in the pan before turning out onto a cooling rack.

When cake is completely cool, sprinkle with a light dusting of confectioners' sugar, using a fine mesh sieve.

Note: If using a standard gluten-free flour blend, add 1/4 teaspoon xanthan gum to the dry ingredients.

# Chocolate Cashew Cake

This cake is absolutely decadent. Although it takes a bit of time, it is well worth the effort.
My sister-in-law introduced this cake to our family. Since then, every birthday cake request has become one for cashew cake! (Thank you, Heather!)
To fit the preparation time into your busy schedule, make the filling and frosting one day then make the cake the following day.

## ingredients:

### Cake

½ cup unsweetened cocoa

½ cup boiling water

½ cup unsalted butter, softened

2 cups sugar

2 eggs plus 1 egg white

1 teaspoon vanilla extract

1¾ cups Wendy Wark's gluten-free
    flour mix (page 181)

½ teaspoon xanthan gum

1 teaspoon baking powder

1 teaspoon baking soda

1⅓ cups buttermilk

1½ cups finely chopped cashews

## frosting:

Six 1-ounce squares semi-sweet
    chocolate

¼ cup Wendy Wark's gluten-free
    flour mix (page 181)

⅔ cup sugar

¾ cup milk

1½ teaspoons vanilla extract

1 cup cold unsalted butter,
    cut into tablespoons

## filling:

¾ cup whipping cream

2 teaspoons vanilla extract

1 tablespoon sugar

## makes three 8-inch rounds

Preheat oven to 350°F. Butter and lightly flour three 8-inch round cake pans.

In a small heatproof bowl, stir cocoa into boiling water. Set aside to cool.

In a large bowl, cream butter and sugar until pale in color and light in texture. Add eggs and vanilla, mixing well. Sift flour, xanthan gum, baking powder, and baking soda in a medium bowl.

Add flour mixture slowly to butter mixture, blending until combined. Add buttermilk and mix thoroughly.

In a small bowl, mix 1⅓ cups of cake batter with cashews. Pour into one of the prepared cake pans.

Add the cooled cocoa mixture to the remaining batter, mixing well. Divide chocolate batter between two remaining cake pans.

Bake for 30-35 minutes, or until a toothpick inserted near the center comes out clean with a few crumbs clinging to it. Let cake layers stand for five minutes before removing from pans. Cool completely on a wire rack before frosting.

*continued:*
**Chocolate Cashew Cake**

**Frosting:** Melt semi-sweet chocolate in the top of a double boiler and cool to room temperature. (Chocolate can also be microwaved in 20 second increments. Stir frequently to avoid burning).

In a small heavy saucepan, combine flour and sugar over medium heat. Add milk and stir until thick and smooth. Cool to room temperature. Add vanilla and butter (3-4 tablespoons at a time) and beat until smooth with an electric mixer. Add chocolate and mix well. Set aside.

**Filling:** In a small bowl, combine whipping cream, vanilla, and sugar. Using an electric mixer, whip on high speed until thick.

Once cake layers have completely cooled, assemble cake in the following order on a serving plate: chocolate cake round, half of the filling, cashew cake round, remaining filling, chocolate cake round. Frost the cake.

*Note: If using a standard gluten-free flour blend, add 1/4 teaspoon xanthan gum to the dry ingredients.*

# Chocolate Cake with Chocolate Glaze

This recipe is adapted from Christopher Kimball's master recipe in *The Cook's Bible* (Little Brown, 1996).
The cake provides complete satisfaction for the true chocolate lover. All ingredients should be at room temperature.

## ingredients:

1½ cups Wendy Wark's gluten-free
   flour mix (page 181)

½ teaspoon xanthan gum

½ cup unsweetened Dutch process cocoa

¼ teaspoon baking powder

½ teaspoon baking soda

¼ heaping teaspoon salt

12 tablespoons (1½ sticks) unsalted butter,
   room temperature

1¼ cups sugar

2 whole eggs

2 egg whites

1½ teaspoons vanilla extract

½ cup espresso

½ cup buttermilk

### Chocolate Glaze

8 ounces semisweet chocolate

1 cup heavy cream

¼ cup light corn syrup

½ teaspoon vanilla extract

## comment:

Chocolate Glaze recipe makes enough for a 12-cup Bundt cake or two 8-inch rounds.

### makes two 8-inch rounds

Preheat oven to 350°F. Prepare two 8-inch round cake pans or one 12-cup Bundt pan by buttering, lightly coating with cocoa, and tapping out excess cocoa.

Sift flour mix, xanthan gum, cocoa, baking powder, baking soda, and salt into a medium bowl and set aside. Using an electric mixer, beat butter on high speed until pale colored. Add sugar gradually and beat until light and airy in texture (about 3 minutes), scraping the bowl often. On low speed, add eggs and whites one at a time, mixing after each addition. Add vanilla and mix briefly. Then add espresso and buttermilk, alternating with the flour mixture until all is added. Blend well but don't overbeat.

Pour batter into prepared cake pans and bake for 25-30 minutes (10 minutes longer if using a Bundt pan), or until a toothpick inserted near the center comes out clean with a few crumbs clinging to it. Let stand for 10 minutes in the pan before turning out onto a wire rack. Cool completely before frosting.

*Note: If using a standard gluten-free flour blend, add 1/4 teaspoon xanthan gum to the dry ingredients.*

*continued:*

**Chocolate Cake
with Chocolate Glaze**

**Chocolate Glaze:**

Microwave chocolate in a glass bowl on medium heat for 20 seconds. Remove from oven and stir with a rubber spatula. Repeat heating in 10-20 second increments, stirring each time you heat to prevent burning, until chocolate is melted. (Chocolate tends to hold its shape even when partially melted; stirring will tell you whether it is actually melted or not.)

Combine cream and corn syrup in a heavy saucepan and heat to a simmer. Remove from heat, cool slightly, and slowly add to melted chocolate. Whisk until well blended and smooth. Add vanilla. Allow glaze to cool. (In a 70°F kitchen this can take a few hours). Lift some glaze up with a spoon and allow it to drizzle back into the bowl; when glaze forms a small mound it is ready to use.

For a Bundt cake, simply pour glaze over cake and allow it to drip down the sides. For a 2-layer cake, pour half the glaze over the bottom cake layer, spreading glaze along cake edges with a knife. Allow glaze to set for 5 minutes, then put top cake layer in place. Pour remaining glaze on top layer, spreading evenly over the cake and down the sides.

To make a thick frosting, add confectioners' sugar and beat until desired consistency is reached.

# Carrot Cake

This cake uses a carrot puree, which is actually less labor intensive than grating raw carrots. You can cook and puree the carrots the day before. Recipe adapted from *The Silver Palate Cookbook*, Rosso and Lukins (Workman Publishing, 1982).

## ingredients:

3 cups Wendy Wark's gluten-free
   flour mix (page 181)
1 teaspoon xanthan gum
3 cups sugar
1 teaspoon salt
1 tablespoon baking soda
1 tablespoon ground cinnamon
1½ cups vegetable oil
4 large eggs plus 1 egg white, lightly beaten
1 tablespoon vanilla extract
1½ cups walnuts, chopped (optional)
1½ cups unsweetened flaked coconut
1⅓ cups pureed cooked carrots
   (about 5 medium carrots)
¾ cup drained crushed pineapple

### Cream Cheese Frosting

16 ounces cream cheese, softened
   (don't use the new spreadable style)
1½ sticks (12 tablespoons) unsalted butter,
   softened
4 cups confectioners' sugar, sifted
2 teaspoons vanilla extract
Juice of one lemon

## comment:

Cream Cheese Frosting recipe makes enough for a two 9-inch rounds. This recipe yields a generous amount of frosting. If you prefer a thinner layer on your cake, you can cut the recipe in half and still have enough.

### makes two 9-inch rounds

Preheat oven to 350°F. Butter two 9-inch round cake pans and line with parchment. Butter inner surface of parchment as well.

Sift flour mix, xanthan gum, sugar, salt, baking soda, and cinnamon into a medium bowl. In a large bowl whisk oil, eggs, and vanilla. Slowly add flour mixture to egg mixture, mixing thoroughly but lightly. Fold in nuts, coconut, carrots, and pineapple.

Pour batter into prepared pans and bake for 50-55 minutes, or until edges pull away from the pan. (A toothpick inserted near the center should come out clean with a few crumbs clinging to it.) Remove pans from oven and let stand for five minutes before turning out onto wire racks. Cool cakes completely (about 3 hours) before frosting.

Cream Cheese Frosting:  In a medium bowl, beat together cream cheese and butter until smooth. Slowly add confectioners' sugar until well blended and free of lumps. Add vanilla and lemon juice and mix until smooth.

*Note: If using a standard gluten-free flour blend, add 1/2 teaspoon xanthan gum to the dry ingredients. Use a half recipe of Royal Icing (page 186) to add some carrot decoration to the top of the cake.*

# Orange Cheesecake

Several different cheesecake recipes were used to develop this version.
You can change the flavor by using cherry brandy or flavored oils (those used in chocolate truffle making - see Sources). Many cheesecake recipes use liqueurs for flavoring; however, as it is difficult to determine their gluten-free status, flavored oils are a better choice. Have some fun and come up with your own creations!

## ingredients:

2 cups gluten-free cookie crumbs
    (molasses cookies work well)

½ teaspoon cinnamon

5 tablespoons unsalted butter, melted

16 ounces cream cheese, softened

1½ cups sugar

4 eggs

2 cups sour cream

2 tablespoons gluten-free flour mix
    (page 181)

1 teaspoon vanilla

1 tablespoon orange zest

2 tablespoons orange juice concentrate

## makes 12-20 servings

Preheat oven to 350°F. Combine cookie crumbs, cinnamon, and melted butter in a small bowl. Press mixture evenly into the bottom of a 9½-inch springform pan. Bake for 5 minutes. Cool completely before filling.

Reduce oven temperature to 300°F. Beat cream cheese and sugar together until smooth and well blended, scraping down bowl several times. Add eggs one at a time, incorporating lightly after each addition. (Be careful not to overbeat.) Blend in sour cream, flour mix, vanilla, orange zest, and orange juice concentrate. Pour into prepared crust. Bake for 60-75 minutes. (Cake should be slightly risen, with a golden top and a custard-like consistency in the center.) Allow cheesecake to cool completely. Refrigerate for at least 8 hours before serving.

*Note: Bake cheesecake in a hot water bath to avoid cracking on top.*

# Pie Crust Dough

Recipe adapted from *Great Gluten Free Goodies* by Rebecca Reilly (Rebecca's Kitchen, 1997)

## ingredients:

1¾ cups (scant) Wendy Wark's
   gluten-free flour mix (page 181)

½ teaspoon salt

1 tablespoon sugar (omit if using crust for a
   savory recipe such as a quiche)

9 tablespoons cold unsalted butter,
   cut into pieces

1 jumbo egg plus one egg yolk, lightly beaten

1½ tablespoons gluten-free
   sour cream or cider vinegar

### makes enough dough for two 9-inch pie shells or a 2-crust pie

Combine flour, salt, and sugar. Using a pastry blender or a fork, work the butter in until small bits the size of peas are distributed throughout the flour mix. Make a well in the mixture and add the egg and sour cream, mixing thoroughly with a fork. If the mixture is crumbly, knead very lightly until the dough just holds together.

Gather half of the dough into a ball and shape it into a 5-inch disk. Repeat with remaining dough. Wrap both disks tightly in plastic wrap and refrigerate for 30 minutes. Follow directions for individual pie or tart recipes.

*Notes: A marble surface provides the ideal cool work surface; however, if you don't have one, place ice or gel ice packs on your countertop prior to rolling out the dough. Once a crust is blind baked, you can freeze it for future use.*

# Pumpkin Pie

This pie stands out from all the rest, with its intensely full, spice-perfumed pumpkin flavor.
I tried many recipes to see if I could find a top-notch pumpkin pie, but nothing beats this one from my grandma and Aunt Judy.

*ingredients:*

*Pie Crust Dough (page 202)*
*One 29-ounce can pumpkin*
*4 eggs, slightly beaten*
*2 tablespoons of any gluten-free flour mix*
*1 teaspoon salt*
*1 teaspoon ground cinnamon*
*¼ teaspoon ground cloves*
*½ teaspoon allspice*
*1 teaspoon ginger*
*2 cups sugar*
*1 teaspoon vanilla extract*
*2½ cups evaporated milk*

*makes two 9-inch pies*

**to bake the crust:** On a cool countertop, between two sheets of wax paper or plastic wrap, roll half the Pie Crust Dough into an 11-inch circle. Remove wax paper from one side. Pick up the crust with your hand on the wax paper side. Place crust into a 9-inch pie plate and remove wax paper. Make a fluted pie edge by tucking the overhanging dough under to make a double edge and pressing the two layers together. Pinch a V shape every ½-inch around the edge of the pie crust. Repeat steps with remaining dough and place in another 9-inch pie plate.

Cover crust-lined pie plates with foil and heap dried beans or pie weights inside. Place pie plates in the refrigerator for 15 minutes while preheating oven to 400°F. Bake crust for 20 minutes, or until edges turn golden. Allow crust to cool for 5 minutes, then remove foil and weights. Return crust to oven for 5 more minutes if a crisp, golden crust is desired. Allow crust to cool for 10 minutes before filling.

**to make the filling:** Reduce oven temperature to 325°F. Blend pumpkin and eggs together in a large bowl. Mix together flour, salt, cinnamon, cloves, allspice, and ginger in a medium bowl. Slowly add the spice mixture to the pumpkin blend. Add sugar and vanilla, mixing well. Add evaporated milk in a slow stream, mixing thoroughly. Pour mixture into prepared pie crusts and bake pies for one hour. Test for doneness by inserting a knife into each pie; it should come out clean.

*Note: A cool countertop is essential to help the dough stay chilled; otherwise, it will stick to the wax paper.*

# Apple Pie

My father made most of the apple pies of my childhood using his mothers' recipe. Their pies are known far and wide (to friends and family) as the best apple pie!

## ingredients:

6 Granny Smith apples

1 teaspoon lemon juice

Pie Crust Dough (page 202)

2-3 tablespoons of any gluten-free flour mix

1-2 teaspoons cinnamon

½ -¾ cups sugar (depending on
   acidity of apples)

1 tablespoon unsalted butter

1 egg yolk

1 teaspoon milk

*Notes: Other apple varieties that work well in pies include Golden Delicious, Jonagold, Newtown Pippin, and Rome.*

*A cool countertop is essential to help the dough stay chilled; otherwise, it will stick to the wax paper.*

## makes one 9-inch pie

Peel, core, and slice apples into bite-sized pieces. Fill a large bowl with water. Add lemon juice and apples.

**to bake the crust:** On a cool countertop, between two sheets of wax paper or plastic wrap, roll half the Pie Crust Dough into an 11-inch circle. Remove wax paper from one side. Pick up the crust with your hand on the wax paper side. Place crust into a 9-inch pie plate and remove wax paper. Make a fluted pie edge by tucking the overhanging dough under to make a double edge and pressing the two layers together. Pinch a V shape every ½-inch around the edge of the pie crust.

Cover crust-lined pie plate with foil and heap dried beans or pie weights inside. Place pie plate in the refrigerator for 15 minutes while preheating oven to 400°F. Bake crust for 20 minutes, or until edges turn golden. Allow crust to cool for 5 minutes, then remove foil and weights. Return crust to oven for 5 more minutes if a crisp, golden crust is desired. Allow crust to cool for 10 minutes before filling.

**to make the filling:** Meanwhile, drain apples in a colander (they should be as free of excess moisture as possible before baking).

Reduce oven temperature to 350°F. Sprinkle a little flour, cinnamon, and sugar on the bottom pie crust. Cover with one third of the apple slices. Sprinkle another layer of flour, cinnamon, and sugar over the apples, and dot with small pieces of butter. Cover with half the remaining apples, followed by another layer of flour, cinnamon, sugar, and butter. Top with remaining apples, flour, cinnamon, sugar, and butter.

Roll out the second crust and place on top of apples (you will have a high mound of apples, but it will settle down). Press edges of top and bottom crust together. Cut slits in top crust to allow steam to escape. Whisk egg yolk and milk together to make an egg wash. Brush liberally over top crust.

Place pie in center of oven and bake for one hour or until apples are tender.

# Apple Tart

This recipe could be short and sweet, but I added a lot of explanation to help the first-time tart maker. I have eaten many pies and tarts with a wheat flour crust that are not nearly as good as this one made with a gluten-free crust. There is no gluten to overwork! Wonderful alone or with a scoop of vanilla ice cream.

## ingredients:

Pie Crust Dough (page 202)

4 pounds Granny Smith apples, peeled, cored, and quartered

3 tablespoons plus 1 teaspoon lemon juice

3 tablespoons plus 1 teaspoon brandy

3 tablespoons sugar

2-3 Granny Smith apples, peeled, cored, and sliced very thin

3 tablespoons unsalted butter, melted

½ cup apricot jam

## makes 10-12 servings

### to bake the crust:

Roll dough into a 12-inch circle on a cool countertop between two sheets of wax paper. (The cool countertop is essential to help the dough stay chilled; otherwise, it will stick to the wax paper.) Remove one piece of wax paper, pick up the crust, and place it into an 11-inch tart pan. Remove top piece of wax paper. Make a double edge by tucking the overhanging dough under and pressing the layers together into the fluted sides of the tart pan.

Let crust rest in the refrigerator for 15 minutes while preheating oven to 400°F. Cover crust with foil and mound dry beans or pie weights on top of foil to keep crust from puffing up. Bake for 20 minutes, or until edges turn golden. Allow crust to cool for 5 minutes, then remove foil and weights. This process is known as blind baking the crust; although it is not an absolutely necessary step, it makes for a crisper crust.

### to make the filling:

Toss quartered apples with 3 tablespoons each of lemon juice and brandy and sprinkle with 1 tablespoon sugar. Spread apples out in a single layer on a roasting pan. Bake at 250°F for 2 hours, stirring occasionally. Let apples cool slightly, then chop into smaller pieces and puree in a food processor. Spread puree evenly over baked crust. Arrange the thinly sliced apples in a circular pattern in the tart pan. Brush apples with melted butter and sprinkle with remaining sugar.

Bake at 350°F for 25 minutes, then place under broiler (watching carefully) for up to 10 minutes.

While tart is baking, heat apricot jam, remaining lemon juice, and brandy in a small saucepan, stirring occasionally with a wire whisk, until heated through and smoothly combined. Brush warm tart with this mixture. Serve tart warm or at room temperature.

# Grand Marnier Semifreddo with Bittersweet Chocolate Sauce and Local Blackberries

### Chef Todd Gray, Equinox – Washington D.C.

Equinox is one of this city's premier fine dining establishments, offering sophisticated, pure American cuisine.
Chef Gray uses fresh, local organic ingredients whenever possible. He is a James Beard Award Nominee for Chef of the Year, Mid-Atlantic, in 2001.
The gluten-free version of this terrific dessert calls for a substitution for the Grand Marnier, unless you are able to determine that Grand Marnier is absolutely gluten-free.
An intense orange flavor can be derived from orange zest or orange extract.

## ingredients:

1½ cups egg yolks (about 18 yolks)

1 cup sugar

½ cup PS Moscato
  (an Italian sparkling wine)

½ cup Grand Marnier or orange juice
  combined with 2 teaspoons of
  orange extract or orange zest

2 gelatin sheets or 2 tablespoons granulated
  gelatin dissolved in ¼ cup of water

2 cups heavy cream, whipped

4-5 cups local blackberries

### Bittersweet Chocolate Sauce

9 ounces bittersweet chocolate

4½ ounces fresh-squeezed orange juice

3 tablespoons butter

1 cup plus 2 tablespoons heavy cream

1 teaspoon vanilla extract

## chef's comment:
Try using fresh, organic eggs from cage-free hens.

## makes 6-8 servings

Combine yolks, sugar, sparkling wine, and orange juice with zest in a stainless steel bowl. Beat over a double boiler, whisking vigorously, until mix is thick, pale, and has doubled in volume. (It will fall in a ribbon when the whisk is lifted from the bowl.)

Remove bowl from heat. Add dissolved gelatin, mix well, and cool. When mixture thickens to the consistency of egg whites, but is not yet firm, fold in whipped cream. Pour into a film-lined terrine mold or jelly roll pan. Cover and freeze overnight.

Bittersweet Chocolate Sauce: Combine chocolate, orange juice, and butter in a large glass bowl. Heat in microwave oven for 30-60 seconds. Whisk mixture to combine thoroughly. (If chocolate has not completely melted, microwave for 30 seconds longer.) Add cream and microwave for about 10 seconds longer, or until slightly warmed. Add vanilla extract and whisk mixture until smooth once again. If sauce is too thick, whisk in additional orange juice and/or cream until desired consistency is reached.

To serve, cut in slices with a knife dipped in hot water. Top with bittersweet chocolate sauce and local blackberries.

# Baked Pears

Such a simple delicacy!

## ingredients:

1 tablespoon sugar

3 Bosc pears, halved and seeded

1 tablespoon unsalted butter

⅔ cup heavy cream

## 4 servings

Preheat oven to 400°F. Butter an 8-inch baking dish and sprinkle with ½ tablespoon sugar. Place pears, cut side down, in dish. Dot pears with butter and sprinkle with remaining sugar. Bake for 10 minutes, then add cream and bake for another 15 minutes. Serve warm.

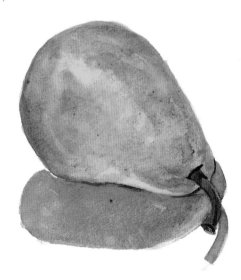

# Cranberry Soufflé

**Chef Hans Bergmann, Cacharel – Arlington, Texas**

Cacharel is a great restaurant situated between Dallas and Fort Worth.
The restaurant has received top restaurant status in the *Zagat Restaurant Survey* as well as in *Condé Nast* and *Gourmet* magazines.

## ingredients:

6 ounces fresh cranberries

7 ounces granulated sugar

2½ ounces butter, softened

¼ cup water

6 ounces egg whites

Dash of salt

Confectioners' sugar

4 ounces whipped cream

## makes 6 soufflés (8 ounces each)

Preheat oven to 450°F.

Place cranberries and 3 ounces granulated sugar in a saucepan. Bring slowly to a boil, then simmer until mixture becomes almost dry. Set aside to cool.

Brush inside of soufflé dishes with soft butter.

In a heavy bottomed saucepan bring water and 4 ounces granulated sugar to boil. Cook until mixture reaches 240°F. (This is the soft-ball stage; when you drop a bit of the hot sugar syrup in cold water you can form a soft ball that will flatten on its own.)

Whip egg whites with a dash of salt and the hot sugar syrup to the soft peak stage. Add cranberry reduction and fold in gently.

Using a spoon, fill the prepared soufflé dishes with the mixture up to the rim and bake in a convection oven for 10-12 minutes until the soufflés rise to double their original size and are cooked in the middle. (If you do not have a convection oven, cooking the time may be longer. Be careful not to overbake, or the edges will burn and the soufflés will fall upon being removed from the oven.)

Sprinkle with confectioners' sugar and serve immediately, with whipped cream on the side.

*Note: If there aren't any fresh cranberries available, substitute frozen. Cranberries are one of the few types of fruit you can freeze without loss of quality.*

# Local Berries with Crème Fraîche

This is a very elegant way to serve local berries. Serve over any fresh in-season berry.
I find this more interesting than ice cream when fruit is at its peak, since the sweetness of the fruit is the focus.

## ingredients:

1 cup whipping cream

2 tablespoons buttermilk

2 cups local strawberries, raspberries,
   or blackberries

## 4 servings

**Crème fraîche:** Combine whipping cream and buttermilk in a glass measuring cup. Stir well and let sit at 70°F for 8-24 hours, or until mixture thickens. Stir, cover, and refrigerate. (It will keep for about 10 days.)

Divide berries between four bowls and spoon ¼ cup of crème fraîche over each bowl.
Garnish with a fresh mint sprig.

# Panna Cotta with Dried Fruit Compote

*Chef Suzanne Goin, Lucques — West Hollywood, California*

Panna cotta is Italian for "cooked cream," a light, silky egg custard served with fruit or chocolate sauce. This version is accented by a dried fruit compote flavored with ginger, citrus, and spices. Suzanne was featured in *Food & Wine* magazine as one of America's Best New Chefs in 1999.

## ingredients:

4 teaspoons unflavored gelatin

2 cups whole milk

1 cup confectioners' sugar

2 cups heavy cream

1 vanilla bean, split down the
    middle lengthwise

1 teaspoon vanilla extract

### Dried Fruit Compote

1 teaspoon black peppercorns

2 cloves

1 teaspoon coriander seeds

4 bay leaves

1 pinch grated nutmeg

1 pinch cinnamon

1 cinnamon stick

3 cups red wine

3 cups port

½ cup sugar

Juice of 2 lemons

Juice of 1 orange

2 pounds high quality dried fruit
    (which may include pears, peaches,
    plums, prunes, figs, and flame raisins)

Hot water

1 tablespoon freshly grated ginger

Zest of one orange and one lemon

## 12 servings

Butter 12 small ramekins and place on a sheet tray.

In a small bowl, sprinkle the gelatin over ¼ cup of the milk and stir to blend. Set aside until the gelatin completely absorbs the milk, 2-3 minutes.

In a large saucepan, combine the remaining 1¾ cups milk, sugar, and cream. Using a small knife, scrape the beans from the vanilla pod and add them to the liquid. Add the scraped pod as well. Bring to a boil over moderate heat and whisk to dissolve the sugar.

As soon as the liquid comes to a boil, remove the pot from the heat and add the softened gelatin-milk mixture and the vanilla extract. Whisk to completely dissolve the gelatin. Strain the mixture through a fine mesh sieve into a container.

Pour the mixture into the ramekins. Cover with plastic wrap and refrigerate until set, about 4 hours.

Tie all spices together in a square of cheesecloth to form a pouch. In a stainless steel saucepan, place spice pouch, red wine, port, sugar, and juice of lemons and orange. Bring to a boil and set aside. This will be the poaching liquid for the dried fruit.

*continued:*

**Panna Cotta with
Dried Fruit Compote**

Cut fruit into slightly bigger than bite-sized pieces. Place fruit in a bowl and cover with hot water. Let fruit plump for 30 minutes.

Drain fruit and place it in the pot of poaching liquid. Simmer fruit for 20-30 minutes, until tender and well flavored by the aromatics in the poaching liquid.

Remove fruit from poaching liquid. Add ginger and zest of orange and lemon to the pot and reduce the liquid down to make a sauce.

Keep the fruit in the sauce, refrigerated, until ready to serve.

To serve, run a sharp knife along the inside of each ramekin to help loosen the cream. Dip the bottom of each ramekin in a bowl of hot water, shaking to completely loosen the cream. Invert onto chilled dessert plates. Spoon the fruit compote around the panna cotta and serve.

**wine suggestion:** a dessert wine such as Vin Santo or Sauternes

*Notes: Panna cotta is also good served with fresh berries marinated in a little sugar and mint.
Sometimes in the manufacturing process, dried fruit is dusted with flour to prevent sticking;
be sure your choices are gluten-free.
You may substitute yellow raisins or any other large raisin for the flame raisins.*

# Floating Islands with Caramel Blood Oranges

*Chef Gerry Hayden, Aureole — New York, New York*

Charlie Palmer's Aureole is revered as a paradigm of progressive American cuisine. It is one of New York's finest restaurants. Restaurant critic Bob Lape says of Aureole, "An elegant dining experience packed with punch … boldly flavored seasonal dishes … theatrically inspired three-dimensional desserts serve to delight all the senses." Chef de cuisine Gerry Hayden taps his experience from some of the finest kitchens in America: the critically acclaimed River Café, Marguery Grill, Tribeca Grill, and Aqua.

### ingredients:

3 egg whites

1½ cups sugar, divided

½ cup water

2 blood oranges, sectioned, juice reserved

1 rosemary branch (optional)

### comment:

This dessert complements Gerry's other contributions to this book, Caramelized Crimini Mushroom Soup with Fresh Rosemary (page 97) and Pan-Roasted Pork Tenderloin with Fennel, Radish, and Arugula Salad (page 98).

### 4 servings

Preheat oven to 250°F. Spray four 4-ounce aluminum cups with a non-stick gluten-free spray.

Combine egg whites and ½ cup sugar in a metal mixing bowl. (If you have a stand mixer, use its bowl attachment.) Set bowl atop a saucepan of simmering water. The bowl should fit snugly on the pot without touching the water.

Whisk the sugar mixture gently until the whites are warm and the sugar is completely dissolved. Remove the bowl from heat and lock in stand mixer. Using the whip attachment, whip until soft peaks form.

Fill a pastry bag, fitted with a large plain tip, with the beaten egg whites and pipe into the center of the aluminum tins. Allow the filling to move outwards from the center. Smooth tops with a spatula, set in a water bath, and cover loosely with foil sprayed with non-stick spray. Bake for 20-30 minutes, until the meringue is firm but still moist. Remove from water bath and refrigerate.

Place remaining cup of sugar and just enough water to moisten a heavy-bottomed saucepan. Bring to a boil and continue to cook until the sugar turns amber. Pour in reserved blood orange juice, rosemary branch, and the remaining water. Bring caramel back to a boil and continue to cook for 2 minutes, then strain over blood orange sections. Cool.

Remove meringues from their molds and place on plates. Spoon blood orange sections and caramel sauce around the meringues.

*Note: If you do not own pastry bags and tips, use a clean plastic bag with one corner snipped off.*

# APPENDIX

# The Gluten-Free Diet

ANY OF THE GLUTEN INTOLERANT SUPPORT GROUPS can provide extensively researched dietary guidelines. I strongly suggest that you contact these groups and request their information (see page 216 for contact information). Shelley Case, Registered Dietitian, has published a highly recommended book called *Gluten-Free Diet: A Comprehensive Resource Guide* (Case Nutrition Consulting, 2002). Shelley has graciously allowed me to use material from her book to help you get started. Her book not only goes into great detail about the diet, it also features over 1600 gluten-free specialty foods, a directory of more than 130 American, Canadian, and international companies, the nutrient composition of gluten-free flours, grains, legumes, nuts, and seeds, and many other resources for the gluten intolerant individual (see Sources).

Every attempt was made to alert the user of *Cooking Gluten-Free!* to ingredients that might include gluten. Questionable ingredients in a recipe are generally preceded with the words gluten-free (i.e. gluten-free sour cream). It is imperative that the user of this book read all product ingredient labels and research the gluten content of any product used in a recipe.

Flours from the following sources are allowed on the gluten-free diet: Rice (white, brown, or sweet), corn, soy, tapioca, potato, quinoa, buckwheat, amaranth, sorghum, arrowroot, teff, nut, millet, and bean.

Both growing and manufacturing should take place in a gluten-free environment.

**Many prepared foods contain gluten. Until you become proficient at reading labels, beware of "hidden gluten" in:**

| | |
|---|---|
| Broth | Sauces |
| Imitation bacon and seafood | Self-basting poultry |
| Marinades | Soup |
| Processed meats | Soy sauce |
| Salad dressings | Thickeners |

**These foods often contain gluten, but are sometimes overlooked by the uninitiated:**

| | | |
|---|---|---|
| Breading | Croutons | Roux |
| Coating mixes | Pasta | Stuffing |
| Communion wafers | | |

Read all labels carefully. If any uncertainty exists about a particular ingredient, call the manufacturer for clarification.

**In addition to Shelly's information on the following page, be aware that the following ingredients may contain gluten:**

- Brown rice syrup (often made from barley)
- Caramel color (it is usually made from corn, but the FDA allows barley as well)
- Monoglycerides & diglycerides (in dry products only) - Check gluten status of carrier agent
- Vegetable gum - Generally not a problem, though the FDA allows it to be sourced from oat gum

Excerpt from *Gluten-Free Diet: A Comprehensive Resource Guide,*
Shelley Case, Registered Dietitian, (Case Nutrition Consulting, 2002).

GLUTEN IS THE GENERAL NAME for the storage proteins (prolamins) in
wheat, rye, and barley. These specific prolamins damage the small
intestine in people with celiac disease and dermatitis herpetiformis. The
actual names of the toxic prolamins are gliadin in wheat, secalin in rye,
and hordein in barley. Up until 1996, the avenin prolamin in oats was
considered to be toxic; however new research indicates that avenin in
oats is not harmful.*** Although corn contains the prolamin zein and
rice contains the prolamin orzenin, these prolamins do not have toxic
effect on the intestine of persons with celiac disease.

Gluten is the substance in flour responsible for forming the
structure of dough, holding products together, and leavening. While
the presence of gluten is evident in baked goods (e.g., breads, cookies,
and cakes) and pasta, it is often a "hidden ingredient" in many other
items such as sauces, seasonings, soups, salad dressings, and candy, as
well as some vitamins and pharmaceuticals. The challenge for individuals on a gluten-free diet is to avoid these hidden sources.

## Gluten-Containing Ingredients To Be Avoided:

| | | |
|---|---|---|
| Barley | Graham flour | Rye |
| Bulgur | Kamut* | Semolina |
| Cereal binding | Malt** | Spelt (dinkel)* |
| Couscous | Malt extract** | Triticale |
| Durum* | Malt flavoring** | Wheat |
| Einkorn* | Malt syrup** | Wheat bran |
| Emmer* | Oat bran*** | Wheat germ |
| Filler | Oat syrup*** | Wheat starch |
| Farro* | Oats*** | |

\* *Types of wheat*
\*\* *Derived from barley*
\*\*\* *Many recent studies have demonstrated that consumption of oats (25-60 g/
day) is safe for children and adults with celiac disease. However, further studies
are needed to determine the long-term safety of oat consumption. Also, the
issue of cross contamination of oats with wheat and/or barley remains a major
concern in North America, therefore, oats are NOT recommended by celiac
organizations in Canada and the USA.*

## Ingredients To Question:

Hydrolyzed plant or vegetable protein (HPP/HVP)
Seasonings
Flavorings
Starch
Modified food starch
Dextrin

Specific labeling regulations in the USA and Canada for these ingredients
can be found in *Gluten-Free Diet: A Comprehensive Resource Guide,* Shelley
Case, Registered Dietitian, (Case Nutrition Consulting 2002).

# Patient Support Organizations

**Gluten Intolerance Group, GIG**
15110 10th Ave. SW, Suite A
Seattle, WA 98166-1820
Phone: 206.246.6652
Fax: 206.246.6531
Email: info@gluten.net
Website: www.gluten.net
Executive Director: Cynthia Kupper

**Celiac Disease Foundation, CDF**
13251 Ventura Blvd., Suite 1
Studio City, CA 91604-1838
Phone: 818.990.2354
Fax: 818.990.2379
Email: cdf@celiac.org
Website: www.celiac.org
Executive Director: Elaine Monarch

**Canadian Celiac Association, CCA**
5170 Dixie Road, Suite 204
Mississauga, Ontario, L4W 1E3
Phone: 905.507.6208
Toll-free: 800.363.7296
Fax: 905.507.4673
Email: celiac@look.ca
Website: www.celiac.ca
Executive Director: Karen Logan

**Celiac Sprue Association/USA, Inc., CSA/USA**
P. O. Box 31700
Omaha, NE 68131-0700
Phone: 402.558.0600
Fax: 402.558.1347
Email: celiacs@csaceliacs.org
Website: www.csaceliacs.org
President and Acting Executive Director: Mary Schluckebier

**Celiac Chat Group on-line** http://forums.delphiforums.com/celiac/start

**The Celiac Disease & Gluten-free Diet Support Page**
www.celiac.com

## Dairy-Free Substitutions

### Foods to remove from your diet:

- All types of milk products, including yogurt, cream, buttermilk, evaporated milk, condensed milk, sheep's milk, and goat's milk
- Butter and most margarines
- All types of cheese (including cottage cheese and cream cheese)
- Milk proteins (as "hidden" ingredients on product labels): casein, caseinate, whey, lactalbumin, sodium caseinate, and lactoglobulin

Always start with high-quality recipes, such as those found in this book, to achieve a moist, delicious result, and to help ensure that the substitution of these dairy-free ingredients work successfully. Check with your physician before using the following substitutions.

### Instead of:

*Cow's milk* — Use gluten-free rice milk or gluten-free soy milk. These types of milk are thinner than cow's milk, so you may need to use about 1 tablespoon less. Coconut milk makes a good non-dairy ice cream.

*Dry milk powder* — Use non-dairy milk powder. Always read product labels to be sure contents do not contain milk proteins. Finely ground nuts can also be substituted in equal proportions (by volume).

*Buttermilk* — Use gluten-free rice milk or gluten-free soy milk mixed with 1 tablespoon lemon juice or cider vinegar.

*Yogurt* — Use soy yogurt. Cookbook authors Knox and Lowman use soy yogurt in many of their recipes in *Lactose-Free* (Fireside, 2000).

*Butter* — Use organic shortening or vegetable oil. Nucoa margarine is an option for margarine lovers.

*Sour cream* — Use IMO or non-dairy versions (available at natural food markets).

*Cream cheese* — Use rice-based versions (available at natural food markets).

Look for gluten-free, tofu-based cheese, yogurt, milk, and margarine as well.

Carol Fenster's book, *Special Diet Solutions* (Savory Palate, Inc., 1997) has an appendix full of substitution ideas for wheat, gluten, dairy, eggs, yeast, or refined sugar.

## Recipe Conversion Ideas

THE PROCESS OF CONVERTING A FAVORITE RECIPE to a gluten-free version is a relatively easy process. Once you learn how to make basics such as gluten-free pizza crusts, biscuits, and flour tortillas, the conversion of a dinner recipe is quite easy. Now that good gluten-free pasta is available (see Sources) you will not be obliged to make it yourself.

### Guidelines for cooking:

- Choose recipes that don't involve French bread, Asian pastes (though many Thai Kitchen products are gluten-free), bouillon cubes, grain-based alcohol, or any other ingredient that is just too difficult to replace with a gluten-free version.

- Get creative. Since I have not found a gluten-free cannelloni shell, I use lasagna noodles and roll them around the filling.

- Thicken sauces with cornstarch, arrowroot, or sweet rice flour.

- You can generally find good gluten-free substitutions for questionable ingredients. Chef Tom Douglas demonstrates this in one of his contributed recipes, replacing the couscous in the original version with brown rice.

*(continued on next page)*

(continued from page 217)

**Guidelines for baking:**

- If you use Wendy Wark's gluten-free flour mix, you are on your way to great baked goods. This flour mix will greatly improve any gluten-free recipe you are now using.
- Follow the guidelines for adding xanthan gum on page 181.
- Add an extra egg white to light-textured cake recipes, but do not add any extra eggs or whites to heavy cakes such as pound cake or coffee cake. Sometimes sour cream cakes benefit from a little extra sour cream; try an extra ¼ cup if you need more moisture.
- In my quest to create a gluten-free "oatmeal" cookie, I replaced the oatmeal with half ground nuts and half quinoa flakes. The quinoa absorbs liquid, so I also added an extra egg white.
- Most cookie recipes require a simple flour replacement and a little xanthan gum.
- Some cookie recipes use a great deal of butter, rather than eggs, to impart moisture. This kind of recipe requires an additional adjustment: replace ¼ of the butter with either sour cream or cream cheese. I discovered this solution when converting the Mexican Wedding Cake recipe. Gluten-free flour doesn't behave like wheat flour does when mixed with some ingredients; this adjustment reduces the amount of spread caused by the butter.

# Helping Children Enjoy Life on a Gluten-Free Diet

THIS IS A DIFFICULT CHAPTER TO WRITE, as children's eating habits can be a very touchy subject. The very essence of the gluten-free diet requires much time, thought, and patience from the parents. Attitude is everything!

At a gluten-free conference, a woman discussed her 13-year old daughter's refusal to adhere to her special diet. Both mother and daughter were understandably frustrated. Food can be such a difficult issue between parents and children; add to that the challenges of a special diet, and you have the makings of a constant struggle.

Every family adjusts to the gluten-free diet differently. In this chapter, I will show you what works for mine. My goal is to inspire parents to have compassion for their gluten intolerant children, and to make cooking a greater part of their daily lives.

It is hard to see the gluten-free diet as a blessing, but it is a healthy way to eat. The trick is to learn how to cook well so that the entire family can enjoy the same meal together. Gluten-free food can rank with that served in a first-class restaurant, and you can make simple versions easily at home!

**Some key points to remember in helping your child with a gluten-free diet:**

- Prepare good, tasty food (yes, it is possible for every meal!)
- Plan "away from home" lunches
- Have your child **try** each item served at dinner
- Be sure your child comes to the dinner table hungry
- Teach your child how to cook, and make it fun for both of you!
- Gather new information and become more involved
- Plan gluten-free evening meals for the whole family (work toward doing this daily)
- Have ingredients for three quick evening meals on hand
- Be sure your child is getting enough B vitamins and folic acid

This may sound overwhelming, so take it a step at a time. It may be a year before you feel as if you have everything under control, but the dividends for your efforts will be great.

## Prepare good, tasty food:

Establish a feeling within your household that a gluten-free diet is delicious and healthy. Remember, your child will develop the same attitude you display. Your child will be more willing to stick to her special diet when you are not around to supervise if the food tastes good. The more you make a gluten-free diet a part of your life, the better off your child will be. Some parents do not fully embrace this diet, and treat the gluten intolerant child as an outsider without realizing it. Food preparation for the special diet is viewed as a huge hassle, and very little creativity is devoted to making meals more than a refueling stop.

To avoid this complication, concentrate on what you do best. For instance, as making a really good loaf of gluten-free bread is difficult, why not focus your efforts on cooking great meals that don't include bread? Some of the best meals are a simple combination of meat, a vegetable, and a starch. You should try going beyond your comfort zone by adding ingredients that you may not have thought of before. For example, add raisins to wild rice as it is cooking, then add toasted pine nuts just before serving for a twist on that "side of rice."

Change your definition of what you consider to be simple food. A dish composed of exotic-looking ingredients might actually be a quick, tasty addition to your household bill of fare! Your family will be pleased, and your efforts will seem like much less of a burden.

## Plan "away from home" lunches:

Encourage your child to prepare a list of things he likes to eat for lunch, and try to keep those items on hand. Inquire at his school about the availability of a microwave, so that he can sometimes enjoy a hot lunch. In our school, office personnel will microwave a frozen entrée in the teachers' lounge. (If you are able to secure this privilege, asking for it once a week or so should be acceptable.) Make special treats and freeze individual portions; they can be packed frozen in a lunchbox, and will thaw by lunchtime. The gluten intolerant child has enough to contend with when he can't eat like the other kids; providing him with snacks that are both healthy and tasty will help make him forget that he is on a special diet. The other children will see your child not as an outcast, but as someone who eats both differently and very well!

## Have your child try each item served at dinner:

If a child thinks she doesn't like something, don't make her eat a whole serving, but do persuade her to try it. As her palate becomes more developed, she will find that something she once hated is now great. It may take 15-20 tries before her taste buds make the adjustment to the new food, but it is worth the effort. Just be sure you handle it in a matter-of-fact way without becoming emotional yourself. When I started sautéing fresh spinach in olive oil, garlic, and lemon juice, my children (6 and 3 years old at the time) said "yuck!" But after several months of having to try it from time to time, they both decided they loved it, and it is now a favorite of theirs. If you do not expose your children to high quality, well-prepared food, they will have a limited range of tastes and preferences. On the occasion that the child refuses to eat a food you know she likes, waiting for the next mealtime is a better lesson than fixing something else that evening.

## Be sure your child comes to the dinner table hungry:

Most kids eat three meals a day and two solid snacks. Some are hearty eaters, while others seem to just pick at their food. Over the course of a week, most kids get the nutrition they need if their parents offer food from the four basic groups. Be sure your children don't take in lots of empty calories from juice or other sugary drinks between meals. Fruit juice lacks the fiber of fresh fruit, and it fills up tummies, making kids "not hungry" when dinnertime rolls around.

While you may be tempted to buy gluten-free junk food and candy to "compensate" for what your child can't have, don't buy it very often. You will find that they end up eating plenty of junk elsewhere, especially once they start school, and candy seems to seep out of the woodwork. My child can easily find gluten-free goodies when he is away from home, as his friends' parents buy these treats especially for him (even though they know all they need to have on hand is fresh fruit). That said, we keep a container of candy in our child's classroom and frozen novelties in the freezer at school for last minute celebrations.

### Teach your children how to cook:

Another important aspect of the gluten-free diet is for children to learn how to cook on their own. When the child is young she can help by dumping a pre-measured ingredient into a bowl and stirring it around. As the child becomes more capable she can contribute more, and by the time she is a teenager she will know how to cook. She will know how scrumptious gluten-free dishes can be, and thus have less desire to cheat. It is important to help the child develop this confidence so she will not feel inferior because of her special diet. The time spent teaching her will represent valuable quality time together, and will be both creative and fun!

### Gather new information and become more involved:

If you don't normally shop at a natural food market, try it sometime. A whole new world of gluten-free products await you. Join patient support groups such as CDF, CSA/USA, CCA, and GIG (see Sources for contact information). Members receive a wealth of information through newsletters and by attending meetings. Every time I am in contact with one of these groups I learn something new.

### Plan gluten-free evening meals for the whole family:

It sounds unrealistic, if not impossible, to those who have never tried cooking a gluten-free meal for the whole family, but the benefits are tremendous. Take it one step at a time and remember that many recipes can easily convert to gluten-free dishes. Reduce your reliance on bread, pasta, and pizza, and explore the recipes in this book. While it is difficult learning a week's worth of recipes in one fell swoop, adding one recipe each week will have your family converted to the gluten-free diet by the end of the year. It is essential to become comfortable with the new way of cooking, and to look upon new recipes and new ingredients as an adventure.

Once you and the rest of the family have converted to a gluten-free evening meal, your child will be a more willing participant. Everyone will benefit, as decreased gluten intake results in more energy and a more finely tuned digestive system. You may take advantage of breakfast, lunch, or snack time (when your child is not around) to indulge in any wheat items you crave.

Our family consumes only gluten-free condiments, jam, peanut butter, etc., which saves precious space in the pantry and refrigerator. A strict "no double dipping" rule is enforced. This means we don't dip a knife back into the jam once we have used it to spread the jam on wheat bread. If more jam is needed, a clean spoon or knife is used, thus avoiding cross-contamination. Additionally, all countertops, cooking utensils, and surfaces are cleaned thoroughly to avoid any stray wheat crumbs. We also have two separate toasters.

**Have ingredients for three quick meals on hand:**

Try to plan three meals in advance. It will take you about 10 minutes to put together the grocery list and about 30 minutes to shop. A little preparedness will go a long way. Always make double the recipe of soups and other freezable meals so as to have "fast food" on hand. Schedule your time wisely throughout the day so as to have more of it to invest in cooking.

**Be sure your child is getting enough B vitamins and folic acid:**

The importance of B vitamins and folic acid is a topic too infrequently addressed with regard to children and celiac disease. In our country, these vitamins are added to wheat bread, pasta, and cereal, but not to the gluten-free equivalents. B vitamins and folic acid are critical to growing bodies. Deficiency of these vitamins causes a host of problems with the nervous system, heart, brain, red blood cell production, and digestive system. A daily multiple vitamin for children is generally sufficient to provide the RDA. Your doctor can recommend the better brands; another good resource is William and Martha Sears' *The Family Nutrition Book* (Little, Brown, 1999). This volume covers all aspects of how food is responsible for the health of the human body. It is fascinating reading for all parents.

And finally, when my son was diagnosed with celiac disease, I became aware of all the chemicals and processed foods we had been eating. The knowledge I gained from reading labels made me glad we weren't eating all that junk anymore. Once you become a gluten-free expert, it is also important to think of the pesticides, hormones, and chemical fertilizers in the food we eat and water we drink. Organic foods, treated water, and hormone free meat make a lot of sense, especially for young growing bodies. By filtering out the impurities through careful buying, you prevent the body from becoming the filter.

## Lunch and Snack Ideas

AT OUR HOME, bread and treats are often times gobbled up more quickly than I can make them. Therefore, it pays to have a variety of ideas for last minute lunches and snacks.

For lunches away from home, it helps to have an insulated lunch box, a small cold pack, and a high quality Thermos that will keep food hot for several hours.

Some ideas listed below require using items left over from a previous meal. For example, when you are steaming green beans, be sure to cook extra for later in the week. (Obviously, all items suggested are gluten-free.)

**No Bread Days:**

On the many days when you will not have bread available for sandwiches, try these ideas:
- Toaster waffles used as bread with peanut butter and jelly sandwiches.
- Crackers served with tuna, hummus, luncheon meat, or cheese. You can make a gluten-free version of the Oscar Mayer Lunchable that the other kids at school bring for lunch. Cut ham and cheese into squares, add crackers, a Capri Sun, and a little Snickers bar and you have a gluten-free "lunchable."
- Quesadillas or corn tortilla chips with black bean salsa (canned black beans, diced tomato, diced yellow pepper, cilantro, diced onion, and lime juice).
- Chicken salad made with leftover chicken (page 55).
- Homemade soup frozen in individual portions, heated, and placed in a warmed thermos. There are also some good gluten-free canned soups.
- Frozen entrées (if your child has access to a microwave) such as Amy's Cheese Enchiladas and Trader Joe's Chicken Taquitos (see Sources).
- Salads are great for older kids. Try lettuce with dried fruit and nuts/seeds, or a Caesar salad (page 41), or a salad with tomato and

cucumber slices. Keep all ingredients packed in separate containers to be assembled at lunchtime.
- Make Buttermilk Chicken (page 87), Sushi (page 88), or Pizza (page 69) for dinner and save some for lunches.
- Carrot sticks and sliced apple are great dipped in peanut butter, and are a favorite with kids.

**Items to add to the lunch box or have for a snack:**

- Dried fruit
- Sunflower seed kernels
- Pumpkin seeds
- Soy nuts
- Apple sauce
- Cheese slices
- Pudding
- Steamed green beans
- Slices of sweet red and yellow peppers
- Carrot sticks
- Granola bars (homemade or from Ener-G Foods)
- Yogurt
- Cottage cheese
- Fresh fruit (apples, satsumas, kiwi, bananas, pineapple chunks, strawberries, grapes, etc.)
- Frozen fruit and vegetables such as corn, peas, and raspberries
- Homemade trail mix with nuts, raisins, dried cranberries, and chocolate chips
- Trader Joe's gluten-free snacks (see in-store gluten-free list)
- Healthy homemade baked goods using quinoa, amaranth, and brown rice flours. Sweet breads with grated carrots, zucchini, pureed pumpkin, etc., are great guilt-free treats.

**Two favorites that can't go in the lunch box but are good after school snacks:**

- Smoothies (page 18). I will often make smoothies at home and take them to after-school pickup so the kids can have a snack in the car; this can fend off grouchiness before it has a chance to ruin a whole afternoon.
- Frozen novelties. Many of the ice cream bars and other frozen treats on the market are gluten-free.

# Outdoor Cooking

COOKING OUTDOORS IS A GREAT WAY to avoid the heat in the kitchen. (There are also fewer pots and pans to wash afterwards!) We like to serve grilled meat, poultry, or fish with simple roasted vegetables to keep cooking time in the kitchen to a bare minimum. Another way to beat the heat is to cook ahead in the morning as much as possible.

Cooking outdoors takes a bit of know-how and skill. It pays to invest in a good grilling or barbecuing cookbook for the best results. Here are a few tips to get you started:

**Grilling Versus Barbecue:**

Most people use these words interchangeably but there is a difference. Grilling is quick cooking over high heat, and works best with tender foods such as fish, chicken, and certain cuts of meat. Barbecue is a slow process using indirect heat and smoke, and is ideal for tougher cuts of meat such as ribs, brisket, tri tip, etc. While gas grills are fine for grilling, a charcoal grill is needed to impart the characteristic smoky flavor of barbecue. Both grilled items and barbecue cooked on a charcoal grill can benefit by the addition of apple wood, cherry wood, mesquite, etc., to the charcoal fire.

## Lighting the Fire for Grilling:

Preheat gas grill on high for 15 minutes to produce maximum heat. (A charcoal grill takes a little longer to get going, but we prefer the added flavor it imparts.) An electric starter is the easiest way to start a charcoal grill without the smell and hassle of lighter fluid. Remove the cooking grate and set the charcoal grate in the upper or middle position (depending on the desired degree of heat). Place the electric starter on the charcoal grating. Pile charcoal into a pyramid shape on top of the electric starter and plug the starter into an outlet. Be sure to use enough charcoal to cook the quantity of food you plan to make. Once coals have started, remove the electric starter and let coals heat until they are covered with a layer of gray ash. Spread out the charcoal in an even layer so that three-quarters of the grill is covered with charcoal. (The remaining cool space can be used for food that is cooking too quickly.) Place cooking grate over hot coals and allow the grate to heat up. Clean the grate with a wire brush to remove any dirt or particles of food. The grill is now ready. If you plan to barbecue, follow your recipe directions for setting up the grill.

## Temperature:

If your grill does not come with a thermometer, be sure to place an oven thermometer on the cooking grate when barbecuing. For grilling, try this test (from *Cook's Illustrated* magazine July/August 2001) to determine when your gas grill or coals are ready: Hold your hand 5 inches above the cooking grate. If you can keep it there comfortably for 2 seconds or less, you have a hot fire. A medium-hot fire is a 3-4 second count. It is important to have a grill with a cover, which shortens cooking time and improves flavor.

## Flavor:

Marinades, spice rubs, and wood chips can be used to add a unique flavor to meat, poultry, and fish. Rubs are the quickest and easiest, as very little advance preparation is needed; simply rub the spices into the meat and grill. Wood chips require a little more preparation. Soak chips in enough water to cover while the charcoal is heating. Drain chips and throw a handful onto the white coals. Let the wood burn for a few minutes before grilling.

## Pantry Basics

IN THE GLUTEN-FREE KITCHEN, there are some basic elements you will want to have to make life easier. Don't rush out and buy everything on the list! Instead, buy what you need to make a specific recipe, and soon your pantry will be well stocked. Cooking will become less time-consuming, allowing latitude for last-minute baked goods, etc.

### Baking Staples:
*(Be sure they are manufactured in a gluten-free environment)*

Brown rice flour (refrigerate)
White rice flour
Potato starch flour
Tapioca starch flour
Quinoa flour
Buckwheat flour
Amaranth flour
Sweet rice flour
Baking soda
Baking powder
Vanilla extract
Chocolate baking squares (sweetened and unsweetened)

Cocoa powder
Walnuts, pecans, almonds, soy nuts, pine nuts, cashews
 (Note: Nuts should be frozen for maximum shelf life.)
Xanthan gum
Active dry yeast (refrigerate)
Cornstarch
Cornmeal
Unflavored gelatin
Honey
Sugar (white and brown)
Gluten-free chocolate chips
Flax seed (store in freezer)
Brown rice syrup (Lundberg's)
Molasses
Maple syrup
Instant non-fat dry milk powder

## Cooking Staples:

*Vinegars:* red wine, rice wine, balsamic, sherry, apple cider vinegar, distilled white vinegar
*Unprocessed Vegetable Oils:* olive, canola, walnut, peanut, sesame, sunflower, safflower (buy small containers of oil and refrigerate to protect from rancidity)
*Wines:* Madeira, Sherry, Port, a bottle each of good inexpensive red and white wine
*Seasonings:* sea salt, fresh ground pepper, fresh herbs when possible
Fresh garlic cloves
Gluten-free chicken stock
Gluten-free ketchup, mustards, pickles, oil cured olives, capers, mayonnaise
Lemon juice (Frozen lemon juice is very handy; once defrosted, it keeps well in the refrigerator.)

Gluten-free tamari (Use to replace soy sauce; it is available most stores where soy sauce is sold.)
Gluten-free Dijon mustard
Finely ground cornmeal for polenta
Variety of your favorite beans
Kombu (Japanese seaweed)
Brown rice, wild rice, pearl or sushi rice, basmati rice, gluten-free buckwheat groats or kasha
Gluten-free pasta
Sun-dried tomatoes, dried prunes and apricots, raisins
Canned goods (refried beans, crushed tomatoes, whole tomatoes, tomato paste, etc.)
Slices of stale bread to make bread crumbs
Artichoke hearts, roasted red peppers (not marinated)

### Dairy (refrigerate):
Butter (unsalted and salted)
Eggs
Cheeses (mozzarella, cheddar cheese, goat cheese, Swiss cheese, etc.)
Milk, whipping cream, half & half, gluten-free sour cream, gluten-free plain yogurt, gluten-free buttermilk

### Frozen Foods:
Homemade gluten-free pasta sauces, pizza sauce, chicken stock, cookie crumbs for pie crust, granola bars, brownies, sweet breads, waffles, pizza crusts, pesto, pecan paste
Juice concentrate
Fruit for smoothies
Vegetables

### Snacks:
There is no end to the number of packaged gluten-free snacks available for your pantry. Choose a few favorites to keep on hand.

# Utensils & Cookware

SINCE YOU ARE GOING TO BE COOKING FOR A LONG TIME, you might as well make it more enjoyable by purchasing the best kitchen gear you can afford. The list is divided up into basics and good things to have. Over time you will discover which cookware works best for your needs. (Note: very few bread machines can make a good gluten-free loaf of bread; therefore, a bread machine is not included in the list.)

**Basics:**

Saucepans (1 quart, 2 quart, 3.5 quart)
Skillets (6-inch, 10-inch, 12-inch)
Dutch oven
Double boiler with steamer insert
  (usually comes with a 2 qt. saucepan)
8-quart (minimum) stock pot
12-inch iron skillet
KitchenAid mixer
  (very important for gluten-free cooking)
2 cutting boards — one dishwasher-safe
  plastic for meat cutting, one wood for
  vegetables
Knives — butcher, slicing, paring, bread,
  boning (German Solingen steel is
  recommended)
Pepper grinder
2 loaf pans and cooling racks
8-inch square glass baking dish
Tube cake pan
Three 8-inch round cake pans
Two 9-inch round cake pans
Colander

Measuring cups (both liquid and dry)
  and spoons
Cheese grater
Wooden spoons
Slotted spoon, spatula for flipping,
  rubber spatula for baking, soup ladle
Long-handled tongs
Toaster dedicated to gluten-free bread
Cookie sheets with edges
Wooden salad bowl with serving spoons
Salad spinner
9 x 13-inch oblong glass baking dish
Mixing bowls
Rolling pin
Garlic press (made of stainless steel,
  not plastic)
Vegetable peeler
Can opener
Meat thermometer
Pot holders
Dish towels
Egg white separator
Basting brush

**Good things to have:**

Wok
Rice cooker
Bundt pan
Mortar and pestle (great for grinding larger
  quantities of pepper and other spices)
Rotary grater (Zyliss has a good reputation for
  ease of use, cleaning, and durability)
2 large pizza pans
Upright poultry roasting column
Glass bowls of all sizes for mise en place
Hand held mixer
Food processor
Large heavy cutting board with moat
  (for meat carving)
Sieve
Zyliss nut chopper or mini-prep Cusinart
Potato ricer
Blender
Deep fryer
Espresso machine
Yogurt cheese strainer
Food mill

# Chef Contributors (alphabetical by chef)

**Hans Bergmann**
Cacharel
2221 E. Lamar Blvd.
Arlington, Texas 76006-7429
Phone: 817.640.9981
Website: www.cacharel.net

**Kathy Casey**
Kathy Casey Food Studios®
5130 Ballard Ave. NW
Seattle, WA 98107
Phone: 206.784.7840
Website: www.kathycasey.com

**Tom Douglas**
Seattle area restaurants:
Dahlia Lounge, 206.682.4142
Etta's Seafood, 206.443.6000
Palace Kitchen, 206.448.2001
Website: www.tomdouglas.com

**Barbara Figueroa**
The Warwick Hotel
401 Lenora Street
Seattle, WA 98121
Phone: 206.443-4300, x256
Website: www.margauxseattle.com

**Suzanne Goin**
Lucques
8474 Melrose Ave.
West Hollywood, CA 90069
Phone: 323.655.6277
Website: www.lucques.com

**Todd Gray**
Equinox
818 Connecticut Ave. NW
Washington D.C. 20006
Phone: 202.331.8118
Website: www.equinoxrestaurant.com

**Gerry Hayden**
Charlie Palmer's Aureole
34 E. 61st St.
New York, New York 10021-8010
Phone: 212.319.1687
Website: www.aureolerestaurant.com

**Christopher Kimball**
*Cook's Illustrated* magazine
P.O. Box 7446
Red Oak, IA 51591-0446
Phone: 1.800.526.8442
Website: www.cooksillustrated.com

**Bob Kinkead**
Kinkead's
2000 Pennsylvania Ave. NW
Washington D.C. 20006
Phone: 202.296.7700
Website: www.kinkead.com

**Michael Kornick**
mk
868 N. Franklin
Chicago, IL 60610
Phone: 312.482.9179
Website: www.mkchicago.com

**Dennis Leary**
Larry Stone, sommelier
Rubicon
558 Sacramento St.
San Francisco, CA 94111
Phone: 415.434.4100
Website: www.myriadrestaurantgroup.com

**Thoa Nguyen**
Chinoise Café Sushi Bar and Asian Grill
Three Seattle area locations
Phone: 206.284.0958
Website: www.chinoisecafe.com

**Marcella Rosene**
Pasta & Co.
Five Seattle area locations
Phone: 1.800.943.6362
Website: www.pastaco.com
Email: pastaco@nwlink.com

**Christian Svalesen**
36° Restaurant and Net Result Fish Market
4140 Lemmon Ave. #134 and #132
Dallas, Texas 75216
Phone: 214.521.4488

**Ludger Szmania**
Szmania's
Two Seattle area locations
Phone: 206.284.7305
Website: www.szmanias.com

**Charlie Trotter**
Charlie Trotter's
816 West Armitage
Chicago, IL 60614
Phone: 773.248.6228
Website: www.charlietrotters.com

**Erol Tugrul**
Café Margaux
220 Brevard Ave.
Cocoa, Florida 32922-7907
Phone: 321.639.8343
Website: www.cafemargaux.com

**Lynne Vea**
Culinary Associate for television show
*Best of Taste* with John Sarich
Food Stylist
Cooking Instructor
Email: lvea@attbi.com

**Linda Yamada**
The Beach House
5022 Lawai Rd.
Koloa, Kauai, Hawaii 96756
Phone: 808.742.1097

## Other Contributers

**Shelley Case**
*Gluten-Free Diet: A Comprehensive Resource Guide*
Case Nutrition Consulting
1940 Angley Court
Regina, Saskatchewan, Canada S4V 2V2
Phone/FAX: 306.751.1000
Email: scase@accesscomm.ca

**Bill Fredericks**
The Chocolate Man
Phone: 206.365.2025
Email: chocolate@chocolateman.net

**Cynthia Lair**
*Feeding the Whole Family*
Moon Smile Press
Phone: 800.561.3039
Website: www.feedingfamily.com

**Dan McCarthy**
McCarthy & Schiering Wine Merchants, Inc.
2401-B Queen Anne Ave. N.
Seattle, WA 98109
Phone: 206.282.8500
Email: msqa@sprynet.com

**Joanne Van Roden**
Wellspring Inc.
Phone: 1.800.533.3561 to find a store near you
    offering Wellspring products

**Wendy Wark**
*Living Healthy with Celiac Disease*
AnAffect Marketing
Phone: 610.524.1253
Email: anaffect@aol.com

**Debra Daniels-Zeller**
Nutritionally-oriented:
Cookbook author
    (vegetarian cookbook in process)
Free lance writer
Cooking instructor
Email: ddanzel@aol.com

# Sources

Ancient Harvest Quinoa
   (flour and quinoa flakes)
Quinoa Corp.
P.O. Box 279
Gardena, CA  90248

Annie's Caesar Dressing
Annie's Naturals
792 Foster Hill Rd.
North Calais, Vermont  05650
Phone: 1.800.434.1234

Barbara's Brown Rice Crisps
Barbara's Bakery, Inc.
3900 Cypress Drive
Petaluma, CA  94954

Birkett Mills (buckwheat flour)
P.O. Box 440
Penn Yan, NY 14527
Phone: 315.536.3311
Website: www.thebirkettmills.com

Boyajian Toasted Sesame Oil
Boyajian, Inc.
349 Lenox St.
Norwood, MA  02062

Cascadian Farm (frozen organic fruits and
   vegetables, organic sauerkraut packed in water,
   and many other products)
Distributed by Small Planet Foods, Inc.
Sedro-Wooley, WA  98284
Website: www.cfarm.com

Chocolate Man
   (a great source for fine chocolate, vanilla
   beans, nut pastes, flavored oils, cocoa,
   chocolate making tools and supplies, tempering
   machine rentals, and truffle making classes)

Bill Fredericks
16580 35th Ave. NE
Lake Forest Park, WA  98155-6606
Phone: 206.365.2025
Website: www.chocolateman.net

DeLaurenti Specialty Food Market
   (offers a wide variety of hard-to-find items
   such as beans, channa dal, capers, oils,
   vinegars, and cheeses)
Phone: 206.622.0141 for mail order information.

Website: www.EthnicGrocer.com
I haven't tried this myself, but their website is full
of unique items from over 15 counties. It looks
like a great source for authentic imports.

Ginger Juice by The Ginger People
   (an easy way to add ginger to any recipe
   without peeling or grating)
Phone: 1.800.551.5284
Website: www.gingerpeople.com

Indian Harvest
   (the ultimate rice, grain, and bean catalog;
   some grains are not gluten-free)
Phone: 800.294.2433
Website: www.indianharvest.com

James Cook Cheese Company
   (offers a wide selection of specialty cheeses and
   a knowledgeable staff regarding cheese
   production — website features truffle oil,
   balsamic vinegar, olives, mustards, and
   chutneys as well)
Phone:  206.256.0510
Website: www.jamescookcheese.com
Email: cookscheese@yahoo.com

*Living Without,* a great magazine filled with
gluten-free product information and articles
P.O. Box 2126
Northbrook, IL 60065
Website: www.livingwithout.com

Lundberg Rice
   (a wide variety of wild rice blends, brown rice, etc.)
Website: www.lundberg.com

Mariani (dried fruit, sun-dried tomatoes)
Mariani Packing Co., Inc.
500 Crocker Drive
Vacaville, CA  95688
Phone: 1.800.774.2678

Muir Glen organic tomato products
(top-notch quality; also makes the best canned pizza sauce)
Website: www.muirglen.com

Mystic Lake Dairy, Inc.
Mixed Fruit Concentrate Sweetener (use in place of refined sugar, corn syrup, or honey)
24200 NE 14th St.
Redmond, WA 98053

Organic Shortening
Spectrum Organic Products, Inc.
Petaluma, CA 94954
Phone: 1.800.995.2705
Website: www.spectrumorganic.com

Papadini Orzo, Hi Protein Lentil Bean Pasta
(the only gluten-free orzo pasta I have found, excellent in minestrone soup — other pasta shapes available as well)
Adrienne's Gourmet Foods
849 Ward Drive
Santa Barbara, CA 93111
Phone 1.800.937.7010
Website: www.adriennes.com

Pasta & Co. offers a wide variety of specialty items: Paradiso Italian-style tomatoes, olives, oils, cheeses, quinoa pasta, etc. Visit their five Seattle area locations or their website.
Phone 1.800.943.6362
Website: www.pastaco.com
Email: pastaco@nwlink.com

Red Star Yeast, Celiac Hotline
Phone: 1.800.423.5422

Rub with Love
(specialty rubs for salmon, pork, and chicken)
website: www.tomdouglas.com

San-J Int'l
Tamari (wheat-free soy sauce)
800.446.5500

Thai Kitchen (offers a wide variety of pastes, coconut milk, and fish sauce)
Phone: 1.800.967.THAI
Website: www.thaikitchen.com
Email: info@thaikitchen.com

Tinkyada Pasta
(the best gluten-free pasta tested in our kitchen)
Food Directions, Inc.
150 Milner Ave., Units 21-23
Scarborough, Ontario, M1S 3R3 Canada
Website: www.tinkyada.com

Trader Joe's – under the direction of the Celiac Disease Foundation, has put together a list of their products that are gluten-free. Store locations are found on their website.
Website: www.traderjoes.com/tj/locations

Wild Salmon Seafood Market ships fresh seafood with ice packs in styrofoam shippers. I buy all my fish here, and the staff are used to answering questions about the method of flash-freezing at sea. They do not dip shrimp and scallops in a wheat slurry prior to freezing (as some do to prevent the pieces from sticking together). Be sure to ask questions to ensure gluten-free seafood.
Phone: 888.222.3474

## Mail Order

THERE ARE MANY MAIL ORDER COMPANIES catering to the gluten intolerant these days. Any of the national support groups can provide you with information about how to contact gluten-free vendors. Shelley Case's book *Gluten-Free Diet* (Case Nutrition Consulting, 2002) offers an extensive list as well. A few companies are listed here to get you started:

Authentic Foods
1850 W. 169th Street, Suite B
Gardena, CA 90247
Phone: 1.800.806.4737
Website: www.authenticfoods.com

*(continued on next page)*

(continued on from page 229)

Dietary Specialties
1248 Sussex Turnpike, Unit C-1
Randolph, NJ  07869
Phone: 1.888.640.2800
Website: www.dietspec.com
Email: info@dietspec.com

Ener-G Foods
5960 First Ave. South
P.O. Box 84487
Seattle, WA  98124-5787
Phone: 1.800.331.5222
Website: www.ener-g.com

Miss Roben's
P.O. Box 1149
Frederick, MD 21702
Phone: 1.800.891.0083
Website: www.missroben.com

The Gluten-Free Pantry
P.O. Box 840
Glastonbury, CT  06033
Phone: 1.800.291.8386
Email: pantry@glutenfree.com

Neither Celiac Publishing or Karen Robertson
received any payment for including these listings
as resources.

# Measurement Conversion Chart

EQUIVALENTS ARE BASED on U.S. liquid measure. This volume standard actually applies to dry measure as well, and is used for not only liquids, but for flour, sugar, shortening, and so on (to name a few of many possible ingredients).

A pinch = a little less than ¼ teaspoon
A dash = a few drops
½ tablespoon = 1½ teaspoons
1 tablespoon = 3 teaspoons
2 tablespoons = 1 ounce = ⅛ cup
4 tablespoons = 2 ounces = ¼ cup
5⅓ tablespoons = 2⅔ ounces = ⅓ cup = 5 tablespoons + 1 teaspoon
8 tablespoons = 4 ounces = ½ cup
16 tablespoons = 8 ounces = 1 cup = ½ pint
2 cups = 16 ounces = 1 pint = ½ quart
4 cups = 32 ounces = 2 pints = 1 quart
16 cups = 128 ounces = 8 pints = 4 quarts = 1 gallon
1 tablespoon minced fresh herbs = 1 teaspoon dried leaf herbs =
     ½ teaspoon powdered herbs

# Gluten-Free Flour

GLUTEN-FREE FLOURS ARE GENERALLY USED in combination with one another to make a flour mix. There is no single gluten-free flour that you can use alone for successful baked goods. The list below will help you understand the characteristics of the various flours.

Cross-contamination at the factory can cause diet compliance issues for the gluten intolerant. Call or write the manufacturers of your preferred flours to inquire about factory and field practices.

**Arrowroot Flour** can be used cup for cup in place of cornstarch if you are allergic to corn.

**Bean Flour** from Authentic Foods and Ener-G Foods is a light flour made from garbanzo and broad beans. When using this flour in your favorite recipes, replace the white sugar with brown or maple sugar (or combine with sorghum) to cut the bitter taste of the beans.

**Brown Rice Flour** is milled from unpolished brown rice, and has a higher nutrient value than white rice flour. Since this flour contains bran, it has a shorter shelf life and should be refrigerated. As with white rice flour, it is best to combine brown rice flour with several other flours to avoid the grainy texture.

**Cornstarch** is similar in use to sweet rice flour for thickening sauces. Best when used in combination with other flours.

**Nut Flours** are high in protein and, used in small portions, enhance the taste of homemade pasta, puddings, and cookies. They are somewhat expensive and difficult to find. Finely ground nuts added to a recipe increases the protein content and allows for a better rise.

**Potato Starch Flour** is used in combination with other flours; it is rarely used in its pure form. (Note: this is not potato flour.)

**Sorghum Flour** is a relatively new flour that is an excellent addition to bean flour mixes. (See Bean Flour)

**Soy Flour** has a nutty flavor, and is high in protein and fat. Best when used in small quantities in combination with other flours. Soy flour has a short shelf life.

**Sweet Rice Flour** is made from glutinous rice (which does not contain the gluten fraction that is prohibited to the gluten intolerant). Often used as a thickening agent. Sweet rice flour is becoming more common in gluten-free baking for tender pies and cakes.

**Tapioca Starch Flour** is a light, velvety flour made from the cassava root. It lightens gluten-free baked goods, and gives them a texture very much like those made with wheat flour. It is especially good in pizza crusts, where it is used in equal parts with either white rice flour or brown rice flour.

**White Rice Flour** is milled from polished white rice. It is best combined with several other flours to avoid the grainy texture rice flour alone imparts. Try to buy the finest texture possible.

**Xanthan Gum** is our substitute for gluten, as it has similar binding properties. See usage information on page 181.

*(continued on next page)*

*(continued from page 231)*

*The following flours are fine for the gluten intolerant, providing you can find a pure source (grown in dedicated fields and processed on dedicated equipment).* Contact GIG, CSA/USA, CCA, and CDF to research these flours further (see Sources for contact information).

**Amaranth** is a whole grain dating back to the time of the Aztecs. It is high in protein (15-18%), and contains more calcium, Vitamin A, and Vitamin C than most grains. The flavor is similar to that of graham crackers without the sweetness. To incorporate amaranth flour into a recipe, substitute amaranth flour for ¼ to ½ of the total flour; the remainder can include arrowroot flour or cornstarch (¼ of the total), with brown rice flour making up the remainder.

**Buckwheat** is the seed of a plant related to rhubarb. It is high in fiber, iron, and B vitamins.

**Millet** is a small round grain that is a major food source in Asia, North Africa, and India.

**Quinoa** (keen-wah), a staple food of the Incas, is a complete protein containing all 8 amino acids as well as a fair amount of calcium and iron. Ancient Harvest, distributed by the Quinoa Corporation in Torrance, CA, is a good source that also carries gluten-free pasta, flour, flakes, etc.

**Teff** is an ancient grain from Ethiopia, now grown in Idaho. It is always manufactured as a whole grain flour, since it is difficult to sift or separate.

# GLOSSARY *of* COOKING TERMS

Selected terms are briefly defined in this glossary. Consult *Joy of Cooking,* Rombauer & Becker (Simon & Schuster, 1997) or *The New Food Lover's Companion,* Herbst (Barron's, 1995) for a more complete reference.

**al dente** — An Italian phrase that describes pasta cooked to the point where it offers some resistance when bitten into.

**barbecuing** — Slow-cooking larger cuts of meat, fish, or poultry on a covered grill for a long period of time. Hardwood or coals are used as the heat source, and low indirect heat (220°F.) is recommended.

**baste** — To periodically brush meat, fish, or poultry as it cooks with sauce, butter, or pan drippings. This process adds color and keeps the food from drying out.

**blanch** — To briefly boil fruits or vegetables and plunge them into cold water to stop the cooking. Blanching helps to easily remove the skin from such fruits as tomatoes and peaches.

**blind baking** — An English term for baking a pie crust before filling by covering the crust with foil, placing pie weights atop the foil, and baking the crust.

**braising** — A method of cooking in which meat, poultry, fish, or vegetables are browned, then simmered slowly in a pot with a small amount of liquid and a tight fitting lid. The slow cooking tenderizes and adds flavor.

**browning** — To cook meat briefly over high heat until the exterior caramelizes. This step adds flavor and color.

**caramelizing** — The browning of sugar that either occurs naturally in food or is added to the food. For example, when vegetables are roasted, their natural sugars are released, causing a nice browned exterior.

**cream or beat** — To combine ingredients on high speed until the mixture is light in color and smooth and creamy in texture.

**cube** — To cut an ingredient into a ½-inch cube shape.

**deglazing** — A cooking method that results in a simple sauce by adding wine or stock to the pan or pot used to cook meat, fish, or poultry. The liquid dissolves the browned bits stuck to the pan and develops into a flavorful sauce.

**dice** — To cut food into ⅛ -to ¼ -inch cubes.

**Dutch oven** — A large pot with a tight fitting lid used for braising and stewing.

**ganache** — A combination of chocolate and cream heated until the chocolate melts, then combined into a smooth mixture. Flavored oils, liqueurs, or coffee are often added. Ganache can be poured over a cake; it can also be cooled, rolled into balls, and dipped in chocolate to make truffles.

**grilling** — A method of cooking by which tender meat, fish, or poultry is quickly cooked uncovered over hot coals.

**jelly roll pan** — A large baking sheet or pan with shallow sides. Size is generally 17-inch x 13-inch x 1-inch.

**julienne** — To cut food into ⅛ -inch thin matchsticks.

**kosher salt** — A coarse grained salt that contains no additives.

**mince** — To cut food into extremely small cubes. This is a much finer cut than dicing, and is preferable to chopping in that the pieces are more uniform in size.

**mise en place** — A French term that means all ingredients are ready up to the point of cooking, thus avoiding last minute problems.

**nonreactive** — Cookware made of a material that does not have a chemical reaction with acidic ingredients such as tomatoes, lemon juice, buttermilk, etc. Glass or plastic is nonreactive. Aluminum and old copper pots are reactive.

**poaching** — A method of cooking food gently in liquid that completely covers the food and is just under the boiling point.

**pressure cooking** — A cooking method by which steam is trapped in a pot with a locked lid; the built-up pressure raises the temperature to cook food in ⅓ the regular cooking time. Old cookers such as the "jiggle top" are not as safe as the new cookers of today.

**puree** — To mash or process (in a food processor) cooked food to a smooth, sauce-like consistency.

**reduce** — To boil down a liquid (sometimes with other ingredients) until evaporation takes place and it achieves a thicker consistency. This process is used to make flavorful sauces.

**roasting** — Cooking uncovered without liquid, resulting in a nicely browned exterior and moist interior.

**roulade** — A French term for a thin slice of meat wrapped around vegetables or other fillings. The exterior is browned before baking or braising.

**roux** — Combining a fat with flour over low heat. Roux is used to thicken sauces or soups.

**sauté** — To cook food quickly in a skillet over medium-high heat with a bit of hot fat (generally a combination of butter and oil).

**scant** — A term used to describe a measurement that is almost as much as indicated.

**sear** — To cook meat, poultry, or fish quickly in a hot pan, browning all sides with the objective of sealing in the juices.

**simmer** — To cook food in liquid over a low heat. At a simmer, bubbles will rise and just barely break at the surface.

**steam** — The process of cooking food in a covered pan over boiling water. Steamed food retains most of its natural juices and nutrients.

**stewing** — A cooking method by which food is very slowly simmered with a small amount of liquid in a pan with a tight fitting lid. Stewing allows meat to tenderize and flavors to meld together.

**stir-fry** — To cook small pieces of food very quickly in a small amount of oil over high heat, stirring constantly. Either a skillet or a wok may be used.

**sweat** — To cook vegetables such as onions, celery, or garlic in a small amount of fat over low heat. Vegetables are covered directly with foil or parchment, and the pot is covered tightly. Sweating produces tender vegetables without browning.

**timbale** — A high sided mold that is slightly tapered at the bottom.

**water bath or bain marie** — A gentle cooking method whereby delicate food such as custards and soufflés are placed in a pan with very warm water and then baked. This helps to prevent cracking and curdling. It is beneficial to place a cooling rack or a dish towel in the bottom of the pan, and to not allow custard cups to touch one another or the walls of the pan.

**whisk** — To combine ingredients vigorously with a wire whip.

# INDEX

KAREN ROBERTSON BEGAN HER JOURNEY into the gluten-free world when her children were first diagnosed with celiac disease in 1997. As a food lover, she was determined to find gluten-free recipes for baked goods that were moist, delicious, and similar to their wheat-based counterparts. Additionally, it was important to develop high-quality meals the entire family would enjoy. Karen has served on the board for the Gluten Intolerance Group, and teaches gluten-free cooking classes in Seattle, Washington.

stance every member has the same immediate goal of total abstinence), along with the creation of a shared social system (in which members may attend several meetings a day, will have the names and phone numbers of other participants on hand, and will be in frequent personal contact with one another in between meetings). By identifying strongly with their distinctive subsociety and its ideology (which places much of the blame for their condition on factors over which they have no control, such as their genetic inheritance), alcoholics begin to feel a lessened sense of shame, guilt, and stigmatization. They also begin to experience an enormous sense of support, not only from the group, but from their sponsor, a nurturing figure who will do his or her best to be continuously available for listening and for guidance.

The self-help experience, then, is informal and open-ended. A.A. members, for instance, can attend any A.A. meeting wherever they may find themselves to be, including a foreign country, and they are free to leave A.A. and to rejoin it at any point they wish. While members are not prohibited from expressing individual concerns and problems, the emphasis is on the mutual goal of maintaining sobriety; hence, any individual problem expressed will be viewed in the light of the threat it poses to that sobriety.

Contemporary trends in psychotherapy continue in the direction of homogeneous, frequently short-term and open-ended groups directed toward helping people who share the same symptom or problem, albeit led by a professional therapist. As we shall point out in our concluding chapter, disease management groups (Roback, 1984), geared to patients suffering from the same illness and their families, offer a typical example of short-term and open-ended group psychotherapy. In their concern with a specific goal (i.e., helping the patient or family member adjust to a difficult reality situation, as opposed to attempting to effect long-term changes in each participant's personality), these groups fall somewhere between the social work and TCI models. They also, perhaps fittingly, return us to group therapy's earliest origins, the disease management group oriented to tubercular outpatients conceived by Joseph Hersey Pratt. Disease management groups, like other short-term psychotherapy groups, also bear out a prediction that we made in the first edition of this book (1974)—that after the looseness and fluidity of the encounter group (which embraced a wide variety of goals, including characterological change), the field of group therapy would return to more "structure, conceptualization, and goal-relevance" (p. 17). We shall have more to say about this issue in our concluding chapter.

# CHAPTER TWO
# THE SOCIAL WORK GROUP

Maeda J. Galinsky
and Janice H. Schopler
*School of Social Work*
*University of North Carolina at Chapel Hill*

Social workers are confronted with a broad range of problems, needs, and demands as they meet with clients in groups. A sampling of current social work groups might include weekly meetings for abusive spouses that focus on ways of controlling and redirecting angry behavior; supportive sessions for relatives of Alzheimer's victims to enable them to gain knowledge of the disease, share different means of coping, and develop community resources; short-term therapy with hospitalized adults to help them learn to identify and master emotional responses; reminiscence groups for residents of nursing homes to review and integrate their life experiences as well as to reinforce effective cognitive functioning; assertion training for mentally retarded young adults living in the community, who must learn to negotiate with salespersons, employers, and oversolicitous family members; and group counselling and recreational programs for children in a residential group home who must come to terms with life together and away from their families. One situation is as "typical" as another.

The diversity of purposes and settings portrayed is indicative of the many different types of groups social group workers must be prepared to lead. Therapy groups, support groups, social action groups, educational groups, recreational groups, task groups, and self-help groups all lie within the realm of social work services. Social group work models reflect the need for versatility in planning and action. At various times the goals of social group work have been geared to social reform; to socialization; to growth and development of normal individuals; to training for participatory democracy; to treatment of individual problems; and to support, education, and social action for common problems. Presently, all of these goals are regarded as appropriate, but they have been emphasized differentially in the various phases of social group work development.

## HISTORICAL BACKGROUND

The history of social group work has, since the latter part of the nineteenth century, been closely linked to the evolution of the social agencies which have developed to handle the needs of people. Beginning as a "cause" devoted to improving the quality of human life in areas such as labor, housing, and recreation, social group work has moved to the status of a professional method with an identified body of social work knowledge and skills. Group work began in settlement houses that were built in the late nineteenth and early twentieth centuries in response to the mammoth social problems of the poor, and often immigrant, slum dwellers. Jane Addams, who founded Hull House in Chicago in 1889, served as an inspiration to settlement workers in this era of progressive reform, when groups were organized to fight for improved housing, better working conditions, and increased recreational opportunities. Education for citizenship and for leisure-time activities was also provided in settlement groups as workers emphasized the values of social participation, democratic process, learning and growth, and cross-cultural contact.

The zeal for reform faded in the atmosphere that existed following World War I as leisure-time and youth-service agencies developed in response to the needs of a growing middle class concerned with preserving the dominant social values and enhancing the human resources of society. Educational and recreational activities were offered through agencies such as the Young Men's and Young Women's Christian Associations, scouting organizations, 4-H Clubs, and community centers. The emphasis was on learning skills and values through the group. Group workers of this period, largely untrained, directed their efforts toward providing socialization experiences for the average, normal citizen. The idea of "treating" people in groups had not yet been developed. Although there was little systematic writing about the extensive work with groups during this period, the practice of group work was greatly influenced by the work of Mary P. Follett, a political scientist who advocated participatory democracy, and the philosophy of John Dewey, who spearheaded the progressive education movement. Dewey's work, in particular, provided a basis for working with small, leisure-time groups, and group workers began to develop a methodology as they stressed principles such as "learning by doing," "individualization," and "starting where the group is."

In the late 1930s and early 1940s, the focus of social group work shifted noticeably. Apparently, closer association with the psychoanalytically oriented caseworkers of this period, as well as the desire of group workers for acceptance by the social work profession, led to the use of groups for treatment purposes. Social group workers began to move into a variety of settings, such as mental hospitals, child guidance clinics, prisons, children's institutions, public assistance agencies, and schools; and the broad, ambitious aims of improving society through group participation were exchanged for a concern with treating individuals, albeit in groups. The writings of Redl and Wineman, Coyle, and Konopka in the 1940s and 1950s contributed greatly to the development of the treatment approach and reflected an increasing integration of social science materials in the growing group work methodology. It was also during this period, in 1946, that the American Association of Group Workers formally united with other segments of the social work profession to become a part of the organization currently known as the National Association of Social Workers. Prior to this time, some group workers had social work training and most had practiced in social agencies, but their identification with the social work profession was a loose one.

By the 1950s, social group workers had become established members of the social work profession. In formulating social work's approaches to groups, they drew heavily on the rapidly developing social sciences—particularly small group theories, sociological theories of deviance, and systems theory. While the methodology associated with using the group for environmental change was more fully developed within the social work speciality of community organization, social group workers were still concerned with the impact of the environment on their clients' lives and with empowering clients to influence their milieu, currently reflected in a systems approach and the use of ecological concepts and organizational theory.

In the past several decades, social group workers have been involved in building their theoretical and practical knowledge through the incorporation of both social science theory and actual field experience. Social group workers, beginning in the late 1950s and continuing into the 1960s and 1970s, concentrated on the development of models of social group work practice. The writings of Konopka, Vinter, Schwartz, Bernstein, Northen, Glasser, Klein, and Shulman were among the most notable of this era. Practitioners adapted these conceptualizations to work with groups in a variety of health and welfare settings.

Social group work models have been designed to be versatile, since they are required to serve a wide variety of purposes. The theoretical approaches must accommodate different types of practice with a broad range of population groups. Some of the concepts offer a perspective compatible with many types of interventions, while others give specific practice directives. At times, practice principles may be "borrowed" from other models, such as gestalt or behavior therapy, when this is deemed appropriate; in fact, some authors, such as Rose (1973) and Rose and Edelson (1987), have combined other models with a particular social group work approach into a framework for practice. Furthermore, social work practitioners, building on a foundation of social group work practice, have maintained a flexible orientation toward their roles as group leaders.

Social group workers in the late 1970s and the 1980s have continued to clarify and expand the theoretical bases of group practice. Publications by Garvin, Henry, Balgopal and Vassil, Sundel et al., and Toseland and Rivas, as well as those of various authors in the journal, *Social Work with Groups,* have further strengthened the conceptual foundations of practice. Social work practitioners have also contributed markedly to recent innovations in group practice, especially to the development of open-ended groups and short-term groups. They have pioneered with self-help groups, educational groups, and support groups and have focused on the potential of groups for the purpose of empowerment. Social group work, grounded as it is in the reality of social conditions and paying special attention to natural and artificially created social networks, is compatible with a focus on individuals' abilities to provide assistance and support to one another and on responding to crisis situations and internal pressures that call for immediate and short-term assistance.

The formulation of social group work presented in this chapter is drawn from a number of models presented in the social work literature. While this is a simplifying strategy there is sufficient commonality among the social work approaches to justify presenting their highlights as a single unitary whole.

## ILLUSTRATION OF A TYPICAL MEETING

In this account, a group of mental patients at a state hospital is meeting together for the fifth time. The social worker has contracted to meet with the group eight times to help the members prepare for discharge. The group's members include: Mr. Aaron, an extremely dependent, middle-aged man who plans to return to his parents' home; Mr. Granger, a rather dependent young man who found employment during a weekend pass; Ms. Jensen, a housewife hospitalized for chronic depression who will be returning to her husband and three teenagers; Ms. Millenson, a young schizophrenic who will be provisionally placed at a halfway house; Mr. Smythe, a man in his thirties recovering from an acute anxiety attack who will be returning to a job his former employer "has waiting for him"; and Mr. Tuttle, a very insecure and paranoid young man who is moving to a semisupervised home and will be working at a sheltered workshop.

> The worker opened the meeting by stating that Mr. Aaron had had a disturbing experience on his weekend home visit and would like the group's help. Mr. Smythe immediately asked Mr. Aaron what happened. Mr. Aaron was visibly upset, rocking in his chair, his voice trembling, as he told the group he had

been "interrogated" by a friend of his father during his visit home. With the worker's prompting, Mr. Aaron related the incident. His father's friend started out by asking if Mr. Aaron's thinking was okay yet. He followed this by a series of questions about "shock treatments" and the "crazy people" at the hospital. Although the friend assured Mr. Aaron outright that he didn't think he was "crazy," Mr. Aaron felt as if he were being attacked and became so upset that he retreated to his room for the rest of the weekend. The worker noted that she could see how this must have spoiled Mr. Aaron's whole weekend and wondered if any of the other members had ever had an experience like this. Ms. Jensen said she knew just how Mr. Aaron felt. When she was at home on the Christmas holiday, her daughter's friends kept looking at her in a funny way; and while shopping, she also ran into a woman from her church who asked her what had been keeping her away from home. Mr. Tuttle shared his feelings of being stared at when outside the hospital. Ms. Millenson then stated that wherever she went, she just told people she was from the state hospital, whether they asked or not, and, as far as she was concerned "they can stare all they want." The worker intervened, pointing out that it sounded as though most of them had been questioned about their stay at the state hospital or had felt like people were wondering about them when they were outside the hospital. She stated that Ms. Millenson had told the group what she did and indicated it might be helpful to know how some of the other members handled this type of situation. The members gave a variety of responses but most of them shared a dislike of talking to others about their hospital experience and two members had tried to deny their hospitalization: Ms. Jensen had told the church member she'd been in the hospital with "female trouble" even though she suspected the lady knew where she'd really been; Mr. Granger had told his new employer that he'd been away, looking for work down south. Ms. Millenson interjected, with some feeling, that Mr. Granger would be in for big trouble if his employer found out, since following a prior hospitalization she had obtained a job without revealing her convalescent status and lost the job for withholding information.

Following her comments, the members became involved in a debate about whether or not people really could identify them as mental patients and whether or not they should reveal their hospitalization. Mr. Granger continued to maintain that you could only hurt yourself by telling people you'd been a mental patient (they would refuse you jobs, expect you to act weird, etc.), but other members were uncertain and were afraid of the consequences of trying to "hide the facts."

The worker helped them summarize, and they tentatively agreed that it's probably best not to hide hospitalization for mental illness if people are at all likely to find out about it. Mr. Aaron pointed out, however, that even when he feels he ought to tell people or answer their questions about the hospital, he gets very upset and doesn't know what to say or what to do. The worker reminded the group that at the last meeting they had talked about feelings related to being a mental patient. Several members commented positively on the previous meeting, and Ms. Jensen, in particular, said that the discussion had really made her feel better. Mr. Aaron interrupted, saying, "Yes, it was a good session, but I still don't know what to say to people." The worker then suggested that the group do some role-playing of different ways of responding to people and helped members structure the situation.

After reminding the group of Mr. Aaron's problem with his father's friend, Mr. Jenkins, the worker offered to act as Mr. Aaron and asked Mr. Aaron to play the role of Mr. Jenkins. Mr. Aaron reviewed the behavior of Mr. Jenkins with the group. The worker then asked the group for help in planning her role as Mr. Aaron. Several members offered suggestions about how she should act when questioned by Mr. Jenkins. First, Mr. Granger said he would turn and walk away from such stupid questions. Ms. Jensen quickly pointed out, "But that's what Mr. Aaron did, and it didn't work at all. Shouldn't he give an honest answer?" Ms. Millenson agreed, saying, "Yes, just tell them you're in the mental hospital but you're not like the rest of the strange people." Ms. Jensen objected: "That doesn't sound right. What you could say is that the patients just have health problems and aren't really crazy like you hear." Mr. Smythe said, "Yes, say it's for mental health, and the social workers and doctors help you see your problems and get better." At this point, Mr. Aaron and the worker role-played the situation with the rest of the group observing.

After the role-play, the worker helped the group to evaluate her responses to the questioning by Mr. Aaron in his role as Mr. Jenkins and to explore Mr. Aaron's feelings. Mr. Aaron said that playing Mr. Jenkins's role helped him understand a little better why Mr. Jenkins asked the questions. Then, with some support from the worker and other members, Mr. Aaron agreed to play himself using the members' suggestions. In this role-play, Mr. Aaron was able to face up to Mr. Jenkins's questions. He admitted he had some problems but said he was getting help for them at the hospital. His performance was enthusiastically rewarded by group members who also made some additional suggestions for handling the situation. During the discussion, Mr. Granger said, "These ideas are just fine for answering the questions of friends and relatives, but they wouldn't be much use when you're out looking for a job." With the worker's guidance the group members considered when and how they would tell a prospective employer about their hospitalization. Then, the group role-played several situations that dealt with conversations with both employers and fellow employees, and all members participated in at least one role-play. In the last few minutes of the meeting, the worker reviewed the various ways that group members had recommended for telling others about their hospitalization. Although some members were still unsure about their ability to handle the situation, at the worker's instigation all the members agreed to try explaining their hospitalization to someone outside the hospital during their weekend away from the hospital and to report back to the group at the next meeting.

## KEY CONCEPTS

**Open Systems Perspective.**  Current formulations of social group work draw on social systems theory in their descriptions of group functioning (Toseland & Rivas, 1984; Germain & Gitterman, 1980; Garvin, 1987). Systems concepts propose a dynamic view of group development and operation, stress the reciprocal nature of relationships among individuals and systems, and alert social workers to the interdependencies that exist between the group and its surroundings. The systems perspective ensures that a social group worker using a behavioral or psychodynamic approach to individual change will not overlook the importance of group dynamics or the members' important family and community relationships; nor will individual responses and member relationships be neglected in groups pursuing social change. In recent years this emphasis on social systems and the duality of the person and environment has been expanded through the use of an ecological framework (Balgopal & Vassil, 1983).

Whether social workers offer their services through a social agency or are in independent practice, they perform a mediating function, facilitating linkage among members and between members and relevant social units outside the group. An open systems orientation directs the worker to explore the impact of client relationships external to the group. Informal exchanges with family and friends and more formal transactions with teachers, employers, and human service professionals influence how members view themselves and how they are viewed by others. These perceptions in turn affect member behavior and the responses of others in their environment.

Social workers may also intervene outside the group to help members obtain needed resources or to facilitate the development of supportive relationships. Often these interventions are directed toward linking clients with formal organizations so that they may receive services such as medical care, training, or financial assistance. At other times, the worker focuses on informal social networks, helping clients make connections with family, friends, and neighbors who can help them achieve their goals and fulfill their needs (Whittaker & Garbarino, 1983). A social worker meeting with a group of sexually abused adolescents recognizes that painful encounters with family, courts, and placement agencies have left members with a heavy burden of guilt and mistrust. While sharing experiences and establishing ties with each other provide a base for regaining self-respect, members also need to build trusting, supportive relationships outside the group before they can lead productive lives.

**The Group as a System.**    Viewing the group as a system with a defined boundary and interrelated parts draws attention to the impact of the reciprocal relations between the worker and group members (Schwartz, 1961; Shulman, 1968; Toseland & Rivas, 1984). An interaction between two members will not only affect each of them but will reverberate through the system, affecting other members as well as the worker. Therefore, in order to understand any one part of the system, the totality of interacting parts must be considered. In the discharge group, Mr. Aaron's recall of his distressing weekend elicited accounts of similar experiences of other group members. This provided the worker with an opportunity to experience with them some of the specific difficulties of the situation; thus the worker was able to help the group activate their mutual need to resolve problems in their relationships beyond the boundaries of the hospital.

**Organizational Influences.** Since most social group work is agency based, a delineation of organizational influences on the group and its members is a common component of social group work models. In this context, the group is regarded as a subsystem of the larger agency organization; and it is recognized that the agency system will affect the group's operation just as the group affects the agency (Garvin, 1987; Hasenfeld, 1985; Toseland & Rivas, 1984; Northen, 1988). An understanding of organizational theory is important to the practice of group work. The agency sanctions group formation and defines acceptable group goals and patterns of operation. The agency must consider the impact of the group's activity and may need to consider reallocating resources or changing policies to facilitate the achievement of group goals. The discharge group might, for example, request a change in hospital rules so the group can practice social and community living skills on shopping trips or eating together at a local restaurant.

**Group Dynamics.** Social workers tend to view the group as an influence system and rely heavily on knowledge about group dynamics (Cartwright & Zander, 1968; Shaw, 1981) as a basis for intervention. Recognition and effective use of small group forces can promote positive outcomes for the group and its members (Garvin, 1987; Vinter, 1985; Roberts & Northen, 1976). Groups that become cohesive units exert a strong influence on their members. If group forces are ignored, the group can drift aimlessly; if misused, members can be harmed (Lieberman et al., 1973; Galinsky & Schopler, 1977).

Throughout the life of the group, the worker must ensure that the group maintenance and task functions are adequately performed (Bales, 1958; Garvin, 1985; Toseland & Rivas, 1984). The group maintenance function addresses the socioemotional component of group functioning. To carry out this function the group worker encourages open expression of both positive and negative feelings, supportive responses to member concerns and contributions, and acceptance of differences. The task function relates to the group's goals, the focus of members' work together. The worker helps the group define appropriate goals, establish priorities, and complete the tasks that will facilitate goal achievements. As the group develops, members share performance of leadership functions. If the group reaches a certain level of maturity, they may rely very little on the group worker for task achievement or group maintenance.

While both functions are essential to group productivity, a balanced approach is sought. Too much attention to socioemotional functioning can cause the group to wander and lose sight of its goals; in similar fashion, overemphasis on task can result in disruption and dissatisfaction if members have no outlet for their grievances and no way to resolve their conflicts. The group's purpose must also be considered in weighing the differential importance of task and maintenance functions. As might be expected, in treatment and support groups, socioemotional needs are a major focus and thus attention to these needs in fact often overlaps with the task function. Educational, action, and other task-oriented groups are more concerned with the task function. Whatever the purpose, however, neither function can be neglected.

Initially the group merely provides the context in which members come together to explore common concerns, seek information, and share experiences. Through the course of worker–member transactions, the group develops a distinct structure with individual and group goals, roles, and norms. Group bonds and patterns of communication emerge. Members share a sense of purpose and have a common commitment to helping each other through established patterns of interaction. Once these characteristics are in place, the group itself becomes a means of influence (Sundel et al., 1985) that can have impact on members and their relationships both inside and outside the group.

**Mutual Aid.**    Ideally, any group can establish reciprocal helping relationships among its members and become a system of mutual aid (Schwartz, 1971; Shulman, 1985/86; Gitterman & Shulman, 1986). As members offer solutions to common problems, make supportive comments, and share in the skill development of fellow members by participating in group exercises, they become committed to helping each other. A beginning sense of mutuality was apparent in the discharge groups as members pooled ideas for handling questions about their hospitalization. In a similar vein, relatives of Alzheimer's patients meeting with a social worker may experience intense relief as they exchange concerns.

In helping the group reach this state, the worker must affirm the members' ability to help each other. Abusive spouses whose behavior has been condemned by society may feel no one is interested in their opinions. Newly diagnosed cancer patients may be caught up in their own personal crises and think they have nothing left to offer. Through the worker's personal encouragement and orchestration of group conditions conducive to sharing, problem solving, and reciprocal influence, members can speak up and experience the benefits of their mutual experiences.

The worker who promotes the group's potential as a means of helping does more than convey interest in each member and the group situation (Vinter, 1985; Schwartz, 1971; Toseland & Rivas, 1984; Garvin, 1987; Northen, 1988). By prompting members' responses and guiding their interaction, the worker helps members form relationships with each other that are direct, purposeful, and invested with feeling. Through the "give and take" of these relationships, each member is strengthened and becomes a part of the productive totality that is the group. Apprehensive child abusers feel less stigmatized as they learn other parents have struck out in anger when pressured or in despair. They learn to face the fact that they have a problem for which they require treatment, and they operate as a unit in seeking solutions for common and unique difficulties. The cancer patients feel less isolated as they have the opportunity to speak openly about their illness and as they assume a helping role with other members. The tone and boundaries of this mutual aid system are first set as the worker and members consider the contract.

**Contract.** The contract defines the relationships within the group system and among the group, the worker, and the agency. Whether it results in a verbal agreement or a written document, whether its formulation is brief or prolonged, the contract represents a transactional process (Schwartz, 1971; Croxton, 1985). During this process the worker and clients come to terms about the goals the group will pursue, group procedures that will structure their work together, and their respective roles. In short-term groups, contracting may even be completed in the beginning session; in longer-term groups, the initial contract may be continually reformulated as the group develops and needs change. When groups have open membership, the contract is reviewed as new members enter and old members leave and becomes a force for maintaining the group's focus and traditions in the face of membership change.

Contracting in social group work is based on ethical considerations and research findings (Northen, 1988; Garvin, 1987). Ethically, social workers affirm the client's right to self-determination. Thus, for members to become partners in a therapeutic learning, or change, process, they must have an opportunity to become fully involved in negotiating the contract. As a result of this process, members gain a clearer understanding of goals and means for achieving them, a factor which increases the likelihood of group success (Schopler et al., 1985).

The nature of the group members' involvement in contracting is geared to their level of understanding and the nature of their problems. A worker can probably elicit more active participation from a group of step-parents who are experiencing difficulty with their "blended" families than from a group of young retarded adults who need help in developing assertion skills or from a group of resistant juvenile offenders. Although the worker may take major responsibility for goal formulation and planning group activities, some degree of client consent is critical. Either verbally or experientially, the worker should provide members with some sense of the group's purpose and the way the group will operate. When there are involuntary clients, such as those who are court-ordered, agreement to attend may be recognized as the only term of agreement initially possible.

In addition to reaching agreement on goals and means, the worker and members must come to some common understanding of their respective roles. Explicit discussion of the rights and responsibilities of the members and worker is required. Questions about confidentiality, attendance, and honesty should be raised. Meeting times and places and fees need to be settled. In addition, members must understand that eventually they will be asked to commit themselves to helping each other. Throughout the experience of contracting, the worker lays the groundwork for mutually beneficial relationships that will promote positive group outcomes.

**Levels of Intervention.**    Social group work models distinguish three levels of intervention: the individual, the group, and the social environment (Vinter, 1985; Garvin, 1987; Northen, 1988). In addition to the spontaneous interactions that are required in any form of group work practice, the social work practitioner frequently prepares in advance the kinds of interventions at the three system levels that may be required, such as giving direct assistance to a new member, building the group system so that it may be used as an indirect means of influence to reach individual group members, or arranging for a substance abuse client to visit an Alcoholics Anonymous meeting. All social group work models have historically given conceptual attention to both individual and group level interventions. More recent formulations of social group work, influenced by the work of Robert Vinter, open systems and ecological perspectives, and networking concepts, also focus on the importance of environmental interventions to support the work of the group (Sundel et al., 1985; Garvin, 1987; Henry, 1981; Balgopal & Vassil, 1983; Toseland & Rivas, 1984; Northen, 1988).

The attention given to each system level varies in practice because of respect for clients' rights, the worker's professional judgments, and agency constraints. A mental health clinic may not have sufficient funds to permit worker contact outside the agency. A pregnant teenager may not want her parents or boyfriend to know about her condition. A worker may decide that members are able to handle external relationships independently without group involvement.

*Individual Intervention.*    Direct intervention with individuals is offered within the scope of the relationship that the worker develops with each client. Individually focused transactions may take place within the context of the group and thus also have an impact on other members or may occur outside the group. The worker may engage members directly to facilitate the achievement of either individual or group goals. On some occasions, members may require guidance, support, or interpretation of an intrapersonal conflict. At other times the worker may need to encourage a member to speak up or to confront a member who has violated a group rule. Social workers have used a variety of personality theories to help guide their work with individuals, most notably psychoanalytic theory, learning theory, and cognitive theory (Garvin & Glasser, 1985; Toseland & Rivas, 1984).

When appropriate, practitioners may intervene following a group session. In a marital couples group, a wife revealed her husband's impotence in an early session. The husband was reluctant to return to the group until he was able to vent his anger and distress in a private session with the worker. An adolescent who wanted to become more independent sought a joint session with her worker and parents to discuss applying for a part-time job. Although sessions with individual members should be evaluated in terms of their impact on the group as a whole, they may be necessary when members face a crisis or require supplementary support.

*Group Intervention.* Throughout the life of the group, the worker focuses interventions on creating and modifying conditions within the group system (Vinter, 1985; Toseland & Rivas, 1984; Garvin, 1987). The group is not only a context within which individual interactions take place, it is also a means to accomplish the work of the group. In contrast to the more direct impact of the worker at the individual system level, worker action at the group level is more likely to affect members indirectly through the group. Using knowledge of group dynamics, the worker intervenes to help the group itself become an influence system, an environment conducive to treatment, and a mutual aid system. Social group work models vary in their classification of group level interventions but generally focus on composition, goals, and group structure and processes.

In making decisions about group composition, the worker uses information about the effects of group size and individual attributes to structure an experience that will benefit members (Bertcher & Maple, 1985; Davis, 1979). The purpose of the group is the primary criterion for determining who should be selected as members. Of course, in many instances the worker has little or no control over the initial formation of the group, and external circumstances may continually alter the membership of the group. In the group of mental patients, membership may include all of the patients ready for discharge. An open-ended group for battered wives may accept all women with abusive spouses and be subject to extreme variations in size of membership. Nevertheless, principles related to size and member selection are still used in understanding the effects of composition on the specific group system.

The formulation of a group goal or purpose from the common concerns and needs of members is a necessary condition for the achievement of individual goals. In the group of mental hospital patients, members' recognition of common concerns about leaving the hospital and their mutual need to make discharge plans provided them with a common focus. Once they had reached agreement on this group goal of planning for discharge, there was a basis for involving the total group in the discharge plans of each member and for motivating members to work on common discharge problems. Goals also served as a guide for choosing group activities and selecting worker interventions. Because all members faced questions and remarks from neighbors, relatives, and employers, the discharge group was ready and eager to role-play as the worker suggested and to discuss their mutual and unique fears and responses.

Group structures, or patterns of relationship in the group, constitute another set of group conditions which can either facilitate or hinder individual change. Building on knowledge of group dynamics, various structures, such as leadership, communication, power, and member roles within these structures, are considered by the worker in using group level interventions. Group processes refer to sequences of behavior or interaction which may encompass a broad range of events. Processes may span a few minutes during a meeting, as a quick decision is made, or cover the lifetime of a group, as in the case of group development. Areas covered under group process consist of such phenomena as conflict and conflict resolution, norms, group cohesion, problem solving, decision making, and changes in group structure. The worker draws upon knowledge of group processes to intervene in the group situation to keep the group actively involved in its pursuit of individual and group goals and to maintain it as a viable instrument for change.

*Environmental Intervention.* Environmental intervention focuses the worker's attention on the social systems outside the group (Vinter & Galinsky, 1985; Garvin et al., 1985). Through interventions with persons, groups, or institutions, the worker may seek environmental changes on behalf of one or more members. A very strict teacher might be encouraged to ignore negative incidents and recognize appropriate classroom behaviors a disruptive child is learning and practicing in group meetings. The substance abuse worker may become involved with a task force to promote the development of a teen center which would provide a positive outlet for group members. A support group for adults who are caring for elderly parents may need the worker's help in making arrangements for respite care. Practitioners intervene in the environment when members need this assistance. However, as much as possible, the workers encourage and enable individuals and the group to initiate such action themselves.

At times the worker may become involved in challenging bureaucratic rules or discriminatory practices that interfere with member rights or opportunities. A mother whose application for emergency assistance was delayed because of a computer error may need the worker to become an advocate on her behalf. When parents complain about the school's failure to respond to the needs of their handicapped children, the worker may help them organize to lobby for a special program.

Whenever the worker contemplates environmental interventions that may have personal consequences for group members, the group should discuss whether or not they wish the worker to proceed. Contact with individuals or systems important in clients' lives may unintentionally lead to negative repercussions or reveal confidences. The worker needs to be certain members are aware of both the benefits and the risks before they make a decision to act. In some situations, the group may wish to take action on its own or request the worker's help in change efforts focused on the environment. Such proposals should be evaluated in light of group and agency goals.

Environmental interventions, or extragroup means of influence, are a critical part of group practice. Members' roles in systems outside the group remain a primary emphasis, and systemic influences, including those of the agency in which the service is embedded, markedly influence the achievement of individual and group goals. An ecological view ensures that important environmental influences will be considered in assessing and responding to clients' needs.

**Programming.** Social group work is clearly distinguished by its frequent use of action-oriented experiences to help clients achieve goals. Since their early days in settlement houses, group workers have been attuned to the benefits of different types of activities. Neva Boyd recognized the importance of games and play as tools for client change and began writing about her observations and ideas in the 1920s (Simon, 1971). Group work's association with education and recreation further strengthened its awareness of the value of activities. Group workers have continuously regarded games, play, structured exercises, role-playing, sensory experiences, cooking, crafts, gardening, artistic expression, and other activities as means to enhance the therapeutic and growth potential of group work. Because social group work was already involved in the use of program activities, it had a readily available framework for incorporating group techniques, such as psychodramatic methods and behavioral homework assignments, from other models of group practice.

*Programming* is the sequential organization of tasks or activities during group meetings. Careful attention is given to the kinds of activities and assignments that will be useful and to the most beneficial way to structure these experiences. A session focused on piecing a quilt, which requires sharing of tools and materials, may, for example, be used to promote cooperative behavior and increase interaction among particular members. In another situation, role-playing interspersed with discussion may be utilized, as in the discharge group, to practice and evaluate responses to difficult situations.

Various frameworks exist for the analysis of the form and content of program activities and their consequences (Vinter, 1985; Middleman, 1968, 1980; Shulman, 1971; Whittaker, 1985). Some of the basic dimensions of activities to be considered are the degree and requirements of participation; the type, number, and distribution of rewards; and the kind and number of essential rules. During a meeting of a parents' group related to handling teenagers' dating behavior, for instance, the discussion could proceed in an informal, unstructured way that would promote friendly, noncompetitive interaction. Further, the program would be likely to be rewarding to all discussants, particularly those who were able to develop new approaches for relating to their teenagers' needs and problems as well as those who were able to offer constructive suggestions. In another group, designed to increase junior high school students' positive behavior and to facilitate achievements in their classroom work, a variation of a T.V. game show might be employed with members following strict rules for responding to questions and the worker enforcing these rules. Competitive behavior would be evoked, and the group worker might need to arbitrate aggressive interchanges. The winners would be rewarded most heavily, but the worker might want to ensure that all participants were given some tangible forms of gratification. In any case, the social group worker, based on an assessment of group and member needs, guides the group in structuring experiences most appropriate to their current level of functioning and their objectives.

Program activities, in addition to fulfilling clients' purposes and enabling the work of the group to proceed, also serve to enhance cohesion. Through participation in engaging activities members build a sense of positive attraction to other members and to the group itself. Thus, chronically mentally ill patients in a group home who have built common memories through the successful planning and preparation of a Thanksgiving feast, overweight young adults who have helped each other practice ways of avoiding night-time binges, and court-ordered, abusive parents who have participated in joint problem-solving exercises in a parent education program may come to value the group for its enjoyment and interpersonal rewards as well as its accomplishments. In this way, program activities can help maintain and strengthen the group, building a sense of commonality and mutual aid and assisting in the socio-emotional aspects of group development.

Programming concepts enable workers to carefully plan and consider alternatives as they help members make the best use of the group experience. A storehouse of possible activities and knowledge of ways to vary the structure of activities and discussion are important for the practice of social group work, and application of programming principles requires creativity and flexibility. Examples of several well-planned programs should serve to give an understanding of the imaginative use to which programming skills and information can be put. In an initial meeting, adult psychiatric inpatients who had difficulty recognizing and expressing emotions were given magazine pictures of people. They were asked to identify the particular emotion displayed and to think of a reason the person might have felt that way, to share their perception with a partner in the group, and then to relay it to the total group. Mentally retarded young adults in a group home participated in a "scavenger hunt" in a shopping mall to test their abilities to compare prices and to practice assertive behaviors. Parents of deaf children spent one meeting with cotton in their ears to better empathize with the world of their child. Virtually any activity or type of discussion can be used in programming to meet group needs; contribution to achievement of group and individual purposes and to group development are the criteria which guide the worker and the members in their programming selections.

## TYPICAL COURSE OF A GROUP

**Group Development.** Despite differences in labelling stages of group development there is sufficient commonality among the various frameworks to present one summary view of expected group occurrences and worker behaviors (for example, see Garvin, 1987; Toseland & Rivas, 1984; Garland et al., 1976; Tuckman, 1965; Tuckman & Jensen, 1977; Sarri & Galinsky, 1985). Conceptually, five distinct phases can be identified: origin or planning; formative or beginning; group growth and revision; maturation or performance; and evaluation and termination.

During the origin or planning phase, the potential client comes or is referred to the agency, the intake process is completed, initial goals for the group are formulated, and group arrangements for meeting place and time are decided. The worker prepares to become involved in the life of the group, developing a kind of preliminary empathy or set, a feel for the ways that members may act and react as individuals and as a group, and decides on possible intervention plans. In a group of recently divorced women who are having difficulties living alone, being solo parents, and finding employment, the worker can "tune in" to probable feelings of helplessness, frustration, loneliness, and uncertainty about their competencies. The group worker may consider teaching them behavioral techniques to use with their children and may plan discussions of ways to find jobs and obtain further schooling, to increase social contacts, and to explore feelings related to their new status. In the discharge group, the worker was attuned to the difficulties mental patients face in interpersonal exchanges on their weekend visits home.

The second phase, formative or beginning, encompasses the group's initial efforts to come together and decide on common goals. It is in this stage that a contract—an agreement on goals for individuals and for the group, on treatment methods, and on roles—is formulated. Members seek to discover how they are alike and different from each other and engage in a type of approach-avoidance behavior before firmly committing themselves to the group and to its goals. A foundation is laid for group cohesion—members' attraction to the group, to other members, and to the objectives. Group norms are established and an initial group structure emerges. The leader's tasks during this period include helping members to explore their common interests and goals, representing the agency's perspective, ensuring that norms and roles are facilitative of group objectives, and fostering members' attachments to the group. Further, the worker completes assessment of member functioning, participates in the process of goal-setting, and makes certain that members clearly understand the terms of the contract.

At this stage in the group's life the leader is frequently active, guiding the group in its first efforts and in its development of a system of mutual aid. During the first few meetings of a couples' group, time may be spent finding out how members are alike and different with respect to their problems, their strengths, and their characteristics. With the worker's assistance members may decide to focus on financial disagreements and on communication skills, and they may determine that each of the four couples will have group time during the two-hour session. In the discharge group, members quickly agreed to work on the various tasks they had to complete before they could leave. Their prior associations in the hospital aided the group in its beginnings.

A third phase, early group growth and revision, is characterized by a certain amount of intragroup conflict, testing of each other and the worker, and crises related to group norms and structure. There is an increase in both positive and negative affect in response to the task and to fellow members. These interactions allow members to challenge as well as to offer support; they signify members' engagement with each other and with the work of the group and their willingness to participate in an open exchange. It is during this time that members frequently question purposes, group structure, and group operations and may revise initial agreements and group conditions.

The group leader must encourage members to express themselves, while at the same time helping the group to maintain itself through stressful times. If members have not mastered satisfactory methods of conflict resolution, the worker may need to intervene to help the group and its members weather conflict; revise group goals, norms, and relationships; and proceed with its work. In a senior citizens group in a retirement center, one member may keep the group focused on complaints about their living situation. Although group members  may have originally agreed to air their gripes and share their feelings, they may quickly tire of this activity and resent the domination of one member. If they want to move on to consider ways of improving the center, the worker can help them become engaged in problem-solving activities and more equal participation, trying to assure that the previously controlling member is given a role if at all possible. In a children's group where a small subgroup may disparage any remarks made by other members, the worker may need to intervene to develop norms of tolerance and mutual respect. When several members in a group of delinquents assigned to participate by the courts reject the goals of finding after-school jobs and attending school, the worker will need to remind them of the consequences of their behavior and help the group to maintain its socially sanctioned goals in the face of this challenge.

The fourth phase of group development, the maturation or performance phase, is directed toward the main work of the group. At this point, the group has an increased ability to plan and act as a unit and to carry out problem-solving processes. Group structure is stable, with clear, flexible, and integrated member roles and a high degree of cohesion. Members are personally involved with one another, operate consistently as a system of mutual aid, and share leadership functions. While conflict and turmoil may occur, the group is prepared to respond to internal and external stress, and the conflicts are less disruptive of the group than previously.

In this phase the worker assists members in using the structure, norms, and operating procedures of the group. Interventions support members' self-direction and activate existing group conditions. If the group is stagnant or retreats from its problem and task focus, the worker and members may need to reexamine their contract. The group leader is also available to members in times of internal group crisis and when pressures from the external environment are too severe. In the later part of this fourth phase, the worker's major responsibility is to facilitate the functioning of a mature and stable group. In a women's support group which has been meeting in a community center for six months the leader may assist members in finding speakers for programs on legal rights in employment and on financial investments. Further, when the group is split into two opposing factions in response to a highly charged political issue the worker may help members with dispute settlement and take a fairly active role in the group until members are able to work on the resolution of the problem more independently. In a therapy group where members have been appropriately confrontive, the leader may need only to intervene with interpretations or facilitative comments when members are too supportive of a man who needs to take greater initiative in dealing with his overprotective parents. In addition, the worker may aid members in examining their own group processes when the group is unable to focus on any member issues for a sufficient length of time or in a meeting which is filled with a series of seemingly unprovoked angry exchanges. It should be noted that many groups never acquire the characteristics of a mature group, and the worker may need to be more consistently active throughout the life of these groups.

The final phase, evaluation and termination, is, as its label implies, concerned with ending the group and helping members to gauge their individual and group accomplishments. Members review their experience, deal with the ambivalent feelings of ending, and prepare for the future. The worker's task is to help members expedite the process of ending. When stated goals seem to have been achieved, the worker tries to ensure the transferability of change to the world outside the group. When goals have not been achieved, the leader assists members in finding alternative means of help. Because termination often arouses deep feelings in members, the leader should try to aid members in expressing and integrating positive and negative emotions. It may be necessary for a worker who has served primarily in a facilitative role in the later group sessions to become more directive if the group has particular difficulties in ending close relationships. For those groups which have ended prematurely or have not progressed in the developmental cycle because of purpose, programming requirements, time constraints, or member limitations, the leader may continue to intervene actively during this period.

In a group of delinquents that has met for two years, termination may arouse feelings of pride in changed behavior; sorrow at losing friends and group support; and intense anger at the worker, the agency, and the community for "forcing" members to disband their special relationships. The worker must attempt to keep the potential for regression from becoming a reality so that the group will end on a positive note. In the illustrative discharge group, presented earlier, the members' major work involved ending their association with the hospital and preparing for new roles in the community within the limit of eight meetings. In a highly structured educationally focused group which has provided for minimal interaction, termination may be relatively easy because of members' lack of investment with each other.

Group development has been portrayed as an orderly and sequential process, but in actuality, there are likely to be shifts back and forth between phases. A variety of factors influences the progression of the group. For example, client distrust may delay assessment and contracting. Goals and worker intervention plans may change as new information is obtained. In later phases, regression of a member, inability of the group to reach solutions to problems, or extreme conflict between members may cause the group to return to earlier stages of development.

The five phases of group development depict the movement of a group with stable membership and a fairly long life. However, in current practice, groups are often of limited duration, and, in fact, some groups are planned for only a single session. Other groups are open-ended with members joining and leaving at various points in the group's history. Because both short-term and open-ended group work are common forms of social group work, their characteristics and patterns of group development warrant special attention.

**Short-Term Groups.**  Groups are frequently constructed to meet for short periods of time (Alissi & Casper, 1985; Rosenbaum, 1983). Short-term may mean as many as six months of meetings for a therapy group or as few as one session for an orientation group. Other groups may be planned for a specific number of times, such as six, eight, or fourteen sessions. Short-term group work has been effective in engaging member participation and in meeting member needs. A preset number of meetings may help members to focus more quickly on their work together and may serve as a motivating force. Group activities may be geared to reaching member goals within a specified period of time. Furthermore, the time-limited group takes account of constraints on client involvement and agency service. The length of service may be dictated by scarcity of agency resources or clients' unwillingness to commit themselves to protracted contact. In any case, the nature of the group experience will be affected by the short period of time members meet together.

Short-term groups have been formed for siblings of handicapped children, for cancer patients, for relatives of hospitalized mental patients, for the aged in nursing homes, for abusive spouses, and for persons with phobias, to name but a few. Their purposes include training, education, support, treatment, and socialization. These groups are sometimes highly prestructured, as in parent education, assertiveness training, or weight reduction programs.

Other groups, designed to operate in a manner similar to the long-term group, are at times less structured.

Because group members do not have the luxury of time for the development of group relations, the worker may be required to take a vigorous and directive role throughout the life of the group. When time is limited, as in the discharge group for mental patients, the worker may find it necessary to "collapse" treatment stages and carry out many activities concurrently. Frequently, short-term groups do not advance to later phases of group development, and the worker may remain active in fostering member bonds, group norms, and group processes.

There are, however, some time-limited groups which pass rapidly through the early stages and into a more mature group phase. For example, a group of couples meeting for six sessions to participate in marriage enrichment may quickly find common bonds and common goals. They may then move along with the work of the group, short-circuiting the conflict processes characteristic of phase three.

A particular case of the short-term group is the single session that lasts from one to several hours. Members may meet for orientation to a correctional institution, for education about a medical treatment regimen and the psychosocial aspects of the disease, or for support and counselling in a temporary disaster relief center. While these groups obviously do not move through the five phases of group development, each single-session group may be viewed as having its own developmental cycle. Each part of the meeting poses different demands and has different implications for worker tasks (Schwartz, 1971). The worker must tune in to member characteristics and concerns, aid members in becoming acquainted and in understanding mutual aims, help the group achieve its purposes, and assist members in terminating. The leader will most likely need to assume control of the group and to set up the kinds of norms and group operations which will facilitate group accomplishments. Thus, a leader may want to plan to structure the form of group interaction and limit the content in a group of foster parents who are meeting for one evening to learn more about teenage physical and psychological development and to discuss common difficulties with adolescent foster children, ensuring that all members are heard and that crucial material is covered. A group worker who is asked to mediate conflict among personnel on a psychiatric ward of a general hospital may present a series of rules to the participants at the outset and monitor their use throughout the session.

**Open-Ended Groups.** Open-ended groups, which allow ongoing membership change throughout the life of the group, are established with the proviso that members may enter the group at any point and attend as long as their needs warrant it. Each group is different in its pattern of implementation; some groups have almost a complete turnover every session and closely resemble the single-session group while other groups meet for years with only occasional membership revisions. Similar to other forms of group practice, the purposes of open-ended groups are for treatment, support, assessment, orientation, and education. Such groups are relatively common in social work practice and operate in a wide variety of settings. They include groups for incest survivors, adolescents in group homes, chronically mentally ill persons in the community, child abusers, caregivers in nursing homes, and couples with marital difficulties. Open-ended groups are particularly helpful for persons in transitions and crises since they can provide immediate, ongoing response to client needs. When groups are open, clients do not have to wait for service and attendance can be adapted to the individual goals of members (Galinsky & Schopler, 1987; Schopler & Galinsky, 1984; Yalom, 1983).

Membership change creates disruption of group structure, processes, and activities. The group must adapt to each new configuration of composition as members enter and exit on a continuous and sometimes unpredictable basis. Groups often establish procedures for handling the arrival of new members and the departure of old ones to ease adjustment to constant change (Galinsky & Schopler, 1985; Galinsky & Schopler, in press).

Because group development is affected by frequent shifts in membership, a cyclical pattern of development can be expected. To some extent, the phases of formation and termination are repeated, even if only for a brief time, whenever the group changes. Some open-ended groups remain in the initial phases of development; others move through the stages and experience only minor alterations with membership change. The disruption to development may be less pronounced when groups have been in existence for a long period of time, when membership change is infrequent, when clearly defined means of incorporating new members or ending with departing ones are in operation, or when there are strong group traditions and a core subset of continuing members. Development in open-ended groups does not have the unitary quality of closed groups where members begin and end together. At any point in time newcomers may be acclimating to membership; old members may be engaged in the work of the group; and members preparing to terminate may have begun to withdraw (Scher, 1973). However, the group itself can progress even though individual members vary in their identification with the group and its process.

The demands on group leadership are high in open-ended groups, requiring continuous and instant assessment and flexible responses to ever-changing situations. The worker must be able to quickly foster member relationships, to create appropriate group conditions, and to alter plans as necessary. Because of frequent membership changes the leader may need to take a directive stance, to structure the meetings, and to retain a central position in the group. However, when a core nucleus remains in the group over a period of time members themselves may assume more of the responsibilities for the group's operation and for passing on the group traditions to new members. Whatever their patterns of development, open-ended groups have become a standard feature of group services and many remain in operation for several years.

A special variant of the open-ended group is the self-help group, currently a common group modality. Because self-help groups have proliferated to a great degree during recent years, and have a number of factors and procedures in common, they merit a separate treatment in their own right and will therefore be presented in Chapter 13. Social workers, along with other professionals, have been active in the development and support of self-help groups (Toseland & Hacker, 1982; Powell, 1987). Most self-help groups have been created to deal with problems of particular populations, such as parents of autistic children, ostomy patients, recovering alcoholics, widows and widowers, and former child abusers, and they remain readily available on a continuous basis to help those who share similar circumstances. An open-ended structure is especially appropriate to the needs of these groups. Leadership most often comes from the members themselves. Professional leaders may play a role in helping the group to initially form in response to member requests or because professionals have identified a common need. Once the group is in process, the professional may continue to serve as a consultant to the group in dealing with group operations, individual members' personal difficulties, intermember conflicts, or factors related to goal achievement; but they do not usually carry a formal leadership role. Self-help groups may remain in operation for many years, depending on their ability to meet needs and attract new members and on the success of the indigenous leadership.

## ROLE OF THE LEADER

At the present time, social group work practice varies widely and the roles assumed by social group workers in their practice do not reflect adherence to a single model. Social group workers may utilize concepts and techniques from a range of social work models and may draw ideas from other models of group interaction. Some models promote a conception of the leader as a director of planned change who uses group methods for the prevention of dysfunction and the rehabilitation of people with problems. In contrast, another prominent approach pictures workers as mediators of troubled transactions between individuals and the systems through which they relate to society. Still other views portray practitioners as consultants or convenors.

However, a review of social work approaches reveals marked similarities in their conception of what social group workers are expected to do. These approaches emphasize the importance of the world beyond the group and, in particular, the individual's and group's relationship to other systems. Social group work authors in all models recognize the impact of the group system on the individual, portraying the group variously as a mutual aid system and a means and context for practice. The social group worker is directed toward using the potential power of this group system and relies heavily on knowledge derived from group dynamics. Group work models also stress a need for clearly established agreements or "contracts" with group members and emphasize the worker's need to know about and use programming to achieve individual and group goals. While the unique contributions of distinct group work models should not be obscured by oversimplification, this chapter has highlighted their considerable correspondence in describing the kinds of activities expected from social group workers.

Selection of appropriate concepts from the different social work approaches is obviously governed by a variety of factors (Schopler & Galinsky, 1972): the needs, problems, and personalities of the clients; the agency setting and purpose; and the worker's own style or composite of personality, skills, and philosophy of life. In the meeting of mental patients described earlier, the worker shows a balanced use of approaches in her work with the group. Her interaction with group members reflects a selection of concepts based on her assessment of unique and common client needs around interactions with inquisitive others, and she calls on the mutual aid system of the group and guides members through a problem-solving process to help them anticipate situations and develop resources. The hospital's influence is apparent in the group's task of preparing for discharge, and the worker's style is expressed in her somewhat structured approach to helping the members resolve their difficulties. Thus, in a variety of ways appropriate to their own styles, client needs, and agency requirements, social group workers select from the concepts provided by models of group interactions as they serve people in groups.

Social work practitioners have pioneered in the use of program activities and, in partnership with other human service practitioners, have continuously promoted new approaches to practice, such as short-term groups and open-ended groups. Social group work traditionally has been responsive to social forces and to the immediate needs of its clients. As new client needs have surfaced and the demands for more efficient and effective services have become apparent, innovative forms of group work, utilizing the group worker as a primary practitioner or as a consultant, have been developed. Professional writings reflect a sense of openness to new knowledge and new demands. The social work models are flexible, since the social workers who use them must adapt their knowledge, skill, and personal style to the needs of an extremely diverse clientele. Social workers offer group services to people of all social classes and cultures whose problems may be related to their personal lives, their work, or their community.

# CHAPTER THREE
# THE PSYCHOANALYTIC THERAPY GROUP

As we saw in Chapter 2, social group work models are concerned with a wide range of therapeutic, socialization, and developmental goals. In the present chapter we are dealing with the psychoanalytic group, our first group model to be considered wholly psychotherapeutic in its structure and purpose.

The introduction of psychoanalytic procedures into group psychotherapy represented a fundamental extension of psychoanalysis, which had up to that point been a method of individual treatment only; indeed, Freud and his immediate followers had not envisaged the possibility of treating two or more people simultaneously. Moreover, despite some attempts on Freud's part to hypothesize about humankind's probable evolution within such fundamental social groupings as tribes, clans, and "civilized" societies (1913, 1922, 1930, 1939), psychoanalysis was, and still is, primarily a theory of individual personality and of personality development, rather than of groups and of how groups develop. Perhaps the closest Freud had come to a small-group psychology was his analysis of family relations; yet even here his approach was oriented more toward the effects of the family, especially the parents, on the developing child, rather than toward the family as a dynamic and coherent "system" in its own right.

It remained to later theorists of psychotherapy, like Gregory Bateson and his colleagues (1956), Jay Haley (1970/71), and James Durkin (1981), to formulate the kind of "general systems" approach in which any small group, whether the nuclear family or the psychotherapy group, is viewed as a *whole,* rather than as an assemblage of discrete personalities. Yet psychoanalysis has in general, despite exceptions that will be noted in Chapters 4 and 9, continued to define itself as a theory of the individual person. Durkin (1964, 1972), for example, points out that psychoanalysis, although not theoretically incompatible with group dynamics or systems theory, does best to retain the person, and his or her unconscious, as its central concern. Consequently, such practitioners of the present model as Wolf and Schwartz (1962) claim that they do not treat groups per se, as do group-dynamic psychotherapists (see Chapter 4), but instead continue to treat an individual patient, as in one-to-one psychotherapy, but this time in the presence of fellow patients (each of whom is also being treated by them). Hence the title of Wolf and Schwartz's formal presentation of their model is *Psychoanalysis in Groups* (1962; underlining ours), as opposed to the psychoanalysis of groups.

The formative role played by psychoanalysis in the field of individual psychotherapy has been paralleled by its similar role within group therapy, where it constitutes the first systematic application of a well-developed body of theory to group treatment; its influence on the practice of group therapy continues to be pervasive. Chapter 1 reviewed the contributions of men like Burrows, Wender, and Schiller, who had begun the process of tentatively applying psychoanalytic concepts to group treatment, and then the work of Slavson, Wolf, and Schwartz, who continued to develop, and to gradually codify, the modern approach to analytic group therapy.

## ILLUSTRATION OF A TYPICAL SESSION

Before introducing some key concepts, we would like to re-create a typical analytic group session, its setting, atmosphere, and content, and, in addition, to show the kinds of interventions the therapist might make. To do so, we will take a wholly fictitious example. Our group has seven members, four men and three women. While fairly similar in cultural background (they are for the most part urban and middle-class), the members differ in age, occupation, and personality characteristics. The youngest member, Marvin (who is silent in the segment below), is a twenty-year-old college student; the oldest is Felicia, a single woman in her early forties. The group has been meeting for two and a half years. Five of the patients have been with the group for all of this time; Mort entered the group ten months previously, and Ralph joined six months ago, both having replaced a member of the original group who terminated therapy.

The group begins without any structuring from Dr. M., who is silent. Ruth, a girl in her early twenties, is talking about the fact that Bob, the man with whom she is living, is probably having an affair with her best friend, Terry. She knows he is attracted to Terry, and each of them has recently, in talking to her about the other, made some ambiguous and erotically-tinged remarks. Ruth doesn't know what to do about this. She is annoyed with herself for being jealous, for she knows that whatever Bob has going with Terry is a purely "physical" thing. He has made it clear to her when they decided to live together that he did not feel sexually bound by conventional notions of a monogamous relationship; yet she feels hurt and betrayed by Terry. Then, at other times, she feels that she is being old-fashioned, that it's obviously just a "sex-thing" for Terry, who is basically interested in another unavailable man.

Mort, a brunette man in his middle thirties, razzes her. He says: That's right, Ruthie; Bob just has too much love in him to share with just one woman; besides, you love both of them so much, this is really an act of generosity on your part—you're giving two people you love to one another!

Ruth reacts with a slight giggle and continues to discuss the problem. Mort continues to bait her. Felicia interrupts at this point, saying that it makes her uncomfortable to see the way Mort is baiting Ruth and the way she allows him to do it.

Ruth interrupts, saying: But what difference does it make? I'm used to Mort's sarcasm. What I'm worried about is Bob. Felicia says: Yes, but you take the same crap from both of them. Mort joins in, saying: Yes, she's so god-damned dumb with those rose-colored glasses on; doesn't she know what the world is like? Boy, she really asks for it.

Ralph then joins in for a moment: She may ask for it, Mort, but I notice you're always there firstest with the mostest to give it to her.

Felicia says in a quiet voice: Ruth isn't happy until she has something to make her really miserable.

Ruth then says: Would everyone stop talking about me as though I weren't here?

Felicia expresses pleasure at Ruth's ability to speak up. Dr. M. then asks Felicia what Ruth's talking up does for her, i.e., Felicia. Felicia shrugs, saying: I don't know, I always like to see the underdog speak up; and I don't like the way Mort speaks to Ruth; he browbeats her.

The therapist says: I notice that you're often speaking up for others— those who get stepped on, those who cannot stick up for themselves, and so on; you're like a cheerleader rallying them on, but I don't hear you asking for something for yourself. Felicia answers: I don't know how to ask for myself. I'd rather play Ruth's big sister, I guess; in fact, I admire Ruth. She talks up a lot and tries to work on her problems.

Ruth says: But I don't get anywhere with them! I've lost every boyfriend I've ever had, and I'm afraid that if I start nagging Bob about Terry he'll leave me too. Mort then says to her: But you're already starting to lose him, you dumb bitch! He's in the hay with Terry, remember? Ruth looks a bit cornered, smiles uneasily, and says placatingly: I know you think I'm being silly, but that's Bob's style; he loves me, and he doesn't see whatever he does with Terry as infringing on his relationship to me.

Mort turns to the group in mock disgust, saying: Oh, god! She's such a dumb martyred freak-out; she's hopeless! Ruth begins to cry, and says: Well explain it to me, don't yell at me. The therapist asks her what she is feeling at that moment. Ruth answers: I don't know—I try, I really do; but everybody winds up getting angry with me. I know I probably do something wrong, like acting too helpless, or showing my insecurity too much, something—Dr. M. asks: You mean you feel angrier with yourself than with Mort right now? Ruth nods and sobs louder.

The therapist says: So right now you're feeling about Mort the way you do about Bob—somehow you're at fault and he's in the right. You just have to find some way of appeasing Mort—or Bob? some way of doing the right thing, even though their behavior makes you uncomfortable and unhappy?

Ruth replies: Yes, I suppose that's true. I don't think I ever really get angry at anybody. Dr. M. asks: Was it always like this, Ruth? Ruth answers: Yes, everyone was always mad at *me* when I was young. I was somehow at fault. My mother hadn't expected me so soon after my sister, and then my father was no longer around; I would try to reassure her that things would be OK, to make it better for her. I was always trying to get people to stop being mad at me.

Ralph then interposes: I know this sounds intellectual, but I think your tears are your anger; I know that has been true of me; and you've cried every time you've been here. Mort says to Ralph: And God forbid you should be intellectual instead of having feelings around here; good boy, Ralph, I can see you're learning to play the group therapy game—a few more months and you'll be a pro at it! The therapist intervenes: Mort, what would you say if you spoke really honestly for once, and put aside your banter and cynicism? Mort answers: Gee, I don't know, doc. I guess I'd say I love you truly, because sometimes when I squint my eyes I have to admit to myself that you look just like my Ma!

A few members laugh: Dr. M. is silent; he doesn't smile. Nelson speaks for the first time, saying to Mort: You've made that crack more than once, maybe there *is* something to it! Mort replies: No, he doesn't really look like my mother; his eyes are darker. Alice says: Mort, you really are unbelievable. Why do you come week after week like this? You're determined to let no one get through to you. It makes me really angry! You're wasting my time too, not just yours.

Mort has a smile on his face and doesn't answer. There is a short silence. Then Felicia speaks up and says: You know, Dr. M., I wonder what you're feeling underneath when Mort razzes you like that. I don't like it when you don't say anything, when you just keep silent.

Dr. M. asks her: What does my silence do to you, Felicia?

Felicia replies: I don't know—it's like what I said earlier about championing the underdog. I feel like my mother took a lot of abuse from my father; I remember watching her and wishing that she'd say something. And I would be wondering when I would be the next to get it—always thinking it was a miracle that I didn't, cause there was no one else around for him to pick on besides her and me, and I knew she wouldn't protect me.

Dr. M.: And you want me to be able to handle myself with Mort, just like you wanted Ruth to?—and just like you wanted your mother to stand up to your father?

Felicia says: I think so. Yeah, I would feel safer if you could—I guess I'm scared of Mort—it's like it was with my father. I'm surprised sometimes that Mort hasn't given me a full dose of his angry sarcasm like he has with the others, and I think that maybe it's because I'm the oldest woman in the group and something about that intimidates him. But I always feel like: My time will come, and I act tough and complain about how he walks over you others, but I make sure not to tangle with him directly.

Mort says to Felicia: You mean you're pretty scared of me? Felicia answers: Yes, I am. You may think I'm kidding, but I'm not—like just now when you said that to me directly I was surprised and I felt my heart begin to race for a second.

Mort answers: But you must get pissed off at me, too, don't you? I don't hear about that. Felicia pauses, then says uncertainly: Well, I don't like it, it makes me uncomfortable, but I'm not sure it really "pisses me off." I guess it's hard for me to get angry. I'm not aware of being *angry* with you; I'm *scared* of you.

Mort answers: That's a lot of crap! Dr. M. says to Mort: I agree that Felicia is much more aware of the anger in you, Mort, than she is of the anger in her- self. But I disagree with your saying she's not scared—I think a lot of people in the group are more scared of you than you think. Just like she doesn't know anger, you don't know fear, so you don't believe people can be afraid of your contempt.

Mort answers disgustedly: I don't know what I believe and don't believe anymore!

And so the session continues. Interaction is fairly lively; interruptions are frequent. By the end of the session, which lasts ninety minutes, all members have spoken up spontaneously, although three have been relatively quiet, and none has "held the floor" for more than a few minutes at a time. The analyst continued to intervene from time to time, but there were periods of seven or eight minutes during which he listened and said nothing whatever.

A discussion of some of the things that the therapist was trying to do in this session will appear in a later section (see "Role of the Leader," p. 62).

## KEY CONCEPTS: THEORETICAL

A complete understanding of the concepts employed by the present model would entail a presentation of the psychoanalytic theory of personality development and of psychopathology. Since such a review is beyond the scope of this book, we will assume some acquaintance with psychoanalytic theory on the part of the reader and will confine ourselves to those concepts that bear on psychoanalytic *method,* especially as it applies to the practice of group therapy.

**Free Association.**   This was the method eventually arrived at by Freud after he discarded hypnosis as too unreliable and too encouraging of suggestibility and dependency on the part of the patient. The analyst instructed the patient to free her mind as much as possible from her typically task-oriented, semirational, day-to-day preoccupations and instead to do something quite different—to report, while facing away from the analyst, her every thought, association, fancy, memory, and revery, however silly, trivial, incongruous, or shocking they seemed. The minimization of outer stimuli, effected by the analysand's lying on a couch and turning away from the analyst, was believed to facilitate this process. The consequent free associations, being less reality bound than the patient's typical thoughts and associations, would give the analyst, and eventually the patient, easier access to the latter's unconscious processes.

Could this most basic of analytic methods be employed within the group context? Seemingly not, since the face-to-face presence of six or seven strangers would surely turn the patient away from her inner life, to the very interpersonal reality from which free association had initially been designed to free her. However, what Wolf, Schwartz, and others (e.g., Durkin, 1964) discovered was that, while free association clearly could never be achieved to the same degree as on the analytic couch, something resembling it in spirit could be duplicated in the group setting.

Patients are not explicitly directed to free associate in a group. However, the therapist, by encouraging group members to discuss what is most on their minds (even if it does not strike them as immediately relevant), by being tolerant of interruptions and distractions, by having a nondirective attitude, and by informing the participants that their fantasies and dreams have a special relevance, can help to establish an atmosphere of permissiveness in which a patient's unconscious dynamics are revealed more vividly and more quickly than in more conventional, task-oriented discussion groups. Foulkes's (1965) term *free-floating discussion* would seem to more aptly describe this kind of verbal interaction than would free association. Moreover, at arbitrary points the leader is always free to intervene and ask a specific patient for free associations (e.g., if the latter has made a slip-of-the-tongue, the therapist might ask: "What is the very first thing that comes to mind when you hear your own error?").

Wolf and Schwartz (1962, pp. 16–18) developed a "go-around" technique as a means of adapting free association to a group context. In it a patient is asked to look at each person in the group and to say the first thing that comes to mind about him or her. The patient is being asked to react spontaneously and along channels that are considered inappropriate to more rationally focused and "purposive" social conversation. The go-around technique might be thought of as involving a kind of *group* free association. (The patient who goes around is rewarded whenever her associations "hit home" by having either the patient to whom she is reacting, or someone else in the group, acknowledge this fact; validation of this sort is especially valuable in the case of inhibited people who tend to mistrust their more intuitive and spontaneous ideas.) The go-around was later adapted to a variety of group models, including the T-group and the gestalt-therapy workshop; the historical data, however, indicate that credit for its first use belongs to Wolf, who was using it as standard practice by 1940.

**Resistance.**   The concept of *resistance* is fundamental to the practice and understanding of psychoanalysis. Resistance is defined by Fenichel (1945, p. 27) as "everything that prevents the patient from producing material derived from the unconscious." Freud first became aware of the phenomenon when he observed the difficulties that his patients experienced in attempting to obey the fundamental rule of free association. He discovered that they continuously, although for the most part unintentionally, used various devices to circumvent his request that they candidly report their spontaneous flow of associations. They asked questions; they challenged the analytic contract and its rationale; and they commented on the physical appearance of the room. Freud soon came to view resistance as a dynamic in its own right—one that the person establishes and exploits, however unwittingly, to protect herself against the intolerable anxiety that would arise were she to become aware of her repressed impulses and their concomitant emotions.

Resistance, then, operates as a defense against anxiety. How, then, is it different from a defense? It is a *kind* of defense, one operating specifically and directly in the treatment situation itself to prevent the analyst and patient from succeeding in their joint task of gaining insight into the dynamics of the patient's unconscious, even though the latter's conscious, healthy self strives to cooperate with the analytic effort. Because resistance refers to any behavior that serves to prevent the therapist and patient from understanding the latter's unconscious processes, it can take many forms. Perhaps the most basic is a direct evasion of the therapist altogether (e.g., the patient is often absent or late). Other, also relatively direct, forms are a conscious lack of cooperation and the expression of distrust and doubt in relation to the analyst and the validity of his procedures.

Resistance can also occur in more indirect and complex ways. One such way is the *transference resistance,* which will be discussed later. Another involves what Reich (1949) was the first to label as *character resistances.* These resistances or character styles were part of the patient's life long before she met the analyst, and they constitute aspects of her habitual, day-to-day, behavioral repertoire in dealing with other people. Such patterns are considered to constitute resistance because (1) they help the person to avoid anxiety and (2) they help her to *resist* becoming a more mature, integrated individual (a step that would doubtless require facing painful anxiety and conflict). Characterological resistances develop early in life and are basic to the patient's defenses and personality structure. Examples would be the cerebral life of the detached intellectual; the denying, "everything's coming up roses" attitude of the Pollyanna; and the clinging, overtly adulatory (but covertly hostile and demanding) orientation of the passive-dependent person. Illustrations of resistances expressed as character styles from the group therapy segment presented before would be Ruth's masochism and Felicia's determination to be consistently helpful to others.

A characterological resistance more difficult to identify involves the open display of a seemingly genuine emotion—like anger. While some patients find it hard to acknowledge their anger, the expression of anger comes relatively easily for others; such people can sometimes use their feeling of anger, and its expression, to resist the awareness of *other* feelings, feelings that they find deeply troubling and have difficulty in admitting to consciousness. For instance, a patient may use hostility as a means of avoiding the rejection and hurt she fears will come her way if she should allow herself to experience, or directly express, tender feelings for another group member. Even when anger is not strictly a defense, its continual, and sometimes histrionic, expression can help to forestall an exploration as to its deeper meaning. This type of resistance is frequently encountered in excessively emotional patients lacking the ability to occasionally take a more detached and reflective attitude toward their own behavior.

A general rule for the analyst in doing both individual and group therapy is to call the patient's attention first to the more readily observable, and treatment-interfering resistances (Spotnitz, 1985), since she is less likely to consider such behaviors as integrally related to her whole style of being; for instance, it is easier for her to accept the analyst's observation that she often changes the subject when beginning to talk about her father than it is for her to acknowledge such character resistances as dependency or authoritarianism. In fact, when doing individual therapy, the psychoanalyst may sometimes wait for extremely long periods of time before beginning to *point out,* much less to interpret, such characterologically embedded resistances.

The group situation, however, is somewhat different. While the *therapist* may still prefer to wait before commenting on the pathological aspects of a patient's character, there is no need for the group members to do so; in other words, the permissive atmosphere of the group makes it perfectly appropriate for the patient's fellow members to react openly to whatever behaviors she manifests. Such characterological attitudes as bravado, covert hostility, and provocative flirtatiousness are bound to stir up feelings of excitement, envy, and irritation in other people. This is an ideal course of events, for the initial reactions of non-therapist peers should be less threatening to the patient than would be the interventions of the authority-analyst. While the precise meaning of these defensive styles, particularly with regard to their connections to childhood events, may await definitive interpretation at the hands of the analyst, the patient will at least begin to be more quickly aware of them.

A distinct advantage of the group context, then, is that characterological resistances can be more readily reacted to in a confrontative way by the patient's peers than by her traditionally somewhat more aloof and more "professional" therapist. This kind of challenging confrontation is especially important when the patient manfests traits (like deviousness) that cause her to violate fundamental group norms or (like withdrawal) prevent her from becoming fully integrated into the group. Another, related advantage of the group is that it enables the therapist to directly observe, for the first time, his patient's interactional style with others; up until this point he has been limited to hearing, in individual therapy, the patient's *reports,* frequently distorted and self-serving, as to what goes on between her and other people.

The therapist can also note other changes in a patient's resistance patterns, or in how they should be handled, as she makes the transition from individual to group therapy (e.g., is the patient habitually late [a treatment-interfering resistance] to group as she was to individual?). In addition to the resistances that could be observed in both individual *and* group therapy (e.g., treatment-interfering resistances), patients could now manifest *group-level* resistances (Fenchel & Flapan, 1985). For instance, some members can "band together," however unconsciously, into a subgroup (as when three people persist in humor and joking while the rest of the group attempts to explore a serious issue) or the entire group-as-a-whole can resist its maturational and therapeutic task (as when all the members mock or scapegoat the leader, refuse to be serious about the subject currently at hand, etc.).

Hence in any single session the group therapist might be faced with a variety of resistances. Member A may have stayed away altogether. B may be very silent and appear dejected. C, D, and E may chat about what they did over the weekend, while F and G say nothing. There are no clear guidelines for the therapist as to what form his intervention should take in such an instance (the one exception to this being when he is faced with a resistance engaged in by the group-as-a-whole; here he is usually encouraged to deal with this group-level resistance before turning to subgroup or individual resistances; see "Interpretation," p. 54). He might focus on B, since the latter is the one whose feelings appear to be most apparent and directly ask what he or she is experiencing. If it is early in the group's development, where the therapist's primary goal is to stimulate interaction, the leader may simply wonder out loud what is happening. He senses, he says, that people are holding back from saying what's on their minds. What are they experiencing?

**Transference.** Like resistance, *transference* is a classic analytic concept. Indeed, it has been stated by more than one theorist that the analysis of resistance and transference lies at the core of psychoanalytic therapy and that any therapy offering systematic handling of these two phenomena may properly be described as psychoanalytic.

Transference manifests itself in individual treatment at that point where "unfinished business" from the patient's past life causes her to distort the present and either misperceive, or behave inappropriately to, the analyst. It is believed that all patients must eventually do this, because their neurosis in itself indicates that attitudes formed in childhood are being inappropriately carried over into adulthood and because the very conditions of analysis—the analyst's neutrality and relative passivity—facilitate transference distortions. Transference is an extremely dynamic force within the analysis. If handled correctly it can play a highly facilitative role for several reasons: (1) It "charges" up the process, since the patient, rather than just *reporting* on her past, begins to *relive* it in the therapy; (2) her "libidinization" of the therapist holds her to the often painful, frustrating, and time-consuming analytic process; and (3) it can be a major source of information for the analyst, who can now learn from the patient's reactions to him a great deal about her internal conflicts, interpersonal problems, and behavior patterns.

Transference is closely related to resistance in that at a particular point in a patient's individual analysis, it can become a form of resistance called *transference resistance* (i.e., when the patient's involvement with the analyst becomes so intense that her original purpose for having entered therapy in the first place becomes lost; she becomes so interested in the analyst that she is more concerned about the latter's regard for her than about changing. This point of intensity is also referred to at times as the *transference neurosis.* Transference resistance is considered to be a very useful form of resistance for the analyst, since it repeats in microcosmic form the way in which the neurosis initially developed. Yet it is one that is very difficult to resolve because the patient has now lost interest in using the analysis to understand herself and her history; instead she wants to exploit it for a quite different and more neurotic purpose (i.e., to gain from the therapist what she wanted but was unable to get from significant people in her past).

Because an examination of the vicissitudes of the therapist-patient relationship was so basic to the analysis, analysts were initially quite concerned about how the introduction of the group parameter would affect transference. Wouldn't the fact that group members continually interrupt one another, and that each of them develops her own particular form of intense transference to the analyst, make it impossible for the latter to systematically follow the subtle evolution of transference in any one patient? After all, one of the reasons why an analyst treating an analysand in individual therapy was able to follow her transference pattern so closely was the sheer amount of time provided for the patient to verbalize without interruption. And wouldn't the presence of so many fellow patients prevent a patient's transference from reaching a point of maximum intensity?

The group situation did indeed alter considerably the original psychoanalytic situation. However, initial experiments with the group method reassured early practitioners of analytic group therapy as to the continued usefulness and applicability of the transference concept. One reason is that in the present model a period of individual therapy almost invariably precedes a patient's placement in the analytic therapy group. As a result, she already will have had a period of time in which to develop a reasonably intense transference to the therapist. To be sure, there was always the chance that once in the presence of others in the group, the patient's transference to the analyst would become somewhat diluted, but this proved to be less frequent than had been anticipated. Besides, if a patient's placement in a group prevented her transference from becoming a full-fledged transference neurosis or transference resistance, this might prove all to the good, since this kind of transference, whether occurring in the context of individual or group treatment, often keeps the patient at a point of such intense dependency that further therapeutic progress is undermined (unless expertly and forcibly handled by the analyst). Indeed, according to Wolf and Schwartz (1962), one of the distinct advantages of the group is that the presence of other members may at times render this kind of regression less likely.

Even more exciting, and not quite predicted, was the discovery that *multiple transferences* regularly occurred within the group—distorted perceptions of other group members (as well as of the therapist)—which could now reveal important material about a patient that had been less available when the patient had worked solely within an individual therapy context. Since analysis in the one-to-one situation emphasizes what Wolf and Schwartz refer to as the *authority vector,* the analyst in individual treatment is mainly related to as a parent figure and is rarely viewed as a sibling. The introduction of the group parameter adds a *peer vector* and because the patient's peer relationships in the group often reproduce her earlier relationships with siblings (if she has had them), the analyst can now gain a firmer sense of the patient's relationships with contemporaries, both past and present, and this will in turn give the patient a chance to explore what she once experienced, and now experiences, in such relationships.

In addition to the peer vector, certain *parent vector* transferences emerged in group treatment that had been difficult to elicit in individual treatment. For example, once a male therapist is experienced as a father by a male patient— let's call him Jeff—it usually becomes harder for Jeff to then develop toward the therapist the kind of feelings and relationship that he had had with his mother. Yet such a shift—from experiencing therapist as father, to experiencing him as mother—is needed for a more complete analysis in which the analyst is able to gain an understanding of all developmental vectors. In this case, the introduction of Jeff to group therapy may provide a solution—once in the group, Jeff finds himself experiencing a strongly transferential reaction to an older woman who reminds him of his mother. It is because of the multiplicity of distinctive personalities present in the group, on whom he can now project various images of the significant people from his past, that any one patient's transference material will usually be more clearly elucidated in group therapy than in individual therapy (Agazarian & Peters, 1981).

Equally surprising for analysts who had begun to do group therapy was the discovery that the introduction of peer figures *did* sometimes lead to a change in the nature of the patient's transference relationship to the analyst, such that, for example, one might note a shift from the patient's-experiencing-analyst-as-father to patient's-experiencing-analyst-as-mother. Just such a transition occurred in the case of Helen (see Wolf & Schwartz, 1962, pp. 33–34). In individual treatment previous to the group, Helen had displayed mildly erotic feelings, combined with some fearfulness, toward the analyst; this essentially duplicated what she had felt toward her father as a child. Then, in an early session of her group treatment, Helen heard the analyst praise George, another patient, for his perceptive reactions to her. Upon hearing this, she sensed George as "preferred," primarily because of his more powerful intellect, and she reacted with both jealousy and hostility. Gradually the therapist understood that he had become mother for her at the point when he complimented George, while the latter suddenly stood for the brother whom she perceived as having defeated her in a bitter competition for their mother's esteem. In her mind George had been successful for two reasons: his greater intelligence and his maleness. The analyst now had a deeper insight into Helen's phallic strivings and her excessive admiration for intellectual accomplishment. It seemed that it had been necessary to introduce a *triadic* element into the analytic situation for her mother transference (still to the authority-analyst, rather than to a participant-peer) to emerge.

The recognition and clarification of transference distortions, especially at the moment of their occurrence, can constitute an important step toward change. The insights that develop in the patient can have a dramatic immediacy in the group setting that they lack in individual treatment because the group members, when they are distortedly perceived by a patient, or treated by her in pathological ways, are usually much more emotionally reactive than is the analyst when he is misperceived in individual treatment. For example, if a woman patient reacts with anger or with hurt at being inappropriately cast in the role of the "bad mother" by a male patient, her immediate sense of injury may prod him into a more intense examination of his perception's validity (and his subsequent concern as to where and how he acquired this perception) than would the more detached reaction of his analyst, whom he cannot come to know in as real a way as he can this other group member.

**Countertransference.**    Here the focus of concern is the *analyst's* emotional state; countertransference traditionally refers to the feelings stimulated in him by the intense transference-projections and fantasies of his patients. For example, if a patient spews out intense, venomous rage toward the therapist, it would be a rare therapist who did not feel *some degree* of resultant irritation or discomfort. It is important that he recognize and understand these feelings, for without such awareness they can often lead to boredom, inattentiveness, or substantial bias toward the patient, such as subtle contempt or an excessive amount of sympathy—both of which will interfere with his maintaining the undistracted, consistently empathic attitude that he should have toward her, as well as toward each of the other group members.

While countertransference is bound to be a potent variable in individual psychoanalysis, group psychoanalysis can only compound its emotional intensity, since the analyst is now confronted with many patients. Not only does this mean one transference multiplied by seven or eight, but it also means the possibility of alliances wherein normally timid patients can use their combined strength, or the presence of an unusually aggressive fellow member, to launch collective attacks against the analyst.

Is this intensification of stimuli for countertransference responses an asset or a liability? Certainly it creates more emotional stress for the therapist. Durkin (1964) sees in this, however, a potential asset: The analyst, confronted by the sheer "weight of numbers" in the group, is forced to confront the fact that some of the negative traits and attitudes that the patients detect in him are actually there, whereas in individual therapy he can more easily discard unflattering perceptions as distorted holdovers from the patient's troubled past. If the therapist can find a way of relinquishing his needs for perfection or omnipotence, these sometimes valid perceptions of himself offered by a group can help him to engage in a more realistic appraisal of his strengths and weaknesses, an appraisal that is bound to eventually benefit his work. Starting in the 1960s and early 1970s, other theoreticians (see Spotnitz, 1985; Epstein & Feiner, 1979; Schafer, 1983), *in addition to Durkin,* began to suggest that the therapist's countertransference could have other beneficial effects, provided that he (1) is aware of them and (2) uses them to further his understanding of the patient. For example, feelings of irritation that well up within him may help him to suddenly see that a female patient has been subtly derogating him, and this insight might then enable both therapist and patient to better comprehend how her unconscious needling of her boss has brought him to the point of seriously considering firing her. (Further analytic work may of course need to be done before the patient can understand the childhood antecedents of her derogating behavior.)

Along with tending to stimulate a greater *amount* of countertransference in the therapist, the shift from individual to group psychoanalytic therapy can produce a wholly unique *kind* of countertransference in the therapist—one that responds to the group-as-a-whole (or to a subgroup), rather than to a particular person (Flapan & Fenchel, 1984). For example, a leader may experience the group as his family, whether it be a loving or hating family, and when he senses the overall group's attitude toward himself as critical or negative, he may unwittingly become distant from, placating toward, or controlling of the group. Again, his awareness is all; so long has he begins to sense these irrationalities within himself, he should be able to apply appropriate correctives to his own behavior.

**Acting Out.**    *Acting out* is a term that has sometimes been broadened beyond its original, more technical meaning to a point where it is equated with engaging in any kind of socially taboo behavior. However, its more restricted and clinical meaning refers to sexual and/or aggressive behavior engaged in by a patient in individual or group therapy that helps the latter to forestall a more painful and direct examination of her problematic feelings and behaviors, along with their earlier origins in childhood. Acting out usually occurs as a response to transference feelings and constitutes a resistance to insight and change (Wolf & Schwartz, 1962). For example, a patient begins to transfer the castration fears he felt in relation to his father to his analyst; rather than face these fears, he becomes sexually promiscuous as a kind of counterphobic bravado, as if to "dare" the analyst to punish him just as he had done with his father in childhood. The sexual activity, which is tension relieving at least for the moment, helps him to avoid the anxiety that would accompany a more direct facing of his problem.

It is usually pointed out that group psychoanalysis increases the patient's opportunities for acting out within the session, for whereas individual analysis virtually immobilizes the patient (she is supposed to lie on the couch and put everything into words, to a point where even her getting up from the couch might be labeled as acting out), group members might chew gum, smoke, occasionally touch, and generally engage in a whole range of "acting out" behaviors designed to relieve conscious and unconscious anxieties. Even in groups where such behaviors are explicitly proscribed by the therapist, patients will probably be able to test these limits to a greater degree, to engage in quasi–acting out behaviors (such as laughing and not paying attention), and to overtly defy the analyst (e.g., socializing outside the group when he has established the rule that they not do so). How the present model attempts to control and restrict acting out will be presented later (see "Limits," p. 57).

**Interpretation.**    Until now we have referred to the analyst's "dealing with" or "handling" various resistances and transferences. The way that he most often deals with them is through interpretations, which are directed toward "helping something unconscious to become conscious by naming it at the moment it is striving to break through" (Fenichel, 1945, p. 25). The psychoanalytic literature has placed great emphasis on the correct *timing* of interpretations. As Fenichel's definition implies, they should be made at a point where the phenomenon to be interpreted is at the center of the patient's attention and close to her conscious awareness. Analytic theory indicates that the most potent interpretations connect a dynamic aspect of the present transference relationship to a remembered childhood situation.

Three very general rules that hold for conducting psychoanalysis, whether group or individual, are: (1) Interpret a treatment-interfering resistance before interpreting a character resistance; (2) interpret a resistance or defense before interpreting the emotion or conflict underlying the resistance or defense (point out, for instance, how the patient's compulsivity serves to bind and contain her anxiety before beginning to discuss the suppressed anger creating her anxiety; and (3) interpret the derivative (or displaced aspect) of a feeling before interpreting the more basic feeling—point to a patient's sense that she received little *attention* from her mother before pointing out her feeling that she never really received love from her.

These rules do not require any major modification in the group setting. However, one dimension that does arise in the group is that the analyst should try to interpret group-level resistances before tackling the character and particularized resistances of individual members (Fenchel & Flapan, 1985). For instance, if at the beginning of a group session, a few members are silent while the remainder of the group discusses a news event of immediate interest, the therapist would probably do best to throw out a question that is addressed to the entire membership: What is the group getting out of the current discussion? And what is the group avoiding?

Finally, recent emphases in psychoanalysis (in particular the contributions of Heinz Kohut and his school of "self-psychology"; see Kohut, 1984) underscore the value of a consistently empathic—as opposed to confronting—approach to a patient's resistances and defenses. The analyst is reminded that the person's character resistances, while seemingly not in the interest of her making maximum use of treatment, initially served an adaptive function in childhood (helping to keep her anxiety in check and frequently enabling her to receive approval from a somewhat neurotic environment) and may even be in the interest of her smooth adaptation to her current adult life (e.g., witness the research scientist's meticulous attention to detail or the energetic, almost manic style of the high-pressure salesperson). Fenchel and Flapan (1985) point out that this kind of respectful approach to the patient's resistance is especially valuable in group therapy, where the patient is often, because of the presence of so many other people (some of them abrasive), under more stress than in individual therapy. "More often than not, character resistances in particular serve to anchor the individual's identity and an attack on them by an interpretation only increases opposition" (Fenchel & Flapan, 1985, p. 35). Hence it is occasionally advisable for the group therapist to wait a long time before interpreting particular resistances, defenses, and transferences. At times change may occur *without* interpretation; time, and the constructive interventions of the patient's fellow participants, plus changes in her outside life that have flowed from her initial improvement (which often occurs early in group therapy and can in turn lead to a further amelioration of neurosis), may prove sufficient.

**Working Through.** This is a key concept in the psychoanalytic theory of cure and can be defined as "the translation of understanding and insight into change" (Caligor et al., 1984, p. 105). Working through thus entails the taking in of many interpretations over time and their cumulative effects on the patient, as she has the opportunity to see the manifold ways in which some of her core conflicts and key defenses emerge again and again—in dreams, in remembrances, in day-to-day problems, and in the fluctuations of her transference resistance. It is as if she is seeing old problems in ever-new clothing, and fresh connections become evident. For example, if the primary psychodynamic focus is on an Oedipal problem, the patient will have a chance to see how this affects his relations to both men and women, superiors and subordinates, and the areas of both competition and affection in his life. No one interpretation dissolves a resistance forever; therefore, resistances, despite newly gained insights, will reappear in different guises and at different characterological levels.

Hence working through requires a fairly long period of time, especially since one of its primary dimensions is a transference relationship that takes a while to build in intensity and then takes further time to dissolve. The application of psychoanalytic method to a group setting does not substantially alter this working through process. However, because of the complexity created by each patient's reactions to both the analyst and other group members, the emergence of the transference becomes more complex and more difficult for the analyst to follow.

## KEY CONCEPTS:  METHODOLOGICAL

**Group Composition.**   The great majority of psychoanalytic group therapists prefer heterogeneous to homogeneous groups. Wolf and Schwartz (1962) suggest several reasons for this preference. A heterogeneous group (1) is a microcosm of the real world, and it is adaptation to the world *as it is* that constitutes the main goal of treatment: The patient must learn to deal in real life with the level of disagreement and pluralism that she will encounter in her therapy group; (2) is less likely to encourage conformity to a uniform standard; (3) offers a greater opportunity than a homogeneous group for multiple transferences on the part of any one group member (for example, the patient may identify a youthful man in the group as her younger brother, an older woman as her aunt, and so on); (4) offers a necessary range of varying characterological styles and defenses (e.g., the talkative patient will be balanced by the listening patient, and the impulsive patient by one who is detached and cerebral). Faced with these obvious differences in group members, each patient begins to have strong reactions to other patients and to see in them some behavioral styles that she would like to adopt, and emulate, for herself.

With regard to the issue of group size, it is generally agreed that the ideal group will comprise between six and nine members. As Whitaker (1985) points out, a group of less than six people usually fails to provide the amount and complexity of interaction needed if the group is to be helpful, whereas a group of ten or more people will more often than not tend to divide into two subgroups, one with active members and the other with relatively passive members who serve as an audience to the first subgroup. Another expert on analytic group therapy, Saul Scheidlinger,[1] gives eight as the "magic number" of participants in the ideally functioning group; eight is less than the potentially troublesome group of ten or more members envisaged by Whitaker, while it at the same time provides a sufficient number of members should one or two of these eight be absent for any particular meeting.

**The Alternate Session.** The alternate session allows participants to meet as a group without the therapist, and it is less frequently practiced and written about than when first advocated by Wolf and Schwartz in 1962. We write about it now, because (1) it can be a useful adjunct to group therapy and (2) it brings to the fore key issues around transference, acting out, and limits (see below).

Standard sessions, with the therapist present, expose the patient to the simultaneity of both an authority vector and a peer vector, and the alternate session, to the peer vector alone. Some participants thereby find themselves more able to talk in the alternate session (where they are no longer inhibited by a fear of the therapist's disapproval), whereas others feel safer in the regular session (where they experience the therapist as a protector). Without an alternate session, there would be no opportunity for such emotional and behavioral contrasts to manifest themselves, hence no opportunity for the patient to become aware of them. In a similar way, negative transference toward the therapist may be expressed in the alternate session, though hidden in the standard session. In other words, a shy patient may be able to talk about her anger toward the therapist only when the latter is absent. However long the patient may wait before bringing this material into a regular session, it will be an important first step in alerting the other members to what she is feeling; they in turn, if they are a well-functioning group, will immediately encourage her to express all of her transference feelings directly to the analyst.

The alternate session can be perceived as a half-way house between the "inner sanctum" of the regular session and the patient's everyday, real-life world. Patients visit one another's homes (which is where the alternate session is customarily held), with the result that they become less anonymous for one another, and, as they take responsibility for the session in the absence of the parent-analyst, they often experience themselves in a more autonomous and adult fashion.

**Limits.** The Wolf and Schwartz model is consistent with the earlier Freudian model of psychoanalysis in emphasizing that limits are essential in treatment (and this includes group treatment), just as they are in life in general. Psychoanalysis has always stressed that frustration is inevitable in life and that maturity entails the ability to withstand it. Limits are immediately inherent in

[1] Personal communication

the group situation when it becomes apparent to the members that sessions will not continue beyond a set time limit, that the group does not accept any new members beyond a certain maximum number, and that physical aggression is not permitted.

An immediate practical concern for the group therapist is the degree to which he will specifically prohibit sexual acting out among group members. Wolf and Schwartz recommend that he take a neutral position on this question, rather than expressly forbid sexual relationships in the group. If the therapist makes a specific prohibition he is duplicating the original position of the parents in forbidding incest, thereby transforming what should be an illusion based on transference (i.e., the therapist as parent) into a reality. Furthermore, he puts himself into an untenable position, for he is proscribing what he cannot enforce. Should the prohibition be made and a patient violate it, she will be successfully flouting the leader's authority at the same time that she will be strongly tempted to conceal her transgression from the group. In subsequent theorizing and writing, Agazarian and Peters (1981) take a quite similar position: Since sexual liaisons need not have a destructive effect on either the direct participants or the group-as-a-whole (so long as they are acknowledged and discussed), the only meaningful taboo is on outside contacts between and among members *that are not later analyzed in the group.*

On the other hand, Agazarian and Peters are not against all limits on either sexual contact among members or on socializing outside the group. What they do is to leave it to the members themselves to decide on whether or not to establish such limits. They believe that this kind of decision making (1) increases the autonomy and maturity of the group (and thereby its therapeutic efficacy), (2) reduces the probability of members' flouting such limits (i.e., acting out), and (3) increases the likelihood that, should acting out occur, its unconscious meaning (both for the actors and the group-at-large) will eventually be brought out and worked through.

**Combined Treatment.**    Combined treatment refers to a situation in which a group patient is simultaneously seen in both group and individual treatment, either having the same therapist for both (which is the more usual), or different therapists. It will have been preceded by a fairly lengthy period of individual therapy, which later serves as a needed preparatory phase for the group (once it has been determined by the therapist that group therapy will probably prove to be a desirable adjunct to the patient's analysis). Combined treatment has become the preferred mode of treatment for most analytically oriented group therapists, their rationale being that individual treatment provides additional time in which a patient can further pursue, with greater intensity and with more emphasis on his or her childhood roots, the complex emotional problems stimulated and expressed in group. Individual treatment also provides an opportunity to initially air intimate material that will eventually be discussed in group, but that is at first too shame-laden to be comfortably shared with more than one other person (Caligor et al., 1984; Rutan & Stone, 1984).

Wolf and Schwartz (1962) provide another, less popular point of view that sees a patient's continuation of individual therapy, after she has begun a group, as a serious dilution of the true potential value of the group. According to them, group therapy is a valid and unique treatment in its own right; too often the analyst seeing a patient in combined treatment regards one as supplementary to the other, with the group usually being viewed as supplemental, and the individual sessions as the core of treatment. In such a situation, the patient may use the individual hour to express feelings about group members that properly belong in the group, and she may similarly use the individual hour to present intense transference material regarding the therapist that she feels too self-conscious to share with him in the presence of the group. Limiting the patient to group treatment will force her to come to terms with the therapist in the company of her peers.

Wolf and Schwartz can see having individual sessions with a patient on a limited basis—to support her during moments of crisis or to see her during an interval in which she feels she must drop out of the group. They also see individual therapy as preparatory for group treatment; indeed, the great majority of their own group patients have had prior individual analysis, some of them for a period of several years.

**Co-Therapy.** Until the mid-1960s, one heard little about the advantages of having two formal leaders in the group, as opposed to one. However, since that time a number of practitioners have cited the usefulness of what is now called *co-therapy* (Agazarian & Peters, 1981; Rutan & Stone, 1984) or *co-leadership* (Whitaker, 1985). Naturally, a therapy group need not be psychoanalytically oriented in order to be led by two therapists; however, it is psychoanalytic group practitioners who have most systematically explored all the complex emotional issues that co-conducting involves, for both the leaders themselves and their patients.

The advantages of co-therapy are usually considered to be the following: (1) It is better to have two points of view than one point of view when it comes to understanding the psychodynamics of any particular patient—blind spots and misjudgments can be corrected; (2) transference issues emerge in a more clear-cut form, for instead of one group therapist's having to represent both mother and father for the patient, transferences can now be split, with one therapist consistently representing mother, and the second one, father; if one co-therapist is female, and the other, male, this kind of separating out of transference material will occur even more readily; (3) there need be fewer interruptions to treatment, since one therapist can be sick or go on vacation without meetings having to be temporarily suspended; (4) patients who during childhood had no opportunity to witness a genuinely collaborative, honest, and rewarding relationship between two adults will be provided a potent model of just such a relationship since most co-therapy models encourage the co-leaders to openly air, without undue aggressiveness, their occasional disagreements before the group; and (5) each therapist can provide an important balancing function for the other—the leader who is attacked by the group can receive necessary emotional support and clarifying understanding from his co-therapist; similarly, the leader who is overly idealized by the group and who therefore begins to overlook his own errors (or even forget that he can make them) will at times miss things that his less emotionally blinded colleague can catch and point out. In general, then, this last point refers to the help that each therapist can provide the other in clarifying significant countertransference issues and in actively intervening at those moments when the other is feeling lost or overwhelmed.

Naturally, all these advantages depend on two therapists who work well together, who are mature enough to share the spotlight with another authority figure, and who are able to comfortably accept criticism from a respected colleague. The moment such collaboration threatens to degenerate into competitiveness or disruptive conflict, the co-therapy relationship has ceased to be advantageous for either the leaders or the group (Agazarian & Peters, 1981; Whitaker, 1985).

## SPECIAL USES OF THE GROUP

Because psychoanalysis in groups involved the first deliberate extension of a model initially created for the purpose of treating a single person, a brief review of what group analysts originally saw (and still see) as the unique advantage of the group parameter is in order. The group helps the patient:

1. To perceive that she is not isolated and alone in having problems; that some others have difficulties remarkably similar to her own; and that still others, although not necessarily sharing her specific problems, have yet other difficulties in living

2. To learn that some of these other people are able to reveal their problems openly and that, in so doing, they gain a measure of relief for these problems; their example emboldens the patient to make similar confidences; apart from the specific help that she may eventually obtain for the concrete problems revealed, the very act of self-disclosing will usually help her to feel better about herself and about being alive (Jourard, 1971)

3. To discover in herself resources for listening to and understanding others that she had not suspected were there; this can be an important source of increased self-esteem

4. To reexperience her early family relationships, but this time in a setting that is conducive to a more favorable outcome

5. To demonstrate to the analyst in a much more direct way than is possible in individual therapy a living example of her usual style of social and interpersonal relating, including the things she does that provoke in others reactions that she then finds problematic or discomforting

6. To experience in a more vivid way her distorted transference perceptions of the therapist, since many of the group members will see the therapist in a different light; in a similar vein, to experience the indiscriminateness of her transferential reactions to one or more fellow group members, since the latter may well be perceived by other participants quite differently

7. To experience, via transferences to fellow patients, early significant relationships that cannot be transferred to the therapist because of many of the latter's objective characteristics—age, sex, physical appearance, personality, and so forth

8. To gain more direct feedback as to the ways in which another person experiences her characterological styles and defenses than is usually possible, either in normal social life or in individual therapy

9. To observe that it is safe and acceptable to express intense anger, even toward the therapist, since if she is timid in this regard she will have the living example of others to spur her on

10. To observe certain kinds of appropriate and attractive behaviors in others that she then decides to imitate or emulate; for some patients, the opportunity to see such behaviors actively demonstrated and to be witness to their visible effectiveness within the group will be a far more dramatic stimulus to adopting them than would be hearing them described or recommended (Agazarian & Peters, 1981)

11. To have a chance to practice newly acquired behaviors in a genuinely social, albeit unusually supportive and protected, environment

12. To have the chance to continue in some form of psychotherapy, should she no longer be able to afford either individual or combined treatment (patients are typically charged less for group treatment than for individual; see Agazarian & Peters, 1981)

13. To wean herself away from the kind of prolonged, excessively self-searching and increasingly dependent relationship to the analyst that can occur in individual therapy; this process occurs by interposing the reality of

other people, who ideally force their way into what might otherwise become a patient-therapist symbiosis.

## ROLE OF THE LEADER

Let us look first at some general principles describing the functions of the group leader within the present model and then consider in more detail how some of these principles are put into effect in the daily life of a psychoanalytic group. The analytic group therapist: (1) sets limits, (2) facilitates the group interaction by helping to establish an atmosphere that is open and accepting, (3) offers support to an individual when she is in need of it and not getting it from the group, (4) is alert to manifestations of resistance and transference in the various participants, as well as to significant countertransference reactions within himself, (5) points out resistance and transference to the patient when the latter is at a point of sufficient awareness to accept and integrate such an intervention, and (6) interprets, at an appropriate time, some of the meanings of these various resistances and transferences, including, if possible, their relationship to crucial childhood events and patterns. Since the criterion for the timing of an interpretation is the patient's ability to accept and truly understand it, considerable exploration must already have occurred before the group analyst is able to make a definitive interpretation and before the patient is able to acknowledge its validity.

One general aspect of the analyst's style of relating to the group, particularly in its early life, involves his abdication of formal leadership. In the absence of his willingness to actively direct the group discussion in any way, or to answer questions concerning the meaning of particular behaviors or the advisability of certain actions, responsibility for how the group will actually proceed to interact is left to its members. More and more they will begin to interact spontaneously, to take responsibility for what occurs in a session, and to eventually become auxiliary therapists as they begin to point out significant motivations and resistances in one another. An illustration of this in our sample session was when Mort pointed out to Felicia that she is much more comfortable in describing herself as frightened than as angry. Wolf and Schwartz (1962), as well as later theorists (e.g., see Yalom, 1985), place considerable emphasis on the specific therapeutic benefit that this behavior has for the patient *offering* such help, since she is able to sense a capacity for resourcefulness, sensitivity, and caring in herself that she had not suspected was there; she also begins to appreciate the transferential dimension in her earlier conviction that only the leader can be a source of therapy in the group.

The group's gradual assumption of responsibility for the session enables the leader to be relatively passive, at least for large segments of time, while he directs his attention to subtle aspects of the patients' statements and interactions. Often this is in the form of questioning: What does this mean to you?

What about this disturbs you so much? While not able to have the same kind of anonymity in the group that he can have in individual treatment, he still is relatively reserved in stating his own immediate feelings about particular members or specific interactions. (If strong feelings of this kind do develop within him, he regards them as constituting countertransference, which will indicate to him that some of his own neurotic difficulties are starting to interfere with his effectiveness.) Hence, Dr. M. in our illustration did not directly react to Mort's attempt to bait him, and when Felicia expressed feelings about his remaining silent in the face of Mort's provocations, he kept the focus on Felicia rather than on himself—that is, he refused to become involved in the *reality* of why he was silent or what he felt, but instead viewed her reaction as a projection of some inner dynamic within herself.

Other characteristic interventions of the analyst in the illustration were the following: (1) Early in the session, he asks Felicia what pleases her about Ruth's "speaking up"; he is focusing on her apparent need to function as an auxiliary therapist. She will comment in a helpful way on what is happening, but not in a mode that reveals the *emotions* in her that have been stimulated by the proceedings. This can be seen as a type of character resistance, and the therapist tries to pinpoint it by observing that he rarely hears Felicia ask for something for herself. (2) Later in the session he tries to get Ruth to see the relationship between the way she deals with Mort in the group and with Bob in her personal life; Ruth is focused on the overt problem with Bob, failing to see that her here-and-now tolerance of Mort's sadism constitutes but another instance of her character pathology. The therapist tries to clarfy Ruth's difficulty in experiencing her anger; as he points out, she prefers blaming herself to striking out at Mort. (3) He encourages Ruth to relate her masochistic way of handling anger to her past by asking her how far back in her life this pattern extends. (4) He confronts Mort's highly indirect way of expressing feelings, but when Mort continues to be provocative, the therapist does not reveal whatever irritation or disappointment he himself might be feeling. (5) At the end of the illustration he states, via an interpretive intervention, his impression that Mort attempts to use counterphobic sadism and attacking behavior as a means of masking his anxiety; this constitutes a situation where the analyst sees anger as a *resistance* to other, less conscious feelings, like fearfulness and despair.

Hence the leader, albeit at times active, is not quite a full-fledged member of the group. While emphasizing the importance of stating one's feelings, he does not express many of his own. His clarifications and interpretations arrive slowly and bit by bit (hence his belief that working through takes time, and his hope that patients will remain in the group and not leave prematurely). With Felicia, Ruth, and Mort he strove to make just one point or one connection. Further clarifications, enlarging on the significance of what he has already pointed out and on its possible relationship to childhood events, remain for future sessions.

# CHAPTER FOUR
# THE GROUP-DYNAMIC THERAPY GROUP

The group-dynamic approach to group psychotherapy is actually a cluster of models, since its major proponents—Whitaker and Lieberman (two Americans who collaborated on the model that we present in this chapter) and Foulkes and Ezriel (each a British psychoanalyst who developed his own distinctive group-dynamics model)—have developed somewhat differing versions of it. Despite these variations, however, these three models have much in common. They are psychoanalytic in their approach to the person in that they emphasize the role of psychosexual stages and of the unconscious in the development of his psychopathology; yet they propose that the psychoanalytic approach to group treatment, in retaining the individual patient as the primary focus of conceptualization, becomes seriously limited in its ability to deal with group processes. As Foulkes put it, "group psychology must develop its own concepts in its own right and not borrow them from individual psychology" (1965, p. 60). According to these group dynamicists an appreciation of social psychology, wherein the group-as-a-whole is regarded as a discrete entity, should be added to the group psychotherapist's store of knowledge.

An English theorist with a similar approach is Bion (1959), whose interest in groups originally developed within the context of psychotherapy, but whose most significant contribution was to be a general theory of small-group processes. Bion was also to create a "small-study," or training, group directed toward helping relatively healthy people become more aware of group dynamics and more adept in handling intraorganizational relations. Bion's small-study group was eventually to become the central component of the Tavistock model, which we survey in Chapter 9.

These group dynamicists—Foulkes, Ezriel, Whitaker, Lieberman, and Bion—whether formally drawing on him or not, owed something to Kurt Lewin and his field-theory approach to understanding the group-as-a-whole (see Chapter 1). A brief review of Lewin's field theory, and of its gestalt psychology background, is therefore in order (Lewin, 1952; Marrow, 1958). This material will also be relevant to an understanding of the gestalt therapy and T-group models (Chapters 7 and 10).

The founders of the gestalt school of psychology, Kohler (1969), Koffka (1935), and Wertheimer (1959), were primarily concerned with developing a theory of fundamental psychological processes, with particular attention to perception. However, their conceptual approach had a strong influence on theoretical developments in the fields of motivation, personality, and social psychology. One such development involved the motivational concepts of Kurt Goldstein (1948), which made a substantial contribution to the "organismic" school of personality theory (Hall & Lindzey, 1978); another was Lewin's field theory, which eventuated in a theory of both personality and group dynamics (1952).

Gestalt psychology originated in Germany in the late 1920s and took issue with the points of view embodied in structuralism and associationism, which until that time had been the dominant schools within academic psychology. Both associationism and structuralism emphasized a "molecular," as opposed to "molar," conception of perception in that they viewed the basic perceptual act as occurring in terms of fundamentally discrete units or elements, which the perceiver then combined—via the effects of learning and of higher mental processes—to form recognizable patterns and configurations. For example, according to structuralism, a table was initially seen in terms of a rectangular plane juxtaposed to four cyclinders; it was only through past experience and learning that these five distinct "elements" were seen as fundamentally related properties of a single functional whole. Indeed, even the rectangular tabletop itself was not necessarily seen as a complete unit, but instead was initially perceived as many discrete bits of sensation that, through past associations to one another and to a functional use, began to be organized as a plane.

The gestalt psychologists, on the other hand, took a "molar" position—they insisted that pattern and organization inhered in perception from the very first, rather than emerging as a secondary or subsequent phenomenon. Stating the well-known principle that "the whole is greater than the sum of its parts," and designing some ingenious visual patterns to illustrate it, they attempted to show that incomplete configurations tend to be seen as complete by the perceiver and that the appearance of an individual element (or, in the language of gestalt psychology, a "figure") can be totally altered by the larger design (or "ground") in which it is embedded. An example of this phenomenon is the popular puzzle found in children's magazines, in which the child is asked to find a hidden figure or person in a large and complex picture. According to the gestaltists, then, the interrelationships among the various components within a visual field have a greater effect on perception than do the individual components themselves.

Lewin's field theory visualized both personality and group processes as patterned "fields" or configurations wherein each element (e.g., in the personality, a need or drive; in the group, an individual) could not be meaningfully viewed in isolation but instead had to be related to every other element within the field. This involved a rather direct application of gestalt perceptual psychology to more complex personality and social phenomena. While Lewin's personality theory did not play an especially formative role within modern personality psychology, his approach to groups enjoys, in many respects, a keystone position in group-dynamic theory. In general, the Lewinian approach to groups places less emphasis than does the psychoanalytic model on what a participant's behavior expresses about his own past, and much more emphasis on how it is a function of whatever tensions predominate within the group at any one point in time. These tensions in turn are influenced by all the significant interrelationships within the group.

Of course the psychoanalytic model of group interaction also gave attention to the effects that members have upon one another, primarily via the concept of multiple transference (see Chapter 3). What the group-dynamics therapist argued is that the group psychoanalyst too often limited his awareness to dyadic and triadic subgroup formations and to what they indicated about each person's history rather than to what any particular interaction revealed about the immediate emotional dynamics of the entire group. As an example, let us take an interaction between Fran and Arthur, in which Fran accuses Arthur of ignoring her by consistently paying more attention to every other person in the group than to her. The group-dynamics therapist has little doubt that Fran's reaction to Arthur has a transferential aspect in that it is in part a function of her past relationships to her father or her brother, and in this sense she is in agreement with the group psychoanalyst. However, she is convinced that she will gain the most therapeutic leverage if she focuses instead on the *group-process* meaning of this dyadic interaction. In attempting to do so, she asks herself the following questions: (1) In what way does the interaction between Fran and Arthur reflect the overall balance of forces within the group at this particular moment? and (2) what does the group either gain or avoid by allowing its tensions and themes to be channeled into this specific two-person interchange?

What the group-dynamics therapist is in effect claiming is that if any significant aspect of the group climate in which Fran accused Arthur were different—for instance, if a new member had not been added the week before—the conflict between them would not have the same content or possibly even take place at all since it is primarily a function of unexpressed tensions within the group-as-a-whole. For instance, a look at what has preceded this interaction reveals that group tensions have been accumulating around the theme of ignoring and being ignored. The group has, since the week before, made persistent attempts to approach its new member, Rick, who has sat tense and withdrawn, responding minimally to its questions. The participants appear to be feeling increasingly helpless and paralyzed in their efforts to come to terms with him. While most of their overt affect has been concentrated on how Rick ignores them, a covert theme expresses anger with the leader for abandoning or ignoring the group at a crucial time of need. It is precisely at this point that Fran accuses Arthur of ignoring her, and the two of them are about to commence a dialogue in which they will attempt to ignore the other patients as they go about exploring the justification of Fran's complaint. For the group dynamicist, then, any concentration on the transferential aspects of Fran's reaction will neglect the major issue. As she saw it, the group context of group therapy transformed the basic psychotherapy situation of the individual patient and his analyst more radically than the psychoanalytic model of group therapy provided for. What was needed, therefore, was a shift from a primarily intrapsychic model of the group to a primarily interactional model.

The one group in which psychoanalysis had shown a distinct interest, from its very beginnings, was the family. However, even here the psychoanalytic model's focus was primarily intrapsychic in that it had tended to confine its attention to the influence that one or two significant people—almost always the parents—had on the developing child. Hence it had remained to a later theorist, like Adler (1927), to formulate a psychology of sibling relationships. Freud had come closest to an interactional focus when he highlighted the three-person system of the Oedipal triangle. Yet even here the main emphasis was more on how each dyadic relationship within this triangle (mother-father, mother-child, and father-child) affected the child's psychodynamics than on the way in which each of these relationships was influenced by, and in turn influenced, the total field of forces within the triangle.

A more total picture of the family would have to leave room for the reciprocal influence that the child has on his parents' marriage. In an interactional framework of this nature, the presence of additional siblings complicates the child-mother-father triangle, and by implication the entire family network, still further. In this conceptual approach the family is viewed as a dynamic configuration in which every member and every relationship make a distinct contribution to whatever degree of equilibrium or disequilibrium characterizes it. This concept has much in common with the theoretical framework of group-dynamics therapy, and it describes the point of view of such "systems" and "communication" theorists as Bateson, Haley, Jackson and Weakland (1956). The group-dynamics therapists have chosen to concentrate their major energies on what Foulkes refers to as "stranger groups" in which patients unknown to one another are treated, while Jackson, Bateson, and Haley have chosen to work mostly in the area of family therapy. Both approaches lie squarely within the framework of what today is known as "general system theory" (Durkin, 1981).

## THE WHITAKER AND LIEBERMAN MODEL

We have opted for Whitaker and Lieberman's approach in choosing a representative group-dynamic model for this chapter because it offers a clearer conceptual structure and more precise guidelines for when and how the leader should intervene than do the other group-dynamic models.

Dorothy Stock Whitaker and Morton A. Lieberman are psychologists who at one time were affiliated with the University of Chicago, originally as graduate students and later as teachers. As social scientists, they have been somewhat more interested in a systematic empirical investigation of the group processes on which their theoretical model rests than have been either Foulkes or Ezriel (see "Methodological Considerations," p. 74). Partly as a result of this, Whitaker and Lieberman offer a carefully articulated framework for conceptualizing group processes, which in their model are analyzed in terms of specific concepts: *focal conflict, theme, group solution,* and *group culture.* Consequently, the group therapist—especially the beginning one—is given unusually concrete guidelines as to both the content and the timing of her interventions that revolve mainly around the axis of "enabling" versus "restrictive solutions" (see "Role of the Leader," p. 75).

The model's authors describe in some detail how focal concerns and themes become elaborated (Whitaker & Lieberman, 1965; Whitaker, 1982, 1985). When Patient A makes a comment, B can pick up on any one of a number of aspects of it. What he responds to is that aspect of A's statement that in some way resonates with him. C does the same in relation to what A and B have said prior to her response. For instance, A may describe the disappointment he experienced at the hands of his father, who never played baseball with him. B also expresses anger toward his father, but he relates the anger to a different facet of the father-son relationship. C's anger is more with her mother; yet she states this symbolically, by talking about the disappointments she experienced in her relationship to her aunt, and some attempts to defuse her rage are apparent in her statement that she feels sorry for this pathetic woman. Hence, while there are idiosyncratic aspects of each one's angry concerns, A, B, and C find themselves coalescing around a single theme involving hostile feelings toward parent and/or authority figures. They have managed to select out what is of common concern to them.

As such motifs generalize to the larger group, there is movement from a shared subgroup concern to a common concern of the entire group. Each member, when faced with the dual track of the private, "there-and-then" preoccupations brought by him into the group, and the "here-and-now" of the group atmosphere and of the overt group discussion, unconsciously interweaves these two strands by expressing those idiosyncratic concerns that are evoked within him by the group session's manifest content. Hence if, in the situation just illustrated, Patient D had come to the session discouraged about his job, A, B, and C's common focus on resentment of authority might well cause him to select, from the several features of his work situation that are dissatisfying to him, those difficulties that revolve around his boss.

Group concerns are normally stated in a disguised fashion. For instance, in the discussion illustrated above, the group's expressed resentment of authority probably reflects a resentment toward the therapist of which the group is not yet aware. Indeed, the patients do not necessarily experience themselves as expressing a shared theme or focus; they may often perceive the group as fragmented, with each participant expressing his own egocentric concerns. The group therapist's skill lies in her ability to ferret out the underlying shared theme, much as the psychoanalyst engaged in individiual treatment attempts to discover an underlying coherence in the analysand's seemingly unrelated free associations.

## KEY CONCEPTS

**The Focal Conflict.** According to this model, all group therapy sessions can be characterized in terms of a single overriding focus or concern; this focus corresponds loosely to what Foulkes often refers to as a theme or shared concern, and to what Ezriel terms the *common group tension*. Whitaker and Lieberman prefer to conceptualize the focus as a conflict between two competing motives, the first termed *disturbing* and the second, *reactive*. Both motives reflect shared concerns of the group members; the disturbing motive is usually conceptualized as a wish, and the reactive motive, a fear. An example cited by Whitaker and Lieberman (1965, pp. 24–32) involved the first meeting of a reorganized inpatient group; we shall refer to this group as Group A. A review of Group A's initial session indicated the gradual emergence of a strong wish on the part of several patients to have a unique and gratifying relationship with the two therapists; equally clear was a motif expressing the fear that such a relationship would invite some sort of retaliation from the therapists.

One might wonder why a particular shared wish must of necessity prove "disturbing" enough to create a counter force. While Whitaker and Lieberman do not answer this question directly, one explanation that is in keeping with their overall point of view derives from the fact that each person in the group has his own aspirations, conflicts, and anxieties. Any unconscious wish that is strongly held by two or more group members and therefore shared by them— whether it is to be singled out by the therapist, to talk about taboo material, to compete sexually, and so forth—is bound to provoke some degree of anxiety and consequent opposition from one or more other group members. Another factor helping to explain why any strongly shared group-wish sets up a counter-balancing group-fear lies in the psychoanalytic conception of personality, wherein all strong wishes (or *cathexes*), because they originate within the instinctual and most repressed part of the individual, invariably set off some sort of defense (or *countercathexis*) that checks or in some way inhibits the wish. Hence, the group member himself is bound to be ambivalent about his strongly felt wishes and for this reason to be almost as ready to abandon or deny them as to gratify them.

**The Group Solution.**    Groups, like individuals, can cope with only certain amounts of tension. Hence a group tries to find some agreed-upon solution for its focal conflict. For example, in the initial meeting of Group A cited above, each patient's effort to establish some sense of uniqueness for himself was consistently blocked, either by challenges from other patients or by what was experienced as the therapists' disapproval. As a result, the members eventually gave up on their attempt to find some partial relief for this disturbing motive and decided instead that they were all fundamentally "alike" in the sense of being essentially friendly people who had some problems, which they were willing to discuss with one another.

For a group solution to be successful, it must (1) be consensually agreed upon, however implicitly, by all its members, and (2) reduce anxiety. An example of how these two criteria operated in a specific instance is seen in another first session cited by Whitaker and Lieberman (1965, pp. 50–57). This inpatient group—let us call it Group B—began with several patients indicating that they would like to reveal their faults to the group (the disturbing motive); also expressed, however, was some fear of the kind of criticism, particularly from other patients, that might follow such self-exposure (the reactive motive). The group was beginning to hit upon a provisional solution wherein a majority of the group was coalescing around the idea that since no one of them was perfect, they should all agree to tolerate one another's shortcomings. This solution was immediately blocked by one patient's insistence that he indeed *was* perfect. Much energy in the group was then directed toward getting the "deviant" patient to change his mind, but he refused to budge. A solution eventually emerged when one patient commented that each of them was a "perfectionist" in the sense of trying to improve himself and this went unchallenged by the deviant. However sophistic and semantically tortured this resolution might appear to be, it seemed to genuinely work as a group solution in that at this point in the discussion tension began to clearly abate; the patients had reached a tentative consensus to the effect that while they constituted a quite superior group in some ways, they could still each hope to gain some personal benefit from the group experience. This solution therefore left room for a further exploration of what some of their individual difficulties might be.

The kind of solution just referred to furnishes an example of what Whitaker and Lieberman term an *enabling solution,* for it helped to relieve the anxiety around the reactive motive—fear of criticism—at the same time that it also paved the way for partial satisfaction of the disturbing motive—the wish to reveal faults. If each patient agreed that he was a perfectionist in the sense of wanting to improve himself in *some* way, a new basis now existed for mentioning those personal areas—however minute or trivial—in which one could conceivably look for change.

Not all solutions are enabling. A *restrictive solution* is one that alleviates the fears involved in a reactive motive without affording any satisfaction of the disturbing motive. It is illustrated by the first session of Group A, in which a wish for each patient to have a unique relationship with the co-therapists (the disturbing motive) was opposed by a fear of retaliation from them (the reactive motive). As we indicated above, any patient's attempt to differentiate himself from the others was successfully countered. For example, a woman who was trying to present herself as an alcoholic was reminded by a second patient that probably each of them had one kind of addiction or another, and to prove his point, he pointed out that Tim—a third patient—obviously had an "addiction" to sleep. And when those patients who had previously been in group treatment showed signs of coalescing as a subgroup around this special status, their stab at claiming uniqueness was inadvertently discouraged by a remark from one of the therapists to the effect that the "new" patients were probably unable to follow their conversation. Therefore the group finally was forced to establish a restrictive solution having the flavor of "We're all basically alike in this group—friendly people with problems that we're willing to discuss"; this constituted a restrictive solution in that the assumption of nonuniqueness altogether thwarted the disturbing motive.

Since groups work best, according to this model, in an atmosphere conducive to enabling solutions—which help members to individualize and reveal themselves—the therapist's intervention just cited (wherein the old members were reminded that they were ignoring the new members) constituted a blunder on her part. Such an error underscores the need for the therapist in this model to always keep in mind the wider implications that each of her remarks will have for the subtle balance between enabling and restrictive solutions (see "Role of the Leader").

Successful solutions—whether restrictive or enabling—end the life of that particular focal conflict to which they constitute a response and pave the way for a new focal conflict to emerge.

**The Group Theme.** A *theme* in the terminology of this model has a rather technical meaning; it refers to a series of focal conflicts that are linked by a similarity in their disturbing motives. For example, if we chart the first four sessions of Group B (Whitaker & Lieberman, 1965, pp. 64–75), we find that the disturbing motive shifted from revealing faults in general, to revealing "bad" impulses, and more specifically—in the fourth session—to revealing angry, hostile impulses and feelings; hence, while there are reasonably clear-cut shifts in focal conflicts as one session follows another (punctuated by various successful solutions), a single theme—the disturbing motive of a wish for self-revelation—connects them. The fifth session was characterized by a highly transitional, anxious, and diffuse quality—it was difficult to specify the nature of its focal conflict—and by the sixth session there were substantial implications that a new theme involving dependent feelings toward the therapist had emerged.

While successful groups can be characterized by a progression of ever-more enabling solutions which permit successively greater amounts of expression on the part of patients (see "The Group Culture" below), the life of even the most successful group is marked by occasional exacerbations of reactive motives, which in turn cause periodic returns to restrictive solutions. Whitaker and Lieberman employ an equilibrium-model for charting these forces; they find that the state of equilibrium at a session's ending has a strongly influential role in what happens in the subsequent session. If a session ends on a note of high anxiety (i.e., with emphasis on the reactive motive), patients are more likely to mobilize their defenses during the interval between sessions, with the result that the following session is characterized by a reduced degree of anxiety and a readiness on the part of the group to institute enabling solutions that successfully cope with the anxiety at the same time that they afford some satisfaction to the disturbing motive. It is as if the group is saying: "O.K., we've suffered enough—let's get down to business so we don't have to keep feeling so afraid." When the session ends emphasizing a disturbing motive—implying that patients have indulged themselves in expressing their dependent, or competitive, or angry, or sexual feelings—they are likely to experience an exacerbation of anxiety between sessions, with a sense of "Should I have gone *that* far?!" In this case, the next session is more likely to stress restrictive solutions in which there is less exposure and more concentration on protection against reactive anxieties.

**The Group Culture.** Whitaker and Lieberman believe that each therapy group gradually establishes its own unique culture, which generally consists of standards defining what is acceptable and unacceptable behavior within the group. A more specific definition, and one that incorporates the model's key concepts, is the following: "The culture of the therapy group is understood to consist of the successful solutions which a group generates to deal with successive focal conflicts" (Whitaker & Lieberman, 1965, p. 96). At any given time, a group's culture consists of whatever solutions are currently operating; since solutions are always being modified, the culture is in a state of constant evolution throughout a group's life.

Some solutions, however, prove to be surprisingly stable. Group B, for instance, was not able to modify the solution it had arrived at in its initial session—namely that all its members were to be viewed as basically alike—until its seventh session. At this time a consensus began to develop to the effect that although the members were *fundamentally* similar, certain surface distinctions did exist among them. This constituted a more enabling solution than the first, since under the umbrella of supposedly "superficial" differences the patients began to allow themselves increased amounts of self-exploration and differentiation. In accounting for this kind of movement in group forces, Whitaker and Lieberman emphasize differences among members as to their varying susceptibilities to either the disturbing or reactive motives. For example, in Group A, where there were both a strong disturbing wish on the part of individual members to have a gratifying unique relationship to the co-therapists and an equally strong reactive fear that such relationships would invite retaliation from the therapists, eventual pressure for enabling solutions permitting more self-expression came from Clifford, who pressed harder than other members in the direction of the disturbing motive, and from Paul, who seemed less affected than others by the reactive motive. Clifford, who found it especially important to claim some sort of uniqueness for himself in the group began to bring out idiosyncratic details about his life, and Paul, who was less afraid of authority figures than some of the other members, indirectly expressed the notion that the punishment that people expect for open self-expression may not always be forthcoming.

Group members typically have to exert much more personal force to influence a solution that has already been established than they do to block an attempted solution before it has been put into effect. For instance, in the example above six sessions had to elapse before the solution that had been initially effected in the group's first session was substantially modified. Hence the model's authors, while cognizant of the role played by personality factors in helping to shape the group's movement, emphasize that the ultimate impact of individual personalities is necessarily influenced, and at times significantly constrained, by the action of specific group-structure variables, particularly the focal-conflict solutions that are in effect at any particular time.

Whitaker and Lieberman (1965, p. 123) cite solutions that typically are encountered early in a group's history: Claim that the friendly feelings that members have about one another don't include sexual ones; find someone who is willing to acknowledge personal difficulties and then aggressively focus on him; talk about hostile and envious feelings only in relation to people outside the group. Hence solutions often impose boundaries on what can or cannot be discussed within the group or dictate which members are permitted to bring up particular topics. Some solutions involve putting pressure on the therapist, as when the group urges her to provide more direction. Certain basic solutions are associated with typical disturbing motives. For example, systematic "turn-taking," wherein group members agree to each become a focus for a certain amount of time (thus precluding a more spontaneous interaction), is frequently a way of defending against competition among the members for "the floor" and also against hostility toward the therapist for not providing more direction. Some solutions by their very nature are less stable than others. A displacement in which one member unconsciously agrees to become a vicarious spokesman for the group by focusing on his own problems will probably be much shorter-lived than will turn-taking, since the latter guarantees each person the floor for at least a while, whereas the former will keep almost all members silent and thereby stimulate competition for the floor; once the members begin to compete the displacement solution is undermined and patients will begin to speak for themselves.

According to Whitaker and Lieberman, therapy groups commonly have an initial formative phase involving a series of critical focal conflicts and themes in which a series of tentative solutions are established and modified. The end of this formative phase, and the beginning of an "extended established" phase typically occurs somewhere between the eighth and twelfth sessions. The ushering in of this second phase is characterized by solutions that successfully deal with fears around criticism and punishment and that afford some degree of gratification for the disturbing motives. At this point the group is beginning to develop a viable culture; members are beginning to feel some sense of comfort, commitment, and hope. The established phase then continues until the group's termination. Two important enabling solutions frequently persist throughout this period. The first involves a basic consensus and confidence within the group as to the therapist's ability to afford a certain minimum of psychological safety, and the second, an assumption of basic similarity among members (an assumption that, as we indicated earlier, can include a tremendous number of supposedly "surface" differences). Restrictive solutions that reemerge from time to time during the established phase typically involve digressions to irrelevant topics, scapegoating, and discussions of purely intellectual issues. Restrictive solutions will always reappear, no matter how successful a group, since under the conditions of enabling solutions patients will engage in considerable amounts of self-exploration that will in turn inevitably lead to periods of anxious pulling-back and regression. Hence the therapist should anticipate occasions when the group may require some sort of restrictive solution as a kind of safety measure or "escape hatch." How she attempts to encourage various enabling and restrictive solutions will be discussed below.

## METHODOLOGICAL CONSIDERATIONS

Because of their emphasis on an empirical verification of their central hypotheses, Whitaker and Lieberman have a somewhat firmer basis for charting the progression of various focal conflicts and themes than is typical in other group-dynamics approaches to psychotherapy. Rather than leaving the specification of the focal conflict to clinical speculation, they have developed a procedure (1965, pp. 37–38) wherein each of two independent raters, working from a verbatim tape, comes to some sort of conclusion regarding what he or she believes the focal conflict in any session to be; the tape is accompanied by a written summary (submitted by a therapist or observer) that includes significant situational features and nonverbal events. The rater includes in a final analysis the steps that he or she went through in arriving at his or her formulation.

The two raters then compare their findings. While agreement is never complete, the results have been somewhat encouraging. Sometimes the intervening steps that each rater went through are similar to each other, while their respective specifications of the focal-conflicts differ; sometimes it is the other way around. For the purposes of Whitaker and Lieberman's research, the two raters argue their respective positions until they come to a common agreement that satisfies both of them. Because of this amount of empirical analysis, generalizations concerning relationships between successive focal conflicts, themes, and group solutions rest on a more solid empirical foundation than is the case with most group models, where the therapist's or leader's formulations concerning processes, patterns, and stages of group development depend on a largely impressionistic and intuitive procedure.

## ROLE OF THE LEADER

Whitaker and Lieberman believe that in order for a therapist to do effective group therapy she must unlearn several of the lessons she has learned in relation to individual therapy. Now her source of therapeutic leverage on the patient no longer lies in the direct therapist-patient interaction, but instead in her ability to influence the group culture. She must be prepared to recognize the fact that she cannot begin to exercise the same degree of control over the therapeutic process in the group that she can in individual treatment, because of the presence of so many other people, and she cannot enjoy the same direct responsiveness to the comments made by an individual patient, whether in the form of questions, clarifications, or interpretations.

However, what she loses in her ability to communicate with patients in the highly individual manner of one-to-one psychotherapy, she makes up for in her ability to guide the forces within the group. According to this model, there are three essential reasons why she is in a uniquely favorable position to alter the subtle balance of group tensions. First, by virtue of the transference attitudes of the group she can relatively quickly, through her reassuring and nonjudgmental manner, reduce some of the more superficial fears of her disapproval, thereby inviting varying degrees of self-revelation. Second, as the leader she has the realistic power to make certain administrative decisions that she knows will increase the group's sense of psychological safety. For example, in a situation cited by Whitaker and Lieberman (1965, pp. 71–73), a therapist in an early session was asked by an inpatient group if it would meet the following week since a World Series baseball game was scheduled for that time. She, knowing that the group was experiencing a high degree of anxiety, informed it that there would be no group session if the game were held. Symbolically she was assuring the participants that she would take their preferences into consideration and that avenues toward occasional psychological withdrawal would not be blocked. Third, the therapist, although empathic, does not participate at the same level of immediacy as do the patients; the intellectual distance that she gains by being able to view the group process as an outsider enables her to understand the group's dynamics in a way that no patient-member can.

The therapist's understanding of the dynamics of the group's culture is especially crucial when she is provided an opportunity for circumventing the institution of restrictive solutions. For example, if a group seems ready to acquiesce to a member's suggestion that they not inquire directly into one another's sex lives, the leader might ask the participants what they believe will be gained by this procedure. Timing here is important because she is in a much better position to block a restrictive solution *before* it is established than afterwards. Despite the general desirability of enabling solutions, it is essential for the leader to remember that there are occasional moments, especially during the formative phase of the group, when anxiety is sufficiently intense for members to need the kind of psychological safety that is afforded by restrictive solutions.

As Whitaker and Lieberman see it, it is the group's unconscious readiness to adjust its level of psychological safety to the combined needs and anxieties of its members that gives it its uniquely curative powers. The patient finds himself increasingly involved in the group as more and more of its focal conflicts, which inevitably involve sexual, angry, and intimate feelings, and their associated dangers, touch on his own unresolved emotions. Although these themes frighten him, some security is provided as consensually arrived at solutions emerge that promise to keep anxiety and conflict within manageable proportions. For example, an adolescent group may implicitly establish that while an exploration of sexual feelings within the group is permitted, discussion of sexual feelings about one's parents is for the time being off-limits. However, without the skilled interventions of the leader, these group forces are not likely to achieve their optimal balance. Her expertise lies in knowing when enabling versus restrictive solutions are called for, and how to facilitate the blocking or adoption of particular solutions at hand.

The fact that the primary direction of the therapist's attention is the group rather than the individual need not mean that she never focuses on a particular patient, for Whitaker and Lieberman point out that one can approach the individual via the group and the group via the individual. For instance, if a leader wants to implicitly challenge a tentative (and restrictive) solution wherein a group has decided to minimize competition, she might encourage a patient to report a dream in the hope that this kind of individual attention will stimulate competitive strivings (here she approaches the group via the individual). On the other hand, a therapist who senses that a timid patient wants to talk about sexual matters but feels inhibited about doing so, might ask the group—assuming that it has not established any prohibition on the discussion of sex—why it has so consistently avoided sexual material during the past few sessions. This way she gives permission for the patient to speak without "putting him on the spot" (here she is approaching an individual via the group).

There may be times that the therapist wants to address herself to a particular patient for the latter's sake. This procedure is permissible so long as she keeps in mind the overall group context and is sure that her individual focusing does not threaten an established group standard (unless, of course, she intentionally wishes to do so). On some occasions the psychological needs of a patient may be so acute that the therapist intentionally interferes with a group's solution, even if it is a potentially constructive one, so as to protect the individual concerned. Whitaker and Lieberman cite an instance where a paranoid man who had willingly held the floor during the previous session was pressured by the group to do so again in the following session (1965, pp. 231–232). The patient probably would have complied out of weakness but was showing signs of considerable disorganization. The therapist asked the group why it preferred to discuss the problem of one particular patient even though he realized that his question would probably forestall a reasonably sound group solution that would have afforded the other members a goodly measure of psychological safety. He was, in a sense, "sacrificing" the interests of the rest of the group in the service of protecting this particular patient, on the grounds that the other members were in a better position than he to deal with their anxiety.

With respect to group composition, Whitaker and Lieberman recommend that group members be reasonably homogeneous in their ability to tolerate anxiety; if not, the group is likely to generate either enabling solutions that stimulate too much anxiety for the highly vulnerable patient or restrictive solutions that do not provide a sufficiently open atmosphere for the intact patient. When it comes to the content of their conflicts and their ways of dealing with tension, group members should not be homogeneous; if they are, they will too readily reach an agreement as to what topics are permissible and what procedures desirable, and these restrictive solutions will go unchallenged.

When it comes to rules governing confidentiality and the permissibility of outside contacts, Whitaker and Lieberman think that it is preferable for a group to be allowed to establish its own standards. A consensually reached agreement is bound to be more effective than a therapist's arbitrary edict, and they find it hard to imagine a group that would establish a standard permitting the violation of confidentiality. Similarly, they believe that outside contact among patients does not usually become a serious problem. Such contact could conceivably emerge as a temporary restrictive solution in an early stage of the group (in that it permits the patients having contact to avoid discussing certain matters in the group), but inevitable shifts in the group's focal conflicts will lead to an eventual modification of these solutions. Like Wolf and Schwartz (1962; see Chapter 3), Whitaker and Lieberman discourage the therapist from having individual sessions with group members, believing that such contacts constitute an evasion of issues that are best explored in the group.

## GROUP-DYNAMIC VERSUS PSYCHOANALYTIC APPROACHES: A CAVEAT

Although acknowledging that group dynamics is a valid field of investigation in its own right and that T-groups can offer a useful means of studying and teaching such dynamics, Wolf and Schwartz (whose version of group psychoanalysis we emphasized in Chapter 3) consistently claimed that using a group-dynamics approach in group therapy constitutes a fundamental misapplication of conceptual frames of reference; for these theorists, the single individual, and his or her unconscious psychodynamics, must always be the primary focus of the group therapist's attention. Indeed, Wolf and Schwartz go on to argue that group-dynamic approaches, by minimizing individual differences and by encouraging tendencies toward mediocrity and conformism, foster a kind of group "mystique" and undermine one of the key goals of any form of psychotherapy—the enchancement of personal autonomy (Wolf & Schwartz, 1962).

We agree with Wolf and Schwartz that the development of subtle collusions and of unexamined norms may at times threaten to encroach upon a participant's autonomy. However, we see this threat as existing in *all* models of group interaction, including the psychoanalytic one, and shall give separate treatment to this problem at a later point (see "Coercion and Manipulation," Chapter 14). What we strongly question is Wolf and Schwartz's assumption that a conceptual approach emphasizing group processes must necessarily coexist with, or lead to, a favoring of the group over the individual in any ultimate, or metaphysical, sense. Indeed, the opposite could be argued, namely that an appreciation of the kinds of social influence processes highlighted by a group-as-a-whole framework renders the group leader *more* wary—not less—of the possible effects, both positive and negative, that a group can have on the individual. A case in point here is Bion who, as a group-dynamics theorist, had a sharp awareness of the regressive and symbiotic forces frequently at work in groups. Obviously no group therapist, whatever his or her theoretical persuasion, can deny the significance of either the individual or the group. If the individual is not important, then why the psychotherapeutic task of the group? And if the group is not important, then why intrude other people into the dyad of the therapist-patient relationship?

Any group event can be conceptualized in terms of either intrapsychic or group-process constructs, and there are fewer and fewer group dynamicists or group psychoanalysts who deny that this is so (Agazarian & Peters, 1981; Schneider, 1982; Scheidlinger, 1984). For example, A's continual domination of the group can be seen in terms of her strong need for omnipotence and whatever light this need sheds on her earlier psychosexual development. Or it can be seen as a reflection of a general concern in the group over who will control and who will be controlled, with A acting out both the group's fear and the group's denial of its fear that it might be annihilated by its leader-therapist. Since A's behavior is a function of both sets of factors, the question of which of the two approaches—individual-dynamics or group-process—eventually results in more effective psychotherapy is an empirical one that can only be answered by the hard data of future research in group psychotherapy. Given the strong commitment that both the psychoanalytic group therapist and the group-as-a-whole therapist have to the validity of their respective approaches, and our own belief—in the absence of definitive evidence—that many different approaches to group therapy work well in the hands of a sensitive and conscientious practitioner, we have little doubt but that both approaches work well with some people some of the time.

To polarize methodological approaches to group psychotherapy in terms of those focused on the group versus those focused on the individual is to introduce a false and essentially misleading dichotomy. The psychoanalytic group therapist who exposes himself to the group-dynamic literature, and who participates in T-groups, probably finds himself becoming increasingly sensitive to such phenomena as group themes, group atmosphere, and group cohesion. Similarly, group-as-a-whole therapists like Foulkes, Whitaker, and Lieberman make it clear that they sometimes find themselves silently conceptualizing the dynamics of an individual's behavior in terms of standard pychoanalytic constructs, and at times they will gear an intervention to a specific individual, and to its likely effect on him, rather than on the overall group process. In fact, Ezriel's group-dynamic approach makes a point of having the therapist indicate, if at all possible, how each patient idiosyncratically contributes to the common group tension (Ezriel, 1973). Therefore, while therapists caught up in this controversy have often felt compelled to identify themselves with one of these approaches over the other, they will probably in actual clinical situations find themselves using various admixtures of both.

# CHAPTER FIVE
# THE EXISTENTIAL-
# EXPERIENTIAL GROUP

Existentialism, although beginning as a formal movement within philosophy, so altered the then-prevalent view of humanity that it was bound to have a critical influence on psychology, psychiatry, psychoanalysis, and the social sciences in general. This it did in the United States, initially through its effect on some psychoanalysts and psychotherapists during the late 1940s and the 1950s and then later through the emergence of an "existential-humanistic" school of psychology that in turn played an important role in the development of the human potential movement in general and the encounter group in particular (see Chapter 11).

Existentialism, which had been foreshadowed in the writings of such nineteenth-century philosophers as Kierkegaard and Nietzsche, reminded the person that beneath the elaborate structure of his or her consensually validated, seemingly knowable, and apparently purposeful world, there remained the palpable, yet indescribable, fact of sheer biological existence; this singular fact (that we "exist") often leads to a felt awareness of "being" that can inspire both terror and awe and that defies succinct verbal articulation. It is this ephemeral quality that accounts for our difficulty in giving words to this existential or ontological level of human experience for, as others have pointed out, our Western languages have many more words for describing and detailing the characteristics of the thing or organism that "is" than it does for elaborating or specifying what we mean when we state that this thing or organism "exists." The kind of phenomenological statements that might begin to approximate existential awareness (though necessarily devoid of their associated emotional content) are: I am; one day I was not; one day I shall once again no longer be.

The philosophy of existentialism, then, cannot be divorced from the situation of the individual person who realizes that her relationship to the world is contingent and finite, and that the world, as experienced by her, will die with her. The more she faces this ultimate aloneness, symbolized by the inevitability of her death, the more she senses that the meaningfulness of life, which might appear to be substantiated by the seemingly purposeful activity ceaselessly taking place around her, can only be confirmed, or refuted, on the most personal and subjective levels. This "decision" as to the meaning of one's life cannot be evaded, since a stance reflecting an ignorance or neglect of the existential problem in itself reflects a kind of intentional act (see Shaffer, 1978), even if it is an action or stance that one takes without full awareness. Hence all of us, born into a universe whose meaning is not manifestly revealed, and given no guidelines indicating what constitutes a legitimate goal of existence (or even a guideline as to whether such a goal or purpose is necessary), find ourselves in an "absurd" situation (Camus, 1955). Yet the fact that no one but ourselves can provide the measure of our life's usefulness, and the possibility that each of us might be able to create his or her own meaning, may be seen as adding elements of dignity and courage to this absurdity.

Experientialism (Mahrer, 1978) played an important role in what gradually became known as *ontology*, or the study of being, for the existentialist's emphasis on the awe that we feel at the simple realization that we are came straight from the data of his or her own conscious experience. In this respect, existentialism was the direct offspring of the modern phenomenological movement in philosophy, which emphasized the importance of paying systematic attention to the precise phenomena of consciousness. Credit for the origination of the phenomenological school is traditionally given to Edmund Husserl (1928), while Husserl was a teacher of Martin Heidegger (1962), who is in turn considered to be the single most influential figure in existential philosophy.

Freudian psychology had developed on a different philosophical basis. It tended to regard conscious experiences as secondary events that were derivative of more fundamental, usually unconscious, complexes and drives. Hence, for the Freudian, the fear of death, made so much of by the existentialists, often represented certain sexual wishes and the defense against them. Just as modern physics approached a physical phenomenon (like a table) in a way that violated the experience of the naive observer (that which appeared to the senses to be a hard plane was actually composed of trillions of subatomic particles in a constant state of motion), the scientific approach to human experience, as it was embodied in psychoanalysis, similarly upset our traditional trust in the primary reality of our own consciousness. Existential phenomenology, on the other hand, strove to give the person back to himself by conceiving him in terms that empathically adhered to his own view of himself and of his relationship to the world. For example, the subjective conviction that most of us have that we have some freedom of choice, despite what we may intellectually know and believe with regard to doctrines of determinism, led the phenomenologist to a belief that we do indeed have some measure of choice, for he refused to endorse a theory that is openly at variance with our fundamental psychological sense of ourselves. It is for this reason that existential-phenomenology eschews a strictly deterministic position.

Existential psychology essentially originated in Switzerland, during the 1930s, through the work of two psychoanalysts, Ludwig Binswanger (1963) and Medard Boss (1963), who had been intimately associated with Heidegger and strongly influenced by his theory of ontology. The phenomenological emphasis in Binswanger and Boss was such that they rejected the usual notions of causality implicit in the predominantly logical-positivistic cast of Western thought and instead saw psychological experience as a "first cause" in its own right. For example, the greedy, incorporative approach to the world seen in a psychotherapy patient whom the Freudian would describe as "oral," was viewed by the existential analyst as a fundamental *dasein* (Binswanger, 1963), or mode of "being-in-the-world" in its own right that did not have to be explained in terms of earlier trauma or prior causes. The greediness constituted the way in which this particular person chose to relate herself to the world and was both a cause and a result; until this mode of experience changed, the world would be perceived by her in terms of food and supplies, and her own self as a void that needed desperately to be filled. This subjective view of herself had elements of a self-fulfilling prophecy; so long as she viewed herself as weak and helpless, she probably felt compelled to establish dependent relations on others and probably sought out people who tended to be dominating. According to the existential school, it was important for the analyst to realize that the world-view of any patient had as much cogency and reality for the latter as did his own world-view for himself, since each of us in attempting to construe the world is constantly in the process of creating his or her own arbitrary meaning. Once the analyst is able to respect the patient's right to choose whatever world-view she wishes, he has more hope of effecting change than does the traditional analyst who, tending to view the patient as an object to be worked on and dealt with, often seemed to believe that the patient could not but change and accept the "correct" view of reality once the right analytic interpretations had been made.

During the 1940s, a few American psychotherapists—among them Whitaker and Malone (1953), and Carl Rogers (1951, 1982)—had already fixed upon a strong experiential approach to treatment, independent of any extensive knowledge of, or specific indebtedness to, European existentialism. Then, in 1958, the publication of *Existence* (which was edited by Rollo May, Ernest Angel, and Henri Ellenberger and which translated three of Binswanger's papers into English) went a long way toward making the ontological approach to psychotherapy intellectually available to a larger number of American practitioners, and May himself was to become one of the major proponents of this approach.

However, few American clinicians seriously and systematically revised their orientation along existential-phenomenological lines, and of those who did, only a small percentage were to develop a particular interest in experiential approaches to *group*, as opposed to individual, treatment. Three people who did specifically address themselves to an existential-experiential approach to group therapy were Thomas Hora (1959), Hugh Mullan (1955), and Milton Berger (1958). At a later point, Rogers began to experiment with an experiential approach to groups (Rogers, 1970), but his work in this area involved encounter groups more than therapy groups (see Chapter 11).

Existential psychoanalysis, as we can see by its very name, saw no need to abandon some of the major concepts of psychoanalysis, particularly those involving unawareness, anxiety, and resistance (although each of these was to some extent redefined, in keeping with shifts in theoretical emphasis). Nor was there necessarily a marked revision of the therapist's techniques (see "Role of the Leader" p. 95), since the existential analyst—whether in individual or group therapy—tended to listen to the spontaneous communications of the patient in order to better grasp their latent meaning. Yet this existential approach, in repudiating Freudian psychology's emphasis on the role of biological drives in human development and in emphasizing instead a cognitive need to give meaning to one's existence, offered a different view of the person's essential life task and of the origins of her psychopathology.

Shifts in attitude that constituted a step away from the orthodox analytic position toward a more existential orientation included the following: (1) a deepened respect for the patient's subjective experiences as constituting valid phenomena in their own right, rather than pale, disguised manifestations of her "real" (unconscious) feelings and thoughts, (2) the belief that the patient's need to give meaning to her life was inextricably linked to her dread of death, and that both these concerns were inherent within the fabric of her being and not necessarily derivative of repressed biological drives, (3) the conviction that a person's unconscious contained within it forces for courage and for creativity, as well as for violence and cruelty, (4) an "I-Thou" conception (Buber, 1958) of the analytic relationship wherein patient and analyst, whatever their respective degrees of expertise and suffering, were more equal than they were unequal since both had to reconcile themselves with the close-to-insurmountable problems of existence (see also Szasz, 1965, 1977), (5) a belief that the analyst's actuality as a person would be a more potent factor for therapy than would be his availability as a transference screen onto whom the patient could project her neurotic fantasies, (6) the therapist's willingness to share significant aspects of his attitudes toward, and fantasies about, the patient (i.e., his countertransference), and (7) a willingness to "let the patient be" (Keen, 1970) in the sense of accepting all aspects of her being, both healthy and pathological, including her freedom to resist the therapist and the treatment.

## ILLUSTRATION OF A TYPICAL SESSION

For our illustration of a typical session we shall take the same group therapy situation that provided the basis of our example in Chapter 3. We are able to do this because the overall setting and basic format of the existential and psychoanalytic models are fundamentally similar. In this way we hope to be able to indicate how, despite these similarities, interventions on the part of the experiential therapist typically have a more direct, sharing, and emotionally involved flavor.

Our fictitious group has seven members—four men and three women—and is reasonably heterogeneous in terms of age, vocation, and personality; with respect to cultural factors, the patients are by and large urban and middle class. They have met for two-and-a-half years, with five of them having been with the group for this entire period of time, and two other members having entered during the previous ten months. Now our therapist is Dr. Alan R.

> The group begins without any structuring from Dr. R. who is silent. Ruth, a girl in her early twenties, is talking about the fact that Bob, the man with whom she is living, is probably having an affair with her best friend, Terry. She knows he is attracted to Terry, and each of them has recently, in talking to her about the other, made some ambiguous and erotically-tinged remarks. Ruth doesn't know what to do about this. She is annoyed with herself for being jealous, for she knows that whatever Bob has going with Terry is a purely "physical" thing. He made it clear to her when they decided to live together that he did not feel sexually bound by conventional notions of a monogamous relationship; yet she feels hurt and betrayed by Terry. Then at other times, she feels that she is being old-fashioned, that it is obviously just a sex thing for Terry, who is basically interested in another, unavailable man.
>
> Mort, a brunette man in his middle thirties, razzes her. He says: That's right, Ruthie; Bob just has too much love in him to share with just one woman; besides, you love both of them so much this is really just an act of generosity on your part—you're giving two people you love to one another!
>
> Ruth reacts with a slight giggle, and continues to discuss the problem. Mort continues to bait her. Felicia interrupts at this point, saying that it makes her uncomfortable to see the way Mort is baiting Ruth and the way she allows him to do it.

Ruth interrupts, saying: But what difference does it make? I'm used to Mort's sarcasm. What I'm worried about is Bob. Felicia says: Yes, but you take the same crap from both of them. Mort joins in, saying: Yes, she's so goddamned dumb with those rose-colored glasses on; doesn't she know what the world is like? Boy, she really asks for it.

Ralph then joins in for a moment: She may ask for it, Mort, but I notice you're always there firstest with the mostest to give it to her.

Felicia says in a quiet voice: Ruth isn't happy until she has something to make her really miserable.

Ruth then says: Would everyone stop talking about me as though I weren't here?

Felicia expresses pleasure at Ruth's ability to speak up. Dr. R then wonders when Felicia is going to start talking up for herself. Felicia at first reacts with defensiveness and confusion, saying: I *am* speaking up.

Dr. R replies: Yes, but on behalf of Ruth, which is your usual way of participating. Perhaps this is partly your way of testing out what you're learning as a social work student. Look, it's okay with me, I like having a co-therapist, but I find myself wishing that you'd find a way to take as well as give; sometimes I sense that underneath that competent, supportive exterior there's a needy, bewildered little girl looking for comfort.

Felicia responds: Yes, I know what you mean, and there are day-to-day problems that I could bring up and at times would like to bring up; but they always seem so insignificant alongside what the others introduce; I guess I'm not ready yet.

Dr. R replies: Okay—I just thought I'd give you a little nudge.

For a few moments everyone is silent. Dr. R asks the group members what they are experiencing. Alice speaks up and says she was thinking about Ruth's problem, and wondering why Ruth was suddenly quiet. Ruth speaks up, saying: I felt criticized by Al in a way—when he pointed out how rarely Felicia brought up her problems, I thought maybe he was also saying that I do the opposite—always take up the group's time.

Dr. R: No, Ruth, I don't feel that way; I feel you have the right to ask for as much from the group as you can.

Ruth: Well, anyway, I don't know what to do about Bob. I guess I should just wait and let this affair between him and Terry blow over—that is, if there *is* an affair; probably if I wasn't so insecure I'd just accept it for what it is.

Nelson: I don't know Ruth—I could see being plenty jealous. I know I would be if Harriet (i.e., his current girl friend) was making it with some guy.

Mort, with heavy-handed sarcasm, says: But Nelson, you're so square, so bourgeois; you have this monogamy hang-up; both she and Bob have complete sexual freedom—the only difference between them being that he can act on his while she can't act on hers; besides, she's supposed to understand that he loves her more than any other woman he screws because he's living with her—so what does she have to be worried about?

Ruth answers Mort: I'm not sure that the idea you ridicule is so crazy, Mort; Bob is a very unusual guy—he's able to love more than one woman at once, and he's made it clear that in many ways I'm very special to him—that's why I get annoyed with myself for being jealous.

Mort becomes angrier and raises his voice, shouting at Ruth: Bob has one helluva good deal with you because you're so fucking blind; he can ball anybody he wants and still be welcomed home by your bleeding heart!

Ralph says: Lay off her, Morty—do you want to help her or destroy her? Ruth then says to Ralph: I don't mind his tone—I just want to figure out if he's right.

Dr. R says: Mort and Ralph both seem to sense the same thing about you, Ruth—that without realizing it you let other people abuse you; Morty is concentrating on how you get it from Bob and Ralph is bothered by how Morty is talking to you.

Ruth asks: But if Mort is right, how is he abusing me?

Alice answers: By speaking to you with contempt!

Ruth says: I think he feels that's the only way he can get through to me; and if he's right—if I *am* being naive with Bob—I want to find out, and I don't care *how* I find out.

Dr. R says: Ruth, you keep so busy trying to figure out what is right and what is fair that you don't instinctively notice that Bob and Mort don't give two damns about whether or not they hurt you. But what impresses me is the irritation and impatience that I am beginning to feel. For just a second now I had the strong impulse to really start yelling at you, to tell you to stop letting everyone treat you like dirt—but then I would have in a sense been doing the same thing myself. So my hunch is that you have some kind of need to provoke anger.

Ruth, seemingly bewildered, asks: But why would I want to provoke you? Dr. R replies: I feel you continuing in the same vein; the innocent young girl, with a perplexed, almost eager expression on your face, still trying to figure it all out.

Ruth asks: But what's wrong with that? Aren't I supposed to discover the reasons for what I do?

Dr. R answers Ruth: Again I'm finding myself starting to become irritated; until you get in touch with what you're feeling right now I don't think we're going to get anywhere.

Ruth is quiet for a minute, while the rest of the group seem attentive. Then she says: I don't know—I guess I feel sad more than anything else, and somehow inadequate; I feel like you're all mad at me, and like you're probably right to be, but I can't figure out just why—mainly that I'm being stupid about something; if I could only figure it out, then I could stop doing it and you'd all stop being so impatient with me.

Dr. R intervenes: So you mainly are aware of our anger with you—not yours with us, right? Ruth answers in the affirmative. Dr. R says: And what you're mainly aware of is your intense need to reason it all out, so you can then find a way to get us to stop being irritated with you.

Ruth says: That's right; and this feels like the story of my life; since I was very young I somehow was doing things wrong enough for my mother to get very mad at me—but somehow I could never be sure why.

At this point Felicia speaks up and says: I can understand that feeling; it's like: I'll be any way you want, so long as you love me. Mort then speaks up, saying: That's very good, Felicia, very empathic. I think we should give you A$^+$ in Casework Methods II for that particular remark.

Alice quickly says: You know, Mort, when you get nasty like that I really feel like killing you. Mort is silent, and no one talks for a minute. Alice suddenly says: So why don't you turn your hostility on me? I'm waiting—my heart is pounding. Mort asks her what she means. She answers: I mean that when I say something like what I just said I expect to get some of your venom, and I imagine some of it would reach its mark and really get to me; so when I don't get it—like Felicia and Ruth seem to—I wonder why am I so lucky? When will my turn come?—and then I resent being so damned afraid of you.

Mort comments: There you all go again; because I say what I think and remind people of the kind of crap that passes for brilliant insight around here and don't play your love-in game, I become some kind of hostile monster who everybody is terrified of.

Dr. R breaks in, saying: Maybe if you allowed yourself to believe that people could be scared of you you'd have to start getting in touch with your own terror. Mort responds: Gee, Doc, you're getting more profound than Felicia—are the two of you in some sort of competition?

Dr. R says: Mort, level with me—do you believe the group when they say they're afraid of you? Mort answers: No. Dr. R. rejoins: Well, I don't know how to convince you that they are; I know that *I'm* feeling it right now—as I often do when I start to tangle with you.

Mort says to him: You're just saying that to make your theoretical point. Dr. R answers: Bullshit! I don't tell you I'm feeling something if I'm not! Mort asks him: But what are you scared of? Dr. R: Probably of what you'll do if your rage gets great enough; I don't feel it right now, but I remember asking myself that same question last session—what *am* I afraid of in you?—and my immediate fantasy was of your going really berserk and wrecking the office—but *completely* wrecking it, and of us standing by helplessly letting you do it.

Mort says to him: I still have the feeling you're putting me on. Dr. R replies: But isn't that your mistrust of everyone? Who does level with you completely as far as you're concerned? Mort answers: I don't know for sure—I'm never sure. Dr. R says: My guess is that if you had to admit that others are terrified, you might have to begin wondering why you never get frightened; you're very comfortable with your anger, but you don't ever express fear.

Dr. R then adds: By the way, Mort, I think my fear of your physical destructiveness is irrational and probably has something to do with some uncomfortableness I still have with my own anger. But I also know that Alice's feeling of being intimidated by you is real.

At this point Mort doesn't say anything; he seems a bit red in the face, as though caught off guard. After a few seconds, Felicia says to Dr. R: I don't think you should have told him your fantasy—it probably will make Mort that much more afraid of his rage. And it sounds a bit pat to me—the same thing as what Mort likes to make fun of you for when you overplay the part of the "for-real," experiential therapist, letting us know just where you "are at" with everything.

Dr. R says: Well, Felicia, I invite you to become your own kind of therapist in your own style real soon—I sure as hell don't have a monopoly on technique; I do know that I felt quite genuine in saying what I did to Mort, and that it also felt great to hear you criticize me like that just now.

Felicia says: I can't imagine ever feeling that way about somebody's criticism of me. Dr. R rejoins: Well, I didn't get there overnight; I can remember in my earlier days not liking it one bit when my patients had something negative to say about me—or when anybody else did for that matter, but I was a rather different person then.

And so the session continues. As was the case in our illustrative psychoanalytic session which concerned essentially the same group (but with a different therapist—see Chapter 3), interaction in the present situation remains reasonably lively, and by the end of the meeting all participants have spoken up spontaneously, although a few have been considerably more active than others. While the analyst, Dr. M, remained silent for periods as long as seven or eight minutes in the psychoanalytic group, Dr. R, our existential-experiential therapist, is more active; for example, from the beginning of the session from which we drew an illustrative segment to its end, the longest period of time during which he said nothing lasted about five minutes.

## KEY CONCEPTS

Since many writers and thinkers formally fall within the existential school of philosophy, a great number of conceptual terms have been introduced into various discussions of ontology. Therefore we shall limit ourselves to a few central and widely encountered concepts which we believe will give some flavor of this approach. These concepts are quite abstract and generalized and involve a philosophical analysis of the human condition, rather than a more specific concern with the process of psychotherapy, whether individual or group. The general implications that the conceptual scheme has for the behavior of the group therapist will be presented in the final section, "The Role of the Leader."

In general, the ramifications that an existential approach has for psychoanalysis have centered on individual treatment, and within the latter framework have largely emphasized the nature of the therapist-patient relationship. In a somewhat similar fashion, the single variable emphasized most in discussions of existential group therapy (e.g., see Mullan, 1955) continues to be the therapist's attitude toward the patient. Consequently, as was the case with the initial psychoanalytic group model, the existential-experiential model tends to neglect the special properties of the group qua group and instead simply transfers a theory of individual psychology and of individual therapy to the group setting. However, the existential therapist did see a specific value of the group in terms of the demands it placed on the individual patient for authentic relating, not only to the therapist (as in individual therapy), but now to other patients as well (Hora, 1959). Hence our discussion of the special uses of the group will be presented below under the concept of "Authentic vs. Inauthentic Existence."

**Being vs. Non-Being.** The concept of "being" can only be grasped on a phenomenological basis. It refers to our felt awareness that we "are," that we "exist"; therefore, it is extremely personal and is difficult to articulate in abstract and symbolic terms. It has many elements in common with what is often called "self-consciousness," since it involves an awareness of physical existence and of individuation (and an envisaging, however vague, of death) that we assume to be unique to the human animal because of our better-developed conceptual capacities.

In short, man *is;* and, with the exception of the alternative of suicide, he has little choice as to when he will no longer be. He has similarly little control over the biological, social, and historical circumstances into which he is born. These accidental conditions surrounding his physical existence—his sex, his race, his bodily features, his century—constitute aspects of what Heidegger (1962) called man's "throwness," and set limits on his existence. Yet they cannot fully determine the shape of his life, for man, despite his throwness and despite social pressures to live "the good life," is able, by virtue of his awareness of some of the influences impinging on him, to say "No" to these influences, or to even attempt to say "No," thereby "transcending" his immediate situation. The person who is open to his sense of "being" feels his future open up before him full of emergent possibilities, some of which will be actualized by him, and some of which will not.

Hence the concept of being has connotations of choice, of identity, and of autonomy. It is an existential, as opposed to essentialistic, concept for it implies that "human nature" is ever evolving and never fixed; a person continues to redefine himself in a continual process of "becoming." The more he experiences himself as a "subject" in the sense of an active agent who has a determining effect on the world, the more he is open to that aspect of his experience subsumed by the concept of being. The more he experiences himself as an "object" who is acted upon, and whose life-pattern is somehow "given," the more his sense of being is attentuated, and the more he experiences himself as approximating the model of man offered by behaviorism (see Chapter 8) and psychoanalysis, both of which—according to the existentialists—tend to regard him as an "object" and thereby rob him of a considerable degree of autonomy.

The price of a well-developed sense of being is the dread of non-being, for the two are in a fundamental and dialectical relationship to each other, much as are the "figure" and the "ground" of gestalt psychology (see Chapters 4 and 7). Each moment of life becomes more precious and more fully "owned" the more one realizes that existence is finite. Just as the figure of a black circle must be contrasted with a lighter background in order to be perceived, so being can only be fully savored in a context that involves the always threatening possibility of non-being or death. Awareness of this threat confronts the individual with existential anxiety (see below); neurosis, and psychopathology in general, are viewed as resulting from efforts to evade existential anxiety.

**Being-in-the-World.**   This concept was originally introduced by Heidegger (1962) and was integral to the theoretical formulation of Binswanger. Again it expresses a dialectical relationship, this time between self and world; hyphens are used to indicate that without self there is no world (at least for the perceiver), and without the world there is no self, for the very notion of a "self" implies some sort of background or "world" against which oneself is figured or contrasted. Hence the expression "being-in-the-world" connotes much more than a purely spatial relationship.

This concept represents an attempt to overcome the subject-object dichotomy, which had bedeviled Western epistemology since Descartes first attempted to distinguish a mind or "soul" that was separate and detached from the sensory input impinging on the organism. According to existentialists, the Cartesian conception fragmented what man had initially experienced as a holistic relationship to the universe into a division between "inner" and "outer" reality, isolating the knower from the known, and alienating modern—or existential—man from the world he inhabits. In this model of reality, two people, each with his essential "self" buried deeply and obscurely within him, can only become indirectly known to each other. Such a view contrasts sharply with the existential notion of an I-Thou, dialogic relationship wherein each person can fully and directly encounter the other; this kind of mutuality ideally characterizes the patient-therapist relationship (see "Role of the Leader" below). In this conception there is no essential self that is secreted away in one's "soul"; instead the self develops and actualizes itself directly through intercourse with the world, and one's access to the world is immediate.

By insisting that each of us constructs his world in the act of perceiving it, existential phenomenology emphasized the creativity and activity involved in man's formation of his own reality. Traditional Western philosophy, in particular logical positivism, had on the other hand devalued subjectivity, implicating it as a source of potential error in man's effort to acquaint himself with "objective" reality. As the existentialists viewed it, at the point where the world pole of the self-world polarity is experienced as more important or more "real" than the self or the perceiver, the "being" aspect of one's existence is starting to become devitalized.

What the existentialist regarded as a person's mode of being-in-the-world, the Freudian saw as his characterology or life-style—for example, an oral, anal, or phallic orientation. And whereas the Freudian was not at all reluctant to distinguish between healthy and pathological life-styles, the existential analyst, in keeping with his phenomenological approach, preferred to grasp the patient's world empathically, without judgment. While the Freudian conceived of the patient's psychosexual orientation as having been "caused" by an earlier collision between the drives and the socialization forces impinging on them, the existentialist bypassed a cause-and-effect analysis altogether and instead perceived the patient as an active agent in constructing her particular mode of being-in-the-world; the patient had created it and therefore only she could change it. According to the existentialist, if the analyst saw himself as someone who, through judiciously timed and worded interpretations, could *cause* the patient's world-view to change, he reinforced the patient's perception of herself as object and as victim, this time with the analyst, rather than the parents, being experienced as the active subject. In a more existential orientation, the analyst might point out to the patient the liabilities involved in the latter's mode of being (for example, if her world is experienced as one in which all good things come at the initiation of others, it follows that she will suffer prolonged periods of deprivation and will often feel powerless), and he might also remind her that alternative modes of being-in-the-world are available to her should she wish to change. Of course the patient may often blame others for her difficulties—for instance, for her dependency and her timidity—but for the existentialist the projection of responsibility onto others constitutes a mode of being-in-the-world in its own right. Such a mode increases whatever feelings of dependency and weakness the patient already has; the analyst's job is to help her see how defining herself as weak eventually makes weakness into a "truth."

If we look to the illustrative session described above, we can describe Ruth's mode of being-in-the-world as one in which she looks to the outside world in an attempt to figure out "correct" or "incorrect" ways of defining sexual relationships; hence she attempts to utilize the group as a means of determining whether she "should" give in to her jealousy, and she turns away from what is happening to her at the hands of Mort in the group. She makes a similar use of Bob and is tempted to substitute his truth (namely a conviction that sexual fidelity is an outmoded ethic) for her own. In this process, she looks to cognition and reason as a way of orienting herself to a locus of values that she experiences as outside of herself.

**Existential vs. Neurotic Anxiety.**   While the threat of non-being provides the most dramatic context for existential anxiety, other contingencies in human existence also account for its emergence. One is the necessity to act and to make choices in the face of uncertainty, with the result that there is no one to blame but ourselves for actions that are bound to have unpredictable consequences; even behavior that is designed to benefit another person can inadvertently bring harm to him or to others. Another source of existential anxiety is individuation, which guarantees that despite the possibilities of communication and empathy, we can never fully discover exactly what it feels like to be someone else.

Existential anxiety is not pathological. It is an inevitable response to a human condition wherein one is required to make decisions in the absence of the clear-cut guidelines provided by religion and other cosmologies in an earlier era. Neurotic anxiety results when a person evades existential anxiety by failing to confront it directly and to make active choices in spite of it. While neurotic anxiety and neurotic symptomatology can take many forms, existentialists usually see it as involving some diminishment of the sense of self-as-subject and a corresponding increase in the self-as-object (Keen, 1970). Hence the individual ceases to relate to the world as an active agent who can structure some degree of meaningfulness for herself; with the breakdown of her usual relatedness to the world, experiences of disorganization, depersonalization, and meaninglessness occur. The more she experiences herself as an object, the more she fears potential abuse or harm at the hands of others.

Hence one fairly frequent symptom of neurosis is overt anxiety attacks. A form of neurosis that is more characterological in nature reflects an experience-mode in which the self is treated more as object than as subject. Here one lives for the expectations and love of others and behaves as she ought to behave in terms of externalized criteria and does not choose her activities on the basis of those that spontaneously appeal to her. In these situations, the self is taken as an object in that it is viewed in essentialistic terms; the self, treated much like a thing, must have particular static characteristics (e.g., punctuality, productivity, courtesy, etc.). Once the self is experienced in more "being" and process-like ways, then what it is to be at any particular moment is determined more by context and by its current state of being-in-the-world.

Again Ruth—from the illustrative session above—provides an example. Experiencing herself as a satellite to Bob, who then becomes the "subject" in her existence, she objectifies her self in that she strives to develop "modern" sexual values that are in conformity to his. Were she more able to experience her self in the sense of "self-as-subject" (Keen, 1970, pp. 17–19) she would probably come into contact with her genuine wish for a nonadulterous relationship. Of course, we don't know what Ruth would choose, since only she herself can make that decision and she has not yet begun to do so in an autonomous way, unclouded by Bob's definition of what she should want. Here again the Freudian and the existentialist clash to some extent, since the latter seems more willing to regard any of Ruth's decisions as "right" for her so long as they are autonomous ones. The Freudian, on the other hand, is more prone to see some sexual orientations—for example, those involving promiscuity or homosexuality—as inherently pathological.

**Existential vs. Neurotic Guilt.** According to the existentialist, orthodox psychoanalysts too often ignore the question of actual guilt and regard a patient's guilt feelings as inappropriate and irrational. For the phenomenologist, however, there is such a thing as ontological or genuine guilt; such guilt is experienced by all of us whenever we neglect certain potentialities within us; since we can never fulfill all our potentials, some degree of existential guilt is inevitable.

As was the case with existential anxiety, ontological guilt, when it is evaded, becomes neurotic guilt. And as with anxiety, the neurotic form of this emotion usually involves a curtailment of the person's sense of herself as an active subject; instead she objectifies herself, blaming herself for having failed to meet arbitrary standards involving fair and loving treatment of others. Of course many of our actions do bring hurt to others, however inadvertently. To the extent to which we take responsibility for these actions and feel pain because we genuinely care about these other people and their unhappiness, we experience either existential anxiety (in anticipating the possibility of hurting them) or existential guilt (after the hurt has occurred). All too often, however, guilt involves a breakdown in the experience of self-as-subject, in which our caring for the other person is paramount, and becomes instead a concern with meeting societal standards of correct behavior and of the way one should be; here the self is taken more as object than as subject.

**Authentic vs. Inauthentic Existence.** The concepts described above pave the way for understanding the existentialist's definition of authentic and inauthentic existence. In authentic existence the person confronts the ever-emergent possibility of non-being, makes decisions in the face of existential doubt, takes responsibility for these decisions, and acknowledges her fundamental "existential isolation" (Yalom, 1980)—the fact that "she is born alone and dies alone" and that she will never directly know or experience another person's consciousness. In inauthentic existence, the person seeks to confirm herself in ways that she hopes will evade the dread of non-being; often these means of self-confirmation are based on grandiose and competitive notions of existence wherein the self is perceived not as an experiencing process that is open to the world and therefore always in flux but as an essence that must achieve certain fixed characteristics. She thinks that once she actualizes this arbitrary self-image she will find security, but since the security she longs for involves protection from the threat of non-being, such a quest is doomed to failure. In attempting to confirm herself inauthentically, such a person keeps "busy" (and thereby reduces existential anxiety) by playing status-seeking games and by conforming to the demands of society; yet in doing so she fails to become what she truly is. To the extent to which others are treated as a means of gaining applause for her life "performance," they are being exploited and "thinged" by her. In a more mutual relationship, which Buber (1958) calls the "I-Thou" relationship, she experiences herself as a subject who actively chooses both the relationship and how she wants to be in the relationship; she is also able to appreciate the other as a "subject" with wants, needs, and a world-view of his own.

Some existentially oriented clinicians (e.g., Nicholas, 1984) have stressed the unique value of group (as opposed to individual) treatment for highlighting four elemental existential themes: one's mortality, freedom, isolation, and need-for-meaning (Yalom, 1980). The presence of other people is especially valuable, first because these are especially tough themes to face on one's own, without direct sharing on the part of another, and second because the average patient usually has not had life experience directly relevant to all four of these themes; for example, a group-therapy patient, Allen, is better able to confront his own inevitable death, which he has hitherto denied, via an extremely serious illness contracted by another group member, Frank. However, it is probably around the concept of *relationship,* the antidote to existential isolation, that group therapy is most especially valuable, simply because it is the multiple relationships of each participant to every other person present, including the therapist, that is the "very stuff" of group therapy.

One way in which to think about relationships in an existential frame of reference is via the concept of authentic vs. inauthentic relating (Hora, 1959). According to Hora, in individual therapy the existential therapist cannot possibly offer so great a range of "dialogic" relationships as is provided in group therapy, because (1) he is but one person and (2) he cannot, despite his greater openness, relate in so full a way as he could if he did not have to attend to his therapeutic task. Since each group member constitutes a different person—and thereby a different mode of "being-in-the-world"—for a patient to relate to, what better laboratory exists for actualizing Buber's (1958) conception of the "I-Thou relationship"? Group therapy can be expected to push inauthentic ways of relating into bolder relief than does the one-to-one relationship in part because the presence of other people typically engenders an unusual amount of anxiety. Silences in the early stages of the group in particular create intense anxiety as members struggle to fill them. The patient is doubtless aware that it is inappropriate to engage in social chatter—an awareness that in itself constitutes another source of anxiety—yet she will find it hard not to fall back on her habitual and inauthentic ways of relating, especially since she is the recipient of more intense interpersonal pressures than are presented by the relatively benign therapist in individual treatment. However, the group will also offer a strong sense of support as the patient strives to find a more authentic base for relating, for each of her fellow patients is embarking upon a similar quest.

The transferential nature of member-to-member relationships within the group are not as emphasized within the present model as they are within the psychoanalytic model of the group. Instead, just as is the case with the leader-patient relationship, the actual and the emotionally committed nature of interpatient relationships receives more stress than do their fantasized or unreal aspects. When the existential group therapist focuses on distorted or inauthentic ways in which patients relate to one another, he attends to the here-and-now aspects of these distortions rather than to their specific genesis in earlier family relationships. Also less pronounced in the existential group therapy model than in the psychoanalytic group model is the distinction between authority and peer vectors, since the special status of the leader becomes less important in the experiential group, where he tends to present himself as another—albeit "most experienced" (see below)—patient.

## ROLE OF THE LEADER

As we indicated earlier, the existential-experiential model tends to take issue with the psychoanalytic one when it comes to theoretical and philosophical concerns regarding the nature of personality development and the origins of psychopathology. Yet the existential group leader's overt behavior—at least to the naive observer—does not necessarily provide a dramatic contrast to that of the psychoanalytic group therapist: In both models the group is itself primarily responsible for initiating and maintaining interaction. Material involving happenings both inside and outside the group is considered pertinent, and, unlike what occurs in the psychodrama and gestalt-therapy models (see Chapters 6 and 7), patients talk about their problems and narrate their life histories in a straightforward fashion. The therapist's primary goal continues to be the enlargement of the patient's awareness, and he attempts to do so within a framework that recognizes such concepts as resistance, transference, and interpretation. Therefore Dr. R., the existential therapist in the illustrative session above, focused on aspects of the patients' behaviors that were similar to those attended to by Dr. M, the psychoanalytically oriented therapist who led the same patient group in Chapter 3's illustrative session: Felicia's reluctance to present personal problems in the group, Ruth's masochistic inability to defend herself against sadistic exploitation by others, and Mort's counterphobic rage.

However, in his role as "the most experienced patient" (Whitaker & Warkentin, n.d.) within the group and in his search for a more spontaneous and mutual involvement with each patient, the existential therapist is more willing than the psychoanalyst to reveal both his immediate experience in the session and various aspects of his own past. This is because he has a tolerant and accepting attitude toward his own countertransference. While he is aware that his countertransference may partly reflect regressive and unworked-through aspects of his personality, he appreciates that it may also include a genuine concern and caring for the patient (feelings that he trusts and that he believes belong to aspects of the therapist-patient relationship that are rooted in reality, rather than in a neurotic repetition of the past). Indeed, some existential analysts go so far as to say that without this care, which represents a kind of love, the patient cannot experience a symbolic rebirth or a true transformation of character, although she may show symptomatic improvement and some change in her relationships.

In his effort to promote an atmosphere within the group of an authentic "happening" in which each person, including himself, feels free to express all aspects of his "being," however realistic or fantastic, however healthy or sick, the experiential therapist strives to ferret out, and even exaggerate, whatever countertransference attitudes and fantasies he may have. For if he is not open to the conflictual aspects of his own character, how can he help the patient to tolerate hers? Hence Dr. R., albeit acknowledging that there is probably a neurotic aspect to his fear of Mort's physical aggression, shares his fantasy of Mort's destroying the office. Other personal actions and experiences revealed by him include his personalized image of Felicia as a needy little girl, his spontaneous pleasure at her ability to criticize him openly, his past difficulties in comfortably tolerating criticism, his momentary anger when Mort accuses him of feigning fearfulness, his immediate correction of Ruth's original perception of him as wanting her to take up less of the group's time, and his subsequent impulse to attack her verbally. Although not *un*interested in the participants' respective pasts, he is most involved in the nuances of their immediate experience—just how each of them is "being-in-the-world" at any one moment. Therefore, unlike Dr. M. in Chapter 3's illustrative session, Dr. R. does not directly ask Ruth whether she can connect her reactions to Bob and Mort with childhood events. Instead Ruth spontaneously remembers her past, a response that often becomes more likely when the patient, as did Ruth, has had a meaningful emotional experience during the session.

The therapist, in his eagerness to be candid about his own experience, must rapidly select those of his subjective reactions that seem intuitively to be most closely related to significant aspects of the patient's being. In this process he would seem to be guided by something akin to Cohn's concept of "selective authenticity" (Cohn, 1972; see Chapter 12) wherein a leader either consciously or preconsciously decides to share those feelings and thoughts that seem most likely to prove helpful in promoting fruitful group interaction. However, any prolonged attention that he might give to the possible self-censoring of material that could prove unhelpful or that could go beyond what a patient "can take" violates the spirit of existential experientialism, which emphasizes the importance of the therapist's freedom and spontaneity and his respect for the patient's ability to take responsibility for whatever reactions he in turn has to the therapist's revelations. Indeed, although it is tempting to discern a specific strategy in the therapist's authenticity (e.g., a modeling function wherein a patient is "shown" how to be more open), this kind of goal-oriented conception, involving as it does the use of a specific means to reach a particular end, would reduce the patient to the status of an object, of one who is "done to" and "done for." Thus experientialism is more accurately viewed as a way of "being with" the patient. This is much more an inevitable concomitant of what the existentialist refers to as the therapist's "presence" (May, 1958, pp. 80–85) than it is a mere therapeutic technique.

This nonmanipulative attitude toward the patient is frequently described as "letting her be" (Keen, 1970, pp. 169–173), and this freedom to be-in-her-world on the patient's part includes all manner of pathology and resistance. Naturally the therapist is equally free to express his own reactions to the patient's chosen mode of being-in-the-world. Indeed, his role as an experiential leader makes it incumbent upon him to do so, though at carefully selected and well-timed moments (letting the patient know, for instance, that her refusal to change, or even try to change, a particular behavior strikes him, the therapist, as self-thwarting and self-damaging). The patient, however, is under no obligation to change for the therapist's sake.

Actually, there was little in Freud's original conception of psychoanalysis that was antithetical to the analyst's taking a noninterfering approach to the patient's resistance. According to the existentialists, orthodox psychoanalysts began over time to move away from this respectful orientation to resistance and to become gradually convinced that their interpretations of resistance, if valid and properly timed, could not help but lead the patient one step closer to insight and therefore to eventual cure—hence the existential therapist's concern that the typical analyst might all too easily lose sight of the patient's inherent freedom to resist his therapeutic efforts. It is this recognition of each group member's right to choose her own mode of being-in-the-world, in the face of any and every therapeutic intervention, that according to this model provides a major stimulus to her continuous growth and individuation.

# CHAPTER SIX
# PSYCHODRAMA

Psychodrama is a group therapeutic approach designed to encourage the expression of feelings that underlie personal problems through the use of spontaneous dramatic role-playing. In its purest form, psychodrama consists of the therapy group or workshop that focuses on acting out emotionally significant scenes from the past, present, or anticipated future for the purposes of catharsis and acquiring new behaviors. The most important aim of the method is to help participants relive and reformulate their problems in dramatic form in order to face their concerns directly and immediately in the living present. Experience in action, rather than the kind of recapitulation in words and thoughts that is characteristic of most psychotherapeutic approaches, is the touchstone of the psychodrama approach.

## HISTORICAL BACKGROUND

The term *psychodrama* and the name of Jacob L. Moreno are so closely tied together that it is scarcely possible to think of one without the other. Psychodrama *is* Moreno's creation, and it has its roots deeply imbedded in his personal history. Moreno was born in 1892, somewhere in eastern Europe. *Who's Who in America, 1966–67* gives his place of birth as Rumania. Moreno, himself (Moreno, 1964), claims that his birth took place on a boat cruising the Black Sea.

Moreno's first experience with psychodrama occurred when he was four and one half years old. While he was playing with some friends in the basement of his house in Vienna, the city in which he grew up, he suggested that they all play God and angels. There was a large table in the center of the room on which a number of chairs were stacked. Moreno climbed to the very top of the chairs and played God while he had other children go around the table flapping their arms as if they were angels. In these roles, the children began to think that they were flying. One of them suggested that Moreno, perched high atop the chairs, fly too: When he attempted to do so, he quickly fell and broke his arm but was left with a sense of exhilaration from the spontaneity of the experience. Both elements—spontaneity and exhilaration—were to become major and central concepts in the later development of Moreno's theory.

The desire to act stayed alive in Moreno throughout his childhood. When he was sixteen and a pre-medical student, he spent time walking in the gardens of Vienna and engaging in fantasy play with the children he met there, acting out fairy tales and stories. He was again struck by the freedom, openness, and creativity of the young people and also began to notice the positive emotional effect that the primitive fantasy play had on them. After earning his medical degree in 1917, he continued to pursue his interest in acting and spontaneous play, an interest that culminated in his opening of the Theater of Spontaneity in 1921. Although interested in drama, Moreno began to view theater presentations with prepared scripts and well-rehearsed actors as stultifying and anticreative. In his initial Theater of Spontaneity there were no scripts; he introduced the concept of "The Living Newspaper" wherein audiences and actors played out events from the daily newspaper in an unplanned and improvisational fashion. At this point in Moreno's work, he made use of unrehearsed drama more as an art form than as a therapeutic effort, but when the personal problems of one of the actresses was brought to Moreno's attention by her fiance, he hit upon the idea of using unscripted role-playing in an effort to resolve personal problems. This fortuitous incident give birth to the therapeutic theater of psychodrama.

When Moreno moved to the United States in 1925, he continued developing the psychodramatic method. Some years later he opened a sanitorium in Beacon, New York, where he built the first stage for psychodrama in the United States. His years in the United States were extremely productive ones. Until his death in 1974, he wrote extensively about psychodrama, sociodrama, sociometric studies, and related areas. He produced a number of books, edited journals, and was extremely active in teaching psychodrama and in demonstrating it throughout the United States and abroad.

Moreno has been frequently credited with introducing the term *group psychotherapy,* and he clearly played an important role in the growth of interest in the field of group psychotherapy in general. The concept of psychodrama, as developed by Moreno, has now been in existence for more than seventy-five years, a fact that clearly marks it as the longest existing specialized group therapeutic technique in current use. There are between fifty and one hundred psychodrama theaters in various institutions around the country, a fact that is often cited as an example of its widespread usage. In addition, psychodrama is, of course, used in situations where no specialized theater has been constructed, and it has frequently been used as a technique adjunctive to other group methods (Siroka et al., 1971; Blatner, 1970). Corsini (1957) developed a modification of the technique that he calls *psychodramatic group therapy,* and an innovative approach to research on attitude change based on psychodrama has been described by Greenberg (1968). Gendron (1980) has produced a valuable and exhaustive bibliography of developments in psychodrama between 1972 and 1980 which illustrates the extremely broad range of uses to which psychodramatic technique in one form or another has been put, including the areas mentioned above as well as marriage and family counselling, teaching of theology, training of psychotherapists, and drug and alcohol treatment. Moreover, a variety of role-playing techniques, all of which have their roots in Moreno's work, have become increasing popular in a number of other group approaches, spanning the broad range from gestalt therapy to behavior modification, and on to eclectic groups. Nonetheless, it is fair to say that psychodrama, as such, is not among the most common group therapeutic techniques in use today, and the great impact that Moreno's techniques and thinking have had on the development of group psychotherapy is less than fully acknowledged.

Clearly one cannot fairly assess Moreno's impact on group psychotherapy by examining only the frequency of use of psychodrama itself; one must also note the influence of his ideas and techniques on the development of other group therapeutic and personal growth methods.

His introduction of an emphasis on action, as opposed to analysis, his focus on the "here and now," and his development of a variety of special techniques for use in groups are all echoed in other group methods that we will be describing. Particularly illuminating in this regard are comments made by Schutz (1971) who is best known for his contributions to the encounter group model (see Chapter 11). When he was scheduled to meet Moreno for the first time, he heard that the latter claimed credit for many of the encounter techniques that Schutz himself had developed. To prepare for the meeting, Schutz read some of Moreno's works; as he did so it became increasingly clear to him that years earlier Moreno had indeed anticipated most, if not all, of the techniques that Schutz was now using in his encounter activities. During their discussions, Schutz acknowledged that many of the methods were derived from Moreno, even though he was unaware of it at the time he developed them. However, Schutz went on to say that he was at least sure that the fantasy methods that he was employing were not derived from the work of Moreno; yet Moreno was quick to point out that even those techniques had been anticipated in articles published many years earlier in his journal, *Sociometry.*

While it is clear that Moreno has had a major impact on the field, it is also true that the impact has been both less than direct and not fully acknowledged. Perhaps some explanation for this fact lies in three characteristics of Moreno and his approach. First is a self-acknowledged immodesty; undoubtedly his manner, his rather overbearing style, and his concern about being properly credited for his productions tended to put people off. Second, although he wrote voluminously, he did not write with the greatest clarity or directness of expression. His writings tend to be rather complex and not very succinct, and they introduce a variety of dramaturgic and philosophical notions that may obscure the main outlines of the group therapeutic and group process conceptualizations underlying his theory. Third, Moreno's emphasis on the nonanalytic nature of the technique, stressing as he did relatively public and conscious attitudes, ran counter to the *zeitgeist* reigning when he produced his major works, which stressed essentially private, intrapsychic, and unconscious data. All of these factors may have contributed to Moreno's writings having been less widely read than might otherwise be expected. In recent years, however, Moreno's contributions to the understanding of group interaction and group therapeutic methods have been more frequently and more fully acknowledged. It is becoming increasingly clear that his influence on the development of group techniques has indeed been an important and insufficiently credited one.

## DESCRIPTION OF A PSYCHODRAMA SESSION

We will describe a session of psychodrama as it might take place in the psychodrama theater in Beacon, New York. The setting is a stage originally designed by Moreno. It is in a small auditorium equipped with seats like a theater but with no proscenium. The stage itself comes close to the first row of seats and is made of three circles of increasingly smaller size, placed one on top of the other, resulting in three different height levels. It has sometimes been described as looking like a three-tiered wedding cake. In addition, there is a semienclosed area in the back of the stage, as well as a balcony. At the back of the auditorium there is a raised area with some simple lighting equipment. The persons who will be participating in the psychodrama include the chief therapist or director; the patient-*protagonist* (or several people who may play that role at various points in the proceedings); and those who will serve as *auxiliary egos* to represent important figures in the protagonist's life, or at times different aspects of the protagonist's self. Additionally, there may be other members of the audience including staff members, visitors, or other patients who are not yet ready to participate. Since spontaneity is of particular importance in psychodrama, Moreno emphasized the importance of having a "warm-up period" to loosen up the members of the group so that they could act in as spontaneous a fashion as possible. This desired effect may be accomplished in a variety of ways. Moreno himself had a charismatic personality and the ability to generate considerable excitement about, and interest in, psychodramatic procedures. This capacity to generate excitement and interest is viewed as a desirable characteristic for all psychodrama leaders. Furthermore, anything that creates laughter or humor that the group can share positively affects the warming-up process. Specific techniques are sometimes used, many of which are quite similar to those later developed for use in encounter groups. For example, a participant might be asked to pick a person who attracts him out of the group and to approach that person and to describe what his reactions are. Techniques involving communication without words, such as picking a person and looking into his eyes, are also utilized. In sum, anything that facilitates participants' expressing themselves openly and directly, as well as creating a feeling of comfort and of shared mutual interest in the group, is a useful element in the warm-up period. Again, it should be remembered that the warm-up should promote the capacity of the individual to engage in action and behave in a spontaneous manner.

The role of the director is of particular importance in the warm-up period and in the initial stages of the psychodrama itself. She must function as a person who makes things happen and who helps people to be comfortable enough to be spontaneous and creative in examining their personal concerns. The director may have already chosen a person to be the first protagonist prior to the beginning of the meeting or she may choose somebody after the warm-up period. If a person has not been previously selected, the director might approach a group member and ask him to bring up a problem he is concerned about and wants to explore further. Using another approach, the director might choose a topic, such as work-related problems or difficulties with family members, and ask those present to say something about concerns they have in that area. After some discussion is generated, the group would focus on the problem of one of the members who would then be encouraged to become the first protagonist. If he were shy or were showing signs of stage fright, the director might try to ease him into the role by asking him to come to the front of the room while continuing to talk with him. The director might continue facing the group and have the member with his back to the group in order to make him feel more comfortable. The director might also try to comfort him physically by touching his shoulder while at the same time easing him up on to the stage.

Once the protagonist is on the stage, the director begins to set the scene. Let us take as an example, a problem whose central focus is a work difficulty, a conflict between the protagonist and his immediate supervisor. The director should rely as much as possible on the protagonist to explain how to play the scene, making certain that the latter provides a description of the situation in which the conflict manifests itself with as much specificity as possible about the setting, how the furniture is arranged, and what other people, if any, are present. Once the scene has been set, a dramatic situation is already underway and the protagonist might begin to "feel" himself in the performance and to experience those emotions associated swith the real-life situation.

Now other participants or auxiliary egos are needed in order to bring the drama to life. Someone to play the supervisor and another person to play a fellow employee are required as additional participants. The auxiliary egos should be chosen by the protagonist but may be chosen by the director if she knows the members of the group well enough to decide who might fit the roles as they have been described; or they may be selected in consultation between the director and the protagonist. Once all the participants have been chosen, the plot needs to be outlined in somewhat fuller detail. The roles of the auxiliary egos have to be explained by the protagonist or the director. The protagonist should give a personal description of the supervisor, including some sense of his behavioral style. Here he describes the supervisor as being gruff and overly critical, loud and overbearing. The protagonist, Donald, outlines the situation in which his boss criticized him in the presence of a fellow worker, Joe, toward whom Donald felt a great rivalry. In the psychodrama, Donald develops a plot in which he "has it out" with his supervisor. He begins by telling him as directly as he can that his criticisms would be much more constructive were they given under different circumstances. The auxiliary ego, playing the supervisor, reacting in terms of his perception of the protagonist's needs rather than according to the role-behaviors described responds warmly, encouragingly, and apologetically, indicating that Donald is quite correct in pointing out the inappropriateness of his behavior. At this point, the protagonist stops the action and explains that his boss would never act that way. He then repeats his description of the boss to the auxiliary ego and gives further instructions as to how the role should be played. Then the role-play starts anew with Donald speaking to his boss.

Donald again begins by telling his boss that he wished he would not embarrass him by "calling him down in front of Joe." The boss this time responds tauntingly, "You'll never amount to anything because you can't take a little honest criticism. You always want to be coddled, to get special treatment." Donald, shaken by the comment, and even more shaken by the memory it evokes of his father's repeated criticisms of him, angrily blurts out, "You're unfair, and you're mean to me in the same way that my father was, never giving me a chance, and never being satisfied with anything I do."

Donald becomes silent, surprised by the feelings that have come to the surface. The supervisor tries to apologize, but the protagonist doesn't respond. After a minute of silence, the director asks why the action has stopped. Donald thinks for a while and then realizes that neither his boss nor his father ever apologized to him for anything, but he is also aware that he has never expressed his anger and his resentment directly to them.

The director takes this opportunity to question the protagonist, who is a shy unaggressive man: "Would you really speak up like that to your boss?" The protagonist replies that he never has and it probably would be very difficult for him to do so and then goes on to say: "I was never aware that my feelings and attitude toward my boss were so much like my feelings and experiences with my father." Donald is clearly impressed by both the emotional release he feels and the insight he gained into his reactions. He begins to wonder whether he encourages his boss to "put him down" by always reenacting the role of the incompetent son that he had played with his father.

A young man in the audience, empathizing with Donald, stands up and says, "I know exactly how you feel because I notice myself overreacting to my boss's comments, and not knowing what provoked it." Other members chime in with personal reactions and advice to Donald.

When the scene has been completed, the protagonist and the others return to the audience. At this point, a variety of alternative activities could be introduced: continuation of the evaluation by the protagonist of his emotional response to the scene with other members of the audience offering their observations or describing their personal reactions or the director might well raise questions or offer interpretations. She might wonder what kinds of gratification Donald might be getting from being criticised or she might focus on what makes Donald so fearful of speaking up for himself. A technique called *sharing* is sometimes used in which members of the audience try to respond to what occurred in terms of relevant experiences of their own. Yet another alternative might be an interpretation of the scene by the director and/or other members of the audience including some suggestions to the protagonist about ways of changing his behavior based on their reactions to his role in the scene.

Following completion of the work on the scene, the same protagonist may move into another scene or a variant of the same scene, or a new protagonist may take center stage. Sometimes, for additional benefit of the original protagonist, the same scene may be replayed with a member of the audience taking the protagonist's role so that he might have the opportunity to observe in a fresh way the experience he has just had.

In the above example catharsis and sudden awareness occurred swiftly and dramatically. Other times, a slower more painstaking effort is required to bring feelings to the fore. The emotional reaction that Donald experienced would, of course, be only the beginning of the psychodramatic work.

## KEY CONCEPTS: PHILOSOPHICAL
## AND THEORETICAL

**Action and Acting.**  In many respects the concepts of *action* and *activity* seem to be Moreno's basic and central theoretical ideas. Like psychoanalysis, psychodrama was developed in Vienna, some years after Freud first began his work. Moreno, however, took the most disparaging view of the passivity of psychoanalytic technique and at times almost seemed to have chosen action because it represented the polar opposite of the psychoanalyst's insistence that the patient remain relatively immobile during the analytic hour and confine himself to thought and fantasy rather than action. Moreno saw the psychoanalytic method as extremely stultifying and constricting, as encouraging a kind of rumination that bordered on the trivial, and as supporting the mediocre and uninspired. Moreno believed that an emphasis on action, on the other hand, made it possible for people to get in touch with aspects of themselves of which they had previously been unaware.

Moreno (1946) suggested that some of the early opposition to psychodrama was due to the widely held belief among mental health workers that action was dangerous while verbal interchange was the tried-and-true method. He suspected that psychodrama received a more favorable reaction in the United States than in Europe because Americans were much more people of action than were Europeans and, therefore, could more readily accept the action orientation to education and behavior change.

Heisey (1982) points to psychodrama's emphasis on the efficiency of action as fundamental to behavior change. Because memory is not only a cognitive but also a physionomic phenomenon and as such is stored in the anatomy and physiology of the body, action precedes words in the development of individuals and in the universal method of catharsis. Heisey follows very closely in Moreno's tradition by underscoring the importance of permitting oneself to act and to learn from the observation of that action.

For Moreno, acting in an open way and acting out one's dreams, desires, wishes, and aspirations, represented a step in the direction of making humans more godlike. Being godlike involved becoming so open and in touch with one's feelings, so spirited and creative, as to be able to extend oneself to the limits of emotion and achievement. Indeed, one of Moreno's basic aims in the development of psychodrama was to help individuals reach a higher state of being than they had thus far attained. In part, his stance developed in opposition to the then current attitude in Vienna's psychiatric circles, one which was becoming increasingly receptive to psychoanalysis. Moreno's orientation had much more in common with the existential-humanistic emphasis on motives such as self-actualization. The firmness of Moreno's conviction that people should be helped to stretch themselves to their creative limits is evident in a description of his one meeting with Freud, a meeting which took place after he heard Freud lecture. Moreno responded to Freud's questioning him about the kind of work he did by saying that the emphasis of his work was opposite to Freud's: "You analyze their dreams, I try to give them the courage to dream again. I teach people how to play *God*" (Moreno, 1946, p. 6).

The concept of *action* represents for Moreno and for psychodrama the conviction that openness and nonconstriction are central characteristics that underlie successful human functioning and creative development.

**Spontaneity and Creativity.**    Closely related to the concept of action, and indeed in many respects overlapping with it, are Moreno's ideas about *spontaneity* and *creativity*. Moreno's first attempt to use psychodrama was in his Theater of Spontaneity, which was originally more closely tied to a dramatic format than to a therapeutic one. He was fond of pointing out that traditional dramatic works, written, directed, and performed in a preplanned fashion, are at best uninteresting and at worst deadening. His approach to theater, stressing experience in the moment and acting out those experiences, was designed to create a vibrant and lively experience, both for actors and observers. In this sense, Moreno's view of traditional theater had much in common with his view of psychoanalysis; he considered both essentially closed and countercreative.

Moreno, impressed by his early experiences of developing impromptu plays in the parks of Vienna with children, was struck by the fact that children, in contrast with adults, are much more ready to act and seem to be much more in touch with their fantasy lives and their feelings, and are better able to enter into a role-playing situation. Children, naturally spontaneous, have not yet stifled their imaginations nor their ability to be creative. Moreno sought to reactivate in adults the capacity to be creative and spontaneous and to experience emotional fulfillment—that is, to revive those characteristics so common in children but so unfortunately rare in adults. Spontaneity, difficult to define as Moreno used it, seemed to have at least two important components for him. One is the ability to experience one's own state of being or feeling, with minimal interference from external impediments or internal inhibitions. The second focuses on an aspect of spontaneity that is truly responsive to reality demands—the wherewithal to respond to new situations immediately, reasonably, and yet creatively. One of the most important functions of learning to be more spontaneous, as one hopefully does in the psychodrama experience or in specific exercises of spontaneity training that Moreno also introduced, is that of freeing a person from stereotyped behaviors rooted in past experience and substituting more creative approaches to current experience.

**Here and Now.**    Like so many of the other developers of group methods described in this volume, Moreno puts great stress on the importance of experiencing in the present, in the moment, in the *here and now*. Psychodrama emphasizes experiencing present problems in action rather than "talking" about them. Therefore, even when one is replaying a situation that in reality is quite similar to an actual event that occurred in the past, or rehearsing one that anticipates a future event, the here-and-now emphasis should predominate since what is important is the spontaneous experience in the moment and dealing with current feelings and emotional reactions. In the role-play example above Donald experienced in the present feelings and emotions about his boss and their connection with feelings about his father that he had never been aware of previously. It was his capacity to experience those feelings in the present that made new learning possible. Psychodrama, then, emphasizes living in the moment and reacting to a situation as it is created in the immediate moment of a psychodrama situation, rather than to a real event as it might actually have occurred in the past or is likely to occur in the future. The emphasis is always on the learning that comes from the reality of the present experience and one's reaction to it, as opposed to verbal rehashing of past events or buried feelings.

**Catharsis.** Moreno's concept of *catharsis* was an extension of an idea originated by Aristotle in his writing on poetry and drama. Aristotle believed that good drama, particularly tragedy, had the power to arouse strong emotions in an audience; experiencing those emotions even in a vicarious way had a purgative effect on members of the audience. Moreno's view of catharsis goes beyond even the Aristotlelian conception. According to him, it is the actors, rather than the audience, in psychodrama who are in the best position to experience total catharsis. Actors in an already written and formulated play are unable to truly experience emotional release since they are not portraying events and emotions from their own experience, and the audience of a formal drama can feel such release only in a secondary or vicarious fashion. The protagonist and to a lesser extent the audience in psychodrama, on the other hand, can develop almost total involvement and empathy and can achieve the attendant cathartic experience because of the immediacy and reality of the enactment.

Moreno saw himself as taking up where Aristotle left off by creating the psychodrama, wherein the participants, as actors, were able to experience total catharsis. In Moreno's view, Freud and Breuer had begun to make headway in the therapeutic use of catharsis when their patients experienced emotional release under hypnosis, but they too quickly rejected it as a useful method, not going far enough in exploring catharsis and casting it aside before they understood its true potential.

Moreno's conception of catharsis is intimately related to his ideas of constructive action and spontaneity—he sees catharsis as most likely to occur in the situation where a person is allowed to deal with real-life experiences and concerns by using an action-oriented technique that facilitates spontaneous expression. In other words, the psychodrama, with proper warm-up that creates a readiness to respond, is an ideal situation for experiencing total emotional release, because the patient or protagonist serves as both the author, who formulates the experience and brings up his own emotional concerns for consideration, and also the actor, who lives out the experience with the help of other actors, who, in turn, experience emotional release from their own involvement in the role-play. The comingling of these two aspects, along with the facilitative role of the director and the receptivity of the audience, serves to set the stage for the most complete cathartic experience.

## KEY CONCEPTS: METHODOLOGICAL

**Protagonist-Patient.**   Once chosen, the protagonist becomes the principle architect of the psychodrama to be played out. In a continuing group where members know each other's histories, backgrounds, and concerns, it is possible to quickly begin the enactment without a great deal of information to set the scene. In a new group, or one that is meeting only for a relatively brief period of time, the protagonist must set the scene by giving some life history information, some description of the problem or concern, and some characteristics of those who will also be portrayed.

The protagonist must literally set the stage, an act that assists in getting into the scene as well as encouraging the involvement of other group members. The protagonist must also select, often with the help of the director, persons from the group to serve as auxiliary egos. Then the protagonist must instruct the auxiliary egos about the specifics of the roles they are to play. These instructions should include identifying characteristics and some background information about the person, guidelines about the role the person plays in the protagonist's life, and his or her particular role in the scene to be portrayed, and a feeling for characteristic behavioral style. Sometimes a protagonist might have to briefly take the auxiliary role to give an idea of how that person acts, or at least how that person appears to the protagonist to act.

The development of the scene itself is, of course, a spontaneously evolving role-playing situation. The experience must grow out of the unrehearsed dramatic playing of both the protagonist and the auxiliary egos and out of the developing emotional feeling among members of the group, particularly among the players of the actual scene. As we saw in the scene with Donald, after an incorrect role interpretation by an auxiliary ego, the protagonist had to stop the action and give additional instructions before the psychodrama could meaningfully develop.

The director or the protagonist may also suggest modifying the central role in the scene in order to see if the protagonist is able to change behavior and observe what effect, if any, changes in that behavior might have on others. The possibility of playing and replaying a scene with various modifications, and of elaborating on it with the assistance of specialized techniques (see p. 110), adds to the therapeutic effect.

Clearly the benefits to the protagonist are the most direct of any group member: the experience of spontaneity, catharsis, reliving of emotionally charged or conflict-ridden experiences, insight into one's behavior in these situations, and the potentiality for learning alternative modes of behavior.

**Auxiliary Egos.**   In the presentation of any psychodrama, unless the protagonist is engaging in a soliloquy, other actors are required in the performance. Moreno termed these persons *auxiliary egos*. In the portrayal of a scene involving the protagonist and other important persons in his life, members of the group are called upon to play roles in the drama. For example, auxiliary egos may play any of a variety of persons in the protagonist's experience—parent, spouse, child, friend, nurse, doctor, and so forth. They are given directions by the protagonist and/or the director as to the characteristics of the persons whose roles they are to play. Those who play the roles of auxiliary egos vary under different circumstances. In a training group or an outpatient group, the auxiliary egos are likely to be other group participants. In working with more disturbed patients, in addition to other group members, specially trained people may function as auxiliary egos. Moreno found that persons who were formerly psychotic and have recovered can be particularly empathic and therefore effective in this role.

Auxiliary egos must both be empathic and observant. First the auxiliary ego must be able to empathize with the protagonist and with the nature of the conflict involved in the scene in order to develop an understanding of the character to be portrayed. Second, the auxiliary ego has to be a careful observer of both self and others, in order to later comment about the experience in the role played as well as reactions to the protagonist, both of which might assist the protagonist in better understanding his conflict. There are some additional special roles for auxiliary egos required by certain specialized techniques that will be described later.

Many of the statements made about the role of protagonist also apply to that of the auxiliary ego—he or she must also get ready to play the role through a warm-up process, be involved in the scene setting, and have a readiness to engage in the spontaneous and creative effort required by the psychodramatic activity.

**The Audience.** The audience in the psychodrama is somewhat similar to the audience in any dramatic presentation. Yet it should be recalled that Moreno viewed psychodrama as going beyond dramatic performance into the realm of psychotherapy and catharsis, such that it had a far greater potential for catharsis than that afforded by observing drama or classical tragedy. The audience of psychodrama may benefit, as may the audience in any effective dramatic presentation, from experiencing empathy with the characters and cathartic emotional release through identification with them.

However, in psychodrama, the role of the audience has other features as well. Because the focus in psychodrama is clearly on human problems and conflicts, there is great opportunity for audience members to empathize and to relate the events to their own life experiences. In addition, the audience has a role in assisting the protagonist and of participating in a variety of alternative follow-up techniques that are available, many of which involve participation of the whole audience. In the sharing following a psychodrama, audience members respond to the scene just played in terms of their own experiences.

When interpretation is focused on the audience, members offer their reactions to what has occurred or make interpretative comments or suggestions to the protagonist.

## SPECIAL TECHNIQUES

Although the basic and central activity of the psychodrama is the spontaneous portrayal of scenes created by the protagonist, a number of special techniques have been developed. The introduction of these techniques is typically at the discretion of the director, who must be alert for occasions when the therapeutic or training effect of the psychodrama would be enhanced by their introduction. Moreno (1953) cautioned that these techniques should not be used to change the spontaneous psychodrama into a static dramatic performance but rather should be used in the same way as the psychodrama itself, to enhance the possibilities of spontaneity, catharsis, and insight. The range of special techniques that might be created is infinite; the director may always spontaneously develop techniques that seem to be facilitative during the course of a particular psychodramatic session. Some of these have been used, modified, and used again and again until they have reached the status of regular parts of the psychodramatic director's armamentarium. Many of the most commonly known techniques have been summarized and described by Zerka Moreno (1959) and J.L. Moreno (1959). We will present a brief description of some of the more widely used techniques.

*Soliloquy.* As its name suggests, soliloquy is a technique in which the protagonist speaks directly to the audience in a spontaneous expression of feeling. Like the soliloquy in the drama, it is a monologue, but unlike it, the soliloquy technique involves a spontaneous emotional expression. The director may elect to suggest that the protagonist try a soliloquy if she thinks that the patient is unable to express his feelings adequately in the psychodramatic scene, or if the intensity of his emotional involvement in the scene is causing him to become unproductive. The soliloquy then provides an opportunity for the protagonist to gain some distance from his emotions and to explore in his own mind the reactions that he has been having.

*Double.* This technique might be employed when the director feels that the protagonist is being overwhelmed by the other characters in the drama or when he is having difficulty in expressing his true feelings. It consists of assigning an auxiliary ego to stand behind the protagonist and act with him and in some instances for him. It requires great empathy on the part of the auxiliary ego to feel what he thinks the patient is experiencing and to help him express it. Sometimes simply standing behind and following the emotions and bodily movements and attitudes of the protagonist is all that is required to give the protagonist additional strength to express himself adequately; at other times the double, or as he is sometimes called, "the alter ego," may react in ways that he thinks reflect what the protagonist is feeling.

*Role Reversal.* The role reversal technique requires the protagonist and an auxiliary ego to switch roles. The director might suggest the use of this technique when she feels that the protagonist would profit from an understanding of how the person with whom he is in conflict is feeling, or when she wants to give the protagonist an opportunity to act the role of a significant person in his life as he would like that person to behave. Since an auxiliary ego is playing the protagonist's role, it also affords the latter an opportunity to gain some knowledge about how others see him.

*Mirror Technique.* This technique emphasizes the previously mentioned function of role reversal, that is, affording the protagonist an opportunity to see himself as others do. The protagonist becomes a member of the audience and an auxiliary ego is assigned the role of the protagonist with instructions to play the role as much like the protagonist himself played it as possible. The director might suggest the mirror technique if she feels that the protagonist could profit from standing back from himself for a while and having the opportunity to see how another person would enact his role. The technique is particularly useful when a protagonist has great difficulty in appreciating the impact that his behavior has on others.

When the protagonist is unable to "get into" his role, the director might suggest a variation of the mirror technique. In this instance, she would instruct the auxiliary ego to deliberately distort the protagonist's behavior through exaggeration of some characteristic with the aim of arousing the latter into becoming more actively involved. The auxiliary ego might exaggerate a whining, demanding quality and thereby arouse the original player to take over his own part again to show how he really behaves.

*Behind the Back.* This is a technique in which the protagonist ceases being an actor but sits with his back to the other group members who then, led by the director, discuss their impressions of him. This, like the mirror technique, is viewed as a method through which the protagonist might learn something about how others see him and react to him.

*Magic Shop.* This technique is considered useful when the protagonist is uncertain or confused or ambivalent about what his real wishes and goals in life are. Either the director or one of the auxiliary egos plays storekeeper in a magic shop that sells not objects but values or personal characteristics or general desires in life, such as success or courage or brilliance or wealth. In the magic shop, however, the method of exchange is not payment for what one wants but bartering. In order to have his wishes granted, the protagonist must exchange some valued characteristic or aspect of himself for what he desires. This technique is seen as giving the person an opportunity to evaluate what is really important to him, as well as what aspects of himself really stand in the way of getting what he wants.

These are just a few of the many techniques that have been developed, all of which endeavor to further the process of exploration and emotional understanding in the psychodramatic setting.

## ROLE OF THE DIRECTOR-THERAPIST

Moreno (1946, 1953, 1964) described the director's role as having three major components: producer, therapeutic agent, and analytical observer. The director is the producer in the sense that she is the organizer of the dramatic situation—warming-up group members and continuing to oversee the proceedings throughout the dramatic presentation. The director is a therapeutic agent in the sense that she helps the patient develop and set the scene; encourages spontaneity, creativity, and catharsis; and subsequently helps in the process of gaining insight and meaning from the experience. As analytical observer the director may have to stop the action for clarification, making certain that roles are being properly enacted, and must also be attendant to the audience members to encourage them to take advantage of opportunities to achieve therapeutic or educative effects from the experience.

The role of the director must vary with the nature of the group membership. For example, in working with a group of regressed patients in the hospital, the director's role has to be an extremely active one. In the warm-up process she must get people involved and willing to participate; it often requires great expenditures of energy and a special ability to enable these patients to become sufficiently relaxed and comfortable to participate in a new and potentially anxiety-provoking experience. A director may have to begin working with a patient around hallucinatory experiences that are occurring in the moment. Then the task will be especially difficult because the patient may be so extremely withdrawn as to give only very minor cues about how to set the psychodramatic scene. In such a situation, the director's ability to empathize with and to tune into the patient's experience, as well as her own charisma and spontaneity are particularly crucial. On the other hand, with a group of outpatients or a group of people using the psychodrama experience for personal growth and development, the director's role in the warm-up period might be a much less active one since the participants already have considerable readiness to participate in the psychodramatic experience.

In a continuing psychodramatic group in a state mental hospital, the patient-protagonist may have been chosen in advance, and the general nature of the scene to be enacted may already have been anticipated. In contrast, in a growth and development group, the major task of the director during the warm-up period might be to find topics of common interest to the group members. The director might also begin by posing questions to the audience at large, or question an individual member of the audience; the director might pick a topic such as problems in marital relations or functioning effectively with supervisors in a work situation and settle on a problem area with a high level of interest among all group members. Such topics as work problems or family conflicts are usually likely to have some meaning for most members of a group.

Once the warm-up is completed and group members are relaxed and ready for the psychodramatic experience, the protagonist is ready to begin the first psychodramatic scene. At this point, the director's role, particularly in groups not involving seriously disturbed patients, becomes much less active and the protagonist assumes the role of setting the scene and, in a very real sense, becoming the creator of the drama to be portrayed. It is the protagonist who chooses those who will serve as auxiliary egos and gives them directions as to how to behave. A director, of course, should keep particularly alert during this period since she must oversee the proceedings and might be called upon to help in giving directions to auxiliary egos or to assist the protagonist in clarifying the scene. Again, with more disturbed patients, the director will have to be more active during this period. In any event, the protagonist needs to trust that the director will be able to provide guidance throughout the psychodramatic experience. It is important that the director remain constantly attentive to what the protagonist is feeling and be ready to intervene should the proceedings take an unproductive turn, or should the auxiliary egos be playing their roles in ways that do not seem to accurately capture the characteristics of the persons to be portrayed in the psychodrama. At some points the director might intervene to suggest a variety of specialized techniques that would add to the cathartic effect and potential insight the scene might afford.

After the scene has been completed, the director might engage in a variety of techniques to extract additional gains from the psychodramatic situation, such as interviewing the protagonist directly in an effort to clarify and make more understandable the scene that was just enacted. Moreno described the protagonist as being in a state of intense involvement immediately following the scene and as having a readiness for further exploration. Since psychodrama is a technique that should always provide benefit for all members of the group, it is seen as important to make efforts to involve those who have not already directly participated in order to enable them to gain something from the experience. One technique to serve this end is sharing. In the sharing period, members of the audience try to relate their own life experiences to what has occurred in the psychodrama by describing similar experiences or emotional reactions of their own and discussing them with the group. Another post-psychodrama technique is an interpretative session in which all members of the group, led by the director, respond to the scene by describing their reactions to the role behavior of the protagonist and/or his auxiliary egos. All of these techniques encourage maximal involvement of the total group. Beyond the emotional release of active participation, they encourage a development of insight into the motivation that underlies the behavior just portrayed in the psychodramatic scene.

## VARIED USES OF PSYCHODRAMA

Starting in the 1960s some psychodramatic techniques, especially role-playing that involves spontaneous expression, have come to be evermore widely employed in a variety of other group intervention modalities (Gendron, 1980). What is particularly striking in a review of recent literature is the emphasis on the variety of different populations considered as appropriate target groups for psychodrama: These include such varied age and diagnostic groupings as borderline personalities (Sidorsky, 1984), latency aged children (Smith et. al., 1985), the elderly in nursing homes (Carman & Nordin, 1984), autistic adolescents (Warger, 1984), prisoners (Schramski & Harvey, 1983), and counselling students in training (Kranz & Huston, 1984).

Throughout all the variety of clientele and purposes to which these groups are addressed, commonly echoed themes continue to be emphasized—spontaneity, creativity, catharsis, and the opportunity to experience and observe behavior in a controlled and benign setting, where the protagonist and others learn new behaviors that can be effectively applied to everyday actual life situations.

## SOCIODRAMA

Another form of spontaneous dramatic experience that Moreno developed is called *sociodrama*. As we have seen, Moreno always had a strong interest in and a desire to contribute to the improvement of the human condition. The creation of sociodrama was inspired by that desire as well as by the wish to put the dramatic expression of spontaneity and creativity to a useful purpose on a large-scale group or social level. Moreno hoped that the use of dramatic methods could increase an exploration of sociocultural difference, through which human conflict might be diminished and understanding among peoples increased.

Although it is difficult to draw a clear distinction between psychodrama and sociodrama, the latter mainly emphasizes group-related needs and issues of general social significance, whereas the former stresses the unique interpersonal concerns of the individual. Yet the two forms are always intermingled to some extent. Individual problems enacted through psychodrama always have a sociocultural aspect; and the social significance of sociodrama is always colored to some extent by unique individual concerns. A useful way to distinguish between the two is to think in terms of the concepts of *figure* and *ground*. In psychodrama, the concerns of the individual are the figure and the group and social concerns the ground, while in sociodrama the reverse is true.

Despite the fact that psychodrama typically occurs in a group setting, the focus of interest is basically on the individual's particular problems. While it is true that members of the group are able to profit from the experience either through playing roles of auxiliary egos or from the various aspects of audience participation that are involved, they are not the center of attention. Sociodrama (Moreno, 1946, 1953, 1964), on the other hand, is viewed as a collective type of group experience that deals with sociocultural parameters. Since the problems dealt with are those of intercultural conflicts, those playing roles in sociodrama are not enacting their own personal problems, but rather serve as exemplars of the problems that affect the group at large or the interface between several groups that are involved in cultural conflict. Sociodrama is the technique of choice when large numbers of people, or all members of a group, or indeed, society as a whole, are faced with a common problem. For example, problems in relating between blacks and whites in contemporary America or conflicts between two groups, one pushing for industrial development and the other for environmental protection would be appropriate topics for a sociodramatic session.

In many respects, sociodrama follows the outline already described for psychodrama in terms of its formal characteristics—the use of the stage, the role of the director, the presence of a protagonist, the use of auxiliary egos, and the like. As already suggested, in sociodrama the emphasis is not on dealing with purely personal concerns, but rather on dealing with the collective experience and group concerns. While the protagonist who plays a role is to some extent affected by his own idiosyncratic approaches and feelings, the actor should try to play the role not for himself, but as an exemplar of the group. Of course, all roles in psychodrama and sociodrama have both their personal and collective elements: One is not only a mother of a particular child but also a member of a particular culture and living in a certain time in a certain place. These factors clearly affect the development of a role in psychodrama and in sociodrama as well as do one's personal idiosyncratic experiences. What is important in differentiating the two is the focus of concern in the group's activity: When the focus is on an individual's concern and personal desire for change, then one is dealing with psychodrama; when the focus is on collective concerns, intergroup relations, collective ideology, group catharsis, and social change, then one is clearly dealing with sociodrama.

Another distinction between the two is the fact that participation of the whole audience is much greater in sociodrama than in psychodrama. In the latter, members of the audience may share personal concerns with the protagonist and achieve a secondary catharsis through involvement in the protagonist's role experience. In sociodrama, the focus is on collective rather than personal roles so that members of the audience are likely to share in common the problems that are of a collective cultural and not personal nature. Obviously the cathartic effect in sociodrama will be the greatest when it deals with issues about which most members of the audience have strong and conflicting feelings, or when there are strong polarities between two subgroups of participants. Many of Moreno's examples of sociodrama deal with intergroup conflicts that focus on racial and religious attitudes or differences. Black-white relations were always of concern to Moreno, and he advocated the use of sociodramatic techniques in helping to achieve group catharsis. Sociodrama as a technique is considered particularly useful under circumstances of very active intergroup conflict, such as the time following a large-scale interracial conflict, or in a preventive way, when intergroup conflict threatens to develop into disruptive outbursts but has not yet done so.

Since the group is the focus of attention in sociodrama, there is no one exactly comparable to the personally conflicted protagonist in psychodrama. Rather, there is a cast of audience members and auxiliary egos who must submerge their personal concerns and play their roles for all members of the culture—a protagonist must be all blacks, all Jews, all Christians, all white Anglo-Saxon Protestants. In fact individuals who are the most emotionally intense about the issues at hand (e.g., those who have been involved directly in a racial disturbance) may be unable to separate their strong personal feelings from shared cultural concerns and therefore may not be effective protagonists. Nonetheless, Moreno suggests that their role in sociodrama is an important one; they may be useful as informants to assist the protagonist or auxiliary egos in playing their roles or serving as persons who help give the audience a feel for what happened in a group conflict. For example, a black woman, extremely angered at being turned down for a job at a white employment agency, may not have enough distance from her anger to be an effective protagonist in a sociodrama. Another person with instructions from her might be better able to play the role in terms of its larger social implications as they touch many in the audience and thus more successfully serve the sociodramatic goal of group catharsis and learning. The relative importance of shared group concerns versus individual problems is highlighted when one considers that the woman who was rejected for employment might eventually want to seek personal catharsis as a protagonist in a psychodrama workshop.

With both psychodrama and sociodrama, Moreno developed a technique which for a long time went relatively unnoticed and unappreciated. In the last several decades—particularly around issues of black-white relations—the technique and derivatives of it have been more widely used, although Moreno has not often been credited for its initiation. For example, many of the confrontation groups that were developed to facilitate communication between intercultural groups in the late sixties and early seventies clearly drew upon sociodramatic technique and theory.

Moreno, himself, also responded vigorously to the outbreaks of violent racial tensions of that period and became an active advocate for the use of sociodrama as a means of understanding the black revolution in the United States as well as for working out intergroup tensions related to it. The *Boston Sunday Globe* in May, 1968, reported a session held at the Annual Meeting of the American Psychiatric Association at which Moreno presented a sociodrama demonstration entitled, "Origins and Causes of the Black Revolution and the Revolution of the Hippies in the United States based on Sociometry, Small Group Research, Sociodrama, and Group Pathology." A large group gathered for the demonstration and many of the members participated. Among the issues suggested by members of the audience were problems such as how to achieve black unity, the problem of the white liberal, and the role of the black middle class "square." The interaction became extremely heated at times, such as when the person playing the role of a black power advocate refused to accept the assistance of a white liberal, and the white liberal couldn't understand why; the black power advocate insisted that at the time it was extremely important that black unity be permitted to develop without the involvement of whites. Many people in the audience spontaneously reacted with angry outbursts around their own ambivalence or their lack of understanding of the attitudes that existed and the strengths of feelings associated with disagreements. All this represented an important first step in dealing with the constant human problem of intercultural conflict. Sociodrama and its derivatives have continued to help people to understand more clearly, in both an emotional and a cognitive way, how many of their strongly held but not well-understood feelings affect their attitudes and behavior vis-à-vis sensitive social issues.

# CHAPTER SEVEN
# THE GESTALT THERAPY WORKSHOP

Gestalt therapy is famous for its founder, Fritz Perls, and for its innovative approach to individual and group psychotherapy, one that involves the patient in a dialogue with herself wherein she gives dramatic expression to the feelings, conflicts, and preoccupations of the immediate moment. When looked at from this purely technical aspect, gestalt therapy would seem to constitute a repudiation of psychoanalysis (and of the latter's emphasis on a more cerebral, discursive, and historically focused dialogue between analyst and analysand) and to be instead an extreme form of experientialism. Indeed, Perls himself made much of his repudiation of psychoanalytic procedure. However, for us, gestalt therapy represents something slightly different: a complex conceptual and methodological "blend" of several influences—some psychoanalytic, some existential-experiential, and some even psychodramatic. These parts combine together to form the unique and coherent "gestalt" that is gestalt therapy.

Until his death in 1970, Fritz Perls and gestalt therapy were synonomous. Credit for the origination of the technique belonged to him, despite the considerable assistance that he received from his wife, Laura, and from the colleagues who were drawn to his unorthodox techniques. Perls lived to be seventy-six years old, and his life, which he described in a book of autobiographical reminiscences (Perls, 1969a), was one of considerable searching, excitement, frustration, and growth. He was in many ways a restless, rebellious person, antagonistic toward entrenched ways of thinking and frequently fighting off boredom and discontent. When the psychoanalytic movement had come to be characterized for him by authoritarian close-mindedness, he set out in a pioneering direction not dissimilar to that taken by Freud many years earlier. Change was a central theme in Perls's personal life, with frequent interpersonal disruptions and geographic shifts, and in his theoretical orientation, which emphasized the constant ebb and flow of healthy, present-centered awareness.

Perls's first dislocation occurred when he left his home city, Berlin, for Frankfurt. The second occurred when he emigrated to South Africa in response to the growing Nazi menace. Still another change involved his move to New York City, succeeded by one to Miami Beach and then to Los Angeles. In 1966 Perls joined the staff of the Esalen Institute in Big Sur, California, and in 1969 he went to Vancouver Island, Canada, where he founded a gestalt community. Although he had published *Ego, Hunger, and Aggression* in 1947 and *Gestalt Therapy* in 1951, it was not until the late sixties, which coincided with his residence at Esalen and with the explosion of interest in the human potential movement, that the man Fritz Perls and his therapy began to achieve national recognition. In the last years of his life Perls led an increasing number of demonstration workshops, and he was an active speaker and participant at the 1968 meeting of the American Psychological Association. In 1969 two additional books appeared—*In and Out of the Garbage Pail* (1969a) and *Gestalt Therapy Verbatim* (1969b). A large number of audiovisual materials demonstrating Perls at work were also produced during these years.

Like most psychoanalytic, experiential, and eclectic therapy groups, the gestalt therapy group often meets on a weekly basis over an extended period of time. However, it can also meet in a noncontinuous time framework (i.e., meeting intensively for a month, a week, several days, or even several hours). Such a format is especially appropriate in a training context, since it enables professionals to be introduced to gestalt methods in a direct and intensive way. During the 1960s, Esalen Institute began to sponsor gestalt workshops on this noncontinuous, usually short-term basis, and it continues to do so. Some of these workshops are primarily for professional therapists and are oriented toward the more technical side of gestalt approaches, and others are geared to nonprofessionals.

The workshop format with which Perls became most identified, at Esalen and Vancouver Island and in the several taped and filmed demonstrations of his work, was noncontinuous; its participants, whether professionals or nonprofessionals, met together from a half-day to several weeks, and their formal contact ceased at the workshop's end. Unlike in psychoanalytic and experiential groups, participants in the gestalt group did not develop a prolonged relationship to the group in which they slowly reconstructed their original relationships to their families of origin, thereby gaining insight into the influence of their past lives. Perls's approach simply required one to focus intensively on her "stream of awareness" via the guidance of a therapist who, much like a Zen master, facilitated this meditative process. Such an approach was bound to have particular appeal for previously analyzed therapists who, while reluctant to reenter formal treatment, wanted to experience some form of brief psychotherapy that would prove vitalizing and reintegrative. Moreover, despite this model's reliance on such terms as *therapist* and *patient,* it departed markedly from the medical model of psychotherapy, in which a "sick" patient suffers from a specific psychological "disease" that is then "diagnosed" and "treated" by a "doctor." Now the patient could be a reasonably healthy therapist who, like all other people, has "problems in living" (Szasz, 1961) or, in the language of gestalt therapy, *blocks* and areas of *avoidance.* These problems could be approached in a workshop setting that, however charged emotionally, bore some resemblance to educational classrooms and seminars. Hence the gestalt workshop, like its psychodrama predecessor, constituted one more step away from long-term group psychotherapy toward a short-term educational-therapeutic experience that would gradually pave the way for the "encounter" model (see Chapter 11).

In an individual therapy setting, gestalt therapy can be practiced in a variety of ways, some more "pure" than others in that they rely on Perls's highly theatrical and unique "empty chair" technique. Here, the patient's direct interaction with the therapist, in the sense of a normal conversational mode in which each addresses statements and questions to the other, is minimal. Instead, the patient is encouraged to translate her moment-to-moment experience into an ongoing, self-enacted psychodrama wherein she personifies, and speaks for, all the body sensations, feelings, and thoughts that she is aware of. Even her concern with the therapist, and with what the latter might be thinking, is directed into a conversation with the therapist-in-the-empty-chair in which the patient's dialogue is with her *fantasy-image* of the therapist, rather than with the actual therapist. Once she has spoken to the therapist-in-the-empty-chair, she is directed to sit in the empty chair and, in the role of therapist (or, to be more exact, her fantasy-projection of this therapist), answer herself back.

On the other hand, individual therapy might proceed in a less puristic fashion, taking on the flavor of a more typically encountered interchange between therapist and patient; as one writer (Flores, 1985, p. 76) put it: "Not all Gestalt therapy is Perlsian." Here the therapist manifests his gestalt orientation by his consistent attention to the patient's nonverbal behavior, his occasionally suggesting various exercises or "experiments" (e.g., "Try exaggerating the motions you are making with your foot and see what you experience"), and in his reminding the patient that he is more interested in the patient's actual moment-to-moment experience than in any arbitrary "program" as to the kind of person she "should" or "should not" become.

In the group setting, the therapist would again have the choice of modeling himself on Perls; if so, he would discourage group members from having spontaneous contact with one another. Instead participants would watch while the therapist engaged in a dialogue with one particular member. Typically Perls would begin the workshop by asking who in the group wanted "to work." Whoever volunteered would then take the "hot-seat," which was the chair facing the therapist. The participant, now a "patient," might start by stating a particular life problem that was disturbing her; if the patient remains silent, the therapist might ask her to express what is in her immediate awareness. Whatever she chooses to express, the focus is on her moment-to-moment, here-and-now experience, and she is encouraged to intensify and exaggerate this experience through a variety of exercises to be described later. The other participants retire to the background and function as a kind of "Greek chorus" (Denes-Radomisli, 1971), resonating and empathizing with the patient so that they gain from her experience via the process of identification. At certain points the group might be called in by the therapist, but usually in a structured way, for the purpose of furthering the therapist's work with the person in the hot-seat (for instance, a go-around exercise might be suggested wherein the patient goes to every participant with the same sentence-beginning—"I want you to like me for my___"—and then is to finish it differently for each group member). The patient might remain in the hot-seat anywhere from ten to thirty minutes; she works until she and the therapist have some sense of closure. Usually from three to six participants would take the hot-seat during any single session.

Since Perls's death, however, more and more gestalt theorists have pointed out the artificial limitations posed when workshop participants refrain from spontaneous interaction and simply observe the therapist at work with a lone individual (e.g., Polster & Polster, 1978; Enright, 1978; Feder & Ronall, 1980). Not only are many gestalt techniques applicable to working with several members at once, but the very notion of a "gestalt," or "whole," depicts the group as a potentially creative entity that is somehow more than the "sum of its parts". (It seems ironic, therefore, that Perls and his immediate disciples preferred to focus on the group solely as a backdrop for individual work; see Kepner, 1980.) This more group-focused approach will characterize the stance taken by the gestalt leader in the illustrative session that follows.

## ILLUSTRATION OF A TYPICAL SESSION

The segment that appears below is drawn from a fictitious all-day gestalt-training workshop for psychotherapists. At the point where the illustration begins, the group has met for an entire morning and is about ten minutes into its afternoon session.

Delia: This morning I was upset by Martin, partly because he reminded me so much of my older brother, Dennis, *seeming* to take an interest in me but really patronizing me and letting me know every step of the way that he doesn't really take me seriously. But then the group, by attempting to interpret my behavior, made me very angry. I thought that in a Gestalt group interpretations were regarded as "head" stuff and from one's "computer" and therefore not to be trusted, and that rather than going with the past, which constitutes a defense, one stays with the immediate feeling.

Therapist (Dan): One thing, Delia, a Gestalt therapist is typically struck by is our unassimilated, incompletely digested "should's" and "shouldn't's." And that's what I'm hearing from you right now—what a Gestalt therapist *should* do and what he *shouldn't* do.

Delia: But isn't that the purpose of the workshop?—to avoid all the cognitive crap that goes on in too many groups. That's what my readings of Fritz Perls tell me.

Dan: And I *should* be more like Fritz?

Delia: Well, frankly, I *am* a bit disappointed with the group so far. It seems too much like my psychoanalytic group back home; I had thought there'd be more confrontation and more opportunity for each of us to do individual hot-seat work with you while the others watched. I even brought in a dream that I had last night, hoping you'd work with me on it, because it seemed as though I had more or less dreamt it for the workshop—being that it's about Dennis and that I dreamt it the very night before the workshop began, just at the point when I had decided that my relationship to him is the major problem in my life.

Lillian: I can't believe you're saying this, Delia. You've already monopolized most of the morning with your relationship to Dennis and now you blithely say you want to bring in a dream that relates to it—it makes me hopping mad! Don't you think it would be fairer to give others a turn?

Delia: If you want the floor you can fight for it right alongside me; I can't monopolize the group without the group's cooperation.

Martin: Screw you, Delia! You always have the right answers.

Dan: Ok—we've heard from Lillian and Martin—how do the rest of you feel?

Frank: I can see that Delia's in a lot of pain, and she has every right to express it, but sure, I had some of the feeling that the others expressed, that the workshop lasts only a day and others should be given a chance.

Rhoda: I agree with both Lillian and Frank—because sure, I can see that there's a problem trying to find enough time for each of us. But I'm also amazed that Lillian is as upset as she is. (Turning toward Lillian) Why does it make you *this* angry, Lillian?

Lillian: Delia makes me feel a bit jealous. I think I probably see in her the demanding child-in-me that would love to demand center stage, if I had the guts to let her.

Dan: Why don't speak to that child and find out what she's all about? Try putting her in the empty chair and let's see what she answers back. (He takes an empty chair that stands just alongside them and places it just inside their circle of chairs.)

Lillian: See, already I feel self-conscious, having everyone's eyes on me this way; I feel like I'm in the fourth grade and performing in my first play.

Dan: So what?

Lillian: Well, it's no fun feeling anxious! (pause) OK—I'll try. (She turns to the empty chair.) Well, little girl, you sit there looking so patient, yet also somehow radiantly expectant. What do you have to say for yourself? (leaves her seat and sits herself in the empty chair).

Lillian-in-the-empty-chair: Oh, wonderful, I was wondering when you would give me a chance to speak! I've been dying to talk all day! But *she* (pointing to Delia) has been jabbering and jabbering all day, hogging the floor and not giving anyone else a chance. Frankly, I was getting bored. Not only did I have what *I* wanted to say, but I want to hear from the rest of you too. Each of you looks pretty interesting and I would hate to leave the workshop without having had a chance to learn who you are, where you live, what your problems are—lot's of different things about you. (Impishly) Gee, Lillian—you look pale and gray. Am I embarrassing you?

Lillian (switching back to her original chair): You certainly are! I guess you say what's on your mind, and you *do* have an impish charm of sorts but I'm uncomfortable with your honesty and your rudeness; perhaps you've said enough? (switches back)

Lillian-in-the-empty-chair: But why should I give up the floor when I've waited so long to have it? I *love* getting all this attention! And unlike you, I don't feel so uncomfortable—it feels natural to want to talk and to let the people know what I'm thinking. You're so damned uptight and careful. You allow yourself to say just so much and no more, lest you offend Person A, or not give Person B a chance to speak because everybody should have their chance. When am I going to have *my* chance?! (switches back again).

Lillian: Well, kiddo, I just gave you a bit of a chance and you've had your moment in the limelight. But just like Delia, you're also going to have to learn to compromise and give other people a chance now and then. Sure, I envy you your ability to let it all hang out and to not have to be like me—Miss Perfection. On the other hand, I think you could use more of my social graces.

Dan: Delia, this might be a good place to break in. How are you experiencing this dialogue between the two Lillians?

Delia: I have more problems with the grown-up Lillian than I do with the child Lillian.

Dan: Could you tell her that directly?

Delia: Sure. Lillian, I like you a lot better as a child than as an adult. You're refreshing, you're spontaneous, (pauses) you're engaging! For the first time I think maybe we could have fun together. When I'm going shopping, I could see us going together, and when I'm planning a party I'd love having you along. From me, that's quite a compliment.

Lillian: The funny thing, Delia, is I stopped being angry with you somewhere along the way, though I don't know just when. Yes, I could imagine having fun with you—I feel a lot more comfortable with you now.

Delia: And I'm glad to see, Dan, from what you just did with Lillian that you *are* willing to do hot-seat work and use the empty chair technique. I like hot-seat work, and I don't care what the rest of you are thinking. I know I'm not Miss-Popular, that some of you find me pedantic and resent my picking Dan's brain, but damn it! I'm here to learn something.

Dan: You're assuming that everybody here resents you for taking over, so in a minute I'm going to ask you to "check out" these perceptions by asking each person how they're experiencing you; some of them have spoken up on this issue and some of them haven't—and some of those who spoke out before may have changed their mind. But first, Delia, I want to directly answer your question to me, because you're all psychotherapists and I know that one of the reasons you've joined this workshop is to learn more about how to use Gestalt techniques in working with groups.

You see, I work somewhat differently from the way Fritz Perls did; for instance, I believe that conscious insight into one's own dynamics can be helpful—as when Delia makes a connection between what she feels here-and-now toward Martin and what she used to feel toward Dennis. And while I sometimes work with one of you in the hot-seat while the rest of the group watches I also, unlike Fritz, like to encourage spontaneous group interaction—like just now, when Delia and Lillian went at each other for just a few seconds and discovered that they are more sisters under the skin than natural antagonists and that they each have something substantial to give the other.

The afternoon part of workshop continues for several hours, with Dan at this point instructing Delia to go directly to each participant in turn, asking what was in his or her mind at the precise moment when she complimented him for his explicit utilization of the empty-chair exercise.


## KEY CONCEPTS

**The Gestalt–Figure–Ground Dynamics.** In reviewing Kurt Lewin's field-theory and its application to group-dynamic psychotherapy (see Chapter 4), we presented the perceptual theory of the three original gestalt psychologists, Kohler, Koffka, and Wertheimer. These theorists had emphasized perception as a process involving the organization of patterned relationships wherein some elements are seen as "figure" and others as "ground," and stimuli are perceived in the context of the overall whole in which they are embedded. For example, a black circle can be clearly perceived as such if it is shown against a white background; however, if it is embedded within a sufficiently complex gestalt involving many lines and patterns, it will for most observers turn out to be "hidden."

Gestalt perceptual psychology was strongly phenomenological in that it regarded one's conscious perceptions of the world as constituting significant and instructive psychological data. It was also holistic in that it emphasized a person's capacity to impose pattern and meaning on discrete events and to organize phenomena into ever-more-complex wholes. Perls extended the phenomenological and holistic principles to personality functioning, for concomitant with his emphasis on immediate experience was his holistic conviction that the therapist's primary task was to help the patient not so much to resolve conflicts as to integrate them in a more coherent, cohesive fashion (e.g., conflicts between thinking and feeling, activity and passivity, etc.). Hence in the illustration above, the therapist attempts to enable the normally sober and somewhat conservative Lillian to become more comfortable with, and accepting of, her fun-loving and exhibitionist side.

Perls was not, however, the first personality psychologist to be influenced by gestalt theory. Along with Kurt Lewin, Kurt Goldstein (1940), one of Perls's teachers, had applied gestalt concepts to the field of motivation, saying that though one's personality might appear to be composed of a random constellation of variously acquired habits, it actually strives for unity and, in so doing, organizes its various habits, predispositions, tendencies, and attitudes into a more or less coherent whole. What made Perls's relationship to gestalt perceptual psychology unusually direct was that, in making the transition from simple perception to the whole gamut of personality functioning, he not only retained the "figure-ground" concepts of the original theory, but concentrated more than any other previous therapist-theoretician on each specific shift in the client's moment-to-moment flow of awareness.

Let's now take the attention that the original gestalt psychologists gave to visual stimuli and extend it to a more everyday life situation, as Perls attempted to do. As a mother listens to her baby's crying, hoping that it will stop, all other noise becomes background of which she is largely unaware. Once his crying has ceased, she may then become aware of a sound that had previously been "ground" (e.g., the whirring of a fan). After the sound of the fan has been "figure" for a while it too will return to the background of her perception, to be replaced by another figure. Usually no one stimulus can be figure for any great amount of time. Human attention doesn't work that way; once a figure reaches a certain point of saturation, it begins to recede into ground. This principle helps to explain some well-known figure-ground reversals (e.g., two white silhouetted profiles face-to-face against a black background that, once reversed, become the silhouette of a black vase against a white background.

What was "perception" for the original gestaltists became "awareness" for Perls. In bringing in the dimension of awareness he extended gestalt phenomenology beyond mere sensation, to feelings and to thoughts. While awareness involves all three elements, Perls claimed that it was within the realm of awareness of *feelings* that the human organism experiences the greatest difficulty. Neuroses, he said, develop at that point in the flow of awareness where feelings that would normally become figure are blocked off by the patient and kept in the background, because of the latter's "phobic" attitude toward them; she "avoids" them because of their unpleasantness. The gestalt therapist's task is to pay careful attention to the patient's "continuum of awareness" and to locate those precise points where she becomes "stuck"; usually these points involve avoidances that disturb the rhythmic ebb and flow of healthy, present-centered awareness. In balanced awareness various emotions, perceptions, and needs intensify to a point where they become clear-cut gestalten. Once fully figured they will obey the law of all perception and eventually become background. If these gestalten involve actual physical needs—like hunger and thirst—the person is functioning most organismically if she turns her attention to those aspects of reality that can best satisfy them; once satisfied, they too, like other perceptions, should gradually fade from awareness.

Perls did not ignore the sensory aspects of the patient's phenomenology. When working with a "stuck" or blocked patient, especially when the latter was caught up in ruminative attempts to discover what she was *really* feeling, Perls often directed her toward the simplest perceptual level: "What do you see? hear? smell?" This was the point of his oft-quoted motto: "Lose your mind and come to your senses!" As the latter statement implies, he was not impressed with the value of thinking per se. Unless it was directed toward genuine problem-solving or scientific pursuits (which Perls claimed it all too rarely was), thinking was largely a form of computing, usually taking the form of fantasies in which we "rehearse" the various roles we intend to play with others in order to impress them. Therefore, for most patients, thinking was in the service of phobic avoidance. For Perls, then, normal awareness, despite its inclusion of feelings and thoughts, would have to take careful account of the physical environment, an account that returned it to the perceptual context in which gestalt psychology had originally developed.

**Now and How.**    These are two central emphases in gestalt therapy theory. The *now* refers to our awareness which—in a fundamental, almost metaphysical sense—must always exist in the immediate here-and-now, however much its content may involve the past or the future. Our specific memories and our anticipations of the future both constitute fantasy-images, however "realistic," occurring in the present; however vivid, they can only remove us from the immediacy of the present in general, and from our sensory and affective experience in particular.

Perls believed that Freud's method of free association was somewhat parallel to his own method in the sense that it too attempted to help patients report on their immediate experience. The problem, according to Perls, was that in asking a patient to report everything that came to her *mind* and in reducing the amount of environmental stimuli available to her (through her placement on the couch), Freud was minimizing the patient's opportunity for genuine contact with the environment. Perls's aim was to help the patient contact her experience with vivid immediacy, rather than to simply talk "about" it. Thus if the patient stated that she was aware of some sadness, the gestalt therapist might ask her: "What does your sadness *say*? *Be* your sadness." Or, if the patient reported: "I think I try to bully people a lot of the time," the therapist might reply: "O.K. Be as big a bully here as you can. Bully me, and go and bully every person in the room." The emphasis is on intentionally demonstrating in the therapy session itself attitudes and behaviors that in psychoanalytic sessions are discussed discursively. Perls argued that in the absence of these intensifying techniques, the patient would all too likely lapse into a useless speculation about *why* she felt sad, *why* she liked to bully, and so on. According to Perls, "why" questions lead to an endless, arid, and cerebral rumination about the past that only serves to encourage the patient's obsessive resistance to present experience. As a phenomenologist, the gestalt therapist has enough to do merely to attend to the *what* of the patient's immediate experience. If past figures are significant, they will probably emerge in the here-and-now work with the patient, either spontaneously ("Now I'm beginning to think about my mother") or through the therapist's alert attendance to cues ("The way you're ordering yourself to 'Start getting down to business!'—does that sound like anybody else's voice? Whom does that remind you of?"). Hence, for the gestalt therapist "What?" "Now," and "How?" replace the psychoanalytic concern with "Why?".

The question of *how* becomes relevant at those points where the patient manifests a phobic attitude toward her experience and attempts to avoid painful affect. Here the therapist must be extremely sensitive to all physical cues; for example, it may be that the patient manages, at the first sensation of tearfulness, to prevent weeping through specific muscular tensions and she may be unaware of this behavior until the therapist draws her attention to it ("Are you aware of your jaw? Try to speak for it.") Or when the therapist notices that a patient breaks eye contact with him, and asks what she experiences at that point, the patient may answer that she becomes preoccupied with an outside concern (e.g., a future event). The therapist now has an important clue as to how the patient uses withdrawal to avoid contacting emotions that are beginning to build in her. It may emerge that the patient breaks contact with the therapist at those moments when her anxiety is beginning to reach intolerable proportions. She has now progressed from knowing only that she was preoccupied with something that she had to do later in the day to being able to connect the emergence of this preoccupation with her moving her eyes upward and with a dim awareness of rapidly mounting tension.

If the patient is aware of the painful affect that she is attempting to avoid, the therapist can urge her to remain with the feeling ("Stay with your emptiness—try to feel as empty as you can!") Through the therapist's reassuring presence, the patient may be enabled to face feelings that she has fought for a long period of time and may find that she has a greater tolerance for them than she had suspected. Also, by allowing the affect to become fully felt and fully "figured," she may learn that no figure (or feeling) lasts forever and may therefore become less afraid of her feelings. The paradox here is that by having repeatedly prevented the affect from becoming fully figured (i.e., by having kept it at a point just below the threshold of awareness), she has held on to, and subtly nursed, her fear.

On the other hand, the therapist can encourage the patient to intensify her avoidance rather than the feelings against which it is directed. Essentially he has no other choice so long as the patient has no idea what the experience is that she wants to avoid. This strategy, although entirely consistent with Gestalt philosophy, also has something in common with what some psychoanalysts view as a "joining the resistance" (Spotnitz, 1969). For example, if the patient says "I feel myself withdrawing; I want to get away from here!" the therapist might encourage her to do just this: "Go in your fantasy to the place you would most like to be in; describe it to me in detail." By "going with" the avoidance and making it as fully figured as possible, the therapist is gradually paving the way for the moment when the need for it will reach a point of saturation and then gradually recede into the background. At this point the patient may be ready for renewed contact with the feelings that she finds hard to tolerate. However, there is another possibility, and this is that the fantasy itself will reveal some of the immediate problems that the patient is trying to avoid. For example, if she imagines herself to be beside the ocean, the therapist can ask her to become, or "speak for," the ocean. If she were to respond: "Shore, I'm going to pound against you and pound against you until you gradually wear away!" She might well be starting to express some of the central conflicts that she initially used the fantasy to evade.

Let us go back to our earlier example in which a patient holds back tears through specific muscle tensions, like the contractions of certain mouth and throat muscles. A typical gestalt procedure at this point would be to ask the patient to intensify her resistance by squeezing these muscles *harder.* Instructing the patient to allow herself to cry would probably be fruitless, since it is unlikely that crying is within her control. However the patient's muscle contractions, once she is aware of them, are within her control. In addition, the therapist's request that she stop her avoidance would tend to repeat the toxic experiences of the past in which the patient's parents refused to accept her as she was. Gestalt therapy embraces the paradox that change is most likely to occur when the patient's right *not* to change is accepted. This tenet reflects the existentialist's emphasis on "Letting the patient be" (see Chapter 5). According to Perls, the patient's attempt to "program" and force change is largely what led her into her neurotic bind in the first place. For the therapist to ask the patient to stop avoiding would encourage the patient to believe that she can control that which she cannot automatically control. However, by asking the patient to intensify her avoidance, the therapist is still paradoxically giving her some control over this behavior, and by making her aware of the behavior, the therapist is also asking her to assume responsibility for it.

It is because it is hard not to read "conscious" for "figure," "unconscious" for "ground," and "defense" for "avoidance" that we stated at the outset of this chapter that we viewed psychoanalysis as one of the significant influences on gestalt therapy. The present model clearly retains the kind of psychodynamic thinking that characterizes psychoanalytic theory, and some terminology—

like "phobic," "projection," and "introjection"—has been incorporated directly into gestalt language. Yet it is equally clear that Perls sought to give a strongly phenomenological emphasis to his theory and to pay more attention to the raw data of actual behavioral events than to theoretical speculation about the contents of the unconscious or about hypothetical connections between a particular constellation of childhood events and later psychopathology. Instead he preferred to concentrate on the minutiae of a patient's overt behavior (e.g., the twitching of a mouth, the averting of an eye), claiming that they embodied all the significant aspects of her experience, even those of which she was unaware. Hence he found a comfortable niche between the intrapsychic emphasis of psychoanalysis and the habit-oriented focus of behaviorism (see Chapter 8); for this reason we find his description of gestalt therapy as a "behavioristic phenomenology" (Perls, 1969b), exceedingly apt.

**Body Language.** The patient's nonverbal cues furnish the therapist with extremely important information, since they often betray feelings of which the patient is largely unaware. "What do your hands say?" is a frequent gestalt question. Or, if the patient is grasping one hand tightly with the other: "What does your right hand say to your left hand? Have them talk to each other." Similarly, the therapist may wish to direct the patient's attention to aspects of her vocal style (e.g., the whine implicit in her voice). As a means of getting the patient away from verbal content and more in touch with her style, the therapist might ask her to intensify aspects of her nonverbal behavior (e.g., "Hear that whining sound in your voice? Could you exaggerate it—just make the sounds, and make noises—don't say words" or "Notice that chopping motion you are making with your arm? Intensify it"). At the point where the therapist gives these directions he has no preconceived idea of where he will go with it; "programming" is antithetical to Gestalt theory since it implies a fantasy of the future. His intent is to stay with wherever the patient is "at" and to follow it as closely as possible. If the patient's arm-chopping becomes a kind of hitting or smashing, he may ask her to accompany it with sounds—so as to intensify the experience for the patient and to enable himself to get a clearer sense of the emotion that the movement expresses. If the patient starts to make angry sounds, the therapist might ask her to give words to the sounds. If the words are: "I hate you!" he may ask the patient who the "you" is; if the patient says "Grandmother" the therapist might eventually encourage the patient to have a dialogue with Grandmother and so on. In this manner, "unfinished business" (see p. 135), ill-buried resentments, and preconscious fantasies are woven into the here-and-now.

The therapist should be especially alert for nonverbal cues that are incongruous with the patient's verbalizations, (e.g., the patient's smiling as she tells the therapist that she is angry with him). The therapist tries *not* to interpret ("You're afraid you'll displease me, so you tell me via your smile that I shouldn't take you seriously") but, in keeping with his phenomenological orientation, simply tells the patient what he sees: "I see that you smile even though you claim to be angry with me." Or he may go a step further and ask that patient to "speak" for her smile, (i.e., to give it words).

**Projection.** The term projection had a broader meaning for Perls than it did for Freud (1911, p. 449) who used the term to refer to the attribution of a repudiated internal feeling or impulse (e.g., I hate him) to another person (he hates me). Since Freud's initial coining of the word, projection has been used in looser ways, as in the term "projective tests," in which *any* aspect of the test-taker's personality (including conscious ones) may be "projected" onto an outside stimulus—like a Rorschach ink blot. Certain totemistic conceptions, in which aspects of nature may be seen as representing forces for good or evil, can similarly be seen as projective in nature. These looser definitions of projection resemble Perls's use of it, since for him *projection* refers to an almost universal human tendency to locate outside the self-boundaries properties of the self that properly belong inside. Indeed, he traces to projection our frequent tendency to view particular people as inherently good or bad, since what we are essentially doing is describing as "bad" that which makes us *feel* bad.

This aspect of Perls's theory receives its most radical expression in his theory of dream formation; for him, every person and even every object in the dream represents a projected, or disowned, aspect of the dreamer. For example, a tyrannical figure in the dream may represent the patient's need to control—the "controller" part of herself. Perls refused to interpret or "explain" a dream, as is the traditional function of the psychoanalyst, and instead helped the dreamer to discover its meaning for herself by having her "play" or enact each of the significant figures in the dream, including both its people and its nonhuman content (e.g., a house). This approach to dreamwork is consistent with two aspects of Perls's philosophy: (1) It discourages the patient from talking *about* the dream and encourages her to become the dream, and (2) it enables the patient—as opposed to the therapist—to take major responsibility for understanding the dream.

In Perls's thinking, the person who experiences frequent self-consciousness is disowning and projecting her own powers of observation and criticism; in giving up her "eyes" she becomes focused on what the eyes of others see in herself. Some gestalt techniques are aimed at helping the patient to "own" (i.e., to reidentify with and reintegrate into herself) her projections. For example, if she perceives the therapist or other group members as critical of her, the therapist might encourage a "reversal" whereby the patient criticizes the therapist or goes around the group making a negatively critical remark to each person in turn. The therapist might say: "Take anything in the other person that is the least bit negative and exaggerate it—blow it up." If the patient claims that she cannot find anything negative in the other person she might be encouraged to "make something up"—play-act it. Through this technique the therapist encourages the patient to begin to exercise once again her now dormant critical faculties.

Another gestalt technique that is often used when a patient claims that others in the group are bored or annoyed with her is to have her "check out" her hypothesis to see if it holds true for the other members. Dan, the leader in our illustration, did just this when he urged Delia to find out if her assumption that all the group members resented her for "taking over" was in fact correct. The checking out procedure helps the patient to distinguish between what is really out there and what her *projections* indicate to her to be there.

**The Empty Chair.** Because of the relative ease most of us having in projecting outward, it should be a fairly simple task to take aspects of ourselves and intentionally externalize them. This is what Perls required the patient to do via his "empty chair" technique. Taking a chair (or stool or hassock), he would place it next to the patient and direct the latter to "put into" the chair an aspect of herself that is presently within her awareness. This is what Dan does (in our hypothetical example) when he asks Lillian, once she has mentioned "the demanding child-in-me," to seat this child in the chair and begin a dialogue with her.

Let's take another instance. Suppose a patient, Jack, is beginning to get in touch with, and to complain about, his greedy feelings. The therapist directs him to first "put" his greed into the empty chair and talk to it and then to switch from the hot-seat to the empty chair. Once in the empty chair, and "speaking for" his own greed, he is to say something back to the hot-seat (which continues to represent "himself," or an aspect of himself). For example, Jack may say to Greed: "Greed, you are the bane of my existence! Go away and leave me alone!" And Greed might reply: "I have no intention of leaving—don't you know my main joy in life is torturing you?!"

This technique can be viewed in several ways. First, it helps Jack to get in touch with his greed on a different level—to *become* it, rather than to merely talk about it. Another is to discourage him from dissociating it—to help him recognize that it is a genuine part of himself, as real a part as the "ego" or "I" that rejects it (as when he says: "*I* don't like my greediness!"). Jack might also begin to sense that his "greed" represents a spiteful, torturing, clinging aspect of himself, perhaps even a specific parental introject. If the therapist senses that this may be true, and observes also that Jack seems to adopt a somewhat different posture and voice when assuming the greed role, he might ask him: "Does Greed remind you of someone you've known? Think back—who talks in that voice?" If Jack replies: "That's Father's voice," the therapist will have Jack sit down in the empty chair and proceed to talk "to himself" in the voice of his father (introject).

As with Perls's "splitting" technique (see p. 136), these dialogues have as their aim the promotion of a higher level of integration between the polarities and conflicts that exist in the healthiest of us. Although Self and Greed face off as if in a life-and-death struggle, Perls's goal was to help them live more comfortably with each other. Too much human effort is directed toward an attempt to *coerce* change; according to Perls, the Self cannot force Greed to disappear, just as Greed cannot force the Self to accept it.

**Introjection.**    This mechanism is the opposite of projection; it involves taking into oneself aspects of other people, especially the parents. Without the ability to take in from others there probably would be no significant forms of interpersonal influence, or learning, in life. Hence Perls implies that some sort of taking-in process is inevitable and even desirable; his frequent use of eating as a biological analog to introjection confirms this impression. For Perls the crucial variable was the extent to which we are discriminatory in our taking-in of others; are we careful to take in only what we value and to discard that which makes us feel anxious and/or hateful? Do we take in because we really want to or because we are overly awed by the power of the significant other? The more selective process, in which unwanted parts can be discarded, is called "assimilation" in gestalt theory.

Uncritical introjection results in inadequately assimilated introjects that can give the organism the psychic equivalent of "indigestion." Especially toxic was that form of the introject termed "top-dog" by Perls; his notion of the top-dog is roughly parallel to Freud's concept of the superego. Tyrannical top-dogs often instigate internal, tense dialogues where the person is told by his top-dog what he "should" be like and how far he falls short of certain ideals. Top-dog is then answered spitefully and defiantly by another part of the personality—by "underdog," who refuses to change, thereby reenacting the role of the disobedient child. This top-dog/underdog struggle helps to explain why our frequent promises to ourselves (e.g., to finish an incompleted task) remain unfulfilled while our procrastination persists: Our underdog continues to evade the moralistic imperatives of our tyrannical and toxic introjects. These kinds of internalized recriminations can result in what Perls described as repetitive and destructive "self-torture" games. This is why he tended to be wary when a patient sat down in the hot-seat with a request that she be helped to rid herself of a troublesome habit or symptom (e.g., smoking, nail-biting, masturbation, etc.). To Perls this sounded like the persecutory demands of the top-dog; the patient was essentially inflicting upon herself a "program" that, in attempting to control that which cannot be controlled (i.e., her own experience and behavior) could only further estrange her from her spontaneous feelings and impulses.

The empty-chair technique offers a ready means for getting a patient to "externalize" an introject. If we take the situation cited above, Perls might quickly have the patient sit in the empty chair, turn back to the hot-seat, and tell "herself" how she must stop procrastinating, smoking, nail-biting, and so forth. Again, one consistent aim of such a technique is to promote integration between conflictual elements within the personality. In this specific situation, though, there may be two additional gains: (1) By "telling off" the introject (let's say it turns out to be Mother), the patient might get into firmer contact with the spiteful, underdog part of herself that has a stake in sabotaging her demands, which are in reality self-imposed demands (e.g., her actual mother may have been long since dead), and (2) she may, particularly if she is prodded by the therapist, begin to get in touch with benign, as well as toxic, aspects of the mother-introject. One means that the therapist has for facilitating the latter process is to ask the patient to tell the mother-in-the-empty-chair what her "appreciations" of her are, as well as her "resentments."

Self-torture games that are linked to introjection can be handled by the therapist in another way, one for which the entire group is essential. The therapist asks the patient to go to each person in the group, to begin the sentence "I want to torture you by...," and to then finish the sentence in a way that seems fitting for each person. This technique has several functions: (1) It directs the patient's inwardly directed aggression outward, where it was doubtless initially directed at some point in her past, (2) it may bring her in touch with the fact that she *still* tries to torture other people (like those who have to live with her endless self-criticism and doubt), but through indirect means: enervating and unproductive self-castigation, (3) it enables her to release energies that have been bound up in self-concern, and (4) should the patient have been working on the hot-seat for a long period of time, this activity forces her to come into contact with the group once again; the request that she finish the sentence differently as she goes around hopefully results in her responding to the unique attributes of each participant. This kind of exercise also leaves the therapist free to "withdraw" for a few minutes should he wish to.

**Retroflection.** "Retroflection means that some function which originally is directed from the individual towards the world changes its direction and is bent back towards the originator" (Perls, 1969c, pp. 119–120). Self-directed love, in the form of narcissism, and self-directed hatred and revenge, in the form of masochism and depression, are examples of this phenomenon. The original impulse is oriented toward contact with the outside world, but contact with the self is substituted because of primitive repressive forces involving fear of punishment, ridicule, and embarrassment.

The patient's frequent self-castigation may express critical, angry attitudes toward others, and her attempts to program and control herself (which can, as suggested above, reflect introjected forces) may retroflect an original wish to dominate and control others. If the therapist suspects that the patient is retroflecting energies that are meant for the environment, he will encourage the patient to turn them outwards, particularly toward the group. The patient may be instructed to criticize each participant in turn, or to dominate them by ordering them to do something. Self-directed aggression, in the form of hitting, scratching, or picking at oneself can in turn be channeled outward;

here the therapist might introduce inanimate objects, like pillows, with the request that the patient perform against the pillow the same actions that a few seconds before were displaced onto the self.

Retroflection has much in common with Wilhelm Reich's notion of "character armor" (Reich, 1949, p. 44). Sensorimotor impulses that are directed toward living, sexual, or angry contact with the environment are opposed by negating and inhibiting impulses. As a result there develops points of chronic muscle tension, consisting of one set of muscles that are set for contact outward and an opposing set that counteract the first; these points of tension are often manifested in characteristic facial grimaces and postural rigidities. The example referred to earlier (see "Now and How" above), in which a patient holds back her tears by contracting the musculature around her jaw, reflects the cancelling-out and balancing effect of a retroflection. Just as in the previous example, the therapist can help to make the patient more aware of her jaw-clenching by instructing her to squeeze these muscles harder.

**The Organismic Self.** Central to Perls's theory is the organismic, autonomous self which, if left to its own natural biological rhythms and not contaminated by the toxic "should's" of a moralistic and pressuring society, can find its way to an aware, authentic existence. The problem lies in actualizing the real self, as opposed to the *self-concept;* the neurotic, in attempting to actualize her self-image, has a need to please others, to live up to external expectations of perfection, and is hereby led to "phony" and role-playing behavior. Perls's emphasis on the person's search for an authentic existence—toward a way of becoming what she fundamentally *is*—owes much to existentialist philosophy and to phenomenology. As we indicated in Chapter 5, this latter viewpoint sees humans as being born into the world without self-evident purposes; our existential task is to cast aside the externalized life-structure imposed by the dominant moral and religious philosophies of our era and by the interaction "games" current in our particular social milieus.

A technique that directly grows out of this concept is the following: The gestalt therapist might ask the patient with whom he is working to identify her primary life-game to each person in the group and to then add in each instance: "And this is my existence!" (e.g., "My main aim is to prove to you how strong and independent I am—and this is my existence!"). The therapist's aim here is to encourage the patient to take full responsibility for this particular "game" and to impress upon her that this is how she chooses to spend the finite amount of time that she has allotted to her in life.

The constant aim of the gestalt group is to enable the patient to function with "self-support" as opposed to "environmental support." The more infantile the person, the more she "plays" helpless and dumb as a means of manipulating others into giving her the comfort and support that she really doesn't need. One way of helping the patient to contact her pseudo-helplessness involves the kind of exaggeration-technique mentioned above: "O.K., be as helpless as you can." Or: "Go to each person in the group and ask him for something that you think you need from him." Should the patient complain that the therapist is not giving her what she needs, a technique occasionally employed by Perls was to direct the patient to go to the empty chair and to "play Fritz." In many instances the patient, as Fritz, was able to give herself quite constructive advice (e.g., "You know, you can take much better care of yourself than you realize," or "You look and act as though you're suffering, but I have the strong feeling that you're not really that bad off!," etc.). The patient, on subsequently returning to her own chair, often reports that she felt less frustrated than she had just before the intervention—despite the fact that it was she who had essentially ministered to her own need.

In the example just cited, one can conceptualize the patient's relief in terms of her having discovered that she was less dependent on the environment than she had thought. Another explanation, one that is consistent with gestalt-introject theory is that the patient is now better able to contact and to use the mothering part of herself. (The gestalt personality-model postulates a constellation of "selves"—male-female; good-mother, bad-mother; etc.—rather than a single "self" or "ego." The more these selves are integrated, the stronger the personality.) One reason that the patient is unable to utilize the mothering, nurturant aspect of herself as a means of self-support might be that she totally identifies the mother introject with the toxic bad-mother. In other words, she is not allowing the positive aspects of her mother-introject to become actualized. One means that the therapist has at his disposal for facilitating the latter process is to help the patient acknowledge whatever appreciation she has for her real mother (see "Splitting" below).

Another very popular device for encouraging a patient to assume more responsibility for herself is to have her change "it" statements into "I" statements. For example if she says "It is trembling" (referring to her hand) or "It is sobbing" (referring to her voice), the therapist encourages him to say: "I am trembling," "I am crying." Whether or not she has volitional control over these responses, they are *hers;* this semantic exercise can at least help her to *begin* to perceive herself as an active agent in her life and to identify with her own feelings.

**Unfinished Business.**   This is a key concept within gestalt theory. It usually involves unexpressed feeling, although highly distinct memories, fantasies, and images may be connected with this affect. Because such feeling has never been allowed to become fully "figured," it stays in the background, is carried over into the present, and interferes with effective "contact functioning" that requires a present-centered, reality-bound awareness of oneself and other people. Since figure-ground relationships are essentially fluid, feelings excluded from awareness would, if they were allowed to become fully figured, eventually reach a saturation point; the ebb and flow of awareness would return and another feeling or "gestalt" would inevitably take its place. This conceptualization also explains Perls's conviction that it is only when we fully accept something about ourselves that it can change; once a disowned characteristic becomes figure and is acknowledged, it too cannot remain a central organizing motif for very long. Hence the gestalt command to the patient on the hot-seat: "Go ahead, be as compulsive, or bitchy, or confused as you can!" Negative qualities, once made figure or "owned," can be more comfortably integrated.

Unacknowledged feelings create unnecessary emotional debris that clutter up present-centered attention and awareness, usually in the form of excessive preoccupation and rumination. The most frequent unfinished business concerns resentment and incomplete separation; a spiteful, clinging, "biting on" attitude toward another person which, according to gestalt theory, often involves unworked through anger toward that person. The irresolution of the anger prevents the possibility of a genuine separation. Unacknowledged grief is another common kind of "unfinished business" and it, too, can prevent a more complete separation from a lost love-object. Therefore "saying good-bye," which often involves placing the living or dead person in the empty chair and speaking to him or her, is an often-employed gestalt exercise. It may include a listing of both appreciations and resentments of that person, since one or the other may predominate in the patient's consciousness and thereby keep its opposite side from reaching awareness—the dead father may be mercilessly blamed and the patient's difficulty therefore lies in acknowledging her good feelings about her father.

**Splitting.** "Splitting" describes hot-seat work that is oriented toward having a patient express both sides of a conflict, polarity, or ambivalence. This is partly the rationale for the therapist's directing her toward stating first her resentments and then her appreciations, or speaking for the greedy part of herself and then the part of herself that rejects this greed. Another frequent kind of splitting involves confusion around a specific decision. The therapist might first have the patient go with one part of the conflict: I want to get a divorce, and then with the other half: I don't want to get a divorce. Going with each side of the conflict may acquaint her in a fuller way with them; in actual life she may be so conflicted that she doesn't let herself experience either side of the ambivalence for more than a few seconds. Psychic integration and *not* specific conflict resolution is the gestalist's aim in this exercise. The person may emerge from it with the feeling that the question of her marital status no longer constitutes the "whole story" of her life—that either way, married or divorced, her life will go on and some of her abiding concerns—children and career—will continue. Such an attitude would seem to indicate a different level of integration; some of the psychological pressure has eased, although the person will eventually have to resolve her indecision one way or the other.

Some polarities, unlike a marital impasse, need never be "resolved." Perls rejected the idea, more characteristic of Western than of Eastern thought, that good and bad, male and female, active and passive, are antitheses. According to him, one did not have to choose one or the other alternative. A splitting exercise aims at a more harmonious combining of these elements within the personality.

**Contact and Withdrawal.**   This last is perhaps the most fundamental polarity within gestalt thinking. Healthy functioning involves effective contact boundaries; this is letting one's own feelings and sensations become fully figured, just as it is letting the reality of other people, unencumbered by distorting projections, become fully figured. Yet there can be no real contact without withdrawal, which provides opportunities for renewal and reintegration. Too often we meet the overly externalized person who permits herself little solitude; here there is a semblance of contact, but the oversatiation often makes genuine contact impossible. The issue for Perls was one of *organismic* regulation, which permits a more aware appreciation of when one wants to be alone—in contemplation, revery, or fantasy—and when one wants to be in contact with stimuli, either human or nonhuman. Too often the question of contact and withdrawal can become a matter of "should's": I *should* spend more time with people, or I *should* spend more time alone.

While withdrawal can be seen as an avoidance of contact, especially in hot-seat work, Perls had great respect for this avoidance, as he did for others. Frequently he allowed the withdrawal to become "figured," so that if the patient said she felt an impulse to leave the situation psychologically, Perls would encourage her to do so and would attempt to accompany her into whatever revery began to absorb her. Again the concept of saturation applies; once the individual's need for withdrawal is *accepted* rather than fought, it too recedes into the background. These paradoxes are reminiscent of Zen thinking; they encourage us to "relax" and "let be," since nothing need last forever. Indeed, it is the Western penchant for forcing, insisting, *making* things happen that can guarantee the kind of fixity we most fear. When the patient is fully ready to return to the here-and-now of the group, and can therefore *choose* to return, the therapist may encourage contact.

As we suggested in an earlier section (see "Now and How" above), a key task of the gestalt therapist is to investigate precisely how and precisely when the patient avoids contact. His aim is to enable the patient to take responsibility for these mechanisms through becoming more aware of them and to help her sense some of the experiences against which they are directed. Let us take a specific example. Suppose a patient tends to often break contact with the therapist by averting her eyes. Inquiry may reveal that she does this at those points where she becomes anxious about what she will say next. If the therapist asks her to speak for this anxiety, the patient might soon reveal fantasy-projections wherein she assumes that if she is silent others in the group become impatient with her. She might then be directed to speak for various group members by imagining what each of them is thinking. In this way the patient is brought into contact with herself, the therapist, and the group. The gestalt therapist is careful to remind the patient that she is fully free to continue to avoid contact and that she is not being told that she *should not* break contact. What he wants to do is to enable the patient to make a more informed and deliberate, and therefore less automatic, choice as to contact versus withdrawal. Despite the codification of Perls's ideas into a formal theory, there can be no law stating that contact is good and withdrawal, bad. The existential spirit of gestalt therapy encourages us to choose to let ourselves experience both contact and withdrawal and to thereby make a more autonomous decision as to which of the two we want at any particular moment in time.

## ROLE OF THE LEADER

The expertise of the Gestalt workshop leader involves his ability to work at both individual and group levels and his ease in moving smoothly back and forth between the two levels. In working with a specific group member, his skill hinges on his ability to suggest techniques that will help the person intensify her experience, in his alertness to nonverbal cues, and in his capacity to identify various projections, introjections, and contact-avoiding behaviors as these are manifested in the patient's behavior. With regard to the overall group context in which the patient is embedded, the leader must be ready to fairly quickly decide when to focus on her individual conflicts (which might entail his recommending that she engage in various exercises of an emotionally intensive nature) and when to work with the group-as-a-whole. For example, in the illustration above the therapist sensed the other members' outrage at Delia's continuing claim for his attention and appreciated that the group, having been in the background for so long, had to be afforded an opportunity to become "figure," if tensions were not to rise to an unbearable degree. Therefore, as other members began to express their reactions to Delia, he permitted them to do so and waited before suggesting further hot-seat work with a specific member, in this case Lillian.

In working with the individual participant, the leader's role is catalytic, demanding a curious combination of activity and passivity. He is active in the sense of constantly instructing the patient as to what to do, much as a stage or film director might; yet it is the patient who typically leads and writes the script, while it is the therapist who follows. Although neither leader nor participant has a program as to precisely where to go, it is the participant who, guided by her awareness, sets the direction. She is the authority on what she senses and feels, and the therapist carefully observes her in an effort to detect specific behaviors of which she may be unaware. Once a particular behavior is pointed out to the participant it is again she who must ultimately lead in attempting to discover its import, and it is the therapist who follows. Suppose, for example, that the participant "leads" in the sense of touching her face; the therapist then "follows" by suggesting that she speak for her fingers as they caress her skin. The patient again leads when she says "I feel a surface that is strangely like clay," and the therapist follows by saying "Speak for the clay." Rarely does the therapist interpret the *meaning* of the patient's experience; instead he tries to create an atmosphere and to facilitate a process whereby meaning emerges in the spontaneous action of the gestalt dialogue, rather than being stated by him in the form of a verbal conceptualization. For instance, in the illustration above, it may soon become clear that the claylike face is essentially a mask; however, it will be the patient who eventually finds this out while speaking for the clay. The gestalt process thus bears a resemblance to the kind of "dreamwork" spontaneously engaged in by the sleeper as he or she dreams, for this process will, if successful, recapitulate via concrete symbols and dramatic action just where the patient "is at," much as the dream, through its own spontaneous artistry, will portray the immediate tensions of the dreamer.

When it comes to sensing where the overall group "is at," the leader needs the kind of feel for group dynamics that we referred to in our chapter on the group-dynamic therapy group (Chapter 4) and that we will refer to again in our chapters on the Tavistock group (Chapter 9) and the T-group (Chapter 10). As he senses which two, or three, participants mirror one another's conflicts, he encourages them to engage in a dialogue, much as our gestalt leader did with Delia and Lillian in our illustration. He must try to sense when hot-seat work with an individual participant bypasses and evades significant unexpressed tensions left over from earlier group work. Once intensive hot-seat work with a specific individual has ended, he should try to elicit specific reactions to this work from the other group members who have just been witness to it.

The participant who does eventually engage in hot-seat work may well be surprised by what evolves, especially if she has begun the hot-seat work with a predetermined idea of the problems she wishes to attack. The therapist, much like a Zen master, disarms her by asking her to do that which she feels she must not do (to bully instead of to stop being a bully), and by showing a benign acceptance of things that the patient might well wish to change. He attempts to demonstrate the absurdity of *all* programs, standing for acceptance rather than control, for what "is" rather than for what "should be." Since all natural processes are characterized by flux, no gestalt—whether an attitude, feeling, need, or specific motor behavior—necessarily remains fixed, particularly if it is allowed to become figure (as opposed to being fought or suppressed).

Nothing need be forever, since there is essentially only the Now. And because no Now can ever be fully determined by previous Nows, it will always contain emergent and creative forces for change; however, it is beyond the patient's power to regulate this change. The gestalt therapist's most fundamental and inclusive task, whether focusing on the individual or the group, is to enable his patient(s) to embrace with more openness and trust the mystery of the eternal Now.

# CHAPTER EIGHT
# BEHAVIOR THERAPY IN GROUPS

Although behavior therapy, like most psychotherapeutic techniques, was initially used in work with individuals, the approach was fairly quickly extended to the group context. This was probably inevitable because the method, with its strong research orientation, lent itself to studies comparing treatment groups with nontreatment control groups, and collecting data was facilitated by actually working with clients in groups. The behavioral approach has had an enormous influence on the development of psychological science, and on the social sciences in general, particularly as they have developed in the United States. Originated by John B. Watson, in the 1920s, and building on Pavlov's historic discovery of the conditioned response, behaviorism viewed personality as a complex constellation of stimulus-response connections learned during the long period of individual development. Because of its foundation in animal learning, studied under precise and controlled laboratory conditions, behaviorism developed as part of experimental psychology with its major thrust in the area of basic research on learning processes. Yet its emphasis on humans as responding both differentially and consistently to environmental stimuli was bound to have important applications to both education and psychotherapy. If a troubled person can learn new and more adaptive responses to stimuli, a potentially powerful therapeutic tool is made available.

Since there is no specific or unified technology of group methods within the behavior therapy framework, there is no single or unified model of behavior therapy in groups. Thus, the organization of this chapter represents to some extent a departure from the format followed in most others—that is, a presentation of a detailed, well-articulated, single group method in its pure form. Nonetheless, because of the considerable interest in behavior therapy and its increasing use in a wide variety of different group modalities, the need for including coverage of it is clear. We attempt to present a general outline of the behavioral approach and to give an account of some of the specific group procedures that have been developed within its framework.

## HISTORICAL BACKGROUND

Behavior therapy, the designation used in Great Britain, or behavior modification, as it is most frequently referred to in the United States, has its roots in the experimental methods of psychology, particularly in learning theories and approaches. Behavior therapy as a widely employed method of working with individuals has a relatively short history, dating back to the early 1950s, although there were clear-cut precursors several decades earlier. As far back as 1924, Mary Cover Jones (1924) described her successful effort in eliminating a fear of animals in a child by using conditioning procedures. She presented a caged rabbit to a boy, placing it some distance from him while he was in a chair eating his favorite food, and through subsequent simultaneous presentations of the positive reinforcement (the favorite food) and the previously feared object (the rabbit) at closer and closer ranges, she succeeded in getting the child to pat the rabbit and was thus able to eliminate his fear of the animal.

The more immediate theoretical precursors of behavior therapy and behavior modification as practiced today came from diverse roots and developed in a variety of places. Pavlov (1941), having introduced the paradigm of classical conditioning, made some initial efforts to apply that method to understanding neurotic behavior. The work of H.J. Eysenck (1960) in London and Joseph Wolpe (1958), originally in South Africa and later in the United States, grew out of the Pavlovian model and the learning theory of Clark L. Hull, as well as the work of Jacobson (1938) on relaxation techniques. Simply stated, they attempted to apply reward or reinforcement and extinction principles derived from learning theory to change or modify overt behavior in individuals. They very clearly eschewed any consideration of underlying dynamics or causes of behavior and proposed that all behavior change could occur through the acquisition of useful new habits and the elimination of problematic ones.

The Pavlovian, or classical conditioning, model posits that learning takes place only under conditions of reward and involves the pairing of two previously unrelated stimuli, one of which reflexively produces a response (e.g., salivation to the stimulus of food). The condition of extinction, on the other hand, deals with eliminating already learned behavior by ensuring that it occurs when no reward is presented. In dealing with human learning, rewards may be material but may also consist of social reinforcement (the desired presence or praise of another individual) or reinforcement in the form of tension or anxiety reduction. Behavior therapy techniques that attempt to eliminate problematic behaviors by replacing them with successful new responses that are incompatible with existing problem responses (e.g., relaxation in place of anxiety) are typically based on a classical conditioning model.

Accounts of the theoretical framework for and the range and kinds of behavior therapy techniques based on this model are available in Bandura (1969, 1986) and Yates (1970). One of the most frequently employed and most intensively studied of these is *systematic desensitization*. The basic strategy is to present a conditioned stimulus for anxiety responses while incompatible responses are being made. The usual procedure involves training in muscle relaxation, the developing of anxiety hierarchies—that is, lists of related objects or experiences in descending order of the degree to which they create anxiety in an individual, and lastly, experiencing the anxiety producing images, from the lowest to the highest while in a state of deep relaxation. In this way, anxiety is reduced by being paired with the incompatible response of relaxation.

Development of behavior modification in the United States followed more directly on the theoretical heels of B.F. Skinner (1938). Skinner's approach was that of *operant* or *instrumental learning*, which requires that the learner take action to get a reward and is most simply seen in the situation in which a hungry rat learns to press a bar for food. The typical experimental situation involves an animal's learning to make a response in the presence of a particular stimulus, such as a sound or the appearance of a light. When the response is made in the presence of that stimulus a reward is forthcoming, and the animal quickly learns to respond only at the appropriate time (i.e., when the stimulus to be rewarded is presented). Most behavior therapy or behavior modification procedures involving the acquisition of new responses have clear roots in the Skinnerian model and involve the use of reinforcement for increasing appropriate behavior and the removal of reinforcement to reduce or extinguish inappropriate behavior.

Because the development of group approaches based on this model was an extension of the procedures developed for individuals, no well-specified or articulated model emerged. Most typically, behavior therapy groups have centered on the introduction of individually oriented techniques into a group setting. In this manner groups have been developed using techniques of systematic desensitization, acquisition of new behavior, behavior control, and more recently cognitive behavioral approaches that had previously been applied to individuals. Although a number of positive effects attributable to the group experience itself were observed, work with groups by behavior therapists was typically initiated for either economy of service delivery or for doing outcome research on various therapeutic techniques. The typical style of group leaders working within the behavior therapy framework is characterized by communication from the group leader to individual members and tends to deemphasize member-to-member interaction. More recently, greater attention has been devoted to behavior therapy groups (Rose, 1977) with a concomitant increase in attention to the importance of member-to-member behavior, especially for support and as a source of social reinforcement. Because much of the impetus for the development of behavior therapy and behavior modification techniques arose from negative reactions to psychoanalytic and psychodynamic approaches, which were based on theories of hypothesized but unsubstantiated internal processes far removed from the concrete reality of observable experience, it is somewhat ironic that the behavior therapy group leader seems most similar to the psychoanalytic group leader (see Chapter 3) in the degree of attention given to individual members and relative inattention to the experience of the group *qua* group.

Behavior therapy approaches to groups share in common theoretical and philosophical concerns of the approach as a whole, characterized by several features which make the approach unique and distinguishable from other psychotherapeutic techniques. One notable characteristic is the high degree of *specificity* in treatment plan wherein the therapist makes a very careful and clear-cut delineation of the specific behaviors, situations, objects, and the like that are problematical for an individual and then attempts to help the person overcome such reactions and behaviors, using any of a broad range of interventions, which are also specified in advance.

A second unique characteristic is the research orientation that has historically been associated with the behavioral approach, especially the emphasis on systematic outcome and follow-up studies to determine the efficacy of techniques used. In focusing on the single case, attempts have been made to study the learning course required to change specific problem behaviors, including efforts to determine the particular conditions that tend to reduce the frequency of or completely eliminate problem behavior and conditions that increase or exacerbate it. Many of these outcomes studies and clinical reports have offered evidence that behavior therapy has a high rate of success, particularly in eliminating specific fears and phobias. However, Lazarus (1981), who had been among the strongest advocates of the behavioral approach, in an extensive follow-up study of individuals treated by behavior therapy techniques, raised considerable doubt about the persistence of change that resulted from behavior therapy. He found a much higher rate of relapse than had been previously reported. Whether or not the behavioral approach is as effective as some of its most ardent supporters insist, it is noteworthy that people working within this framework tend to give a higher priority to evaluation of their techniques than have the proponents of virtually all other psychotherapeutic approaches.

Below we shall describe four rather distinct categories of group approaches developed within the behavioral therapy framework: systematic desensitization groups, behavioral practice groups, specific behavior control therapy, and cognitive behavioral therapy groups.

## SYSTEMATIC DESENSITIZATION GROUPS

As described by Wolpe and Lazarus (1966), desensitization groups represent a direct application of individual techniques in a group setting. The basic structure of the desensitization procedure involves three steps beginning with group members being given instruction in the process of deep muscle relaxation. In this procedure the therapist suggests that the patient get as comfortable as possible and try to let go of all of the tension that he is experiencing. Next, the patient is told to tense up and fully experience heightened tension and then to stop tensing and experience the feeling of relaxation and *the contrast between the two states.* Through a series of practices and successive approximations to total relaxation with a heavy dosage of hypnotic-like suggestion, most group members are able to become quickly relaxed in therapeutic sessions. The second task is to construct an anxiety hierarchy, most easily illustrated in the case of a person with a specific phobia, for example, a snake phobia. Someone with such a phobia is likely to be made most anxious by the actual physical presence of a snake, by having to look at or perhaps touch the snake. Further on down the hierarchy would be anxiety created by knowing that a snake might be present or seeing pictures of snakes, while still less anxiety provoking situations are those where one thinks he might see a snake such as entering a zoo or museum, knowing that there might be live or stuffed snakes in the area, hearing someone talk about snakes, or picturing a snake in one's mind. Lowest on the hierarchy, creating only minimal anxiety, might be reading the word "snake." In constructing an anxiety hierarchy, it is important to make certain that the patient is able to imagine "scenes" of the items. The third step in the systematic desensitization procedure requires the patient to relax as fully as possible and then begin imagining the scenes on the hierarchy, step by step, progressing up the hierarchy of anxiety provoking stimuli, beginning with the weakest. At the point at which a patient begins to feel anxious and lose the state of relaxation, the procedure stops and the patient is helped to induce the relaxed state once again; when relaxed again the patient begins imagining the ascending series of scenes on the hierarchy another time. The effectiveness of this procedure is based on the assumption that anxiety responses will be weakened if antagonistic responses (in this case, relaxation) can be evoked when stimuli usually creating anxiety are present.

Lazarus (1961), one of the first to describe the use of systematic desensitization in groups, advocated its use for patients who are made anxious or fearful by specific objects or situations. His group approach consisted basically of an individual procedure carried out in a group setting, with members typically having very similar fears or anxieties. In general, advocacy for use of such groups is in terms of greater efficiency or economy when compared with individual treatment, although the effect of the group atmosphere as a supportive and reinforcing agent has also been noted, in that members support one another in their efforts at change in behavior outside the group and reinforce each other for successes. Furthermore, the successful group member gives evidence to others in the group that change is, in fact, possible and thereby gives additional encouragement to work for change.

Fishman and Nawas (1971) focused almost exclusively on a desensitization procedure wherein all participants proceed through their total anxiety hierarchy within a specified period of time. Working with individuals with snake phobias, they developed a standardized anxiety hierarchy and followed a standardized time schedule, which is realistically possible only when all group members present the same symptom. Desensitization groups of this type last five to six sessions, with the first session devoted to members' learning deep relaxation following the Jacobson (1938) method. In subsequent sessions the hierarchy is presented and the desensitization procedure followed in the standardized manner described. Each member is given one minute for imagining the scene, and each scene is presented about six times in this period. In this approach there is little or no group interaction or patient participation in developing hierarchies or any other mutual group activities.

A second type of desensitization group has emphasized greater interaction among members, but group discussion typically is limited to a period at the end of the session and is essentially directed by the leader. McManus (1971) and Paul and Shannon (1966) provide descriptions of this broader approach, which is distinguished by the fact that participants more commonly exhibit diffuse anxiety rather than specific phobias. While McManus worked with college students experiencing test anxiety, and Paul and Shannon worked with social anxiety, stage fright, and fear of speaking in public, we shall generally describe how such desensitization in groups works.

Desensitization groups typically last for six to ten sessions and begin with members discussing similarities in how they experience anxiety, while the therapist emphasizes these similarities, refers questions to the group as a whole, and attempts to apply the comments of each member to others in the group.

The relaxation training period is begun in the first session and is followed by group members sharing their reactions to the experience with one another. In the following session, the group begins to construct a desensitization hierarchy that will be usable by all members, provided of course, they have a common presenting problem. In constructing a group hierarchy care has to be taken to find mutually meaningful and acceptable wording so that all members can successfully apply the items to themselves. After additional training in relaxation later in the session, the leader begins to instruct participants in visual imagining of scenes from the anxiety hierarchy, after which members evaluate their ability to employ imagery.

In the third session, the anxiety hierarchy is completed, further training in relaxation occurs, and desensitization proper begins. Remaining sessions are characterized by induction of the relaxation experience, while simultaneously presenting items on the hierarchy, followed by group discussion of the experience. Using desensitization in groups requires gearing movement through the hierarchy to the pace of the slowest member of the group—that is, the group should not move on to the next higher item on the hierarchy until all members are completely relaxed in the presence of the anxiety producing scene they are presently imagining.

Both the group desensitization procedures of McManus and of Paul and Shannon were conducted in the context of experiments designed to determine whether such procedures were in fact effective. In the McManus study, a follow-up indicated a significantly greater increase in grade point average of those who participated in the group desensitization experience when compared with the no-treatment control group. Paul and Shannon's subjects, who were anxious about public speaking, were also evaluated by a battery of personality and general anxiety measures. This group, when compared with the control group and with groups offered other treatment alternatives, showed a significantly greater decrease in anxiety and a decrease in other indices of personality dysfunction. Moreover, a two-year follow-up study (Paul, 1968) revealed greater continued positive effects of the group desensitization procedure when compared with the other group methods.

In summary then, group desensitization involves the application of a common procedure to all group members. When compared to most of the other group approaches described in this volume, it is more highly structured and has more clearly specified goals that emphasize specific desired changes in behavior. Typically, such groups are suggested for persons having similar problems or anxieties, although it is possible to compose such structured groups of patients with different problems, in which case each member would be required to work on a separate individually developed hierarchy.

Although there have been many innovations in behavioral treatment approaches during the past decade, Berk and Efran (1983) note that group systematic desensitization has continued to be used effectively and to attract both clinical and research attention.

## BEHAVIOR PRACTICE GROUPS

Behavior practice or behavior rehearsal groups are designed to help individuals develop more effective ways of functioning in interpersonal interactions, or more specifically, to learn new and more appropriate responses to situations that have been problematical for them. Focusing on role-playing or practicing new interpersonal skills in order to overcome behavioral deficits or inadequacies, such groups often target behaviors such as the inability to assert oneself effectively or to express feelings openly.

Despite rather striking differences in orientation and approach between psychodrama and behavior therapy, the role-playing in behavior rehearsal groups has clear-cut roots in Moreno's method, described in Chapter 6. In behaviorally oriented groups, role-playing is devoted almost exclusively to practicing behaviors that participants have been unable to perform successfully, whereas in psychodrama the aim of reliving, for the purpose of catharsis, emotionally charged past or present life situations is of equal or greater importance. In the behavior rehearsal group, leaders assist group members in specifying and clarifying the nature of ineffective behaviors, the kinds of situations in which they are evoked, and in determining what responses would be more effective. Group members then role-play new responses to these problem behaviors, discuss the strengths and weaknesses of the role-play, and evaluate the performance of the member whose problem is under consideration. Provided with opportunities to rehearse a situation a number of times, members continue to get feedback about where their performances need improvement. Sometimes the group leader will play the role of coach by directly modeling the desired behavior while engaging in the role-play activity. Group members, having applied new behaviors to actual life situations outside the group, often discuss their successes and their problems in performance in subsequent meetings. Relaxation training is often included as part of the group's activity to serve as an additional aid in counteracting unrealistic anxiety experienced in social situations.

Perhaps the most highly developed version of the behavioral practice group is the kind that has been termed the *assertiveness training* or *expressive training* group. Lazarus, (1968) and Fensterheim (1972; Fensterheim & Glazer, 1983) have provided extensive descriptions of this approach, which originally focused on difficulties in direct communication of annoyance and displeasure and subsequently included work with inhibition in expressing warm, tender, and other positive feelings as well.

Assertiveness training groups, composed of eight to ten members of homogeneous background, typically continue for six or more sessions of two hours duration. Like most behaviorally oriented groups, assertiveness training is characterized by a fairly high degree of leader-provided structure. Since members are selected on the basis of a history of difficulty in asserting themselves, the first session addresses this issue by beginning with a didactic presentation on the nature of unrealistic social anxiety. To set the stage for forthcoming behavior change activities, the point is underscored that members have learned to be unrealistically anxious in situations that do not present any actual danger; the focus then becomes that of unlearning these interfering internal responses and subsequently learning new assertive behaviors. Following the initial presentation, members introduce themselves and the introductions are tape-recorded; next, the introductions are played back so that members may get the group's comments on the ways in which their performance was less than successful. Such discussions tend to focus on the manner in which the individual's anxiety and defensiveness were in evidence in the actual behavior in introducing oneself to the group. When relaxation procedures are included, relaxation training usually begins at the end of the first session.

In the second session there is further training in relaxation and attention is given to members' description of behaviors that they feel are particularly problematical. One member might, for example, complain that she is unable to tell a waiter in a restaurant that her dinner is unsatisfactory and another might describe how he finds it difficult to say that he has other plans when his boss asks him to work late in the evening. After all members have described problematical behaviors around assertiveness, they commit themselves to attempt to carry out the previously avoided behaviors during the coming week.

In the third session members describe the assertive behaviors they attempted since the last meeting and evaluate the degree to which they were able to carry them out. Since these first attempts are typically not entirely successful, the group turns its attention to the core activity of the assertiveness training group—role-playing. For example, if the member who had problems in asserting herself with waiters angrily blurted out a volley of dissatisfactions to the waiter so that she got only an angry response back, the group using role-play, would work on modulating her behavior to help her achieve a more desirable reaction. After further portrayal of the scene, a discussion of its successful and unsuccessful aspects would follow, with suggestions from other group members or from the leader about how to improve the behavior. Role-playing the scene again, this time incorporating the group's suggestions, would conclude the session. The fourth session is very similar to the third in that there is additional relaxation training and further discussion of attempts to engage in assertive behavior outside the group meeting, followed by analysis of the behavior in role-playing. From the fifth session on, the process is much more dependent upon the specific needs of members, and on the particular assertive activities that concern them. Sometimes, groups tend to focus regularly on role-playing procedures; other groups devote more effort to discussing the attitudes and values that underlay interference with engaging in assertive behaviors; still others are characterized by an equal combination of both role-play and discussion.

Lazarus contended that assertiveness training groups are successful and useful for between fifteen and twenty sessions, after which they tend to become rather repetitive. Efforts to decrease the length of these groups have been attempted by employing less input of specific member problems and using canned or "prescripted" scenes in which assertive behavior is appropriate but difficult for members to successfully achieve. Incidents such as being kept waiting by a friend for an hour or being brought by a cab driver to a wrong address by a circuitous route are employed. Members, working in dyads practicing scenes, are offered suggestions by the leader who also makes observations about the degree to which they are successful in being assertive. Other groups, using specific scripting with actual dialogue provided for group members, create the opportunity for behavioral practice without requiring participants to generate responses. Such approaches have been more frequently used with relatively less well-educated and less verbally facile clients. In these latter groups the leader plays an especially active role in directing the activities of the group, with the expected result that the degree of interaction among members is minimal, except for the role-playing interaction within the dyad.

## SPECIFIC BEHAVIOR CONTROL THERAPY

This type of behaviorally oriented group therapy is concerned with alleviating specific behavioral excesses, such as extreme overeating or excessive smoking. Composed of members with similar unwanted behavior patterns, such groups typically involve a direct application of individual behavior therapy techniques, such as stimulus saturation (see below) in a group setting. As might be expected, the majority of the interaction in these groups occurs between the therapist and the individual member or between the therapist and the group as a whole. However, in some groups discussion of difficulties and discomfort encountered seems to be valuable in providing group support and encouragement to continue participation in the experience. Moreover, group approval or disapproval can also be highly potent as positive or negative reinforcement.

Penick and his colleagues (1971) proposed a group oriented technique for working with obese patients; the main focus of the approach is to help group members become better observers of their eating behavior and then to learn new ways of controlling the behavior more effectively. The group met weekly for three months for a five-hour program that included a two-hour behavior therapy session, an exercise session, and a low-calorie lunch. The therapist began by asking members to describe their eating behavior and the circumstances surrounding it. After the first meeting members were required to keep records of the time and place of eating, the speed at which they ate, the kinds of food they consumed, as well as any discernible emotional and attitudinal reactions related to eating. This procedure had two important effects: (1) It required group members to become cognizant of many characteristics of their eating behavior that previously had gone unnoticed, and (2) it directed their attention to the attitudes and emotions that seemed to accompany excessive eating behavior, for example, noticing that when feeling angry one eats even more than usual.

After the gathering of information about the circumstances and external stimuli related to eating behavior, attention was directed toward efforts to control stimuli governing eating activities. Patients were instructed to see to it that their eating did not occur in the random way that they had observed. For example, it was suggested that group members confine eating to one place in their homes, that they eat at certain specified mealtimes rather than whenever they felt like it, and that they separate their eating experiences from other activities such as watching television, talking on the telephone, or engaging in other distracting activities. In addition, members were instructed in techniques for controlling the act of eating itself, by counting each mouthful, by putting forks on their plates after a specified number of bites, and by chewing more slowly. Although no effort to encourage group interaction was described, group sessions included members' recounting difficulties in maintaining eating schedules, sharing with each other "tricks" that they played on themselves to help them stick to their schedules, mentioning successes that they achieved in lowering food intake, and describing problems encountered in performing self-observation homework assignments. When compared with traditional discussion therapy groups focused on weight problems, patients in these groups show significantly greater weight loss, with 50 percent of the members losing twenty pounds or more.

Controlling excessive smoking is another specific behavior that has been dealt with extensively in behavior control groups (Marrone et al., 1970). A commonly used technique, *stimulus saturation,* requires group members to engage in smoking behavior continuously over an extended period of time with so great a frequency that the pleasurable aspects of smoking become overshadowed by the discomfort created by excessive usage. Sessions were arranged in two formats in two different groups: Group One had twenty-four hours of treatment in a forty-hour period, and Group Two had ten hours of treatment in a thirteen-hour period. Patients were permitted to engage in any kind of group activities they wished with one proviso—they had to smoke continuously throughout the period, with a one dollar fine charged if a patient was seen not holding a cigarette or inhaling at least once every two to three minutes. Obviously an important leader task was constantly monitoring the smoking behavior of patients, who typically became nauseous and in about 50 percent of the cases vomited during the treatment period. This form of aversive conditioning led to the majority of members of both groups giving up smoking initially; follow-up after four months showed that Group One had significantly more nonsmokers than group two, with 60 percent of the former's members continuing to abstain.

Behavior practice groups have become widely used for a wide variety of problem behaviors, including smoking, use of alcohol and drugs, overeating, and the like. With greater emphasis on promoting healthful behaviors, it is anticipated that self-management groups will become even more frequently used in clinics and agencies, as well as in the workplace.

## COGNITIVE BEHAVIOR THERAPY

Cognitive behavior therapy interventions represent a broad array of approaches that focus on the use of verbalizations and thoughts as mediators between what stimulates behavior and the response that emerges. As has been noted, much of the early work in behavior therapy, particularly that based on the classical conditioning model, took pains to emphasize stimulus-response connections through reinforcement and to avoid any consideration of verbal mediators. As experimental psychologists began to emphasize studies in cognition, particularly in the 1970s and 1980s, conceptualizing behavior from a cognitive perspective was again considered not only acceptable but even desirable. As the cognitive trend became increasingly influential, with its primary emphasis on thoughts and beliefs as factors that influence behavior, a variety of established and novel approaches were put forward as new forms of cognitive behavior therapy.

One of these, *rational emotive therapy* (RET), developed by Albert Ellis in the mid-1950s, had been on the scene for many years before it was labeled as a cognitive behavioral approach. The fact that behavior therapy put such great emphasis on differentiating itself from more "mentalistic" approaches by espousing its adherence to learning principles and eschewing any relationship to cognitive functioning created an obvious difficulty when making a theoretical justification for using cognitive concepts. Nevertheless, it has been noted that many of the changes attributed to conditioning-based behavioral interventions seemed to have arisen more from so-called "nonspecific" factors—that is, therapist behaviors common to all psychotherapy and extrinsic to the actual procedures themselves, including sympathetic attention, skill in self-observation, and explanations of or rationales for the problem. Furthermore, the recognition that many clients' complex human problems did not seem amenable to a reductionistic conditioning approach led to the emergence of cognitive behavior therapy.

Cognitive behavior therapy, in essence, represents an amalgam of methods and approaches which often have little in common with specific learning paradigms or modalities, other than the fact that they attempt to describe in specific terms cognitive patterns that result in faulty or inaccurate beliefs, such as negative self-statements, overgeneralizations, and overconcern with bi-polar opposites (e.g., right-wrong, good-evil, black-white). In fact, cognitive behavioral methods really represent a mix of behavioral and psychodynamic modalities. They take from the behavioral a focus on behavior change, graded task assignments, scheduling, and behavioral rehearsal, and from the psychodynamic the importance of understanding internal dialogue and bringing ideas into "conscious" awareness. A description of the approaches of Ellis and Michenbaum will illustrate how the cognitive approach operates in practice.

Albert Ellis developed RET after having come to believe that psychoanalytic and psychodynamic modes which he practiced were ineffective and not directly responsive to interferences with effective functioning. Because he found both free association and an emphasis on reconstructing history to be too passive and too focused on the past to challenge clients' current views of themselves and their experiences, his new approach was designed to directly confront their belief systems and irrational ideas and attitudes.

RET essentially consists of identifying one's irrational beliefs and having them actively or directly challenged by the therapist and the group with the aim of developing more realistic beliefs. Ellis suggests that much psychopathological behavior results from an inaccurate interpretation of the relationship between events and consequences. For example, Ellis (1982) suggests that if at point A a person experiences some undesirable or unpleasant event (such as social rejection) and at point C the individual begins to feel unhappy or anxious or depressed, the interpretation he typically makes is that A is the cause of C because one preceeded the other. Ellis believes that this is largely an inaccurate perception because the most important factor is the unrecognized existence of point B which intervenes between A and C. B represents the individual's *irrational beliefs or attitudes.* While social rejection contributes to some of the resultant unpleasant feeling or reaction, the individual's irrational belief system is the more important determiner of that reaction. In this case, he has an irrational belief, such as "I am unattractive," "I am a failure," or "nobody will want to have any kind of relationship with me." Because this belief is unarticulated and, therefore, not clearly in the awareness of the individual, it remains unchallenged. Therefore, although event A—someone's rejecting you because they don't like you—may be unchangeable in that particular situation, it probably also has to do with characteristics of the individual you met, the circumstances, and so forth and would not, in and of itself, call for such a strong reaction. It is the intervention of B, negative self-statements, that causes the extremity of the reaction. What is striking is that B is almost always changeable, because it is an unexamined belief held by the individual and therefore is capable of change and modification, after it is revealed and its irrationality exposed.

RET, then, essentially consists of identifying irrational beliefs, of working toward changing them with the assistance of a therapist and other group members, and of eventually replacing them with more realistic beliefs. Ellis suggests that there are some fairly widely held irrational beliefs such as: "*I must* perform well and be approved for doing so, and it's *awful* if this is not true. What a rotten person I am" and "Conditions under which I live *must* be easy and give me precisely what I want exactly when I want it; and it's *terrible* when they aren't. Poor me! poor me!" (Ellis, 1982, p. 384). It is the task of the therapist and the group not only to question and challenge these beliefs but to unearth new irrational beliefs, which are usually denoted by very strongly held *shoulds, oughts,* and *musts,* with all their characteristics of perfectionistic strivings.

Although Ellis states that spontaneity in groups is encouraged, RET groups are usually highly structured and organized. In a typical group session, after each member presents a current problem such as feelings of depression, anxiety, loneliness, or some maladaptive behavior, the group focuses on one member's problems by first identifying its activating circumstances (A) and the subsequent maladaptive response (C), after which attention is turned to identifying the most powerful and controlling irrational beliefs (B) that sustain C. Members of the group then vigorously dispute these beliefs and encourage the individual to do so as well, both within the group and when he experiences such emotional responses outside the group. In addition, group members or the leader will often suggest cognitive and/or behavioral homework to help eliminate irrational beliefs. For example, a socially isolated man may be given the assignment of initiating a conversation with at least one person a day. Compliance with homework which is checked on in subsequent sessions seems to be greater when it is assigned in groups rather than in individual therapy perhaps because of the size of the audience to which to report as well as the additional component of peer pressure provided by other group members.

Actually, RET group sessions often contain an amalgam of strategies that enable clients to reveal and confront irrational beliefs, including structured exercises such as role-playing and self-disclosing. Ellis finds role-playing particularly effective in evoking emotion and eliciting productive critiques from other group members. The RET therapist, who tends to be extremely active and directive during sessions, has the responsibility to see that only one person speaks at a time; to push untalkative, inhibited individuals to reveal themselves; to assure that no member is too talkative or domineering; and to ensure that members bring up serious problems and that the group stays productive rather than becoming apathetic or disorganized. In addition, the leader is often the most vigorous disputer of irrational beliefs.

In summary, then, Ellis's efforts are directed toward using the group to help the clients replace damaging irrational beliefs with more reasonable ones—that is, to help them react to situations on the basis of their actual impact rather than on the basis of the way in which they seem to confirm a failure to live up to an irrational set of ideal expectations.

While the approach of Meichenbaum (1977) overlaps to some extent with that of Ellis, the former attempts to combine cognitive approaches with more traditional behavioral approaches such as relaxation training. He emphasizes self-instructional training wherein the individual makes positive coping statements to himself, statements that are incompatible with the negative self-statements under whose influence the client has been operating. A description of a cognitive behavioral group for test anxiety (Meichenbaum,

1972; Meichenbaum & Genest, 1977) illustrates how the method combines both cognitive and more traditional behavioral approaches. A group composed of eight students met for eight one-hour weekly sessions and began by exploring the behaviors, emotions, and cognitions experienced by group members before and during a test-taking situation. After having completed a stress-inducing test before the session, group members reviewed and reflected on the self-defeating and irrational aspects of their self-statements and the behavioral and emotional effects of the statements. Among the thoughts and feelings expressed were (1) worry about performance, including ideas about others doing better; (2) ruminating about which answer to choose; (3) becoming preoccupied with bodily reactions to anxiety during the test; (4) ruminating about negative consequences of poor test performance, including lowered self-esteem, disapproval from others, and damage to academic records; and (5) other less specific thoughts and feelings of inadequacy.

Also in the first session an effort was made to provide members with a rationale for the therapeutic approach to help them see their problem as solvable and to outline steps that are needed to solve it. In this group the rationale was based on the idea that emotionality, worry, and difficulty in focusing attention are the primary factors in test anxiety, which has both a physiological and cognitive component, both of which would be dealt with in the group. Thus the groundwork was laid for a combined therapeutic approach that included learning relaxation skills *and* ways of examining and controlling one's thoughts and attention. With regard to the latter, being aware of producing negative self-statements serves as a cue to produce different and positive thoughts as well as providing signals to challenge and dispute negative self-statements. Clients were encouraged to believe in their capacity to achieve these changes.

Once the group was in session, direct work was begun on changing clients' negative self-statements by describing various aspects of the test-taking situation and using the group members' earlier reported experiences and reactions to them. After the negative cognitions were outlined, efforts were made to develop more adaptive cognitions, many of which were self-instructions that group members produced, such as "make no negative statements," "just think rationally"; "don't get lost in detail"; "look at the big picture." To deal with feelings of being overwhelmed, suggestions include statements such as "just try to keep anxiety manageable" and "just take one question at a time." The group also suggested some self-reinforcing statements, such as "it's working"; "I can control how I feel"; "I am in control."

In addition to the cognitive restructuring activities, the group engaged in relaxation exercises geared to controlling those aspects of anxiety that had previously been labeled as physiological. The emphasis in these exercises was on slow deep breathing and stressed the way in which this controlled and carefully observed process of inhaling and exhaling could produce a sense of relaxation and warmth. Suggestions were made to the effect that breathing techniques can create a feeling of relaxation and that the capacity to feel relaxed was under each individual's own control.

This group technique of Meichenbaum's was employed in a controlled study that compared the above described procedure with systematic desensitization and showed that it was more effective than the latter in reducing test anxiety, when measured in a variety of ways, including self-reports after treatment, one month follow-up, and subsequent grade point averages. Subjects offered this procedure did not differ at follow-up from previously low test anxious students on several measures of anxiety.

In addition to the specific content areas mentioned above, group cognitive behavior therapy has been employed in a wide variety of areas including patient compliance with medical regimens, alcoholism, obesity, depression, speech anxiety, and obsessions and compulsions.

## KEY CONCEPTS

**Focus on Overt Behavior.**    In contrast with most group methods, the behavioral approach eschews constructs dealing with hypothesized internal motivational states and instead concerns itself as much as possible with overt and observable behavior. The basic therapeutic questions become: What are the behaviors the individual wishes to change or eliminate, and what are new behaviors to learn? For example, the assertiveness training group focuses on practicing behaviors that members have been unable to perform. Oftentimes, what is required is very careful observation of the patient's actual behavior, paying close attention to its subtle characteristics as well as to related situational factors that have previously gone unnoticed. Such close observation was required in the obesity group described, where group member's keeping close track of all circumstances in which eating took place was emphasized. The main therapeutic concern is with identifying and observing problem behavior and then with creating the means of changing it.

**Specificity.**    Closely related to the focus on overt behavior is an emphasis on detailing conditions that control behavior and specifying as clearly as possible the nature of the problematical behavior under consideration. The behavior therapist is never satisfied with a general statement of a problem; instead she requires a careful delineation of its nature, the circumstances under which it occurs, and of its unsatisfactory concomitants. Vague descriptions of problems are unacceptable. The behavior therapist would not allow a patient to describe himself as anxious and let it go at that, but would rather inquire into the specific behaviors that the patient is referring to when using that adjective. Knowing when, how, where, and the manner in which a feeling is experienced is quite relevant. Thus, becoming aware of the specific conditions that elicit problematic behavior, so that new conditions may be created to facilitate behavior change, is a central principle.

**Determining Treatment Goals.**    Behavior therapists would view many of the treatment models previously discussed as vague and undelineated and as having extremely amorphous goals, so that whether they are achieved or not always remains unclear. In sharp contrast, the behavior therapy approach attempts to state in very concrete ways the kinds of behaviors that an individual finds problematical and wishes to change; it also attempts to detail the nature of the change that needs to take place. This approach is typically directed toward one or another of the following goals or some combination of several of them: acquiring behavior, maintaining behavior, strengthening behavior, and eliminating behavior. There is, of course, a range of specificity of goals within the behavior therapy model, with very delimited changes such as stopping smoking or losing a predetermined number of pounds in a certain period of time at one end of the scale and feeling more comfortable in social situations at the other. But even the latter would not remain so vaguely described but would be broken down into identified observable behaviors that need attention, as we saw in the development of anxiety hierarchies in the desensitization group for students with fears of speaking in public and of being in social situations. Behavior therapists contend that changes in delimited problematical behavior or elimination of specific symptoms have additional unanticipated positive effects that go beyond an alleviation of the specific symptom. For example, general anxiety level is diminished when only one specific phobic area is focused on in the treatment situation. A number of variables centering around the general level of personal comfort, greater ease in social situations, and feelings of increased adequacy occur along with the achievement of more circumscribed treatment goals.

**Treatment Plan.**    After developing specific goals, it is necessary to choose the most appropriate method for successfully accomplishing them from among the diversity of approaches that come under the behavior therapeutic rubric. Careful analysis of an individual's overt behavior should lead to a reasoned choice of method by which to help the individual change the behaviors of concern. Specific interventions have become primarily associated with certain problems, such as desensitization techniques with phobias and other circumscribed anxieties and behavior practice techniques with behavioral deficits, as in the use of assertiveness training to increase the ability to express oneself straightforwardly. While a particular technique may be commonly used with a given problem, it is important to emphasize that customizing the technique and treatment plan to the specific needs of each individual is an important task of the group leader.

**Objective Evaluation of Outcome.**    A great emphasis in the behavioral approach has been placed on evaluating the effectiveness of techniques used and continuing to carefully reexamine and improve them. Many behavioral techniques have evolved in the context of controlled studies, which compare them with either other treatment approaches or with no-treatment conditions. This emphasis on evaluation clearly articulates the roots of the behavioral approach in the experimental-scientific method.

## ROLE OF THE LEADER

Let us now summarize the leader characteristics that we have pointed to throughout our discussion of group behavioral approaches. The leader in the behavior therapy group frequently fills the role of teacher or expert, employing a style that is typically very authoritative but hopefully not authoritarian. Because the majority of behavior therapy groups focus on identified problem behaviors, not surprisingly the leader tries to come across as knowledgeable about the problems under consideration, frequently has didactic information to impart, and in general is the organizer of the proceedings. Group interaction is characterized by instructions and comments from the leader to a particular individual in the group or to the group as a whole, although there are some exceptions, notably in those instances where group discussion plays a relatively prominent role. Rose (1977) indicates that the leader has a variety of important roles to perform, including organizing the group, orienting members to the group, assessing problems and ways of resolving them, monitoring behavior identified as problematical, evaluating the progress of treatment, planning for specific interventions, and creating means for transfer and maintenance programs that will occur outside of the group itself. Given this set of leader characteristics and expectations, clearly the major activity of the behavior therapy group leader is directing and organizing group flow.

In contrast with group process or group psychodynamic approaches, characterized by a high degree of member-to-member interaction, low frequency of input by leader, tolerance for periods of long silence, the leader in the behavioral approach is typically quite intent on keeping the proceedings going and leading the group through a predetermined set of specified activities related to an identified and agreed upon set of goals. The leader is active and directive and is looked to by the members for instructing, pacing, and sequencing and assuming overall responsibility for the proceedings.

# CHAPTER NINE
# THE TAVISTOCK
# APPROACH TO GROUPS

The Tavistock approach to training in group dynamics, like that of the T-group and laboratory method to be discussed in the next chapter, typically involves an institute, or conference, in which several distinctive types of groups are organized. However, just as Chapter 10 will focus on the T-group as *the* core learning experience within an overall laboratory, the present chapter will emphasize one particular kind of Tavistock group, the *small study group,* as that which is central to the overall Tavistock approach even though a Tavistock conference will often include additional groups, such as the *large group* (see p. 166) and the *institutional event* (see p. 167).

The small study group is the unit that meets most frequently over the course of a conference's life and is the one about which Tavistock trainees tend to have the strongest feelings. It is also the group that, more than any other Tavistock group, dramatically manifests the latent forces that Wilfred Bion, the model's founder, believed to be characteristic of all groups. Therefore, when we mention the *Tavistock model,* we shall be primarily referring to the small study group.

The Tavistock model bears important similarities to the three group-dynamic therapy models presented in Chapter 4. Like them, it reflects a unique blending of concepts derived from both psychoanalysis and Lewinian field theory. However, unlike them, it is not a psychotherapy model and is geared toward relatively healthy people who wish to learn more about group processes, especially as they relate to problems of leadership within bureaucratic organizations.

Credit for the development of the Tavistock model is usually given to Bion, whose theory of small group dynamics provided the model's basic conceptual foundation and eventually led to the development of the small study group. Later, A.K. Rice and Margaret Rioch were to become prominently involved in the design and administration of Tavistock conferences, where other kinds of groupings were added to the small study group.

Bion's intensive work with groups had begun during World War II when, as a British army officer, he had the dual responsibility of selecting candidates for office training and of heading a hospital unit of psychiatric patients (de Maré, 1985). In connection with the latter task, he became heavily involved in group treatment and soon was impressed with its therapeutic potential. For him its value lay not so much in its efficiency as in the way in which it recapitulated, in microcosmic, living form, each patient's fundamental problem in becoming integrated into the larger society. In this respect, Bion's perspective is reminiscent of that of Foulkes, who viewed the individual as a sociobiological unit and her psychopathology as an inability to adapt to the interdependence needed for effective role functioning in the modern community. Just as the patient's difficulties had developed within a sociocultural matrix, so must the treatment and cure take place within such a matrix.

Bion's fascination lay with the ways in which groups continually form resistances to the reality demands of the task-at-hand (Bion, 1959). These resistances take the form of "basic assumption" matrices wherein a group regressively looks for magical solutions to the hard work before it (König, 1985). While such resistances were observable in therapy groups, Bion's thinking was essentially that of a generalist who saw the specific phenomena before him as instances of considerably broader and more universal principles. Hence the ways in which the therapy group resisted its essential task (i.e., the resolution of its members' psychological difficulties) was but a concrete example of the general tendency for all groups to engage in similar avoidances. Not many more steps were needed before Bion was to arrive at the idea of the small study group, whose primary task was to study its own behavior. The role of the leader, or "consultant," would be to interpret at selected moments the latent meaning of the group's behavior, much as a psychoanalyst might do with an individual patient. The small study group began as a means of training group therapists and other mental health professionals; several such groups were run by Bion at the Tavistock Clinic in London and were his first civilian training groups after the war. Because of the association of study groups with the Tavistock Clinic, and later with the Tavistock Institute of Human Relations, they became known as "Tavistock groups." Then, starting in 1948, there was a seven-year hiatus during which small study groups were discontinued at the

Tavistock Clinic, which had begun instead to focus on group therapy and on other kinds of professional education.

A major revival of the small study group took place in 1957 at a conference organized under the joint auspices of the University of Leicester and the Tavistock Institute of Human Relations, and Tavistock conferences and Tavistock groups have been occurring ever since. Between 1957 and 1965, seven additional such conferences were run under the same organizational collaboration, while others were sponsored by the Tavistock Institute in cooperation with other organizations, and still others by the Institute alone. Prominently involved in the organization and directorship of these conferences was A.K. Rice, an Englishman who had been associated with Bion's first civilian training group at Tavistock, and whose background included many years as a government administrator in both Africa and India. It was this latter work that had initially led to Rice's interest in organizational psychology and to his wish to learn more about the psychodynamics of leader–follower relationships.

Primary credit for the introduction of Tavistock thinking into America belongs to Margaret Rioch, a psychoanalyst on the faculty of the Washington School of Psychiatry. Rioch attended a Tavistock conference held at the University of Leicester in the early sixties, returned home, and stimulated enough interest in some of her colleagues for them to attend a subsequent Tavistock conference in Great Britain. The first such conference held in the United States occurred in 1965, on the campus of Mt. Holyoke College, and was sponsored by three organizations: the Washington School of Psychiatry, Yale University's Department of Psychiatry, and the Tavistock Institute. Such conferences have been held annually at Mt. Holyoke since 1965, and other national conferences based on the Tavistock model have taken place at Amherst College. An important organizing influence behind these Group Relations conferences has been a semiautonomous institute within the Washington School of Psychiatry; this unit was formally named the A.K. Rice Institute in 1970, one year subsequent to Rice's death.

In addition to sponsoring conferences, the Rice Institute offers management consultation to interested organizations. In 1971 a somewhat similar group was incorporated in New York City; calling itself the Institute for Applied Study of Social Systems and existing on a nonprofit basis, this institute provides consultation services and holds roughly four training conferences per year. Parallel organizations in England are the Grubb Institute and what is now known as the Tavistock Center for Applied Social Research. While businesses and schools have shown an interest in this model, psychiatric and psychoanalytic institutes have also been particularly receptive to its theory. For this reason, such groups as Mt. Zion Hospital (in San Francisco) and the Menninger Institute (in Topeka, Kansas), along with Yale's Psychiatry Department, have become informal centers for Tavistock learning.

Bion's unique contribution to the Tavistock conference was the original small study group. The gradual elaboration of other conference events around the basic unit of the small study group to a large extent represents the contribution of Rice (1965). We shall first describe the course of a typical Tavistock conference, after which we shall present the key concepts involved in Bion's conceptual framework.

## DESCRIPTION OF A TYPICAL CONFERENCE

The nature of Tavistock conferences is most succinctly and comprehensively described in Rice's *Learning for Leadership* (1965). In order to cite concrete examples of what an actual conference is like, we will occasionally refer to a weekend meeting sponsored by the Institute of Applied Study of Social Systems in New York City that had as its specific theme the "Exploration of Male–Female Work Relations in Group Settings," which one of us attended. Its format was consistent with those of previous Tavistock institutes and turned out to be a forerunner of a number of subsequent such conferences, each devoted to the effects of both gender and age on role expectations and role performance in occupational settings (Gould, 1985).

The typical Tavistock conference begins with a relatively brief Opening Plenary, which is acknowledged to have some ritualistic aspects (Rice, 1965). Yet it also serves to bring the entire membership together for the first of what may be several plenary review sessions. Moreover, at those conferences where members live in residence, certain important "housekeeping" details, like meals, will be mentioned and the conference's Administrative Secretary introduced. The purpose of the conference is summarized in a brief statement that also appears in whatever written brochures or program-announcements participants are given. This statement serves to establish the set for all the group events that follow and is very rarely repeated by the consultants: Members are told that the institute's main task is to explore covert processes, especially as these relate to issues of authority, and they are reminded that there is no specific prescription as to what anyone will learn. Conference participants are encouraged to assume active responsibility for what they get from the experience and to relinquish any expectations that their primary learning will occur via specific cognitive inputs, or "lessons," from the staff.

**The Small Study Group.**    The small study group is composed of from eight to twelve people. The number should be small enough for every member to feel some degree of personal relatedness to each of the other members and large enough so that no one member need feel continually pressured to speak or to be "on stage." Conference planners try to ensure that members are not known to each other beforehand, so that group life can start "from scratch," with a minimum of conventional customs carried over from members' prior associations with one another in either formal or informal settings.

The small study group almost always convenes shortly after the Opening Plenary. It is thought that it should constitute the first primary group event because (1) it is the most frequent and most intensive event of the conference (it may meet approximately six times during a three-day conference), (2) it is the event about which members usually have the most anxiety, and (3) as a face-to-face-group, it can offer the participant a primary group identification with which to approach subsequent conference events. The schedule is arranged so that the study group will stop meeting before the official conference ends. Hence this group, which meets both regularly and often during the first three-quarters of the conference's life, will normally drop out altogether during its final quarter. It is believed that this procedure enables the participants to have an initial separation-termination experience that helps them to realistically anticipate, and therefore better prepare for, the eventual conference ending. Through this procedure participants avoid having to simultaneously lose both their small study group, which gradually has come to offer a strong sense of support and affiliation, and the entire conference membership. Furthermore, Rice and others think that ending the conference with group events that more closely resemble outside life—like the application group (see p. 171) and the institutional event (see p. 167)—helps to provide a smoother, less abrupt transition as members move from the relatively cloistered and intense conference experience to their "back-home" existence.

At the first small study group meeting, the study group's leader-consultant will usually make no formal introduction to the group; instead, he simply waits for members to begin to speak and to interact. One reason for this silence is his wish to establish a culture within the group that is divorced from the more formal culture of most task groups, where the leader tends to take on an authoritative and directive role. Another reason is the fact that the conference's primary objective, the study of covert processes, had already been outlined in the opening session and in the literature sent out before the conference and did not need to be explicitly stated or reviewed by him.

As Rice defines it, the goal of the small study group is to "provide an opportunity to learn about the interpersonal life of a group as it happens" (1965, p. 57); consequently, the focus is on immediate, here-and-now events. Individual behavior is seen and interpreted in terms of what it expresses about the underlying group forces currently at work. This is *not* to say that the remarks of a particular participant—let's call her Diane—have nothing to do with her own personality dynamics or personal history; for example, Diane's preoccupation with separation and loss may reflect her recent divorce as much as it does the fact that her small study group is soon to disband. However, what the consultant-leader chooses to emphasize is how Diane's communications express that which is common to the membership (that which, so to speak, "carries on" the work of the group) rather than that which renders her unique or differentiates her from the rest of the members (Eisold, 1985). In this respect, the model takes an even more extreme position than the group-dynamic therapy model (see Chapter 4), where the leader, although eager to make interpretations at the group-as-a-whole level will also direct interpretations, when appropriate, to individual participants within the group.

The consultant's interventions are almost always referred to as *interpretations* in the Tavistock literature. This term, however, is a broad one and covers a variety of different interventions that might be made. Although many of the consultant's interventions are interpretations in the traditional sense of exploring what particular behaviors may mean, others are behaviorally oriented in that they point out overt aspects of the interaction without speculating about their covert meaning. For example, after about twenty minutes of random, seemingly innocuous discussion, a leader observes that the group conversation has revolved around outside affairs without any reference to the immediate situation. However, while the overt level of the leader's intervention refers to behavior evident to all, its covert effect is to sensitize the group to the possibility, if not the probability, that these behaviors constitute defenses against anxiety. There is a direct parallel to psychoanalysis, where an analyst's interpretations will point out a patient's resistances and avoidances, particularly during the early stages of treatment.

According to Tavistock theory, the primary experience against which most study-group resistances are directed is the participants' here-and-now feelings and fantasies concerning the leader. Consequently, when a group led by Rice (1965, p. 59) began with the participants discussing a murder that had recently been featured in the press, Rice eventually broke in, stating that as far as the here-and-now was concerned, *he* was the murder victim, for the group was by its consistent and rigorous ignoring of his presence effectively killing him and any help that he might be able to offer.

Much of the group's initial activity involves attempting to get the consultant to tell it what to do, just as in outside task groups there is often a similar tendency to expect magic from the leader. He is seen as the person to blame when things go badly in the group. Similarly, he is perceived as the source of good feelings in the group whenever there are good feelings. However, the actively managerial role that the leader tends to play in real-life task groups mitigates against the likelihood of the group's ever becoming aware of these dependent tendencies within itself (since the members' dependency on him is, in sense, "realistic" and legitimized). The small study group is unique in this respect: Just as in group psychoanalysis, the participant's attention is turned away from outside stimuli and diversions and is directed instead toward examining the normally unexplored data of group life, including feelings. The leader-consultant, by not fulfilling a participant's expectations, helps to make her aware of infantile fantasies that in ordinary groups are usually masked.

How does the leader accomplish this? By refusing to satisfy the group's demand for direction, and by instead interpreting its behavior as a childlike attempt to avoid working at its true task. At the same time, the leader, by means of his interpretations, implicitly demonstrates an ability and an activity that should be available to each group member (if only she can find her way to it): namely, the capacity to make rational sense of her own behavior, as well as that of her fellow participants. The consultant is in effect saying: "I have no special magic to wield; what I do have is the power of observation, and the ability to use it to understand what's going on. I invite you to use *your* capacities for observation and logical analysis in a similar way."

Following an initial period of discouragement and confusion, members often take strength from the consultant's dispassionate, almost clinical, attitude. There is no aspect of their collective mental life that cannot be explored—no fear or wish, however primitive, that in the cool light of day does not appear to be but another aspect of "the human condition." In addition, the fact that whatever participants reveal about themselves is interpreted as something that they all share in common as a group (rather than something that distinguishes each of them from one another) also helps to reduce their defensiveness.

After a while members may begin to value the group for its candor and permissiveness, and gradually there is an expression of positive feelings toward the leader for having made these developments possible. Yet the leader is unequivocal in his pursuit of analytic understanding, for he interprets the group's lauding of itself and of him as an effort to deny the fact that theirs has been an essentially mixed experience, that all learning and progress is uncertain and incomplete, that the members have had, and probably still have, some intensely hostile feelings toward him, and that they must at some point prepare for the pain of the group's dissolution. The consultant is in effect continuing in his role as frustrater: He refuses to collude with the group's "patting of itself on the back" and instead underlines it as a behavior that, constituting a defense against anxiety, might well characterize much of the day-to-day functioning of the participant's back-home work groups.

The theory of how learning takes place in the small study group receives an implicit, not explicit, statement in the Tavistock literature; such learning is conceived along lines that are similar to the theory of change in psychoanalysis. One Tavistock assumption, for example, is that learning is maximized in an ascetic atmosphere wherein needs for approval and structure are denied and powerful fantasies and affects are mobilized. Distortions will be thrown into relief by the consultant's nonauthoritarian behavior, feelings become less fearsome as they are openly expressed and accepted, and members are presented with a leadership model that shuns omnipotence in favor of a more limited (but nonetheless useful) ability to observe, to weigh possibilities, and to come to tentative conclusions.

**Lectures.**  A Tavistock conference sometimes includes a series of lectures, perhaps one per day, in which an attempt is made to provide purely cognitive content. Often the series is divided into two parts, the first relating to theories of group behavior and the second to an application of these theories to actual work settings. Although the overt purpose of these presentations is didactic, the lectures, by bridging the gap between traditional approaches to education and the strongly nondirective, experiential approach employed by the conference itself, can help to render the conference atmosphere slightly less foreign and anxiety producing for the membership.

American conferences, especially the briefer ones, tend to omit straight lecture presentations. This omission is possible since participants have become increasingly sophisticated about the experiential approach inherent in the Tavistock orientation and are therefore less likely to expect that they will be "taught" in a format even remotely akin to that of the academic classroom.

**The Large Group Event.**  The large group event includes all the conference participants, with the result that it may include anywhere from 100 to 150 people. The consultant leading the large group is on the conference staff and may be a leader of one of the small study groups. His role in leading the large group does not differ markedly from that of leading the small study group; yet his interventions will occasionally rely less on interpretation for reasons that we will cite below. Because members have already been informed of the group's purpose, he makes no formal introduction and instead silently waits for someone to start the discussion; once people have begun to speak he will make interventions at those points that he deems appropriate.

As the participants move from the small study group event to the large group event several difficulties emerge that did not exist in the small group (Rice, 1965): (1) While the anticipation of exposing oneself to a group of any size will usually create *some* degree of anxiety, the reduced intimacy of a large group intensifies this feeling for many; (2) once a member succeeds, despite her anxiety, in gathering up the courage to speak she might well feel guiltier about taking up the time of a large group because of the greater number of people competing for the floor; (3) an added source of anxiety is the fact that usually there is either a greater actual potential, or a greater felt potential, on the part of the group members for panic, anarchy, or a kind of "mob psychology" in a large unstructured group than in a small one (Freud, 1922; Milgram & Toch, 1969); and (4) at the same time that the large group is a source of increased tension, it also maximizes opportunities for defensive hiding, since a participant's silence is less likely to be noticed or commented upon. A rise in anxiety, when combined with increased opportunities for avoidance or hiding, is bound to make it less probable that an atmosphere of genuine authenticity wherein members feel able to express themselves freely will be created.

Marked tendencies toward diffusion and fragmentation constitute another problem facing the large conference group. These tendencies originate from at least three sources: (1) by virtue of its greater size, the large group is less likely than is the small group to unite behind a coherent defensive-regressive strategy for resisting the group task (see "Basic Assumptions Groups," p. 173), (2) the things that large groups in real life tend to have in common, and that give them a sense of a collective identity (a well-defined purpose, a motto or flag, a parliament or governing counsel, a common heritage or enemy) are not available to the conference's large group, and (3) the one source of identification readily at hand for each group member, the particular small study group to which he or she belongs, is more a source of fragmentation than of unity because in most instances (the exception being the fellow members of their particular small study group) members belong to *different* study groups. Once the large group is experienced as more diffuse and fractionated, it is more easily distorted, thereby becoming a readier target for a member's disowned and projected hostile feelings and thereby becoming yet another source of anxiety (Main, 1985).

A paradox that results from all these factors is that the large group is frequently forced to *unite* around the theme of the contending parties and fragmentations within it. The perceptive consultant might well interpret this phenomenon as follows: "It seems we can be united only if we are split; we can become one only if we are more than one" (Bion, 1959, p. 80). The participants often act on, and act out, this feeling by pointing out that things would probably prove more manageable if the large group were to divide into two or more smaller groups. Once this suggestion is made, a subgroup typically emerges that is opposed to this idea; with this subgroup in formation, the group does not have to follow such a suggestion by actually splitting into separate groups, for it now has an issue that emotionally divides it.

What does the consultant do with these complex dynamics? While his main function in the small study group is to interpret them, this may be less helpful in the large group, which is already rife with tension. For in this context, the inherent ambiguity of interpretations (e.g., who can prove them right or wrong?), plus their tendency to make the participants' hidden feelings and intentions their primary focus, might well provoke a close-to-unbearable degree of anxiety. Therefore, at least one Tavistock practitioner, Main (1985), recommends that the consultant to the large group event offer direct statements of his own feeling reactions to what is happening within the group. By maintaining a less intellectualized and distanced position, he can help to offset tendencies inherent in the large group toward fragmentation ("We, the staff, versus you, the members") and excessive competition ("We, the staff, know more than you, the membership").

**The Intergroup Event.**   After the large group has met once or twice, the intergroup exercise will usually begin. At this point a member has faced her small study group, plus a large group situation in which all the study groups have been brought together. Now, with the intergroup exercise (Gould, 1985), she is thrown into an even more complex situation wherein she must, as a member of a small group called a "membership group" (having a different composition from that of her study group) start some formal negotiations with similar membership groups, along with the staff, which will constitute its own membership group. All conference members participate in the intergroup event, and the number of membership groups will be roughly equivalent to the number of small study groups. The learning to be promoted in the intergroup event encompasses those group events and processes that typically occur when groups negotiate with other groups. For the first time in the conference, participants are presented a task that goes beyond the study of group process per se; now they must try to communicate with *other* groups. Here the conference planners are trying to simulate the kinds of problems—involving organization and the distribution of power—with which the participants are usually faced in their daily work situations.

At the outset of this exercise, members are told that their primary agenda involves studying the relationships between the staff group and the various membership groups and among the membership groups themselves. Just what the membership groups will do to accomplish this task, what messages they will send to other membership groups, and how they will set up the political machinery needed to send these communications and to make various decisions constitute the formidable problems that the participants face.

To illustrate how this exercise is typically introduced, we take as our example the three-day residential conference on male-female work relationships referred to earlier. For the initial, brief orientation to the intergroup event, men and women met separately to highlight the conference theme (this was the only instance where groups formed along gender lines). Members were told that directly after the orientation, staff-consultants would be available in specifically assigned rooms, one consultant to each room, in order to help members in their performance of the intergroup task.

The task in this initial postorientation session was for the members to form groups among themselves and to then study the kinds of relationship behaviors that occurred between and among their groups as they attempted to interact with one another. Members were free to form whatever membership groups they wished to form by going to a room in which there was a particular consultant, or by forming face-to-face groups *without* the presence of a consultant in rooms specifically set aside for this purpose. Starting with the second session and for the remainder of all subsequent intergroup events, the staff would constitute itself as a separate membership group and would meet in its own specifically designated room. Staff members would be available as consultants to separate membership groups or to meetings between membership groups. (In other words, unlike both the small and large study groups where a consultant-leader is always present, the utilization of a consultant in the intergroup event constitutes an option which a membership group—or two or more membership groups meeting together—can either accept or reject).

The members were also informed that a membership group, if and when it prepared to send one of its members as an emissary or representative to another group, could give this person three different levels of representativeness: (1) observer status—here the representative could try to observe and to gain information from other groups but was not empowered to articulate viewpoints or to act on behalf of her group; (2) delegate status—here the representative could deliver a message in the name of her group or state her group's opinion on a particular issue; however, she could not modify these messages, no matter what she learned once she left her group, nor could she take any further action without returning to her group for consultation, (3) plenipotentiary status—here the representative had flexible negotiating powers in that she was allowed to take action and to make decisions on behalf of her fellow group members without referring back to them for consent.

One can well imagine the kinds of basic political problems that membership groups face as they go about attempting to set up a structure for dealing with other groups. As soon as representatives from other groups begin to knock at a group's door (or, in Tavistock lingo, "to cross boundaries"), the group is forced to make a fundamental decision as to whether to receive such messages and whether to admit observers and possible new members to its meetings. It might decide to station a "gatekeeper" at the door and to leave these decisions to her, but even to do this the group must develop some basis for arriving at a consensus. Once a group has sent out a plenipotentiary it must come to terms with the amount of power it has given her; a Tavistock plenipotentiary has had the experience of returning to a group only to find that it had in her absence decided it no longer is to be bound by whatever commitments she may have made to other groups on its behalf. And a group, on the other hand, sometimes has learned that its delegate overstepped the bounds of her authority by firmly committing it to an intergroup decision without returning for consultation.

As groups go about constructing this elaborate machinery for negotiating with one another, they are still left with the basic question of how to fulfill the function of the exercise. Should they set before the conference a petition demanding that one of its female consultants have her status enhanced by being designated as a co-director of the conference? Should they form larger groups for the discussion of male-female relationships? Since the theme was men–women relations, our actual Tavistock conference considered both these possibilities. Despite their intellectual realization that they are free to adopt any agenda they wish and are responsible for their own learning, members tend to become convinced that the staff has some definite notion as to what will constitute successful task performance; once they are so convinced, some members will attempt to formulate a program that will "please" the staff whereas others will "rebel" against the exercise by evading its instructions altogether. Yet the membership, however struggling, uncertain, and awkward it may appear to be in its efforts to meet the task, *cannot but perform* it, for from the moment a group selects a representative from among its ranks it is beginning to engage in some form of intergroup relations. Whenever a member observes what is happening in a concerted attempt to draw conclusions from it, she is studying the intergroup process at the same time that she is engaged in it.

The membership is also free to utilize this exercise for learning about relationships between membership and management, since the latter, from the second session on, constitutes itself as a separate group. Staff is the one membership that meets throughout the intergroup event, whereas other members are free to "cut" the exercise altogether, to leave their groups, or to reorganize into new groups. Members are allowed to observe the staff meetings at any point. The staff can serve as a model in two distinct ways: (1) It will hopefully illustrate some adaptive ways of making decisions, of delegating authority, and of expressing feelings; and (2) it can, through its errors, its blind spots, its dissensions and disruptions, demonstrate that conference leaders, as they assume membership in their own group, are as vulnerable to the irrational forces of group process as are conference members.

As we indicated above, membership groups have the option of calling in a consultant at any point that they decide that his services might be useful. Consultants leave the staff meetings one-by-one during the intergroup exercise, usually in alphabetical order. They are committed to consulting with a particular group only insofar as they perceive the group as having a legitimate need for consultation. It is important to remember that the authority-membership mistrust is such that members may well have as their unconscious purpose in requesting consultation a wish to in some way weaken the staff and to "win over" the consultant to its cause. If paranoid enough, a group may begin to feel that the consultant, while seemingly interested in helping, is actually attempting to sabotage its attempt to fulfill the task. Furthermore, since the staff is prey to its own irrational hostilities and projections, these "paranoid" fears on the part of a group may occasionally be justified.

Increasing the tensions and confusions that already exist on the basis of task ambiguity, membership frustration, and staff-member hostilities, are severe time and space "boundaries" (see "Key Concepts," p. 172). Staff is extremely punctual in beginning and ending the intergroup events, and some rooms are available only for *intergroup* meetings (as opposed to a meeting of a single membership group). In the Tavistock conference in which we participated, these tensions were heightened by the staff's further limiting space resources by suddenly removing a room from the list of available rooms. Membership anger eventually reached such proportions that one group acted out its defiance by "occupying" the staff's room during a coffee-break and refusing to yield it upon the staff's return. As Rice points out, the entire intergroup event is a kind of game or charade that is supposed to mirror its real-life organizational equivalent. Yet, as the just-cited behavior demonstrates, it is a game that mobilizes tremendous emotion and that most members play in deadly earnest.

**The Plenary Reviews.**   The Opening Plenary, which begins the conference, was described earlier. Typically there is a second plenary event or plenary "review" toward the end of the conference, the purpose of which is "to provide opportunities for ending work relationships between members and staff without applying closure to the learning of the conference" (Lawrence, 1979). It is here that the entire membership will have a chance to explore collectively its brief history as a group, to review the meaning of its various crises, and to integrate some of these emotionally charged events with conceptual material. Before the large group event was devised, there had been a tendency for the plenary session to take on some of the functions of that experience; once this role was no longer needed, the plenary reviews could now concentrate more directly on a summarizing and integrative function.

Currently plenary sessions seem to be viewed by Tavistock leaders in a ritualized and ambivalent fashion. This ambivalence is hardly surprising when one recalls that Tavistock theory views learning in a way that challenges traditional conceptions of the student-teacher relationship. For this reason it is usually difficult for a Tavistock staff to directly satisfy the learning needs that typically manifest themselves at such a session, where members will tend to want intellectual presentations of Tavistock concepts and direct answers to their questions. For instance, at the conference on male–female work relations, staff consultants were reluctant to share their understandings of previous conference events and instead confined themselves to interpreting the here-and-now events of the plenary session itself, especially the membership's need to know how the staff had conceptualized earlier conflicts and crises. This need was interpreted as the members' exaggeration of their leader-dependence as a way of avoiding a more autonomous approach to learning (see "Basic Assumption Dependency Group," p. 174). The staff's preference for focusing on latent meanings was increased by the fact that this particular conference, in omitting large group events, had not provided any other vehicle for the processing of large-group behavior.

**The Application Group.**   If not actually the final conference event, application groups come very close to a conference's end. They have as their explicit focus an exploration of what had been learned and the application of this learning to a member's vocational setting. For this reason an attempt is made to keep the group homogeneous (i.e., to assign to it people from similar occupations). The placement of this event at the conference's conclusion is designed to help ease the members' emotional transition to their outside lives. (These groups are sometimes also referred to in Tavistock literature as "review groups," "role-relations consultation groups," or "role analysis groups"; see Lawrence, 1979 and Gould, 1985).

Because the consultant makes a concerted effort here to be more cognitive and didactic than in other conference events, this group is often experienced by members as "flatter" than the previous groups (Rice, 1965, p.

117). Members are instructed to remember back to their significant learning experiences and to relate them to analogous events and situations in their work environments. Rice believes that the group leader need not be particularly familiar with members' respective employment specializations to do this. What is important is that he be able to grasp some sense of a member's unique organizational situation from the member's description of it, and that the consultant is then able to help her relate insights developed during the conference to what she describes as her day-to-day work tasks and work problems.

## KEY CONCEPTS

Bion's theory of group behavior was primarily set forth in a collection of his papers called *Experiences in Groups* (1959). Bion's highly abstract concepts are usually several steps removed from the concrete data of everyday life and are, therefore, frequently hard to grasp. However, there are secondary sources that help to clarify and explain them (see Rioch, 1970; Pines, 1985).

**The Work Group.**    Bion thought of any group as simultaneously consisting of two groups, or as having two coexisting aspects: a work group and a basic assumption group. At any point in time a group's behavior expresses a balance between these two groups, sometimes weighted toward the work group, and sometimes toward the basic assumption. The more a group functions toward the work-group end of the continuum, the more it is rationally and maturely focusing on the performance of its proper task in as efficient a manner as possible; the more it functions toward the basic assumptions end of the continuum, the more it is behaving in a regressive fashion wherein the group takes on primitive, familial connotations for its members by beginning to be used for emotional gratification and tension release.

If a task group were to function solely as a work group, the number and contents of its meetings would be determined only by the nature of its task. Its leader would be chosen, not by virtue of his charisma, but in terms of his ability to do the job, and his leadership would last only so long as that job remained to be completed (Turquet, 1985). Members would have a strong enough sense of autonomy and individuation to cooperate without fearing loss of self and without undue competitive feelings. Because their interest in the task would outweigh their libidinal interest in either the leader or one another, they would not allow either emotional gratification or emotional deprivation to interfere with effective task performance.

If the Tavistock small study group were to perform within a pure work-group culture (a state of affairs that can exist only in theory), its consultant would not need to intervene, since the group would quickly begin to process its own data without any avoidances or regressions. For example, he wouldn't have to ask why the group ignores him, since the group would either not be ignoring him or, if it were, would comment on this behavior by itself, and by so commenting would already have begun to pay attention to him.

**Basic Assumption Groups.**   When a group is in a state of emotional regression it acts *as if* it believes certain things to be true that really aren't true (and in Bion's theory a group is always in such a state to one degree or another). For example, if the group is behaving in accordance with the basic assumption of dependency, it assumes that the leader is omniscient. Basic assumptions are oriented toward the way we would like reality to be, rather than toward the way it is; therefore, they constitute resistances to the rational task of the work group (Schermer, 1985).

In the typical task-group situations of everyday life, several factors tend to obscure these basic assumptions to a point where they function in an implicit and partially disguised fashion. These factors are: (1) As Freud (1922) (1975) discovered many years before the emergence of the Tavistock model, most people tend to be unaware of the more infantile aspects of their emotional life; (2) since basic assumptions are essentially *shared* fantasies, they belong more to a group's unconscious than to any single individual's unconscious; as such they constitute a kind of "collective unconscious" (Jung, 1917) and therefore are *even more easily* denied by an individual than are his more personalized and idiosyncratic unconscious fantasies; (3) task group leaders do not as a rule encourage their groups to pay attention to the more subtle aspects of their fantasy life and instead direct their attention onto concrete projects that focus the members' attention outward rather than inward; and (4) the fantasy needs of the typical task-group leader have enough in common with the fantasies of his followers for him to collude with the group's fantastic expectations of him; since he tends to go along with these expectations, the discrepancy between fantasy and reality is less marked and the group member consequently has less chance to gain insight into the infantile nature of her attitude toward authority.

The small study group is a special kind of task group, however. Although the study group's consultant can do little in the way of a direct modification of the first and second factors listed above, he attempts to directly offset the third and fourth factors. He gives the group no task other than the understanding of its own emotional processes (factor number three), and by flatly refusing to meet the group's emotional needs, he directly attempts to foil— and thereby highlight more dramatically—their fantasies (factor number four). For example, while the fantasy lying at the heart of basic assumption fight-flight (see below) is that the leader will rally the group against a common enemy, the consultant refuses to do this. Hence it would seem that the role of basic assumptions in the small study group is almost the precise theoretical counterpart of the role played by transference resistance in psychoanalysis, both individual and group. However, a basic assumption is characteristic of a group as a whole, while a transference resistance is from a conceptual point of view the property of an individual.

Bion distinguished three main kinds of basic assumption groups. Like the more general concepts of the work group and the basic assumptions group, these specific basic assumption states do not emerge in an absolutely total way. At any particular point in the group interaction, some members may be operating more in accordance with one kind of basic assumption, and other members, with another. However, careful attention to the group process will usually reveal one of the three basic assumptions to be predominant.

*A. The Basic Assumption Dependency Group.* To the extent to which a basic assumption of dependency prevails, a group lives for and through its leader. He and his infallibility are the source of all wisdom, comfort, and security; neither one's own resources nor those of one's peers count for very much. The leader's observations are regarded more in religious terms involving unswerving faith than in scientific terms involving balanced and empirically oriented judgments. The primary axis of relatedness for each member is between herself and the leader, and it is only in this context that other members have significance for her. Hence the person who presents herself to the group as weak or sick may be eagerly confirmed in this position by her peers, who vicariously use her to force some display of nurturance from the leader. Since members relate in a greedy and demanding manner and since their infantile expectations cannot be completely met, considerable jealousy, disappointment, and resentment are activated, however much suppressed.

*B. The Basic Assumption Fight-Flight Group.* While the main focus in basic assumption dependency is a fantasy relationship with the leader, the primary focus in this second example is the preservation of the group through some kind of action, either fight or flight. Both fight and flight stem from the same motivational dynamic (i.e., a defensive escape into activity for its own sake). Bion implies that whichever of the two is chosen in any particular instance may relate more to incidental factors than to the basic dynamics of the group; it is as if the group is ready for some kind of action and will seize on whatever comes its way. Therefore if a member who has been absent from the group returns, she may be attacked (fight), whereas if a particularly charismatic member begins to talk about a well-publicized event outside the group at a time when it is ready for such a diversion, it will most likely mobilize around and pursue this digression (flight).

Bion does not make clear what events or stages are needed to prepare for the emergence of the fight-flight culture. One senses that it requires some degree of group identity and cohesiveness. Once aroused, this group spirit acts as a strong force, with the result that members struggle to preserve the group at all costs. Since a group is more than the sum of its parts, each member is able to imagine its surviving intact despite the fact that some of its other members have been hurt or destroyed in the process. Unlike the dependency culture, then, which treats the ailing individual with compassion in the hope that she will arouse the leader's sympathy, the fight-flight group can be ruthless in its disregard for her welfare, much as a retreating army may leave its wounded behind to die. Indeed, there may be times when the group's "fight" is directed toward one of its own, now scapegoated, members. Since this group culture is oriented toward action, it is responsive to the kind of leader who rallies it against a common enemy (e.g., a team-captain, an Army sergeant, etc.), but unresponsive to a leader who embodies the values of intellectuality, introspection, and understanding (e.g., the study group consultant).

How realistic is the group's concern with its own survival? To qualify as a basic assumption it must be primarily irrational. If this need to preserve itself physically were actually the main basis of the group's existence together, as in the case of an army platoon under attack, the fight-flight orientation would begin to constitute a more appropriate basis for a work-group culture and in this sense would no longer offer a pure example of a basic assumptions culture. Indeed, in situations where a group is under physical attack, the basic assumptions group and the work group tend to converge, and the basic assumption of fight-flight can—in the hands of an effective leader who knows how to harness and exploit it—prove quite supportive of the group's real task.

However, most groups need not survive beyond the rather limited purpose that called them together (e.g., the development of a marketing plan, the writing of some legislation, etc.) and should they find they are not "making a go" of that which has united them, their most adaptive response would be to disband. Yet the fantasy element in any fight-flight group culture, whatever the group's real purpose and situation may be, is the individual's assumption that her survival and that of the group are completely synonomous and codetermined, that she will die if the group should die. It is probably when we are very young that we most consistently and most consciously perceive our survival as inextricably linked to the survival of our "small group"—our family—and in this parallel we see the strongly archaic pull of the fight-flight culture.

*C. The Basic Assumption Pairing Group.* Here the individual member-to-individual-member axis becomes paramount. One possible indication that a pairing culture is in the making is the group's gradual focusing on a colloquy between two particular people; in the group's unconscious mental life there begins to arise the hope that this "pairing" will in some way affect the life of the group for the better. Pairing is more obvious if the dyad consists of people of the opposite sex, and if their conversation is relatively personal and intimate. Yet the pairing basic assumption may exist when the two people are of the same sex and seem to be focusing on something relatively innocuous—for example, what the group should discuss at that particular moment. The basic assumption then, is that "there could be no possible reason for two people's coming together except sex" (Bion, 1959, p. 62). The second basic assumption is that out of this sexual relationship something or someone is to be born—perhaps a new idea, or a new leader—that will "save" the group. An atmosphere of attentiveness and optimism gradually permeates the group—the sense of a Utopia-about-to-be-born that will extricate it from its present frustration, irritation, and uncertainty. Even without direct evidence of a distinct member-to-member pairing, feelings of hopefulness are almost always a clue as to either the existence of a basic assumptions pairing group or its imminent emergence. A second, slightly less reliable sign is the way in which the group allows one particular dyad to become prominent; it would seem that somewhere in the group's attentiveness there is some expectation, however submerged, that this interaction will bring something different, and hopefully something better, to all. This is why the group nurtures the dyadic focus—it promises something for everyone.

In order for the pairing culture to persist, it is essential that the *promise* (and not the actuality) of a new idea or a new leader be present; should such a Messiah or idea emerge he or it will inevitably be rejected and hope be killed, for the "complete solution" that the group longs for exists only in fantasy. Real "solutions" are all too temporary and incomplete; whatever understanding that could be reached would gradually be replaced by confusion as the group began to focus its attention on new tensions and new problems; whatever good feelings come into the group would gradually dissipate. Such is the life of groups on earth; what the pairing culture strives for is group-life as it is commonly imagined to exist in Heaven.

As we have described the three basic assumption groups, we have moved from themes of being nurtured and supported (dependency), to mobilization and aggression (fight-flight), to reproduction (pairing). Hence, while the Tavistock literature does not contain a reference that directly links the three basic assumption cultures to Freud's three psychosexual stages (oral, anal, and phallic), this correspondence seems to us to be fairly clear. Moreover, the three basic assumptions are almost always described in the order in which we listed them, even though Bion does not imply that in any given group they will necessarily emerge in this order, or that one kind of basic assumption is more mature than any other. We mention the parallel in order to indicate the extent to which fundamentally psychoanalytic notions prevail within this model and also to show how the laws of group behavior are considered to directly embody and continue, albeit at another level, the same archaically determined dynamisms that account for the laws of individual behavior.

**"Sophistication."**    Thus far we have primarily viewed basic assumption groups as having negative effects in that they interfere with the goal of the work group. However, some basic assumptions, if put to a "sophisticated" use, can be supportive of the work group. For example, as we indicated above, the army platoon's assumption that it must fight to the death to preserve itself might well make it more effective in combat, just as the parishioner's dependency on his pastor might help to strengthen the effectiveness of their church. And the one group in social life that ideally has pairing, reproduction, and the maintenance of hope as its essential functions is the family. In these situations, where the goal of the work group requires some of the primitive affect released by the basic assumptions groups, it is the leader's skill in mobilizing and channeling these emotional forces that most often makes the difference between success and failure in the task. To be effective, he must actually embody some of the qualities that the basic assumption culture wants in its leader, though he can never possess them to the degree that the archaic mentality underlying basic assumptions demands (Rice, 1965, p. 72). In other words, the basic assumption dependency group yearning for an infallible leader might settle instead for one who is nurturant; the fight-flight culture longing for an unconquerable leader might accept one who is merely courageous, and the pairing culture, wishing for a leader who is "marvelous but still unborn," might manage to live in reality with one who is only "creative" (Rioch, 1970, pp. 64–65). Since the work-group aspect of any task group is always in force to some degree, along with whatever basic assumptions groups exist, these sophistications and compromises are often possible.

What is the role of the basic assumption cultures in the small study group, and can they too be exploited in a sophisticated way? On the surface they would seem entirely unadaptive and unsophisticated. Surely they are treated as such by the consultant. According to him, the group's inappropriate expectation that he will save it from its confusion only postpones the point at which it might begin to take responsibility for itself and make some sense of what is occurring. He is equally quick in challenging the group's magical conviction that fighting, or escaping into trivia, or pairing will somehow extricate it from the morass of frustration and despair into which it is sinking. Hence it would seem that the leader, rather than harnessing these basic assumptions, is instead exposing them as infantile attempts at delay and avoidance.

Yet there is a paradox here, for if no basic assumptions existed within the study group there would be no reason for the group's existence. The study group convenes in order to better understand the irrational forces of group life and the way in which it can most effectively do this is to observe these forces as they emerge within the life of its own here-and-now group. If the emergence of basic assumptions did not threaten the life of work groups, task groups in business and government would go about their projects with maximum efficiency, group dynamics would not be particularly complex, and there would be no need for the Tavistock model. In essence, then, the work group that the consultant repeatedly tries to summon into existence is an inherently unrealizable ideal; if it were ever to actually exist in a prolonged and stable form the study group would no longer have meaningful data to process. In this respect the basic assumption concept again parallels the concept of resistance in psychoanalysis, for resistance is claimed to "impede" the work of free association, just as the study group's basic assumptions are said to interfere with the work group's task. Yet both methods exploit and indeed depend on these "impediments," for at the point where the patient can free associate with complete success (again an unrealizable ideal) she has adequate access to her unconscious and is therefore "cured." Similarly, once the study group is able to do what the consultant asks it to do from the outset—to effectively work at the task of understanding its own data—it is at the end of the process rather than at its beginning. Thus it turns out that the study group, like the family, the army, and the church, is quite adept at making a sophisticated use of basic assumptions, albeit in a paradoxical and surprising fashion. Indeed, we would argue that it makes an unusually sophisticated use of the sophistication principle in that it not only manages to make constructive use of *all three* basic assumptions, but also denounces them at the same time that it exploits them.

**Valency.**   Individuals differ in their propensity for subscribing to any one of the three basic assumptions: Dependent people will be more responsive to a dependency culture, antagonistic ones to a fight-flight culture, and sexual ones to a pairing culture. Bion (1959) used the term *valency* to refer to a person's predisposition to respond in terms of a particular basic assumption. Knowledge of a person's valency can be useful in determining which groups she should join as a member. For example, groups with a preponderance of antagonistic people would be overly likely to go in the direction of a basic assumption fight-flight group, leaving too little room for aspirations toward dependency and pairing.

   A leader might well have reciprocal valencies in that he is readier to respond to certain basic assumptions than to others. In this sense, particular kinds of leaders can be matched with particular kinds of members (e.g., a leader with a high valency nurturance would best be placed with a group where several members already tend to have a high-valency dependence).

**Boundaries.**   According to Bion and to the Tavistock leaders who subsequently implemented his model, effective functioning of the work group depends on a clear-cut appreciation of boundaries and limits (Singer et al., 1979). For example, a work group is most likely to be actualized if its task is clearly delimited and if each member has a well-defined role to perform; members will then resist activities that detract from efficient task performance. Here, Bion's constructs for group-life are analogous to similar constructs employed by Freud to account for an individual's psychological functioning: the work group parallels Freud's "secondary processes" (Munroe, 1955, p. 35) which, in their acknowledgment of fixed categories of time and space and in their ability to differentiate fantasy from reality enable a person to function more effectively. Basic assumption groups, on the other hand, resemble Freud's "primary processes"; in their search for effortless fluidity they tend to deny the distinction between task performance and emotional gratification, and between the individual and the group.

In addition to boundaries involving tasks and roles, other boundaries are important to the work group, including those between one task group and another and those involving time and space. The press of basic assumptions is such that the work group may all too quickly: (1) lose sight of why the group is convening in the first place (*task* boundaries), (2) forget that it has at its disposal only a finite amount of time and space resources (*time and space* boundaries), (3) want the leader to step "out of role" to a point where he gives emotional nurturance (*role* boundaries) or is expected to engage in the same degree of self-disclosure as are the group members (*staff–member* boundaries; see Lawrence, 1979), (4) attempt to deny its members' individual identities through a cozy, warm, oceanic coming together wherein each member becomes the group and the group becomes one (*member-group* boundaries), (5) cast aside the selectivity required to determine how other groups can best be used, and communicated with, in the pursuit of the work task and thereby approach other groups in an overdependent and indiscriminate manner (*group* boundaries), (6) flee from contemplating the possibility and advisability of action into "acting out" (*intrapsychic systems* boundaries; see Durkin, 1982), (7) confide too much about how the issues discussed in the group relate to their personal lives outside the group, losing sight of the fact that the conference's goals are educational, rather than therapeutic (*education vs. therapy* boundaries; see Gould, 1985).

The fact that effective task organization, and life itself, will always involve *some* boundaries need not mean, however, that each and every boundary is sacred and need never be revised. The creative work group is willing to redefine and revise a boundary that, if rigidly adhered to, might easily impair the competent performance of its task (Lawrence, 1979).

## ROLE OF THE LEADER

Because the function of a consultant to a small study group is different from that of a consultant to a task group (such as the groups involved in an intergroup event at a Tavistock conference), we shall consider these two roles separately.

**1. The Small Study Group Consultant.**    The role of the study group consultant is best understood in the context of three theoretical assumptions or premises basic to the Tavistock model: (1) Any comments made by a participant reflect concerns that are shared to some degree by all other members (along with idiosyncratic meanings peculiar to her alone); it is to this shared, *group-as-a-whole* meaning that the consultant's interventions are to be addressed; (2) the single most difficult and emotionally charged issue facing any group involves coming to terms with its leader and the authority that he symbolizes; and (3) transference feelings and needs expressed in the group are to be for the most part interpreted rather than gratified.

Based on a Freudian model that views peer and sibling relationships as a reaction to, and as a way of handling, far more powerful and emotionally crucial parent–child axes, the Tavistock orientation views the leader as a recipient of extremely ambivalent and primitive feelings. He is loved as wise and grand, feared as powerful and potentially destructive, competed with as a rival, and hated as the source of all the bad feelings in the group. Member-to-member issues primarily reflect the vicissitudes of the member–leader relationship, and the group interaction is conceptualized as a dynamic oscillation between the expression of feelings about authority and an attempt to defend against them. The participants' irrational fantasies about authority emerge as especially inappropriate and paradoxical in view of the fact that, just as the consultant has been voluntarily hired by the group, he can as easily be fired by it. His degree of power over group members is minimal, for they are free to do as they like (including leaving the group) and he gives no direction as to what should be talked about. In actuality, his rather limited authority lies in his expertise in understanding and analyzing the group's underlying dynamics (and even here they are free to either ignore or disagree with him).

Although the consultant is in a formal sense a member of the group, he holds himself separate from it. For example, he rarely expresses his feelings directly, especially as they involve particular participants. However, he tries hard to be silently aware of these feelings so that he can use them to infer what the group is unconsciously experiencing at any one moment, just as the individual and group psychoanalyst tries to employ his countertransferential reactions in a similar fashion (see Chapters 3 and 5). His interventions often take the form of interpretations, with these interpretations being pitched to the group level and sometimes couched in highly metaphorical terms (e.g., the group might be likened to an animal wallowing in its own excrement); consequently, they are often, at least initially, experienced by participants as cryptic and deliberately obscure.

The leader is relatively formal in manner, careful not to step "out of role," and scrupulous in his attention to time boundaries. It is clearly not in role for him to reinforce particular behaviors, either through praise or disapproval. As Rice puts it, "learning is its own reward; lack of learning its own punishment" (1965, p. 67). His essential function is to interpret (the single exception being the large group event, where he may choose to be less interpretive; see above and Main, 1885); how the group opts to use these interpretations is its own decision. This is by design a somewhat aloof role and for this reason Tavistock consultants, even outside the confines of the study-group setting, are usually careful to limit their overt fraternization with conference members. Essentially the leader is a firm and remote figure; he respects the autonomy of each member, frequently reminding the membership that it bears the major responsibility for what it does and doesn't learn; he refuses to evaluate the amount of learning that has occurred, and he embodies as his primary value an interest in understanding the "truth" of the group's unconscious, however unflattering this truth may be.

Recently, however, there has been some questioning from within the Tavistock school itself as to the need for so much seriousness and asceticism in the consultant's stance. First, Rioch (1985) wondered if there is not room for a greater sense of play and playfulness in the leader's approach to the small study group, and for less concern on his part with the validity of each and every interpretation. Second, Gustafson and Cooper (1985), similarly viewing the traditional stance of Tavistock consultant as overly remote, claim that it is through his emotional availability and consistently accepting attitude that a collaborative and "safe" group atmosphere can best be promoted.

**2. The Task Group Consultant.**  The sole function of study groups is the understanding of their own internal processes. The groups involved in the intergroup event, on the other hand, resemble traditional task groups in that they have a tangible agenda directing their attention outward toward other groups in an effort to coordinate a specific program or project. In attempting to accomplish this goal, they are forced to make some concrete decisions.

For instance, let's say that in the intergroup event described above, plenipotentiaries meet to design a large-group session bringing together all the face-to-face groups involved in the exercise, and they then find themselves mired in the question of how their divergent ideas are to be resolved into a coherent consensus. Now that it is no longer so necessary for the consultant to foil, and to throw into relief, the basic assumption dependency group via a nonauthoritarian stance (as in the small study group), he is willing to share his knowledge concerning organizational life and organizational procedures. Should he notice that a group has difficulty maintaining its group boundaries (e.g., it is allowing members to walk out and visitors to walk in) he will share this observation. Other things that he might note and direct to the group's attention can include any one of the following: the group's failure to provide maximum role differentiation of its members (with the result that there is no formal designation of a leader); its ambivalence about delegating authority (with the result that plenipotentiary powers are granted, then subsequently revoked); its lack of precision in defining the responsibilities of its representatives; its inefficient use of time and space resources; the absence of any unanimity as to the definition of the task facing it; and so forth.

The task group consultant consistently emphasizes the point that the group's task is no longer that of studying its own dynamics. The oft-observed resistance of the task group to its new agenda, which is a function of its eagerness to remain with the old one of group-processing, stems from two factors, one cognitive and the other emotional. On the cognitive side, there is the fact that up until now trainees have been involved in study groups, either large or small; consequently, the processing of its own behavioral dynamics is the single activity with which the groups are most familiar. In addition, the task of the intergroup event tends to be ambiguous and hard to grasp, and almost any group prefers sticking with a known task than trying to grapple with an unfamiliar one.

On the emotional side, the intimacy and the opportunity for self-revelation inherent in the study group exert a strong pull on the membership. After an initial period of resisting the demand for analyzing their own group dynamics, participants are beginning to experience the emotional payoffs that come from a lowering of defenses and a sharing of feelings, and they strongly prefer to continue with this activity. The task group consultant is at pains to ensure that he does not abet this resistance to the task in any way; therefore, if asked by a task group to help it better understand its own processes (which is the purpose of the *small study* group, not the task group), he refuses to do so.

A leader also declines to consult with a task group when he suspects that it wants to use him in the service of basic assumption needs. Such a possibility is particularly likely in the intergroup event, where angry feelings toward the staff, and the chance to act them out, are maximized. For example, what if a membership group becomes enmeshed in a fight-flight culture that has defined the staff as its common enemy? The group might then believe that by requesting a consultant (which would remove him, however temporarily, from the staff group) the staff will thereby be weakened. If such a request is in fact made, the consultant will refuse to heed it. On the other hand, once a consultant determines that the task group *is* trying to fulfill its assigned task, he will remain with the group until he reaches a point where he has given it all the rational help he can.

Complex emotional dynamics and basic assumption cultures will of course continue to arise in task groups, as in study groups, and the consultant must be aware of them. However, he is at pains to remember that an awareness of these group dynamics is no longer the task group's primary goal, and he therefore discourages it from examining such processes *for their own sake.* Consequently, he highlights latent processes only when they have become serious impediments to the group's effective implementation of its agenda.

Whether functioning as a consultant to either the small study group or to the task group, the Tavistock leader is generally rather aloof, notwithstanding the caveats issued by Gustafson and Cooper (1985), as well as by Rioch (1979). The majority of the leader's remarks are addressed to the group-at-large and frequently take the form of an interpretation. Rarely is his participation extensive or prolonged. In the next chapter we explore the T-group, an alternate approach to group-dynamics training where the influence of psychoanalysis has been considerably less and where the leader's style of relating consequently becomes more personal and emotional.

# CHAPTER TEN
# T-GROUPS
# AND THE LABORATORY
# METHOD

Since their inception in 1946, T-groups (T standing for "training")—or as they have alternatively been called sensitivity training groups and human relations laboratories—have been among the most widely attended "educationally focused" group experiences. The T-group may be described as an intensive experience in interpersonal self-study and as a method of learning how to improve interpersonal skills and to understand the phenomena of group dynamics by participation in a group.

## HISTORICAL BACKGROUND

In a very real way, Kurt Lewin is the spiritual father of the T-group method, which is based on group dynamics and action research, an approach that encourages making decisions by using information from relevant and well-analyzed data. Lewin continually stressed the use of valid data as both the basis for action and a means for studying the impact of that action, thereby generating more useful data on which to base future decisions. These conceptual formulations provide the background and undergirding of T-group theory.

The T-group emerged almost by accident during a workshop designed to help community leaders implement the Fair Employment Practices Act. The workshop was held in Connecticut in 1946 under the direction of the Research Center for Group Dynamics at M.I.T., with Kenneth D. Benne and Leland P. Bradford, both with backgrounds in adult education, and Ronald Lippitt, a social psychologist, in charge of the training, with Lewin and Lippett directing research on the conference experience. The format of the conference, distinctly different from what subsequently emerged as T-group training, began with a series of discussions about how to comply with the act. Participants presented experiences that had caused them problems in dealing with its provisions, while other group members tried to develop solutions to the problems raised.

Interestingly enough, the format of the T-group developed not in the context of the conference but instead grew out of evening meetings originally planned for staff members to discuss observations that researchers made as the conference progressed. Several participants who had free time asked if they might observe and were permitted to attend. Thereupon, the unusual circumstance of the Group Dynamics staff discussing observations about conference members in their presence occurred. As might now be obvious, but then came as a surprise, group members questioned the accuracy of the research staff's observations. While these discussions became quite heated, they were also extremely fascinating to both staff and participants; before long all participants began attending the evening meetings, some of which lasted for several hours. Thus, in an unexpected way, the training staff of the Research Center for Group Dynamics hit upon the idea for an extremely powerful educational tool, the now widely known method of learning about group process and one's impact on others through observing one's own behavior in a group session and receiving feedback about that behavior from other group members. Until this time, Lewin's research on group process had not directly involved group participants in examining the data of their own experience. Heretofore, group members had engaged in their group task activities, and researchers had gathered data on how group process variables affected the work of the group. The T-group brought these activities together in a strikingly unique way; the very same participants produced data and then processed and examined those data in an effort to learn about group dynamics from their own group experience. An entirely new way of studying group process had been discovered.

Although much of the impetus for the development of T-groups came from the work of Kurt Lewin, and although he was present when the work was conceived, he died early in 1947 before the T-group format was fully developed. As a follow-up to the initial experience, participants of the conference met again in 1947 at Bethel, Maine, a town whose name subsequently became almost synonomous with laboratory training. Here the idea of the "basic skills training group" (a forerunner of the T-group) was developed, a group which had two broad purposes: (1) to serve as a medium for learning how to encourage planned change in social systems and (2) to provide an opportunity to understand and facilitate individual and group growth and development.

As the laboratory method evolved, the functions of the basic skills training group were divided and assigned to two separate groups: T-groups, which focused on learning about small group dynamics and interpersonal styles by studying the group's own behavior; and A-groups (or action groups) which focused on strategies for social action and social change in large social systems, employing the more traditional method of didactic presentations and group discussion of reading and lecture material. The attention to interpersonal dynamics that had become characteristic of T-groups had so powerful a lure for most participants that its style of analysis tended to spill over into the A-groups, resulting in the two becoming very similar in format. Despite a variety of efforts to resolve problems around the different aspects of learning in the laboratory method and efforts to retain the two distinct groups, the A-group was finally abandoned and a laboratory format that combined T-groups with other didactic experiences evolved.

The educational backgrounds of the participants who developed the T-group at Bethel played an important role in the way the approach became formulated. The original group that developed the laboratory method was comprised almost entirely of social psychologists, who, following Lewin's action research model, were basically concerned with using group dynamics to influence social change and with discovering more effective ways to function as agents of social change. When new staff members with backgrounds in clinical psychology and psychiatry were invited to participate, T-groups began to focus on processes of individual behavior change, in addition to their original orientation around group dynamics, group development, and decision-making processes. When the more clinically oriented participants began to have a major influence on the development of T-groups, learning about oneself, that is, learning how one behaves in groups and the impact one's behavior has on others, soon became a major group focus.

The interpersonal learning emphasized in T-groups grew out of the desire to make large-scale bureaucratic organizations more humane and more productive. While many T-groups continued to focus on effective and creative functioning within large-scale organizations, more and more they came to emphasize learning about interpersonal interaction for its own sake, divorced from its role in the improvement of organizational functioning. This, of course, was a major departure from the original action research and social change orientation of Lewin and his group, a change which also was no doubt influenced by the *zeitgeist*. When T-groups were developing—the late 1940s and the 1950s, psychoanalysis and other dynamic theories of personality had a major influence on developments within academic psychology, as well as a tremendous impact on the public at large. These factors undoubtedly contributed importantly to the manner in which the T-group's interpersonal focus became more clearly emphasized.

## DESIGN OF A RESIDENTIAL LABORATORY

The essential form of the laboratory experience may be best observed in the two-week residential laboratory that came to be the prototypical T-group experience. Detailed descriptions of such laboratory experiences are provided by Benne, Bradford, and Lippitt (1964) and Schein and Bennis (1965).

Because an important feature of the residential laboratory is the creation of a *cultural island,* it is typically located in a bucolic setting where participants are removed from their everyday work and familial props and demands. Being removed to such a cultural island may have a variety of effects on participants, but two characteristics are considered to be of especial importance: (1) removal of participants from a setting with built-in expectations and props for behavior enables them to be more open to new input and experience and (2) the unusual character of the setting serves to heighten anxiety and uncertainty about the laboratory experience. While didactic sessions dealing with small-group theories, large general meetings, and social activities are part of the residential laboratory, the T-group sessions are considered to be its major learning vehicle.

Removing participants from everyday life experience enhances the residential laboratory's capacity to encourage learning a different style of approach to problems. Perhaps this can be most vividly imagined if one thinks of the typical participant in the T-group experience as a person from middle management in a large organization whose typical personal style emphasizes activity and productivity. Because the T-group presents an unstructured situation with no clear-cut expectations, with no agenda or guidelines as to appropriate behavior or expectations of others, it presents an antithesis of the prototypical participant's everyday life experience. Although the T-group has a designated leader, it is someone who functions not as a chairperson or an authority figure, but rather as a facilitator or helper in the learning process. In fact, one of the roles of the leader is to create a vacuum which participants must fill with their own behavior, which in turn is analyzed by the members of the group and serves as a major source of the learning experience. The behavior that emerges and the understanding of that behavior in its multifaceted forms becomes the basic content of the learning, but the fact that members' own behavior is the grist for the learning mill is not evident to participants as they embark on their group experience. Although the typical laboratory experience starts out with an overview and explanation of what the T-group experience will be like, it is presented at a fairly high level of abstraction; furthermore, participants are often unable to incorporate the knowledge presented in a way that will not be meaningful to them until they experience the T-group itself.

A typical T-group might begin with a "trainer" stating that she imagines that group members have come to learn about how people behave in groups by learning from their own experience of becoming group members. The leader offers neither agenda nor any suggestions as to how to proceed, thereby creating a vacuum in which group members begin to act in their characteristic ways. Some may try to provide structure by suggesting that an agenda be created or that a chairperson be elected; others may complain about the leader's failure to provide guidance; still others may comment about the anxiety that the lack of structure creates in them. Because these comments are likely to be interspersed with periods of silence, group members often experience a good deal of tension as they attempt to cope with the ambiguity of the situation. Although many suggestions may be offered by group members as to how to proceed, typically none is followed up, as the group looks to the trainer for guidelines, while she in turn reflects back the group's desire for structure.

Finally, a member may suggest some easily agreed upon action, such as all the members' introducing themselves, and the group, seizing on it, agrees to proceed in this manner. The first session typically ends with members feeling confused and bewildered about what happened during the session and about how to proceed. The following several sessions provide further evidence of group members' efforts to cope with the frustrations of ambiguity and lack of structure. Abortive attempts at leadership develop; the group may become divided into two camps—those who very much want leadership and structure and those who are opposed to organizing until the group decides what it wants to do. When the trainer suggests that members explore their feelings of frustration at their inability to get the group going, the comment is typically ignored. Often there are a variety of other abortive attempts to organize, set up committees, elect chairpersons; the sense of frustration continues to grow. Eventually the group responds to the trainer's suggesting that it consider how members contribute to the lack of group progress.

This juncture marks a shift to examining member behavior and members' interpersonal styles. Attention might first be directed to a member who has been particularly active in an earlier effort to elect a chairperson. For example, Alex, a hard-driving production manager who has played a similar role in the group begins to get feedback about the bossy and authoritarian way in which he insists his procedure is correct. His inability to consider alternatives once he has formed an opinion and his attacks on those who stand in the way of his drive for leadership are also pointed out. He initially acts defensively, unwilling to consider the comments, but several sincerely concerned members convince him that the comments are meant to help him in his exploration and are not the cruel attack that Alex seems to believe them to be. With this supportive attention, he is able to look at his overconcern with performance, with getting the job done properly, at his distrust of others' capabilities, and his consequent inability to share responsibility. In a similar fashion, characteristics of other members are explored, sometimes at the member's own initiation, at other times with assistance, prodding, or feedback from other members or the trainer. Don, another member, who had vacillated about supporting a number of alternative ways to proceed earlier, spontaneously begins commenting on his inability to take responsibility and his constant hedging and avoiding, an observation that was touched off by his awareness of how starkly his own style contrasts with Alex's. Others chime in with concerns about being either too aggressive or too passive, too involved or too cool, too emotional or too stolid. Finally, Ned, a member who has been quite inactive, is turned on by the group for not wanting to reveal his feelings, for not being willing to let other people know him.

The mutual support members have given each other during the period of feedback may lead to a great deal of expression of positive feelings among members; for example, Don may be lavishly praised for his willingness to take a good hard look at himself. Group cohesiveness is now at its height. The concern of the group often then turns to comparing individual members in terms of their degree of involvement, and efforts are made to "bring in" those who seem insufficiently involved. Ned again becomes the focus of attention as members make an effort to make him feel more a part of the group. As the session draws to a close, attention is turned to evaluating and examining what members have gained from the group, both in terms of greater awareness of the nature of their impact on others and of knowledge about how group process works.

The foregoing description illustrates the fact that learning in T-groups is different from the typical learning mode that most participants experience in their everyday vocational and personal lives. Learning in the T-group involves observation and examination of one's own behavior and of the interaction among members in the group. It requires a radically different approach from the usual interpersonal style of the middle management participant, which often is the antithesis of learning that emerges from the ferment of the immediacy of experience. In other words, didactic instruction alone about the same content could not result in acquisition of knowledge about individual and group phenomena in usable form. Nonetheless, laboratory training does include theory sessions that are kept separate from experiences in the T-group; each is expected to have a mutually useful and productive effect on the total learning of the individual, but the experiential component provided by the T-group experience is seen as crucial for learning in an emotionally meaningful way.

Because the residential laboratory model considers informal contacts among participants as important to the learning process, members typically share rooms, take their meals together in groups, have arranged cocktail hours, and a considerable amount of free time available for "bull sessions." In addition, informal dress is encouraged and usual status and role props, such as formal styles of address and the use of organizational or educational titles, are discouraged. To provide a break in the experience, members at a two-week residential laboratory will typically have the weekend between the two weeks free either to return home or spend some time away from the residential setting in a nearby city.

Each of the two weeks of the residential laboratory has a special role in the experience. The main task of the participants (or as they are sometimes called, delegates) in the first week is to become immersed in the laboratory culture, with its demand for a whole new style of learning how to observe oneself and others. After this immersion has occurred, the group turns to applying this new style to real experiences. To facilitate this process, didactic sessions in the second week stress applying learning to actual life circumstances facing the participants, although the T-group experience continues to emphasize learning in the "here and now." While the laboratory method involves a number of different kinds of experiences—T-groups, lectures, and intergroup activities, the major focus of the experience is on the T-group itself, whose meetings vary from one to three two-hour sessions per day, concentrated most heavily at the start of the laboratory experience. In a typical laboratory, there is a total of about fifty participants, divided into four T-groups of from ten to fifteen members each.

In addition to T-groups, there are also theory sessions that provide didactic information about the underlying learning principles of T-groups and focused exercises that frequently involve intergroup competition. Theory sessions are designed to complement the experiential part of the learning that occurs in the T-group by offering didactic material on group process, communication, and observation of behavior. Offered this kind of conceptual framework, the participant is helped in understanding ongoing T-group experiences and in maximizing learning opportunities. Tasks used in intergroup competition require cooperation among members within each T-group (e.g., producing as many greeting card verses as possible or developing a system for democratizing autocratic organizational structure). Observations on how well the group deals with the task may then be analyzed in subsequent T-groups sessions.

Most experiences of personal change are difficult to describe; T-group experiences are no exception, but a great deal has been written by and about participants and their reactions. Participants frequently say that they feel different, that they have learned a great deal, but find it difficult to classify precisely what they learned or in what ways they have changed. Many participants in laboratory experiences come away with very positive feelings, with feelings that they have changed, and that important learning has taken place. Some have suggested that the experience of intimacy and mutuality in the group is a very important component of their positive reaction. Feelings of freedom and openness to other people and to new experiences seem to characterize the response of many participants.

Klaw (1961) writes graphically about the laboratory experience from the viewpoint of an observer not trained in group leadership. He recounts reactions of participants that range from initial anxiety created by the ambiguity of the group, to efforts at dealing with issues of openness and trust, to how one learns about interpersonal impact. Yet he remains skeptical about whether people are really changed by the experience.

Because there are many similarities between T-groups and Tavistock conferences (Chapter 9)—setting, length, purpose of learning about group dynamics—some comments about differences between the two approaches might be useful here. The points of divergence involve the degree to which the leader: (1) focuses on the idiosyncratic behavior of each member, as well as on the overall group process, (2) is interested in exploring member-to-member as well as member-to-leader relationships, and (3) is willing to make interpretations about the meaning of the group's behavior. The T-group trainer is more willing to respond to each of these three variables; these differences are directly attributable to the theoretical underpinnings of each model.

The T-group model is not nearly as concerned with the group's unconscious processes as is the Tavistock model. Instead it places its main emphasis on the rational aspects of group life and on certain characteristics that are conducive to ideal functioning in the group—that is, openess and trust, authority based on competence, maximum task involvement, and genuinely democratic values. The egalitarian emphasis is such that participants are encouraged to gradually accept the leader as another member of the group and one another as potential sources of competence and expertise. While the trainer is aware that the typical member has irrational expectations of her, she demonstrates to participants by her own behavior that they are in fact only fantasies. In psychodynamic terms the trainer, rather than examining the group's "transference-resistance," attempts to demonstrate by her behavior its inappropriateness.

In the Tavistock model, directly descended from psychoanalysis, the leader emphasizes continually interpreting for the group the most unconscious and regressive fantasies that it has about itself in relationship to her; she believes that any gratification of these fantasies will only cause them to be held onto more vigorously. As a result the Tavistock leader is aloof from the group, less likely to step "out of role," and less willing to be viewed as another member of the group. The leader's interventions are always directed toward the group rather than to individual members, are focused on achieving insight, and make little attempt to actively encourage behaviors—like collaboration, and exchange of feedback—that might be useful in the work group to which the member will return. The participant is expected to internalize whatever understanding he has gained of unconscious group processes and to use it however he deems fit once back on the job. This is a lonelier, more isolating conception of what a group can give an individual than one finds in the T-group, where group participation is seen in more open, gregarious, and optimistic terms.

## KEY CONCEPTS: PHILOSOPHICAL
## AND THEORETICAL

**Value Bases.** In studying the evolution of the T-group, it becomes clear that although the method had its roots in social science theory, its development has been based more on practice and experience factors than on systematically developed theory. The idea for the T-group came directly from the action research in group dynamics emphases of Kurt Lewin and was based on the group's analysis of data that it produced itself. Theoretical concern about the relationship of personal change to interpersonal or group influence, and to variables such as cohesiveness and equilibrium, also grew out of Lewinian theory. However, by the time the format of the T-group had become set in the early 1950s, it had already become one that was based on practice and little invested in using the group experience for theory development and data collection about interpersonal and group processes. Therefore, despite initial hopes, no fully articulated theoretical structure was produced to undergird T-group technology. Among T-group practitioners there has been considerable interest in studying aspects of group process—ranging from anecdotal and observational to quite rigorously controlled—but no systematic or inclusive theory of group processes has emerged from this work.

There is, however, fairly general agreement (e.g., Schein & Bennis, 1965; Bradford, Gibb, & Benne 1964; Schein, 1985) on the kinds of value bases that formed the ideological underpinnings of the T-group at its inception and of the important values that T-groups hope to inculcate. A focus on organizational change through the impact of individual efforts aimed at modifying hierarchical structure, it will be recalled, was a prominent concern of Lewin and his group.

*Science and the Scientific Method.* The creators of the T-group sought to introduce behavioral science concepts, particularly group dynamic ones, into the day-to-day thinking, planning, and frames of reference of responsible people in organizations. The underlying hope was that through greater knowledge of behavioral science a more rational approach to organizational development and a greater openness to inquiry might be introduced into the system. Being open to experience, allowing oneself to utilize all relevant information in making decisions, being aware of how one's values can influence the way in which one views a situation are all aspects of this approach.

*Democratic Orientation.* Because many of the participants in T-groups came from organizational structures that were at best hierarchically structured and, at worst, extremely authoritarian, an emphasis on practicing more democratic values was deliberately stressed. Early research by Lewin and his colleagues supporting the superiority of democratic decision making in groups bolstered this belief (e.g., Lewin, Lippitt, & White, 1939). While it was clear that bureaucratic structures were unlikely to change to the point that all members of the organization could participate in all decisions affecting them, nonetheless the belief was held that a greater degree of cooperation, and the minimization of the kinds of covert dissatisfaction that hamper productivity, would be achieved through an increase in each member's level of participation. If the T-group experience could heighten awareness about how cooperation and collaboration facilitates group functioning and, in the larger sense, total organizational functioning, and if that learning were carried back to the work situation, it would have a positive impact on larger organizational structures when group members returned to them.

*Genuine Concern for Others.* The desire to introduce a greater sense of "humanness" into large impersonal organizations was central to T-group theory; the introduction of this humanness constituted a main goal for the originators of T-groups. Caring for others, being willing to help them, being concerned with other's feelings, rather than hindering productivity in organizations, all facilitate it, while at the same time enriching the lives of its members. The T-group became an arena for learning how people profit from genuine caring human interaction.

**Goals.**   Attempts to articulate T-group goals range from those at a very general level of analysis to highly specific and articulated outlines with a number of subgoals suggested. For some representative discussions see Benne, Bradford, and Lippitt (1964), Schein (1985), National Training Laboratories (1962), and Golembiewski and Blumberg (1977). Although there are minor variations in emphasis among T-group theorists, the central core of characteristics will be described and discussed.

*Learning How to Learn.* The most basic and almost universally mentioned goal is the central concept of *learning how to learn.* In the course of our educational experience, most of us are taught to look to experts for accepted knowledge and to view teachers as authorities and pupils as absorbers of information. While in the T-group, a participant has the opportunity to learn that he has the wherewithal to generate new and useful knowledge and information himself. One comes to "learn how to learn" by using one's powers of observation, by stretching one's imagination, by listening to what others are saying, by responding to others and observing their reactions to those responses, and finally by examining the impact of one's own behavior on other people. In our example of a typical T-group, Alex, during the early sessions, constantly looked for structure, demanded that trainers provide it for him, and finally offered his own suggestions for structure—that is, that the group make an agenda and follow it. After he received feedback from others and had to deal with the single-mindedness of his preoccupation, he became much more attuned to his own inner experience and to others' reactions. In this way participants have the opportunity to develop their acuity in observation and to increase their ability to observe both their own and others' behavior.

*Self-Knowledge.* Increased self-knowledge, self-awareness, or insight can be considered as a special subcategory of learning how to learn (i.e., learning how to learn about oneself—one's own behavior and one's own reactions). The T-group provides an opportunity for participants to come to know themselves better by learning in an atmosphere of openness about how others react to them, and by having the opportunity to observe themselves more carefully than they typically do. Such self-observation would include attending to one's own feelings and responses to other people, as well as observing one's own behavior more carefully. Don, in our example, was able to experience his passivity because of its sharp contrast with Alex's style. In this way, he began to learn something about how his characteristic stance had an effect on him and had an impact on others.

*Effective Participation in Group Functioning.* In order to help people become more effective in dealing with others in group settings, the T-group provides an opportunity for emotional give-and-take in a setting where one gets constant feedback about how he is perceived. This experience in turn helps to make one more observant both in the T-group itself as well as in subsequent group interactions. As members become more aware of the range of needs of people in the group and the variety of techniques that they have for dealing with them, as well as more aware of and responsive to their own needs and desires in the group context, they learn to monitor and to modulate their own behavior in group settings in more effective ways.

*Leadership Techniques.* Experience in the T-group is also designed to help members become more responsive to the needs of others—to the needs of persons both subordinate and superordinate to them in a hierarchical structure. This kind of learning is designed to help members become better leaders in any organizational or managerial functions they perform. Developing a leadership style that is nonauthoritarian, responsive, caring, and attentive to the wants and desires of others helps create a working atmosphere wherein the needs and feelings of all are taken into account. Such an attitude has a softening effect on the dominant depersonalizing task orientation that often exists in organizational structures and in the long run may increase both productivity and the quality of performance or output.

*Impact on Organization.* Although less directly related to the actual activities of the T-group, one of the important motivations for development of the method was the desire to influence positively how people function in organizations. Therefore, one of the goals of T-group, particularly when a number of individuals from the same organization are involved, is to have an impact on the quality of human relationships within that organization. When sufficient numbers of organization members become more self-aware, more concerned about the needs of others, and more effective as group members and group leaders, they cannot help but eventually have a positive influence on the total function and structure of any system. This kind of organizational impact clearly emerges from the T-group value bases of democratic orientation and concern for others.

## KEY CONCEPTS: OPERATIONAL

In our attempt to describe the important events, activities, and processes that occur in a typical T-group we have selected a limited number of operational concepts to discuss from an extremely broad array of dimensions described by writers in the field. We have chosen those emphases that we judge to be most central and germane, and about which there was most consensus, although not all writers have referred to them in the same terms as ours.

**Here-and-Now Focus.**    Learning in the T-group is extremely dependent upon observing and responding to what is, in fact, occurring in the group itself. Underlying the here-and-now focus is the assumption that learning about interpersonal style can most effectively occur when observing immediate experience and reacting to its emotional impact. Because attending to feelings as they are felt and understanding what evokes those feelings is central, long digressions into problems that members face on their jobs, into historical events in their personal lives, or into attempts to explain dynamics of present behavior in terms of past relationships are strongly discouraged. One learns from participating in the group process, from observing that process, and from reflecting on it. The here-and-now focus of the T-group experience is an essential ingredient in learning about group dynamics.

**Unfreezing.**    *Unfreezing* denotes freeing people from their standard and typical ways of behaving and viewing themselves and others in interpersonal situations. It is a complex process that occurs under conditions of abrupt and dramatic change. The cultural island of the residential laboratory both contributes to the unfreezing process and then, once it occurs, exploits it as a vehicle for learning. Because the T-group has a lack of structure and the absence of any formal agenda, it provides an opportunity, indeed a demand, to take a fresh look at one's typical style of functioning. Ambiguity about structure, the absence of role and status props, uncertainty about expected, desired, or appropriate behavior in the group, all contribute to the unfreezing of a group member.

**Group Support and Atmosphere of Trust.** Although the process of unfreezing helps to put members in a position to view things in a new way, the motivation, willingness, and feeling of security sufficient to do so is primarily a function of the developing group process. Concern of members for each other, toleration of failure or mistakes in others, the leader's attempt to create an atmosphere of psychological safety, and the encouragement of risk taking—all are important elements in fostering trust among members. Undergirding all of these is the support of each member for the other because they all find themselves in common circumstances foreign to their previous experience, which renders them particularly needful of each other's care and concern.

**Disclosure.** A basic assumption is that, to a greater or lesser extent, all members are motivated to learn in the T-group setting. Yet, at the same time there exists a counter-motivation created by anxiety resulting from ambiguity and uncertainty, from fear of emotional involvement, and from concern about exposing one's weaknesses. Because the T-group fosters the norm of self-disclosure—of revealing one's personal reactions and feelings—the participant is emboldened to overcome his anxiety and to allow his motivation to learn to become prepotent. Because there is a danger that this expectation will create great pressure on members to disclose more than they can comfortably reveal, the trainer needs to be alert in guarding against such occurrences. While members can only learn from each other by openly revealing their reactions, there must necessarily be some limit to *how much* is revealed, since the T-group is a time-limited nontherapeutic group. Therefore, central to effective learning in the T-group is the development of realistic norms concerning the appropriate degree of self-disclosure.

**Feedback.** Feedback—the communication of a member to other members and *their* response to *him*—is the *sine qua non* of learning in a T-group. An honest, straightforward, helpful sharing of reactions to one another provides basic, but rarely available (in most everyday life situations) information about how one is affecting others. In the example of the T-group described above, members' telling Alex about their reactions to his authoritarian manner and *their convincing him of their genuine concern for him at the same time* illustrates a highly desirable feedback style. When feedback is given in an atmosphere of interested concern, of trust, and of shared disclosure, an optimal condition to use it for personal growth and change clearly obtains. Moreover, feedback given in a hostile manner, in a way that the recipient cannot accept, or in a way that distorts the behavior of the individual in terms of the respondent's own perceptions, creates conditions that undermine the effective use of this powerful tool. Therefore, an important task of the trainer is to help the group create norms that discourage destructive feedback.

**Developing Group Norms.** Most of the typical norms that develop in T-groups grow out of the value bases and out of other group process emphases (e.g., the here-and-now orientation described on page 194). Yet it is possible for the group to develop idiosyncratic norms that may be detrimental to effective group functioning. For example, the usual norm of openness and concern for others' feelings may at times become distorted to a norm of "Don't give any negative feedback." The leader should be alert for norms enabling members to collude in avoidance and should question the group about any counter-productive norms (whether implicit or explicit), such as systematic turn-taking, excessive politeness, or overprotection of a member.

## ROLE OF THE LEADER

The trainer in the T-group has to bring a special set of role characteristics to the experience, because she is not in the usual sense a teacher, a group therapist, a chairperson of the proceedings, or a group leader. Rather, the trainer is viewed as the facilitator or helper in the learning experience. Because the leader provides few procedural suggestions, a kind of vacuum of structure and expectation is created, a vacuum that is inevitably filled by members' behavior in deciding how the group should function. That behavior, and its analysis, becomes the basic content of the group experience.

A central aspect of the trainer's role is creating an atmosphere for effective learning, a task that involves a complex set of activities and characteristics. Setting the scene by making clear that she will not serve as an authority and by helping the group to develop goals of its own is important. Just as central is the continual modeling of behavior as a good group member—openness, responsiveness to others' needs, eagerness to understand and explore ongoing group phenomena, and requesting and offering constructive feedback. Attending to and anticipating changes in group process and keeping the group focused on that process in the present instead of becoming overly involved with personal concerns are also important trainer skills.

Let us examine several special categories of leader characteristics that have been shown to be important in the T-group process.

**Facilitation of Learning.** The most frequently mentioned aspect of the trainer's role lies in providing members with the opportunity to behave in a group setting and to observe their own behavior. The fact that the leader does not offer structure, respond to member demands to assume authoritative control, or offer specific action guidelines forces members to act in characteristic ways, which, in turn, assist the trainer in her role as facilitator.

**Protection.** Helping to create a climate of trust in the group is another important aspect of the leader's role. At times she may have to intervene when feedback from one member to another becomes so hostile, ill-timed, or inaccurate as to put the recipient of the feedback in the position of great anxiety or distress. For example, if in one of the early group sessions a very shy member begins to talk haltingly about how anxious the uncertainty of the situation makes him feel and is quickly attacked by a boisterous member for being perfectly absurd, the trainer might first turn to the rest of the group to elicit similar feelings of anxiety; if she fails to do so, she might then tell the shy member that she can readily understand why he feels that way.

**Balancing the Role of Helper, Member, and Expert.** The trainer's role includes elements of a number of subroles, among which the helper or facilitator role is perhaps the most important. In addition, the trainer functions as a member; particularly when a group develops a more truly egalitarian atmosphere, a greater degree of sharing with other members on an equal basis becomes possible. In order for participants to observe those attributes that constitute good member behavior, the trainer should serve as a model of openness, concern for others' feelings, and response to behaviors in the here-and-now. At the same time, the trainer must function as an expert; she is more knowledgeable about group process and group dynamics than is the typical member, a fact that is better acknowledged than denied. Furthermore, certain aspects of the trainer's role clearly involve specific expertise—for example, presenting role-playing techniques or introducing training exercises, such as competition among T-groups in producing greeting card verses. Of major importance is the fact that flexibility, balance, and the ability to shift from one role to another—from helper, to member, to expert—is necessary for an effective training repertoire.

**Group Process Orientation.** In order to be in the position to make interventions that are useful to the here-and-now learning of the group and to develop hypotheses about the nature of group movement, the trainer must carefully observe interaction among group members. In our example, once Alex had accepted the fact that his overbearing attitude created discomfort in others, the trainer might have taken the opportunity to help group members explore their reactions to such demands from one individual, while at the same time anticipating that for some members the structuring aspect of that stance remained a very positive lure. Being oriented toward the immediate process in the group also helps the trainer to avoid several pitfalls of the training experience: becoming too directive, or too clinically oriented, or too invested in the there-and-then rather than the here-and-now. The group process orientation, then, is particularly facilitative of the kind of learning that the T-group is designed to provide—that is, learning about group interaction and one's impact on others in a group. Here again, trainer behavior in pointing to group process issues serves as a model for the development of similar orientation among members.

**Controlled Interventions.**  Whether the group is better served by trying to find its own way or by trainer intervention is a matter that requires constant attention during the course of the group. At issue is the question of balance, of the trainer's not taking on too much responsibility for intervention facilitative of group functioning. For example, if a group member suggests electing a chairperson and making an agenda, the experienced trainer knows that the suggestion will come to naught, but she also knows not to cut off discussion of the issue lest the group feels that she is impeding its progress in an autocratic way. The trainer must let the group consider the issue until enough members are sufficiently disenchanted with the idea to begin to examine how efforts at structuring result from their fleeing from ambiguity.

## VARIED USES OF T-GROUP

Almost from its inception, the T-group expanded from its original group-dynamic focus into a concern with personal growth and development, which was clearly reflected in changing terminology, such that by the mid-1950s the term *sensitivity training* became increasingly common. That general trend continued despite the tremendous variation that existed from group to group, leader to leader, and situation to situation. Indeed, some consider that by the 1970s T-group trainers had broken into two camps—one focused on organizations which eventually created the field of organizational development (see page 199), while the other more pointedly stressed growth and change of individuals.

Another way to examine the range of uses of the laboratory method is to review situations where T-groups have been utilized. The two groups that have most frequently made use of the laboratory method are business organizations on which much of the initial work was focused (Blake & Mouton, 1985) and groups in the helping professions trying to learn more about ways to function effectively in their work (e.g., psychologists, social workers, psychiatrists, school counselors, and nurses). Later still, use of T-groups in community action organizations, cross-cultural groups, and interracial groups became more common. An additional emphasis has been on training graduate students from the behavioral sciences in small group dynamics and interpersonal skills.

During the 1970s T-groups with a personal development emphasis began to draw participants from the population at large. In these groups there often was considerable overlap in method and technique with other models—for example, nonverbal techniques identified with encounter groups (see Chapter 11). National Training Laboratories began to sponsor groups or workshops with specific themes that tended to create overlap with theme-centered groups (see Chapter 12) and included topics such as: ( *1* ) *Developing Individual Potential—A Personal Growth-Oriented Experience to Promote Authentic, Honest, Trusting*

*Relationships in the Context of the Small Group Experience; (2) Couples' Interaction—An Effort to Learn New Creative Ways of Sharing Life Together; (3) Being a Woman—An Opportunity to Develop a Personal Sense of Identity Outside of the Expectations of Husband, Children, and Parents; (4) Family Relationships—Participation of the Whole Family in Learning Better Ways to Express Needs, Anger, and Affection; (5) Between the Generations—An Opportunity for Younger and Older People to Get Together and Examine the Generation Gap.* Because many of these groups introduced a variety of nonverbal exercises and techniques and employed leadership styles of great variation, it might not be quite accurate to refer to them as T-groups. In fact, both their style and format make them relatively indistinguishable from the encounter groups of that same period.

What was characteristic of the emphases described above was both a focus on individual growth and development and freedom in human interaction, as well as on specificity of content and targeting of audience for those workshops. Whereas earlier the themes of laboratories were much less specific in focus and context, and generally were concerned with functioning in occupational roles, the emphasis that developed in the seventies and to some extent continues in workshops currently is on learning to broaden and enrich certain very universal and non–work-related roles—husband and wife, youngster, woman, member of the family, older person. At the same time, the second thrust in the development of T-groups was in the direction of working entirely within a single organization to develop better team performance. It is interesting to follow the history of a movement whose initial concern was with helping people to personalize roles, especially work roles in presumably authoritarian structures, and then observe a move to develop workshops concerned with roles that have historically been presumed to be the most highly personal. Considering the proliferation of such workshops during the 1970s one may assume that many people did not find the degree of satisfaction in openness to intimacy in their daily lives that they wished.

In more recent years, emphasis in T-groups has moved again in this two-channeled direction with the one concerned with organizational development and the other with personal development, with the latter once again focusing on work-related roles, such as the group for students of behavioral science described above.

## ORGANIZATIONAL DEVELOPMENT

Initially, T-groups emphasized working with people from business organizations, especially middle management. Groups were most often made up of people functioning in comparable roles, but in different organizations; alternatively several members of an organization at different levels in the hierarchy might attend the same T-group at a site away from their usual place of employment. Subsequently T-groups were brought into an organization and involved participation by a group of people who all knew each other or at least had worked together—usually at different levels in the hierarchy—in the same organization. The ways in which such groups blurred lines of authority raised concerns about subsequent working relationships being compromised because co-workers, particularly those of lower status, might be fearful of expressing themselves freely lest they be subject to future sanctions. This concern along with the recognition that the T-group alone might not be sufficient for developing greater productivity in a corporation led to the broadening of the concept into organizational development (Patten, 1981; Bennis, Benne, & Chin, 1985).

Organizational development focuses on working with managerial staff within existing organizations and makes use of a variety of techniques, including T-groups, to increase cooperative human effort to meet individual as well as organizational objectives. It includes a variety of activities designed to improve managerial styles, enhance employee commitment and morale, develop new ideas for problem solving, and create meaningful work objectives. In this way the T-groups of an earlier era which took place in a cultural island away from the workplace have given way to a more comprehensive approach to human relations within organizations.

With the advancement of organizational development, the T-group phenomenon has become a part of a larger process with a practical objective of building an efficient managerial organization. Organizational development has also been extended to other settings for a variety of purposes. For example, in schools (Derr, 1974) such interventions have been used to facilitate desegregation and in hospitals (Margulies & Adams, 1982) to promote inter-staff cooperation and to improve patient care.

While it is clear that organizational development is not a group intervention or training modality per se and goes beyond the scope of the kind of group interventions on which we have focused, it is also clear that it is an outgrowth and extension of a model that originally grew out of the group-dynamic focus from which T-groups emerged. In this sense it represents a logical development of the same desire to enhance human functioning in large organizations that underlay the original impetus for the T-group's creation.

# CHAPTER ELEVEN
# THE ENCOUNTER GROUP

As we indicated in Chapter 1, the encounter group is best viewed as an outgrowth and compendium of all the group models that preceded it. It flourished during the 1960s and early 1970s, occupying a keystone position in the human potential movement and receiving vast amounts of media publicity. The encounter group movement probably did more to make the public aware of the existence of groups for helping people, even though such groups had already been in existence for roughly thirty-five years, than any other group model before or since. Despite this fame and popularity, however, the overall encounter movement has become moribund, and by the 1980s Esalen Institute, which had done more than any other organization to make encounter famous, no longer included encounter group within its weekly curriculum of seminars and workshops (Goleman, 1984).

The encounter group, however, continues to exist in various forms. Religious organizations in particular have utilized encounter groups, certainly in spirit, if not in actual name or label. For example, congregations are frequently offered a variety of retreats (for couples, teenagers, families, or single individuals) that, in their combination of a weekend away from one's normal environment and their use of several intensive small-group meetings, strongly resemble the kind of short-term group experience that Esalen provided in the heyday of encounter (Yalom, 1985). (In a seemingly similar vein, in the

1970s both Jewish and Christian groups began to sponsor a widely known and widely employed *marriage encounter* program; however, the similarity here lies more in the label than in the actual structure of the experience, for the primary emphasis is on a husband and wife encountering each other, alone and apart from other couples, with all the couples convening into a single group only much later in the experience; see Larsen, 1986).

The encounter group model has also influenced the development of *large group awareness programs* (Lifespring and est are two examples), which offer a time-limited, emotionally intense experience that lasts from two to three days and consists of formal presentations, frequently of an inspirational nature, plus smaller encounter groups into which the entire assemblage is divided. Yalom, a frequent observer of the group psychotherapy scene, estimates that as of the mid-1980s over 650,000 people had attended either the Lifespring or basic est workshops. "So, although the movement is over and an encounter group *qua* encounter group is hard to find, more people than ever before are having an encounter group experience" (Yalom, 1985, p. 488). He also points out that since many group therapists have not had either the inclination or the opportunity to be patients in a long-term therapy group, it is probably via membership in an encounter group that they have any direct small-group experience whatever.

The encounter group, at least in the *open encounter* version developed by Schutz at Esalen, is also of considerable *historical* importance, because of (1) its use of innovative (especially nonverbal) techiques, some of which were adopted by psychoanalytically oriented group therapists (see Mintz, 1971, 1986), (2) its publicizing of earlier group methods, like gestalt and psychodrama, that had not yet become widely known, (3) its influential role in the formation and development of self-help groups (see Chapter 13) and medically oriented groups, whether short- or long-term (see Chapter 14), (4) its raising of the time-intensity issue with more focus and clarity than any other model before or since (i.e., the possible therapeutic value of having a group meet almost constantly over a period of a day or more), and (5) its important influence in helping to reduce the traditional distinction between a growth and development group on the one hand and a psychotherapy group on the other. Because Schutz's open encounter was responsible for all the influences and developments just reviewed, and because it is reasonably representative of other forms of group encounter, the comments and examples to appear below, with the exception of our "Historical Background" section, will apply to the open encounter group.

## THE OPEN ENCOUNTER GROUP

The open encounter group originally provided an intensive group experience designed to put the *normally* alienated individual into closer contact—or "encounter"—with herself, with others, and with the world of nature and pure sensation. Consequently, members of an Esalen encounter group, along with whatever interpersonal exchanges that their group membership provided, took part in various sensory awareness exercises in which they were encouraged to touch, feel, taste, and look (not only at one another, but at their lush physical environment, in its every detail). In this respect, the encounter group had a clearly educational and programmatic thrust: Its leaders wished to "turn on" the participant to capacities within herself for feeling and for energy that she had not suspected were there and to turn her on to the world at large. Hence the title of Schutz's first book about encounter was *Joy* (1967), referring to the joy of simply being and feeling. If the participant wished, in addition, to use the experience as a means of exploring unfinished business from childhood, this was a legitimate choice and her group leader had a variety of techniques, frequently nonverbal, with which to facilitate this process.

The focus of the open encounter movement went beyond the individual, however. In its heyday it constituted a social movement (Back, 1972). In its original form this model, more than any other we have presented, expressed a distinct ideology comprising a rejection of a rational-bureaucratic society and an embracing of new values for guiding one's day-to-day existence outside, as well as inside, the group. This ideology included an emphasis on spontaneity, on absolute honesty, and on body-awareness (as opposed to cerebration), with Schutz insisting that it is the absence of these values that leads to alienation from one's feelings, from one's body, and from one another, an alienation so widespread in our society that there is no one who does not suffer from it to some degree or other. He went on to offer specific suggestions as to how various social and political structures (including families, schools, and even the United Nations) could function more productively and more humanely, almost always recommending that each person within the organization make an honest presentation of herself—her feelings, fantasies, intentions, and even her most agonizing self-doubts.

These points help to explain the widespread appeal of encounter during the 1960s and early 1970s, which constituted an era when a rebellious "counterculture" that rejected traditional authority, repudiated the need to be concerned with standards of "appropriate" behavior, and championed the importance of experience for its own sake held sway (Roszak, 1969; Reich, 1970). People doubtless were (and still are) burdened by the powerful demands of an increasingly externalized and materialistic society and frequently missed the emotional outlets provided by opportunities for ritual and celebration that an earlier, simpler time made more available. Moreover, the encounter experience promised something akin to a feeling of mutual concern and of a close-knit community that seems to be lacking in our increasingly fragmented urban culture, a culture in which most people find themselves participating in a wide variety of *disparate and isolated* reference groups—familial, occupational, social, civic, and religious. Encounter seemed to give the individual a chance to immerse herself in an intensive group experience in which she came as *herself*, rather than as a representative of a particular social or vocational role; moreover, she did not have to present herself as a patient having specific psychological symptoms. Members were encouraged to stop striving to impress one another and instead to simply let themselves "be," to the point where the real person behind the facade, and the actual body underneath the clothing, could be revealed. (Hence, during the 1960s, the nude encounter [Bindrim, 1968]—a variation of the open encounter—seemed a logical, concrete, and perhaps inevitable extension of this idea.)

Schutz has continued to lead encounter groups and, unlike others, does not see the encounter movement as moribund. In fact, it is Schutz's belief that the 1980s has witnessed a renaissance of curiosity about encounter, "especially by professionals too young to have lived through its evolution" (Schutz, 1986, p. 365). Many of the curious, particularly therapists, are introduced to encounter via five-day workshops similar to those that Schutz led at Esalen, but this time held in the form of private workshops or retreats (see our illustrative session below). However, most of the encounter groups currently led by Schutz (1984, 1986) have shifted back to the organizational focus originally inherent in T-groups, and for this reason take place within a work setting. It continues to be Schutz's conviction, though, that no behavioral change will occur without crucial changes in a person's self-concept; in this respect, he still views his role as similar to that of the group psychotherapist and encounter as a form of group therapy. Moreover, as a holist, Schutz believes that changes made in the participant's workplace consequent to the group experience will inevitably spill over to her entire "encounter" with the world. In working with organizational teams, Schutz's emphasis continues to be on ruthlessly honest personal disclosure; he points out that the most creative work groups tolerate, and even encourage, dissent and disagreement, and he thinks that competition within the team need only become destructive when it is suppressed rather than openly stated (Wieder, 1985).

Before tracing the history of Schutz's model, we want to give the reader some sense of what an open encounter session, as it might have been led by Schutz in the mid-1960s, was like. The setting for the illustration below is a five-day encounter workshop at Esalen Institute. These groups traditionally had their first session on a Sunday evening and would then continue through the morning of the following Friday.

## ILLUSTRATION OF A TYPICAL SESSION

A total of fifty-two people are taking the five-day workshop that Schutz is leading for General Foods Corporation. Those selected represent middle-management staff who the corporation, in consultation with Schutz, have decided will have most to gain from the encounter experience; the corporation's goal in sponsoring the workshop is the enhancement of each participant's interpersonal competence. On the first evening of the workshop the participants assemble for their initial *microlab* session, which will involve the entire workshop membership. The microlab's purpose is to introduce them to the kind of communication exercises that they will engage in during the five days, to prepare them for what will at times prove to be emotionally intense interactions, and to help them feel more comfortable about direct physical contact with one another. The leaders begin by directing participants in a variety of exercises. For instance, one will involve initial, nonverbal encountering of others ("Now gently brush against anyone you come across; do not talk, just make slight physical contact with people as you keep walking"); one will require more extensive and aggressive contact with another person ("Now claim your space as you keep walking; if there is someone near you—get them out of the way"); and another will encourage both self-reflection and potentially competitive interaction with others ("Think of whether you consider yourself a dominating or a submissive person; if you feel that you are dominating, go to the front of the line, if you feel you are submissive, go to the back of the line") (Schutz, 1984, p. B19).

Following the microlab, the fifty-two participants are split into five encounter groups, each having ten or so members. One of these groups is to be led by the leader of the microlab session, and the remaining ones by four other leaders, graduates of the training program for encounter leaders and supervised by Schutz himself. The small group now constitutes the primary medium of the participant's encounter experiences and will meet throughout the remainder of the week, usually with the leader, but on rare occasions without him. General sessions involving all 52 participants, scheduled for the middle of the next four afternoons, will demonstrate particular techniques or methods (e.g., body movement, graphics, Yoga). In one of the afternoon sessions the theme of encountering the world of nature will be introduced, via Esalen's famous *blind walk* exercise in which a blindfolded person is walked around the grounds by her partner, who presents many natural objects to her through nonverbal means, including touch, taste, and smell. The two will then reverse roles. In this exercise the issue of trust is admixed with a sensory dimension.

As our illustrative excerpt from the opening of one of the small groups will show, many of the open encounter sessions have a specifically therapeutic focus. However, the overall encounter experience aims for nonprogrammed personal growth in the most general sense of this term. The emphasis is on an individual's expanding her awareness along any one of many dimensions and also on her own responsibility in choosing which of these dimensions is most important to her. Since most encounter proponents believe that the contemporary citizen of the Western world has overdeveloped his or her intellectual faculties at the expense of bodily and sensory experience, the major stress is on the latter, leading to a better balance between the two. Once concentration and contact with the inner self is sufficiently strengthened, the possibility of achieving experiences that are variously described as "peak," "mystical," or "transcendental" is increased. Again, peak experiences can occur in a variety of ways. However, they are most likely to occur in moments when the participant allows herself to live fully in the immediate present and to feel at one with others in the group or with nature. Situations where the participant experiences herself as truly cared for and nurtured by fellow members can be especially intense (see Mary and the *roll and rock* exercise below).

Let us follow one of the smaller groups as it meets in its first session with its designated leader, Ted. It is now about ten-thirty in the evening, and the group is composed of eleven people—six men and five women—ranging in age from nineteen to fifty-five. They are seated in an informal circle on the floor of a relatively bare, but carpeted, lodge. The leader begins by reminding each participant that she bears the primary responsibility for what happens to her in the session; if she wishes to either go with or resist group pressure, to let herself get injured physically, to become extremely upset, to enjoy herself—the decision is hers. This is stated, in part, to bring home to participants the fact that they have both more responsibility for, and more personal control over, their own behavior than they usually realize.

The leader now suggests a warm-up exercise in which people give their first impressions of one another. He stops, giving no further directions, while the group is silent for a few moments. Then Alex, a man in his mid-forties who has had some previous encounter experience, leaps up and positions himself in the center of the group. Other participants begin to make spontaneous comments, not necessarily going in order. "You try to look kind, but I have a sense that you could stab me in the back," says one man. "You're sexy," says a woman. From another woman: "I sense a scared little boy underneath." When almost everyone has been heard from, Alex returns to the circle and is replaced by Meredith, a pretty girl in her early twenties, who stoically seats herself before the group as though steeling herself for the worst. Again the participants offer comments in no particular order. Several participants, most of them male, make some appreciative comments about her attractiveness. Participants replace Meredith in the center of the room in random order; Doris, who follows Meredith, laughingly says that it makes no sense to drag out the anxiety, so she "may as well get it over with." The exercise is over once each participant who wants to has taken his or her turn in the center of the circle. (The encounter leader can start off the session with any one of a number of warm-up exercises. Some leaders prefer to begin in a totally unstructured fashion, much as in the T-group format. Once the group atmosphere is sufficiently loose, encounter exercises are introduced in a more discriminating and specifically therapeutic way in that the leader will usually introduce them only when he thinks they will facilitate the work of a particular group member.)

At this point Ted, the leader, asks the participants for their reactions. Alex leads off by saying that he was hurt that more than one person had reacted to him as a frightened little boy. He knows that this is an aspect of himself, but it is one that he has been trying to change, both through psychotherapy and previous encounter groups, and he expresses disappointment that this part of him still shows through so strongly. Mike, a husky, vital-looking man in his early thirties, begins to show impatience with Alex and says that the latter, by his whining and self-pitying behavior, is still acting the role of the little boy and subtly asking the group for sympathy and reassurance. "If you were really a man," says Mike, "you wouldn't need us to tell you you are!"

Alex's initial reaction to Mike's irritation is one of feeling hurt and defensive, but as Mike continues to needle him, he becomes increasingly attacking. Finally he lights into what he calls Mike's "cocksureness" and says that Mike has the same self-doubt as he, Alex, does but chooses to cover it over with a face of super-virility. After continued discussion that seems to be going nowhere, Ted interrupts and suggests the *high noon* exercise (Schutz, 1971, pp. 140–141), which requires the two men to go to opposite corners of the room and face each other. Their instructions are to refrain from speaking and to slowly walk toward each other. Once they have approached each other, they are to spontaneously let their bodies lead and to go wherever their impulse tells them. As the two men begin to follow his directions, he reminds them to not plan their actions beforehand and encourages the group to remain silent as the exercise proceeds.

Once the two men are opposite each other at the room's center, they pause. Alex stands rigidly still, as if determined that it be Mike who makes the first move. The latter seems awkward and uncertain; he reaches out as though to hit Alex playfully on the shoulder, but then impulsively embraces him. Alex seems surprised, then responds by putting his arm around Mike. The latter hugs harder and harder, and then, with his head on Alex's shoulder, begins to weep.

Ted moves over to the two men. As Mike's sobbing subsides, Ted asks him what he is experiencing. Mike, still crying, says that he thinks about the gulf of antagonism that has always existed between him and his father. He feels suddenly in touch with the positive aspects of the relationship that existed between them when he was very young, and he is recalling the longing for affection and comradeship that he felt in relation to his father long ago. Ted, sensing that Mike has begun to meaningfully explore these feelings toward his father but does not know where to go next, invites him to try a psychodrama activity. "Mike, would you talk to Alex as though he was your father, and express some of these feelings?" Mike does so and finds himself trying to explain to his father why it seemed that they could never get together. Suddenly he lashes out: "It was Mom who didn't want us to be friends—somehow she kept spoiling it." Ted intervenes and asks "How?" Mike responds: "By speaking about him derogatorily to me, and by tearing him down in front of me—and you—you schmuck" (here he turns back to Alex) "you let her!"

Ted asks Mike to select from the group the woman who most reminds him of his mother. He picks Mary, a youthful-looking woman in her mid-fifties. Ted tells Mike to begin to express his feelings toward his mother. He instructs Mary to listen and to respond as she senses Mike's mother might have. Mike begins to upbraid his mother for her behavior toward him and his father; taking his cue, Mary responds in a slightly scared and defensive way. Mike corrects her and says "No, my mother would counterattack much more forcefully," and for a moment he takes the mother role in order to show Mary how he perceives his mother to behave. Mary resumes her role-playing with a more forceful manner as Mike struggles to get his anger out. Perceiving him as too timid, several members of the group, without any direction from Ted, spontaneously assume alter-ego roles and try to shout down his mother. Mike begins to shout too, but in a few minutes turns to Ted in frustration, saying: "I still can't get it out—I'd like to kill her, the bitch!"

Ted suggests that he go to the couch that is against the wall, that he stand next to it with his feet about a foot apart, and that he begin to beat it as hard as possible, all the while shouting at his mother whatever angry words come to mind. Seeing that Mike is querulous, Ted tells him that the activity might seem artificial at the beginning, but that he should proceed in an attempt to see what feelings emerge. Mike begins. As he starts to throw his body more and more into the beating, he pounds more savagely, his cries become louder, and his curses against his mother more vehement. After several minutes of this, his pounding gets weaker and he complains of exhaustion. When Ted asks if he feels finished, Mike indicates that he does.

The group is silent for a few minutes while Mike continues to lie by the couch, breathing heavily. Doris comments that Mary seems to be in great pain. With encouragement from Doris, Mary begins to talk about some of the feelings that she experienced during her role-playing with Mike, and about how she was reminded of the guilt that she feels in relation to her daughter, Nancy, who died several months ago at the age of thirty. Mary feels that most of the criticisms that her daughter had begun to direct at her during these past few years had been valid ones. She expresses regret that she had not been a better mother and that Nancy had probably died without realizing how much Mary loved her.

Ted asks Mary if she would like to work on these feelings. She says yes, and Ted encourages her to proceed in a gestalt therapy exercise (see Chapter 7) in which she places Nancy in the empty chair and speaks to her. She begins by describing for Nancy the loneliness she has felt since her death; as Nancy, she directs angry complaints against her mother. Once again in the role of herself, Mary expresses, and is surprised by, the anger Nancy's accusations arouse in her; she defends herself and states her love for Nancy. Returning to the role of Nancy, she expresses great wonderment at the extent of her mother's love, which she had never permitted herself to fully feel before. At this point, as she plays Nancy in the empty chair, Mary is overwhelmed by her feelings and begins to sob uncontrollably. Once she has regained some composure, Ted suggests she continue the gestalt therapy dialogue and say good-bye to Nancy.

At the end of this exercise Mary is softly weeping. Ted quietly gestures toward the other participants, who slowly gather around her. Performing the *roll and rock* exercise (Schutz, 1961, pp. 145–146), the group lifts Mary to her feet and forms a circle around her. Ted instructs her to close her eyes and to let herself go completely limp; as she does so, the other participants gather closely around and pass her around the circle. After a while, they move her to a horizontal position and lift her above their head. Holding her in this position, they rock her back and forth for several minutes, while softly singing a lullaby. Then they continue their rocking motion, while they slowly lower Mary to the floor.

By now it is two o'clock in the morning. Nothing is said while Mary continues to lie on the floor with her eyes still shut. Her face appears to be in gentle repose. Some participants continue to gently touch her to stay close by her side. Other members are off to the side, either singly or in groups of two or three. Most seem relaxed; all are silent. Ted asks if anyone has some reaction or feeling, encouraging the others to speak of their own reactions. When they are finished, he reminds them that they are to reassemble in the same place at ten o'clock that morning, and he bids them goodnight.

Save for the elimination of warm-up sessions, the format of the small-group sessions does not change during the remaining four-and-a-half days. The leader waits for members to spontaneously bring up problems and concerns. Many of them do so in response to the work of other participants, much as Mary, in her role as Mike's mother, had been moved to speak of her own personal anguish. While participants are given free rein to talk about the past, they are encouraged, through the use of gestalt therapy, psychodrama, and other techniques, to connect these concerns to the immediate present, to their fellow participants, and to their shared group experience. By Friday morning every participant has revealed something of his or her own life circumstances, through having had a chance, like Mike and Mary, to take "center stage."

## HISTORICAL BACKGROUND

As we have already indicated, the encounter model is best viewed as a logical extension of all the group models that preceded it. The social work group and psychoanalytic group models had taken the initial steps in encouraging participants to shed their more social and stereotypic masks in order to reveal the more authentic person underneath. The experiential model had made another significant step when it encouraged the leader-therapist to do the same. Then came psychodrama and gestalt therapy, which claimed that therapeutic results could be gained in a time-limited framework and encouraged participants to stop talking *about* their difficulties and to instead act them out in more expressive and vivid ways. At a subsequent point there emerged the T-group, offering an experience in interpersonal sensitivity that was explicitly for normal people and that, like psychodrama and gestalt therapy, could impart something valuable to a participant within a relatively brief time period.

As the growth and development group that had inaugurated the sensitivity-training movement, the T-group was the most conspicuous and immediate predecessor of the encounter group. At first, the T-model was relatively strict in maintaining two distinct foci (see Chapter 10). The trainer was to (1) encourage the group to become intentionally aware of its own processes and (2) ensure that the group consistently concentrate on the here-

and-now. By prohibiting the introduction of there-and-then material (especially past events from a particular participant's life), the trainer avoided the kind of individual focusing that could be seen as constituting psychotherapy. For reasons that we reviewed in Chapter 1, T-group leaders, starting in the mid-1950s, gradually began to relax their adherence to these two parameters; at this point the first distinct introduction of an encounter thrust into sensitivity groups occurred.

Other steps toward a strong encounter focus, in particular an emphasis on nonverbal contact, soon followed. In retrospect it can be argued that once the explicitly personal focus of group therapy models was introduced into groups designed for nonpatients, once the spirit of experientialism was interpreted to grant the leader complete freedom to be himself (to the point of having physical contact with the participant), and once the more expressive and less verbal procedures involved in psychodrama and gestalt therapy were brought into a sensitivity-training format, the relatively unstructured encounter group was an inevitable outcome.

However, the path taken by sensitivity training, as it proceeded from the more structured and social science oriented T-group to the more loosely organized and experiential encounter group, involved several disparate developments. One step in this sequence involved the work of Carl Rogers (1970, 1980) who developed what he called his *basic encounter group* and introduced into the group experience a strongly humanistic and personalized emphasis. A second step involved the *marathon model* developed by Bach (1966, 1967) and Stoller (1972), two psychoanalytically oriented therapists who, although proceeding from a different theoretical orientation, hit upon a time-limited group format with significant similarities to Rogers's approach. A third and final step in this sequence involved the evolution of what is sometimes referred to as the *Synanon* or *attack* approach to group interaction. Despite the fact that the Synanon group met on a long-term basis as part of a treatment plan for drug addicts, its encouragement of a highly confrontational approach, whether on the part of the leader or fellow participants, played an influential role in the movement toward open encounter. In addition, Synanon groups were eventually organized for "straights," as well as for addicts. Following is a summary of each of these three approaches.

**Rogers's Basic Encounter Model.**    Rogers's orientation to working with groups is a clear-cut outgrowth of his "client-centered" approach to individual therapy (Rogers, 1951). His group model, like his individual model, emphasizes a strongly phenomenological dimension wherein the therapist or leader responds in terms of the client's internal frame of reference and refrains from imposing his own interpretations of the latter's experience (Rogers, 1980). It is a pervasively humanistic orientation, predates by many years the emergence of all encounter methods, and has much in common with the existential-experiential model (see Chapter 5). Indeed, Rogers's initial experience with groups goes back to 1946, when he began to work with counselors-in-training on a group basis. In developing his group model, which he later labeled "encounter," Rogers bypassed both the psychoanalytic and T-group models and instead remained remarkably consistent in his basic approach to the people with whom he is working.

Three distinct aspects of Rogers's basic encounter helped to place it within the mainstream of what, at that time, was a rapidly developing encounter movement (Rogers, 1970): (1) He did not worry about making a distinction between growth and developmental goals and psychotherapy goals, leaving the participant free to talk about past, as well as present, events; (2) he emphasized the value of honest confrontation, even if the feedback presented seemed negative or potentially hurtful; (3) he had little interest in directing the group's conscious attention to its own processes. This is not to say that he had little awareness of, or respect for, group-dynamic processes. On the contrary, he emphasized that a trusting and cohesive group climate— which he, as a leader, continually attempted to facilitate—is one of the most therapeutic properties of the basic encounter. However his preference was to exploit these group-dynamic properties (rather than to explicitly analyze them for the group, or to prod the group into analyzing them) to a point where his interventions could become minimal and each participant could become, at key moments, a facilitator or therapist for other participants in the group.

Rogers has come to view encounter as offering an extremely effective antidote to alienation and as therefore one of the truly important sociocultural inventions of our time. As a result of his enthusiasm, and also as a test of it, he helped to form special encounter groups having conflict resolution as their central aim. For instance, at Immaculate Heart College in Montecito, California, he used encounter to promote an active dialogue between faculty and students, and in Northern Ireland he placed within a single group Irish Catholics and Irish Protestants, plus some participants from England. He concluded that both experiments were successful (Evans, 1981).

**Stoller and Bach's Marathon Encounter.**   Fred Stoller (who died in 1970) and George Bach, two psychoanalytically oriented group therapists, were interested in extending the format of conventional group therapy to the point of having participants remain in one another's presence for periods of time ranging from twenty-four to forty-eight hours. Because of an emphasis on the time factor, Stoller and Bach initially called these groups (which they co-led) *marathons;* within three years, perhaps influenced by the already budding encounter movement, the term *marathon group encounter* was being used (Bach, 1967; Stoller, 1972).

Rogers had come to encounter from a client-centered tradition that deemphasized the role of both diagnosis and interpretation in doing treatment. By contrast, because Stoller and Bach had emerged from a strongly psychoanalytic and clinical tradition, their shift toward an encounter approach represented a dramatic transition in their thinking. No longer did they deem it necessary for the group therapist to have a detailed knowledge of the patient's past or for the patient to have intellectual insight in order to change. In their thinking, the "working through" phase of psychotherapy, so integral a part of the psychoanalytic method, could be accomplished by the participant on his or her own in the weeks following the marathon (though it had doubtless begun via new or changed behavior during the marathon experience itself) with the expectation that significant personality change could occur on the basis of a single marathon experience. In other words, traditional features of conventional treatment underlining the importance of a treatment plan and of careful support of defenses until the patient was ready to relinquish them were slipping away. Instead, these two therapists stressed the positive forces for autonomous growth, reparation, and reintegration that existed within each group member. This emphasis on the need for the participant to assume responsibility for her own welfare—as opposed to her placing this responsibility in the hands of either the leaders or the group—was to become a fundamental feature of the encounter model.

Similarly novel was Bach and Stoller's belief that if change were to occur it must occur *now.* This shift in emphasis wherein the emitting of new behavior was made primary, and the understanding of old behavior secondary, philosophically had much in common with the behavior therapy model and reversed the traditional priorities of psychoanalysis, which claimed that meaningful change could occur only in the context of a patient's emotional and intellectual appreciation of her own dynamics.

Rogers had been used to working with groups on the basis of an intensive and time-limited format and therefore did not stress this aspect of his approach to encounter. Stoller and Bach, on the other hand, made much of the time factor, because for them it was a distinct departure. As they saw it, the extended time format had several advantages: (1) The prolonged nature of the marathon tends to produce fatigue, which in turn leads to a weakening of defenses; (2) paths of retreat that in traditional group therapy are normally open to patients who feel hurt by the negative reactions of others are less available in the time-extended group, where no participant is likely to escape the group's attention during the long session; (3) the fact that the group does not have to anticipate breaking within an hour or so (as in conventional group meetings) helps it to be less wary that there will be an insufficient amount of time to deal with the hurt and angry feelings attendant upon confrontation, thereby enabling its members to take greater risks in leveling with one another; (4) the participant has a considerably greater opportunity to see that her reaction-style — which she likes to think is primarily determined by either the situation or her mood of the moment—is recurrent and patterned in that it cyclically repeats itself throughout the extended marathon sequence; and (5) the dramatic and keenly anticipatory nature of the marathon helps to create an atmosphere of crisis and expectancy; this climate has within it elements of a self-fulfilling prophecy wherein the participant, expecting a breakthrough for herself, works hard to make it happen. Where she does not, her fellow participants, realizing that she has come for a distinct reason and has a strong investment in the outcome, are quick to remind her that there will be no next session to which pressing emotional issues can be deferred.

Initially, Stoller and Bach were so impressed by the time-intensity and fatigue factors that they advocated nonstop twenty-four hour sessions in which the group was given no opportunity for sleep. Later this position relaxed, and marathons ran late into the night and then broke until the next morning, thereby giving participants a chance to sleep. This is the procedure that Schutz followed in his Esalen open encounter.

**Synanon and Attack Therapy.**    Synanon, a residential setting for the rehabilitation of drug addicts, was initially established in Santa Monica, California, in 1958 by Charles Dederich, a recovered alcholic and nonprofessional who conceived of a unique approach to the treatment of addicts (Casriel, 1963; Yablonsky, 1955). Those wishing to enter the program were required to live at Synanon, to keep strictly "clean," and to abide by a number of house rules. The direct participation of professionals was kept to a minimum, in part because Dederich's intention was to create a self-help community in which an autocratic family structure would help to provide a source of control and stability for the initially anarchic and dependent addict (hence Synanon was to provide one of the earliest precursors of the self-help group model; see Chapter 13). Important components in this process involved the chance to model the behavior of addicts who were higher within the organizational hierarchy and who had had a longer record of "clean days" and to participate in the leaderless small-group sessions, or *synanons,* which were the primary setting for the group approach known as *attack therapy.*

Synanons meet continually throughout the life of the house, but their membership is not fixed. One advantage of this arrangement is that it prevents the kind of collusion that can develop among members of a fixed, ongoing therapy group in which members sometimes establish an unwritten pact to refrain from exposing particular vulnerabilities in one another. The average Synanon member will participate in about three such groups a week.

The attack phase of a synanon refers to an interaction sequence wherein a particular participant is cross-examined, ridiculed, and berated for certain aspects of her behavior or attitudes that are felt to be impeding her path toward greater self-reliance. Characteristics focused on might include excessive self-pity, undue dependency on outside family figures, false humility, or laxness in performing a job. Once under attack, the victim usually attempts to defend herself, but her defenses are exposed as the rationalizations and excuses they are. A therapeutic confrontation requires a good deal of skill in that the attacker must know when to back off and when to offer support.

To the outside observer, a prolonged attack may appear to be a sadistic "third degree" or inquisition. Synanon proponents, however, make several arguments in support of its effectiveness: (1) One of the addict's problems is that she has been treated too laxly in the past and with too little recognition of her potential for toughness and strength; (2) the victim gradually learns that it is her *problem* that is being attacked, rather than her basic "self"; (3) she might even realize that what seems like an overt attack is frequently an expression of caring and of genuine regard; (4) sometimes an addict's emotional blocks are of such an intensity that she can be reached in no other way; (5) attack therapy teaches the addict verbal ways of handling stress that are considerably more effective than her previous reliance on acting-out; and (6) new members slowly appreciate that while the content of an attack is valid to the attacker, the attack format is something of a game, with its own rituals and rules of play, including exaggeration.

Although Dederich has pointed out that attack approaches may work only within the very particular context of Synanon, the Synanon approach to group therapy had a strong influence on the encounter movement. One manifestation of its impact has been the belief, on the part of many encounter proponents (including Schutz), in the effectiveness of lay, or "grass-roots," leaders who would run face-to-face groups in their own communities, with the purpose of increasing a sense of both consensus and of emotional intimacy. Another has been the increased use of confrontational styles, in which group members at times feel free to fight with each other physically, as well as verbally. Also reminiscent of the synanon is the quite common interaction pattern wherein each encounter member will "take a turn" and become, for a prolonged period of time, the primary focus of the group's attention.

**Schutz's Open Encounter Model.**    The developments recapitulated above take us through the mid-sixties and helped to pave the way for Schutz's open encounter model. One additional event that was to prove instrumental in this model's final emergence occurred in 1967 when Will Schutz joined the staff of Esalen Institute. Esalen had been established in 1962, when two Stanford University graduates, Michael Murphy and Richard Price, decided to use sixty-two acres belonging to Murphy in Big Sur, California, for the development of a center that would devote itself to the exploration of human potential (Anderson, 1983). Murphy and Price, both nonprofessionals, were convinced that Esalen, if it were to remain consistent with its humanistic orientation, had to be nondoctrinaire. Therefore, while they wished to study further the sensitivity-training procedures initially developed by the National Training Laboratories, they were receptive to other techniques (including gestalt therapy, Yoga, meditation) and to non-Western religions and cosmologies; hence, there was an emphasis on Eastern philosophy, Zen Buddhism, and mysticism in general. Starting with weekend retreats, Esalen's Big Sur program and facilities grew to a point where by 1968 it offered year-round events, had a permanent live-in staff, and ran two to three simultaneous workshops lasting anywhere from weekends to several months; it was also in the process of developing a San Francisco branch that within a year would be sponsoring shorter workshops on a nonresidential basis. In this way, Esalen came to spearhead and to epitomize the human potential movement and to develop into a prototype for scores of growth centers that subsequently sprang up throughout the United States.

At the point when Schutz arrived on the scene, some of Esalen's workshops were centered around a particular technique, like Yoga or meditation; others were thematic in nature and might concern marriage, divorce, loneliness, intimacy; still others had no specific focus apart from the kind of interpersonal exploration that is the general aim of all growth and development groups. These were workshops that were called "encounter," and it was their development, along with the creation of a program for leaders-in-training, that became Schutz's primary responsibility.

Schutz was a social psychologist with a strong grounding in psychoanalysis. While on the faculty of Harvard, he wrote a book, *FIRO* (1958), that attempted to coordinate psychoanalytic approaches to group dynamics with the psychoanalytic theory of personality dynamics. He also received some training in group leading during this time from the National Training Laboratories at Bethel, Maine, and from Elvin Semrad, a Boston psychoanalyst whose theoretical orientation to work with groups was in the Bion-Tavistock tradition (see Chapter 9). In 1963 Schutz joined the faculty of the Albert Einstein College of Medicine in New York City. In New York he came under the tutelage of Alexander Lowen, the founder of Bioenergetic Analysis, a school of psychotherapy emphasizing the essential unity of mind and body; bioenergetics stresses the necessity of reawakening whole areas of a patient's body, often through extremely vigorous exercises involving thrusting and pounding movements of the entire skeletal musculature. According to Lowen (1967), this kind of body work permits the patient to get into renewed contact with long-suppressed emotions; until these affects are felt and released, latent energies within the body are so blocked as to prevent a real feeling of aliveness. Lowen in turn had been a disciple of Wilhelm Reich, whose theory of character armor postulated that each emotional repression or blockage within us has a specific site of muscular tension associated with it (Reich, 1949); as a result, many aspects of our posture both embody and signal (to the sensitive observer) our defensive and/or characterological stance, and psychological treatment that ignores the body is bound to be superficial. During this period, Schutz, albeit impressed by the intellectual insights of Freud and his followers in the dynamics of human character formation, began to believe that formal analytic technique was usually unsuccessful in achieving any genuine transformations of character. His experience in personal analysis up until that time had done nothing to convince him otherwise. The Reichian and Lowenian emphasis on physical action and body-work seemed to hold some promise for a more potent means of reawakening long-dormant feelings.

Given this background, Schutz was in an ideal position to integrate theoretical strands emanating from Freud, Reich, and Kurt Lewin into the unique amalgam that he eventually labeled open encounter. He did not abandon a psychoanalytic understanding of character formation, but instead of exploring these processes in a purely verbal way with a participant-patient, he was eager to approach them through more immediate physical and bodily means. Similarly, he had both a theoretical and intuitive command of group dynamics and respected them as important phenomena, but instead of desiring to help the group explicitly label and understand these processes, he preferred to employ them in such a way as to build a cohesive, trusting atmosphere wherein each participant could begin to liberate herself from the devitalizing effects of her chronic alienation.

## KEY CONCEPTS

**The Centrality of the Body.**    Following in the tradition of Wilhelm Reich and Alexander Lowen, Schutz makes the body the single overriding concept in his theory of encounter. While the gestalt therapy model, in its careful attention to body language, had earlier taken significant steps in this direction, Schutz's model was to go even further. Once Schutz was aware of a particular emotional constellation within a participant-patient, he would consistently urge her to translate her feelings into a physical activity that expresses it in a direct and concrete fashion. For instance, if a participant expresses a sense of immoblization and constriction, the leader is likely to suggest the *breaking out* exercise (Schutz, 1971, p. 142), which requires the group to lock arms around her and to forcibly prevent her breaking through their tight circle to the outside. If she expresses mistrust, she is encouraged to engage in the *falling back* exercise (Schutz, 1971, p. 138), which has her falling back with the trusting conviction that the person behind her will catch her. (In the illustrative session above, both the high noon and rock and roll exercises are attempts to put into the realm of physical action whichever emotions are in the forefront of the group's immediate attention.) According to Schutz, the body cannot lie or hide: "When nonverbal techniques are used, real feeling tends to emerge spontaneously" (Schutz, 1986, p. 371).

Implicit in Schutz's thesis is the following: Our earliest experiences originate in the body before we have any symbols, other than body language, with which to encode them. The earliest emotions, including feeling good (which probably relates to feeling loved and cared for), feeling bad, and feeling angry, begin as *body* feelings. Therefore, there is no more basic way of experiencing ourselves, and our being, than through bodily sensations. No amount of "head" talk to the woman who wants to break through her self-containment (e.g., discussing why she feels so constrained or what she might do to feel less constrained) is likely to offer a learning experience equivalent to her expressing her problem motorically, and there will be a higher probability of her experiencing the full extent of her rage (and of realizing how she sabotages herself through a premature giving up) in the breaking out exercise than there will be in conventional group interaction, which almost always proceeds via verbal symbols or dialogue. Furthermore, any actual success that she eventually has in escaping from the group-circle will help her to feel more intensely the exhilarating possibility of breaking out in the larger emotional sense, again because the body furnishes the most powerful encoding of a sense of expansiveness and of self-transcendence.

These techniques reverse the psychoanalytic method, which limits the patient's behavior in the analytic session to verbalization and reflection and discourages overt action in the actual session (the patient is directed to lie on the couch and to speak). Although convinced of the limitations of verbal interpretation when employed by itself, Schutz did not oppose its use altogether, claiming that such an interpretation, if combined with body movement and body action on the participant's part, can serve an important role in helping the latter to consolidate, understand, and integrate an intensely emotional experience or conflict.

**The Facilitative Role of Fantasy and Inner Imagery.**   As indicated above, one way to give an emotional conflict more concrete form is to translate it directly into physical activity. Another way is to direct it into *imagined* physical activity, for according to Schutz, even a *fantasy* of physical activity will have a greater chance of rendering a problem emotionally alive than will discussing it in a more discursive or abstract manner. As a means of encouraging the imaginative process, Schutz—once he becomes acquainted with a participant's central dilemma—will suggest a specific image that she then uses to get started in her fantasy. Should she become stuck at some later point, he will intervene to supply further help. Schutz refers to this procedure as the *guided daydream* (Desoille, 1965; Leuner, 1965).

Let us cite a specific example that Schutz uses to illustrate his technique (Schutz, 1986, pp. 374–376). Peony, a good-looking woman in her late twenties, was a member of one of his five-day encounter groups. Raised in Great Britain in a small-town community, she had been a quiet child who avoided social relationships. Her reasons for entering the group involved an intellectual curiosity about groups and a wish to better her relationship with her boyfriend, who was a participant in the same group.

Schutz introduced Peony into the guided daydream after she had already done considerable work using other techniques to relax her defenses so that she had been able to weep and to have some degree of emotional contact with each of the other participants. But now Peony was experiencing her deepest feelings, particularly her terror, and Schutz thought that it was time for her to work more on her own, apart from the group. He encouraged her to have a fantasy in which she would go into her body and proceed to that part where she felt her terror to be.

Peony first felt herself to be an extremely tiny person within a large cave, went down her legs into her feet, felt sand under her feet, and then proceeded out into the sea ("I'm swimming slowly—it's calm and warm and feels good"). Peony went back into her feet and legs and then into her stomach, where her terror was greatest. She felt extremely awkward here, primarily because she experienced herself as in limbo, "in between the front and the back. I'd like to fill up the space and stop feeling backless." Peony could feel her back from the outside—something that Schutz facilitated by touching her on the left side—but not from the inside. Encouraged by Schutz to try to feel her back from the inside, she was eventually able to do so ("I'm beginning to, it feels warm, and *the front and back are together*"; italics added).

Peony told Schutz that she was not yet ready to come out of her body. Schutz said, "There's a mountain—can you see it?" Peony responded "Yes" and pointed to her stomach. Encouraged by Schutz to go up the mountain, she did, saying that the climb became harder toward the top, where the air was thinner and where she had to breathe more deeply. Because of the precipitous drop at the summit, she then decided to come halfway down the mountain, where she discovered a soft shelf, which provided her an opportunity to rest for a few minutes and to find a means of breathing adequately. Peony was now able to leave her body, to ease herself out of her fantasy, and to become emotionally reintegrated with the rest of the group.

Had Schutz wished to introduce a cognitive dimension into the resolution of Peony's defensive blocks and inhibitions, he could have ventured various *interpretations:* "Your being able to feel your front and back together represents your beginning to feel more whole and integrated; indeed, it represents the integration of your body with your mind, your feeling self with your thinking self"; or, "Your ability to climb the mountain, to find enough air to breathe at the top and then reduce your anxiety by discovering a more comfortable spot halfway down means that you are now able to soothe yourself and need no longer depend solely on the soothing of others." Yet in part because he could not be completely sure of the validity of such interpretations, and even more because he sensed them to be superfluous, he did not offer them. His assumption is that in Peony's unconscious, any mastery that she experiences within her fantasy will generalize to, and ease, areas of her living wherein she experiences herself as similarly terrified and blocked.

Schutz's conceptualization here is not an unusual one. For example, some child therapists have always encouraged a reworking of a child's neurotic solution by addressing comments to the child's fantasy *without* indicating the parallel between the fantasy and the child's actual life situation ("I wonder if the sister-doll wouldn't need the brother-doll so much if she could find some friends of her own."). Like Schutz, these therapists assume that the patient will unconsciously apply the fantasy solution to her own emotional dynamics.

The guided daydream, which offers a quite representative example of how Schutz liked to use mental imagery in his work with individual participants, constitutes an alternative to the overt physical activity involved in an encounter game such as breaking out. For instance, Peony's successful climbing of the mountain is the imaginative equivalent of another participant's *actually* succeeding in breaking through the group circle. Although here the activity involves an act of imagination, it is experienced by the imaginer so vividly as to seem real; for Peony it is as though she has broken through an actual physical impediment. As Schutz sees it, this immediacy makes for greater therapeutic effectiveness than can any verbal, and inevitably logical, discussion of the childhood dynamics underlying her avoidance of solid emotional contact with others.

**The Dissolution of Blocks.**   All of the examples above can be seen as attempts to resolve one kind of block or another: mistrust, which blocks one's way to closer relationships; devaluation of the body, which blocks one's way to a fuller enjoyment of it; feelings of constriction, which block one's path toward a sense of expansiveness; and so on. Schutz seems close to Carl Rogers (and to an organismic theorist like Kurt Goldstein; see Chapter 7) in assuming that the fundamental human drive is toward growth, with the result that once blocks are removed the organism will resume a temporarily interrupted movement toward greater and greater degrees of self-realization. Growth will not necessarily continue uninterrupted; hence, the encounter participant is free to seek out future encounter groups, or other kinds of growth-promoting experiences. Indeed, within this framework the encounter experience can be viewed as a psychotherapy technique for "normal" people that is available on a lifelong and periodic basis.

The body work that Schutz does in the group can be conceptualized within the framework of block dissolving; since body tensions are thought of as blocks against feeling. Reducing tension in specific body parts can help to bring about emotional release. And certain feelings, like hostility, can serve as blocks against other feelings, like affection. The most fundamental way to help a person contact body feelings, and feelings in general, is through a relaxation and deepening of her breathing. Another technique involves *unlocking*, in which people with shallow breathing and cramped postures (usually indicating resistances against interpersonal contact) are encouraged to uncross their arms and/or legs and to breathe deeply. These are relatively "quick" techniques aimed at blocks closer to the surface of the personality. Other techniques are geared toward "deeper" levels of the personality (e.g., feelings of compulsive friendliness, which may constitute a block against the experience of anger, and so on).

**The Energy Cycle.**    This is a concept that is partly derived from George Herbert Mead (1938) and is closely related to Schutz's emphasis on both the blocking and the discharge of tension. As a need is activated, energy is mobilized and begins to flow into muscle fibers. If a person's energy has been adequately discharged, she is left in a relaxed state. If not, it might express itself in various signs of chronic tension or nervous activity, like headaches, clenched jaws, or tapping fingers.

Schutz uses the energy concept to describe how the open encounter leader makes decisions regarding which individuals, and which group issues, are most in need of attention at any given moment ("Dull groups result from the pursuit of energyless issues" [Schutz, 1986, p. 369]). He encourages the leader to sense where the group energy is strongest and to avoid going after issues and feelings that will turn out to be superficial and lifeless. For example, the leader should hesitate before focusing on a participant who seems relaxed, since the latter at such a moment is unlikely to be experiencing very strong feelings. If the leader turns his attention toward someone who seems tense and constricted, he should try to activate more energy within this person before beginning intensive work (usually through some of the block-dissolving techniques cited above, such as breathing and unlocking exercises). Just as the leader must know when an energy cycle is probably ready to begin, he must also be able to sense at which point it is about to reach closure, lest he linger over an emotional experience after it has begun to wane.

**The Inclusion-Control-Openness Trichotomy.**    This concept is derived from earlier empirical research done by Schutz (1958) which integrated personality dynamics with group dynamics. He has found that the concept describes what a participant typically experiences as she goes through the beginning, middle, and termination phases of an encounter experience (Schutz, 1984). Originally called the *fundamental interpersonal relations orientation* [FIRO] (Schutz, 1958), this conceptualization cites three fundamental issues that predominate in human relatedness: inclusion, control, and openness. While these concepts are applicable to an individual's personality style (i.e., people can usually be characterized in terms of which of these three issues is most salient in their emotional living), they also can be applied to group dynamics in that any particular interaction segment within a group may have one of these interpersonal orientations as its central emotional dynamic.

*Inclusion* is perhaps the most fundamental and primitive issue in that it involves feelings of acceptance by other people. If we apply it to the encounter group, inclusion touches on the question of the degree to which a participant feels that she is either "in" the group or "out" of it. Exercises requiring her to "break into" a physical circle formed by the group members attempt to reflect this dimension.

The second interpersonal issue is *control;* issues predominating here involve power and authority, and in the encounter group this orientation will focus on dominance and competition for leadership within the group. A specific exercise serving to highlight control issues is *dominance*, in which members line up, each of them being directed to take the position that she believes will reflect her order of dominance within the group. A key question here is: Am I on the top or the bottom?

The third issue involves *openness* to another person; it corresponds to Erik Erikson's concept of intimacy (1964) and Freud's of genitality. As participants become enmeshed in this issue, the group-as-a-whole oftens recedes in importance and concerns involving pairing, and specific dyads, become paramount. Illustrating this dimension is the *high school dance* exercise (Schutz, 1971), in which a large group of people are asked to select partners for a dance. The key question for each participant is: To whom do I feel close, and from whom do I feel distant? When contrasted with inclusion, openness includes giving, as well as receiving, and is more discriminating as to who is loved.

Schutz believes that as a group progresses in time, it moves from an initial concern with inclusion to a focus on control and finally to affection. Sensing which of the three issues is predominant at any particular point can help the leader determine which intervention would be most facilitative. For instance, if he perceives that the men in the group are competing for the most attractive women, he might wish to select an exercise that forces the latent competition among them to surface. And by highlighting this problem, he would also enable himself to gain access to whatever competitive feelings exist among the women as to which of them are considered desirable by the men. During the earlier stages of the interaction he would need to be alert to those participants who don't yet feel included by the slowly coalescing group.

## ROLE OF THE LEADER

As with almost all our group models, the open encounter leader is to be viewed as a catalytic agent who helps to facilitate the group interaction. However, because of the looser format of open encounter, the leader has an unusual degree of freedom regarding the kinds of methods he can use and the kinds of issues he can pursue. For example, while the group psychoanalyst almost always relies on verbal and discursive forms of communication, the open encounter leader feels free to introduce psychodrama, gestalt, body movement, and imagery exercises at points where he believes they will facilitate either interpersonal communication or individual catharsis. While the Tavistock leader confines his interventions to those that highlight what the group is doing *as a group*, the encounter leader may make comments that are addressed to a specific individual, as well as to the group-as-a-whole. And while the T-group trainer strives, when dealing with a particular participant, to avoid focusing on the latter's unconscious processes, lest this activity be construed as constituting psychotherapy, the open encounter leader is not at all reluctant to do so.

In Schutz's perception of the leadership role, as in Rogers's, the leader does best to eschew making the group consciously aware of the forces promoting or impeding its cohesion and instead guides these forces in such a manner as to produce a strongly felt sense of closeness and group cohesiveness. (For instance, his understanding of the inclusion-control-openness trichotomy enables him, during the earliest stages of the group, to focus primarily on the degree to which a member feels accepted by, or included in, the group, and it is only during the later stages that he will explore issues of rivalry or affection between specific members.) In Schutz's view, the individual and the group reciprocally interact, with genuine catharses on the part of individual members serving to intensify the group's feeling of closeness, and with increased feelings of group closeness in turn enabling members to feel that much more emboldened to reveal themselves. As individual members' defenses are penetrated, and the overall level of cohesion thereby heightened, the similarities among group members become much more marked than do their differences. The resultant sense of communality may enable participants to realize that in a fundamental sense they are more alike than unalike, giving a mystical feeling of unity to the group experience (as though the members are somehow merged; Schutz, 1971).

In deciding which specific participants to approach, and when, the leader is alert to those people and those dyads where energy is most mobile (see "The Energy Cycle" on page 220). Once he has determined with whom to work, his skill lies in sensing what emotional issues he should concentrate on and in selecting those methods that will most facilitate his work; here the talents and intuitions of the experienced psychotherapist are probably most relevant. Wherever possible, the open encounter leader strives to have core emotional issues expressed via the body; hence affection becomes translated into touching and holding, hostility into shoving and pushing, possessiveness into clutching, and so on. Personal qualities in the leader that doubtless are of considerable help in enabling him to make these kinds of moment-to-moment interventions are self-trust, imaginativeness, and flexibility.

The open encounter leader encourages each member to share with the group whatever problems and concerns have led her to seek out an intensive group experience. However, he endeavors to respect the member's right to not participate and also emphasizes each participant's personal responsibility when it comes to critical decisions regarding interpersonal confrontation and physical expressiveness. Although setting some (usually implicit) limits on the destruction of physical property, the leader tries to leave it to the participants themselves to determine how much they can take in terms of verbal or physical confrontation. Once group cohesion has started to develop, he typically trusts other members to monitor their own affective and aggressive behavior.

In summary, the open encounter leader attempts to provide an intensive emotional experience for as many participants as possible. In doing so, he is careful to remind them that they have the main responsibility for trying to gain something for—or to protect—themselves. He refuses to make precise distinctions between personal growth and psychotherapy, instead trusting the member's autonomous capacity to either disregard the experience or use it for further growth.

# CHAPTER 12
# THE THEME-CENTERED INTERACTIONAL METHOD

The theme-centered interactional model (or TCI, as it has come to be known both in the United States and abroad) has as one of its major innovations the setting of a clear-cut theme that the group is kept consistently aware of in a noncoercive way by the leader. This theme may be quite personal, and in such instances the group might resemble sensitivity-training groups; however, the theme is explicitly stated (e.g., "Letting the 'Real Me' Show Through"). In other instances the theme may be relatively impersonal, as in traditional groups formed around a specific task or learning purpose, such as committees, staffs, seminars, and academic classes (Gordon, 1985); here the theme might be: "Understanding *Huckleberry Finn*" or "Planning Next Year's Curriculum." However, a TCI approach to these latter themes, unlike that of other orientations, regards digressions from the overt theme as appropriate and even desirable, for what is aimed for is an *optimum,* rather than maximum, amount of theme-centeredness.

The theme-centered group leader, then, will at times encourage her group to pursue issues going beyond its formal theme, particularly if the discussion until then has been so theme-focused as to have excluded an expression of the participants' more personal reactions—to the theme or task, to the leader, to one another, or to what has transpired during the session thus far. Especially relevant would be *distractions,* as when a participant finds himself too preoccupied with other concerns to concentrate on group interaction, and *resistances,* as when a student has not done the class assignment or feels no interest in the lesson at hand. What the TCI format brings to sensitivity-training contexts, then, is a more structured approach in which the leader more sharply defines and delimits the group's learning goals by focusing on a specific theme. What it introduces to task and education groups is a more psychologically aware and humanistic orientation wherein goals and purpose are pursued in a more open, communicative, and enlivened atmosphere (Gordon & Liberman, 1972).

The present model was primarily inspired by Ruth C. Cohn, a European-born psychoanalyst and group psychotherapist. She was trained at the Zurich Psychoanalytic Institute and fled Germany in the thirties. Following her emigration to the United States in 1941, she began a private practice in New York City. It was in the context of a supervision group for psychotherapists that Cohn first began to practice the approach that was later to evolve into TCI. Called "The Countertransference Workshop," and initially sponsored by the National Psychological Association for Psychoanalysis, her group was geared toward helping therapists become more aware of how unresolved aspects of their own conflicts and feelings interfered with their helpfulness to patients. What quickly became apparent was the frequency with which a therapist's personal difficulties with a patient became in some manner reflected or reenacted in his behavior within the group. For example (Cohn, 1969), a presenting therapist's inability to recognize the rebellion and anger implicit in his presented patient's nonpayment of fees was paralleled in the workshop by his difficulty in perceiving that he and a co-participant, by getting into a discussion of the case before he had finished presenting it, were rebelling against the leader's authority and the overall workshop structure (which prohibited discussion of a case until *after* all pertinent material had been presented). Since the workshop's general theme was countertransference, what we see in our example is a parallel between the countertransference theme (the therapist's need to promote rebellious acting out in his patient) with a specific group interactional dynamic (the therapist's own rebellious struggle—which included his having encouraged a similar acting out on the part of a co-participant—against the structure of the workshop and the authority of its leader).

Cohn gradually began to see her task as that of keeping the workshop's focus evenly balanced between the countertransference theme and the emotional interaction of the participants (these two motifs, rather than being separate or independent aspects of the group process, were turning out to be interdependent, dynamically interrelated forces, just as in the illustration above). If the therapist's countertransference themes and preoccupations were described and discussed only as they affected life with his patient in his consulting room, they might at times interest, and even enlighten, his co-participants (who are also therapists), but they would still remain somewhat abstract and somewhat "there-and-then" in their focus; however, if these same countertransference problems became directly manifested within the here-and-now of the group process, how much livelier the overall group interaction would become, and how much more emotionally significant the learning that could occur.

Thus far the only group or workshop theme that Cohn had directly experimented with was that of countertransference, the only learning theme that of how to do pychotherapy more effectively. Her excitement in watching what had developed within these workshops, however, was such that she began to wonder if her technique could work with themes other than countertransference, and with learning groups other than countertransference workshops. For example, doesn't a history class have a common history as a distinct group in time? What if a literature seminar reading a poem on loss has recently lost one of its members? And perhaps the task group attempting to solve the organizational problems of its company finds itself facing not too dissimilar organizational problems within its own committee structure. In each of these situations, the alert group leader would be "hitting pay dirt" whenever she could find a point of direct contact between a workshop's theme (e.g., "Understanding History") and an immediate event in the group that highlighted and illuminated this theme (a significant historical event within our own history as a group—the illness of our first, somewehat problematic teacher and her replacement by a much better-liked and warmer one).

But why, Cohn asked herself, stop with classroom groups? What about couples workshops for people trying to improve their marriages? groups for single parents struggling with child-rearing? and neighborhood groups seeking to resolve racial and class tensions? If the theme-centered approach could work in these contexts, then it would enable Cohn to finally find workable community applications for psychodynamic and psychotherapeutic techniques that had hitherto been effective in their ability to treat individual neuroses, but unable to bring about change in humankind's more social and collective ills (Cohn, 1969).

The next application of this gradually evolving model was to an industrial situation; Cohn was asked to tackle some of the organizational problems confronting a large company (Cohn, 1969). What she had hoped for and anticipated in fact emerged—the here-and-now focus and process interaction of her group at times reflected in bold relief tensions and conflicts existent within the larger administrative structure of the overall company; hence, the theme and interaction dialectic of the countertransference workshop had proved transferable to another setting. In this particular situation, the theme that Cohn eventually set, "Management Relations," was not stated by her at the workshop's inception, but instead slowly evolved over several sessions. It soon became evident, however, that it was preferable to state a theme clearly at the beginning of a workshop, since this theme, once established, will typically exercise a strong influence on the participants' initial set and on their subsequent orientation. Hence a milestone was reached in a 1963 weekend workshop sponsored by the Los Angeles Society for Clinical Psychologists when for the first time a noncountertransference theme was explicitly stated in advance—"Training in Emotional Skill."

Cohn was slowly discovering that the thematic aspect of her approach provided an exceptional degree of versatility, since the number of themes that could be set for a wide variety of groups, each with its own unique purpose, was virtually unlimited: psychotherapists might find themselves interested in "Freedom and Control in the Psychotherapy Relationship," parents in "The Teenage Drug Culture," writers in "Freeing Creativity," teachers in "Living Learning vs. Dead Learning," and so on. Principles and procedures that had evolved through an inductive, trial-and-error phase were now sufficiently experience tested to be codified into a tentative model, which could in turn be taught to leaders-in-training. For example, Cohn and her colleagues found that a workshop proceeded best if a leader first opened it with a formal statement of its theme and then asked the participants to listen silently to her guiding questions and directions in order to come into deeper contact with the theme both intellectually and emotionally. Noncoercive "ground rules" were developed that provided a framework to help members relate to one another as autonomously and richly as possible. In addition, certain balancing principles were built into the model. Leaders were reminded to keep both thematic and interactional motifs in proper proportion, so that neither was focused on to a degree that proved detrimental to the other. Similar balances were to be established between a concentration on cognition versus feeling in the group, on intrapsychic awareness versus interpersonal awareness, on the here-and-now of the immediate group experience versus the there-and-then of one's past and the outside world (Cohn, 1969). And so the model was born.

In 1966 an organization devoted to the teaching and implementation of the theme-centered interactional method was founded. Called the Workshop Institute for Living-Learning (W.I.L.L.), it was established in New York City. Within the next several years branches were started in Atlanta, Georgia; in Pittsburgh, Pennsylvania; and in Basel, Switzerland. Since that time, a consolidation of the various branches has occurred, so that there is now a W.I.L.L. America and a W.I.L.L. Europe. W.I.L.L. offers ongoing training programs (in the TCI method) for professional and community leaders, consults with community groups and agencies in order to help them develop appropriate workshops within their local settings, and offers time-limited workshops on a wide variety of themes for the general public.

In 1968 Ruth Cohn made her first trip to Western Europe for the purpose of giving TCI workshops. The method seemed to catch hold in Europe with especial strength, in part because other, competing group methods, like gestalt and encounter, had never gained a strong foothold there; in part because many of her participants were teachers (the theme-centered model is probably more applicable to classroom discussion than is any other model), and in part because Cohn herself had been forced to flee some of these very same countries thirty-or-so-years earlier. In 1974 Cohn was invited to take residence in Switzerland as a TCI consultant at the Ecole d'Humanite, an international boarding-school run according to humanistic principles and located in Hasliberg-Goldern, Switzerland. There she has continued the work she had begun in the United States, with particular emphasis on training leaders from within the ranks of education, religion, and industry.

Although theme-centered workshops are usually time-limited, the time span involved may range anywhere from a single afternoon to an entire semester. The latter might be the case in a classroom, or in a course given by the Workshop Institute for Living-Learning. For a course or seminar, an overall theme will describe the content of the entire course, and specific subthemes are then set for each session. While the overall theme is normally determined ahead of time by the educational objective of the course, there is no reason why subthemes cannot be flexible or need be determined by the leader alone. She may invite participants to join her in a consideration of possible themes, and within this context, "Choosing Future Themes" might well constitute an appropriate subtheme for one or two sessions; such is the flexibility of the method.

Some theme-centered group settings are relatively open-ended, with members leaving and joining; the countertransference workshop is an example of such a group. And some psychotherapists have experimented with an application of theme-centered methodology to group therapy, where the therapist sets themes, either beforehand or spontaneously, in accordance with the predominant mood or concerns of the group (Gordon & Liberman, 1983).

## ILLUSTRATION OF A TYPICAL SESSION

In order to give a feeling for what a segment of a typical theme-centered session might be like, we will take as an example a workshop for psychotherapists with the theme of "Freedom and Control in the Psychotherapy Relationship."

> Let us say that a young psychologist Bob, in the context of what has been a relatively intellectual discussion about the concept of freedom, has begun to talk about his relationship to one of his female patients, Sylvia, because he wonders whether some of the limits that he has been trying to set for her—which could be viewed, said Bob, as attempts to constrain her freedom—have really been very effective. Sylvia, a highly labile woman with a severe character disorder, had made some dangerous suicidal gestures in the past month. Bob had strongly encouraged her to "talk out" rather than act out her feelings of depression and desperation, and emphasized his availability to her, at least by telephone, at all times. When Sylvia made a subsequent suicide attempt Bob told her that if this happened again hospitalization would probably be necessary. He had

hoped that her shaky sense of self-control might be buttressed by his firmness. Yet Sylvia had become angry, and when she provocatively asked what would happen if she refused to agree to be hospitalized, Bob had surprised himself by replying, "Then I won't be able to treat you."

Bob had not yet gotten to the denouement of this situation when he was interrupted by Alice, who immediately began to mention Sylvia's marked similarity to one of her own current patients. Bob, who had earlier expressed some discomfort with the theme-centered format, since he was looking for a more formal group-supervision structure, then turned to the leader, Helen, saying in effect: You see what's wrong with these workshops?! There's no rule as to who should speak and when—I like it better when there is a formal case presentation where the therapist first gives all the information and then everybody can discuss it.

At this point the leader asked the rest of the group what they thought about the issue Bob had raised. Joan said that although she didn't want quite that strict a format, she had felt annoyed when Alice inappropriately jumped in. Dorothy said that people should be able to speak whenever they felt like it—after all, wasn't that an advantage a workshop had over a seminar? Jim said: Yes, of course nobody can tell you when you can talk and when you cannot, but there are still rules of common propriety; if everyone felt free to utter his every random thought the result would be chaos. Roger then spoke, saying he was bored with the whole wrangle and wished the group would settle it so he could proceed to discuss a problem that had begun to concern him in relation to his own practice.

The leader said it was her impression that Roger wanted to talk about his problem right away, but was reluctant to speak lest he offend the group, which was struggling to define when it was appropriate to speak and when it wasn't. Roger said it was more simple than that—he didn't want to start talking when he felt that others weren't yet ready to listen. Joan remarked suddenly: You know it's true—the rules here don't give us any guidance as to what to do; they don't even tell us we have to stick with the theme; the funny thing is that Bob wants us to do with Alice what he is trying to do with Sylvia: He wants to make a rule as to when Alice can interrupt, just as he wants to give Sylvia a rule about not acting out and about following his recommendations for hospitalization.

Bob then answered Joan somewhat heatedly: I can proceed in any way I want; I don't have to—and shouldn't—see a patient who's making me too angry and too uncomfortable to be of help! Dorothy laughed, saying to Bob: I guess that's the paradox of freedom—that you're *free* to control others, or at least to try to control them; but you're reacting to Joan as though she had given you orders as to what procedures to follow with Sylvia and what procedures not to follow; if she did that she'd be attempting the same control with you that you seem to try with Sylvia; I know that *my* feeling is that you make an error in not acknowledging her right to make her own free choice, even the choice to die, but that doesn't mean I'm insisting you follow my advice.

After a brief silence, the leader turned to Alice and told her that she, Helen, had been very aware of her silence. Roger then came in angrily, wondering why Helen had chosen this point to intervene when the group was obviously very much interested in the interchange among Bob, Joan, and Dorothy, which had been left hanging; furthermore, said Roger, Helen was over-solicitious of Alice; if Alice had hurt feelings she could doubtless take care of them herself. Alice then said: No, I have been smarting and feeling foolish and embarrassed; Helen made it easier for me to come in just now when she singled me out. Alice went on to report that she often spoke out at the wrong moment, probably as a means of getting attention, and she suddenly remembered some incidents in early adolescence when her mother had become very angry at her for the very same thing and shared these memories with the group. Alice added that even as a therapist she erred in the direction of overactivity and overintrusion into the patient's stream-of-consciousness.

Roger at this point asked the leader if she had been annoyed when he had criticized her intervention. She reminded him of a ground rule suggesting that participants try to state the thoughts and feelings behind their questions. He replied that she had looked slightly angry to him, and that this made him quite uncomfortable, since he always wanted to feel that people in authority liked him. Helen acknowledged that she had been somewhat irritated by his telling her how she "should" lead the group, and wondered if his comments hadn't reflected an overall group concern, perhaps inspired by the freedom vs. control theme, as to how other people should behave: Sylvia should stop her acting out, she as a leader should have both imposed a stricter format on the group and refrained from commenting on Alice's prolonged silence, Alice should not have interrupted, and Bob should not have attempted to set limits on his patient. Bob then smiled and said: That reminds me—I never did get to finish my story about Sylvia and the hospital! This remark produced considerable laughter and appeared to relieve tension in several of the members.

The concepts to be formally presented below apply to, and help to explain, certain key features of the illustration just presented. For instance, the methodological principle of "Dynamic Balancing" (see p. 238) encourages the leader to link the freedom and control theme, which nominally applied to the participants' work with their psychotherapy patients, to the here-and-now of the group interaction. This could be conceived of as establishing a balance between "content" and "process." Other kinds of balances were also evident. Some of the material was cognitive, as when Dorothy wondered about what she thought to be an authoritarian attitude on the part of Bob toward his patient; other material was emotional, like the anger of Roger and Bob, and Alice's hurt feelings. And though the balance between an in-depth focusing on a specific individual and fluid group interaction favored the latter, Alice had said enough about herself to indicate the kind of person she was and Bob had had a chance to discuss specific clinical material in some detail.

## KEY CONCEPTS: PHILOSOPHIC

**Autonomy and Interdependence.**   These two concepts are not unique to the model presently under consideration. They have been attended to by psychological theorists, by philosophers, and by humanists for centuries. *Autonomy* refers to the "I-ness" of my experience and to all experiential phenomena relating to self-awareness and selfhood. As the receiver of all sensations emanating to me from the outside world and as a reactor to these sensations (I feel good about what I perceive, or I feel bad about what I perceive), I am at the center of my universe. I, in my awareness of you, am still at the center of my universe, although you are now part of my universe too. I am autonomous with regard to you in that I can choose the kind of relationship with you that I most want and can attempt to implement that desired relationship; you are autonomous in that you have a choice as to whether to accept, reject, or modify my definition of our relationship. Interdependence exists because my autonomy is not sufficient to the satisfaction of all my needs. Without another person or other persons with whom I can be intimate I will feel lonely; without a sexual partner I will not be able to procreate. This other person does not have to be you—to the extent to which I feel that *only you* can satisfy my needs, I have exchanged my interdependence for symbiosis. We are each separate, yet connected, and Donne's classic "No man is an island...." remains a most poetic statement of this human connectedness (Ronell, 1980).

Autonomy and interdependence are existential givens that can only be denied at the expense of one's fundamental sense of reality; the person who claims helpless and passive dependence blots out his sense of autonomy, just as the isolated, grandiose paranoid attempts to avoid a sense of interdependence. The theme-centered interactional model elevates these two concepts to a place of central importance in its theory and practice by making it incumbent upon the leader to promote both the felt autonomy and interdependence of each participant; we say *felt* autonomy and interdependence because they belong to each member, whether he chooses to acknowledge these aspects of his being or not. The model's structure directs the attention of each participant to his own thoughts and feeling awareness (his autonomy) and to his relatedness to others within the group (his interdependence). How the leader, through certain technical procedures, puts these aspects of the model into operation will be discussed later .

Cohn has always claimed that the theme-centered approach leaves more room for ethical and spiritual concerns than do most group models, and it is via the concepts of autonomy and interdependence that something in the way of an ethical-political, perhaps even spiritual, philosophy is most clearly expressed. A person's autonomy is sacred and inviolable; therefore, he is given great leeway in what he feels and believes, including intense idealism and/or a belief in some kind of higher being. Yet the spiritually oriented person (the "I," if you will), if he is to respect and acknowledge the autonomy of the other (the "Thou") must be ready to grant the latter *his* right to hold to antithetical, materialistic values. In the ensuing dialogue, both the person and the other should strive to maintain an attitude of mutual respect reminiscent of Buber's I-Thou relationship (see Chapter 5).

According to Cohn, it is in part for this reason that various churches in both Switzerland and West Germany have demonstrated, and continue to demonstrate, an intense interest in TCI, frequently sending clergymen, religious education teachers, and student pastors for training in its method. And in assessing why there is this particular connection among TCI, ethical-spiritual concerns, and its particular attractiveness to many Europeans, it should be remembered that TCI was being introduced to West Germany and Switzerland by a Jew who had been forced to flee these very same countries thirty-five years earlier. These countries were, when Cohn arrived, first beginning to truly come to terms with the reality and meaning of the Holocaust.

**The "I-We-It" Triangle.**    This aspect of the model, in combination with the *globe* (a concept to be explained in more detail below), can be conceptualized in visual-spatial terms: What one sees is a flat, two-dimensional triangle (the three points of which represent the I, the We, and the It) bisecting a three-dimensional sphere which represents the globe.

The "I," "We," and "It" are essentially logical constructs, or theoretical abstractions, subsuming specific aspects of the group interaction; each is of equal importance, and each must be kept in mind by the leader as she conducts the group. The "I" encompasses the experience of each person at any point in time, whether or not this experience is directly verbalized or expressed. The "We" refers to the interrelationships within the group at any one point in time and to an awareness, on the part of at least some participants, that they form a distinct, unique group with its own particular dynamics, interconnections, and concerns. The "We," then, subsumes the issue of the group's cohesiveness (or lack of it), and it is via the concept of the "We" that theme-centered theory handles the group-as-a-whole concept that we have already taken up in discussing the group-dynamic group, the gestalt therapy group, and the Tavistock group. It can also be stated that the "I" aspect of the triangle roughly parallels the concept of autonomy, while the "We" focuses on interdependence.

The "It" point of the triangle refers to the theme, or task, that the group meets to consider. It might be thought that the "It" relates only to theme-centered groups, where a theme is formally presented for consideration. However, one of the major tenets of the theme-centered philosophy is that all groups gather with some sort of focus, however implicit, and that the more this focus is explicitly stated and intentionally kept in the forefront of the consciousness of both leader and participant, the more successful will be the group process and outcome. The implicit theme of a psychotherapy group is: I want to feel and function better; of an encounter group: I want to get more in touch with the world inside me and the world outside me. The present model's proponents see as one of its major contributions the explicit attention given to both the emotional-experiential-interactional aspects of the group on the one hand (the "I" and the "We"), and to the group's cognitive-task-learning function on the other (the "It"). Traditional groups (e.g., the committee meeting or the classroom) pay too much heed to the overt task without sufficiently encompassing the affective and interpersonal components of the group (e.g., who is angry? bored? excited?). In contrast, sensitivity groups give too much attention to the "I" and the "We" aspects of the group without giving enough structure and cognitive attention to the specific learning-agenda of the group. For instance, the T-group model's approach to teaching about group dynamics and interpersonal relations is almost entirely experiential; most trainers explicitly discourage an academic or intellectual formulation of group-dynamic principles in the T-group. On the other hand, a theme-centered approach to such learning might well entail a leader's introducing some conceptualization into the discussion, but only at a point where the group process had been sufficiently intense and involving for these group-dynamic concepts to be meaningfully understood and integrated. Relevant here is the motto of the Workshop Institute for Living-Learning, "Sensitivity is Not Enough," which was designed to indicate that people, while sensing and feeling, also think and that self-awareness, albeit important, cannot by itself constitute a solution to the problems confronting today's world. What is also required is the kind of rational planning, political action, and program development that is traditionally encompassed by the concept of "task," and in theme-centered terms, by the concept of "It."

*Content* is another term that is traditionally applied to what theme-centered leaders call "It," whereas *process,* which is usually contrasted to content, is embraced by the theme-centered concepts of "I" and "We." For a certain segment of a group's session its members may find themselves attending to content. For instance, parents of autistic children participating in a workshop with the theme of "Constructively Parenting a Disturbed Child" might talk about the difficult parental situations that they share in common, especially in the early stages of the group; here the "It" or content aspect of the triangle would predominate, though with some attention to the "I" since participants are bound to include at least a few of their personal thoughts and feelings about the problems they face at home. During another segment of the time, process, or "We," aspects of the group may become salient, with participants finding themselves in a discussion of what has been transpiring in the group. For example, a female participant might observe that it is the women in the group who have been the talkers; another member might wonder if this is because they, as mothers, feel more fundamentally related to the child, and still another member might suggest that another important factor is the leader's also being a woman. This "We" segment becomes more strongly tinged with an incipient "I" focus at those moments when a participant begins to elaborate on his personal reactions to the group process. The reader may well wonder when a theme-centered leader views the group process as focused on the "I" point of the triangle with minimal saturations of either the "We" or the "It." Her answer would probably be: whenever an individual, with little overt reference to either the theme or the other people in the group, talks about aspects of his life outside the group–his past, his work, his problems, and so forth.

Usually content and process will coincide at several points within the group interaction; these connections involve the dovetailing of thematic and interactional motifs described at the beginning of the chapter. Let us say that in the parent group mentioned above Lorraine describes herself as overly protective of her child. Ralph then points out to her that she tends to play the same mother-hen role in the group; several other participants agree, and one of them, Cynthia, states that this behavior tends to irritate her. At this point Lorraine begins to talk about her chronic anxiety, which usually manifests itself in a compulsive concern with the welfare of others. In this segment of the group scenario we have an intersecting of "I" (Lorraine and her anxious feelings), of "We" (the other members are giving her feedback as to her role behavior in the group and the feelings that this behavior engenders in them), and of "It" (Lorraine's overly anxious treatment of her child was also briefly in focus).

The "I," "We," and "It" are not all-or-none phenomena; they must always be a matter of n.ore or less. For instance, at a point where a mother in the example above talks about the problems faced by all parents of autistic children she is being relatively abstract and is therefore centered on the "It"; nevertheless her statements are inevitably tinged with an "I" aspect since it is *her* statement and *her* thought. At the point where she expresses her deeper feelings about her particular situation and her child, the "I" focus becomes larger and tends to balance the "It." At a point where she leaves the theme altogether and discusses an experience she had on the way to the workshop that upset her, the "I" focus becomes even larger, while the "It" begins to diminish. If, after a few minutes, another person interrupts her in order to express some of his feeling response to her, the "We" focus, which has thus far remained dormant, starts to enlarge. In attempting to explain these triangle points we have found ourselves envisaging them as three spotlights reflected through a lens-diaphragm; they may expand and they may contract to a mere pinpoint of light, but they never completely go out.

**The Globe.**  The *globe* is an extremely inclusive concept, for it encompasses any aspect of a workshop's environment (including the world-at-large) that is likely to impinge on a participant's awareness or affect his overall orientation to the workshop. This may include the immediate physical environment; the workshop's geographic location, its schedule, the circumstances surrounding its origination, its perceived purpose; and the degree to which members have had prior contact or acquaintanceship with one another. The globe may also include more remote national and international issues, so long as these are in some way a matter of concern to many—if not all—in the group.

The leader needs to be especially alert to those aspects of the globe that may be in some way discomfitting or confusing to the participants; these are the factors that will have to be dealt with explicitly in the workshop. If a serious international crisis has developed the day before the workshop, this fact cannot be ignored. Sometimes there are extreme physical factors that affect the globe (e.g., a breakdown in air-conditioning on a hot summer day). Typically it is more immediate elements, such as the participants' goals and expectations, that become salient aspects of the globe. For example, the participants may be co-workers on the same job who feel that there has been some subtle coercion to join the workshop on the part of their supervisor, even though their entrance into the workshop was supposed to be a matter of free choice. These circumstances do not have to be changed for the workshop to be successful, but it is important that the leader know about them so that she can help the participants to reveal some of their apprehensions, suspicions, and resentments. In some instances the straightforward presentation of relevant information on the part of the leader can go a long way toward "clearing" the emotional atmosphere. In a workshop where participants are co-workers, the leader's explicit statement that she will not give any information as to its proceedings to their supervisor might prove helpful.

Globe factors involving possible feuds, hierarchical constellations, subfactions, and contrary purposes within the group become especially crucial. Such situations are more likely when the leader is an outsider coming into an ongoing agency and/or institutional setting. Whose decision was it that the workshop be held? If it was an administrator's, to what extent has the latter consulted participants as to their feelings about the workshop and been reasonably frank as to his own expectations? To become aware of such factors the leader must do a fairly intensive amount of investigation and information-gathering before the workshop proper. There are no guidelines as to what she does with regard to any or all of these global features. Again, her awareness is all; being aware, she can help participants to contact and express their respective awarenesses of these same factors.

## KEY CONCEPTS: METHODOLOGICAL

**Theme-Setting.** Theme-setting concerns the selection of a theme and its precise wording. It may strike the reader as a relatively straightforward procedure and therefore of not major methodological consequence; yet theme-centered practitioners claim that it is far less simple than it appears and hence have given it considerable emphasis in their conceptual structure.

Advertised workshops provide a situation where theme-setting is a relatively direct affair, since the leader knows the themes in which she is most interested—"Marriage and I," "Overcoming the Generation Gap," and so on;

she, or her sponsoring organization, then attempts to attract a group of people, most of whom are strangers to each other, to a workshop centered on the theme. Situations in which a subcommunity, like a school, agency, or church, call in leaders for help with a concrete situation are more difficult. Here the workshop planners must attempt to diagnose the problem, since the agency directors, being close to the situation, may not be the most expert in labeling their interests and/or difficulties. Consequently, the workshop planner, who will not always be its eventual leader, should be knowledgeable about organizational dynamics; an assessment of the problem precedes her selection of a theme. Is the difficulty one of indirect or faulty communication among the staff members? Or is the problem one of perceptions that are distorted but nonetheless clearly communicated?—two factions, let's say administration and staff, may unrealistically regard each other with antagonism and suspicion and communicate quite accurately to each other this feeling of threat and hostility. Or is the perception a realistic one?—administration and staff have genuinely competing interests, and so long as they do they will not feel comfortable with each other and will look to replace the other with a new set of people. Themes involving empathy and communication would seem most appropriate to the first situation, themes involving prejudiced, stereotyped, and distorted perception to the second, and themes involving a redefinition of goals and expectations to the third. The reader may wonder why theme-centered theorists make so much of the theme, yet it must be pointed out that their rationale is consistent; if it is true that the theme has an important effect on the kinds of things that members bring up for discussion, then the extent to which the theme fits the circumstances and needs of the people attending it is extremely important.

Once the theme is selected there still remains the problem of its precise wording. Theme-centered leaders find that specific words, like overall themes, can have an important effect on participants' expectations. Therefore they have developed several specific guidelines. One is that themes should be worded positively rather than negatively; for instance, "Overcoming the Generation Gap" would probably prove to be a better wording than "Faulty Communication between Parent and Teenager." A second guideline is that the use of the pronoun "I" and the "-ing" form of verbs helps themes to become more personal and more energizing; for example, "Being Myself at Work" might well turn out to have a less deadening effect than would "The Impersonal World of Jobs."

Setting themes within a classroom can also require intensive consideration. The overall theme of a course is usually fairly clear, since it will in most instances correspond directly to the course's purposes as stated in a formal curriculum. More difficult is the session-to-session setting of subthemes. As we mentioned earlier, there is no reason why the teacher cannot invite the participation of the students in setting themes for at least some of the sessions. Ideally a subtheme will reflect the content of what is being taught and read, be broad enough to leave room for varying student reactions to the material at hand, and yet explicit enough for it to evoke meaningful associations and feelings within each student. "Erik Erikson's Eight Stages of Man: Their Meaning in My Life and My Living" would be an example (Erikson, 1964).

**Introductory Procedures.** The theme-centered group leader, in beginning her group, proceeds in a more structured way than does the T-group leader, the group therapist, or the gestalt-workshop leader. She resembles somewhat the encounter leader who chooses to begin his group with some specific "microlab" or nonverbal exercises involving milling, touch, groping with eyes closed, and so forth. In contrast to the encounter leader, however, the theme-centered group leader's procedures are usually verbal. She has two primary aims: (1) to get the group to focus on the theme in a total, thinking-feeling way and (2) to reduce anxiety as much as possible. Her main means of minimizing anxiety, once the group interaction has started, is to respond in a somewhat positive and empathic way to the initial comments of participants. This kind of paraphrasing responsiveness is very similar to that mode of intervention encouraged by Carl Rogers (1951) in his model of client-centered psychotherapy. It helps members to feel less threatened, and it is especially useful in the early stages of a group, when a participant's initial statements are likely to receive no answering comment from another member; the participant's remarks (which however innocuous on the surface may have cost him dearly in the sense of premature exposure and personal vulnerability), unless quickly responded to by the leader, may instead be greeted by a deafening silence which only increases his discomfiture and probably acts as a deterrent to those who are silently debating whether or not to speak up.

One way that theme-centered group leaders like to begin their groups is through a period of silence in which the participants are asked to let their minds revolve around and associate to the theme, which is clearly stated by the leader at the inception of the group. The "triple" silence, wherein the participant is encouraged to internally relate the theme to both his past and the here-and-now, is a favorite of Ruth Cohn and her associates. It will be described and illustrated below. It is important to remember, however, that because silence can severely increase the anxiety of group members, it works best with relatively sophisticated and motivated groups. Where groups are characterized by considerable apprehension and mistrust, the leader can begin in a somewhat informal way, asking people to introduce themselves and to state what meaning the theme has for them and what their expectations are in joining a group concerned with this particular theme. In a workshop entitled "Living Creatively," participants could be asked to discuss those areas of their lives in which they feel themselves to be least creative.

The three steps of the triple silence ask the participant to perform three tasks: (1) to think about the theme, (2) to try to be in contact with, and to intensify, how it feels to be in the group, and (3) to connect a theme-oriented task with the present group. Let's take Ruth Cohn's example of a workshop for counselors and state as its explicit theme "Improving My Counseling Skills" (Cohn 1972, p. 856). In step one, the participant is asked to shut out outside stimuli and to get into himself, especially in relation to his feelings about himself as a professional counselor, both past and present; in order to intensify the experience of turning inwards, he is sometimes asked to close his eyes. This procedure invites a connecting of the "I" and the "It," but not the "We," since the group aspect of the experience is temporarily held in abeyance. In step two, the "I" is linked with the "We." If the participant has had his eyes closed he is asked to open them, to become aware of how it feels physically and emotionally to be in this room with these co-participants. One way of implementing step three, which attempts to link the "I," the "We," and the "It," is to give the following directions: "Please remain silent and choose one of the participants to be your personal counselor. Tell him why you came to visit him and what you want to gain from this visit. Then reverse the situation. Choose another group member whom you would like to counsel. And imagine any reason why this counselee has come to you."

Following the silence, the leader invites the group to interact. One way of offering this invitation that embodies several of the theme-centered ground rules (see below) without listing them in a formal way proceeds as follows (Cohn, 1972, p. 856):

> Let us now communicate about whatever we want to—the theme, my suggestion to you, your experiences, thoughts, feelings, whatever you want to communicate about. Please be your own chairman and try to get whatever you want to get from the group and to give whatever you want to give. I will do the same being my own chairman, and the chairman of the group. Do interrupt when you are bored, distracted, angry or anything else which prevents you from full participation.

In most instances, these introductory procedures will be sufficient to produce some initial interaction around the theme. Subsequent leader-interventions are geared toward maintaining and deepening these processes.

**Dynamic Balancing.** Dynamic balancing refers to the leader's activity in making sure that the group process does not remain overly focused on any one part of the "I-We-It" triangle. Her skill lies in detecting those decisive points at which the group is becoming stuck and is therefore most ready for a shift of some kind (e.g., from "I" to "We"). Her conceptual understanding of the triangle and an ability to sense which of its three aspects is being most seriously neglected will facilitate her ease in balancing.

Certain techniques are helpful in making these transitions. One such technique, the snap-shot device, is often useful in enabling a group to know where each of its members "is at." It works in the following way: The leader creates a "stop-action" situation by snapping her fingers and saying: "Please try to pinpoint just where you were at the moment I snapped my fingers and stopped the action. Now go around, each in turn, and give a *brief* statement of what your inner experience was at that point." It is important that this exercise be handled in a disciplined way; each member is to be as brief as possible, and each person should proceed in order without spontaneous interaction. In other words, even though Member X's experience may have involved negative thoughts about Y, Y is not given a chance to reply until a formal "go-around" has taken place. This is a relatively easy way to introduce a "We" focus and is designed to promote a greater sense of group cohesion.

Encounter techniques can be of aid in intensifying dyadic interactions; two participants experiencing conflict and tension vis-à-vis each other could be asked to come to the center of the room and to engage in verbal or non-verbal dialogue. Here too the "We" focus will be intensified, though now its scope will be reduced to two people instead of the entire group. If the formal theme relates to interpersonal relations, this technique will simultaneously strengthen the "It" point of the triangle. Should the group seem ready for a shift to "I" at a slightly later point, the leader's focusing on a particular individual—should it meet a positive response—will effect such a movement. In the example of the freedom vs. control group cited above, this was precisely what was done when the leader commented on Alice's prolonged silence.

Expertise in the thematic area on the part of the leader is useful, but not absolutely necessary. It is rare for the skilled group leader to have as great an understanding of "Management Relations" as do the executives she is leading. The teacher who uses the theme-centered model in her classroom is conversant with her subject area, but we can imagine a sensitive group leader being brought into a high school class in order to lead a group discussion around poetry, so long as she—along with the participants—has read the relevant poems. Co-leading can be a tremendous aid in the dynamic balancing process, since it permits a division of labor wherein one leader takes primary responsibility for attending to the theme or task aspect of the group process, and the other the interactional aspect.

Themes like "Training Empathy" or "Understanding Group Dynamics" are directly related to here-and-now interpersonal processes. They are what might be described as "sensitivity" themes and in such contexts content and process tend to overlap (as contrasted with a situation where the theme might be "Understanding French Poetry"). The merging of the "I" and the "It," or the "We" and the "It," can make for greater excitement, but also more difficult group-leading, since it is harder to keep the three points of the triangle in distinct focus. The leader is able to introduce an "It" emphasis whenever she focuses on aspects of an emotional interaction that relate to the theme. For example, where the theme is "Training Empathy" she might ask two participants who are in conflict with each other to role-play each other as a means of helping each to connect with what the other is feeling (thereby bringing the group back to the empathy theme); where the theme is "Understanding Group Dynamics" she might ask the group to conceptualize in dynamic terms the interaction that is occurring at that very moment (thereby bringing the group-dynamics theme explicitly into focus).

**Ground Rules.**  In conducting a theme-centered interactional workshop, the leader states several "rules" or procedures that participants should keep in mind in pursuing their dialogue. With the exception of the "Be Your Own Chairperson" rule, which is often stated at the beginning in the manner already indicated (see "Introductory Procedures" above), these guidelines are usually introduced where they are appropriate. For example, the "Speak One At a Time" rule would probably not be mentioned at the beginning of a group but would only be introduced at a point where several members were speaking at once, or where two members were making comments to each other secondary to the main group interaction. Participants sometimes view these rules as coercive restraints; however, it is thought that if the leader presents them with the right spirit, they will be seen as *facilitators* of the group interaction rather than as arbitrary impediments to it. Actually, there is no coercive power behind the rules; any participant is free to "break" them at any time. The leader can only try to make him aware that he is doing so and wonder what his need to flout them might mean. The five rules are as follows:

*1. Be Your Own Chairperson.*  It is an existential given for all group models that the participant, not the leader, has primary responsibility for what he does or doesn't obtain for himself during the session. However, a unique feature of the theme-centered model is the fact that the group leader, as chairperson of the group, is expected to occasionally remind the participant of this existential fact and to in this way attempt to prod him into an ever greater degree of self-chairpersonship. For example, a leader might wonder aloud if Participant X, who has remained silent, is getting from, and giving to, the group as much as he would like. She might even encourage X to take a few moments, while the group waits, to silently develop his own "agenda" as to what he would ideally like to see happen within the remainder of the session—either in relation to himself or others. The leader might then, once X has had the fantasy, encourage him to do his utmost to make whatever he fantasized actually happen.

The ultimate choice of whether or not X begins to overtly participate belongs to X (autonomy), although he may, of course, as a result of the facilitator's encouragement, begin to participate more fully (interdependence). From one point-of-view, the leader's intervention here can be construed as an *interference* with the participant's autonomy; however, from a theme-centered perspective it is an enhancement of it, for the participant's existential freedom and autonomy is such that he may respond to the intervention in any way he wishes, including ignoring it. The leader should also be at pains to remember that a group member's decision to remain silent can be as authentic, or "free," as the choice to speak.

*2. Speak per I.* This guideline is directed toward an attempt to encourage each participant to state his own experience as clearly as possible. Participants very often mask their statements in such a way as to appear to be making generalizations about human behavior; for example, "You find that as you get older…," "One never likes to…," and so forth. Even when a participant is instructed to speak from his own experience and to begin his statements with "I," he frequently—after some initial compliant behavior—finds himself lapsing into "You" statements. When the leader hears a second person statement ("You don't want to be cut off from your family, so you start giving in on small points") she may suggest that the participant try to speak for himself only. Perhaps some of the other people in the group have the same feelings, perhaps not; the participant concerned can always try to find out if others have had the same experience. Some people may argue that the tendency to begin statements with "You" is a habit of syntax, but the theme-centered approach argues that on a deeper psychological level such linguistic customs represent somewhat defensive attempts to project out and to collectivize, rather than to fully *own* and assume responsibility for one's experiences and convictions.

*3. Give the Statement behind Your Question.* Like rules number one and two, this rule encourages each participant to take as much responsibility for his own actions, beliefs, feelings, and concerns as possible. Most questions that one person asks of another hide an unstated concern or curiosity; for example, the very common question of "What do you do?" may mask a more authentic statement of: I feel competitive and am wary lest you have higher status than I—or it might even imply the less complex feeling: I am made more and more anxious by this silence between us. Often in groups, X's emotional reaction to Y becomes obscured by an attempt to "interview" him. For example, X may ask "Do you often get this nervous in a group?" The leader may then intervene with, "X, could you try to state what Y's nervousness does to you? How it makes you feel inside?" We do not wish to imply that all such questions on X's part betoken an egocentric concern; some questions addressed to another group member proceed from a genuinely felt, empathic response to this other person; yet rather than this feeling of closeness being stated more directly, it frequently becomes protectively "embedded" in an inquiry that tries to make the recipient, rather than the questioner, the focus of interest.

*4. Disturbances Take Precedence.* This rule recognizes the fact that no participant can be fully involved in the group process so long as he is acutely bothered by something or experiencing emotional interference. This becomes an especially important issue in nonsensitivity groups like classrooms and committee meetings where it is often assumed that everyone is attending to the theme at hand. The leader, through the "disturbance" rule, encourages each participant to let the group know when he is too distracted or preoccupied to partake fully in the group discussion. However, this kind of autonomous self-responsibility, which is a difficult affair at best, becomes especially burdensome at those moments when a member is upset; therefore it is important for the leader to be alert to the signs and signals of a disturbance in anyone and to encourage him to express his concern to the group. It is often sufficient for a member to simply talk about his feeling, especially if he then receives some sympathy and/or support from other members. At other times, this kind of direct catharsis might not be enough, and certain encounter or gestalt games might prove appropriate. For example, the participant who feels overwhelmed by a sense of group rejection might be encouraged to go around to each member and begin his statement with "I want you to like me for my..." which he then completes differently in each instance. The leader attempts to limit the expression of each disturbance to the here-and-now context as much as is possible, since the workshop's purpose—as a nontherapy group—is *not* to resolve disturbances originating in the past, but to temporarily relieve the participant of his distress to a point where he can return his attention to the group. This is not to say that participants do not find workshops therapeutic in their effect—but many experiences in life are "therapeutic" without constituting formal psychotherapy.

During those moments that the leader works with a "disturbed" participant, the "I" aspect of the theme-centered triangle becomes paramount; yet to the extent to which the leader can get other members to join in (as in the Gestalt-therapy games cited above) or link the disturbance to the group's explicit theme (for example, the participant feels rejected by the group and the theme is: "Collaboration vs. Alienation in Today's Society") a "We" or an "It" focus might also emerge.

*5. Speak One at a Time.* This ground rule is, in a sense, the most practical of the five cited. It constitutes an attempt on the part of the leader to avoid mass confusion in situations where several participants speak simultaneously. All those wishing to speak could be encouraged to "fight for the floor," or the leader could instead ask each of them to say quickly what he wants to say, much like the snap-shot technique mentioned earlier.

This rule is also invoked when there is only one participant speaking as part of the formal group interaction and two or three members have a whispered conversation that constitutes an aside to the "main action." The leader often encourages such members to make their statements to the group at large, since they obviously reflect an unsuccessfully suppressed response to the group process, and as such, are an invaluable part of the group process. Even if the overt content of this side conversation is totally "irrelevant" to the group interaction, such content is usually an implicit statement of boredom and annoyance on the part of the conversers. To the extent to which the conversers are asked to share their side conversation in the spirit of an admonishment they will of course be reluctant to do so; to the extent to which they are asked to in the spirit of making the interaction as meaningful as possible, they might find their embarrassment at being asked to share their experience with the rest of the group less acute.

**Selective Authenticity.**   This concept involves the extent to which the leader shares with the rest of the group her own inner here-and-now experiences, especially as they involve emotional reactions to specific participants. The leader, as chairperson of herself as well as of the group, finds that she, like other participants, has to monitor personal needs for giving and getting; for example, she may be tempted to express hostility toward someone who irritates her and to seek out positive feedback from others. Yet the expression of some of these needs conflicts with her leadership role since they may well impede the group process. Hence the idea of *selective* authenticity: The leader selects from her stream of inner awareness those experiences that help to either facilitate the group interaction or to amplify the theme and states them; she inhibits or delays the expression of those that do not.

An example of selective authenticity was provided in our initial session-segment, when Roger asked the leader if she had been angered by his criticism and she acknowledged that she had been irritated. Her directness doubtless facilitated the group interaction, since any evasion on her part would not only have frustrated Roger and made him that much more anxious lest she dislike him, but also have discouraged other participants from being candid in their expression of feeling. Three other factors could be seen as helping her in her decision: (1) She knew that her feelings were of direct interest to at least one participant (i.e., Roger); (2) the fact that her anger was not intense made it easier for her to be straightforward with Roger; and (3) her reaction was shared at a point where the group cohesion was sufficiently great for some negative feelings, even on the part of the leader, to be expressed.

It is difficult to formulate very general rules as to when authenticity on the part of the leader is growth-promoting for a participant or for the group and when it is not—partly because successful instances of a leader's authentic sharing depend on a subtle balance of many factors existing at a unique moment in a group's progression, and such moments are rarely repeated. A few guidelines, however, seem possible and we will state them within the framework of the "I-We-It" triangle.

It is with respect to the "It," or theme, that the leader has most leeway in sharing herself, particularly when she relates to aspects of the theme that are more intellectual or that relate to her experiences outside the group. For example, in a workshop having marriage as its theme she might wish to share some of her own experiences as a married person; in a theme on "Freedom and Control in the Psychotherapeutic Relationship," the therapist-leader might wish to discuss some of her own cases. Especially in the classroom, it is in the theme area that the teacher-leader usually has most to give to her students. If, for instance, the topic under discussion were "Appreciating the French Novel," her own thoughts about the theme—along with those of her students—would be very relevant.

Greater sensitivity would be demanded in the areas of the "We" and of the "I." With regard to the "We," the leader would be expected to confine herself to observations that are conducive to the greater cohesion of the group; therefore, if she experiences feelings that she suspects are shared by at least some other members and that seem to be impeding cohesiveness, she might want to express them. In the case of her reactions to a specific participant, she tries to confine herself to feelings and observations that will promote the ego-integrity of that person. As in any encounter involving people, whether it be therapy, counseling, or group leading, considerations of tact, timing, and sensitivity are paramount. As was indicated in the discussion of "Introductory Procedures" above, the leader has to take greater care in keeping all her responses positive toward the earlier stages of the group. We can envisage situations where a leader's statement of some irritated feelings toward a particular participant could be constructive—if it helps the latter to attain a deeper understanding of his effect on others without unduly wounding him. Also, the leader might want to share her fantasies about a participant—in a theme discussion involving marriage, the leader might say: "When I imagine you with your spouse I picture you behaving in such-and-such a manner." Here the leader is functioning much as a therapist might—in the sense of using her inner life as a source of hypotheses—but her aim is to deepen the participant's experience in relation to the theme. It would not be appropriate for her, in the example just cited, to share her fantasy about how the participant behaves with his boss or with his daughter.

It might also be appropriate for a leader to occasionally share her own "disturbances" with the group, particularly if these genuinely prevent her from attending closely to the discussion. Many factors would enter into such a decision, including the nature of what is bothering her, the cohesiveness of the group, the emotional maturity of its members, the group's theme, and so forth. Given a sufficiently trusting group atmosphere and a comfortableness on the leader's part with regard to sharing herself personally, this kind of authenticity can prove helpful: It might relieve the leader, at least temporarily, of her burdensome preoccupation and it might enable others to more readily identify with her, thereby promoting a feeling of closeness with the group.

## ROLE OF THE LEADER

By means of its "be your own chairperson" guideline, each participant in a theme-centered workshop is given primary responsibility for making sure that he tries to get something for himself from the discussion, and the leader's role, as "chairperson of the group" is to constantly encourage members to exercise this autonomy. A second leadership role involves an enforcement of the ground rules, wherein members are asked to state their feelings and ideas as directly as possible, and a third requires the leader to keep certain dynamics in a state of relative balance. These dynamics can be briefly summarized as involving: (1) the "I-We-It" triangle, (2) cognition and affect, (3) the here-and-now and the there-and-then, and (4) the intrapsychic and the interpersonal. Ruth Cohn has likened the leader's task in this respect to that of an organist who, through a skillful use of hand-stops and foot-pedals, which soften some sounds and resonances and amplify others, tries to make the richest music possible. Just as the organist's music must bear some relationship to the composition played and to the instrument he is playing, the group interaction, no matter how skilled the leader, cannot be independent of the theme, the globe, and the people participating.

If every person in the group were truly his own chairperson, to the point of saying what was on his mind most of the time, minimal leadership would be necessary and the leader's sole function would be to enforce the ground rules, particularly the one that asked people to speak one at a time. Because members would be actively involved, interaction would be fluid. And, given a diversity of members—some having intellectual interests and some looking for an emotional experience, some tending to be self-involved and some preferring to draw out others, some preferring to stay with the theme and some wanting to digress from it—the group would dynamically balance itself.

In actual experience such a group is rare. The over-talkative member is not necessarily interrupted—at least not soon enough; a digression is not offset by members wanting to find their way back to the theme; and the silent, suffering person who searches for contact does not have his need answered by another participant. Here the interventions of the leader are crucial, and her willingness to be quite active is often the key. If one or two people consistently monopolize the discussion, she might wonder aloud what is happening in the group that twelve people appear willing to listen, in apparent stupefaction, while two persons dominate. If she notices concerted efforts to avoid the theme, she would share this observation with the group; in fact, proceeding on the basis of selective authenticity, she might even express a growing conviction that the theme was either poorly selected or phrased and attempt to rectify this.

The leader has no goals more specific than the balancing ones we have mentioned, especially when the theme under consideration does not involve a specific task or agenda. When it does, she usually hopes for task completion, but the latter will be as much a result of the members' efforts as of her own, and she can have no clear idea ahead of time as to what the final task-product will be. Where personal and learning themes are concerned, the leader strives to enable the group to have a maximally enriched experience around the theme wherein each member feels free to express his thoughts and feelings about it, and to relate to others as they similarly struggle to connect with, and associate to, the theme. Whatever learnings or significant experiences occur around such interchanges are necessarily somewhat amorphous and not easily measured, as is true for all the models of group interaction we have presented. This kind of unprogrammed and experiential learning, which gives considerable responsibility to the learner for what he gains, may appear to be closer to psychotherapy than to education; yet educators increasingly advocate that classroom learning involve a group-discussion process in which learning consists not so much of memorizing facts as of incorporating the ability to see relationships between events and things in ever more novel and diverse ways (Postman & Weingartner, 1969).

The leader relates to a participant's emotional needs only insofar as they either interpenetrate with the theme or distract the participant from the theme. To deal with personal needs other than in the context of the theme would take the workshop into the realm of psychotherapy, which is not its purpose. For example, in the sample session first presented, Roger, after having attacked the leader, worried lest he had incurred her disapproval. In a group therapy context, it would be entirely appropriate for the leader to point out the paradox involved in Roger's acting provocatively toward a transference figure from whom he wants a positive response, but in the theme-centered setting the leader intentionally bypassed this dynamic. Had Roger behaved similarly in a workshop having a theme more relevant to this behavior—for example, "Learning to Express My Needs"—the leader would be more justified in commenting on the paradox. Even here, however, her efforts would be better directed toward helping Roger focus on how he frustrates himself in satisfying conscious needs, like his wish for approval, than on his unconscious need for aggression.

The leader strives to keep the theme in clear, but not perpetual, focus throughout the workshop. A major tenet of the theme-centered method, and it is one that is closely allied to theoretical aspects of Gestalt therapy, holds that a continual theme focus would produce oversaturation and fatigue. Just as the natural rhythm of the perceiver is such that he cannot keep a stimulus "figure" for too long without its become "ground," the theme-centered participant can better attend to a theme if it is occasionally allowed to recede into the background. Spontaneous interactions unrelated to the theme, statements of disturbance, humor and laughter, brief "snap-shots" in which each participant states whatever he was experiencing at a particular moment regardless of whether or not it is theme relevant—all have a place in the workshop. The leader's task is to return the group to the theme—sometimes subtly, sometimes obviously—but only when this is not done by the spontaneous behavior of the participants themselves.

# CHAPTER THIRTEEN
# THE SELF-HELP
# GROUP

*Self-help groups, peer psychotherapy groups,* and *mutual support groups* are interchangeable terms referring to the same phenomenon. Alcoholics Anonymous (to be reviewed in a historical survey, see p. 251) is the earliest example, while Synanon, a program for the rehabilitation of drug addicts cited in Chapter 11 as a precursor of the encounter group, is a more recent prototype.

Self-help groups have long existed as an independent development, parallel to, but outside of, the group therapy movement. There are several reasons for this: (1) Self-help groups tend to avoid professional leadership and affiliations; (2) they consist of a highly homogeneous membership that shares a common problem, affliction, or deviant status; (3) they meet outside such traditional therapy settings as hospitals, clinics, and private practices; (4) they involve an open-ended membership wherein the group's composition is rarely constant (some members might attend every meeting, some might participate sporadically, and some might come to a single session, never to return); and (5) in addition to regularly scheduled sessions, self-help groups provide an informal social network that often involves the participant in a large variety of informal member-to-member contacts, sometimes viewed as more therapeutic than the formal group meetings.

On the other hand, certain developments within the formal group therapy movement, which we enumerate below, have in some ways paralleled key aspects of self-help groups, whether independently or as a direct result of the self-help movement and its influence:

1. The creators of one of the earliest models, the psychoanalytic group, considered from the outset the possibility that members might benefit from "alternate" sessions during which the analyst-leader was absent. One of this session's main purposes was to permit participants to discover what it felt like to be in the company of patient-peers without the presence of the therapist.

2. Chapter 2 described recent developments within social work groups wherein the precise composition of the group changes from meeting to meeting and where the patient's family is also welcome to attend. We also saw how some social work groups become homogeneous to a point where all the participants suffer from a common, frequently chronic, physical disease.

3. In Chapter 9, we described the Tavistock model, which places the small-group session at the center of its learning conference and then extends the range of group experiences offered so as to include a large group event, an intergroup exercise, and a plenary review. In this fashion, the participant is offered a larger range of informal contacts with other participants than is the case with many other models.

4. Chapter 10 described how the laboratory-training experience transplants participants to a "cultural island" where they enjoy constant interaction with fellow participants (with whom they eat and live) in addition to the actual T-group meetings.

5. In Chapter 11, we explored the possibility of grass-roots, nonprofessional leaders who might conduct within their communities encounter groups based on shared interests; in this kind of community group, it is difficult to determine just where formal interactions sessions leave off and informal "rap" sessions begin.

6. Finally, in Chapter 12, we described the theme-centered model. Setting forth a straightforward theme and readily understood guidelines (e.g., "Speak One at a Time" and "Give the Statement behind Your Question"), this is a model whose simplicity renders it applicable to a wide variety of groups in which participants share common concerns. In a paper written in the late 1960s that now seems prophetic of the self-help movement, Cohn and Malamud (1969) encouraged people to form within their communities face-to-face groups that would identify, and help them to deal with, their shared needs and shared dilemmas. Such meetings worked best when there was a preset theme and a designated leader who would be selected from among the participants themselves. Although resting on a theme-centered model, the community-based group envisaged by Cohn and Malamud strongly resembles a contemporary self-help group, where the facilitator is usually drawn from the membership itself, and where, like the leader of Cohn and Malamud's neighborhood and community groups, he is neither a psychotherapist nor a professional facilitator. Instead, he is the person who helped to found and organize the self-help group and normally is a constant figure from one session

to the next; only occasionally will he have received some training in leadership skills. (Although some proponents of self-help groups go so far as to recommend that they have *no* leader—see Ernst & Goodison, 1981—the number of truly leaderless self-help groups is extremely small).

Each of these six developments, whether by deemphasizing the importance of the leader's being a trained professional, selecting a homogeneous—and open-ended—membership, or stressing the helpfulness of member-to-member contacts outside, and apart from, formal group sessions, seems in retrospect to have in part *followed* the model set forth by the earliest self-help groups (e.g., Alcoholics Anonymous; see pp. 251–254), but also, via a process of reciprocal influence, to have in turn helped encourage, and set the stage for, the later proliferation of self-help groups that occurred in the 1970s. In this respect, the group therapy and self-help movements are best envisaged as two distinct, but still parallel and interdependent, tracks.

## ILLUSTRATION OF A TYPICAL SESSION

What appears below is the beginning segment of an actual taped session (with some changes—e.g., names are fictionalized) of a self-help group called Mothers Without Custody, which was founded in 1982 and which by 1986 had fifty chapters throughout the United States (credit is to be given to the California Department of Mental Health for permission to quote this dialog and for funding the film from which it came). At this particular meeting, which takes place in a local church, eight members are present, two of whom are new.

> Jane: My lawyer suggested this group, that maybe it would help me. The first time I came I couldn't talk—I cried the entire time I was here, and that was the cleansing I think I needed. I was able to let it out with people who knew where I was coming from. I gave up custody of my kids because my ex-husband—just like talked me into it. I signed them over and I went back last March and I tried to get them back and I lost by a jury decision.
>
> Ann: My situation was what I call voluntary coerced, which means I didn't fight back for my kids because, for one reason I didn't have any money to fight for them, and I was kind of intimidated by the whole situation—I don't think my lawyer did that good a job for me, but really it was because I didn't tell him what I wanted.
>
> May: I was very young and very ashamed of what I had done. Even though in my heart I knew it was the best for my son, I felt like, what is it that society's going to say about me if I gave him to his father?!
>
> Ann: It's not like you're not their mother anymore and that you don't like them—that has nothing to do with it. Because sometimes it takes a strong and courageous woman to decide that this is what's best for her child, instead of looking at her own selfish interest in it, which would be "I don't want his *father* to have him" when actually he usually has the financial means to take care of the child and you don't. But rather than people looking at what you did as

courageous, they look down on you just because it's the norm. People ask questions, and you get real smart with them, like—(here Ann's voice takes on a strongly exaggerated and ironic tone)—sure, I was a drug addict and a prostitute!! (Much laughter.)

Jane: My ex-husband and I are not on good terms; we haven't spoken in three months. You know, he's remarried, and his wife told me on our last conversation that I was not their mother, that *she* was their mother. (to May) Didn't you have the same experience, May? I believe it was you that said that your ex-husband's current wife said that you were not the children's mother? (May nods.) That *is* very upsetting!

Louise (who is serving as the facilitator of today's session): What were you feeling when that happened, May?

May: Almost hatred; I mean, nothing personal against this woman—after all, I don't know her—but who is *she*? Who does she think she is to say anything like that?!

Jane: I was on the verge of insanity for three weeks after that, it upset me that bad; it wasn't until I came into this group that I got back on an even keel.

Randy: Well, as most of you realize, I'm a new member and I feel like if I don't jump in now and say something, and start to tell you a little bit about *my* story, it's going to get harder and harder for me to talk. When my daughter was three years old her father ran away with her. I tried to find her, and couldn't, so when I finally got back to town I went to see his lawyer. He said: Everything's settled; and they had the papers for me to sign, and if I didn't I would never see my child again, so I signed. When I walk into a baby store (becomes visibly tearful) I see a stroller, and I say I'm gonna get that for her, but I can't anymore—she's already fourteen! And I never had that time with her, when I *could* buy all the things she wanted.

Jane: There's something—I don't know the exact name of it, but it's a family law center, and they don't charge to represent you when you go.

Randy: But that's why I lost her—the lawyer that I had at the time was at that center (her voice trails off while others interrupt with nervous laughter).

Jane: She's fourteen now and they can bring her in and she can tell the judge what she wants, and really! Nine times out of ten...

Randy: We've tried everybody, and what they ask her is: Does your father abuse you? They consider physical abuse the only thing that's dangerous, and if it's mental or emotional abuse, they say: She's a teenager, she'll be OK.

Miranda: I'm doing what I can do with the court process; it's taken me two years to get where I am, and I'm still not finished, and then I have to look and face the reality that I may lose anyway just because of circumstances—money, lawyers, judges, who paid who...and, uh, it's very hard to keep on top of that, you know....

Louise: But you're doing it.

Miranda: Yeah, I am...and this group helps!

The group continues in its session for roughly another sixty minutes and will meet again the following week. The group has a core of seven or eight constant members, while prospective new members are always encouraged to attend a meeting and to then continue as active, on-going participants.

## HISTORICAL BACKGROUND

Any account of the self-help movement must begin with a description of Alcoholics Anonymous, which was the earliest, and most prominent, precursor of today's self-help groups. Its evolution and format proved prototypical of many of the mutual-help groups that followed and it continues to be the largest and best-known self-help network extant in the world today.

## ORIGINS

The first person responsible for the existence of Alcoholics Anonymous was Bill Wilson, age 39, a man who although a problem drinker during most of his adult life had five months earlier successfully renounced drinking, in part through his "drying out" in a New York hospital, and in part through a profound spiritual revelation that he had experienced there. His spiritual awakening had led to his active association with the Oxford Group (an international religious organization advocating a return to the pristine vision and faith of Christianity at the time of its birth) and had left him convinced of both his belief in God and of the fact that one of his best ways of remaining sober lay in his actively helping other drunkards to become sober (Gellman, 1964; Robertson, 1988).

What led to Wilson's co-founding of A.A. with Bob Smith, a man sixteen years his senior and a fellow alcoholic, was his finding himself sorely tempted to drink again while on a business trip to Akron, Ohio. He decided to go to a church directory at his hotel, hoping to locate a member of the Oxford Group. The clergyman whom he chose to telephone, Walter Tunks (a name that he was never to forget), did not belong to the Oxford Group but fortunately knew some people who were, none of whom were available on this particular Saturday afternoon. Wilson's series of phone calls eventually led him to Henrietta Seiberling, a divorcee and member of the Oxford Group who, while not an alcoholic herself, had an interest in saving alcoholics, particularly one alcoholic to whom she had become especially devoted, Dr. Robert Smith, a proctologist (Robertson, 1988).

When Wilson stated that to maintain his sobriety he probably had to speak to a fellow alcoholic, Seiberling, a devoutly religious woman, became persuaded that Wilson's call was a direct result of God's intervention; she proceeded to invite both men to her home. Smith was too drunk to come that day, but despite a hangover appeared at Sieberling's home with his wife the next day (which happened to be Mother's Day). Smith had made his wife promise that they would stay for no longer than a quarter-hour; their visit, however, led to dinner, after which the two men adjourned to the library, where they conversed past eleven o'clock:

They had spent six hours together, most of it alone. No one will ever know exactly what they said to each other. But each told the gist of it later, in countless conversations with other alcoholics. It is clear that the dialogue between the two men who became founders of Alcoholics Anonymous set a pattern that has been followed by millions of drunks all over the world, desperate to be well. (Robertson, 1988, p. 34).

This, and other, conversations between Wilson and Smith helped them to appreciate the value of mutual confession and mutual support, which along with the theme of spirituality gradually coalesced into the heart and center of the organization that they began to found. The sole criterion for membership would simply be that the prospective member have a genuine wish to stop drinking, and because they believed it important that the member be guaranteed the right of anonymity, it was decided that no membership cards would be issued or rosters kept. Thus was Alcoholics Anonymous born. Initially established in 1935, by 1941 it had become an international organization with eight thousand members.

**The Structure and Format of A.A.**    The most frequent and well-attended A.A. sessions consist of what are called the *open* and *closed* meetings. Both alcoholics and the general public are free to attend the open meeting, which is usually held at night. The chairperson of the evening typically begins by telling his "story," which will describe how he initially became a drinker and how he eventually found his way into the organization. He is then followed by the first speaker, who does the same thing. It is the open meeting that a prospective member will first attend. Once the latter has been sober for three consecutive months, he is eligible to speak at an open meeting, and his debut as a speaker is considered to be a significant event by both the membership and himself.

The closed session is open to alcoholics only; it is the A.A. meeting bearing the closest resemblance to the kind of group interaction sessions one encounters in most self-help groups, including the Mothers Without Custody group illustrated above. According to Gellman, this "closed meeting is an authentic form of group psychotherapy and is referred to by many members as the 'workshop' of A.A." (Gellman, 1964, p. 89). Leadership of the closed meeting is rotated, so that no one leader conducts the same group twice during the same one-year period. The leader begins the closed meeting by briefly recounting the history of his recovery from alcoholism, after which the discussion part of the session begins. Here a series of questions are submitted by the members (e.g., "Can alcoholism be viewed as a disease of the personality?"). After the leader makes his own responses to the questions, members are invited to freely comment upon, or revise, the answers thus far offered. The practice of offering various topics to participants for general discussion was to become incorporated into the format of many later self-help groups.

Once a neophyte has joined A.A., he need not confine his participation to one particular group but may decide to attend a wide variety of different groups. Typically a new member will identify primarily with one specific group, but his allegiance need not prove binding. Because members are encouraged to attend several meetings weekly and because no one group meets more than once or twice a week, affiliates of one unit will often visit other units on an evening when their group is not meeting. A similar kind of informality and loose structure has tended to characterize many, if not most, post-A.A. mutual-aid groups.

**The Role of A.A.'s Informal Network.** While open and closed meetings are one part of the program in A.A., the informal contacts continually taking place among members between sessions also constitute an indispensable aspect of the recovery process.

It is usually through contact with an A.A. member at a critical moment that the neophyte comes to attend his first meeting. The crisis is usually similar to the countless ones preceding it. Yet now, via a fortuitous combination of circumstances leading to a direct plea for help from A.A. (let's say from his family or a friend), two of the organization's members come to his home, wait patiently until he is sober, and explain A.A.'s aims and procedures. The absence of a judgmental attitude on the part of the visitors can help the prospective new member to feel more hopeful about his condition than ever before.

The suffering alcoholic may well have to be hospitalized and detoxified before he is ready to attend his first meeting. If hospitalized, he might be visited by one of the members who visited him at his home, and this person will eventually become his sponsor. The latter's responsibilities include helping him to get to his first meeting, to continue to attend meetings as regularly as possible, and to remain sober. The sponsor is encouraged to be as available as he can possibly be, at any time of day or night. Hence "telephone therapy" (Gellman, 1964, p. 138) is an integral ingredient in the newcomer's rehabilitation, and when his sobriety becomes more certain, he will gradually grow independent of his sponsor and may himself eventually become a sponsor for the next new member.

In this way, the continuity of the organization is maintained, and the links comprising its informal network—a member's intimate knowledge of other members, many of whom will belong to local groups other than his own—are thereby extended and strengthened. Behavior that previously led to condemnation and isolation is now openly acknowledged and in fact becomes a bond uniting the membership. Consequently, much of the stigmatization usually attached to deviant behavior is bypassed, and a substitute social order, supplanting that of outside society, established. Appreciating how therapeutic for the individual the removal of stigma can sometimes be, Gellman was in 1964 able to accurately predict the increasingly prominent place that self-help model organizations would occupy in the overall group therapy scene during the coming decade, in part due to the extraordinary influence of the A.A. model:

To whatever extent A.A. has demonstrated its success in dealing with one form of widespread deviance, it is conceivable that its principles may be applicable in other areas. In the next decade many more self-help and lay organizations may emerge as important factors in coping with certain complex social problems. May it not be that the accomplishments of A.A., customarily attributed to spiritual factors, reside instead in the character of the unique social organization of the fellowship? (p. 174).

**The Unfolding of the Self-Help Movement: Later Developments.**  Gellman's prediction proved to be accurate: By the mid-1970s, Katz and Bender (1976) had judged the number of peer psychotherapy groups on the North American continent to be at least a half-million, while Katz's subsequent research (1981) indicated the earlier estimate made by Bender and himself to have been far too conservative. By 1984, there were groups for parents of runaway children, gay children, and disabled children; single parents and abusing parents; Vietnam Veterans; couples choosing to be childless; ex-prisoners; previously hospitalized psychiatric patients; gamblers and drug addicts; and people suffering from any of the approximately two hundred diseases enumerated by the World Health Organization. There were even groups for caseworkers serving the elderly, and it may turn out that similar groups, for professionals who are beginning to experience burnout, will constitute one of the significant trends characterizing the self-help phenomenon during the coming decade (Gartner & Riessman, 1984).

For some distressed people self-help groups provide opportunities for the emotional support, mutual identification, and information that they are unable to get from traditional mental health services. Single parents find themselves discussing the day-to-day problems of finding appropriate baby sitters and day-care centers, and gays still uncomfortable with their sexual orientation talk over problems of "coming out" and of how to present themselves when trying to secure a job. The therapeutic value of such groups was acknowledged in a report prepared for President Carter by his Presidential Commission on Mental Health (1978) emphasizing the constructive role played by self-help groups in meeting the emotional needs of vast segments within our national population and recommending that communities develop "clearinghouses" on mutual support groups, which would make available directories listing the names and locations of specific self-help groups (see "Role of the Mental Health Professional and of the Self-Help Clearinghouse," p. 260).

## KEY CONCEPTS

Some of the main concepts and principles involved in self-help have already been mentioned, such as the therapeutic value of informal member-to-member contact in general and the availability of "telephone therapy" in particular. Another key principle evolves from self-helpers' having been able to found their organization and set it going without any administrative or professional help from outsiders, a fact that engenders a strong sense of group identity, group morale, and group autonomy—"We can do it ourselves" (Lakin, 1985, p. 184). Yet another key principle involves the concept of advocacy, wherein group members are encouraged to work for the kinds of legislative and socioeconomic change that can improve their status and reduce the effects of their disabilities or life circumstances, again a process that encourages them to feel more autonomous and less passive, as separate individuals and as a group. Three additional key concepts are reviewed below.

**The Role of Ideology.**   Ideology, particularly ideology around adversity (why it happens and how it's best dealt with), plays a role in all self-help groups. We saw an example of this in our Mothers Without Custody illustration, when Ann, in coping with potential humiliation and perceived social derision at her loss of custody, developed a comforting rationale (unchallenged by her fellow members) to the effect that their decision to relinquish their children was based on strength and on a genuine concern for the children's welfare. Ideology has an especially central part to play when it comes to behavior control and/or anonymous groups, where members deem some of their behaviors undesirable and as needing to be changed. As Antze puts it, the self-help group aiming for behavior change often "claims a certain wisdom concerning the problem it treats" and "has a specialized system of teachings that members venerate as the secret of recovery" (1979, p. 273). While such "wisdom" is doubtless important in all groups, it is especially needed in a self-help group because of the absence of a therapist who normally symbolizes and embodies it (Lieberman and Borman, 1979); it is most particularly necessary in a behavior-change self-help group, for here members are under constant severe temptation and therefore in need of something reasonably tangible to restrain them—like their "teachings," which are concretely available via books and pamphlets.

Another reason why an explanation-oriented cognitive system is especially therapeutic for some mutual-help groups is the fact that participants here, unlike those in more traditional, heterogeneous groups, share the same status or symptom; therefore, each member can apply the explanation taught by the group as to how the affliction came about (e.g., in a group for overeaters) and how it can best be responded to.

However, the paramount reason accounting for the especially central role of ideology in behavior-control self-help groups involves the sense of stigmatization, or of a "spoiled" personal identity that frequently accompanies *any* addiction (Goffman, 1963). For the group to be effective in removing the sense of stigma and in restoring the participant to a more intact sense of identity, it must help to retell the "story" of how he came to his present state and of what he can do about it. (Probably all therapy groups help to do this for each individual member to some degree, but self-help groups do it in a much more intentional and explicit fashion.) To explain this process more clearly, let us look at the role played by ideology with reference to Alcoholics Anonymous.

A brief review of the clinical data (Antze, 1979) relevant to the alcoholic is needed before we can apply Goffman's stigmatization theory to the functioning of A.A. It has been found that the alcoholic, despite his weaknesses, frequently has a grandiose side in that he possesses an exaggerated feeling of power over the world (a sense of power that, although unrealistic, has some basis in the degree to which he seems able to inflict suffering on those around him). Consequently he often develops an inflated, self-dramatizing guilt over his failure to remain sober. His guilt alternates with an extreme touchiness in response to others' accusations about his drinking, a touchiness wherein he reverses things and accuses them of persecuting *him*. His touchiness now leads to elaborate and poorly rationalized attempts at self-justification. This cycle leads to extreme pain for the alcoholic (as well as for those around him), pain that is handled through the only means the alcoholic has at his disposal for pain reduction—renewed drinking.

A.A. ideology is responsive to these dilemmas in three distinct ways: (1) It teaches the drinker that alcoholism is a disease, one that renders his physical response to alcohol different from that of the average person, thereby relieving him of guilt over his unsuccessful efforts to break his habit; (2) it teaches him that he *can* cease drinking, but only through a reliance on a "higher power." Once he accepts his dependence on a power outside himself, this dependence helps to reduce his grandiose sense of what his will can accomplish; it also helps to diminish his profound feelings of loneliness, because the higher power is presented as a warm, accepting personage. Also assuaging his loneliness and isolation is the mutuality, support, and brotherhood of the overall A.A. network; (3) A.A. encourages the neophyte to engage in a "moral inventory" wherein he takes careful stock of his strengths and weaknesses; he then confesses his wrongs to the group and makes active attempts at restitution vis à vis the people whom he has hurt in his personal life. In the process, his guilt is again alleviated, while his interpersonal relationships are strengthened.

With his grandiosity diminished and with others more available for support, the problem drinker can now engage in a more realistic appraisal of the connections among intention, action, and outcome. According to A.A. ideology, if he is persevering, fortunate, and relentlessly *modest* about his own strengths, he may be able to stay sober. In this fashion, his earlier stigmatization is in part undone and his spoiled identity in part restored. His success at this, however, is portrayed as never to be taken for granted and must be rewon on a daily, if not hourly, basis.

**The "Helper-Therapy" Principle.**    The founders of the psychoanalytic therapy group described the helper-therapy principle (Riessman, 1965) when they pointed out that one advantage of group therapy over individual treatment was the opportunity it afforded a patient to behave in active and helpful ways toward other participants (see Chapter 3). This principle should apply to all groups in which members openly interact with one another. However, it has special applicability to the present group model, where participants are the *only* source of help for each other. This is very different from a traditional therapy group, where no matter how helpful or therapeutic members may be, there will almost always be a tendency to see the therapist as the most potent force for change within the group.

Some of the mechanisms accounting for the therapeutic value of acting in the helping role are: (1) The helper lessens his feeling of dependence on others; (2) he gains an increased sense of interpersonal competence; and (3) as he behaves in a new role, he begins to take on the characteristics of that role:

> The entire helper-therapy concept is derived from role theory, whereby a person playing a role tends to carry out the expectations and requirements of that role. In effect, as a helper the individual displays mastery over the afflicting condition—plays the role of a non-addict, for example—and thereby acquiring the appropriate skills, attitudes, behaviors, and mental set. Having modeled this for others, the individual may see himself or herself as behaving in a new way and may, in effect, take on that role of his or her own. (Gartner & Riessman, 1984, p. 20).

Our previous analysis of the role played by ideology in self-help groups enables us to grasp yet another aspect of the helper-therapy principle—the fact that a participant, in the process of retelling his life story to a new participant, modified in a way that is in keeping with his newly discovered and internalized ideology, becomes further persuaded of its validity. In this way *he himself* becomes one of the persons whom he is helping. For example, a recent joiner of A.A., sober for three months and serving as one of the main presenters at an open meeting, finds that in the process of relating his life tale he becomes even more convinced of the truth of what he is saying. His earlier belief, to the effect that he could easily stop drinking without the help of others, he now sees as unbridled arrogance, and his former denial of a higher power, as dangerously irreverent. This phenomenon illustrates a well-replicated experimental finding of social psychology that goes back at least three decades (Festinger, 1957)—namely that when a communicator attempts to persuade others of something, the person with whom he will usually succeed best is himself. Two ideas reviewed earlier also relate to the helper-therapy principle: (1) the therapeutic importance of a self-help organization's having been founded and administered by the self-helpers themselves and (2) the psychological value of the advocate role that self-help groups frequently play in attempting to create social and political change. In both instances the self-help participant, by becoming an active agent in both his own and the group's behalf, helps himself.

**Prevention.**    There are many documented cases of people who, once they have been put into active touch with their unresolved problems by means of the mutual-aid experience, go on to seek formal psychotherapy (Willen, 1984). However, there are also cases where the group experience seems to have proved sufficiently helpful to prevent further emotional deterioration in the afflicted person so that professional help is not needed. The preventive thrust of self-help groups is especially apparent when the group is designed for people experiencing a sudden loss, like the death of a spouse or child. To the degree to which the person is spared the development of psychological symptoms (which might include serious psychosomatic diseases), those around him, some of whom might be quite vulnerable (e.g., young children), are also spared the impact of his symptoms. In this way, the family members of an afflicted person (e.g., a woman who has recently undergone a mastectomy) might also fare well enough to not have to require mental health services.

Two telling illustrations of the preventive role played by mutual-aid groups involve a group for mothers whose babies were delivered via a Caesarian birth and another for parents of short-statured children. Previous findings had indicated that Caesarian birth, especially when it had been totally unanticipated, was a source of stress for many mothers (and also, therefore, a potential stressor for their newborn child). Through a mutual-support group, women who had experienced a Caesarian birth were provided an opportunity for emotional cartharsis wherein they grieved for the natural birth experience they had looked forward to and been denied. This emotional release enabled them to become more accepting of their infants, and through interactions with mothers who had had similar experiences, to feel less "different" and less alienated. Two other important sequelae tended to follow from the mother's improved emotional state: a lessening of tensions between her and her husband and a much more positive attitude toward the prospect of having another child, who might have to be delivered via a Caesarian procedure (Lipson, 1982).

In our second example, average-sized parents of either newborn or young dwarf children were helped by having contact with other parents in the same situation by joining a local chapter of the Parents Auxiliary of the Little People of America (Ablon, 1982). Even more important than the information they received concerning concrete services, like special classes for their child, was the opportunity to observe other parents who, by means of their reasonably high level of self-esteem and the obvious emotional adjustment of their children, were able to demonstrate that people could come through this experience intact—feeling good about themselves, about the parenting experience, about their dwarfed children, and about their children's futures.

Especially important was the new members' eventual willingness to grant their child more independence than previously, and their gradual acceptance of the fact that no amount of zeal on their part could totally protect their dwarfed child from sometimes insensitive and humiliating responses from other people. For some members, these group interactions were so intense and so relieving that they found themselves laughing *and* crying as they shared the sometimes outrageous, sometimes ludicrous experiences they had had at the hands of the "well-meaning" outside community.

## ROLE OF THE LEADER

The indigenous leader of a self-help group normally has fewer guidelines and a less explicit methodology than does the leader of more traditional therapy groups, where professional leadership training and the learning of a clear-cut theoretical structure are involved. Often the nonprofessional leader of a self-help group is encouraged to do "what comes naturally" and in this sense will operate within a largely common-sense framework. In general he is expected to help as many members as possible express themselves, to discourage unnecessary and random interruptions of the person speaking (particularly when the latter is narrating his or her life story), to keep the discussion going, and to maintain a supportive atmosphere. Some self-help groups leave the nonprofessional leader to his own devices, assuming that he will, after an initial trial-and-error period, hit upon a leadership style that feels comfortable. Other self-help organizations encourage leaders to undergo a period of training, however brief, and to read various manuals and other materials. What follows is based on leadership manuals prepared for self-help facilitators by two separate organizations—Parents Anonymous (1982) and Family Service America (Mallory, 1984). The guidelines that we enumerate represent a culling and combining of the primary principles enunciated in both these manuals; much of what appears in one manual repeats, and is concordant with, what appears in the other.

Facilitators are encouraged to remember that groups do best when: (1) Members have a strong commitment to the group and tend to take responsibility for it, not leaving it to the facilitator to constantly "carry the ball"; (2) older members are encouraged to introduce new members into the folkways and by-laws of the group; (3) every member is heard from at least once during any particular session (however, the facilitator should never actively pressure a silent participant to speak); (4) discussion "monopolizers" are tactfully reminded that other members doubtless have something to say; (5) participants are encouraged to speak *personally* and from "gut feelings," rather than to engage in abstract theorizing; (6) members refrain from attempting to analyze one another's hidden motivations or unconscious strivings; (7) participants learn to *actively* respond to one another's statements (e.g., "Try not to just listen quietly to what Fred says; instead let him know, once he has finished, just what thoughts and feelings his comments stimulate in you"); (8) the facilitator himself models the behaviors that he wishes to encourage in others, including openness, responsiveness, empathy, and emotionality; (9) group members are encouraged to enter into informal contracts wherein they agree to work hard on a problematic attitude or behavior (and the group is then encouraged to hold a member to his/her contract as much as is humanly possible); (10) the leader, though always loving and caring, is willing to actively confront a participant whenever the latter manifests behaviors destructive to the group-at-large; (11) a time for informal social interaction is added at the end of formal meetings or in between them (e.g., parties, picnics, and trips); (12) the leader helps the group to establish definitive norms and limits.

With regard to the last point, what kinds of limits are most essential? In setting limits, the facilitator is encouraged to keep four key issues in mind: (Mallory, 1984) (1) confidentiality: members are not to discuss the group, or its interactions, with outsiders; (2) timekeeping: each participant should be given a chance to present whatever his/her significant feelings, thoughts, or experiences of the week have been, without undue interruption from others; (3) leaving the group: groups tend to work best when any member who is thinking about leaving first discusses this with the group and then, should he decide to stick to his plan, attend a final session in which he will have an opportunity to say good-bye to every other member; (4) conflict and cooperation: direct expression of anger is crucial and not to be evaded; however, the leader should never permit the release of hostility to reach threatening proportions lest this prove too anxiety provoking for the group and too disruptive of its hard-won cohesiveness.

## ROLE OF THE MENTAL HEALTH PROFESSIONAL AND THE SELF-HELP CLEARINGHOUSE

Because self-help groups tend to bypass mental health professionals in the leading of their groups and in the governing of their overall organizations, there has been some ambiguity on their part as to how best to perceive, and relate to, these professionals. One way is to take an antagonistic view of the mental health professional, a not uncommon attitude, particularly when the self-help group succeeds where traditional mental health services have failed— as has often occurred, for example, in the case of treating addictions (Sugarman, 1974).

Nevertheless, it is most often beneficial for the self-help leader and the mental health professional to work in a complementary, rather than competitive, fashion for each has something to offer the other (Gartner & Riessman, 1984). For example, if we look at an alcoholic who is involved in ongoing psychotherapy, we see that the self-help group is able to offer him an immediate social support that his therapist cannot provide; hence this therapist will often refer him to A.A., and his family to Alanon or Alateen. In a reciprocal fashion, the mental health professional has something to offer the self-help group, particularly if it is just getting started. He may well have ideas as to how to recruit members for a beginning group, how to publicize its first meeting, and how to organize its initial sessions. When impasses occur in later stages of the group, he may have concrete suggestions concerning their possible resolution. In fact, Parents Anonymous goes so far as to build into its structure a professional sponsor for each local chapter, who acts as a resource person and consultant for the chairperson-parent leading the group, and as an authority who can appropriately refer parent-members to outside services and resources should this prove necessary (Lieber, 1984). In addition, professionals have been able to make a contribution to the research literature on self-help groups. Using the actual data of various groups, they have formulated theories concerning what tends to work and to not work in running a group, and as to why in certain situations self-help groups are more effective than professionally led ones. On the basis of these findings, they have made recommendations regarding the future role that the self-help movement should play in the delivery of mental health services to the general public (Borman & Lieberman, 1979; Lavoie, 1984).

The self-help clearinghouse, which typically functions under the aegis of professionals offers some of the services just mentioned. For instance, let's say that John Doe, suffering from kidney disease and recently placed on dialysis, finds himself feeling lonely, depressed, and eager to meet and talk with others in a similar situation. He may feel that he has been coping reasonably well but also senses that he could cope still better. In addition, he has learned practical techniques for dealing with his disability that he is eager to share. If there is no existing self-help group for renal-disease patients in Doe's locality, he might want to establish such a group. When he approaches a clearinghouse for help, he will find a place where he can advertise his group, learn the names of other people also on dialysis, enter classes in group leadership, have announcements and mailings photocopied, and perhaps even secure a meeting room for the group. (As the group's founder, it is probably Doe who will become its indigenous leader; whether or not there will be co-leaders, or alternate leaders, will be something for the gradually evolving group to decide).

For the person seeking an on-going group—for example, a recently bereaved widow, Mrs. Y—the clearinghouse can provide a slightly different service. For her appropriate groups are likely to already exist and it is a matter of matching Mrs. Y with the most suitable group. This is not always an easy task, since in an urban area she may well have more than one group to choose from. The first might be indigenous to the local area, while the second is a local affiliate of a national organization. In consultation with the clearinghouse, Mrs. Y will decide which group would seem to serve her needs best. Should her initial choice prove unsatisfactory, she may wish to try a different group, and should she desire further consultation as she goes about selecting another group, the clearinghouse will again be available to help.

# CHAPTER FOURTEEN
# INTEGRATION
# AND PERSPECTIVES

In this final chapter, we return to the global orientation of our introduction in order to view our models from a broader perspective focusing on their commonalities. First we will briefly review the therapeutic processes inherent in group psychotherapy in general, then we will explore some of the ethical and procedural dilemmas characterizing all the models, and last we will make some predictions as to probable future trends within the group psychotherapy movement.

## THERAPEUTIC PROCESSES IN GROUP PSYCHOTHERAPY

Until this point, we have had as our primary aim describing the special characteristics—historical, conceptual, and methodological—of each model presented. In addition, we have compared a number of the group modalities in several instances, particularly when there seemed to be striking commonalities or clear-cut differences among them.

Now it seems worth turning our attention to the common features of *all* these approaches. A number of theorists, most notably Yalom (1970, 1975, 1985), as well as Scheidlinger (1982), Rutan & Stone (1984), Roback (1984), and Lakin (1985), have attempted to systematically identify the therapeutic factors inherent in *any* form of group therapy, particularly factors that characterize therapeutic activity in a group, as opposed to individual, setting.

We have synthesized the most frequently cited factors into five categories, which we have labeled (1) observation of self and others, (2) identifying and practicing new behaviors, (3) recasting problems and developing strengths, (4) group support, and (5) therapist's observations.

The first category, observation of self and others, includes several factors. The group experience affords each member the opportunity to learn that he is not alone in having problems, a fact that becomes abundantly clear as members have opportunity after opportunity to describe their life circumstances and painful experiences. The group also allows the participant to observe other member's capacity to self-disclose, which in turn will encourage him to make similar self-disclosures. In addition, members inevitably become aware, often in a dramatic fashion, of how distorted their particular perceptions of the therapist are, since fellow members will undoubtedly perceive and respond to the therapist in quite different ways. Finally, the group creates a setting in which multiple transferences become possible, because of the presence of members of different ages and genders. Transference reactions that are sometimes difficult to achieve in individual therapy become more possible when additional stimuli, in the form of group members, are provided.

The second set of characteristics centers around the many chances that a group provides for a patient's identifying and practicing new behaviors. To begin with, members typically receive more feedback about how others react to them than is available in either individual therapy or normal social living. At the same time members have an opportunity to observe appropriate and attractive behaviors in others—behaviors that they may then decide to emulate. Emotional learning becomes possible, too, as participants learn, via observing other participants, that it is all right to express intense feelings, including hostility—even hostility toward the therapist. Finally, participants can practice their still tentative new behaviors in the protected environment of the group setting.

The third set of characteristics, recasting problems and developing new strengths, is probably best exemplified by the fact that members find themselves being empathic with others in the group and learning that they have resources for responsive understanding that they had hitherto been unaware of. The group experience reawakens issues originally experienced within their childhood family settings; however, within the group, members are able to reexperience these feelings and relationships in an environment that facilitates a more favorable outcome.

Group support is most clearly illustrated by the concept of *cohesiveness,* which refers to both the intensity of interrelationships among the participants and to the group's overall attractiveness for its members in general. Cohesiveness plays a facilitative role for other therapeutic factors rather than constituting a therapeutic factor in its own right; for instance, the more cohesive a group is, the more it encourages disclosure on the part of each member. As self-disclosure increases, both interpersonal learning and growth become more likely. Another group support characteristic is the instillation of hope. While a therapist can of course offer and embody hope for a client in one-to-one psychotherapy, entry into an already functioning group surrounds patients with people who have already been helped and who are able to share information about that help in a concrete way that few therapists are able to do.

Our final characteristic notes that working in a group enables the therapist to observe vividly a patient's typical style of interacting with a variety of people—all the other members in the group—that is not possible in individual work. In our experience many therapists who have worked with a particular patient intensively through a period of individual therapy express frequent surprise at a patient's behavior once he or she has joined a psychotherapy group. Patients who appear relatively confident are shy and reserved with their fellow members, while the self-described introvert may display charm, ease, and humor. In addition, the new patient in the group may suddenly develop an intense and unpredicted transference in relation to a specific member.

## ETHICAL ISSUES IN GROUP PSYCHOTHERAPY

Now that we have concentrated on those processes that tend to be most *helpful* to the group patient, we can turn to a second issue common to all the models—namely the factors inherent in the group therapy situation that appear to put him at risk and those ethical procedures or stances on the part of the leader that best minimize or offset this risk. An ethical focus at this point is especially important, first because it has not been fully addressed in the group therapy literature and second because ethical issues become more ambiguous and more complex as one moves from individual therapy to group therapy. Why more complex? First, in the group situation there is a far greater number of persons who can have a potentially destructive effect on the patient. Second, the advent of two recent models—encounter and self-help—increases the likelihood of group leaders' having received a minimal degree of training, when it is just such training that can best sensitize them to ethical dilemmas, increase their appreciation of the subtle effects that group patients have on one another, and improve their skills in making interventions that minimize the risk factors to be explored below.

Another reason, less often mentioned, as to why ethical soundness on the leader's part is so crucial lies in the moral dimension inherent in the kind of change patients ideally undergo in both group and individual therapy (London, 1964; Szasz, 1965). Whether viewed in terms of Freud's "genital character" (who is capable of loving in an altruistic, nonpossessive way) or the importance of a person's gradually internalizing, as he or she develops, a healthy "superego" or conscience, many therapists believe that while they strive to eschew *specific* goals for a patient (e.g., marrying, divorcing, having children, changing jobs, etc.), they hold a generalized aim of helping him or her relate to others in a caring, nonexploitive fashion. Hence, if a group therapist fails to relate to a patient in these ways or permits other members to similarly fail, she does not furnish an appropriate model of mature, protective behavior for the group-at-large. One would of course hope to see a patient shield himself from abuse at the hands of a fellow participant without requiring the therapist's aid, but for many patients, if not the majority, the ability to do this is more likely to *follow* an experience in group therapy than to precede it.

According to Lakin, the group should be led in a fashion "that does not denigrate members, assail their dignity as humans, or exploit their needs" (1985, p. 228). We present below the ethical dilemmas that most typically confront the group's leader as she goes about fulfilling this task.

**Pregroup Screening and Informed Consent.** Ethical guidelines established by the Association for Specialists in Group Work (1980), which is in turn a branch of the American Personnel and Guidance Association (APGA), require that group leaders conduct pregroup screening sessions for prospective participants in order to ensure that they are appropriate candidates for the group and, if so, to orient them as to what is likely to happen in the group.

With regard to orientation, some general points that a leader will do well to touch on are: potential risks (e.g., possible changes in lifestyle that can occur as a consequence of group participation), information about any unanticipated procedures to be used (e.g., nonverbal exercises), any formal recording or taping of sessions that will take place, expectations of confidentiality, and finally what the group can, and cannot, reasonably be expected to accomplish. The leader should also remind prospective members that participation in the group is entirely voluntary whenever this is in fact the case. When it comes to preparing prospective members for just what occurs in a specific group meeting, the leader should attempt to steer a fine line between overpreparing them for an experience that is hard to describe beforehand (a preparation that can increase, rather than diminish, anxiety) and giving them no orientation whatever. Preparation for group experiences is therefore simplest when it grows out of a model involving rather specific methods, techniques, and exercises which can be fairly easily explained and illustrated (such as psychodrama, gestalt, behavioral, and encounter). Where the group interaction appears to be more conventional and conversational (as in social work, psychoanalytic, and existential), it is harder to help the novice grasp how such group interactions differ enough from those of everyday life to be unique and therapeutic. Here the leader probably does best to give a general sense of the kinds of interactions that typically occur and of what her role will be in responding to them and to then acknowledge that beyond this only the inter-action itself can fill in the details of what the group experience will involve, particularly in terms of its emotional flavor and impact.

With regard to the selection of candidates for the group, such a proce-dure is more essential when the leader has had no prior exposure to a prospec-tive participant than when, as in the psychoanalytic situation, the candidate is already known to the leader via a previous period of individual therapy. Where members have not been previously known to the leader, she must be alert for the kind of emotionally fragile person who is overwhelmed by intense feelings in others, who would appear to be especially susceptible to being scapegoated, and who cannot adequately express himself (Lakin, 1985); here the leader's responsibility is to block, however gently and tactfully, the prospective member's entry into the group.

**Confidentiality.** It is expected that whenever a group's privacy is abrogated by a formal recording of the group interaction, each group member should be apprised of this, along with information concerning how the recorded material will be used and whether such use will in any way compromise his anonymity.

The confidentiality issues involved in formal recording are straightfor-ward and easily enforced when compared with what is usually meant by con-fidentiality—namely, how much each participant reveals about the group to people outside the group. A conservative interpretation of this guideline states that nothing should be revealed about the group interaction, even if the iden-tities of those involved are kept hidden. A more relaxed interpretation sug-gests that a member will from time to time of course reveal interesting happenings within his group—to spouses and to friends—but this is all right provided that the members' anonymity is protected. Whichever interpretation one uses, the rule of confidentiality would appear to be one that is as much honored in the breach as in its adoption; this has been our own personal ob-servation, as well as that of others (e.g., see Lakin, 1985).

There are several reasons why confidentiality is not always maintained: (1) It constitutes a rule that is virtually impossible to enforce; (2) the fact that a member can tell other people about events within the group without reveal-ing the identity of those involved permits him the rationalization that he is still remaining within the spirit of the law, if not its letter; and (3) members may have as many positive reasons for wishing to break confidentiality (e.g., want-ing to share an important emotional experience) as negative ones (e.g., in-directly releasing hostility felt toward another participant, or toward the leader, by "gossiping" about them).

Despite the factors just enumerated, it is important that the leader keep the rule in the forefront of the group's awareness by frequently mentioning it and by attempting to check from time to time as to how carefully it is being main-tained. The more this is done in a nonauthoritarian manner that encourages each participant to be responsible for his own behavior, the greater is the likelihood that confidentiality will not be flagrantly violated (Lakin, 1985). Although some members claim that it does not matter to them if strangers whom they will probably never meet "know my business," others state that only with an assumption of confidentiality can they risk maximum self-disclosure. Hence, if the group is to provide an atmosphere wherein *each and every* participant can comfortably reveal himself, it is in the mutual interest of the entire group that the confidentiality of their interactions be protected. The leader needs to assert and reassert this principle, although aware that confidentiality can never be fully guaranteed. The more the leader observes the rule, the higher the probability that the participants will, for it is highly unlikely that a leader who does not take a group norm seriously can effectively maintain it.

**Coercion and Manipulation.** *Coercion* refers to the fact that in certain instances group membership is not voluntary, as when a sexual abuser is sent by a family court to a group for incest offenders. The fact that group participation is involuntary need not prohibit the group from being therapeutic; however, it is imperative that the leader acknowledge the fact of coercion and ensure that the participants feel free to explore how they feel and what their questions are about it (Lakin, 1985). For example, members will doubtless tend to wonder about how and when they may leave the group. If we use our incest offenders group as an example, a participant may also have serious concerns about confidentiality—what will his leader say when asked by the court about his readiness for supervised visitation with the child whom he molested? Since this procedure almost always occurs in situations involving incest, the leader needs to spell out in detail ahead of time what information she will and will not reveal.

A more frequent concern than coercion is that of potential *manipulation* of a participant, either by the leader or by the group. When emanating from one's fellow members, this kind of manipulation or influence constitutes the well-known phenomenon of *group pressure.* Any group situation renders a person susceptible to influence, whether by interpretation, advice, support, confrontation, or exhortation. (This fact has received ample demonstration in widely publicized research indicating that, in order to conform with the expectations of others, some people will claim to see something different from what they actually see and will perform actions about which they have grave ethical reservations; see Asch, 1952; Milgram, 1974.) Indeed, if a group were unable to exert *any* influence on a participant, there would be no point in placing him in the group in the first place! However, it had been the hope of early practitioners of the social work and psychoanalytic group models, just as it had been the faith of Lewin and his co-workers in founding the T-group, that participants would be changed by, and benefit from, their respective groups without any serious injuries to their autonomy. This viewpoint characterizes all of the models presented in the previous chapters, since each rests on the assumption that the group can have a valuable impact on the participant without seriously compromising his individuality.

Focusing on the participant's sense of autonomy or personal integrity provides us with a useful means for differentiating between the helpful and potentially harmful effects of a group (Lakin, 1985). For instance, let's say that a participant, Louise, has acknowledged to her group that there is something in her past about which she feels extremely ashamed; part of her would love to unburden herself by confessing it to the group, but another part is terrified to do so. What if the group then says to Louise something like: We respect your right to keep something private if that is what you must do, but we also hope that you will eventually trust us with your secret because you seem to want to do so more than not do so, because we think you will probably feel relief in doing so, and because we believe we will not dishonor your trust. This constitutes a situation in which a group supports and encourages an individual *without* attempting to unduly pressure or manipulate her.

Let us take as a second hypothetical example, Sheila. Sheila has been a member of a five-day workshop billed as "an encounter experience designed to increase interpersonal sensitivity and group awareness," which has involved spontaneous group interaction, plus some use of games and exercises. Although each of the other seven members has "taken a turn" in allowing the group's attention to fall on him or her for a prolonged period of time (in which the person, either via gestalt or psychodrama exercises, reveals a significant childhood conflict or trauma), Sheila has chosen not to do, claiming that she does not yet feel sufficiently comfortable with the group and has some reservations about the leader's trustworthiness. She adds that because she is currently in individual therapy she does not feel the strong need to work on personal issues; her primary motivation in joining the group was to experience what it was like, to learn something about group process, and to see if she could improve her interpersonal and communication skills. Several group members then challenge her, saying "Everyone has had an opportunity to get out feelings but you—it's your turn" and "You're obviously very angry, and the only way you're going to help yourself is by expressing your anger!"

Surely, Sheila has every right in this situation to choose *not* to take a turn. Her ability to hold distinct opinions about herself, about what she is ready for and needs, and to *trust* these self-perceptions, seems a healthy development— one that should be nurtured and validated by the group. We also wonder how peer participants are by themselves able to make a clinical determination to the effect that a patient's core dynamic problem is anger, and even if they are correct, how are they to decide if it is therapeutic for this anger to be *immediately* expressed? In all potentially manipulative situations of this kind, the leader or therapist's role is crucial and whether or not she chooses to actively intervene, her behavior will have an influence on the group.

Indeed, extremely few groups are able to act in ways that are consistently protective of a fellow member's integrity without the active watchfulness or intervention of its leader, for even in the most therapeutic groups members will sometimes behave toward one another in pressuring and unhelpful ways. The overt stance that the leader takes in relation to these potential influences is crucial; it is our feeling, as well as that of others (Lakin, 1985), that she must at times assertively intervene in order to protect a member's personal integrity, particularly at that point where the member seems tempted to succumb to the group's pressure. For instance, if the group is pressing the member to do something dramatic (e.g., participate in a gestalt or psychodrama exercise), the group leader would do well to ask "Would you go ahead and still do this if you could know for sure that the group and I would like you just as well if you didn't?"

Sometimes *the leader* attempts to pressure a participant, and if the latter is already vulnerable to the influence of fellow participants, he is probably that much more so to the leader's influence. Ironically, leaders too can be pressured and influenced by group members; when members have come with high expectations of dramatic breakthroughs and are already in a state of high affective arousal, the leader may feel compelled to "push" those members, like Sheila, who have not yet achieved a dramatic catharsis of one sort or another. "[I]nsofar as members take on the attributes of an audience,...the leader is induced to produce increasingly dramatic displays for them" (Lakin, 1985, p. 241).

All these factors make it abundantly clear that the ultimate responsibility for a group's ability to confuse a member about who he really is, or what he really wants, lies more with its leader than with its peer participants. While the presence of fellow members, in addition to a therapist, can at times help to dramatically confront a patient with aspects of his character that are highly bothersome to others, the leader will at times have to act to protect the patient from feedback that is stated in an overly brutal fashion, that is unjustifiably critical, or that is, from her (i.e., the leader's) point of view, inaccurate.

**Casualties.** A group *casualty* refers to an emotional breakdown, or severe emotional crisis, occurring in a person as an apparent result of his having participated in an intensive group experience. During the height of the human potential movement, such incidents were said to have happened in connection with short-term groups, whether labeled as an "encounter" or "marathon," and one empirical investigation cited an 8 percent casualty rate for people who had had membership in such groups (Lieberman, Yalom, & Miles, 1973). Although some have disagreed with this estimate (Rogers, 1970; Gibb, 1971), there has been a consensus to the effect that casualties can and do occur, in however small a number (Lakin, 1985).

Why might a small-group participant become a casualty? In citing reasons, we refer the reader to the immediately preceding section, where we spelled out some of the ways in which a member might be at risk. Did he say or do things that he now regrets, or hear something—an interpretation, or a piece of feedback—that he now finds difficult to integrate with his self-concept? If so, there is always the possibility that he will become extremely upset. While such distress is theoretically possible in long-term therapy groups, it seems more likely in short-term groups, particularly encounter groups, where there is pressure for immediate, frequently dramatic results; where the facilitator (unlike the T-group leader, for example) embraces openly therapeutic goals and does not avoid an exploration of one's past or one's unconscious; where the participant has far less opportunity to integrate, understand, and work through, in session after session, what he has experienced and learned in the group; where the participant, after a period of intense psychological exposure and intimacy, will find himself suddenly bereft, emotionally and sometimes geographically, of both his facilitator and his fellow group members; where the leader has not always received intensive training—as either a psychotherapist or a professional group leader. Furthermore, the encounter leader, like the encounter participant, is under pressure for fast results without having the chance to become well-acquainted with each other; knowing the participants, less thoroughly, the leader is in a weaker position to estimate the degree of his emotional vulnerability in general or his special sensitivities in particular.

What can a leader do to minimize the likelihood of serious distress in a particular individual? All the caveats mentioned in the preceding section seem relevant, including her carefulness in checking how a participant is specifically reacting to feedback. Most important of all, the leader must do whatever she can to make herself available to a group participant, should the latter begin to experience extreme emotional vulnerability or discomfort following an intensive group experience. This was a unique advantage that we found to exist in Mintz's encounter model, since she is almost always in a position to offer geographic proximity to a participant subsequent to her marathon weekends (see Chapter 11). Where a leader is not able to be geographically available, she should be reachable by telephone and in a position to make as effective a referral as she can within a reasonable radius of the participant's home. The participant should also, at both the outset and conclusion of the group, be told that there is some possibility, however small, of this kind of adverse reaction and of where he will be able to contact the group leader following the group's disbanding.

**Professional Accreditation.**    Although group leaders can be certified through the Association of Specialists in Group Work and the American Group Psychotherapy Association (one purpose of such accreditation being to ensure an appreciation of ethical issues, as well as to ensure other competencies and skills), many group therapists have expressed pessimism regarding our ability to hold leaders ethically accountable (Lakin, 1985). The reasons for this are: (1) The guidelines for the training of group leaders and therapists are even more ambiguous than those already vague guidelines defining the training and practice of individual therapy; (2) in some group models (e.g., self-help) leaders need to have received minimal, if any, training; and (3) teaching and talking about ethical issues to someone does not guarantee that he or she will behave ethically. Even so, it seems clear that discussing ethical issues and guidelines with the potential group practitioner will not make her *less* ethical, while there is every chance that such discussion might render her more thoughtful and concerned about each of the issues mentioned above. Therefore it is our recommendation that the kind of general guidelines presented by us be shared and discussed with anybody who will have some degree of responsibility for planning and/or leading any of the kinds of groups reviewed in this book.

## CURRENT TRENDS IN GROUP PSYCHOTHERAPY

Current developments have borne out the predictions we made in the first edition of this book (1974), where we anticipated a decreasing emphasis on adherence to specific models and a greater blending or merging of models in which there would be an eclectic usage of aspects of various approaches. Probably this is most clearly seen in self-help groups, described in Chapter 13, which typically do not draw on a particular theoretical orientation or adhere to a specific model but instead make use of a variety of techniques and approaches, in an effort to discover ways of helping people cope with common life stresses or problematic behaviors. Other indications of this trend are seen in a lessening of enthusiasm for either the pure encounter group or for other broadly focused growth and development groups, and an increasing emphasis on task-oriented, frequently short-term groups (e.g., behavior modification, theme-centered, and T-). We shall have more to say below concerning this issue of overly amorphous versus clear-cut and concrete group tasks.

In a parallel fashion, Scheidlinger (1982) predicted an emphasis on short-term group modalities that are well-suited to the unique problems shared by particular (frequently disadvantaged or stigmatized) subgroups within our society (e.g., substance abusers and the elderly). In this volume we have tried to anticipate, and point the way toward, this same trend: In Chapter 2, we stressed the flexibility and eclecticism of the social work model; in Chapter 12, we underscored the theme-centered model's ability to adapt its format to a wide variety of issues and populations; and in Chapter 13, we described how people in immediate crisis sometimes use peer groups, with peer leaders, to find emotional support and, if needed, concrete social services. The predominant contemporary development within group psychotherapy, then, is the emergence of homogeneous groups—either short-term or open-ended—devoted to the special needs of a particular population (Rosenbaum, 1984). Such groups, while varying in their theoretical orientation, would seem to resemble, and in some way combine, the social work, theme-centered, and/or self-help models.

*Disease management* groups, a term devised by Roback (1984) and describing groups created for patients having the same illness offer an excellent example of the kind of short-term, frequently open-ended group we have been describing. Such groups attempt to show patients in concrete ways that they are not alone, help to instill hope, create some degree of empathy and mutual identification around shared physical discomfort, suggest coping strategies (e.g., how to deal with a specific handicap), and at times impart vitally needed information (e.g., counteracting the false belief that multiple sclerosis will, over time, impair the patient's intellectual functioning). This group is also appropriate for family members who need to cope not only with the patient's reactions, both physical and psychological, to his or her disease, but with their own stress and not infrequent despair. Roback prefers to see his model as novel and unique, without ties to previous models, and in describing the leader's role highlights such leader functions as "information disseminator," "catalyst," "orchestrator," and "model for learning." However, in terms of its frequent open-endedness, its concern with providing cognitive information as well as emotional relief, and its encouragement of strong member-to-member ties (which gradually replace the need for active direction from the group facilitator or leader), the disease management group clearly falls somewhere in the range of groups encompassed by the social work, theme-centered, and self-help models, thereby supporting our contention that differences between and among various group models have over time become less and less marked.

What we have witnessed, then, since this book's initial edition, which reviewed the group psychotherapy scene in the mid-seventies, is a lessened interest in the quest for intimacy, community, and self-actualization characterizing the growth and development groups—especially encounter—that flourished in the late 1960s and through much of the 1970s. For although encounter groups, and those groups resembling them, were in fact short-term (like the homogeneous groups more commonly seen today), they brought together people of frequently dissimilar backgrounds who had generalized aims of becoming more sensitive, more intimate or "related," and more fulfilled; surely such people constitute a quite different group from recently bereaved widows and widowers brought together to discuss their common plight. What might prove initially perplexing is that this transition, from groups having a generalized and amorphous agenda to groups having a much more clear-cut one, has occurred despite the fact that a strong motivating factor for encounter, and similar groups, would seem to still hold true today: widespread alienation which in the 1960s and 1970s led to the search for roots and community, for intimacy and connection, that encounter and similar groups appeared to satisfy if only temporarily. We shall attempt to explain this paradox.

One possible reason for the lessened popularity of encounter revolves around the question that we raised at an earlier point (Shaffer & Galinsky,

1974) of whether *any* small-group structure, encounter or otherwise, can have as an overt goal the creation of a genuine and intimate community, however attractive this goal might be. For all of the small-group experiences that we have surveyed will end, and none of them entails a true living together for twenty-four hours a day; the critical issue then becomes the degree to which the participant has been enabled to transfer to his outside living whatever sense of community, and of cooperative give-and-take, he has gained from the group experience. A true community, whether large or small, must unite its members in a way that goes beyond emotional sharing for its own sake; it must provide for health and safety, see to the education of its children, and so on. It is interesting to recall in this regard that Fritz Perls's solution to the problem of building "community" into his gestalt therapy model was for his workshop participants to actually live together in a commune that he founded on Vancouver Island during the last years of his life. His efforts in this direction would seem to have reflected a similar conclusion on his part.

Another possible reason for the decline of encounter, at least as a social movement, revolves around a second question: Can a group meaningfully offer as one of its primary purposes the creation of intimate connections among its members? This is not to say, of course, that intimacy doesn't develop as a group goes about fulfilling what is its main purpose or task—giving and receiving feedback in the case of a T-group, or discussing how it feels to have a debilitating illness in a disease management group. What was unique to the encounter model, however, was that it frequently made the creation of intimacy one of its primary goals and then went on to equate intimacy with openness, the assumption being that the more openness there is in the group, the more intimacy. It strikes both us and others (e.g., see Back, 1972) that there is something strangely impersonal—or at least unselective—about this kind of group intimacy, since what one reveals is not necessarily a function of a particular relationship between persons who know and care about one another. Instead the encounter participant is expected to quickly want to share his confidences with every person within the group and with whatever group he finds himself in. Even in long-term therapy groups (e.g., psychoanalytic groups), intimacy is usually not made an end in itself, but develops over time, as members go about fulfilling their primary aim, which is to feel better and to function more effectively. Feelings, thoughts, and events about which a member feels deeply ashamed may take a long time to emerge and the competent group leader rarely pressures, or attempts to hurry, such revelations. In fact, we can envisage certain cases where a particular patient, overly gregarious and frequently impulsive, needs to be directed toward relating with *less* rather than greater intimacy—or at least with a more discriminating style of involvement with others.

Intimacy is probably not a viable goal in itself, but usually evolves as an outgrowth of other engagements and other efforts. Even in marriage it is often an accompaniment to, and consequence of, joint endeavors involving child-rearing and household management. Hence it strikes us that another reason for the declining interest in short-term groups emphasizing intimacy and self-fulfillment is the fact that such groups, in abandoning the clearer structure and goals of earlier group models, left themselves with an insufficient context in which to function. It is precisely along this dimension of a viable agenda that we see such groups as social work, T-, theme-centered, and self-help as having more structure and meaning for their participants, because in such groups whatever sense of intimacy, community, or satisfaction develops is a *byproduct* of the group's attempt to accomplish a tangible goal.

We have yet another reason to offer for the diminished prominence of what were earlier called encounter, sensitivity, self-actualization, or growth and development groups. While no one seriously suggests that we see before us a less alienated society today (statistics detailing the incidence or crime, sexual abuse, and substance addiction certainly don't indicate otherwise), we have witnessed since 1974 a diminution in the overt and openly intense yearnings for community and for intimacy that so strikingly embodied the spirit of the sixties. What the historical factors are that have contributed to this change are not entirely clear, but they have to include the impact of a major recession at the beginning of the 1980s, a clear turn in the direction of embracing a more politically conservative ideology within the U.S. population, and a concomitantly greater emphasis on financial success and security—an emphasis that had fallen into disfavor during the sixties and seventies, but that developed a renewed vigor in the eighties.

Alongside traditional long-term therapy groups, therefore, we anticipate a continuation of the trend toward more purposefully focused and structured groups having concrete and clearly explicated goals. This direction is likely to continue, at least until the concerns of our larger society should once again move toward encouraging citizens to reflect on their alienation (from both self and others) in groups having more amorphous self-actualization goals. Yet even then, for all the reasons cited above, we would have serious reservations concerning the long-term viability of this particular group model.

# REFERENCES

## CHAPTER ONE

Bion, W.R. (1959). *Experiences in groups*. New York: Basic Books.

Burrow, T.L. (1927). The group method of analysis. *Psychoanalytic Review, 14,* 268–280.

Calame, B.E. (1969). The truth hurts. *The Wall Street Journal,* July 14.

Cohn, R.C. (1969). From couch to circle to community: Beginnings of the theme-centered inter-action method. In H.M. Ruitenbeek (Ed.), *Group therapy today.* New York: Atherton Press.

Cohn, R.C., & Malamud, D. (1969). Be your own chairman: Participating in small groups. An un-published manuscript.

Denes-Radomisli, M. (1971). Gestalt group therapy: Sense in sensitivity. Unpublished paper, Adel-phi University/Postdoctoral Program in Psychotherapy: 1971 Conference on Group Process Today.

Durkin, J.E. (Ed.). (1981). *Living groups: Group psychotherapy and general system theory.* New York: Brunner/Mazel.

Ezriel, H. (1973). Psychoanalytic group therapy. In L.R. Wolberg & E.K. Schwartz (Eds.), *Group therapy: 1973.* New York: Intercontinental Medical Book Corporation.

Feder, B., & Ronall, R. (1980). *Beyond the hot seat: Gestalt approaches to group.* New York: Brun-ner/Mazel.

Foulkes, S.F. (1965). *Therapeutic group analysis.* New York: International Universities Press.

Lewin, K. (1952). *Field theory in social science.* London: Tavistock.

Marrow, A.J. (1969). *The practical theorist: The life and work of Kurt Lewin.* New York: Basic Books.

May, R., Angel, E., & Ellenberger, H.F. (Eds.). (1958). *Existence.* New York: Basic Books.

Pines, M. (Ed.). (1985). *Bion and group psychotherapy.* London: Routledge & Kegan Paul.

Polster, E., & Polster, M. (1973). *Gestalt therapy integrated.* New York: Brunner/Mazel.

Reich, C.A. (1970). *The greening of America.* New York: Random House.

Roback, H.B. (1984). Introduction: The emergence of disease management groups. In H.B. Roback (Ed.), *Helping patients and their families cope with medical problems.* San Francisco: Jossey-Bass.

Rogers, C.R. (1967). The process of the basic encounter group. In J. Bugenthal (Ed.), *Challenges of humanistic psychology.* New York: McGraw-Hill.

Roszak, T. (1969). *The making of a counterculture.* New York: Doubleday.

Schilder, P. (1936). The analysis of ideologies as a psychotherapeutic method especially in group treatment. *American Journal of Psychiatry, 93,* 601–617.

Schutz, W.C., & Seashore, C. (1972). Promoting growth with nonverbal exercises. In L.N. Solomon & B. Berzon (Eds.), *New perspectives on encounter groups.* San Francisco: Jossey-Bass.

Shaffer, J.B.P., & Galinsky, M.D. (1974). *Models of group therapy and sensitivity training.* Englewood Cliffs, NJ: Prentice Hall.

Slavson, S.R. (1950). *Analytic group psychotherapy.* New York: Columbia University Press.

Spotniz, H. (1961). *The couch and the circle.* New York: Knopf.

Sullivan, H.S. (1953). *The interpersonal theory of psychiatry.* New York: W. W. Norton.

Wender, L. (1936). The dynamics of group psychotherapy and its application. *Journal of Nervous and Mental Diseases, 84,* 54–60.

Whitaker, C.A., & Malone, T.P. (1953). *The roots of psychotherapy.* New York: Blakiston.

Whitaker, D.S., & Lieberman, M.A. (1965). *Psychotherapy through the group process.* New York: Atherton.

Wolf, A., & Schwartz, E.K. (1962). *Psychoanalysis in groups.* New York: Grune and Stratton.

Wolf, A., McCarty, G.J., & Goldberg, I.A. (1970). *Beyond the couch: Dialogues in teaching and learning psychoanalysis in groups.* New York: Grune & Stratton.

Yalom, I. (1985). *The theory and practice of group psychotherapy,* 3rd ed. New York: Basic Books.

## CHAPTER TWO

Alissi, A.S. (Ed.). (1980). *Perspectives on social group work practice: A book of readings.* New York: The Free Press.

Alissi, A.S., & Casper, M. (Eds.). (1985). *Time as a factor in groupwork.* New York: The Haworth Press.

Bales, R.F. (1958). Task roles and social roles in problem-solving groups. Pp. 437–447 in E.E. Maccoby, T.M. Newcomb, & E.L. Hartley (Eds.), *Readings in social psychology,* 3rd ed. New York: Holt, Rinehart and Winston.

Balgopal, P.R., & Vassil, T.V. (1983). *Groups in social work: An ecological perspective.* New York: Macmillan.

Bernstein, S. (Ed.). (1976). *Explorations in group work: Essays in theory and practice.* Boston: Charles River Books.

Bernstein, S. (Ed.). (1976). *Further explorations in group work.* Boston: Charles River Books.

Bertcher, H.J., & Maple, F. (1985). Elements and issues in group composition. Pp. 180–202 in M. Sundel, P. Glasser, R. Sarri, & R. Vinter (Eds.), *Individual change through small groups,* 2nd ed. New York: The Free Press.

Cartwright, D., & Zander, A. (1968). *Group dynamics,* 2nd ed. New York: Harper & Row.

Coyle, G. (1948). *Group work with American youth.* New York: Harper & Row.

Croxton, T.A. (1985). The therapeutic contract. Pp. 159–179 in M. Sundel, P. Glasser, R. Sarri, & R. Vinter (Eds.), *Individual change through small groups.* New York: The Free Press.

Davis, L.E. (1979). Racial composition of groups. *Social Work, 24,* 203–213.

Follett, M.P. (1934). *The new state,* 4th ed. New York: Longmans, Green & Co., Inc.

Galinsky, M.J., & Schopler, J.H. (1977). Warning: Groups may be dangerous. *Social Work, 22,* 89–94.

Galinsky, M.J., & Schopler, J.H. (1985). Patterns of entry and exit in open-ended groups. *Social Work with Groups, 8,* 67–80.

Galinsky, M.J., & Schopler, J.H. (1987). Practitioners' views of assets and liabilities of open-ended groups. Pp. 83–98 in J. Lassner, K. Powell, & E. Finnegan (Eds.), *Social group work: Competence and values in practice*. New York: Haworth Press.

Galinsky, M.J., & Schopler, J.H. (in press). Developmental patterns in open-ended groups. *Social Work with Groups*.

Garland, J., Jones, H., & Kolodny, R. (1976). A model of stages of group development in social work groups. Pp. 17–71 in S. Bernstein (Ed.), *Explorations in group work*. Boston: Charles River Books.

Garvin, C.D. (1985). Group process: Usage and uses in social work practice. Pp. 203–225 in M. Sundel, P. Glasser, R. Sarri, & R. Vinter (Eds.), *Individual change through small groups*, 2nd ed. New York: The Free Press.

Garvin, C. (1987). *Contemporary group work*, 2nd ed. Englewood Cliffs, NJ: Prentice Hall.

Garvin, C.D., & Glasser, P.H. (1985). Social group work: The preventative and rehabilitative approach. Pp. 35–49 in M. Sundel, P. Glasser, R. Sarri, & R. Vinter (Eds.), *Individual change through small groups*. New York: The Free Press.

Garvin, C.D., Glasser, P.H., Carter, B., English, R., & Wolfson, C. (1985). Group work intervention in the social environment. Pp. 277–293 in M. Sundel, P. Glasser, R. Sarri, & R. Vinter (Eds.), *Individual change through small groups*. New York: The Free Press.

Germain, C., & Gitterman, A. (1980). *The life model of social work practice*. New York: Columbia University Press.

Gitterman, A., & Shulman, L. (Eds.). (1986). *Mutual aid groups and the life cycle*. Itasca, IL: F.E. Peacock Publishers.

Glasser, P., Sarri, R. & Vinter, R. (Eds.). (1974). *Individual change through small groups*. New York: The Free Press.

Hasenfeld, Y. (1985). The organizational context of group work. Pp. 294–309 in M. Sundel, P. Glasser, R. Sarri, & R. Vinter (Eds.), *Individual change through small groups*. New York: The Free Press.

Henry, S. (1981). *Group skills in social work: A four-dimensional approach*. Itasca, IL: F.E. Peacock Publishers.

Klein, A.F. (1970). *Social work through group process*. Albany, NY: School of Social Welfare, State University of New York at Albany.

Klein, A.F. (1972). *Effective group work*. New York: Association Press.

Konopka, G. (1949). *Therapeutic group work with children*. Minneapolis: The University of Minnesota Press.

Konopka, G. (1963). *Social group work: A helping process*. Englewood Cliffs, NJ: Prentice Hall.

Lieberman, M., Yalom, I., & Miles, M. (1973). *Encounter groups: First facts*. New York: Basic Books.

Middleman, R.R. (1968). *The non-verbal method in working with groups*. New York: Association Press.

Middleman, R.R. (1980). The use of program: Review and update. *Social Work with Groups, 3*, 5–23.

Northen, H. (1969). *Social work with groups*. New York: Columbia University Press.

Northen, H. (1988). *Social work with groups*, 2nd ed. New York: Columbia University Press.

Powell, T.J. (1987). *Self-help organizations and professional practice*. Silver Spring, MD: National Association of Social Workers.

Redl, F., & Wineman, D. (1952). *Controls from within: Techniques for the treatment of the aggressive child*. Glencoe, Illinois: Free Press.

Roberts, R.W., & Northen, H. (Eds.). (1976). *Theories of social work with groups*. New York: Columbia University Press.

Rose, S.D. (1973). *Treating children in groups*. San Francisco: Jossey-Bass Publishers.

Rose, S.D., & Edelson, J.L. (1987). *Working with children and adolescents in groups*. San Francisco: Jossey-Bass.

Rosenbaum, M. (Ed.). (1983). *Handbook of short-term therapy groups*. New York: McGraw-Hill.

Sarri, R.C., & Galinsky, M.J. (1985). A conceptual framework for group development. Pp. 70–86 in M. Sundel, P. Glasser, R. Sarri, & R. Vinter (Eds.), *Individual change through small groups*. New York: The Free Press.

Scher, M. (1973, July). Observations in an aftercare group. *International Journal of Group Psychotherapy, 23,* 166–169.

Schopler, J.H., & Galinsky, M.J. (1972). Criteria for model selection in social group work. Paper presented at the Annual Forum of the National Conference on Social Welfare, Chicago.

Schopler, J.H., & Galinsky, M.J. (1984). Meeting practice needs: Conceptualizing the open-ended group. *Social Work with Groups, 7,* 3–21.

Schopler, J.H., Galinsky, M.J., & Alicke, M.D. (1985). Goals in social group work practice: Formulation, implementation, and evaluation. Pp. 140–158 in M. Sundel, P. Glasser, R. Sarri, & R. Vinter (Eds.), *Individual change through small groups.* New York: The Free Press.

Schwartz, W. (1961). The social worker in the group. Pp. 146–177 in *The social welfare forum, 1961.* New York: Columbia University Press.

Schwartz, W. (1971). On the use of groups in social work practice. Pp. 3–24 in W. Schwartz & S.R. Zalba (Eds.), *The practice of group work.* New York: Columbia University Press.

Schwartz, W., & S.R. Zalba (Eds.). (1971). *The practice of group work.* New York: Columbia University Press.

Shaw, M.E. (1981). *Group dynamics,* 3rd ed. New York: McGraw-Hill.

Shulman, L. (1968). *A casebook of social work with groups: The mediating model.* New York: Council on Social Work Education.

Shulman, L. (1971). Program in group work: Another look. Pp. 221–240 in W. Schwartz & S.R. Zalba (Eds.), *The practice of group work.* New York: Columbia University Press.

Shulman, L. (1985/86). The dynamics of mutual aid. *Social Work with Groups, 8,* 51–60.

Simon, P. (Ed.). (1971). *Play and game theory in groupwork, a collection of papers by Neva Leona Boyd.* Chicago: The Jane Addams Graduate School of Social Work at the University of Illinois.

Sundel, M., Glasser, P., Sarri, R., & Vinter, R. (1985). *Individual change through small groups,* 2nd ed. New York: The Free Press.

Toseland, R.W., & Hacker, L. (1982). Self-help groups and professional involvement. *Social Work, 27,* 341–347.

Toseland, R.W., & Rivas, R.F. (1984). *An introduction to group work practice.* New York: Macmillan.

Tuckman, B.W. (1965). Developmental sequence in small groups. *Psychological Bulletin, 63,* 384–399.

Tuckman, B.W., & Jenson, M.A.C. (1977). Stages of small group development revisited. *Group and Organization Studies, 2,* 419–427.

Vinter, R.D. (1967). *Readings in group work practice.* Ann Arbor, MI: Campus Publishers.

Vinter, R.D. (1985). The essential components of social group work practice. Pp. 11–34 in M. Sundel, P. Glasser, R. Sarri, & R. Vinter (Eds.), *Individual change through small groups.* New York: The Free Press.

Vinter, R.D. (1985). Program activities: An analysis of their effects on participant behavior. Pp. 226–236 in M. Sundel, P. Glasser, R. Sarri, & R. Vinter (Eds.), *Individual change through small groups.* New York: The Free Press.

Vinter, R.D., & Galinsky, M.J. (1985). Extra group relations and approaches. Pp. 226–276 in M. Sundel, P. Glasser, R. Sarri, & R. Vinter (Eds.), *Individual change through small groups.* New York: The Free Press.

Whittaker, J.K. (1985). Programs activities: Their selection and use in a therapeutic milieu. Pp. 237–250 in M. Sundel, P. Glasser, R. Sarri, & R. Vinter (Eds.), *Individual change through small groups.* New York: The Free Press.

Whittaker, J.K., & Garbarino, J. (1983). *Social support networks: Informal helping in the human services.* New York: Aldine.

Yalom, I.D. (1983). *Inpatient group psychotherapy.* New York: Basic Books.

## CHAPTER THREE

Agazarian, Y., & Peters, R. (1981). *The visible and invisible group: Two perspectives on group psychotherapy and group process.* London: Routledge & Kegan Paul.

Bateson, G., Jackson, D.D., Haley, J., & Weakland, J.H. (1956). Toward a theory of schizophrenia. *Behavioral Science, 1,* 251–264.

Caligor, J., Fieldsteel, N.D., and Brok, A.J. (1984). *Individual and group therapy: Combining psychoanalytic treatments.* New York: Basic Books.

Durkin, H.E. (1964). *The group in depth.* New York: International Universities Press.

Durkin, H.E. (1972). Analytic group therapy and general systems theory. In C.J. Sager & H.S. Kaplan (Eds.), *Progress in group and family therapy.* New York: Brunner/Mazel.

Durkin, J.E. (Ed.). (1981). *Living groups: Group psychotherapy and general system theory.* New York: Brunner/Mazel.

Epstein, L., & Finer, A. (Eds.). (1979). *Countertransference.* New York: Jason Aronson.

Fenchel, G.H., & Flapan, D. (1985). Resistance in group psychotherapy. *Group, 9,* 35–47.

Fenichel, O. (1945). *The psychoanalytic theory of neurosis.* New York: W. W. Norton.

Flapan, D., & Fenchel, G.H. (1984). Countertransference in group psychotherapy. *Group, 8,,* 17–29.

Foulkes, S.H. (1965). *Therapeutic group analysis.* New York: International Universities Press.

Freud, S. (1913/1938). *Totem and taboo.* In A. A. Brill (Ed.), *The basic writings of Sigmund Freud.* New York: Random House. 1938.

Freud, S. (1922). *Group psychology and the analysis of the ego.* London: Hogarth Press.

Freud, S. (1930). *Civilization and its discontents.* London: Hogarth Press.

Freud, S. (1939). *Moses and monotheism.* New York: Alfred A. Knopf.

Haley, J. (1970/71). Family therapy. *International Journal of Psychiatry, 9,* 232–242.

Jourard, S. (1971). *The transparent self,* 2nd ed. New York: Van Nostrand Reinhold.

Kohut, H. (1984). *How does analysis cure?* Chicago: University of Chicago Press.

Reich, W. (1949). *Character analysis.* New York: Orgone Institute Press.

Rutan, J.S., & Stone, W.N. (1984) *Psychodynamic group psychotherapy.* Lexington, MA: D. C. Heath.

Schafer, R. (1983). *The analytic attitude.* New York: Basic Books.

Spotniz, H. (1985). *Modern psychoanalysis of the schizophrenic patient,* 2nd ed. New York: Human Sciences Press.

Whitaker, D.S. (1985). *Using groups to help people.* London: Routledge & Kegan Paul.

Wolf, A., & Schwartz, E.K. (1962). *Psychoanalysis in groups.* New York: Grune & Stratton.

Yalom, I. (1985). *The theory and practice of group psychotherapy,* 3rd ed. New York: Basic Books.

## CHAPTER FOUR

Adler, A. (1927). *The practice and theory of individual psychology.* New York: Harcourt, Brace, & World.

Agazarian, Y., & Peters, R. (1981). *The visible and invisible group: Two perspectives on group psychotherapy and group process.* London: Routledge & Kegan Paul.

Bateson, G., Jackson, D.D., Haley, J., & Weakland, J.H. (1956). Toward a theory of schizophrenia. *Behavioral science, I,* 251–264.

Bion, W. (1959). *Experiences in groups.* New York: Basic Books.

Durkin, H.E. (1964). *The group in depth.* New York: International Universities Press.

Durkin, J.E. (Ed.). (1981). *Living groups: Group psychotherapy and general system theory.* New York: Brunner/Mazel.

Ezriel, H. (1973). Psychoanalytic group therapy. In L.R. Wolberg & E.K. Schwartz (Eds.), *Group therapy: 1973.* New York: Intercontinental Medical Book Corporation.

Foulkes, S.F. (1965). *Therapeutic group analysis.* New York: International Universities Press.

Foulkes, S.F. (1973). The group as matrix of the individual's mental life. In L.R. Wolberg & E.K. Schwartz (Eds.), *Group therapy: 1973.* New York: Intercontinental Medical Book Corporation.

Foulkes, S.F., & Anthony, E.J. (1965). *Group psychotherapy,* 2nd ed. Baltimore: Penguin Books.

Goldstein, K. (1948). *Language and language disturbances.* New York: Grune & Stratton.

Hall, C.S., & Lindzey, G. (1978). *Theories of personality,* 3rd ed. New York: John Wiley & Sons.

Koffka, K. (1935). *Principles of gestalt psychology.* New York: Harcourt, Brace.

Kohler, W. (1969). *The task of gestalt psychology.* Princeton, NJ: Princeton University Press.

Lewin, K. (1952). *Field theory in social science.* London: Tavistock.

Marrow, A.J. (1958). *The practical theorist: The life and work of Kurt Lewin.* New York: Basic Books.

Scheidlinger, S. (1984). Individual and group psychology—are they opposed? *Group, 8,* 3–11.

Schneider, P. (1982). Interpreting analytical group psychotherapy, more specifically the individual interpretation and the group interpretation. In M. Pines & L. Rafaelson (Eds.), *The individual and the group: boundaries and interrelations,* Vol. 1. New York: Plenum Press.

Wertheimer, M. (1959). *Productive thinking,* enl. ed. New York: Harper.

Whitaker, D.S. (1982). A nuclear conflict and group focal conflict model for integrating individual and group level phenomena in psychotherapy groups. In M. Pines and L. Rafaelsen (Eds.), *The individual and the group: boundaries and interrelations,* Vol. 1. New York: Plenum Press.

Whitaker, D.S. (1985). *Using groups to help people.* London: Routledge and Kegan Paul.

Whitaker, D.S., & Lieberman, M.A. (1965). *Psychotherapy through the group process.* New York: Atherton.

Wolf, A., & Schwartz, E.K. (1962). *Psychoanalysis in groups.* New York: Grune & Stratton.

## CHAPTER FIVE

Berger, M.M. (1958). Nonverbal communication in group psychotherapy. *International Journal of Group Psychotherapy, 8,* 161–178.

Binswanger, L. (1963). *Being-in-the-world: Selected papers of Ludwig Binswanger.* New York: Basic Books.

Boss, M. (1963). *Psychoanalysis and daseinsanalysis.* New York: Basic Books.

Buber, M. (1958). *I and thou.* New York: Charles Scribners.

Camus, A. (1955). *The myth of Sisyphus.* New York: Alfred A. Knopf.

Cohn, R.C. (1972). Style and spirit of the theme-centered interactional method. In C.J. Sager & H. Kaplan (Eds.), *Progress in group and family therapy.* New York: Brunner-Mazel.

Durkin, H.E. (1964). *The group in depth.* New York: International Universities Press.

Heidegger, M. (1962). *Being and time.* New York: Harper & Row.

Hora, T. (1959). Existential group psychotherapy. *American Journal of Psychotherapy, 13,* 83–92.

Husserl, E. (1928). Vorlesungen sur phaenomenologic des innern zeitbewusstseins. (Halle a.d. Saale, 1928).

Keen, E. (1970). *Three faces of being: Toward an existential clinical psychology.* Englewood Cliffs, NJ: Prentice Hall.

Mahrer, A.R. (1978). *Experiencing: A humanistic theory of psychology and psychiatry.* New York: Brunner/Mazel.

May, R. (1958). Contributions of existential psychotherapy. In R. May, E. Angel, & H.R. Ellenberger (Eds.), *Existence: A new dimension in psychiatry and psychology.* New York: Basic Books.

Mullan, H. (1955). The group analyst's creative function. *American Journal of Psychotherapy, 9,* 320–334.

Nicholas, M.W. (1984). *Change in the context of group therapy.* New York: Brunner/Mazel.

Rogers, C.R. (1951). *Client-centered therapy.* Boston: Houghton-Mifflin.

Rogers, C.R. (1970). *Carl Rogers on encounter groups.* New York: Harper & Row.

Rogers, C.R. (1982). *A way of experiencing.* Boston: Houghton-Mifflin.

Shaffer, J.B.P. (1978). *Humanistic psychology.* Englewood Cliffs, NJ: Prentice Hall.

Szasz, T.S. (1965). *The ethics of psychoanalysis.* New York: Dell.

Szasz, T.S. (1974). *The myth of mental illness,* rev. ed. New York: Harper & Row.

Whitaker, C.A., & Malone, T.P. (1953). *The roots of psychotherapy.* New York: Blakiston.

Whitaker, C.A., & Warkentin, J. *Spontaneous interaction in group psychotherapy.* Atlanta: Atlanta Psychiatric Clinic.

Yalom, I. (1980). *Existential psychotherapy.* New York: Basic Books.

# CHAPTER SIX

Blatner, H.A. (1970). *Psychodrama, role-playing, and action methods.* Thetford, England: Howard A. Blatner.

Carman, M.B., & Nordin, S.R. (1984). Psychodrama: A therapeutic modality for the elderly in nursing homes. *Clinical Gerontologist, 3,* 15–24.

Corsini, R.J. (1957). *Methods of group psychotherapy.* New York: McGraw-Hill.

Dietz, J. (1968). Psychodrama: Possible answer to the nation's race problems. *Boston Sunday Globe,* May 19, 1968, p. 50.

Gendron, J.M. (1980). *Moreno: The roots and the branches and bibliography of psychodrama, 1972–1980; and sociometry, 1970–1980.* Beacon, NY: Beacon House.

Greenberg, I.A. (1968). *Psychodrama and audience attitude change.* Beverly Hills, Calif.: Behavioral Studies Press.

Heisey, M.J. (1982). *Clinical case studies in psychodrama.* Washington, DC: University Press of America.

Kranz, P., & Huston, K. (1984). The use of psychodrama to facilitate supervisee development in master's level counseling students. *Journal of Group Psychotherapy, Psychodrama and Sociometry, 37,* 126–133.

Moreno, J.L. (1946). *Psychodrama, Vol. 1.* Beacon, NY: Beacon House.

Moreno, J.L. (1953). *Who shall survive?* Beacon, NY: Beacon House.

Moreno, J.L. (1959). Psychodrama. In Silvano Arieti (Ed.), *American handbook of psychiatry,* Vol 2. New York: Basic Books.

Moreno, Z.T. (1964). *Psychodrama,* Vol. 1 (Rev. ed.). Beacon, NY: Beacon House.

Moreno, Z.T. (1959). A survey of psychodramatic techniques. *Group Psycho-therapy, 12,* 5–14.

Schutz, W. (1971). *Here comes everybody.* New York: Harper & Row.

Schramski, T.G., & Harvey, D.R. (1983). The impact of psychodrama and role playing in the correctional environment. *International Journal of Offender Therapy & Comparative Criminology, 27,* 243–254.

Sidorsky, S. (1984). The psychodramatic treatment of the borderline personality. *Journal of Group Psychotherapy, Psychodrama and Sociometry, 37,* 117–125.

Siroka, R.W., Siroka, E.K., & Schloss, G.A. (1971). *Sensitivity training and group encounter.* New York: Grosset & Dunlap.

Smith, J.D., Walsh, R.T., & Richardson, M.A. (1985). The Clown Club: A structured fantasy approach to group therapy with the latency-age child. *International Journal of Group Psychotherapy, 35,* 49–64.

Warger, C.L. (1984). Creative drama for autistic adolescents: Expanding leisure and recreational options. *Journal of Child and Adolescent Psychotherapy, 1,* 15–19.

*Who's Who in America* (1966). Vol. 34, 1966–67. Chicago: A. N. Marquis Co.

# CHAPTER SEVEN

Enright, J.B. (1978). Gestalt therapy in interactive groups. In F.D. Stephenson (Ed.), *Gestalt therapy primer.* New York: Jason Aronson.

Feder, B., & Ronall, R. (1980). *Beyond the hot seat: Gestalt approaches to group.* New York: Brunner/Mazel.

Flores, P.J. (1985). Group psychotherapy as taught by the Polsters and the Gouldings. *Journal of Contemporary Psychotherapy, 15,* 74–93.

Freud, S. (1911/1959). Notes upon an autobiographical account of a case of paranoia. In S. Freud (E. Jones, Ed.), *Collected papers,* Vol. III. New York: Basic Books.

Goldstein, K. (1940). *Human nature in the light of psychopathology.* Cambridge: Harvard University Press.

Kepner, E. (1980). Gestalt group process. In B. Feder & R. Ronall (Eds.), *Beyond the hot seat: Gestalt approaches to group*. New York: Brunner/Mazel.

Perls, F.S. (1969a). *In and out of the garbage pail*. Lafayette, CA: Real People Press.

Perls, F.S. (1969b). *Gestalt therapy verbatim*. Lafayette, CA: Real People Press.

Perls, F.S. (1969c). *Ego, hunger, and aggression*. New York: Random House.

Perls, F.S., Hefferline, R.F., & Goodman, P. (1951). *Gestalt therapy*. New York: Julian Press.

Polster, E., & Polster, M. (1973). *Gestalt therapy integrated: Contours of theory and practice*. New York: Brunner/Mazel.

Reich, W. (1949). *Character analysis*. New York: Orgone Institute Press.

Spotniz, H. (1969). *Modern psychoanalysis of the schizophrenic patient*. New York: Grune & Stratton.

Szasz, T.S. (1974). *The myth of mental illness*, rev. ed. New York: Harper & Row.

## CHAPTER EIGHT

Bandura, A. (1969). *Principles of behavior modification*. New York: Holt, Rinehart and Winston.

Bandura, A. (1986). *Social foundations of thought and action*. Englewood Cliffs, NJ: Prentice Hall.

Beck, A.T. (1976). *Cognitive therapy and the emotional disorders*. New York: International Universities Press.

Berk, S.N., & Efran, J.A. (1983). Some recent developments in the treatment of neurosis. In C.E. Walker (Ed.), *The handbook of clinical psychology: Theory, research, and practice*, Vol. II. Homewood, IL: Dow Jones-Irwin.

Ellis, A. (1982). Rational-emotive group therapy. In G.M. Gazda (Ed.), *Basic approaches to group psychotherapy and group counseling*, 3rd ed. Springfield, IL: Charles C Thomas.

Eysenck, H.J. (1960). *Behavior therapy and the neuroses*. London: Pergamon.

Fensternheim, H. (1972). Behavior therapy: Assertive training in groups. In C.J. Sager & H.S. Kaplan (Eds.), *Progress in group and family therapy*. New York: Brunner/Mazel.

Fensternheim, H., & Glazer, H.I. (1983). *Behavioral psychotherapy*. New York: Brunner/Mazel.

Fishman, S.T., & Nawas, M.M. (1971). Standardized desensitization method in group treatments. *Journal of Counseling Psychology, 18,* 520–523.

Goldfried, M., & Davison, G. 1976. *Clinical behavior therapy*. New York: Holt, Rinehart & Winston.

Jacobson, E. (1938). *Progressive relaxation*. Chicago: University of Chicago Press.

Jones, M.C. (1924). A laboratory study of fear: The case of Peter. *Journal of Genetic Psychology, 31,* 308–315.

Lazarus, A.A. (1961). Group therapy of phobic disorders by systematic desensitization. *Journal of Abnormal and Social Psychology, 63,* 504–510.

Lazarus, A.A. (1968). Behavior therapy in groups. In G.H. Gazda (Ed.), *Basic approaches to group psychotherapy and group counseling*. Springfield, IL: Charles C Thomas.

Lazarus, A.A. (1981). *The practice of multimodal therapy*. New York: McGraw-Hill.

Marrone, R.L., Merksamer, M.A., & Salzberg, P.M. (1970). A short duration group treatment of smoking behavior by stimulus saturation. *Behavior Research & Therapy, 8,* 347–352.

McManus, M. (1971). Group desensitization of test anxiety. *Behavior Research & Therapy, 9,* 55–56.

Meichenbaum, D. (1972). Cognitive modification of test anxious college students. *Journal of Counseling and Clinical Psychology, 39,* 370–380.

Meichenbaum, D. (1977). *Cognitive behavior modification*. New York: Plenum.

Meichenbaum, D., & Genest, M. (1977). Treatment of anxiety. In G.G. Harris (Ed.), *The group treatment of human problems: A social learning approach*. New York: Grune & Stratton.

Paul, G.L. (1968). Two year follow-up of systematic desensitization in therapy groups. *Journal of Abnormal Psychology,* 71. 124–135.

Paul, G.L., & Shannon, D.T. (1966). Treatment of anxiety through systematic desensitization in therapy groups. *Journal of Abnormal Psychology, 71,* 124–135.

Pavlov, I.P. (1941). *Conditioned reflexes and psychiatry* (trans. by W.H. Gantt). New York: International Universities Press.

Penick, S.B., Filion, R., Fox, S., & Stunkard, A.J. (1971). Behavior modification in the treatment of obesity. *Psychosomatic Medicine, 33,* 49–55.

Rose, S.D. (1977). *Group therapy: A behavioral approach.* Englewood Cliffs, NJ: Prentice Hall.

Skinner, B.F. (1938). *The behavior of organisms.* New York: Appelton-Century-Crofts.

Wolpe, J. (1958). *Psychotherapy by reciprocal inhibition.* Stanford, CA: Stanford University Press.

Wolpe, J., & Lazarus, A.A. (1966). *Behavior therapy techniques.* New York: Pergamon.

Yates, A.J. (1970). *Behavior therapy.* New York: John Wiley and Sons.

## CHAPER NINE

Bion, W.R. (1959). *Experiences in groups.* New York: Basic Books.

de Maré, P.B. (1985). Major Bion. In M. Pines (Ed.), *Bion and group psychotherapy.* London: Routledge & Kegan Paul.

Durkin, H. (1982). Boundaries and boundarying: A systems perspective. In M. Pines & L. Rafaelsen (Eds.), *The individual and the group,* Vol. 1. New York: Plenum.

Eisold, K. (1985). Recovering Bion's contributions to group analysis. In A.D. Coleman & M.H. Geller (Eds.), *Group relations reader 2.* Washington, DC: A.K. Rice Institute.

Freud, S. (1922). *Group psychology and the analysis of the ego.* London: Hogarth.

Freud, S. (1975). *Three essays on the theory of sexuality.* New York: Basic Books.

Gould, L.J. (1985). Men and women at work: A group relations conference on person and role. In A.D. Coleman & M.H. Geller (Eds.), *Group relations reader 2.* Washington, DC: A.K. Rice Institute.

Guereca, D. (1985). A manager's view of the institutional event. In A.D. Coleman & M.H. Geller (Eds.), *Group relations reader 2.* Washington, DC: A.K. Rice Institute.

Gustafson, J.P., & Cooper, L. (1985). Collaboration in small groups: Theory and technique for the study of small-group processes. In A.D. Coleman & M.H. Geller (Eds.), *Group relations reader 2.* Washington, DC: A.K. Rice Institute.

Jung, C. (1917). *Collected papers on analytical psychology.* New York: Moffat, Yard, and Company.

Konig, K. (1985). Basic assumption groups and working groups revisited. In M. Pines (Ed.), *Bion and group psychotherapy.* London: Routledge & Kegan Paul.

Lawrence, W.G. (1979). Introductory essay: Exploring boundaries. In W.G. Lawrence (Ed.), *Exploring individual and organizational boundaries.* New York: Wiley.

Main, T. (1985). Some psychodynamics of large groups. In A.D. Coleman & M.H. Geller (Eds.), *Group relations reader 2.* Washington, DC: A.K. Rice Institute.

Milgram S., & Toch H. (1969). Collective behavior: Crowds and social movements. In G. Lindzey & E. Aronson (Eds.), *The handbook of social psychology,* Vol. IV, 2nd ed. Reading, MA: Addison-Wesley.

Munroe, R.L. (1955). *Schools of psychoanalytic thought.* New York: Dryden Press.

Pines, M. (Ed.). (1985). *Bion and group psychotherapy.* London: Routledge & Kegan Paul.

Rice, A.K. (1965). *Learning for leadership.* London: Tavistock Publications.

Rioch, M.J. (1970). The work of Wilfred Bion on groups. *Psychiatry, 33,* 56–66.

Rioch, M.J. (1979). The A.K. Rice group relations conferences as a reflection of society. In W.G. Lawrence (Ed.), *Exploring individual and organizational boundaries.* New York: Wiley.

Schermer, V.L. (1985). Beyond Bion: The basic assumption states revisited. In M. Pines (Ed.), *Bion and group psychotherapy.* London: Routledge & Kegan Paul.

Singer, D.L., Astrachan, B.M., Gould, L.J., & Klein, E.B. (1979). Boundary management in psychological work with groups. In W.G. Lawrence (Ed.), *Exploring individual and organizational boundaries.* New York: Wiley.

Turquet, P.M. (1985). Leadership: The individual and the group. In A.D. Coleman & M.H. Geller (Eds.), *Group relations reader 2.* Washington, DC: A.K. Rice Institute.

## CHAPTER TEN

Benne, K.D. (1964). History of the T-group in the laboratory setting. In L.P. Bradford, J.R. Gibb, & K.D. Benne (Eds.). *T-group theory and laboratory method.* New York: John Wiley & Sons.

Benne, K.D., Bradford, L.P., & Lippitt, R. (1964). Designing the laboratory. In L.P. Bradford, J.R. Gibb, & K.D. Benne (Eds.), *T-group theory and laboratory method.* New York: John Wiley & Sons.

Bennis, W.G. (1969). *Organization Development: Its nature, origins, and prospects.* Reading, MA: Addison Wesley.

Bennis, W.G., Benne, K.D., & Chin, R. (Eds.). (1985). *The planning of change,* 4th ed. New York: Holt, Rinehart & Winston.

Blake, R.R., & Mouton, J.S. (1985). *The managerial grid, III.* Houston: Gulf Publishing Co.

Bradford, L.P., Gibb, J.R., & Benne, K.D. (1964). *T-group theory and laboratory method.* New York: John Wiley & Sons.

Derr, C.B. (Ed.). (1974). *Organizational development in urban school systems.* Beverly Hills: Sage Publications.

Golembiewski, R.T., & Blumberg, A. (1977). *Sensitivity training and the laboratory approach,* 3rd ed. Itasca, IL: Peacock.

Klaw, S. (1961, August). Two weeks in a T-group. *Fortune Magazine,* pp. 114–117.

Lewin, K., Lippitt, R., & White, R.K. (1939). Patterns of aggressive behavior in experimentally created "social climates." *Journal of Social Psychology, 10,* 271–299.

Margulies, N., & Adams, J.D. (1982). *Organizational development in healthcare organizations.* Reading, MA: Addison Wesley.

National Training Laboratories. (1962). *Issues in human relations training.* Selected Readings Series, No. 5. Washington, DC: NTL.

Patten, T.H. (1981). *Organizational development through teambuilding.* New York: John Wiley & Sons.

Schein, E.H., & Bennis, W.G. (1965). *Personal and organizational change through group methods.* New York: John Wiley & Sons.

Schein, E.H. (1985). *Organizational culture and leadership.* San Francisco: Jossey-Bass.

## CHAPTER ELEVEN

Anderson, W.A. (1983). *The upstart spring: Esalen and the American awakening.* Reading, MA: Addison-Wesley.

Bach, G.R. (1966). The marathon group: Intensive practice of intimate interaction. *Psychological Reports, 18,* 995–1002.

Bach, G.R. (1967). Marathon group dynamics: I. Some functions of the professional group facilitator. *Psychological Reports, 20,* 995–999.

Back, K.W. (1972). *Beyond words: The story of sensitivity training and the encounter movement.* New York: Russell Sage Foundation.

Bindrim, P. (1968). A report on a nude marathon. *Psychotherapy: Theory, research, and practice, 5,* 180–188.

Burton, A. (1969). *Encounter.* San Francisco: Jossey-Bass.

Casriel, D. (1963). *So fair a house: The story of Synanon.* Englewood Cliffs, NJ: Prentice Hall.

Denes-Radomisli, M. (1971). Gestalt group therapy: Sense in sensitivity. Unpublished paper, Adelphia University/Postdoctoral Program in Psychotherapy: 1971 Conference on Group Process Today.

Desoille, R. (1965). *The directed daydream.* New York: Psychosynthesis Research Foundation.

Durkin, H.E. (1964). *The group in depth.* New York: International Universities Press.

Erikson, E.H. (1964). *Childhood and society,* 2nd ed. New York: W. W. Norton.

Evans, R. (1981). *Dialogue with Carl Rogers.* Springfield, MA: Praeger.

Freud, A. (1946). *The ego and the mechanisms of defense.* New York: International Universities Press.

Goleman, D. (1984, December 10). Esalen wrestles with a staid present. *The New York Times,* p. C1.

Henry, J. (1963). *Culture against man.* New York: Random House.

Larsen, E. (1986). A program for couples. *Marriage encounter, 15,* 19.

Leuner, H. (1965). *Initiated symbol projection.* New York: Psychosynthesis Research Foundation.

Lieberman, M., Yalom, I., & Miles, M. (1973). *Encounter groups: First facts.* New York: Basic Books.

Lowen, A. (1967). *The betrayal of the body.* New York: Macmillan.

Mead, G.H. (1938). *The philosophy of the act.* Chicago: The University of Chicago Press.
Perls, F. (1968). Gestalt versus encounter. Unpublished paper delivered at the meetings of the American Psychological Association, 1968.
Reich, C.A. (1970). *The greening of America.* New York: Random House.
Reich, W. (1949). *Character analysis.* New York: Orgone Institute Press.
Rogers, C.R. (1951). *Client-centered therapy.* Boston: Houghton-Mifflin.
Rogers, C.R. (1967). The process of the basic encounter group. In J.F.T. Bugenthal (Ed.), *Challenges of humanistic psychology.* New York: McGraw-Hill.
Rogers, C.R. (1970). *Carl Rogers on encounter groups.* New York: Harper & Row.
Rogers, C.R. (1980). *A way of being.* Boston: Houghton-Mifflin.
Roszak, T. (1969). *The making of a counterculture: Reflections of the technocratic society and its youthful opposition.* Garden City, NY: Doubleday.
Schutz, W.C. (1958). *FIRO: A three-dimensional theory of interpersonal behavior.* New York: Holt, Rinehart & Winston.
Schutz, W.C. (1967). *Joy: Expanding human awareness.* New York: Grove Press.
Schutz, W.C. (1971). *Here comes everybody.* New York: Harper & Row.
Schutz, W.C. (1984). *The truth option: A practical technology for human affairs.* Berkeley, CA: Ten Speed Press.
Schutz, W.C. (1986). Encounter groups. In I.L. Kutash & A. Wolf (Eds.), *Psychotherapist's casebook.* San Francisco: Jossey-Bass.
Stoller, F.J. (1972). Marathon groups: Toward a conceptual model. In L.N. Solomon & B. Berzon (Eds.), *New perspectives on encounter groups.* San Francisco: Jossey-Bass.
Wieder, R.S. (1985, February). Dr. Truth. *Success Magazine,* pp. 57–58.
Yablonsky, L. (1965). *The tunnel back: Synanon.* New York: Macmillan.
Yalom, I. (1985). *The theory and practice of group psychotherapy,* 3rd ed. New York: Basic Books.

## CHAPTER TWELVE

Cohn, R.C. (1969). From couch to circle to community: Beginnings of the theme-centered interactional method. In H.M. Ruitenbeek (Ed.), *Group therapy today.* New York: Atherton.
Cohn, R.C. (1972). Style and spirit of the theme-centered interactional method. In C.J. Sager & H.S. Kaplan (Eds.), *Progress in group and family therapy.* New York: Brunner/Mazel.
Erikson, E.H. (1964). *Childhood and society,* 2nd ed. New York: W. W. Norton.
Gordon, M. (1985). *How to plan and conduct a successful meeting.* New York: Sterling.
Gordon, M., & Liberman, N. (1972). *Theme-centered interaction.* Baltimore: National Education Press.
Gordon, M., & Liberman, N. (1983). Theme-centered interactional therapy. In G.M. Gazda (Ed.), *Innovations to group psychotherapy,* 2nd. ed. Springfield, IL: Charles C Thomas.
Postman, N., & Weingartner, C. (1969). *Teaching as a subversive activity.* New York: Delacorte
Rogers, C. (1951). *Client-centered therapy.* Boston: Houghton-Mifflin.
Ronall, R. (1980). Intensive Gestalt workshops: Experiences in community. In B. Feder & R. Ronall (Eds.), *Beyond the hot seat: Gestalt approaches to group.* New York: Brunner/Mazel.

## CHAPTER THIRTEEN

Ablon, J. (1982). The Parents' Auxiliary of Little People of America: A self-help model of social support for families of short-statured children. *Prevention in Human Services, 1,* 31–45.
Antze, P. (1979). Role of ideologies in peer psychotherapy groups. In M.A. Lieberman & L.D. Borman (Eds.), *Self-help groups for coping with crisis.* San Francisco: Jossey-Bass.
Borman, I.D., & Lieberman, M.A. (1979). Conclusion: Contributions, dilemmas, and implications for mental health policy. In M.A. Lieberman & L.D. Borman (Eds.), *Self-help groups for coping with crisis.* San Francisco: Jossey-Bass.

Cohn, R.C., & Malamud, D. (1969). Be your own chairman: Participating in small groups. An unpublished manuscript.

Ernst, S., & Goodison, L. (1981). *In our own hands: A woman's guide to self-help therapy.* Los Angeles: J.P. Tarcher.

Festinger, L. (1957). *A theory of cognitive dissonance.* New York: Harper & Row.

Gartner, A.G., & Riessman, F. (1984). *The self-help revolution.* New York: Human Services Press.

Gellman, I.P. (1964). *The sober alcoholic: An organizational analysis of Alcoholics Anonymous.* Schenectady, NY: New College and University Press.

Goffman, E. (1963). *Stigma: Notes on the management of spoiled identity.* Englewood Cliffs, NJ: Prentice Hall.

Hill, K. (1983). *Helping you helps me: A guide book for self-help groups.* Ottawa: Canadian Council on Social Development.

Katz, A.H. (1981). Self-help and mutual aid: An emerging social movement? *Annual Review of Sociology, 7,* 129–155.

Katz, A.H. (1984). Self-help groups: An international perspective. In A. Gartner & F. Riessman (Eds.), *The self-help revolution.* New York: Human Sciences Press.

Katz, A.H., & Bender, E.I. (Eds.), (1976). *The strength in us: Self-help groups in the modern world.* New York: New Viewpoints.

Lakin, M. (1985). *The helping group: Therapeutic principles and issues.* Reading, MA: Addison-Wesley.

Lavoie, F. (1984). Action research: A new model of interaction between the professional and self-help groups. In A. Gartner & F. Riessman (Eds.), *The self-help revolution.* New York: Human Sciences Press.

Levy, L.H. (1979). Processes and activities in groups. In M.A. Lieberman & L.D. Borman (Eds.), *Self-help groups for coping with crisis.* San Francisco: Jossey-Bass.

Lieber, L.L. (1984). Parents Anonymous: The use of self-help in the treatment and prevention of family violence. In A. Gartner & F. Riessman (Eds.), *The self-help revolution.* New York: Human Sciences Press.

Lieberman, M.A., & Borman, L.D. (1964). *The sober alcoholic.* New Haven: College and University Press.

Lipson, J.G. (1982). Effects of a support group on the emotional impact of Cesarian childbirth. *Prevention in Human Services, 1,* 17–29.

Mallory, L. (1984). Leading self-help groups: A guide for training facilitators. An unpublished manuscript/Family Service America. New York, N.Y.

The Parents Anonymous Chairperson-Sponsor Manual. (1982). Torrance, CA: Parents Anonymous, Inc.

President's Commission on Mental Health. (1978). *Commission report,* Vol. 1. Washington, DC: U.S. Government Printing Office.

Riessman, F. (1965). The "helper-therapy" principle. *Social Work, 10,* 27–32.

Robertson, N. (1988). *Getting better: Inside Alcoholics Anonymous.* New York: William Morrow.

Schutz, W.C. (1971). *Here comes everybody.* New York: Harper & Row.

Silverman, P.R. (1980). *Mutual help groups: Organization and development.* Beverly Hills: Sage Publications.

Sugarman, B. (1974). *Daytop village—a therapeutic community.* New York: Holt, Rinehart & Winston.

Willen, M.L. (1984). Parents Anonymous: The professional's role as sponsor. In A. Gartner & F. Riessman (Eds.), *The self-help revolution.* New York: Human Sciences Press.

## CHAPTER FOURTEEN

Asch, S. (1952). Effects of group pressure upon the modification and distortion of judgments. In G.E. Swanson, T.M. Newcomb, & E.L. Hartley (Eds.), *Readings in social psychology,* 2nd ed. New York: Holt, Rinehart & Winston.

Back, K. (1972). *Beyond words.* New York: Russell Sage Foundation.

*Ethical Guidelines for Group Leaders.* (1980). A pamphlet published by the Association for Specialists in Group Work, a division of the American Association for Counseling and Development. Alexandria, VA.

Gibb, J.R. (1971). The effects of human relations training. In A.E. Bergin & S. Garfield (Eds.), *Handbook of psychotherapy and behavior change.* New York: Wiley.

Lakin, M. (1985). *The helping group: Therapeutic principles and issues.* Reading, MA: Addison-Wesley.

Lieberman, M., Yalom, I., & Miles, M.B. (1973). *Encounter groups: First facts.* New York: Basic Books.

London, P. (1964). *The models and morals of psychotherapy.* New York: Holt, Rinehart & Winston.

Milgram, S. (1974). *Obedience to authority: An experimental view.* New York: Harper & Row.

Roback, H.B. (1984). Introduction: The emergence of disease management groups. In H.B. Roback (Ed.), *Helping patients and their families cope with medical problems.* San Francisco: Jossey-Bass.

Rogers, C.R. (1970). *Carl Rogers on encounter groups.* New York: Harper & Row.

Rosenbaum, M. (Ed.). (1984). *Handbook of short-term therapy groups.* New York: McGraw-Hill.

Rutan, J.S., & Stone, W.N. (1984). *Psychodynamic group psychotherapy.* Lexington, MA: D.C. Heath.

Scheidlinger, S. (1982). *Focus on group psychotherapy: Clinical essays.* New York: International Universities Press.

Shaffer, J.B.P., & Galinsky, M.D. (1974). *Models of group therapy and sensitivity training.* Englewood Cliffs, NJ: Prentice Hall.

Szasz, T. (1965). *The ethics of psychoanalysis: The theory and method of autonomous psychotherapy.* New York: Dell.

Yalom, I. (1970). *The theory and practice of group psychotherapy.* New York: Basic Books.

Yalom, I. (1975). *The theory and practice of group psychotherapy,* 2nd ed. New York: Basic Books.

Yalom, I. (1985). *The theory and practice of group psychotherapy,* 3rd ed. New York: Basic Books.

# NAME INDEX

# SUBJECT INDEX